W9-BEV-396

The Revolutionary Guide to Assembly Language

Vitaly Maljugin

Jacov Izrailevich

Semyon Lavin

Aleksandr Sopin

WROX PRESS ®

The Revolutionary Guide to Assembly Language

© 1993   Vitaly Maljugin
          Jacov Izrailevich
          Semyon Lavin
          Aleksandr Sopin

All rights reserved, no part of this book may be reproduced, stored in a retrieval system or transmitted in any form or by any means - electronic, electro static, mechanical, photocopying, recording or otherwise without the prior written permission of the publisher, except in the case of brief quotations embodied in critical articles or reviews.

The author and publisher have made every effort in the preparation of this book and disk to ensure the accuracy of the information. However, the information contained in this book and disk is sold without warranty, either express or implied. Neither the authors, Wrox Press nor its dealers or distributers will be held liable for any damages caused or alleged to be caused either directly or indirectly by this book or disk.

Published by Wrox Press Ltd. 1334 Warwick Road, Birmingham, United Kingdom.

Printed in the UK by Unwin Brothers Limited.

ISBN 1 - 874416 - 12 - 5

About the Authors

Vitaly Maljugin is head of the Research Bureau at the Regional Center of New Information Technology Voronezh University, Russia. He is the author of educational texts on FORTRAN and Mainframe Operating Systems.

Jacov Izrailevich is a lecturer in mathematics at Voronezh University, where he is head of the computer laboratory. He is the author of a Russian bestselling mathematics title, he currently gives seminars on using software on PCs.

Semyon Lavin is head of the CAD department at the Voronezh Institute of Building. He is an experienced programmer in AutoCad, C, Clarion and Clipper, and has written educational books on algorithmic languages and operating systems.

Aleksandr Sopin is head of the system programming department at the Voronezh Institute of Automated Machine Design. As a software developer he has produced a dialog environment for mainframes and PCs using FORTRAN and Assembler.

Technical Editor **David Lachlan**

Technical Adviser **David Maddock**

Language Editor **Victoria McCluskey**

Editorial Consultant **Ivor Horton**

Beta Testers **Mark Harley and Mark Phillips**

Book Design **Nina Barnsley and Ewart Liburd**

Cover Design **Ewart Liburd and Paul Hougham**

Acknowledgements

Thanks must go to our families for their patience and understanding during the production of this book. Thanks must also go to Sergei Landsberg for his help throughout this project.

The relevant Timings and Encodings are reprinted by permission of Intel Corporation, Copyright/Intel Corporation 1993, and Microsoft Corporation.

Trademark Acknowledgements

Wrox Press have endeavoured to provide trademark information about all the companies and products mentioned in this book. Wrox Press cannot guarantee the accuracy of this information.

MS-DOS, MS, QuickBASIC, QuickC, CodeView, Microsoft, Microsoft BASIC, Microsoft Pascal, Windows and QBasic are registered trademarks and trademarks of Microsoft Corporation.

IBM, OS/2 and PC XT and AT are registered trademarks and trademarks of International Business Machines Corporation.

Borland, Borland C++, Turbo Assembler (TASM), Turbo Pascal and Turbo C++ are registered trademarks of Borland International Inc..

Clipper is a trademark of Computer Associates Inc..

Intel is a registered trademark of Intel Corporation.

CP/M is a registered trademark of Digital Research Inc..

Norton Commander is a trademark of Symantec Inc..

Periscope is a trademark of The Periscope Company Inc..

Xtree is a registered trademark of Xtree Corporation.

PC Tools is a registered trademark of Central Point Software Inc..

DESQview is a trademark of Quarterdeck Office Systems.

Contents

Appendices

Who is This Book For?

This book is primarily designed for programmers who already have experience with a high-level language and now would like to increase the power and flexibility of their programs. It is also suitable for novices who are going to use assembly language as their first computer language. As the native language of computers, assembler will help both these groups to exploit the full potential of their hardware and software.

This book will show you how to use assembler to control elements of your hardware that are inaccessible to high-level programs. Incorporating small assembler modules into your high-level language programs will give you access to BIOS and DOS services which are difficult or even impossible to use directly. Along the way, you will also gain a clear understanding of the PC's hardware design and operation.

What is Covered in This Book

This book gives comprehensive coverage of assembly language for IBM-compatible PCs. Although there are several different assemblers available, we'll concentrate on Microsoft Macro Assembler (MASM) versions 6.0 and 6.1 being run under Microsoft Disk Operating System (MS-DOS) version 4.0 or higher.

We have aimed to produce an attractive and easy tutorial to assembly language, and then tried to cover its most useful applications in detail. The book concentrates on the practical aspects of using MASM, discussing the various software and hardware components involved.

You will learn how to write programs in assembly language using the most suitable commands, how to create finished and ready-to-run programs, and then how to debug them if they don't work. In doing this you will learn how to use Microsoft Macro Assembler, Microsoft Linker and Microsoft CodeView debugger. Having learnt about such assembly language features as directives and macros, we will then use them to create assembly language procedures. Finally we will learn how to store these in libraries, which can then be called from high-level language programs written in C, C++, BASIC, Pascal, Clipper or FORTRAN.

There is also in-depth coverage of controlling the basic hardware components such as the keyboard, video system, disks, printer, and mouse. The book also covers using BIOS and DOS services, writing TSR programs and interfacing between assembler modules and high-level programs. Where appropriate we have tried to explain any problems not fully described in the standard documentation.

The program disk which accompanies the book includes some original programs that both illuminate the subject matter covered, and also form the basis of a useful library for assembly language programmers.

What isn't Covered in This Book

It is impossible to cover every aspect of assembly language in one book. Nor would it be sensible to try, as many more advanced topics have a special audience and warrant a separate book.

Therefore this book doesn't discuss floating-point operations, protected-mode programming, advanced graphic operation, extended memory management and programming in 32-bit mode. While some may be disappointed, we are confident that the scope of the material we have included will allow most readers to get everything they want from assembly language.

Why Do You Need Assembler?

Assembly language directly reflects a computer's structure and its native instruction set. Assembler is often called a one to one level language, meaning that generally one machine command is produced by one assembly language statement. It is because of this feature that only assembly language gives a programmer full control over every machine instruction in the program being created. Therefore anybody who wants to use every feature of the PC's hardware and software has to master assembly language.

Those with some experience can reasonably ask if there is any need for assembly language when such powerful high-level languages and database systems are available? It is true that many programmers can successfully solve their problems using these systems. However, it's important to realize that this software exists more or less thanks to assembly language. Usually the first programming product created for a new type of computer has to be an assembler. Thus, software, firmware and even hardware designers and developers all have to master assembly language.

But why should a user who is not a professional programmer or a computer designer use assembly language? There are three very good reasons:

1. To use hardware features that are not supported by other software or to use hardware in a non-standard way.

2. To use program products for which there is no interface to a certain system, eg. using C++ or BASIC libraries in Clipper programs.

3. To make high-level language programs run faster and take up less memory.

This is not an exhaustive list of the potential uses of assembly language. However, you can be sure that every programmer will come across one of them eventually.

There are of course some fanatics that consider assembly language the only language worth using at all. Such people regard all other languages as unnecessarily parasitic intermediates between programmer and computer. We don't anticipate that you are one of those, but we are certain that a thorough knowledge of assembler, and through that of your computer itself, will make you a better programmer no matter what language you are using.

Assembly language can make your programs efficient, flexible, and fast - that is make them as perfect as possible. And you will never regret that you started to learn assembly language, because above all it's incredibly interesting.

What You Need to Use This Book

First of all you need an IBM compatible PC. Throughout the book we have deliberately covered what we regard as the most common standards, so you can get by using an 8086 machine with an EGA display and a small hard disk. Although we will mention 386/486 machines and VGA displays etc, every program in the library will run on the minimum configuration.

You will also need appropriate software - i.e. MS-DOS (or another compatible operating system, for example DR-DOS, OS/2), MASM 6.0 or higher and CodeView.

The Structure of the Book

The first part of the book (Chapters One to Five) is an introductory tutorial to MASM and assembly language, and is designed to be read as a whole. It begins with a brief introduction to PCs, MS DOS, assembly language and MASM itself. In reading this you will get acquainted with the most important DOS components, and become familiar with MS Assembler, Linker, Debugger and MS Library Manager. Those readers not comfortable with binary and hexadecimal arithmetic should read Appendix A, which gives a quick tour of the key concepts.

This first part also describes the process of creating a program step by step, from deciding what the program must do up to the moment when the program is ready to use. Memory organization and data addressing methods are covered, as well as using various techniques for controlling program flow.

By the end of Chapter Five you will be like a carpenter with a full bag of tools, ready to move on from learning how to use a hammer, to how to design and build your own furniture. The second part of the book (Chapters Six to Twelve) is about what you can do with assembly language.

It starts by covering the basic concepts of BIOS and DOS services, and how they enable you to control your PC hardware and software effectively. We also look into the system data fields and find out how they relate to the operation of the machine.

In separate chapters we learn to control the keyboard, disks and video as well as other hardware elements such as the mouse. We have covered TSR programming in a chapter on its own, recognizing this as one of the most exciting applications of assembly language. Finally we provide a guide to interfacing your assembly language programs with high-level languages such as C, Pascal and BASIC.

The third part, the Reference Section contains the description of the most often used BIOS and DOS services, machine instructions, ASCII codes and keyboard scan codes.

How to Use the Book

This book is intended to be used as both a tutorial and a reference. Each chapter is broken into three separate sections

Fundamental Knowledge

Gives you the background required to make sense of the subject. It explains how the machine itself works, and what that means for you, the programmer. You can read this section without turning your machine on if you want to get the lay of the land.

Tools

In this section all the instructions, directives and system functions that are available to accomplish the task in hand are reviewed. The emphasis here is on practical techniques that can be used in your own programs. You will often refer back to this section.

Library

Here we have tried to incorporate into useful programs as many of the techniques and ideas discussed in the chapter as possible. We have struggled to make every program valuable in its own right. The source and executable code of every example is on the program disk.

We recommend that you begin by working through Chapters One to Five to get a good grounding in assembly language. Then, depending on your area of interest, work your way through Chapters Six to Twelve. By the end of the book you will be able to accomplish most tasks thanks to your understanding of assembly language and the library of programs you have assembled along the way.

Installing the Disk

The disk with this book has two parts:

▲ The Revolutionary Tutorial Program
▲ The source code for the programs in the book

You install each part separately. The tutorial program is installed into a directory called **ASMTUTOR** and the source code is installed into a directory called **ASMCODE**.

The files are compressed. To decompress the source code onto your C: drive, type **A:ASMCODE** at the C:\> prompt and press <ENTER>. To decompress the Tutorial Program onto your C: drive, type **A:ASMTUTOR** at the C:\> prompt and press <ENTER>.

To summarize, the two files can be installed onto the C: drive as follows:

      C:\>**A:ASMCODE**<ENTER>
      C:\>**A:ASMTUTOR**<ENTER>

The Tutorial Program

To run this tutorial you will need an EGA/VGA monitor. First you should install your mouse if you have one. Then go into the **ASMTUTOR** directory by typing **CD \ASMTUTOR** at the C:\> prompt. Type **ASMTUTOR** and the program will start.

In summary, start the program as follows:

      C:\>**CD \ASMTUTOR**
      C:\ASMTUTOR>**ASMTUTOR**

The tutorial has an opening menu which lists the topics covered. At the bottom of the screen is the menu selection for using the mouse. Once in a topic, information on that topic is displayed on the screen. If you move around the screen you will see subjects highlighted in green. These have further information which you can view by clicking with the mouse or pressing RETURN. To exit from the program click on ESCAPE or press ESC.

Function	Action	
	With Mouse	Without Mouse
Scroll up/down the screen	Scroll bar	Cursor keys
Move page up	Click PG UP	PgUp
Move page down	Click PG DN	PgDn
Move to a green highlight	Move Mouse	TAB (forwards)
		SHIFT-TAB (back)
Select a topic/subject	Click	ENTER
Go to next topic (chapter)	Click NEXT	END
Go to previous topic (chapter)	Click BACK	BACKSPACE
Go back to main menu	Click MAIN	HOME
Exit to DOS	Click ESCAPE	ESC

The Structure and Usage of the Source Code

The source code for the programs in the book will be installed into the following directories:

Chapt1-5

Source and executable modules of programs included in Chapters One to Five, BAT-files and an auxiliary program VIEW.EXE used in BAT-files for viewing assembler listings.

Chapt6

Examples for Chapter Six "Using BIOS and DOS", the program for determining the location of primary handlers for all interrupts.

Chapt7

Examples for Chapter Seven "Using the Keyboard", the keyboard buffer extender, several versions of a program determining scan and ASCII codes for all keys on the standard and enhanced keyboard.

Chapt8

Examples for Chapter Eight "Using Video", demo programs for controlling video in text and graphics modes.

Chapt9

Examples for Chapter Nine "Using Disks", service programs for reading/modifying sectors on floppy and hard disks, a utility for reading/assigning the disk label which allows you to use all ASCII characters in disk labels.

Chapt10

Examples for Chapter Ten "Controlling the Hardware", demo programs for working with the mouse, the program for determining the keyboard scan codes using the low-level technique of controlling hardware.

Chapt11

Examples for Chapter Eleven "Writing TSRs", the full version of the screen blanker described in this chapter, the resident program for controlling the process of copying information onto floppy disks.

Chapt12
   Examples for Chapter Twelve "Interfacing with High-level
   Languages", object libraries for usage with the MS C/C++, Turbo
   C, Turbo C++ and Borland C++ programs.

If you want to use the BAT-file from the disk for compiling your
assembler programs, you need to copy these BAT-files into the directory
included in the PATH command in your AUTOEXEC.BAT file.

CHAPTER 1

The Assembler
Environment

In this chapter we will introduce the basic ideas behind assembly language, and how it relates to your system. We also will examine the tools of the trade for the assembly language programmer and how to get the best out of them. Finally, we will show you some DOS batch files that will make the process of creating a finished program easier.

If you are completely new to assembly language and do not have much experience with the lower-levels of your PC, then some of the material here may be heavy going. Don't worry! We have deliberately put all this information together as you will often refer back to it as you become more experienced. What may not be completely clear now will fall into place as you get more hands-on experience. For now, think of it as a quick tour round the factory.

Fundamental Knowledge

Assembler as a Programming Language

Assembly Language was arguably the precursor of all programming languages because it was the first tool which relieved programmers from dealing with zeros and ones, and enabled them to use meaningful names for instructions and operands. In fact, the first Assembler was simply a system for representing machine instructions with simple mnemonics. Its main advantage was in automatically assigning values to instruction addresses. This meant that you no longer had to change all your jump commands after inserting one byte of data or an instruction into the program!

Since one statement of an assembly language generated one instruction or one element of data, assembly language was known as a *one to one level* language.

The next stage was the development of more compact languages in which a sequence of machine instructions could be represented by one statement. An example of this is any macro language - it allows programmers to use standard instruction sequences known as macrocommands, and even to define their own sequences and store them for further use.

These languages were defined as *one to many level*, and were sometimes known as macrogenerators (this is not strictly correct; more recent macrogenerators can usually pass information between macrocommands, and sometimes more than one line of source text generates part of the resulting code). Their popularity lasted quite a long time, and in fact they are still sometimes used as elements of more complex languages. For example, Assembler/370 for IBM mainframes and many assemblers for IBM-compatible PCs, such as MASM, have a built-in macrogenerator.

The languages most widely used today are *many to many* level. This means that several statements of source code produce several machine instructions. So for example, the following simple Pascal statement

```
a := b + c(i)
```

cannot be translated into machine code without knowing additional information about a, b, c and i. To pass this information to the compiler you would write something like:

```
Var a, b : real;
    i: integer;
    c: array[1..10] of real;
```

You may well ask where modern assembly language fits into all this: the answer for PC assembly language might seem surprising - all three levels!

The PC's Assembler is:

▲ A **one-to-one** level language because it includes a symbolic denotation for each machine instruction and allows you to define any data.

▲ A **one-to-many level** language because it has a built-in macrogenerator which allows you to create statements that produce several machine instructions.

▲ A **many-to-many** level language because later versions such as MASM 6.0 include new features such as IF-THEN-ELSE or DO-WHILE constructions which are common to high-level languages such as C or Pascal.

Machine Code and Assembly Language

A program is a sequence of commands (instructions) that the computer performs one by one. The execution of each individual command is completed in four steps, namely:

1. Getting the instruction from the memory
2. Decoding the instruction
3. Executing the instruction
4. Proceeding to the next instruction

Every instruction in the program is represented in memory as a sequence of ones and zeros. So the instruction which moves 0 to the register BX looks like

```
1011 1011 0000 0000 0000 0000
```

Obviously it's not that easy to write (or read) programs in this form. Assembly language solves the problem by having a **mnemonic** to represent each microprocessor instruction, with other symbols to represent its registers. Hence the machine instruction given above would look like this in assembly language:

```
    MOV   BX,0
```

It's certainly an improvement.

Each line of machine code corresponds to a line of assembly language written using mnemonics. Of course, nobody (other than a small minority of so-called hackers) converts machine code programs into assembly language programs. Actually, quite the opposite is true. Typically, programs written in assembly language are translated into machine code, but thankfully not by hand.

In fact, this one-to-one correspondence is not strictly true. Certain lines (directives) in assembly language do not have corresponding instructions in the assembled machine code program. These directives are used to show HOW the assembly language program should be translated. Besides, different machine code instructions may correspond to one and the same assembly language mnemonic instruction executed in different situations.

Nevertheless assembly language gives full control over each instruction of machine code program.

Assembler as a Software Component

As a programming language, Assembler provides more complete access to the system's resources than any other language. How important these features are to a given task determines whether you use Assembler as a separate programming language, or employ its unique capabilities in components of programs written in other programming languages.

We are by no means suggesting that you abandon all other programming languages immediately and write all your programs solely in assembly language. This obviously isn't the quickest way of creating software, although it does produce the leanest and fastest programs. The most realistic approach is to just write parts of your program in Assembler and combine it all using a linker. Which parts of a program should be written in Assembler depends on your overall objectives, but there are some common reasons for writing certain modules in Assembler which you can use as a guide:

▲ It can give access to system resources which are not directly available through your chosen programming language; for example, Clipper doesn't provide direct access to the video memory or extended memory.

▲ If you want to access DOS and BIOS services but your programming language doesn't include corresponding built-in or library functions.

▲ If you need your program to run at the highest speed possible using the most efficient instructions for memory and register access.

Assembly components can also be employed without using special software such as MASM or TASM. Many high-level languages now have a built-in Assembler which allows you to insert Assembler code directly into your program, known as in-line assembly. In this book we'll give practical examples of both ways of using assemblers.

Creating Programs at a Glance

The process of creating a program starts with building a sequence of statements known as the **source code**. The text file containing the source code is referred to as the source module. The source code can be written in any programming language such as Assembler, Pascal, BASIC or C.

A working computer program is a sequence of elements which can be interpreted and executed by a processor. Since the purpose of a computer program is to execute your code, this form of the program is called **executable code**. The file containing the executable code of a program is referred to as an executable module.

Turning source code into executable code consists of the following stages, shown in Figure 1.1.

Creating the source module
Creating one or more object modules from the source module
Linking object modules into one executable module

Once the executable module has been built, it can be run directly, or under the control of a debugger.

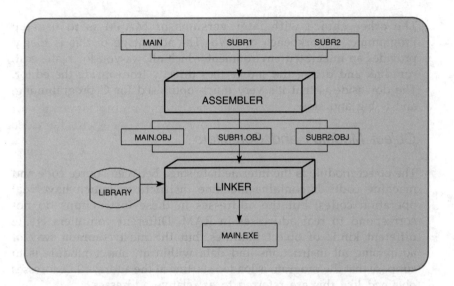

Figure 1.1
**Creating An
Executable
Module**

At least, that's the theory! In practice, the different stages are not always completed in that order, and some are missed out altogether. For example, some BASIC or xBASE systems do not build an executable module. Instead, they transform statements, of a program into an executable form and immediately perform one by one. Although this approach means you can keep the interpreter small, simple and fast, it decreases program execution speed. Having said that, all assembly language programs are compiled into executable code via object modules.

Source Code and Text Editors

We'll start by looking at the **source module**. This is a file that contains the program text in assembly language. You can create this file using either a text editor or a word-processor. The text editor program does quite a simple job - it reads text, inserts, deletes or replaces lines, searches and replaces symbols and so on. A classic example of this is the MS-DOS 5 editor EDIT.

If you're already used to a particular text editor or word processor, then stick with that. However, there are a few potential problems you need to watch out for. If you use a word processor like WordStar or WordPerfect you must save your Assembler programs as DOS text files, without formatting them, otherwise it will insert special formatting codes into the text which Assembler does not understand.

The other choice with later versions of MASM is to use the Programmer's Workbench or PWB. The advantage of this is that it provides an integrated environment which allows you to create, edit, run, link and debug the source files directly from inside the editor. The downside is that it's very much optimised for C programming, and is big and slow.

Object Modules and Compilers

The object module is the intermediate stage between source code and machine code. It contains machine instructions which have real operation codes, but the addresses in these instructions do not correspond to real addresses in RAM. Different compilers create different kinds of object modules, but the most common way of addressing all instructions and data within an object module is to suppose that the program is loaded starting at the address 0. Addresses obtained like this are referred to as relative addresses.

Before running, relative addresses must be replaced with real addresses which are determined by the location of the program in the memory. This task is performed by the link editor, covered later in this chapter.

An object module usually corresponds to one program unit - either the main program or a subroutine. If your program does not call any other routines, a single module can simply be converted into executable form, and run. If your program does call other routines though, you have to find them and combine them together.

The Relationship Between Modules in a Program

There is usually a clear distinction between the main program and any sub-programs, although the same unit can sometimes be used for both purposes. They are defined as:

▲ Main program - a module that can be called by the operating system; for example, all external MS-DOS commands such as FORMAT, EDIT or DISKCOPY are main programs.

▲ Sub-program - a module which can be called by another module; for example, the function SIN included in the library of most compilers.

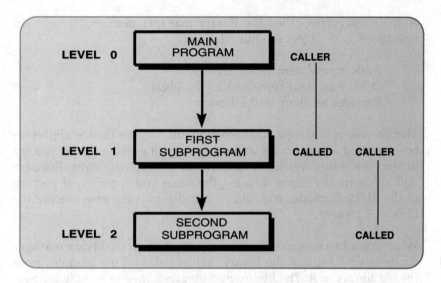

Figure 1.2
**Relations
Between
Program Units**

We will also use the terms **caller** (calling module) and **called** sub-program. If you look at Figure 1.2 you'll see that it shows the relationship between the three program units: Main Program, First Subprogram and Second Subprogram .

When writing relatively large programs you will need to combine several program units. There are often hundreds (or even thousands) of units of this type. The process of uniting modules is made easier by creating libraries which contain a set of object modules. You then only need to deal with the library when creating the executable modules.

Object Libraries and Library Managing

If you are already using a high-level language system such as C, BASIC, Pascal or FORTRAN, look at the files included in that system. Some of them will probably have an extension .LIB which denotes object module libraries. If you don't have these files, don't worry. There are different kinds of libraries which, although similar in purpose, have different structures and naming conventions. For example, libraries created by Turbo Pascal are stored as files with the extension .TPU, and dynamic libraries used in Windows and OS/2 have the extension .DLL. We will cover those libraries which are used in Microsoft compilers (C/C++, Pascal and FORTRAN) and can be processed by other systems such as Turbo Assembler, Turbo C/C++ or Clipper.

A special program called the **library manager** performs three main operations with object module libraries:

> Adds a new item to the library
> Deletes an item contained in the library
> Replaces an item in the library

The process of adding a new object module to the library applies to both creating a new library and expanding an existing one. If you try to process a library which does not actually exist yet, the library manager will automatically create it, using the name you specified. If you are in the dialogue mode, you will be asked for confirmation before the library is created.

When you add a new module to an existing library, the library manager creates a new copy of the library and includes all the modules from the old library in it. The library manager then tries to include the new module in this newly created library by first checking whether a module with the same name is already present. If it is, the library manager outputs an error message and exits, otherwise it includes the new module in the new copy of the library. It then changes the extensions in the names of the new and old libraries: the old library gets the extension .BAK and the new one - the original name of the library.

A new library is also created when you remove an object module from a library. In this case, the library manager copies all modules, except the module which has to be deleted, into this new library. The new library and the original are then renamed in the way described above.

Executable Modules and Link Editors

The process of creating an executable program is performed by a special utility called the **link editor** or **linker**. Most early MS-DOS systems contained a simple free version of this utility, LINK.EXE, and you'll meet more powerful versions of it in programming systems such as C, Pascal or Assembler. We'll cover the most common linkers in more detail later in this chapter, but for now we'll concentrate on the more general functions of the linker by looking at what it does and how to use it.

You can probably guess the two main purposes of the linker from its name - *link editor*. First it *links*, which means that it connects several program units (possibly written in different languages) into one executable program. Second it *edits*, which involves changing the representation of the program. Let's look at these functions more closely.

The link editor reads two different kinds of input data - object modules and object libraries. If it cannot find an input module, the editor stops working and outputs a critical error message. The object module itself contains three main types of information - the program code, entry point labels and external references:

▲ **Program code** contains a special representation of machine instructions and data, which is an intermediate form between source code and machine code as it is presented in the memory. It also includes information about program segments, their types and location.

▲ **Program entry points** (or simply entries) are labels which can be used by other modules to call this module. Each module has an entry point which corresponds to its first executable instruction, and has the same name as the module.

▲ **External references** define the modules which can themselves be called from this module. They correspond to library procedures and functions or to other modules of the program which were compiled separately and possibly written in other languages.

The object module can also contain optional information about line numbers in the source program, internal variable names and other information, depending on compiler features and the compilation parameters.

The Linking Process

To create an executable module, the linker has to assign real addresses to all entries and external references. The first part is simple because the offsets of each entry from the program start are stored in the allocation table. The only requirement is that each entry must be defined only once. This means that each object module that you include in your program must have a different name. Note, however, that entries of a certain type, such as COMMON blocks in FORTRAN, can be mentioned in several object modules in one program, but the first occurrence is taken to be the definitive one.

The process of finding the relevant entry for each external reference is more complex. This process, known as resolving external references is complete only when all of the external references have a corresponding entry. When the linker finds an external reference, it first of all looks for the corresponding entry in any list of object modules entered at the command line. If this process fails, the linker searches the specified libraries. If a corresponding entry is still not found, the linker reports an error. When this happens some linkers abandon the process of creating an executable module, while others create a module with an unresolved external reference. Even in cases where such a module is created, you should think twice before running it because the results are unpredictable. If the unresolved external reference corresponds to a procedure or function that is called, control will be passed to the memory area which contains instructions or data belonging to the previously executed program. If the unresolved reference corresponds to common data, your program will use data that has not been initialized.

When the process of resolving external references is complete, the linker combines all object modules into one module which uses a common address counter.

Two Kinds of Executable Modules

When the linker has successfully finished its work, you are left with an executable module. If you look at your DOS directory you will see modules with the extensions .COM and .EXE. Although they look different, these are both executable modules. DOS treats all modules with .COM and .EXE extensions as executable, but distinguishes between them not by their file extensions, but by using a special signature present in the EXE-module. Modules without this signature are treated as COM-modules. This means that DOS will still process a module correctly even if you assign the extension .COM to an EXE-module.

COM-modules are the simplest kind of executable modules owing to the fact that their structure is inherited from CP/M an operating system which is the predecessor of MS-DOS. These programs are literally "ready to use" and contain the exact image of the memory area occupied by a program. The only disadvantage for their usage is that they cannot occupy more than 64K of memory.

EXE-programs require an additional job from an operating system in order to run them. They begin with a special header containing information about memory allocation for the program and have to be re-distributed before they are run. We will take a more detailed look at the structure and purpose of executable programs of both types in Chapter Three.

Loading Programs and System Blocks

In order to execute a program, DOS starts by allocating the Memory Control Block - MCB. The most important information it contains is the size and start address of the memory allocated to the program. The MCB block is undocumented in standard DOS, but is worth knowing about to help understand memory allocation and usage in general. Figure 1.3 shows a program and its control blocks loaded into the memory. In this diagram the letter n denotes the address in memory that DOS has chosen as the start address of our program. This will almost always be different every time the program is loaded.

The system information for the program is located in a special memory block called the PSP - Program Segment Prefix. This block usually (in fact always for COM-programs) precedes the memory allocated to the program itself. The PSP block contains information which DOS passes to the program. Later in this chapter we'll give you a table that details the contents of this block.

In order to understand how these system blocks are addressed by the processor, we need to take a quick tour around the system architecture, and in particular the registers.

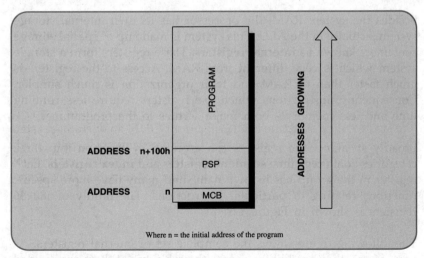

Where n = the initial address of the program

Figure 1.3
**A Program and
Corresponding
System Block
in Memory**

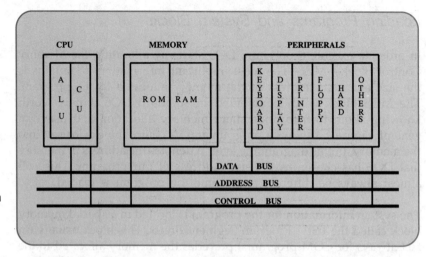

Figure 1.4
Block Diagram of the Computer

The Processor and its Internal Registers

A microprocessor performs two main functions: it processes information stored in RAM, and controls external devices such as the keyboard, screen, disks and other peripherals. It has two main units which enable it to do this: the Arithmetic Logical Unit (ALU) and a Control Unit (CU).

Besides the system RAM, the processor has its own internal storage system, actually in the ALU. This system is made up of special storage containers known as **internal registers**. These registers form a storage system which is very different from RAM. Access to the registers is much faster than to RAM and their organization is much simpler. Consequently, instructions which use registers require less running time and less memory - both major virtues to the programmer.

Broadly speaking, the registers can grouped by function into three categories : **data registers**, **segment registers** and **index registers**. Each register in the group has its own name and many have more specific functions relating to particular instructions. The family of i80x86 registers is shown in Figure 1.5

The following figure shows the complete set of internal registers. As you can see, they are 16-bits wide, although some of them are divided into two 8-bit registers.

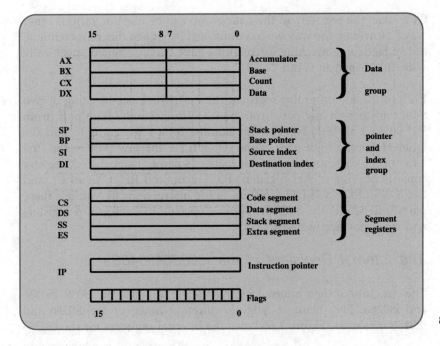

Figure 1.5
Internal Registers of 8086/88, 80286

Data Group Registers

For the time being we will only look in detail at the data group registers - we will cover the others in the next chapter in our first programs.

The main purpose of registers AX, BX, CX, DX is to contain the initial data for, and the results of, arithmetic or logical instructions. By convention, each has a primary usage:

▲ **Accumulator** AX is the best general purpose storage for the data used by the current operation.

▲ **Base** BX is most commonly used to point to certain data arrays used by the program.

▲ **Count** CX is frequently used as a counter to organize cycles.

▲ **Data** DX is used to store information about the peripherals while input/output instructions are being performed, or to record components of data in multiplication and division.

Of course, the registers in the data group can be used in various other ways. However, the way we have outlined is not just the most common, but in fact some machine instructions have been designed specifically with this usage in mind.

Each of these data group registers can be treated as consisting of two 8-bit registers - a low part (from bit 0 to 7th bit) and a high part (from 8th bit to 15th bit). The rule for naming 8-bit registers is to add the letter **H** for the high part or the letter **L** for the low part to the first letter of the corresponding 16-bit register's name. Thus, the AX register consists of AL and AH registers, BX - of BL and BH, CX - of CL and CH, DX - of DL and DH registers. Some instructions let you use these parts independently. This property is specific to data group registers and does not apply elsewhere.

The Internal Registers of the i80386/i80486

The structure of their internal registers is the same for the i8088, i80186 and i80286. The picture is slightly different however for i80386 and i80486 machines. Figure 1.6 shows the internal registers for the i80386

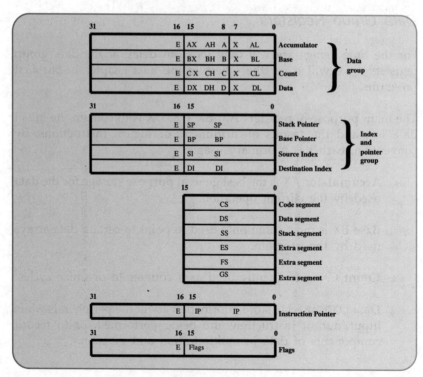

Figure 1.6
Internal Registers of i80386 / i80486

and i80486. Registers AX, BX, CX, DX can be accessed either as a single 16-bit register or as two 8-bit registers. However, in these processors, each of the 16-bit registers AX, BX, CX, DX has a further 16-bit extension. These extended 32-bit registers EAX, EBX, ECX, EDX (E here means Extended) can be used for manipulating 32-bit data.

The Program Segment Prefix - PSP

The actual code of a program is loaded into memory immediately after a special system block - the PSP. Figure 1.7 shows an example of typical memory distribution for programs loaded. The word *prefix* in the title Program Segment Prefix refers to the fact that operating systems like CP/M and earlier versions of MS-DOS put this control block just before the program. In more current versions, MS-DOS can keep the program itself separate from the control information, but in most cases PSP is still the *prefix* of the program.

There are basically two types of memory distribution and initial register settings, those for -COM and those for -EXE modules. The difference between these two is minimal really, especially when an -EXE program is located within one physical segment (64K bytes). The only significant difference in this instance is that when a -COM module is loaded, all segment registers point to the start of the PSP, while for an -EXE module, the CS register points to the start of the code segment. The contents of the segment registers for the simplest type of -EXE and -COM modules is shown in Figure 1.7.

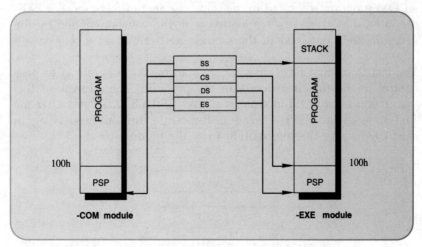

Figure 1.7
-EXE and -COM Module Loaded

Offset	Meaning
00h	The instruction INT20h for exit to DOS; can be used for finishing a program by passing control here; often is considered as PSP signature (hex codes 0CDh 20h)
0Ah	The full address of the exit routine address (the address of the system routine which will gain control when the program finishes)
2Ch	Segment address of the block containing the copy of the environment area (environment variables created by the DOS command SET)
5Ch	FCB blocks for two files passed as parameters; can be used as work area
80h	The length of the parameters passed in the command line (the command tail)
81h	The text of the parameters in the command line

Table 1.1
The Most Frequently used Fields of the PSP

Table 1.1 details the meaning of the most important fields in PSP.

The main code of a program is usually located immediately after the PSP, which occupies 100h bytes (256 in the decimal system). DOS sets up the DS and ES registers to point to the beginning of the PSP for all modules. When DOS passes control to the COM-module, it sets the CS and SS registers to the start of the PSP as well, as every part of a COM program is located in the same segment of memory. For EXE-modules, these registers are loaded with the values assigned by the program and contained in the module header.

The last thing that DOS does before starting the program is to pass control to the first instruction in the program. The address of this instruction for a COM-module is always CS:100h (256 bytes after the first byte of the PSP). For an EXE-module, this address is again calculated using the information from the module header.

Tools

Compiling Programs

The two most frequently used assemblers are MASM (**M**acro **AS**se**M**bler) from Microsoft and TASM (Turbo **AS**se**M**bler) from Borland. Although they look different, they actually share many features, so we'll consider them together. The name of the main TASM module is, of course, TASM. The name for MASM in versions before 6.0 is MASM; in version 6.0 and 6.1 it's ML. MASM version 6.0 does however contain a module called MASM for compatibility with the earlier versions.

To start the assembler, type its name then the names of the source module, object module and file for listing. If the name of the object module and listing are not defined, Assembler uses the default names for these files. By default, Assembler gives an object file the same name that the source file had but changes its extension from .ASM to .OBJ. No listing file is generated. For example, the command line

```
masm myprog
```

has the same effect as the line

```
masm myprog.asm,myprog.obj,nul.lst
```

The most important parameters of the Microsoft Macro Assembler (MASM) version 6.0 are detailed in Table 1.2, MASM version 5.1 - in Table 1.3 and Borland Turbo Assembler - in Table 1.4.

Value	Meaning
AT	Enables tiny memory model needed for building .COM files
c	Compile only, not to call a linker (create object module
Cp	Preserve case of identifiers (useful for linking with C programs)
Cu	Convert all identifiers to upper case
Cx	Preserve case of identifiers declared as PUBLIC and EXTRN

Table 1.2
Parameters of MASM 6.0

Fe\<file\>	Create the executable file and write it as FILE.EXE
Fl[file]	Create the listing and write it as FILE.LST
Fo\<file\>	Create the object module and write it as FILE.OBJ
Fpi	Generate code for i80x87 instruction emulation
G\<c|d\>	Generate procedures call according to C or Pascal conventions
Gz	Generate procedures call according to STDCALL conventions (MASM 6.1 only)
I\<path\>	Use the additional path for INCLUDE directives
Sp\<n\>	Set the page length to *n* lines
Sc	Display timings in listing (MASM 6.1 only)
X	Do not use the value of INCLUDE environment variable
Zd	Include line numbers in the object module for debugging
Zi	Include in the object module the full information for debugger
Zm	Provide the compatibility with MASM 5.10
Zs	Perform syntax checking without building an object module

Table 1.2 (Continued)
Parameters of MASM 6.0

Value	Meaning
I\<path\>	Use the additional path for INCLUDE directives
l	Generate the listing of source and object code
Ml	Preserve case of identifiers (useful for linking with C programs)
Mx	Preserve case of global identifiers
Mu	Convert global identifiers to upper case
w*n*	Output messages for error level *n*: 0-none, 1-serious, 2-warnings
z	Include line numbers in error messages
Zi	Include in the object module the full information for debugger
Zd	Include line numbers in the object module for debugging

Table 1.3
Parameters of MASM 5.1

Besides the parameters listed in Table 1.2, MASM 6.0 can pass parameters to the linker called from within MASM directly. These parameters have to be typed in the command line after the keyword /link, for example:

```
ml mod.asm /link /exepack
```

Value	Meaning
I<path>	Use the additional path for INCLUDE directives
l	Generate listing
la	Generate expanded listing
ml	Preserve case of identifiers (useful for linking with C programs)
mu	Convert all identifiers to upper case
mx	Preserve case of global identifiers
mn	Perform up to n passes for forward references resolving
w-	Disable all warnings
w+	Enable warnings
wn	Set warning level to n; $n=0$ - none, $n=1$ or $n=2$-all
z	Include line numbers in error messages
Zd	Include line numbers in the object module for debugging
Zi	Include in the object module the full information for debugger

Table 1.4
Parameters of Turbo Assembler

In this example, MASM creates the object module then calls the linker, passing the parameter *exepack* to it. This has the same effect as the command line:

```
link mod.obj /exepack
```

We'll explain what exepack does along with rest of the parameters for LINK.

Managing Libraries

Every assembler programming system comes with a library manager: the Microsoft Library Manager (LIB) for MASM and the Borland Turbo Librarian (TLIB) for TASM. Although the object modules created by MASM and TASM are compatible, there are some structural differences, mostly connected with debugging. The structure of the libraries used by MASM and TASM is fortunately the same, so in most cases the library managers are interchangeable.

Value	Meaning
IGNORECASE	Don't distinguish case on names
NOEXTDICTIONARY	Don't create extended dictionaries
NOIGNORECASE	Distinguish case on names
PAGESIZE:n	Use the library block size n bytes

The parameters of the Microsoft Library Manager are detailed in Table 1.5. Borland Turbo Librarian has only two parameters:

/C which forces TLIB to service the case-sensitive library, and
/E which causes the creation of an extended dictionary.

Both Microsoft Librarian and Turbo Librarian can execute the same set of commands given in Table 1.6.

Creating Executable Modules

Like library managers, a linker is included in each Assembler programming system. Thus, MASM includes the Microsoft Overlay Linker called LINK, TASM - the Borland Turbo Linker TLINK. The functions performed by these programs and the rules for calling them are practically the same. The basic parameters of the Microsoft Linker are detailed in Table 1.7, the parameters of TLINK - in Table 1.8.

In Table 1.7, the uppercase characters show the minimum abbreviation which LINK will recognise. For example, parameters "/co", "/code" and "codeview" are all valid and carry the same meaning: prepare an executable module for debugging with CodeView.

Table 1.6
Commands Executed by Library Managers

Command	Meaning
+name	Add object module to the library
-name	Delete object module from the library
-+name	Replace object module contained in the library
*name	Extract object module from the library into separate file
-*name	Extract object module and delete it from the library

Value	Meaning
Codeview	Prepare an executable module for debugging
Exepack	Reduce the size of module by packing repeated bytes
Farcalltranslation	Optimize FAR calls within the segment
Map	Generate MAP file
NODefaultlibrarysearch	Don't search libraries named in object modules
NOIgnorecase	Preserve case in identifiers
PACKCode	Group code segments with the same attributes
PACKData	Group data segments with the same attributes
Stack	Change the size of the stack from the default
Tiny	Create a COM-module instead of EXE-module

Table 1.7
Parameters of Microsoft Linker

Value	Meaning
m	Generate map file
x	Don't generate map file
l	Include source line numbers into an executable module
n	Don't search libraries named in object modules
d	Output warning when duplicate entries found in libraries
c	Preserve case in identifiers
v	Include full information for debugger
t	Create a ACOM-module instead of EXE-module

Table 1.8
Parameters of Turbo Linker

TLINK parameters are denoted by their first character and are passed through the command line. The order of parameters is the same for both LINK and TLINK. For example, the following command line will generate the executable module PROG from object modules MOD1 and MOD2:

```
link mod1+mod2,prog
```

Note that you do not need to type the extensions .OBJ and .EXE. To produce the COM-module using Turbo Linker, type the parameter /t in the command line:

```
tlink com-mod /t
```

The following command line illustrates preparing the executable module for debugging with CodeView:

```
link deb-mod /co
```

Output from the Assembler

By now you are familiar with the main files that an assembler system deals with:

Source texts - files with the extension .ASM
Object modules - files with the extension .OBJ
Executable modules - files with the extension .EXE or .COM

In addition to the files listed above, an assembler can generate other files which contain information that you should really know about. Figure 1.8 shows the full set of files produced by MASM 6.0. Most of these are also generated by other assembler systems such as TASM.

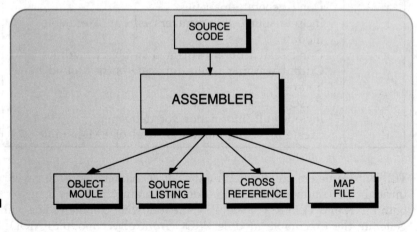

Figure 1.8
Files Generated by Assembler

Source Listing - The .LST File

It doesn't take much to work out that the source listing contains the text of the source program. As you'll see in a moment, it also contains additional information which can be useful for debugging assembler programs. The content of source listing generated by MASM 6.0 for the program given in Listing 1.1 is shown below:

```
.model  tiny
.stack
.data
Msg     db  'This is a very simple'
        db  'program',0Ah,0Dh,'$'
.code
.startup
Begin:  mov  ah,09
        lea  dx,Msg
        int  21h

Finish: mov  ax,4C00h
        int  21h
        end
```

Listing 1.1 An Example of a MASM Program

```
Microsoft (R) Macro Assembler Version 6.00      02/06/93 11:15:09
simobj.asm                                      Page 1 - 1


                     .model            tiny
                     .stack
0000                 .data
0000 54 68 69 73 20 69        Msg      db 'This is a very simple
                                       db 'program...',0Ah,0Dh,'$'
     73 20 61 20 76 65
     72 79 20 73 69 6D
     70 6C 65 20 70 72
     6F 67 72 61 6D 2E
     2E 0A 0D 24
0000                 .code
                     .startup
0100                 *@Startup:
0100 B4 09     Begin:           mov ah,09
0102 BA 0000 R  lea             dx,Msg
0105 CD 21                      int      21h

0107 B8 4C00   Finish:          mov ax,4C00h
010A CD 21                      int      21h
                                end


Microsoft (R) Macro Assembler Version 6.00      02/06/93 11:15:09
simobj.asm                         Symbols 2 - 1
```

```
Segments and Groups:

Name                        Size   Length Align Combine Class

DGROUP . . . . . . . . . . . . GROUP
_TEXT  . . . . . . . . . . . . 16 Bit  010C  Word  Public  'CODE'
_DATA  . . . . . . . . . . . . 16 Bit  0023  Word  Public  'DATA'
STACK  . . . . . . . . . . . . 16 Bit  0400  Para  Stack   'STACK'


Symbols:

Name                        Type    Value    Attr

@CodeSize . . . . . . . . . . .  Number  0000h
@DataSize . . . . . . . . . . .  Number  0000h
@Interface . . . . . . . . . .   Number  0000h
@Model . . . . . . . . . . . .   Number  0001h
@Startup . . . . . . . . . . .   L Near  0100        _TEXT
@code . . . . . . . . . . . . .  Text    DGROUP
@data . . . . . . . . . . . . .  Text    DGROUP
@fardata? . . . . . . . . . . .  Text    FAR_BSS
@fardata . . . . . . . . . . .   Text    FAR_DATA
@stack . . . . . . . . . . . .   Text    DGROUP
Begin . . . . . . . . . . . . .  L Near  0100        _TEXT
Finish . . . . . . . . . . . .   L Near  0107        _TEXT
Msg . . . . . . . . . . . . . .  Byte    0000        _DATA


   0 Warnings
   0 Errors
```

We'll now go over the main parts of this source listing.

The first part is the title, giving information about the assembler - its name, version and date of production.

The section following this is usually the largest. It contains source and object codes listed in two columns (bi-listing). It shows the object code created from the source program, line by line. Each instruction or data field is preceded by its address. All addresses in assembler listings are relative, that is, they only show the relative location of code and data in a program; the absolute addresses are assigned later by the linker. In certain situations however, the relative addresses can be the same as the absolute ones. This only happens if:

> The program contains only one module.
> The address of the first instruction is set by the PRG directive.

You can use this trick when creating special programs such as device drivers or TSRs.

Next comes information about groups and segments. Using the data in the column titled Length, you can estimate the size of the program. The column Align tells you which boundary the segment starts at (byte, word or paragraph) and the column Combine Class informs you how the segments in different modules will be united by the linker.

The Symbols section describes program objects such as labels and variables. It gives you the name of the object, as well as its location and type. For example, you can see that the label Begin has a relative address 100h and is a Near Label which means that within one physical segment, only references to this label are allowed.

Finally, the listing contains two lines which detail the number of errors and warnings found by Assembler while translating your program.

Debugging Programs Using CodeView

It is not unheard of to create a program that is free of syntax errors, works, and to the best of your knowledge outputs the right results. Do not immediately assume though that this is the happy ending you deserve. On the contrary, it is quite reasonable to expect that your program contains a bug (and sadly - not just one). If you have experience of high-level languages, you are probably familiar with the process of debugging. If this concept is new to you though - read on!

The only real way to debug a program is to find out what's going on inside it. You can do this either by following the execution of every instruction, or more efficiently by examining the critical parts of the program in detail, and letting the program run uninterrupted between these points.

MS-DOS has a built-in tool for debugging. It will probably not come as a great surprise to learn that this utility is called DEBUG. It includes practically all the features needed for effective debugging, letting you start your program and run it in the step-by-step mode. This means that you can watch the changes in the memory and registers content after each instruction. However, DEBUG has an obsolete command-line interface and is rarely used for large scale work now, although we will use it to explore the system later in the book.

MASM offers a powerful full-screen debugger called CodeView which is also used together with other Microsoft compilers such as C, Pascal and Basic. This debugger allows you to run the program in step-by step mode, set breakpoints and watch the effects on variables, registers and memory areas. In addition it has some advanced features which use special PC resources such as the coprocessor, extended memory and 386/486 instructions.

The Command CV - The CodeView Debugger

There are many versions of Codeview that run under MS-DOS, OS/2 and other operating systems. Each version differs slightly, but their main features are the same. Figure 1.9 shows the initial screen of CodeView 2.2 which comes with the Microsoft Macro Assembler 5.10. Figure 1.10 shows the initial screen of CodeView 3.14 which comes with the Microsoft Macro Assembler 6.0.

The finer details of the CodeView screen depend on which version you have and which windows you have chosen to view, but the essence is still the same. The screen consists of windows, each of which has its own name and purpose. We'll start with CodeView 2.2 that comes with the Microsoft Macro Assembler 5.10. The main screen of the CodeView debugger is divided into windows. A good place to start for debugging assembly language programs is with the following windows since they are the ones most commonly used:

    The source text window
    The registers' window
    The command window

We will now describe these in turn.

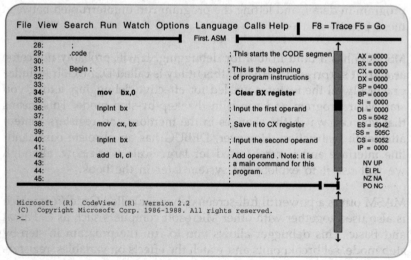

Figure 1.9
The Main Screen of CodeView

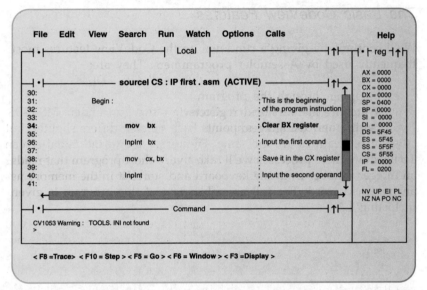

Figure 1.10
Main Screen of CodeVeiw 3.14

The **Source window** contains the text of your program in assembly language and the line numbers. When CodeView executes one command in your executable module, it highlights the corresponding line in your source code in the Source window. To execute one command, press the **F8** or **F10** key.

The **Register window** reflects the current state of the registers and flags. The registers are represented by name (AX, BX and so on) and their hexadecimal values. Flag values however have symbolic denotation (NZ, OV and so on). The Register window is situated on the right side of the screen. This window appears when you press the **F2** key and disappears if you press it again.

The **Command window** is intended for controlling the debugging process. The cursor is usually located in this window, indicating that you can type in commands.

If you were to suddenly find yourself in a strange room, what is the first thing that you would look for? The exit - of course! Since we share this feeling, the first Codeview command we'll explain is the **q** command, which means **Quit**. This command finishes the debugging process, and returns control to MS-DOS. The next most useful command is the **h** command, which means **Help**. Use this command to get online information about CodeView commands, parameters and features. These two commands are practically all you need to start working with CodeView.

The Basic CodeView Features

We'll continue by giving a rundown on the CodeView features most frequently used by Assembler programmers. They are:

Stepping through the program
Watching memory and registers
Setting and using breakpoints

To illustrate these processes we'll take a very short program that reads an integer number from the keyboard and stores it in the memory as an unsigned word. The full assembler text of this program is given in Listing 1.2

```
 1
 2 .model  small
 3 .stack
 4 .data
 5 UnsWord dw     0
 6 Hex     dw     16
 7 .code
 8 .startup
 9 NextCh:mov   ah,01      ; function 01h - keyboard input
10        int   21h        ; DOS service call
11        cmp   al,0        ; special character?
12        jne   NotSpec     ; if not - process character
13        int   21h        ; read code of special character
14        jmp   FinProg     ; finish program
15 NotSpec:cmp  al,'0'      ; compare character read to"0"(number?)
16        jb    FinProg     ; if not, don't process
17        cmp   al,'9'      ; compare character read to"9"(number?)
18        jb    ProcNum     ; if cypher - process
19        cmp   al,'A'      ; compare   to "A"(hex  number?)
20        jb    FinProg     ; if not, don't process
21        cmp   al,'F'      ; compare  to "F" (hex number?)
22        ja    FinProg     ; if not, don't process
23        sub   al,7        ; prepare characters A - F for converting
24 ProcNum:sub  al,30h      ; convert character to number
25        mov   bl,al       ; copy character read into BX
26        mov   ax,UnsWord  ; hex number into AX
27        mul   Hex         ; one hex position to the left
28        mov   UnsWord,ax  ; store result back into memory
29        add   UnsWord,bx  ; add current hex digit
30        jmp   NextCh      ; read next character
31 FinProg:mov ax,4C00h     ; function 4Ch - terminate process
32        int   21h        ; DOS service call
33        end
```

Listing 1.2 The RdNum Program

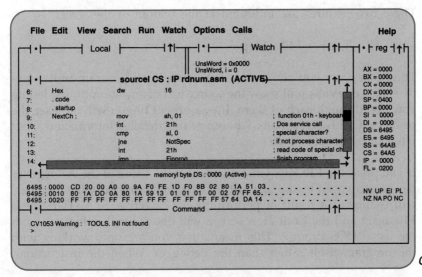

Figure 1.11
*Program RdNum
-The Initial
CodeView Screen*

Start by preparing this program for debugging by compiling, and linking it. Then, start the executable module obtained under the CodeView debugger.

On your disk are specially prepared batch files designed to make the assembly process easier. They are fully documented in the Library section of this chapter, but for the moment if you want to use the BAT-files from your program disk for this, type the following command lines:

```
asm RdNum /d <enter>
run
```

When the program is activated, you'll see the initial CodeView screen. The finer details depend on the intial CodeView mode you have set up, but it will be similar to Figure 1.11.

Now let's get on with the exciting process of hunting for bugs!

Stepping Through Programs

CodeView offers two approaches to stepping through the execution of a program - one examines each instruction including subroutine calls, the other only steps through the current program unit. The first of these is useful for debugging complex programs that have several subroutines, while the second is useful for analyzing how a particular program unit works.

These two features are indicated at the bottom of the screen:

F8 - Trace   F10 - Step.

The **F8** key lets you run every instruction in all program units step-by-step. CodeView will show the source text of any subroutines, letting you step through each of them. If you press **F10** you will only see the results of CALL instructions, without getting detailed information about what the subroutines do.

If you press the **F10** key, you will see that the value of the AX register has been changed by the first instruction of the program. Other registers will change as a result of performing the directive .STARTUP. Press **F10** again and the CodeView screen will disappear, leaving you with the usual DOS prompt. This means that you are now working with the program itself rather than the debugger. When the instruction

```
int 21h
```

is performed, CodeView passes control to the corresponding DOS service and the program continues to work in the usual way. When the I/O operation is finished, control is returned to the debugger and you can analyze the results of this operation. The instructions in lines 9 and 10 are designed to read a character from the keyboard. Each time the instruction in line 10 is performed, the character read appears in the AL register (in the register window on the right of the screen).

Watching Variables

Although the contents of the registers are very important for understanding what is going on within the program, often it is also necessary to know the current value of internal variables in a program. As an example, let's look at the program RdNum that converts a character string typed on the keyboard into a hexadecimal number stored in the variable UnsWord. Using CodeView, you can watch all the stages of this process. To see the current value of a variable, make the source window active (press the **F6** key until you can see that the cursor has moved into the source window). The scroller will also appear on the right side of this window. Next, move the cursor to the line that contains the name of the variable you want to watch and press Ctrl-W. A dialog box containing the name of the variable will appear on the screen. An example of the CodeView screen when the "Watch" dialog box is active is shown in Figure 1.12.

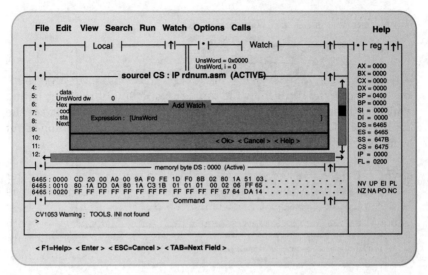

Figure 1.12
An Example of the " Watch " Dialog Box

If you press Ctrl-W when the Source Window is active, CodeView takes the text at the current cursor position as the name of the variable. Otherwise, you have to specify this name explicitly, typing it in the dialog box. The default form for displaying the value of a variable is hexadecimal, but Codeview can also use decimal, ASCII and so on. For example, pressing Ctrl-W and the name of the variable will let you watch the variable UnsWord in hexadecimal form. To make this value decimal, specify the name of the variable as

```
UnsWord,i
```

where *i* stands for integer.

Watching Local Variables - The Local Window

As you will see in later chapters, routines written in Assembler can use special variables. An example of this is using local variables which are allocated by Assembler when it meets the special directive LOCAL in a program. These variables are allocated within the stack on entry to a routine and deleted on return. Since it may be important for debugging a program, CodeView provides a special feature for watching these variables. When entering a procedure, CodeView shows the value of local variables allocated within this procedure in a special window entitled the Local Window. If a procedure being debugged calls another subroutine, the local variables of the subroutine are shown in this window. When control is returned to the calling procedure, the content of the Local Window goes back to reflecting the actual values of the local variables of the caller.

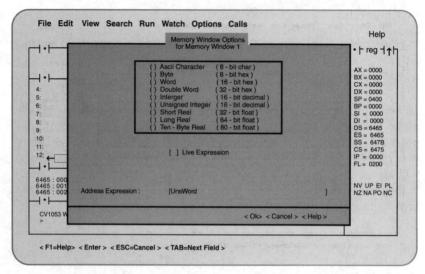

Figure 1.13
The Dialog Box for Memory Window Initialization

Using the Memory Window

Another way of examining the memory content is to use the Memory Window in CodeView. This window displays the current contents of a particular part of the memory in a specified format. Initially, the memory window displays the memory starting at the address contained in the DS register, i.e. the content of PSP. To display another part of the memory, you must specify its starting address in the special dialog box shown in Figure 1.13.

For example, to watch the changes in the memory area starting at the address which corresponds to the variable UnsWord, specify its name as shown in Figure 1.13.

The Memory Window is usually used for examining relatively large objects such as strings or arrays, while the Watch Window is fine for observing byte, integer, logical or character variables.

Using Breakpoints

Running programs in the step-by step mode lets you follow exactly how each instruction is executed. Naturally this takes a ridiculously long time on big programs, especially if they contain long cycles. Fortunately, CodeView debugger has a feature called BreakPoint which means you can select which parts of a program you want to consider in detail. When an instruction that you have singled out is performed, CodeView debugger halts program execution and waits for a command. This gives you time to decide what you want to do - output or change registers or variables, set or delete variables you want to check and so on.

To set a breakpoint, make the Source Window active by pressing **F6**, move the cursor to the line you want to mark as a breakpoint, and press **F9**. What happens next depends on the state of the line before you pressed F9. If the line was not marked previously, a breakpoint will be set and the line will be displayed on the screen, highlighted. If the line had already been marked, pressing F9 again disables the breakpoint.

Library

A Set of BAT-Files for Dealing with Assemblers

There are several assemblers (for example, MASM and TASM) which can be used for assembling programs. Similarly, object modules created by an assembler can be processed by several linkers. Furthermore, you can use a number of different debuggers which are either included in the assembler package (CodeView or Turbo Debugger) or sold separately, like Periscope. Although the parameters of different assemblers, linkers and debuggers do vary, they perform the same tasks - assembling, running and debugging process. This means that it is possible to create a tool that allows programmers to use different assemblers, in the same way.

Here are a set of batch files you can use to simplify the process of compiling, linking, running and debugging assembler programs.

        ASMSw - sets the assembler parameters up
        ASM   - compiles the source program
        RUN   - links and runs one or more object modules

As all these procedures use the DOS environment variables to pass information, they should be run directly from DOS. This means that a procedure might not work properly if it is started from a shell such as Xtree or Norton Commander because shells usually create a new copy of an environment block for each new process.

ASMSw - Choosing an Assembler

The procedure ASMSw is intended for setting the initial values of the environment variables used by other procedures described in this chapter. It has only one parameter that defines which assembler, linker and debugger will be used. The text of this procedure, in batch file control language, is given in Listing 1.3. If the parameters which describe the location of your software differ from those given in this procedure you can change them on your hard disk using any text editor.

```
@Echo off
If %1. == 5. GoTo Masm5
If %1. == 6. GoTo Masm6
If %1. == 61. GoTo Masm61
If %1. == tasm. GoTo Tasm
If %1. == TASM. GoTo Tasm
```

```
:Masm5
Set AsmPath=d:\masm5\bin
Set LnkPath=d:\masm5\bin
Set DebPath=d:\masm5\bin
Set AsmPg=masm
Set AsmOpt= /Zd
Set AsmListF5=,%tmp%\Obj.Obj,%tmp%\Lst.Lst,Nul
Set AsmListF6=
Set AsmListFT=
Echo.
Echo Microsoft Macro Assembler 5.10 and CodeView 2.3 will be   used
Echo.
GoTo EndMas
:Masm6
Set AsmPath=d:\masm\bin
Set LnkPath=d:\masm\binb
Set DebPath=d:\masm\bin
Set AsmPg=ml
Set AsmOpt= /Zd /c
Set AsmListF5=
Set AsmListF6= /Fo%tmp%\Obj.Obj /Fl%tmp%\Lst.Lst
Set AsmListFT=
Echo.
Echo Microsoft Macro Assembler 6.0 and CodeView 3.14 will be used
Echo.
GoTo EndMas
:Masm61
Set AsmPath=d:\masm61\bin
Set LnkPath=d:\masm61\bin
Set DebPath=d:\masm61\bin
Set AsmPg=ml
Set AsmOpt= /Zd /c
Set AsmListF5=
Set AsmListF6= /Fo%tmp%\Obj.Obj /Fl%tmp%\ Lst.Lst /Sc
Set AsmListFT=
Echo.
Echo Microsoft Macro Assembler 6.10 and CodeView 4.0 will be used
Echo.
:EndMas
Set AsmOptD= /Zi
Set LnkPg=link
Set DebPg=cv
Set SetDeb= /CO
GoTo FullEx
:Tasm
Set AsmPath=d:\tasm
Set LnkPath=d:\tasm
Set DebPath=d:\tasm
Set AsmPg=tasm
Set AsmOpt= /l
Set AsmOptD= /zi
Set LnkPg=tlink
Set DebPg=td
```

```
Set SetDeb= /v
Set AsmListF5=
Set AsmListF6=
Set AsmListFT=,%tmp%\Obj.Obj,%tmp%\Lst.Lst
Echo.
Echo Borland Turbo Assembler and Turbo Debugger will be used
Echo.
:FullEx
```

Listing 1.3 The Procedure ASMSw - Setting the Assembler Environment

This procedure sets or changes the meaning of the following environment variables:

AsmPath - the name of the directory containing the assembler used
LnkPath - the name of the directory containing the linker used
DebPath - the name of the directory containing the debugger used
AsmPg   - the name of the assembler main program (ML for MASM 6.0 and 6.1)
AsmOpt   - assembler default options
AsmListF5 - parameter list for MASM 5.1
AsmListF6 - parameter list for MASM 6.0 and 6.1
AsmListFT - parameter list for TASM

You can change the default value of these variables to match the location of the files on your hard disk using any text editor.

ASM - Compiling Programs

The ASM procedure is intended for compiling assembler programs. The full text is given in Listing 1.4.

```
@Echo Off
Set _SavPath_=%path%
Path %AsmPath%;%_SavPath_%
Set Comp=ASM
Set DebMode=N
If %1. == .  GoTo Noparm
If %1. == ?. GoTo Help
If %1. == /H. GoTo Help
If %1. == /h. GoTo Help
If %1. == /d. GoTo Debug1
If %1. == /D. GoTo Debug1
If %2. == /d. GoTo DebOth
If %2. == /D. GoTo DebOth
If %3. == /d. GoTo DebOth
If %3. == /D. GoTo DebOth
```

```
If %4. == /d. GoTo DebOth
If %4. == /D. GoTo DebOth
GoTo Working
:Debug1
Shift
:DebOth
Echo.
Echo Flag /d was specified - module %1.asm will be ready for debugging
Set debmode=Y
GoTo Working
:NoParm
Echo.
Echo No parameters specified - "HELP" action assumed
Echo To standard HELP function type "%0 /h" or "%0 ?"
Echo.
Echo %0 - command to ASSEMBLY program(s) compilation
Echo.
Echo Usage: %0 source [object] [listing] [/d]
Echo.
Echo Parameters:
Echo.
Echo source  - source module name (without "ASM" extension)
Echo        Default : NONE (parameter needed)
Echo object  - object module name (without "OBJ" extension)
EchoDefault : obj.obj (if %%TMP%% environment variable was
Echodefined - %tmp%\obj.obj
Echo listing - compiler listing file name (without "LST"extension)
EchoDefault : lst.lst (if %%TMP%% environment variable was
Echodefined - %tmp%\lst.lst
Echo /d     - flag to setting "debugging" compiler option
Echo.
Echo Example:
Echo.
Echo %0 c:\myprog\kwakwa,,c:\mylist\kwakwa
GoTo Exit
:Working
If %tmp%. == . set tmp=e:\tmp
Del %tmp%\obj.obj > nul
Del %tmp%\lst.lst > nul
Echo.
Echo Compilation ASSEMBLY program %1.asm
Echo.
Echo Use "ESC" key to exit from "FVIEW" command
Echo after end of compilation.
Echo.
Set Options=%AsmOpt%
If %DebMode%. == Y. Set Options=%Options% %AsmOptD% %AsmPg%
%Options% %PrmAsm% %AsmListF6% %1.asm%AsmListF5%%AsmListFT%
Set Options=
:EndComp
Shift
If %1. == /d. GoTo Deb2
If %1. == /D. GoTo Deb2
GoTo NoDeb2
```

```
:Deb2
Shift
:NoDeb2
IF ERRORLEVEL 1 GOTO ERR
Echo.
Echo Successful compilation
IF %1. == . GOTO NoObjCp
IF %1. == .. GOTO NoObjCp
Echo.
Echo Object module file will be named %1.obj
COPY %tmp%\obj.obj %1.OBJ > nul
GoTo :NoObjCp
:Err
Echo INVALID PROGRAM - COMPILATION DELETED
:NoObjCp
Shift
If %1. == /d. GoTo Deb3
If %1. == /D. GoTo Deb3
GoTo NoDeb3
:Deb3
Shift
:NoDeb3
IF %1. == . GOTO NoLstCp
Echo Source listing file will be named %1.lst
:NOLST
COPY %tmp%\lst.lst %1.LST > nul
:NoLstCp
:FINIS
FVIEW %tmp%\lst.lst
:Exit
Path %_SavPath_%
Set _SavPath_=
```

Listing 1.4 The ASM Procedure - Compiling an Assembler Program

The ASM procedure assembles programs either with the environment variable DebMode on or off. The RUN procedure then analyzes the value of this variable to either select the debugger, or start the executable module directly.

In the command line which runs ASM, you can specify a special parameter /D that stands for Debug. The slash "/" is the usual notation for system parameters in MS-DOS. By typing the parameter /D you are preparing your program for debugging. For example, to compile the program **FIRST.ASM** using the debugging mode you should type the following command line:

```
ASM FIRST /D
```

This procedure activates the assembler and creates the object module and the source listing. It then shows you the source listing by displaying the file using the file browsing utility. To look through this listing press the arrow keys on your keyboard.

FView - The File Browsing Program

The program FView lets you look through the contents of a file. The executable module of the program, the file FVIEW.EXE, is stored on your program disk and is used in the BAT-files, for viewing listings created by Assembler. When you run the program, you must specify the name of the file you want in the command line. You can move through the text using the following cursor control keys:

PgDn	scroll one screen down
PgUp	scroll one screen up
Home	display the first 23 lines of the file
End	display the last 23 lines of the file
↓	scroll one line down
↑	scroll one line up
→	scroll one position to the right
←	scroll one position to the left
Ctrl+Home	scroll contents displayed to the left, placing the first character in each line in the first left-hand column of the screen.
Esc	finish working and return to MS-DOS

A full description of FVEIW can be found in Chapter Eight, "Using Video".

RUN - Running and Debugging Programs

The RUN procedure uses the linker to produce an executable module and then either passes control to that module directly or calls the debugger, depending on the parameter set by the previous ASM procedure.

```
@Echo Off
Set Work1=
Set Work2=
Set _Path_=%Path%
Path %LnkPath%;%DebPath%;%Path%
If %tmp%. == . set tmp=c:\tmp
If %1. == . GoTo Noparm
If %1. == ?. GoTo Help
If %1. == /H. GoTo Help
If %1. == /h. GoTo Help
If %1. == /d. GoTo Debug1
If %1. == /D. GoTo Debug1
If %2. == /d. GoTo DebOth
If %2. == /D. GoTo DebOth
If %3. == /d. GoTo DebOth
If %3. == /D. GoTo DebOth
If %4. == /d. GoTo DebOth
If %4. == /D. GoTo DebOth
GoTo Working
:Debug1
Shift
:DebOth
Echo.
If %comp%. == clip. GoTo EngDebC
If %comp%. == CLIP. GoTo EngDebC
Echo Flag /d was specified - CodeView debugger will be used
GoTo ContDeb1
:EngDebC
Echo Flag /d was specified - Clipper debugger will be attached
:ContDeb1
Set DebMode=Y
GoTo Working
:NoParm
Echo.
Echo No parameters specified - last compiled module will be  linked
GoTo Working
:Help
Echo.
Echo %0 - command to object module linking and execution
Echo.
Echo Usage: %0 object [[executable] map-listing]] [/d]
Echo.
Echo Parameters:
Echo.
Echo object      - object module name (without "OBJ" extension)
Echo              Default : %tmp%\obj.obj
Echo executable - executable program name (without "EXE"extension)
Echo    Default : go.exe (if %%TMP%% environment variable was
Echo              defined - %tmp%\go.exe
Echo map-listing - linker listing file name (without "MAP"extension)
Echo     Default : map.map (if %%TMP%% environment variable was
Echo              defined - %tmp%\lst.lst
Echo /d  - flag to setting "debugging" LINKER option
Echo.
```

```
Echo Example:
Echo.
Echo %0 c:\myprog\kwakwa,c:\myexec\kwakwa
GoTo Exit
:Working
Set Work1=%1
If %Work1%. == . Set Work1=%tmp%\Obj
:NoPrm1
DEL %tmp%\go.* > nul
DEL %tmp%\map.map > nul
Echo.
Echo Linking OBJECT program %Work1%.obj
Echo.
If %DebMode%. == Y. GoTo DebComp
%LnkPath%\%LnkPg% %Work1%,%tmp%\Go,%tmp%\Map.Map,%prlib%%PrmLnk% ;
GoTo EndComp
:DebComp
If %comp%. == clip. GoTo ClipDeb1
If %comp%. == CLIP. GoTo ClipDeb1
%LnkPath%\%LnkPg% %Work1%,%tmp%\Go,%tmp%\Map.Map,%prlib%%PrmLnk%
%SetDeb% ;
GoTo EndComp
:ClipDeb1
Set Work1=%Work1%+%ClipDeb%
%LnkPath%\%LnkPg% %Work1%,%tmp%\Go,%tmp%\Map.Map,%prlib% /Noe
%PrmLnk% ;
:EndComp
Shift
If %1. == /d. GoTo Deb2
If %1. == /D. GoTo Deb2
GoTo NoDeb2
:Deb2
Shift
:NoDeb2
IF ERRORLEVEL 1 GOTO ERR
Echo.
Echo Use "ESC" key to exit from "BROWSE" command
Echo after end of linkage editing.
Echo.
Echo Linkage editing complete.
Set Work2=.Exe
If Exist %tmp%\Go.Com Set Work2=.Com
IF %1. == . GOTO NoObjCp
IF %1. == .. GOTO NoObjCp
Echo.
Echo Executable program will be named %1%Work2%
GoTo EndRus2
COPY %tmp%\Go.* %1.* > nul
GoTo :NoObjCp
:Err
Echo INVALID OBJECT MODULE - EXECUTABLE PROGRAM NOT CREATED
:NoObjCp
Shift
If %1. == /d. GoTo Deb3
```

```
If %1. == /D. GoTo Deb3
GoTo NoDeb3
:Deb3
Shift
:NoDeb3
IF %1. == . GOTO NoLstCp
IF %1 ==  GOTO NoLstCp
Echo Map listing file will be named %1.map
:NOLST
COPY %tmp%\map.map %1.MAP > nul
:NoLstCp
:FINIS
Rem Browse %tmp%\map.map
If Not Exist %tmp%\Go.* GoTo NoExec
Echo.
Echo Results of program's running:
Echo.
If %DebMode%. == Y. GoTo ExeDeb
%tmp%\Go
GoTo Exit
:ExeDeb
If %comp%. == clip. GoTo ClipExe
If %comp%. == CLIP. GoTo ClipExe
%DebPath%\%DebPg% %tmp%\Go%Work2%
GoTo Exit
:ClipExe
%tmp%\Go
:Exit
:NoExec
Set Work1=
Set Work2=
Path %_Path_%
Set _Path_=
```

Listing 1.5 The Procedure RUN - Creating/Debugging an Executable Module

This procedure checks whether the previous **ASM** procedure was executed using the **/D** parameter and passes the corresponding parameters to the linker. Then, it either runs the executable module created by linker directly or involves the CodeView debugger to debug this module. The **RUN** procedure can actually do a lot more than this, but we'll consider its advanced features later on. To get a basic idea of how the **RUN** procedure works, you can run it (if you'll excuse the play on words) using parameters **?** or **/H** as follows:

```
RUN ?
```

or

```
RUN /H
```

Summary

This chapter has covered the basics of the assembler environment and shown how you can use it for creating programs.

You can now use Assemblers such as MASM and TASM and with the help of our examples you should be able to use both standard documentation and the assembler itself more effectively.

The object module libraries will make your life easier when it comes to creating large programs involving several programming languages and help you to combine modules created by different compilers.

The batch files we have included should help automate the process of setting up and using the assembler components.

As we said at the beginning, you will probably refer back to the information in this chapter as you become a more proficient assembler programmer.

CHAPTER
2

From Instructions to Programs

In this chapter we will introduce the nuts and bolts of assembly language programming - how an algorithm is translated into statements, and how we can control the execution of those statements using such devices as loops and jumps.

We will create our first real program, and then watch it execute under Codeview, seeing how it interacts with the system.

Fundamental Knowledge

The Basic Elements of Programming

Niklaus Wirth, the inventor of Pascal and Modula (you knew his name sounded familiar, didn't you?), made an important contribution to computer science:

algorithms + data structures = programs.

How does this relate to Assembler? Well, an assembly language program is made up of at least two basic types of statements: those that define or manage data structures, and those that together form an algorithm. We will begin by looking at assembly language instructions in general, and then at the ways of stringing them together into a real program.

Preliminaries - Instructions and Directives

Every instruction has its own name, or mnemonic, which consists of three or more letters. Most of these instructions have one or more operands. As a rule, any instruction can work with various kinds of operands, for example registers of different sizes. Appendix D gives details of the most important assembly language instructions.

Instructions and directives are the main elements of assembly language program statements. Directives are mostly used to control the assembly process while instructions are actually executed by the processor when the program runs (i.e. during run time). Both instructions and directives are written in lines and have similar structures.

The set of instructions available is determined by the kind of processor you have, for example an i8086 has a set of about 100 instructions, while a i80386 has over 150. The set of directives depends on which Assembler you choose, both MASM and TASM currently having over 150 directives, most of which are common to both in one form or another.

The basic structure of an instruction is as follows:

```
Label    OperationCode    Operands    ; Comment
```

Note that all the fields are optional, but at least one of them must be present. For example, all the following instructions are valid:

```
        cli          ; disable interrupts - only instruction code used
        push ax      ; place content of AX onto stack - one operand used
        mul  bl      ; multiply Al by BL - one operand assumed
TstEsc: cmp  dl,1Bh  ; check symbol in DL for Esc - both operands used
Nothing:             ; this is used only to refer to next instruction
```

Let's consider the fields which make up an assembler instruction.

The first ELEMENT in a line of assembler code is the label which is used to refer to this particular instruction. In other words, a label is the name given to a line containing an instruction. To create labels you can use the characters A - z (Assembler usually doesn't distinguish between upper and lower case letters unless you specify this explicitly).

The exact rules for creating labels are slightly different depending on which Assembler you are using. However, in all PC assemblers labels must be seperated from instruction code by the character ":" (colon) and cannot start with numbers or special characters. The maximum length of a label is also different in different assemblers. In MASM 6.0 the maximum is 247 characters. For example, both the following labels could be used in a program written in MASM 6.0:

```
A:
```

```
Very_long_but_not_very_meaningful_label_which_is_nevertheless_valid:
```

The instruction code defines which machine command (or, sometimes, commands) is generated by Assembler when it processes this statement.

Operands specify which objects are processed by this instruction. They can refer to the registers or memory addresses of a microprocessor. Note, however, that if an instruction has two operands, they cannot both refer to memory addresses at the same time.

Comments are used in assembler programs because these programs are not only designed to be processed by Assembler but also to be read by people. If you are used to writing programs in a high-level language, the only thing that you need to learn about comments in assembler programs is that they begin with the character ";" and can be put either after the last operand of an instruction or on a separate line.

Note that assembler programs usually need more comments to be easily understood. For example, compare the Pascal statement:

```
Income := Salary - Tax :
```

with the equivalent assembler instructions:

```
mov    ax,salary
sub    ax,tax
mov    income,ax
```

Assembler directives are designed for defining data, controlling memory allocation and program flow and describing the program organization. Some directives do not generate machine instructions while others generate sequences of instructions or affect the way Assembler generates instructions. The basic structure of a directive is as follows:

```
Name  DirectiveCode     Operands    ;  Comment
```

Directives which affect the process of the code generation directly usually begin with the character "." (period). The following example shows some of the most commonly used directives:

```
.model small       ; describes the method of memory distribution
Message DB'Hello!' ; defines text data to be used in the program
.386               ; allows assembler to generate i80386 instructions
.code              ; starts part of program containing instructions
.data              ; starts part of program containing data
   public ThisProg ; makes label ThisProg "visible"
```

Operands and Data

Many assembly language instructions have no operand or argument, while those that do can accept a variety of different kinds. Some of the operands may contain initial data for the instruction being performed, or point to such data in memory.

If an instruction has two operands, the first one is called a **destination operand** and the second one is called a **source operand**. The source operand always contains initial data or points at such data, while the destination operand always contains (or points at) the result of the operation which has just been performed. However, in some instructions the destination operand may be used for both purposes. In either case the destination operand is given a new value which is generated by the instruction which has been performed.

There are three classes of data which you can use as operands in instructions: immediate data, register data and memory data.

▲ **Immediate data** is data which is written exactly as it is in the instruction, eg. 2, A0h, 'A'.

▲ **Register data** is data which is allocated in the register and is used by writing the name of the register in the instruction.

▲ **Memory data** which is held at some particular location in memory. There are a number of different ways of addressing this kind of data, which we will consider in the next chapter.

For example, in the instruction

```
mov    bx,0
```

the source operand 0 is an immediate data type (the value zero) and the destination operand BX is a register. MOV is the mnemonic for the move instruction, probably the simplest and most frequently used instruction of all, followed by the tools for basic arithmetic such as ADD, SUB, MUL, DIV.

However, it is not the syntax of the instruction set that is the essence of programming, but the way in which those instructions are combined into an algorithm.

The Instruction Pointer and Program Flow

An algorithm can be represented by a **flow chart** that graphically exposes the program flow. See Figure 2.1 for the basic elements of a flow chart.

The flow chart of the program FACTR in Listing 2.2 is illustrated in Figure 2.2.

The flow of a program describes the order in which the executable statements are performed. The sequence of execution coincides with the order of statements in the program, unless it is changed by conditional or unconditional branches and loops. The demo program FLAGS in the library section of this chapter executes every statement in the order they are written down, which is suitable for the purposes of the demonstration but is hardly a triumph of functionality.

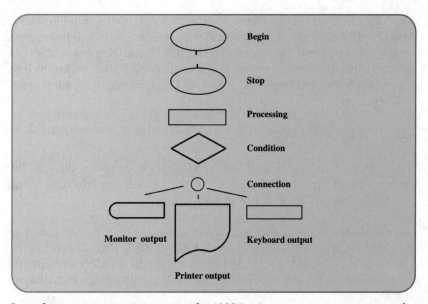

Figure 2.1
**Basic
Elements of
a Flow Chart**

In order to execute a program, the i8086 microprocessor computes the address of the next instruction to be fetched from the memory and executed. This address is stored in the CS and IP registers and can be calculated as CSx16+IP. All full addresses in i80x86 machines take up two registers, and in the case of IP, the first part of the address is always assumed to be in CS. We will go into addressing in detail in the next chapter, but for the time being you can treat CS:IP as the full form of the instruction address.

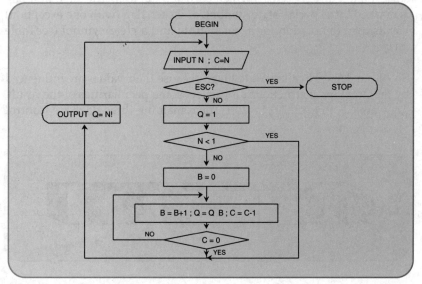

Figure 2.2
**The Flow Chart
of the Program
FACTR**

The value in IP cannot be changed directly by an instruction like MOV. Usually, IP is increased automatically by the length of the instruction which has just been performed, so that CS:IP contains the address of the next instruction. However, some instructions, such as jumps and loops and the instructions CALL and RET, do change the natural order of execution.

Jump into the Loop

The simplest tool that enables us to change program flow is the unconditional branch. In assembly language, this is performed using the **JMP - unconditional jump** instruction.

A conditional, as opposed to unconditional, branch is performed in two steps - first of all a given condition is tested, then depending on the outcome, a jump is performed. Such a test will usually communicate its outcome by setting or clearing one of the many flags available on the PC.

Flags

The i8086 microprocessor has 9 flags which are located in the 16-bit **Flag Register** FL (see Figure 2.3).

Each flag in the i8086 processor is a single-bit wide memory container with its own name and one of two possible values: **set**, which corresponds to 1, or **clear**, which corresponds to 0. The state of a flag is marked by a special **state symbol**, and each flag (with one exception) has its own denotation for a **set symbol** and a **clear symbol** (seeTable 2.1).

Six of the flags are called **State Flags** because their values are influenced by the previous instructions and reflect some peculiarities of the result. They are CF, PF, AF, ZF, SF, OF. The remaining three flags are **Control**

Figure 2.3
The i8086
Flags

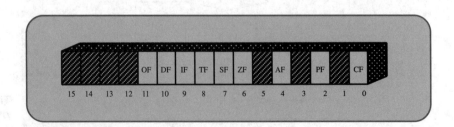

Position in FL	Abbrev-iation	Name	State or Control	Set Symbol	Clear Symbol
0	CF	Carry	S	CY	NC
2	PF	Parity	S	PE	PO
4	AF	Auxiliary	S	AC	NA
6	ZF	Zero	S	ZR	NZ
7	SF	Sign	S	NG	PL
8	TF	Trap	C	-	-
9	IF	Interrupt	C	EI	DI
10	DF	Direction	C	DN	UP
11	OF	Overflow	S	OV	NV

Table 2.1
Flags of i8086/ i8088 Microprocessors

Flags so called because their purpose is to control the execution of certain instructions. They are TF, EF, DF.

The picture is slightly different for 80286,80386,80486 microprocessors (see Figures 2.4 and 2.5). The i80286 processor also has a 16-bit flag register but it has two additional flags, one of which is 2-bits wide. Figure 2.4 shows the flags for the i80286 microprocessor.

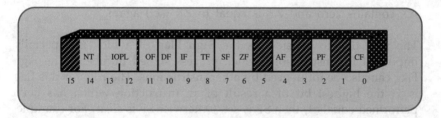

Figure 2.4
The i80286 Flags

i80386/i80486 microprocessors have a 32-bit wide flag register. The i80386 processor has two additional flags RF and VM, which are not present in earlier models and the i80486 has one further flag AC. Since these flags can only be used in protected mode we are not going to cover them in this book.

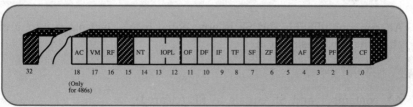

Figure 2.5
Extra Flags of i80386 /i80486 Microprocessors

Which flags are affected depends on the instruction used. Some instructions (MOV for instance) do not influence any flags at all. The effect of each instruction on the flags is detailed in Appendix D. Let's continue by having a detailed look at the flags themselves.

State Flags

We'll start with the **Zero Flag** ZF, as it's the easiest to understand. If the result of an arithmetic or logical instruction which has been performed equals zero, then ZF is set, otherwise ZF is cleared. This means that after the instruction

```
SUB AX,AX
```

AX is equal to zero and the Zero Flag is set, i.e., ZF becomes equal to 1 which is denoted as ZR. After the following instruction

```
ADD. AX,1
```

AX equals 1 and ZF is equal to NZ (cleared), and after the next instruction

```
ADD AX,0FFFFh
```

AX contains zero and ZF is equal to ZR (set) again.

The next flag to consider is the **Sign Flag** SF which is especially important for instructions which process signed numbers. The Sign Flag can also be influenced by other instructions. The rule for this flag is: if the highest bit of a result of an instruction which has been performed equals 1, then SF is set. Otherwise SF is clear. For example, after the instruction

```
SUB AX,AX
```

AX = 0 and the Sign Flag is equal to PL (cleared, positive), after the following instruction

```
SUB AX,1
```

AX contains 0FFFFh and SF is now equal to NG (set, negative), and after the next instruction

```
ADD AX,2
```

AX contains 1 and SF equals to PL (cleared).

Next in line is the **Carry Flag** CF which indicates the carry from, or the borrow to, the highest bit of the result of an arithmetic instruction. The value of the Carry Flag (1 if set or 0 if clear) is also used in performing arithmetic operations with long binary numbers.

Let's look at some simple examples. After the instruction

```
SUB AX,AX
```

the Carry Flag is equal to NC (is cleared, no carry), after the instruction

```
MOV AX,0FFFFh
```

the Carry Flag remains unchanged, after the following instruction

```
ADD AX,1
```

the value of the Carry Flag is CY (set, carry - yes!), and after

```
ADD AX,0
```

the Carry Flag takes the value NC (cleared).

The Carry Flag can also be used as an indicator by certain DOS and BIOS routines. In this case its value is changed by special instructions - STC (SeT Carry) and CLC (Clear Carry). We'll consider this use of the Carry Flag in Chapter Six, when dealing with the BIOS and DOS services.

The **Auxiliary Carry Flag** AF is similar to the Carry Flag. It is designed for operations with BCD numbers, so it marks whether there have been carries from or borrows to bit #3 (counting from the right - don't forget about bit #0) of the result. For example the instruction

```
SUB AX,AX
```

makes AF equal to NA (cleared), the instruction

```
MOV AX,8
```

does not change the AF flag, the following instruction

```
ADD AX,8
```

makes it equal to AY (set), and

```
ADD AX,0
```

makes the Auxiliary Carry Flag equal to NA (cleared).

The **Overflow Flag** OF, together with other state flags, reflects peculiarities of arithmetic operations. Firstly, it is set after the addition or subtraction of signed numbers if the result does not fit into the operand, otherwise it is clear. In other words, when adding integers of the same sign, a carry from the (n-2)-th bit to the (n-1)-th bit (i.e., the sign bit) will result in the Overflow Flag being set. Similarly, a borrow from the sign bit obtained while subtracting two integers of opposite signs will set the Overflow Flag. Secondly, if the high half of the result of a multiplication is not equal to zero, then both CF and OF are set, otherwise they are both cleared.

The sequence of instructions below should help you to understand the OF flag:

```
SUB AX,AX      ; Clear AX - OF must be NV(cleared)
MOV AL,128     ; OF is unchanged
ADD AX,128     ; OF is set i.e. equal to OV
```

The next flag - the **Parity Flag** is rarely used nowadays, which is probably why it is often misunderstood.

The rule for the Parity Flag PF is a bit unusual, but very simple: if the lower byte of the result of the instruction which has just been performed has an even number of bits equal to 1, then PF is set, otherwise it is clear.

This means that the instruction

```
MOV AX,0F001h
```

does not change the Parity Flag, whereas the instruction

```
ADD AX,2
```

sets the PF flag to PE (set), and the next instruction

```
ADD AL,5h
```

makes the PF flag equal to PO (cleared).

You will find examples of all these in the program printed in Listing 2.1 and the source code of the program is stored on your program disk. We suggest that you check all these examples using the CodeView debugger as explained later on in this chapter.

Control Flags

Whereas the purpose of state flags is to reflect the state of the program execution process, the control flags TF, IF, DF are designed to enable you to control the flow of the program. Consequently, there are a set of instructions which allow you to manipulate the control flags DF and IF directly.

The **Trap Flag** TF enables step by step execution of a program, which is very useful for designing debuggers like CodeView, Debug and Turbo Debugger etc; you use the Trap Flag while debugging your programs step by step, even though you might not be aware of its existence. Some copy protected programs also use this flag to prevent hackers from breaking their shield.

This is clearly illustrated in the program DetStep included in the Library section, so we'll only give a brief description of the method used here. The program tries to set the Trap Flag, then checks whether this operation was successful. DOS usually ignores the state of the Trap Flag and doesn't prevent programs manipulating it. However, debuggers working in the step-by-step mode start executing an instruction by setting the Trap Flag, then clearing it immediately after the instruction has been performed. If a program is performed in the step-by-step mode, the Trap Flag is always cleared by the debugger, even in situations when the program has set it.

Since programmers rarely operate with the Trap Flag in everyday programming, there are no special instructions for setting or clearing it. You can set and clear this flag using POPF instructions.

By way of compensation for this restriction, you can do whatever you want with the Carry Flag. This was a wise move on behalf of the Intel designers as it means that the Carry Flag is quite safe, letting you do a lot of useful things.

The **Direction Flag** DF and the **Interrupt Flag** IF are exceptionally useful, but for the time being we will limit ourselves to a rather superficial description. The Direction Flag determines whether, when performing repeated string manipulation instructions like **REP**, **REPE** and other REP*'s, the addresses are automatically increased or decreased. If DF is cleared, the memory is processed from lower addresses to higher ones, and vice versa if set.

The Interrupt Flag IF allows the microprocessor to respond to special situations called interrupts when it is set, or to ignore them when IF is cleared. When the Interrupt Flag is set, the system can pass control to a designated routine or interrupt handler in response to the appropriate keystroke or hardware event.

Additional Flags of i80286 and i80386/i80486

These flags have been designed to set different options for i80286, i80386 or i80486 microprocessors. Two of the flags - NT and IOPL - are present in all three of these processors.

The **Nested Task Flag** NT enables multitask work. It is set whenever an interrupt, or any other event, causes a task switch.

The **Input/Output Privilege Level** IOPL occupies two bits. It indicates the privilege level (from 0 to 3) that enables a procedure to execute input/output instructions: IN, INS, OUT, OUTS, CLI, STI.

The i80386 has two further flags - VM and RF. When the **Virtual 8086 mode** VM is set, it makes it possible for you to use 80386/80486 as multiple 8086 microprocessors. Consequently, you can run a number of 8086 tasks, as each of them is running on a separate 8086 computer.

The **Resume Flag** RF is designed to control program interrupts used for debugging ("debug exception").

The i80486 microprocessor has yet another flag - the **Alignment Check** AC. When AC is set, it uses some of the advantages of 80486 memory access, which increases the processing speed.

Tools

MOV Instruction

The move instruction format is

```
MOV     operand1,operand2
```

The purpose of the MOV instruction is to copy information from operand2 to operand1 (here in Russia we can only guess at why our American colleagues decided to name this instruction MOV instead of COP...). The operands in the MOV instruction may be either register data, memory data or immediate data of 8-bits, 16-bits and (for i80386/i80486) 32-bits. Both operands have to be the same size.

Data group registers can be used quite freely in the MOV instruction. See Appendix D for an exact description of MOV instructions.

Here are some practical examples of the MOV instruction.

The following instructions copy immediate data into the 8-bit and 16-bit registers (BL and AX, respectively):

```
MOV     BX,0
MOV     AX,4C00h
```

The instruction

```
MOV     DX,BX
```

copies the number stored in the BX register into the DX register.

The following instructions copy data from one register to another:

```
MOV     CH,AL
MOV     DS,AX
```

ADD and SUB - The Simplest Arithmetic Instructions

These instructions perform arithmetic operations on binary numbers. The format of the instructions is the same:

```
ADD     operand1,operand2
SUB     operand1,operand2
```

The purpose of the ADD instruction is to add the contents of operand2 to the contents of operand1, and to put the result obtained into operand1. The SUB instruction subtracts the contents of operand2 from the contents of operand1, and also puts the result into operand1. These instructions can operate integers up to the maximum length available for the microprocessor used. Note that immediate data cannot be used as the destination operand (operand1). Both instructions can work with both signed and unsigned numbers. A detailed description of the ADD and SUB instructions is given in Appendix D. Here we will give you some simple examples of their usage:

```
add  al,bl     ; add numbers in BL and DL registers
add  si,2      ; increase the value in SI by 2
add  ax,Charge ; add value of variable CHARGE to content of AX
sub  ax,Tax    ; subtract the value of variable TAX from content of AX
```

MUL Instruction

There are two assembly language instructions for the multiplication of integers: MUL for unsigned integers and IMUL for signed integers. Their syntax is not as simple as that for the ADD instruction.

The accumulator registers are always involved in MUL instructions. The MUL instruction has only one operand, which denotes one of the two factors to be multiplied. So where is the other factor hiding? The MUL instruction assumes that it is contained in AL or AX (or possibly in EAX for i80386/486).

If the first factor is stored in the 8-bit register then the second one is stored in AL. And where is the result? It is allocated automatically in AX. There is enough room in the 16-bit register AX to contain the product of two 8-bit factors (see Figure 2.6). For example, in the instruction

```
MUL  CL
```

the number stored in CL, is multiplied by the number stored in AL; the result overwrites the AX register. Figure 2.7 shows the work of the MUL instruction with an 8-bit factor: 32x16=200h=512..

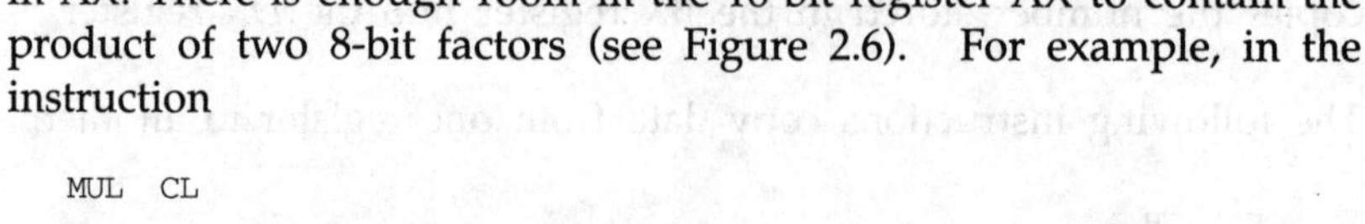

Figure 2.6
The Product of Two 8-Bit Factors

1111 1111   1111 1111 = 1111 1110 0000 0001

Before performing the MUL CL instruction	AH 0	AL 20h=32	CL 10h=16
After performing the MUL CL instruction	AH 2	AL 0	CL 10h=16

Figure 2.7
The Work of the MUL Instruction with an 8-bit Factor

If the first factor is allocated in the 16-bit register, then the second one is allocated in the whole AX register; the 32-bit result is stored in the DX:AX pair of registers (the first portion, consisting of high 16 digits, in DX and the second one, consisting of low 16 digits, in AX). The data which had been stored in DX and AX earlier is overwritten by the result of the MUL instruction. For example, the instruction

```
MUL CX
```

works in the way shown in the Figure 2.8, which illustrates the work of the instruction with a 16-bit factor: 512x128=10000h=65536.

The i80386/486 processor treats the EDX:EAX registers in the MUL instruction in a similar way. The result of the

```
MUL ECX
```

instruction is the product of integers stored in ECX and EAX 32-bit registers; it overwrites the contents of the EDX:EAX registers.

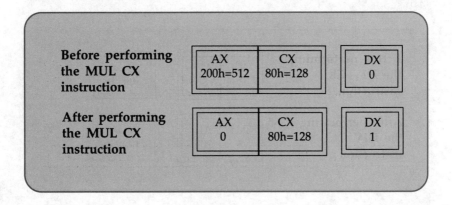

Before performing the MUL CX instruction	AX 200h=512	CX 80h=128	DX 0
After performing the MUL CX instruction	AX 0	CX 80h=128	DX 1

Figure 2.8
The Work of the MUL Instruction with a 16-bit Factor

Take time to examine the descriptions of the IMUL instruction, and then the descriptions of DIV and IDIV instructions.

DIV Instruction

Once you understand assembly language instructions for multiplication, you will find it is easy to master the instructions for division. There are two instructions for this, **DIV** for unsigned integers and **IDIV** for signed integers.

The **DIV** instruction has one operand which denotes the divisor. If the register is 8-bit, then the contents of the AX register are processed as the dividend. The quotient then overwrites AL and the remainder overwrites AH.

For example, the instruction

```
DIV CL
```

divides the number stored in AX by the number stored in CL; the quotient is written in AL and the remainder is written in AH. The instruction

```
DIV CL
```

is shown in Figure 2.9. The figure demonstrates the work of the DIV instruction with an 8-bit divisor: 515=203h divided by 16=10h equals 32=20h with remainder 3.

If the operand of the **DIV** instruction is a 16-bit register, then the number contained in DX:AX registers is divided by the contents of the operand. The quotient is then stored in AX and the remainder in DX.

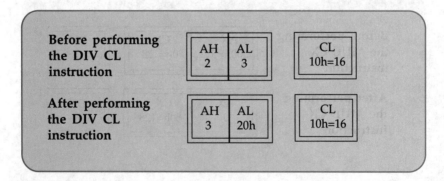

Figure 2.9
The DIV Instruction with an 8-bit Divisor

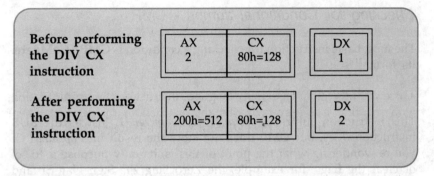

Figure 2.10
**The DIV
Instruction
with a 16-bit
Divisor**

See Figure 2.10, which shows the work of the DIV instruction with a 16-bit divisor: 65538=10002h divided by 128=80h equals 512=200h with remainder 2.

The **DIV** instruction for i80386/i80486 works with 32-bit extended registers in a similar way.

You shouldn't have any difficulty mastering the **IDIV** instruction (see Appendix D).

JMP - Unconditional Jump

This instruction has several forms, but we'll start with the simplest of them which uses a label:

```
JMP Label
```

where *Label* is an identifier used to mark a place in a program. When it is used as a marker, it has a colon after it. However, when used in an instruction like **JMP** to point where the program flow should jump, it is written without a colon. If we take an example:

```
Next:
 ...........
JMP next
```

you can see that the **JMP** instruction switches the program flow, causing the part of the program marked by the label Next to be executed again and again.

Checking for Conditional Jumps - CMP

The most basic instruction for checking a condition is **CMP - CoMPare**. Its format is

```
CMP operand1,operand2
```

This instruction subtracts *operand2* from *operand1*, just as the **SUB** instruction does, but **CMP does not** store the result into *operand1*. If you're wondering what the point of this is, its only purpose is to set or clear the flags; for example, the Zero Flag ZF, Sign Flag SF and Overflow Flag OF. Certain instructions like **JE - Jump if Equal** check the state of these flags, which influences whether they make a program flow branch or not. We'll demonstrate this by looking at the **JE** instruction. One possible format is

```
JE JmpAddr
```

Other forms of the jump instruction are given in Table 2.2.

The distance between the jump instruction and the instruction labelled JmpAddr is the signed offset from the address of the jump instruction. Since only one byte is reserved in the instruction for storing this value, it cannot be more than 128 bytes. However, MASM 6.0 processes this instruction in a special way, allowing you to use a jump distance up 32767 bytes, which we'll look at later in this section.

You can calculate the distance between two instructions using the listings generated by Assembler. This distance is measured in bytes of machine code program, so unless you are an experienced assembler programmer able to estimate the distance in machine code exactly, give yourself some leeway in your calculations.

To make a jump safely, at any distance, you should perform it in two steps. The fragment given below will only work when the distance between the label Found and the jump instruction is no greater than 128 bytes.

```
        cmp    dl,0Dh      ; compare code in DL with value "0Dh"
        je     Found       ; jump to label FOUND if equal
    .................
    Found:
```

If the jump distance is greater than 128 bytes, assemblers earlier than MASM 6.0 will indicate an error while compiling the program.

Mnemonic	Condition	Brief Description
JB/JNAE	CY	below/not above or equal
JAE/JNB	NC	above or equal/not below
JBE/JNA	CY or ZR	below or equal/not above
JA/JNBE	NC AND NZ	above/not below or equal
JE/JZ	ZR	equal/zero
JNE/JNZ	NZ	not equal/not zero
JL/JNGE	SF <> OF	less/not greater or equal
JGE/JNL	SF = OF	greater or equal/not less
JLE/JNG	ZR and SF <> OF	less or equal/not greater
JG/JNLE	NZ and SF=OF	greater/not less or equal
JS	NG	sign
JNS	PL	not sign
JC	CY	carry
JNC	NC	not carry
JO	OV	overflow
JNO	NV	not overflow
JP/JPE	PE	parity even
JNP/JPO	PO	parity odd

Table 2.2
The Conditional Jump Instructions

The following example shows a long-distance conditional jump, performed in two steps. First of all the near conditional jump, then the unconditional jump. Note that the condition in the first jump instruction is the reverse of the condition in the first example.

```
        cmp   dl,0Dh    ; compare code in DL with value "0Dh"
        jne   Cont      ; jump to label CONT if not equal (continue)
        jmp   Found     ; jump to label FOUND if equal
Cont:
.................
Found:
```

The whole process is a lot easier with MASM 6.0 since it automatically creates machine code in line with this two-step technique when required.

As you'll see below, conditional jumps are often used together with the compare instructions for building constructions of the **WHILE ... DO ...** and **REPEAT ... UNTIL ...** type, popular in structured programming.

Pseudo High-Level Language Constructions in Assembler

If you have any programming experience, you will have frequently used loops to perform a task repeatedly until some condition is fulfilled. High-level languages provide a variety of different WHILE-DO and REPEAT-UNTIL tools, the equivalents of which can be constructed in assembly language.

Figure 2.11 shows the flow chart of the WHILE-DO construction which includes 4 steps:

1. Test the condition

2. Continue to step 3 or exit

3. Execute

4. Return to step 1

Figure 2.12 shows the flow chart of the REPEAT-UNTIL construction which includes 3 steps:

1. Execute

2. Test the condition

3. Branch to exit or return to step 1

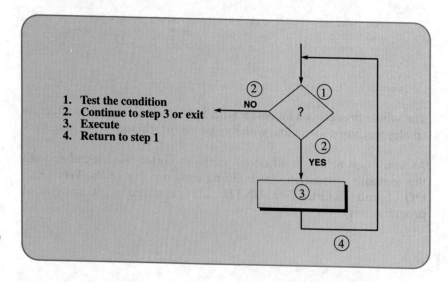

1. Test the condition
2. Continue to step 3 or exit
3. Execute
4. Return to step 1

Figure 2.11
The While-Do Loop

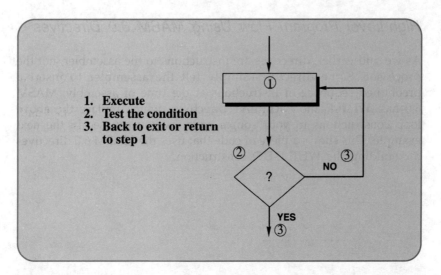

1. **Execute**
2. **Test the condition**
3. **Back to exit or return to step 1**

①

②   ③

?   NO

YES
③

Figure 2.12
**The Repeat-
Until Loop**

Let's have a look at how these constructions can be used in an assembler program. The fragment below shows an example of the WHILE-DO construction.

```
.....................
BegLoop: cmp    ax,AMAX  ; compare AX to the maximum value
         ja     Cont     ; conditional jump to continue program
         inc    ax       ; prepare next performance
;.....................
;        The cycle body goes here
;.....................
         jmp    BegLoop     ;to the next step
Cont:
.....................
```

Note that the condition is tested before the cycle body is executed.

Conversely, in the example below, which illustrates the REPEAT-UNTIL construction, the condition is tested after the cycle body and as a result, the cycle will be performed at least once.

```
BegLoop: inc    ax           ; prepare next performance
;.....................
;        The cycle body goes here
;.....................
         cmp    ax,AMAX   ; compare AX to the maximum value
         ja     Cont      ; conditional jump to continue program
         jmp    BegLoop    ;to the next step
Cont:
```

High-Level Program Flow Using MASM 6.0 Directives

As we said earlier, directives are instructions to the assembler, not the processor. Some directives simply tell the assembler to insert a predefined sequence of instructions at the time of assembly. MASM 6.0 has **.WHILE** and **.REPEAT** directives, which replace the above loop constructions in your source code, as you can see in the next example. This shows a piece of code that uses the MASM 6.0 directives for building the WHILE-DO construction.

```
        .WHILE    AX <= AMAX
        inc       ax
;.....................
;       The cycle body goes here
;.....................
        .ENDW
```

The operands of the .WHILE directive are a logical condition which can be written using the operators listed in Table 2.3, which shows the runtime operators for decision and loop runtime directives. The same operators are used for creating the REPEAT-UNTIL and IF-THEN constructions.

As you might expect, the REPEAT-UNTIL construction is also simpler in MASM 6.0. The following fragment displays an example of the REPEAT-UNTIL construction similar to the one on the previous page.

```
        .REPEAT
        inc       ax
;.....................
;       The cycle body goes here
;.....................
        .UNTIL    ax > AMAX
```

The assembly language decision directive .IF is similar to the "if" construction in high-level languages. Its format is as follows:

```
        .IF        condition1
                   statement1
    [.ELSEIF condition2
                   statement2]
    [.ELSE
                   statement3]
        .ENDIF
```

For example, the fragment of the program that converts the binary

Operator	Description
==	is equal to
!=	is not equal to
>	is greater than
>=	is greater than or equal to
<	is less than
<=	is less than or equal to
||	logical OR
&&	logical AND
&	bitwise AND
!	negation
CARRY?	Carry flag CF is set
OVERFLOW?	Overflow flag OF is set
PARITY?	Parity flag PF is set
SIGN?	Sign flag SF is set
ZERO?	Zero flag ZF is set

Table 2.3
The Runtime Operators

numbers 0 to 0Fh into characters and replaces numbers greater than 0Fh with a blank, could look as follows:

```
.IF (AL < 10)
    add   al,'0'
.ELSEIF (AL < 16)
    add   al,'A'
.ELSE
    mov   al,' '
.ENDIF
```

Figure 2.13 shows how this is constructed.

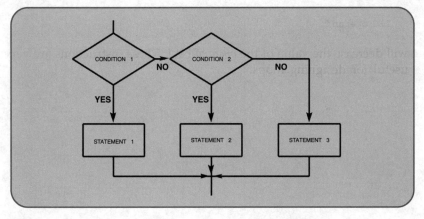

Figure 2.13
IF-THEN-ELSE-IF-ELSE Construction

Simple Loops

The best way of constructing a simple loop is using one of the **LOOP***
instructions - the most basic of these being the **LOOP** instruction:

```
LOOP JmpAddr
```

In the same way as with the conditional jump instruction, the label
JmpAddr must be placed no further than 127 bytes from the **LOOP**
instruction. The instruction automatically decreases the value of CX
by 1. If the value of CX is not equal to 0, execution proceeds to the
place in the program marked by the label JmpAddr. If the value in
CX is equal to 0, execution proceeds to the next instruction (i.e., the
instruction that comes immediately after **LOOP**).

In the example below, a factorial n! of a positive integer n placed in
CX is evaluated and stored into BX.

```
       mov    bx,0
Mult:  mov    dx,0      ; Clear the high part of result
       inc    bx        ; Increase the work register
       mul    bx        ; The next result
       loop   Mult      ; Continue the cycle
. . . . . . . . . . . .
PrtRes:
```

You can change the value of a register using instructions **INC** and
DEC. The **INC**rement instruction

```
INC operand
```

will increase the value, while the **DEC**rement instruction

```
DEC operand
```

will decrease the value of the *operand* by 1. These instructions are very
useful for designing loops.

Library

A Demo Program to Illustrate Using Flags

We have included a program on your program disk which is intended to show you how certain commands affect certain flags. When you run this program under the debugger you'll see how flag values change straight away. For explanation purposes we have assumed you are using MASM and CodeView, and that you will compile and run this program using the BAT-files from your program disk. If you have not installed your program disk yet, refer to the installation instructions placed in the introduction.

To compile the program type the following command line:

```
asm flags /d
```

then, to execute this program under CodeView, type

```
run
```

Figure 2.14 shows the first screen display that you will see running this program under CodeView. Running this program in debug mode,

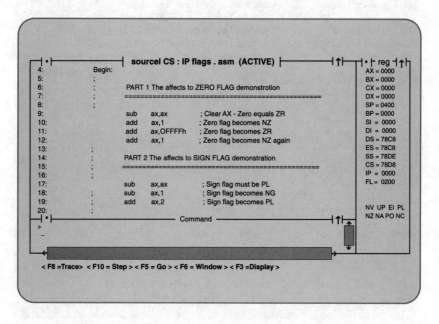

Figure 2.14
**The Initial
CodeView
Screen**

step by step, you will see how flags are changed after performing certain instructions. Comments included in the program text will tell you, what particular results you should see. The full text of the FLAGS program is given in Listing 2.1.

```
 1  Page 60,132
 2  .model small
 3  .code
 4  Begin:
 5  ;
 6  ;    PART 1 The effects to ZERO FLAG demonstration
 7  ;    ==========================================
 8  ;
 9      sub ax,ax      ; Clear AX - Zero equals ZR
10      add ax,1       ; Zero flag becomes NZ
11      add ax,0FFFFh  ; Zero flag becomes ZR
12      add ax,1       ; Zero flag becomes NZ again
13  ;
14  ;    PART 2 The effects to SIGN FLAG demonstration
15  ;    ==========================================
16  ;
17      sub ax,ax      ; Sign flag must be PL
18      sub ax,1       ; Sign flag becomes NG
19      add ax,2       ; Sign flag becomes PL
20  ;
21  ;    PART 3 The effects to CARRY FLAG (CF) demonstration
22  ;    ===============================================
23  ;
24      sub ax,ax      ; Clear AX - CF must be NC
25      mov ax,0FFFFh  ; Carry flag is not affected
26      add ax,1       ; Carry flag becomes CY
27      add ax,0       ; Carry flag becomes NC
28      sub ax,1       ; Carry flag becomes CY
29  ;
30  ;    PART 4 The effects to AUXILIARY CARRY FLAG
31  ;    =======================================
32  ;
33      sub ax,ax      ; Auxiliary Carry gets NA
34      mov ax,8       ; Flag is not affected
35      add ax,8       ; Auxiliary Carry gets AC
36      add ax,0       ; Auxiliary Carry gets NA
37      sub ax,1       ; Auxiliary Carry gets AC
38  ;
39  ;    PART 5 The effects to OVERFLOW FLAG demonstration
40  ;    ==============================================
41  ;
42      sub ax,ax      ; Overflow flag must be NV
43  ;                  ;
44  ;    Addition
45  ;                  ;
46      mov al,128     ; Overflow flag is not affected
47      add al,128     ; Overflow flag becomes OV
```

```
48 ;
49 ;  Subtraction
50 ;
51     sub  ax,ax       ; Overflow flag becomes NV
52     add  ax,8000h    ;
53     sub  ax,7FFFh    ; Overflow flag becomes OV
54 ;
55 ;     Multiplication
56 ;
57     sub  ax,ax       ; Overflow flag must be NO
58     mov  al,16       ; The first factor into AL
59     mov  bx,16       ; The second factor into BL (BH=0)
60     mul  bl          ; Product=256 in AX, Overflow flag is OV,
61                      ;   Carry flag = CY
62 ;
63 ; PART 6 The effects to PARITY FLAG demonstration
64 ; ============================================
65 ;
66     sub  ax,ax       ; Parity flag must be PE
67     add  ax,1        ; Parity flag becomes PO
68     add  ax,10h      ; Parity flag becomes PE
69     add  ax,0100h    ; Parity flag unchanged
70 ;
71 ; PART 7 Finish the program
72 ; =========================
73 ;
74     mov  ax,4C00h    ; AH - Dos service number,
75                      ; Al - Return code
76     int  21h         ; Dos service call
77     .data
78     .stack
79     end begin
```

Listing 2.1 The Demo Program FLAGS

Calculating Factorials

Having acquired a few simple tools to let us examine data and change
the order in which instructions are executed, we'll now look at a small
program that shows these tools in practice. As an example, we'll take
a program which will calculate the mathematical function **factorial** -
n!. To calculate its value we have to multiply the numbers from 1 to
n together with each other. The formula for this is:

```
n! = 1x2x...x(n-1)xn
```

We'll go through the program **FACTR** line by line. Don't worry about
the unfamiliar commands. At the moment you will probably only
understand lines 41 - 51 completely. The full text of the program **FACTR**

with line numbers is printed in Listing 2.2. The source code for this program is also stored on your program disk.

```
 1 .nolistmacro
 2 Page 60,132
 3 ;
 4 ;              Program   FACTR
 5 ;              _____
 6 ;
 7 ;            Voronezh, 26 November  91
 8 ;            _____
 9 ;    This  is  a  sample of an assembler program which
10 ;    calculates the function called  n-factorial.   It
11 ;    shows commands for organizing cycles and for data
12 ;    examination.  To run the program enter the number
13 ;    after  the  cursor  and then the separator symbol
14 ;    (for example the factorial symbol "!").  To  exit
15 ;    the program press the ENTER or ESC key instead of
16 ;    the number. You may meet commands  that  you  do
17 ;    not   fully  understand   even   if  you  are  an
18 ;    experienced user. Don't worry about  them.   All
19 ;    commands will be explained in later chapters.
20 ;
21 ;
22 .model SMALL               ; This defines memory model
23     IF1                    ; On first pass
24     include maclib.inc     ;  open macro library
25     ENDIF                  ; End of macro including block
26 ;
27 ; _____ C O D E   S E G M E N T _____
28 ;
29 .code
30
31 Begin:                     ;
32 Next:                      ;
33                            ;
34    InpInt cx               ; Enter the number to compute
35                            ;
36    cmp   dl,0Dh            ; Check the ENTER key
37    je    ExCycle           ; Exit if pressed
38    cmp   dl,1Bh            ; Check the ESC key
39    je    ExCycle           ; Exit if pressed
40                            ;
41    mov   ax,1              ; The initial value of factorial
42    cmp   cx,1              ; Check the input value
43    jl    Prtres            ; Skip the calculating if the
44                            ;  number is less than 1
45    mov   bx,0              ; Clear the work register
46                            ;
47 Mult:                      ;
48    mov   dx,0              ; Clear the high part of result
49    inc   bx               ; Increase the work register
50    mul   bx               ; The next result
```

```
51    loop  Mult              ; Continue the cycle
52                            ;
53 PrtRes:                    ;
54                            ;
55    OutInt ax               ; Put result on screen
56                            ;
57    NewLine                 ; Move cursor to the next line
58                            ;
59    jmp   Next              ; Proceed next number
60                            ;
61 ExCycle:                   ; This label marks end of program
62                            ;
63    mov   ax,4C00h          ; AH register contains 4Ch code that
64                            ;is a DOS function number, AL register
65                            ;    contains return code 00.
66    int   21h              ; Dos service "Terminate program"
67                            ;
68 .stack                     ; This line defines the STACK segment
69    end   Begin
```

Listing 2.2 The Program FACTR

The first line is a directive that tells the assembler not to list the macro extensions (statements, which are generated from the macros). Don't worry about this now, we'll explain macro extensions in later chapters. The next line is again a directive that makes the assembler list 132 symbols in a line and 60 lines per page.

The next lines (lines 3-21 on the listing) are the comments that make up the program header.

The line after this is the directive to define a method of using the memory. Every assembly language program has to tell the Assembler where to put all the bits of the program in memory, with the SMALL model being the best for simple programs like this. We will cover all the options when we discuss memory in more detail.

The following three lines give the program access to the macro library. This library is stored on your program disk, supplied with this book. At the moment, that's all you need to know about macro libraries. You will find out how to create and use single macros and macro libraries in Chapter Five. If you have used a wordprocessor like MS WORD or WordPerfect, this denotation of a macro will be familiar. If you have used high-level languages such as PASCAL, FORTRAN, C and so on, you'll find that macros are something like subroutines or procedures in these languages. Briefly, a macro is a sequence of frequently used operations that as a group have been given a name and are invoked every time this name is used. Basically, it's a customised instruction. As we shall see later, they are tremendously powerful and are a significant feature of MASM (Microsoft **Macro** Assembler). If the term "macro" still sticks in your throat, don't waste time over it here. For the time being just think of these lines as a necessary part of a program, like please and thankyou in your speech. You'll meet a macro soon enough in the program we're going to look at.

The following line (except the comments lines 26-28) is the directive that starts the code segment, telling the assembler that the subsequent lines 30-66 constitute the **program body** - i.e, the assembly statements which produce the executable machine commands.

You should now be able to see two labels: **BEGIN** and **NEXT**, which precede the first assembly statement. It wouldn't be unreasonable of you to ask - isn't it enough to have one label for one command? Of course it is, but we believe that sometimes it is better to give more than one label to one statement if this statement plays more than one role. The first label, BEGIN, is given to the first instruction of the program and is used in the END directive to indicate where DOS must pass control when the program is loaded. The second label, NEXT, marks the first instruction of the cycle body - an instruction which must gain control when the cycle is repeated. Therefore, the statement

```
InpInt cx
```

is the first executable statement in our program, and it is also the first statement in the main processing cycle. This statement calls the macro which writes the integer number you type on the keyboard into the BX register. When you enter this number you should type the symbol "+" after the last digit. This symbol and certain others like "=", "-", etc. indicate the end of the number. Do not press **ENTER** after the symbol "+".

What you can see next is a block that is designed to decide whether work should be continued. Statements 36 - 39 are intended for this purpose. The macro InpInt places the last symbol you have entered from the keyboard into the **DL** register. Line number 36 compares this code and the code 0Dh. This is the ASCII code that corresponds to the **ENTER** key. All keys have a corresponding code, all of which are explained later in Chapter Seven and are listed in Appendix C If the **ENTER** key has actually been pressed, line 37 passes control to the label **ExProg** that marks the end of the program.

Lines 38 and 39 do the same job for the code 1Bh, which corresponds to the **ESC** key. In other words, this block terminates the program when you press the key **ENTER** or **ESC** instead of a number.

The next block includes lines 41 - 43. This block checks whether the number you have entered is 1 - the value of the function *n!* that corresponds to the argument 1 is 1. If so, then line 43 passes control to the label **PRTRES** without performing any action and leaves the initial value of the result unchanged. Note that the initial value 1 is stored into the AX register after the command in line 41 has been performed.

Line 45 clears the BX register, which is used as a work register. The program uses this register to accumulate the factor during calculation.

The next block which includes lines 47-51 is the main block for this program and starts with the label **MULT**. The result of the MUL function is always stored in the AX register and this register is also used as the first factor in the MUL operation . This block works according to the formula $AX = AX \times BX$ after which the value contained in the BX register increases by 1. The highest part of the result is stored in the DX register and this register is cleared before each iteration. This means that you can simplify this block but limits the result up to number that can be stored in one word (2^{16}=65536).

You are now looking at two macros which put the result onto the screen. This part of the program starts with the label **PRTRES** in line 53. The first macro **OUTINT** (line 55) puts the integer value onto the screen and the second macro **NEWLINE** (line 57) moves the cursor to the next line to avoid mixing the results on the screen.

The command JMP Next in line 59 passes control to the part of the program which reads the next number you want to use as an argument of the function *n!*. At this point you can stop the program by pressing **ENTER** or **ESC**.

The last block which completes the program's work and returns control to DOS, begins in the line 63. Most programs finish in the same way. This block uses the standard DOS service "Terminate program" which is available using the DOS interrupt 21h. We'll explain DOS interrupts in detail later, but for the moment you can just copy this section of code into your own programs as it stands.

For further practice you could write a program calculating factorial using the CX register simultaneously as a loop counter and work register for storing a factor.

Using Flags - Detecting the Step-by-step Mode

Having introduced Codeview in the previous chapter, we'll now look at the debugger in action by looking at a program that uses the control flags to determine whether it is executed under the debugger. The program DetStep shown in Listing 2.3 operates the Trap Flag discussed earlier. This program illustrates the technique of determining whether the program is run in step-by-step mode or in the usual way. The program should output the message "The Trap Flag is set successfully. No active debugger found." If you run this program under debugger, it must detect that the debugger clears the Trap Flag after performing each instruction. You can use a similar algorithm for preventing your programs from being analyzed by people who are too inquisitive.

```
1
2  page 55,132
3  .model small
4  .stack
5  .data
6  TitMsg  db    'Program demonstrating how the Trap Flag '
7          db    'works.',0Dh,0Ah, 0Dh,0Ah,'$'
8  NotSet  db    'Cannot set the Trap Flag - program works '
9          db    'under debugger.'0Dh,0Ah,'$'
10 IsSet   db    'The trap flag is set successfully. No active '
11         db    'debugger found.'0Dh,0Ah,'$'
12 .code
13 .startup
14         lea  dx,TitMsg      ; address of initial message
15         mov  ah,09          ; function 09 - output text string
16         int  21h            ; DOS service call
17         pushf               ; push original flags
18         pop  ax             ; copy original flag into AX
19         or   ax,0100h       ; set bit 8 - Trap Flag
20         push ax             ; push flags value to be set
21         popf                ; pop flags with TF set
22         pushf               ; push new flags value
23         pop  ax             ; copy new flags into AX
24         and  ax,0100h       ; separate bit 8 - highlight TF
25         lea  dx,IsSet       ; address of message "TF is set"
26         cmp  ax,0           ; is bit 8 clear?
27         jne  OutMsg         ; if not, output message
28         lea  dx,NotSet      ; address of message "cannot set TF"
29 OutMsg: mov  ah,09          ; function 09 - output text string
30         int  21h            ; DOS service call
31         pushf               ; push original flags
```

```
32        pop  ax                ; copy original flag into AX
33        and  ax,not 0100h      ; clear bit 8 - Trap Flag
34        push ax                ; push flags value to be set
35        popf                   ; pop flags with TF clear
36        mov  ax,4C00h          ; function 4Ch - terminate process
37        int  21h               ; DOS service call
38        end
```

Listing 2.3 The Program DetStep - Manipulating the Trap Flag

The program starts by outputting an initial message. The statements from lines 6 to 11 are the data segment of the program, and use the db directive to place the strings of characters in memory at a location labelled by TitMsg, NotSet and IsSet respectively. Lines 14 to 16 output the first string by pointing at it using the LEA (load effective address) instruction and calling the DOS output function.

The functional part of the program begins in line 17. This instruction pushes the contents of the flag register onto the stack using PUSHF and then pops it into the AX register with POPF. The stack is just a special area of memory, which we use here to overcome the inability of the processor to load the flags directly into another register.

The program then sets bit 8, which corresponds to the Trap Flag and pushes the result back onto the stack. The final step is to pop the contents of the flag register back off the stack, which in turn will set the Trap Flag. The contents of the flag register are then pushed onto the stack again and popped in the AX register. This means that we have copied the contents of the flag register into AX. Finally, the program checks bit 8 of AX which corresponds to the Trap Flag.

If the program is not working in step-by-step mode, bit 8 of AX will be equal to 1, indicating that the Trap Flag was set. If it is run under debugger, the picture is very different. The instruction POPF (line 21) will set the Trap Flag, but this flag will be immediately cleared by the debugger. So, the value of the flag register pushed onto the stack corresponds to the Trap Flag when it is clear. This effect is what lets you establish whether your program is really working in the step-by-step mode.

That's the theory anyway! If you experiment with the program DetStep it won't take you long to find out that a result telling you that a program is working in the ordinary mode is not necessarily correct. Oh dear!

There's a good reason for this though - remember that the CodeView debugger allows you to set breakpoints. Using this feature you can run all but two instructions - POPF (line 21) and PUSHF (line22) in the step-by-step mode. The first of these instructions loads the flag register with the value of the bit 8 equal to 1 (the Trap Flag set) and the second pushes that value back onto the stack.

To see how this works for yourself, set the breakpoint at line 23 by moving the cursor to this line and pressing the F9 key. Then perform the instructions step-by-step by pressing the F10 key. After line 20 has been executed, press the F5 key which means "GO" (run the program without stopping). The debugger will perform the critical part of the program in the usual way before returning to the step-by-step mode at line 23 (the breakpoint). Run the program up to the end and the message you see will tell you that this program is not running under a debugger - despite the fact that you know better!

Summary

This chapter has introduced some simple assembly language instructions, and highlighted the difference between these and directives.

In order to combine these into useful programs, we then looked at different methods of controlling program flow. As a result, you now know about the flags in CPU and the role they play in program control.

We explained how branching and loops are constructed in assembly language, looking at the JMP*, CMP* and LOOP* instructions.

In addition, those of you with MASM 6.0 will now understand the high-level language directives .WHILE, .REPEAT, .IF that this version offers.

The programs in the Library demonstrate a simple loop construction and illustrate the role of the flags.

Memory and Data

In this chapter we will look at the layout of the memory, the basic principles for addressing it, and the tools available for defining and controlling the memory fields. We will also explain the concept of **segment** and **offset**. The result of all this is that you will be able to create programs which use the memory to store and operate data and to access important system information.

Fundamental Knowledge

Memory - Purpose and Structure

So far you have been storing and processing data mainly using registers. Although programs which use this technique do work, you will soon find that you need a slightly more sophisticated approach for writing really useful programs. In Chapter One we examined the structure of a computer. In the diagram we looked at, we included an important component - RAM, that is Random Access Memory. This area is specifically intended for storing machine instructions and data.

IBM-compatible PC's usually have at least 1MB of RAM. Most new machines today will have 4 to 16 MB, while there are still some early machines with 512KB or less. We will start by considering the memory organization and allocation for a typical configuration of 1MB of memory.

Every byte in RAM has its own unique **address**, so that the microprocessor never confuses them. Figure 3.1 illustrates the most simple example of typical memory allocation. The first byte in memory has an address equal to 0. Since addresses from 0A0000h to 0FFFFFh are reserved for internal system usage, the last byte available for DOS programs has an address 9FFFFh or 655,359 in the decimal system. Other operating systems such as OS/2 or UNIX can use all the available memory, but DOS programmers can only use 640K of memory directly - the "640K DOS barrier". In practice it is slightly less because user programs have to share this memory with DOS itself and any TSR (terminate but stay resident) programs that may be installed.

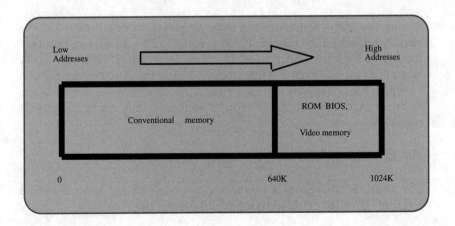

Figure 3.1
Typical Memory Allocation

The number 1,048,576 (1M) can be represented as 2^{20}. In Appendix A on number systems, you can see that n bits are needed to store 2^n numbers from 0 to 2^n-1. It would be logical therefore to assume that a 20-bit address is needed to access the full 1 MB. The problem here is that the i8086, the original processor for which DOS was written, has a 16-bit wide data bus, making it impossible to store an address up to 1MB in one 16-bit register. If we can overcome the problem inside the processor, then we are able to address the full 1MB as the i8086 does have a 20-bit wide address bus. The concept of **segment addressing** was invented to solve this problem.

Segment Addressing

We'll explain this using a simple analogy. Imagine a city where each house has its own unique number. To ensure that a letter is delivered to the right address, we have to give the name of the city and the number of house within that city. Now imagine that the city is arranged into streets of the same length and the houses within each street are renumbered. Finally, imagine that each street is served by its own post office. In this case, we only need to indicate the number of the house in the street to send a letter to the right street. It follows that if the postman knows that all the letters he must deliver are being sent to the same street, he can deliver them to the right house knowing only the number of this house.

While this might be an interesting concept for postmen and frustrated letter writers, how does it relate to our subject - the memory of a PC? The fact is that the microprocessor works in exactly the same way. Instead of a city, streets, post offices and houses however, we are dealing with the memory, segment registers and bytes respectively.

Taking the i8086, segments can have a maximum of 65536 bytes. We already know that the number 65536 is equal to 2^{16}-1, so to store numbers from 1 to 65535 we only need 16-bit wide registers. You can easily work out that a conventional memory is made up of 10 segments, each of which has a capacity of 64k bytes. Now let's consider how we can address each byte in the computer memory only using the 16-bit registers.

An Effective Address

The absolute address of a location in memory, that is unique to that location, is called its **effective address.** Since the maximum memory address for the i8086 processor is 1M or 2^{20}, an effective address for any i80x86 is at least 20 bits wide. It is this address which is used by the memory controller to reach a byte of memory and defines the width of the address bus. The i80x86 processors therefore have a 20-bit wide address bus at least (24-bit in the protected mode for i80286 and 32-bit for i80386/i80486). The most commonly used addresses are therefore 20-bits wide. Let's have a look at how the microprocessor creates 20-bit addresses using only 16-bit registers.

Let's go back to our post office analogy. Suppose that each block consists of 10 houses and all the blocks are numbered from 0. If this is the case, the definitive number of a house can be calculated as

$M \times 10 + n$

Number of the Block x 10 houses in each block + Number of the house

For example, the definitive number of the 7th house in the 12th block, will be equal to

$12 \times 10 + 7 = 127$

This number is made up of two components - 120 and 7, which are referred to in computer terms as the **segment** and **offset**. The **segment:offset** notation is used specifically for addresses which comprise two components. It has the following form:

SSSS:OOOO

where SSSS is the segment part (the number of block) and OOOO is the offset part (the number of house in the block). So for the last example, the address of the house would be 12:7. In the PC, each component can have from 1 to 4 hexadecimal numerals making it a maximum of 16 bits wide.

An effective address is therefore calculated by multiplying the segment address by 16 (2^4), and adding it to the offset:

$EA = segment \times 16 + offset$

Note that shifting a hexadecimal number by 4 bits to the left is the same as multiplying it by 10h (16 in the decimal system).

Forms of Segment:Offset Notation

The segment:offset notation has a feature which might seem somewhat strange - a particular memory location can be denoted in several different ways. In the context of our analogy about the city, this means that the number of a house depends on what we take to be the beginning of the street. Similarly, the address of a byte in segment:offset notation depends on where the segment that contains this byte starts. Since we can start the segment at any paragraph boundary, one byte can belong to several segments. This fact is illustrated in Figure 3.2. Note that the effective address of a byte is unique, as it is measured from a fixed point - the start of the memory (the byte at location 0000:0000h).

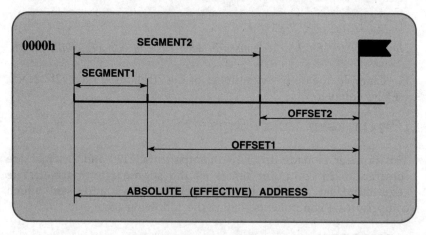

Figure 3.2
Addressing a Byte in Segment:Offset Form

Let's do something with all this theory now and look at the address of some important system information - the Keyboard Flag, which indicates the keyboard's state. Its absolute address is 00417h, which in segment:offset notation can be written in several different ways:

```
41hx10h+ 07h  =417h
40hx10h+ 17h  =417h
..............
 0hx10h+417h  =417h
20hx10h+217h  =417h
```

The first of the forms listed above is referred to as *standard* or *canonical* notation. In this form, an offset value can vary from 0 to 0Fh. The canonical form of segment:offset denotation for the address 00417h is therefore 41h:7h.

In practice, the most convenient or logical form of representation is used. For example, the most commonly used form for the address of the Keyboard Flag, considered in our example is 40h:17h. This is because all DOS programmers know that the segment address 40h is the beginning of the BIOS data area.

In more recent microprocessors, segments have been put to a more sophisticated use. The i80286 and later microprocessors can work in protected mode which allows programs to use the full address range (24 bits for i80286 and 32 bits for i80386/i80486). These microprocessors have extra segment registers which allow them to work in multitasking mode without jeopardizing or affecting data belonging to different programs. An effective address in this case can be written as GGGG:SSSS:OOOO where the component GGGG is stored in an extra segment register. This allows two or more programs to use the same effective address SSSS:OOOO but still refer to the different physical addresses, each of which has the unique component GGGG. Unfortunately, a detailed discussion of this subject is beyond the scope of this book.

Physical and Logical Segments

So far we have discussed how the PC's memory is broken down into segments. However, the notion of a segment, referring to part of something, has more than one meaning in the computing world.

On one hand, it can refer to part of the computer's memory. In this context we are talking about a **physical segment**. A physical segment is a group of bytes which have sequentially increasing addresses. Such a group can be from 0 to 65,535 bytes long.

On the other hand, when writing a relatively complex program, it will help if you think of it as a sequence of parts - the data block, command block, working memory and so on. These parts of a program are **logical segments**. You will often meet terms like code segment, data segment and so on.

Although physical and logical segments are different, they are usually connected in some way. It is common practice to group similar objects in separate areas of the memory - commands in one area and data in another. So, when we talk about the code segment and the memory segment we are really using both senses of the word segment: we are using a particular part of the memory (physical segment) for storing information which belongs to a particular part of the program (logical segment).

As we explained in previous chapters, i80x86 processors have registers which are specifically intended for dealing with segments. These registers are used for creating effective addresses of objects located in different segments. Thus, the registers CS and IP are used to store the effective address of instructions (or more precisely, of objects located in the active CODE segment). The register pair SS:SP identifies objects in the STACK segments, which we'll come back to later in this chapter. The data segment registers DS and ES are used in combination with the SI and DI registers for accessing data (again, to be exact - for accessing objects located in DATA segments). Now let's consider the different types of segments included in a typical assembler program.

Program Segments

If you have read every word in this book so far, you will have no problem answering the question - "Which segments should a typical program contain?" Logically, you can expect that there will be three main parts to a program, each of which occupies a separate area of the memory:

▲ A data area which contains data used in the program and intermediate data.
▲ A code area containing executable instructions for the program.
▲ Areas reserved for use by system functions.

The actual structure of a program is very close to this. Although there are several ways of organizing programs, there is a commonly used scheme which includes three main segments:

Data segment
Code segment
Stack segment

The Data Segment

It doesn't take much to work out that the data segment is intended for data! The implication is that memory areas intended for storing variables, buffer work spaces and so on should be grouped into one logical segment. If necessary, a program can contain more than one data segment. The i80x86 microprocessor has two segment registers which are commonly used for accessing data segments: DS (Data Segment register) and ES (Extra Data Segment Registers). Most instructions for processing data use the DS register for storing the segment address of data. So, if your program contains the instruction

```
mov    ax,Field1
```

it is treated by the microprocessor as

```
mov    ax,DS:Field1
```

unless you specifically tell the instruction to use another register, for example

```
mov    ax,ES:Field2
```

Some instructions use both DS and ES segment registers. Take the MOVSB instruction which moves strings for example. Before performing this instruction you have to load four registers - two segment registers, DS and ES and two index registers, SI (Source Index) and DI (Destination Index). The following example shows a complete program which processes data located in different segments:

```
.model large

ExtDat    segment 'DATA'          ; this defines extra data segment
;..............................
StringD  db 'This must have enough space to fit a source string'
;.......
ExtDat    ends
;..............................

.data
; this is ordinary DATA segment
;..............................
StringS  db    'This is the source string'
LSource  equ  $ - StringS
;..............................

.code
..startup
          mov  ax,seg StringS     ; load segment address of StringS
          mov  ds,ax              ; DS points to segment of StringS
          mov  ax,seg StringD     ; load segment address of StringD
          mov  es,ax              ; ES points to segment of StringS
          mov  si,offset StringS  ; DS:SI point to StringS
          mov  di,offset StringD  ; ES:DI point to StringD
          mov  cx,LSource         ; load length of StringS into CX
rep       movsb                   ; copy strings (size in CX)
;..............................
.exit
          end
..............................
```

The MOVSB instruction copies the string, whose initial address is stored in the DS:SI register, into a string specified by the contents of the ES:DI register. Note that this instruction is preceded by the REP prefix. Unlike labels, prefixes have no character ":" after them and are used for repeating an instruction depending on certain conditions. The simplest form of the repetition prefix used in this example causes the MOVSB instruction to be repeated n times, where n is the value in the CX register. Each repetition of the MOVSB instruction involves transferring one byte from the memory location specified by an address in DS:SI to the target byte at the address ES:DI. When you use the MOVSB instruction, the length of the string being processed is contained in the CX register.

The DS and ES registers are not the only segment registers you can use in data processing instructions. For example, if you want to calculate the size of a particular fragment of a program, you could use the following sequence of instructions:

```
......
        mov     ax,offset cs:FirstInstr
        mov     cx,offset cs:LastInstr
        sub     cx,ax
.....
Firstinstr:
......
LastInstr:
```

This piece of code calculates the distance between the instructions labelled FirstInstr and LastInstr and places this value into the CX register. This kind of technique is widely used for calculating the size of the memory area required for a certain part of a program.

You can also use the data segment registers in instructions which control program flow, such as jumps or calls. For example, suppose that the NewInstr label is located in a data segment. In this case, the instruction:

```
jmp    ds:NewInstr
```

is valid, but it behaves unexpectedly - the segment address of the next instruction to be performed is still in the CS register but the offset address is equal to the offset of the NewInstr label in the data segment! This is because the Assembler is "too clever" and always tries to generate the most compact machine code possible. Therefore, by default, it treats the instruction JMP as JMP SHORT which always uses the CS register as a segment register. If you want to write a program which creates a new executable code in a data segment and then passes control to that code, use the FAR JMP instruction:

```
jmp    far ptr ds:NewInstr
```

Note that we have told Assembler explicitly how to calculate the effective address of the instruction. By default, program flow control instructions such as JMP or CALL use the CS register as an address segment. The specifier FAR PTR (Far Pointer) tells Assembler to use the segment register given in the instruction rather than the default one.

This trick will work if the data located where control is passed can be interpreted as valid machine instructions. Make sure that these instructions do not perform tasks such as low-level formatting of a hard disk or transferring all your data through communication ports.

The Code Segment

The code segment is not only the main segment of a program but quite often the only one. It contains machine instructions generated from the source code. Although you can put both data and work areas in the code segment, we don't advise it, unless you are writing a special program intended for working in a limited memory area such as a device driver or TSR.

The default segment register for all the objects in the code segment is the register CS. As a result, all the instructions which deal with commands (jumps, calls and so on) treat the short form of an address *label* as *CS:label*. For example, the instruction

```
jmp    MyLabel
```

is treated as the instruction

```
jmp    cs:Mylabel
```

To use other segment registers for accessing objects belonging to the code segments, you must assign the relevant values to these registers.

The Stack

The stack is widely used in high-level programming languages. Initially it was introduced as an array, accessed in the LIFO (Last In - First Out) manner. The first time you met something like the stack is probably much longer ago than you imagine.

Remember one of your first toys - the pyramid? (See Figure 3.3) This toy is made up of a set of rings of different colors and sizes which you can put on and take off. The ring you put on last (ring 1 in Fig 3.3) is on top of the stack so it has to be taken off first. To remove the ring at the bottom of the stack (ring 5 in Figure 3.3) you have to remove all the rings above it (rings 1-4), starting with the first one.

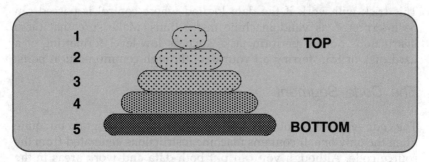

Figure 3.3
The Stack Prototype - The Child's Pyramid

It's just as well that we don't shed "toys" like this along with our childhood, although several generations of oriental sages who have worried over a task called "The count of eternity" (based on the notion of the stack) may have had an easier life if we did! More prosaically, stacks are widely used in programming for storing immediate data, passing parameters to and from procedures, processing symbols and so on. One particularly useful application is for creating re-entrant and recursive procedures - procedures which can be called more than once at the same time and even can call themselves. You will also remember how in Chapter Two we pushed the flags register onto the stack in order to copy its value into another register.

The hardware of IBM-compatible PCs is specially adapted to support stacks and includes stack manipulation instructions such as PUSH and POP and registers such as SS and SP. Figure 3.4 shows the part of the memory known as the stack segment.

Let's consider the process of pushing data onto and reading it from the stack in more detail. Suppose that the

PUSH AX

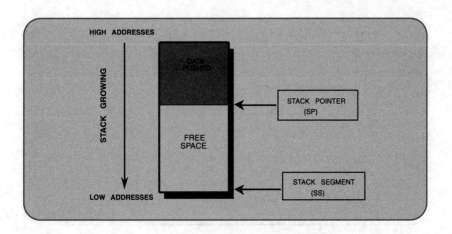

Figure 3.4
The Stack Segment

instruction is performed when the stack is empty. This process involves the following steps:

Takes the current value of the SS and SP registers
Stores one word at the address SS:SP
Decreases the value of the SP register

The process of popping data from the stack is very similar, the difference is that data is read from the memory and the value of the SP register is increased.

Note that the stack pointer decreases once data has been pushed onto the stack - it grows from high to low addresses. This is shown in Figure 3.5. This technique might seem a bit strange, but it does have its advantages. The alternative organization of the stack does not tell

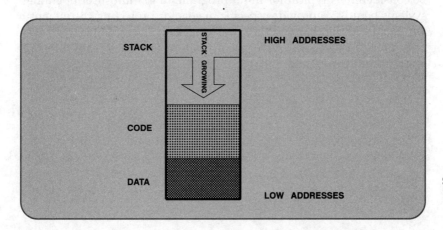

Figure 3.5
Stack Memory Allocation on the PC

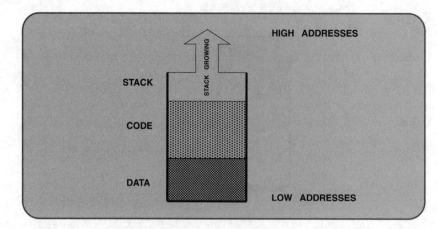

Figure 3.6
**Alternative
Stack
Arrangement
Growing to
Higher
Addresses**

you how much memory your program will require to run. Figure 3.6 shows how the memory layout looks when the stack grows to higher addresses. As you can see, you cannot determine the end of the program since the size of the stack can vary during program execution.

Figure 3.5 shows the typical memory distribution for a program on IBM-compatible computers. The size of the program is a constant value and can be calculated before the program starts. Moreover, this value remains constant until the program is finished.

When used on DOS PCs, this technique simplifies the process of allocating memory and helps to detect attempts to modify memory which is not allocated to the program.

A surprising feature of the PC is that on the one hand, the stack can be considered as typical for multi-programming, multi-user operating systems because it provides specific means for protecting the memory yet on the other hand, PCs were originally designed as *personal* computers and as such were not actually intended for any kind of multitasking processing!

Tools

Creating a Program - Starting with the Bare Bones

We have already had a brief look at program structure. In this section we'll expand on this with a short guide to writing the basic parts of a program. Since every program can be divided into segments (this covers any meaning of the term "segment" discussed in this chapter - logical or physical) we'll use this as our starting point.

A program usually consists of three segments - code, data and stack. In order to access objects located in a segment, the microprocessor calculates their effective addresses using the values stored in the segment registers. For this reason, the program must know which segments are controlled by which register and the initial value of this register. Don't forget though that this information only tells Assembler how to use the segment registers - you have to load their correct initial values.

Putting together the most simple program skeleton involves:

> Defining the memory model
> Defining the stack segment
> Defining the data segment
> Defining the code segment
> Describing the use of segment registers
> Initializing these segment registers
> Performing the functional part of the program
> Returning control to DOS or calling program
> Defining the starting point of the program

This is a general outline only - not all these elements are always necessary, for example you don't need a data segment if your program only uses registers. Furthermore, it does not cover all the elements required for more sophisticated programs where you may need to define several data or code segments, or other kinds of segments, for example shared data.

Having said that, we'll stay with our general scheme and look at how it can be used for writing real programs. Since there are two common kinds of executable programs (-COM and -EXE modules), we'll consider their organization separately.

EXE Program Template

There are two main types of program which can be executed under MS-DOS: .EXE-programs and .COM-programs. You should really decide what kind of executable program you want to obtain before creating the assembly language program, since there are differences even at this stage. These differences are mainly in their segment organization, which is best illustrated by examining an example of each. To begin with we'll consider an assembly language program which will create an .EXE-program. This program, shown in Listing 3.1 will say "Hello!" to everybody.

```
        TITLE   Hello1 Example Program 1; title is not necessary
OurCode SEGMENT PARA PUBLIC 'CODE'              ; declare code segment
        ASSUME  CS:OurCode, DS:OurData, SS:OurStack
Start:  MOV     AX,OurData   ; copy address of data
        MOV     DS,AX        ; segment into DS
        LEA     DX,Hello     ; address of message
        MOV     AH,09h       ; DOS service "output text string"
        INT     21h          ; DOS service call
        MOV     AH,4Ch       ; DOS service "terminate process"
        MOV     AL,00h       ; return code zero
        INT     21h          ; DOS service call
OurCode ENDS                 ; end of code segment

OurData SEGMENT PARA PUBLIC 'DATA'       ; declare data segment
Hello   DB      'Hello!$'               ; define string to display
OurData ENDS                            ; end of data segment

OurStack SEGMENT PARA STACK 'STACK'      ; declare stack segment
        DB      64 DUP (?)              ; reserve 64 bytes
OurStack ENDS                           ; end of stack segment

        END     Start                   ; end of program
```

Listing 3.1 Hello1 - An Example of .EXE Program

The first thing you can see is the program title (on the same line as the TITLE directive) which is optional. The program is then divided into three parts, each of which starts with the SEGMENT directive and ends with the ENDS directive. These parts are the code segment, the data segment and the stack segment, marked by the words 'CODE', 'DATA' and 'STACK' respectively. Finally, the END directive marks the end of the program and points to the execution start point - every assembly language program must include this line.

Every .EXE-program must contain one stack segment and at least one code and one data segment. However, this rule, like all rules, has some exceptions. You don't need to define the data segments in a program which uses no memory data. Similarly, you don't need stack definition if you are sure that your program does not use the stack (some DOS services may use the stack for internal purposes and any CALL and INT instructions use the stack for storing the return address). And finally, you don't need code segment definition for programs which don't contain any executable instructions (for example, if your module only contains shared data used by other routines).

As their names indicate, the code segment contains the code of the program and the data segment contains data definitions, while the stack segment temporarily stores various data during program execution - the more complex a program is, generally speaking the larger the stack has to be.

Each of these logical segments must be contained in one physical segment, which limits the size of a logical segment to 64K bytes. If you need a larger data segment, you must divide it into sections of no more than 64K bytes and treat these as separate data segments. You can then switch between these parts by changing the value of the corresponding data segment register (DS or ES).

As you see, the SEGMENT directive in the example given above contains two parameters: PARA and PUBLIC. The first parameter defines the **segment alignment** - the memory boundary corresponding to the beginning of the segment. This can be one of the memory unit definitions such as BYTE, WORD, DWORD or PARA (which stands for paragraph). The second parameter, PUBLIC, allows a linker to combine all segments which have the same name and are located in different modules into one contiguous segment.

Physical segments can overlap or even be the same, depending on the value of the corresponding segment registers such as DS, ES and SS. The values of these registers can either be assigned by the programmer explicitly or by MASM, using the simplified segment directive .CODE, .DATA and .STACK. If you use the SEGMENT directives rather than the simplified MASM directive, you must tell Assembler which segment contains the object used in an instruction. This is done using the directive ASSUME which has the following format:

```
assume   register:segment
```

where register is one of the segment registers CS, DS, ES or SS. For example, to tell Assembler that it must use the ES register to calculate the addresses of objects located in the segment BIOS_SEG you would write:

```
assume    es:BIOS_SEG
```

Note that MASM 6.0 always uses the CS register to address the current segment. This means that if your program consists of only one segment, you will not need to mention the CS register in the ASSUME directive. Note that earlier versions of MASM and some other Assemblers do need the ASSUME directive for addressing all segment registers used in a program.

An important characteristic of the ASSUME directive is that it does not generate machine instructions. This means that you must load the segment registers with the addresses of the corresponding segments manually. To do this, use the MOV instruction as follows:

```
    assume    es:EXTRA_DAT    ; assembler will use ES to calculate
                              ; addresses of objects in EXTRA_DAT
......
    mov       ax,EXTRA_DAT    ; load address of EXTRA_DAT
    mov       es,ax           ; ES now points to start of EXTRA_DAT
```

The next example we'll look at shows how the simplified segment directives included in MASM 5.0 and later versions can be used to write more compact source code for defining segments. The Hello Example Program 2 shown in Listing 3.2 is essentially the same as the Hello Example Program 1, it is significantly shorter though because simplified MASM directives have been used. The order of the segments in the program has not changed.

```
TITLE   Hello2 Example Program 2        ; title is not necessary
.MODEL  SMALL                           ; declare memory model
.CODE                                   ; declare code segment
Start:  MOV   AX,@Data                  ; copy address of data
        MOV   DS,AX                     ; segment into DS
        LEA   DX,Hello
        MOV   AH,09h                    ; define DOS function number
        INT   21h                       ; call DOS function to display
        MOV   AH,4Ch                    ; define DOS function to exit
        MOV   AL,00h                    ; with code zero
        INT   21h                       ; exit to DOS

.DATA                                   ; declare data segment
Hello   DB    'Hello!$'                 ; define string to be displayed
.STACK                                  ; declare stack segment
END           Start
```

Listing 3.2 The Modification of the Hello Program

The first line in this listing is the .MODEL directive describing the method of memory distribution in a program. The parameter SMALL indicates that the program can only include one logical segment for each basic type (code, data and stack) and all these logical segments must be located within one physical segment. Near references are used to access all labels and variables.

The predefined symbol @DATA is used to refer to the name of the data segment and is used in the same way the label Our_Data in the previous listing.

COM Program Template

The two main differences between .EXE-programs and .COM-programs are:

1. A .COM-program is a relatively small program that cannot occupy more than 64K of memory, while an .EXE-program is not restricted in this way

2. A .COM-program is organized so that it can be loaded into RAM and executed slightly faster than an .EXE-program with similar code.

A .COM program has only one code segment, and no data segment. All data definitions are in the code segment. Even if you use the .DATA directive to define the data segment, MASM places that logical segment in the same physical segment with the code. You don't have to worry about the stack, as MASM will organize that itself. Listing 3.3 shows the Hello Example Program 3 which is the .COM-version of its .EXE prototype.

```
TITLE    Hello Example Program 3           ;title is not necessary
OurProg  SEGMENT PARA 'CODE'               ; declare code segment
         ORG    100h                       ; 100h byte for PCP
         ASSUME CS:OurProg, DS:OurProg,
                ES:OurProg, SS:OurProg     ; information on program
                                           ; structure
Start:   JMP    Begin                      ; jump over data definition
Hello    DB     'Hello!$'                  ; define string to display
Begin:   LEA    dx,Hello                   ; DS:DX - effective address of string
         MOV    AH,09h                     ; function 09h - output text string
         INT    21h                        ; DOS service call
         MOV    ax,4C00h                   ; function 4Ch - terminate process
         INT    21h                        ; DOS service call
OurProg  ENDS                              ; end of program segment
         END    Start
```

Listing 3.3 The -COM Version of the Hello Program

Note the ORG directive that points to the offset of the start of the program; the line

```
ORG    100h
```

must be included in every assembly language program that is designed as a .COM-module unless your Assembler generates this directive automatically. This directive sets the initial value of the instruction pointer to 100h - the address of the byte that immediately follows PSP. Since MS-DOS treats the first byte of a -COM program as its starting address and passes control to this instruction, your program must have an executable instruction at the beginning. There are two possible ways of ensuring this condition:

▲ Begin your program with the JMP instruction that passes control to the executable part of the program

▲ Put the executable part of the program first and all data and work areas after the last program instruction.

Maybe once, a long time ago, programmers had a reason for choosing the first technique as the basic one. Today, although this way makes your programs at least two bytes longer, it is still the most common:

```
            ......
            org    100h
    Start:  jmp    Begin
    ;
    ;..... data and work area goes here
    ;
    Begin:                          ; executable code starts here
            ......
            mov    ax,4C00h         ; function 4Ch - terminate process
            int    21h              ; DOS service call
            end    start
```

The second option lets you make your program shorter by one instruction:

```
            ......
            org    100h
    Start:                          ; executable code starts here
            ......
            mov    ax,4C00h         ; function 4Ch - terminate process
            int    21h              ; DOS service call
    ;
    ;..... data and work area goes here
    ;
            end    start
```

Note that in -COM programs you don't need to set up the value of the segment registers - DOS puts the segment address of the PSP into the CS, DS, ES and SS registers automatically when the program is loaded.

Using Simplified Directives - General Template

We gave a brief description about initializing segment registers earlier in the chapter but here's a slightly more detailed account of the initial values of the segment registers for -COM and -EXE modules.

The picture for -COM modules is very simple. All the segment registers point to the start of the PSP and the initial value of the Instruction Pointer is 100h. Generally speaking, you do not need to change the value of segment registers until you want to use data located in other physical segments, for example in the BIOS data area which starts at the address 0040:0000h. Another reason for changing the value of segment registers is when you want to have several logical segments in your program. The Command Segment register CS for -COM programs always points to the start of the PSP.

When an -EXE program is loaded, the CS register points to the start of the code segment, the SS register to the start of the stack segment and both DS and ES registers point to the start of the PSP. If you intend to use a data segment in your program, you need to load the relevant value into the DS and ES registers. You can do this using either the predefined variable @DATA or the MASM simplified directives.

The example below uses the simplified directives provided by MASM 6.0 for creating an -EXE program template:

```
.model    small ; This model permits the use of one physical segment
                 ; only
.stack    1024  ; stack area occupies 1024 bytes
.data
;.......data definition goes here
.code
.startup
;.......functional part of the program goes here
.exit           ; this finishes the program with the return code 0
.end
```

Although it does not actually do anything, this is a genuine and most importantly, correct program that you can either assemble and run as it stands, or use as a skeleton for other programs. The template for the -COM variant of this program is:

```
.model    tiny  ; This model permits the use of one physical segment
                ; only
.stack    1024  ; stack area occupies 1024 bytes
.data
;.......data definition goes here
.code
.startup
;.......functional part of the program goes here
.exit           ; this finishes the program with the return code 0
.end
```

Although this program looks very similar to the previous one (the only difference is that the memory model is TINY), the object code is slightly different. Instructions generated by Assembler from the directive .STARTUP, initialize the segment registers as required by -COM modules. Let's look at another remake of the program HELLO as an example of using the simplified MASM directives for creating a -COM program:

```
TITLE  Hello Example Program 4   ; title is not necessary
.model tiny
.data
Hello  DB     'Hello!$'          ; define string to display
.code
.startup
       LEA    DX,Hello           ; DS:DX - effective address of string
       MOV    AH,09h             ; function 09h - output text string
       INT    21h                ; DOS service call
       MOV    ax,4C00h           ; function 4Ch - terminate process
       INT    21h                ; DOS service call
       END
```

Listing 3.4 Using Simplified Directives for Creating a -COM Module

The .STARTUP directive introduced in MASM 6.0 makes the lives of us programmers a lot easier as it sets up the address counter and generates instructions for loading segments registers. Using this directive we can convert the example above into the -EXE module by just changing *one* word in the source code - replacing the word TINY with the word SMALL. Note, however, that you also need to tell the link editor which kind of executable module you would like to get.

To create a -COM module, make sure that the parameter /t is specified in the command line for running the link editor. To create an -EXE module you should do the opposite to be sure that this parameter isn't present in the command line involving the linker. If your linker cannot create -COM modules directly, then using the /t parameter causes an error and you need to use the DOS utility EXE2BIN to convert an -EXE module into a -COM module.

Defining and Using Data - EQU

It is virtually impossible to imagine a program that does not deal with data. Even when a program consists of only a few instructions like the program Hello considered in this chapter, it still contains data. The simplest type of data is immediate data - numbers or characters. For example, the following two lines of code are intended to finish a program:

```
mov   ah,4Ch              ; function 4Ch - terminate process
int   21h                 ; DOS service call
```

These lines contain immediate data 4Ch and 21h - hexadecimal numbers of one byte in length. The constant 4Ch defines the DOS function "Terminate Process" and the constant 21h is the number of an interrupt which provides the DOS service (don't worry about the term "interrupt" here, in a few chapters time it will seem like a life long friend).

In practice, programs usually contain significantly more constants than the examples we have considered might suggest. For this reason, it will come as a relief to learn that assembly language includes the directive EQU which lets you give meaningful names to constants. This directive has two parameters - the name of a constant and of an expression, the value of which will be assigned to that constant. For example, we can assign the name TermProc to the constant 4Ch and the name DosServ to the constant 21h, then rewrite our program as follows:

```
TermProc    equ   4Ch        ; This defines constant
DosServ     equ   21h        ; This defines constant
......
            mov   ah,TermProc
            int   DosServ
```

The text of the program is now easier to read, isn't it? The following examples show how to use the EQU directive for defining symbolic constants.

```
Cr        equ      0Dh    ; Carriage Return
Lf        equ      0Ah    ; Line Feed
EndMsg    equ      '$'    ; End of message for DOS service 09h
......
TextMsg   db       'This is the text string',Cr,Lf,EndMsg
```

Constants defined by EQU can also be used to make your programs more flexible. Suppose you have a table of a particular length which you process sequentially, element by element - the typical fragment of code designed to do this is:

```
TablBeg   db       1,2,3,4,5
......
          mov      cx,5   ; set cycle counter to the table length
ProcTab:
;......
;   the cycle code goes here
;......
......    loop     ProcTab
......
```

However, if you change the table, it can mean that you have to change the line of code that sets up the cycle counter as well. The following example shows how to get round this:

```
TablBeg   db       1,2,3,4,5
TablLen   equ      $-TablBeg
......
          mov      cx,TablLen   ; set cycle counter to table length
ProcTab:
;......
;   the cycle body goes here
;......
......    loop     ProcTab
......
```

The named constant TablLen is calculated by the Assembler while compiling the program and is changed automatically if the size of the table changes. Note that the $ character in the line defining TablLen denotes the current value of the instruction pointer, which at the time of calculation will be at the byte after the end of the table.

The EQU directive can be a very powerful tool, doing much more than we have just shown. For example, take a look at the next piece of code:

```
Nlines          equ 65
NChars          equ 50
CharsonPage     equ Nlines*Nchars
```

Good use of this directive can make your assembler programs close to high-level ones in style, easier to read and consequently, easier to use.

Defining Data with the DB Directive

No programming language would be complete if it did not include the concept of a **variable** - one of the most useful tools as far as programmers are concerned. Variables were introduced in early versions of symbolic coding languages to give meaningful names to certain memory areas. Assembler has kept this original meaning of the term "variable", as well as taking on the understanding typical of high-level languages. For example, MASM supports all types of simple variables - bytes, words and double words as well as strings, arrays and structures.

You can define a variable in your program using one of the **data definition directives** - **DB**, **DW** and **DD (define B**yte, **W**ord, Double-word). The format of the DB directive is:

```
    Name DB immediate_data
```

where *Name* is a label (written without a colon at the end) which denotes a variable, and *immediate_data* is a number or a character usually the size of one byte. As you will see in a short while, the DB directive can be used to define data that occupies more than one byte.

This kind of directive, when written in the proper place (usually in the data segment of the program) enables you to use the variable *Name* in your program. The variable it creates will have the value *immediate_data* until you change it using an instruction. For example, the

```
    Apple1  DB 2h
```

directive defines the **Apple1** variable and gives it an initial value 2h=2.

You can also include a character value in the variable. In this case, the character must be enclosed by double quotes or apostrophes. For example, the directive

```
Banana2    DB    '2'
```

allocates memory for the **Banana2** variable and assigns the initial value '2' to that variable. Note that the value '2' is represented by the ASCII code 32h=48=00110010b which is different to the integer number 2. Something that might strike you as odd is the fact that you can define a variable length which is significantly greater than one byte. You can do this using the DB directive. For example, the directive

```
MsgText    DB    'You have an '
```

defines the **MsgText** variable which has the value of the "You have an " string. This directive ensures that the Assembler reserves the right amount of bytes in the memory for storing the string. It also connects the address of the first of these bytes with the variable name (label). This means that you can treat the **MsgText** variable as an array of bytes and manipulate it accordingly. This very powerful feature of assembly language allows you to build complex data structures, which is the subject of the next chapter.

If you need to include an apostrophe in a character string, you can do it in one of three ways. Firstly, you can use double quotes for defining these strings, secondly, you can denote an apostrophe by writing it twice. For example, both of these character strings are valid:

```
Msg1    db    "That's a string with double quotes"
Msg2    db    'That''s another form of defining an apostrophe'
```

The third option is based on the fact that you can mix ASCII codes and numbers in the string definition. For example, the line

```
MixMsg    db    'It',39,'s an apostrophe'
```

is valid and defines the string "It's an apostrophe". Note that the number 39 (27h) corresponds to the ASCII character "'" (apostrophe).

DW and DD Directives

These directives are similar to the DB directive. DW stands for **Define Word** and DD stands for **Define Doubleword**. Hence the DW directive defines a variable of one or more words (16 bits). Similarly, the DD directive defines a variable of one or more double words (32 bits).

You can use the symbol ? in the DB, DW and DD directives instead of immediate data. This symbol tells the directive to just reserve memory for those variables listed, without giving them initial values.

Although the DB directive on its own lets you define any data, using it together with the DW and DD directives gives you more flexibility. For example, you can define the constant 0FFFFh using either of the following directives:

```
Const1      db      0FFh,0FFh
Const2      dw      0FFFFh
```

In this example, the constant Const2 consists of two equal bytes. The following example shows how to define a slightly more complex constant, where constant 1 is stored as a word. The following example shows how to define it using the DB, DW directives.

```
ConstB      db      0,1
.......
ConstW      dw      1
```

Assembler uses the information about the length of constants and variables while generating instructions for storing and loading data. For example, the instruction

```
mov         ax,ConstW
```

will load the constant 1 into the AX register but the instruction

```
mov         ax,ConstB
```

is invalid because its operands are different sizes. The solution to this problem is to specify the size directly, for example:

```
mov         ax,word ptr ConstB
```

However, this gives us another headache - the result in the AX register is 10h instead of 1! This is because of the way memory is organized on IBM-compatible PCs. Remember that the highest byte of the word is stored at the highest address, so to define the constant 1 stored as a word, we need to write:

```
Const1      db 1,0
```

This has probably convinced you that it's much easier to use the directives included in MASM to define memory fields of a required size!

Addressing Your Data

Earlier on we explained that an effective address is calculated by multiplying the segment part by 16 and adding the offset part to the result. The actual process involves different registers, and the particular method applied depends on which registers are used. Here we'll consider the basic methods of addressing and how they can be presented in assembler statements.

The simplest kind of addressing involves using immediate operands, so not surprisingly it is called **immediate addressing**. For example:

```
mov    ax,4C00h
```

This instruction uses two kinds of addressing: immediate (the constant 4C00h) and **register addressing**. The register operand is simply the name of the register (8-bit, 16-bit or extended 32-bit register on 386/486 computers).

The next type is **direct addressing**, used to move data between the memory and registers. The following instruction copies the value stored in the variable RetCode into the AL register.

```
mov    al,RetCode
```

The variable RetCode must be defined by the corresponding directive (in this case by the DB directive).

Another type of addressing is **register indirect addressing** which uses the base and index registers for calculating effective addresses. This type of addressing usually involves the BX, SI and DI registers. The most significant aspect of this type of addressing is that you specify the names of the registers containing the addresses rather than the addresses themselves. The following example loads the value from the memory into the AX register. Unlike the previous example, this type of addressing uses the value stored in a register as an offset address of an operand.

```
mov    ax,[bx]
```

Note that square brackets are used to tell Assembler that the value of the BX register is treated as an address.

The DUP Prefix

Suppose you want to create a relatively large variable and fill it with something simple like the symbol "=" or blanks. You do not need to count the quantity of symbols in the string:

```
"=============================="
```

You simply need to write the directive

```
LongSign    DB 32 dup ('=')
```

This directive defines the LongSign variable, 32 bytes long, where each of these bytes contains the ASCII code of the symbol "=" that is, 3Dh. This is very useful when defining the size of the stack for a program. You can write the DB directive without a variable name but still include the DUP prefix and place this directive in the stack segment of your program as follows:

```
.STACK
                db 128 dup (0)
```

In this example, a stack of 128 bytes size is defined and filled with zeros.

The LEA Instruction

The abbreviation LEA stands for **Load Effective Address**. Its format is:

```
LEA destination,source
```

where *destination* can be any 16-bit register of the data group or pointer&index group of the internal registers. For i80386 and i80486, this includes the 32-bit extended registers.

The *source* must be a memory operand and can be addressed in any valid way.

The **LEA** instruction places an offset address of the *source* into the *destination*.

Hence, the instruction

```
LEA   SI,I386
```

writes the offset address of the I386 variable into the SI register. Similarly, the instruction

```
LEA   DX,MsgText
```

writes the offset address of the **MsgText** into DX.

Note that the **LEA** instruction works with the offset address which is only part of the full address. The **LDS** and **LES** instructions copy both the segment address and offset address into given registers.

Instructions Which Work with the Stack

Instructions which work with the stack are extremely useful when handling subroutines. They are usually used for saving the values of registers and flags etc on entry to the subroutines and for restoring these values on return. This means that the procedure called can use the registers for its own purpose and the original values used in the main program will remain unchanged. Most programming languages also use the stack for passing parameters between program units, organizing nested cycles and similar processes.

The PUSH instruction pushes data onto the stack. Its format is:

```
PUSH operand
```

where operand denotes data. For example, the instruction

```
PUSH DX
```

places the value contained in the DX register onto the stack.

The POP instruction does exactly the opposite. It transfers data from the stack into the register or variable. The format of the POP instruction is

```
POP operand
```

where operand denotes the register or variable where the value is transferred. For example, the

```
POP     DX
```

instruction places information from the stack into the DX register.

Note that you can only write information onto and read it from the stack using 16-bit units of information - words. As a result, the commands PUSH AL, PUSH AH and PUSH AX work in the same way. Even if you push an 8-bit register such as AL or BL onto the stack, the value pushed will be 16-bit.

The PUSHF and POPF instructions are quite similar to the two instructions considered above. The difference is that they work with the flag register as a whole, and consequently, do not need any operands. The format of PUSHF instruction is

```
PUSHF
```

This instruction places the information contained in the flag register onto the stack. This action is reversed by the POPF instruction which has the following format

```
POPF
```

This instruction takes the 16-bit value from the stack and places it in the flag register.

Remember that the stack is a LIFO structure i.e Last In - First Out. Later on you'll see how useful this is for saving information while performing nested calls of subroutines.

Stack and Flags

Any information stored in the memory or common registers can be accessed by instructions such as MOV. Unfortunately, there is no instruction which allows you to deal with the flag register as a whole. You can change certain flags using instructions like CLD (Clear Direction), you can choose which instruction will be executed depending on the flag value (conditional jump) but you can neither change the value of more than one flag nor check the value of more than one flag simultaneously. However, you *can* work with the values of flags if you copy these values into the memory or registers, as we did in the program DetStep in Chapter Two.

The command set of i80x86 microprocessors contains two instructions intended for saving and restoring flags:

PUSHF   - writes the flag register onto the stack, and
POPF   - restores the flag register from the stack.

On the 80386/80486, these instructions were developed for operating with the extended 32-bit flag register. These instructions are PUSHFD and POPFD for saving and restoring the 80386/80486 flag registers.

The instructions PUSHF and POPF were originally intended for organizing the interface between separate parts of the program called procedures. We will come back to this later, for the moment we will remind you how to change the value of the flag register using the PUSHF/POPF instructions.

The PUSHF instruction stores the value of the 16-bit flag register in the stack. You can then read this value into a register using the instruction POP, process it and store the new value back in the stack using the PUSH instruction. Finally, you can assign a new value to the flag register by popping one word from the stack (the instruction POPF) or two words for 80386/80486 processors (the instruction POPFD).

Library

Inputting and Outputting Numeric Data

We'll now look at an example of a complete program that includes most of the aspects of assembly language considered in this chapter. The program NumIO given in Listing 3.5 reads a numeric string from the keyboard, converts it into a binary number and stores it in the memory. The program then takes this number, converts it back to a character string and outputs this string to the screen.

```
 1
 2 .model small           ; small memory model - one segment only
 3 .stack                 ; stack of default size
 4 .data                  ; this starts data segment
 5 CR      equ  0Dh        ; Carriage Return
 6 LF      equ  0Ah        ; Line Feed
 7 EndMsg  equ  '$'        ; End of message
 8 MsgIn   db   CR,LF,'Enter a number less than 65536: ',EndMsg
 9 MsgOut  db   CR,LF,'You have entered the number ',EndMsg
10 UnsWord dw   0          ; number to be output
11 Ten     dw   10         ; constant for obtaining decimal digits
12 .code                  ; this starts code segments
13 .startup               ; this initializes segment registers
14         mov  ah,09h     ; function 09h - output text string
15         lea  dx,MsgIn   ; address of message into DX
16         int  21h        ; DOS service call
17 NextCh: mov  ah,01      ; function 01h - keyboard input
18         int  21h        ; DOS service call
19         cmp  al,0       ; special character?
20         jne  NotSpec    ; if not - process character
21         int  21h        ; read code of special character
22         jmp  OutNum     ; output number
23 NotSpec:cmp  al,'0'     ; compare character read to "0" (number?)
24         jb   OutNum     ; if not, don't process
25         cmp  al,'9'     ; compare character read to "9" (number?)
26         ja   OutNum     ; if not, don't process
27 ProcNum:sub  al,30h     ; convert character to number
28         mov  bl,al      ; copy character read into BX
29         mov  ax,UnsWord ; hex number into AX
30         mul  Ten        ; one decimal position to the left
31         mov  UnsWord,ax ; store result back into memory
32         add  UnsWord,bx ; add current hex digit
33         jmp  NextCh     ; read next character
34 OutNum: mov  ah,09h     ; function 09h - output text string
35         lea  dx,MsgOut  ; address of message into DX
36         int  21h        ; DOS service call
37         mov  ax,UnsWord ; place number to be printed into AX.
38         mov  cx,0       ; clear counter of digits
39 NexDiv: mov  dx,0       ; clear high part of number
40         div  Ten        ; divide number to be printed by 10
```

```
41           push dx       ; push remainder (current digit) into stack
42           inc  cx       ; increase counter of digits
43           cmp  ax,0     ; result is zero? (number was less than 10)
44           jne  NexDiv   ; if not, continue process (get next digit)
45           mov  ax,0200h ; function 02h - output character
46 OutSym: pop  dx       ; pop current digit from stack
47           add  dl,30h   ; convert digit to character
48           int  21h      ; DOS service call
49           loop OutSym   ; to output next digit
50 FinProg:mov  ax,4C00h ; function 4Ch - terminate process
51           int  21h      ; DOS service call
52           end
```

Listing 3.5 The NumIO Program

This program reads characters from the keyboard, converts them into decimal numbers 0 - 9 and then forms the result using the formula

$$N = N \times 10 + I$$

where N is the decimal number stored in the memory and I is the character currently read. The program is written using the simplified MASM directives and includes the following elements of MASM discussed in this chapter:

> The EQU directive for defining named constants
> The DB and DW directives for defining variables
> The simplified MASM directives for defining segments and initializing the segment registers.

When it starts working this program outputs an initial message using the DOS service "Output text string" which was introduced in Chapter Two.

The line labelled NextCh is at the beginning of the block which reads a character from the keyboard using the DOS function 0h. This function returns an ASCII code for each key pressed or 0 if this key is a special key such as a function key or cursor control key. In this case you need to call this function again to get an ASCII code for that key. This technique allows you to distinguish between character keys and special keys which generate the same ASCII codes, for example the F1 key and the character key ";".

The program then checks whether the key that has been pressed is a character key in the range "0" - "9" (ASCII codes "30h" - "39h").

To do this, the program compares the code returned by the DOS service in the AL register with the values '0' and '9' and then passes control to the relevant instruction using the conditional jump instructions - JA (Jump if Above) and JB (Jump if Below). These conditional jump instructions are especially useful for dealing with unsigned integers and character codes. If the character read from the keyboard is out of the range, the program outputs the number obtained so far and finishes its work.

Once a character has been read the block beginning in the line labelled ProcNum converts it to a decimal digit and adds this digit to the result. Table 3.1 shows the ASCII codes for the characters '0' - '9' which are converted into one-byte unsigned integers by subtracting the value 30h.

Character	ASCII Code	Character	ASCII Code
'0'	30h	'5'	35h
'1'	31h	'6'	36h
'2'	32h	'7'	37h
'3'	33h	'8'	38h
'4'	34h	'9'	39h

Table 3.1
ASCII Codes for Characters Representing Decimal Digits

The program stops inputting when it meets the first non-digit character and moves on to outputting the result obtained.

To convert the value of the binary number stored in the UnsWord variable (which is the result of the process described) the program divides this number by 10 and pushes the remainder onto the stack. The result is then written back to the UnsWord variable and the process is repeated until the value 0 is obtained. For example, the process of converting the value 12345 can be represented as follows:

```
12345 : 10 = 1234 (5)
 1234 : 10 =  123 (4)
  123 : 10 =   12 (3)
   12 : 10 =    1 (2)
    1 : 10 =    0 (1)
```

Values in brackets are remainders which are pushed onto the stack in order from top to bottom. Then, performing the POP instruction, we get them in reverse order, in other words 1, 2, 3, 4 and 5. If we convert each of them into a character by adding the value 30h and output the character obtained, we get the character string representing the number processed. This is done in the block starting in the line labelled NextDiv.

Using Flags to Determine the Type of Processor

Now that you understand what flags are and how you can use them in conjunction with the stack, we'll show you how to create a program that will prove useful for routine work. We'll look at Listing 3.6 which shows a program that detects what type of processor is in use and generates a corresponding return code. We will explain how it works after the full listing:

```
 1
 2          page 55,132
 3 .model small
 4 .stack
 5 .data
 6 InMsg  db   0Dh,0Ah,'You have an i80$'
 7 FinMsg db   ' microprocessor.',0Dh,0Ah,'$'
 8 i86    db   '86$ '
 9 i186   db   '186$'
10 i286   db   '286$'
11 i386   db   '386/486$'
12 .code
13 .startup
14 ;===   output initial message
15         mov ah,09     ; function 09h - output text string
16         lea dx,InMsg  ; address of initial message into DX
17         int 21h       ; DOS service call
18 ;=== Try to clear bit 15 (to put 0 into it)
19         pushf         ; push original flags
20         pop ax        ; copy flag register into AX
21         and ax,7FFFh  ; keep all bits but 15 (clear bit 15)
22         push ax       ; push value with bit 15 clear
23         popf          ; load flags (bits 0-14 original), bit 15 = 0
24         pushf         ; push flag register
25         pop ax        ; read flags into AX
26         shl ah,1      ; if bit 15 is set CF will be set
27         jc  Less286   ; processor not 286 or above
28 ;=== Processor is 286 or above
29         pushf         ; push original flags
30         pop ax        ; copy flag register into AX
31         or  ah,40h    ; set NT flag (bit 14)
32         push ax       ; push value with bit 14 set onto stack
33         popf          ; copy this value into flags (set NT flag)
34         pushf         ; push flag register onto stack
```

```
35          pop ax        ; copy flag register into AX
36          and ah,40h    ; check bit 14 (NT flag)
37          jnz Det386    ; if it is actually set-at least 386 found
38   ;=== Processor is 286
39   Det286:lea dx,i286  ; address of message "286" into DX
40          jmp FinPgm    ; to finish program
41   ;=== Processor is 386/486
42   Det386:lea dx,i386  ; address of message "386/486" into DX
43   FinPgm: mov ah,09h   ; function 09h - output text string
44          int 21h       ; DOS service call
45          lea dx,FinMsg; address of message "microprocessor found"
46          int 21h       ; DOS service cal
47          mov ax,4C00h  ; function 4Ch - terminate process
48          int 21h       ; DOS service call
49   ; Processor is lower than 286
50   Less286:lea dx,i86   ; address of text "86"
51          mov ax,1      ; set bit 1 of AX
52          mov cx,32     ; shift counter = 32
53          shl ax,cl     ; shift AX to the left by 32 bits
54          jz  FinPgm    ; if AX is clear - i8086 found
55   ;=== Processor is 186/188
56          lea dx,i186   ; otherwise - i80186/i80188
57          jmp FinPgm    ; to finish program
58          end
```

Listing 3.6 The DetProc2 Program

This program uses the following algorithm to determine the processor type:

▲ Tries to clear bit 15 of the flag register; in i8086/i8088s and i80186/i80188s the bits 12-15 are always set. If you are able to clear it means that you have an i80286 processor or higher.

▲ If bit 15 of the flag register is set, the program tries to determine whether it works on i8086/i8088 processors by shifting the contents of a register to the left by 32 bits; if the register is clear after this operation, this means that the microprocessor is an i8086/i8088, otherwise it is an i80186/i80188.

▲ To distinguish between i80286 and i80386/i80486 the program tries to set bit 14 of the flag register which corresponds to the NT flag which is only present on i80386 and higher processors; if this fails, then the microprocessor is an i80286.

To set and clear separate bits of a register the program uses the logical instructions AND and OR. To work with the separate flags the program uses the same technique as the DetStep program described in Chapter Two. The flow chart for the program is given in Figure 3.7.

To set and clear separate bits, this program uses the logical (bitwise) operations OR and AND, respectively. You are probably familiar with the denotations for logical (or, sometimes, boolean) constants and variables used in high-level languages and the operations AND and OR used for creating logical expressions. The assembler instructions AND and OR perform the same tasks for separate bits,bytes or words.

The AND instruction performs the operation of bitwise AND, also known as logical multiplication. The result of this operation can be evaluated in the same way as for multiplication operations in the binary system:

0 AND 0 gives 0
0 AND 1 gives 0
1 AND 0 gives 0
1 AND 1 gives 1

As you see, the result of the AND operation is equal to 1 only when both operands are 1. The AND instruction performs this operation on

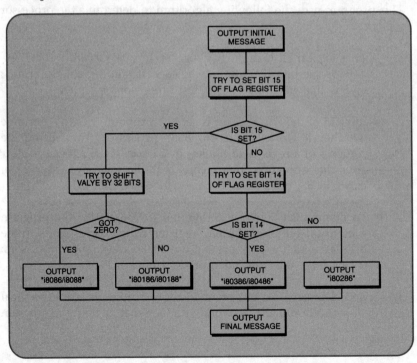

Figure 3.7
**The Flow
Chart of the
DetProc2
Program**

all bits in its operands. For example, the following instructions write the value 4 into the AX register:

```
mov   ax,1234h
and   ax,5
```

To find out how this result is obtained, let's look at the binary representation of the operands:

```
      1234h = 0001 0010 0011 0100
  AND
          5 = 0000 0000 0000 0101
          ────────────────────────
              0000 0000 0000 0100
```

As you see, only bit 2 is set in both operands, so the result is 4. In general, to evaluate the result of the AND instruction you need to perform the bitwise AND operation on corresponding bits of operands. Note that the result of performing the AND instruction is 0 in case at least one of its operands equals 0. For example, the instruction

```
and   ax,0
```

can be used for clearing the AX register.

If one operand of the AND instruction has all its bits equal to 1, the result of the instruction is equal to the second operand. For example, the following instruction does not change the value stored in the BX register:

```
and   bx,0FFFFh
```

The OR instruction performs the operation of logical (boolean) addition or bitwise OR in accordance with the following rules:

```
0 OR 0 gives 0
0 OR 1 gives 1
1 OR 0 gives 1
1 OR 1 gives 1
```

As you see the result of this operation is 1 if at least one of its operands is equal to one. Like the AND instruction, the OR instruction performs the bitwise OR operation on all bites of the operands. For example, the OR instruction processing the values 52h and 25h gives the result 77h:

```
      0101 0010
OR
      0010 0101
      ─────────
      0111 0111
```

It's quite funny that in fact the OR instruction gives the same result as the usual addition in binary system. However, although the tables for logical and binary addition only have one line different, the next example proves that you shouldn't mix them up:

```
      1010 0101
OR
      1010 0101
      ─────────
      1010 0101
```

As you can guess by looking at the table of logical addition, when one operand of the OR instruction is 0, the result is equal to the second operand. If one of the operands have all bits set, all bits of the result are also set. For example, the next instruction puts the value 0FFFFh into the AX register:

```
   or ax,0FFFFh
```

The following instruction sets bit 0 (the rightmost bit of the BL register):

```
   or bl,1
```

Sometimes AND and OR operations are referred to as "if all" and "if any", respectively. Having looked at the examples given you can understand why these terms are used. You can see that the result of the AND operation is 1 only *if all* its operands are 1 while the OR operation gives 1 *if any* one its operands is 1.

Another kind of operation used in this program is shifting which is performed by two assembler instructions - SHR and SHL. The format for these instructions is

```
SHR  destination,  source
```

or

```
SHL  destination,  source
```

The operand *destination* specifies the value to be shifted and the operand *source* defines the shift count. The last character of the instruction name defines the shift direction - R stands for Right, L stands for Left. The source operand on i8086/i8088 processors can be either CL or 1. On later processors, it can also be an 8-bit immediate constant, for example:

```
shr   ax,cl        ; this is valid for all microprocessors
shl   bx,1         ; this is valid for all processors too
shr   MemVal,cl    ; this is again valid
shr   dx,5         ; this can be used on i80186 and higher only
```

This program uses the fact that not all microprocessors perform the shift instructions in the same way. The i8086/i8088 microprocessors allow any value for the shift counter although it doesn't make sense to use values greater than 32 since the maximum size of an operand is 32 bits. The later processors use only bits 0 - 4 of the shift counter. This means that they treat shift counter 32 as 0, 33(21h) as 1, 34(22h) as 2 and so on. Therefore, we can see that the following instruction sequence will give different results on different processors:

```
mov   cl,33        ; shift counter 33
mov   ax,1         ; bit 0 of AX is set
shl   ax,cl        ; shift AX by 33 bits to the left
```

On i8086/i8088 processors the result will equal 0 because bit 0 of AX becomes bit 32 which is out of the register capacity and therefore is lost. Later microprocessors treat the shift count 33 as 1 and therefore the result will equal 2.

Summary

This chapter has given you basic information about memory organization, addressing and usage.

We looked at how a microprocessor calculates an effective address for objects located in different segments involving different registers, as well as the basic types of addressing.

If you are using a recent version of Assembler such as MASM 6.0, use the simplified directives whenever possible. The corresponding templates for -COM and -EXE modules are given in this chapter. Note that the -COM variant is preferable for programs that can be allocated within one segment.

The EQU directive we explained allows you to give meaningful names to constants, helping to improve readability.

The basic forms of addressing explained in this chapter can be used for accessing objects located in different storage units - memory and registers.

The full assembler text of all the programs we have discussed is stored on your program disk.

CHAPTER
4

Data Structures

Remembering Nicklaus Wirth's assertion that:

Algorithms + data structures = programs

It's now time to look at data structures in more detail.

In this chapter we will learn how the tools we covered in Chapter Three can be used to create really useful data structures that mirror more closely the way we use information in the real world.

Fundamental Knowledge

Strings

Anyone who has written a computer program cannot have avoided the concept of a **string**. Any program that outputs text longer than one character processes strings. In earlier chapters we also used strings, although we didn't define the term properly.

Even the infamous program that outputs "Hello, world!", is actually designed to process strings. In most programming languages this can be written in one line, for example in Pascal:

```
Program Hello (output) ; Begin Write ('Hello, world!' ) ; End.
```

This single line both defines the string constant 'Hello, world!' and calls the Pascal procedure Write, which outputs a text string onto the screen. In Chapter Three we saw how to do the same thing in assembly language. In this chapter we'll discuss string operations which are more complex than just outputting a string.

2

A string is a sequence of characters, and since each character occupies one byte, it follows that a string is a sequence of bytes. In Assembler, quotes are used to define a value stored in a certain part of the memory that should be treated as a string (i.e. represented in ASCII code). For example, constants 5 and '5' are not the same. If you look at the listing generated by the Assembler, you will see that these two values are represented differently:

```
......
0000         .data
0000 05      DecConst db 5
0001 35      StrConst db '5'
......
```

The first line defines the decimal value 5, stored in one byte, while the second defines the byte containing the value 35h - the ASCII code for the character "5". Note that in Assembler, StrConst is a string variable 1 byte long. Strings can be written in quotes,

```
Quot  db 'This is a string'
```

double quotes

```
DQuot db "This is a string too"
```

or in some special cases, angle brackets

```
< This is also a string >.
```

You can also include quotes or double quotes inside a string. Note though, if you use the same character inside the string as you have used as the delimiter, it must appear twice in the string text, for example:

```
'That''s a string'
"But that's also a string"
'Say "cheese", please'
"Please, say ""cheese""!"
```

Unlike most high-level languages, in Assembler, a string only contains information which is directly relevant to the string itself. If you process strings created by a high-level language, you need to know their structure. If this string includes additional information such as the NUL character in C programs, or the actual length of the string as in Pascal you need to process this information in your program. Assembler strings are simply sequences of bytes and do not contain any additional information.

Declaring Strings

Defining string variables in Assembler requires very little effort. If you are used to BASIC or Pascal, it will seem inordinately simple since assembly language does not have special directives or signs for declaring string variables (although there are directives intended specifically for defining string constants). You just need to write the name of the variable and specify the DB directive, followed by the string enclosed by delimiters:

```
var_name    DB    'Nice string'
```

The total length of an initialized string can be up to 255 characters which can be divided into several lines, making it more readable:

```
long_string    DB    'This is',' a very long,',
                     ' long,',' long,',
                     ' but not longer than ',
                     ' 255 characters ', ' string.'
```

Don't be put off by the fact that the maximum length is only 255 bytes, it doesn't stop you from writing a long string. For instance, the following example defines a sequence of bytes which can be treated as one string:

```
Really_Long_String     db 'This is a really long,'
                       db ' long, long, long, long, long,'
                       db ' long, long, long, long, long,'
                       db ' long, long, long, long, long,'
                       db ' long, long, long, long, long,'
                       db ' long, long, long, long, long,'
                       db ' long, long, long, long, long,'
                       db ' long, long, long, long, long,'
                       db ' long, long, long, long, long,'
                       db ' long, long, long, long, long,'
                       db ' long, long, long, long, long,'
                       db ' long, long, long, long, long,'
                       db ' long, long, long, long, long,'
                       db ' long, long, long, long, long,'
                       db ' long, long, long, long, long,'
                       db ' long, long, long, long, long,'
                       db 'string.'
```

What we have done here is to use several DB directives which in fact define several strings. Only the first directive is labelled, the other lines define unlabelled variables. The trick is that all these variables can be considered as one adjoining sequence of bytes, which means that they make up **one** string! However, since most assembler instructions cannot operate strings longer than 255 bytes, we don't recommend using this technique unless absolutely necessary.

When a string variable is declared by the DB directive, the corresponding text is stored in RAM as a sequence of bytes. If you want to reserve storage for a string variable without initializing it, you can do so using **?** together with the DUP operator:

```
var1     DB     100 DUP   (?)
var2     DB     10 DUP ('KWA')
```

The first line reserves 100 bytes which are then used for storing the string. The initial values of these bytes are undefined, which means that their contents do not change when the program is loaded. The second directive reserves 30 bytes and stores the string "KWAKWAKWAKWAKWAKWAKWAKWAKWAKWA" in this area.

Processing Strings

Once a string has been declared and possibly initialized, you are then free to process it. Up to now we have only mentioned string operations which deal with the string as a whole, for example input/output operations on complete strings. These operations transfer strings between RAM and peripheral devices such as the screen and keyboard. Later on when dealing with the video and peripheral devices we'll discuss string-oriented I/O operations in more detail, but for now let's look at processing strings located in the memory.

There are four main string processing operations:

1. Copying/moving strings located in different memory areas
2. Comparing strings
3. Searching strings for a character or character sequence (sub-string)
4. Processing string elements (characters)

Copy/move operations allow you to move a sequence of characters from one memory location to another. For example, when your program is loaded by DOS, it can read the parameters passed to it in the command line. It is often necessary to copy this string from its original location in the PSP into the work area, thereby avoiding changing the original copy. This is even more important when dealing with strings in ROM, from which you can of course only read information.

String comparison works by comparing the string elements one by one. Strings are equal when all the elements of both strings are the same. Note that in Assembler you can only compare strings of the same length.

String searching is useful in text processing and business applications. For example, any text editor should be able to find a sequence of characters within the text file. The operation of copying a string can then be used to replace the sequence found. A special utility for performing this task is included in DOS - an external command FIND.

On a PC, string processing instructions usually use the DS:SI and ES:DI register pairs to point to the source and destination strings respectively, while the CX register usually takes its traditional role as a cycle counter. Since a string usually contains more than one character, a string processing operation is a cyclical process, with certain prefixes causing instructions to be performed repeatedly. In the Tools section we'll consider a set of prefixes used for the unconditional (fixed number of times) and conditional (depending on the value of a string element) repetition of string processing instructions.

String processing operations need not be used purely for processing characters. Since any sequence of bytes can be treated as a string (or maybe as a number of strings, if it is long enough), string processing operations are useful for processing any type of data.

Most i80x86 instructions are able to address the individual elements of memory in a variety of different ways. In Chapter Three we looked at indirect register addressing, which allows you to access the memory location determined by the index register. In this chapter we'll discuss the most powerful ways of addressing - based and indexed indirect addressing.

Arrays

Besides defining a sequence of bytes using the DB directive, you can use other directives to create data groups of different sized elements, such as words or double words. Such sequences are known as **arrays** - groups of data elements. Unlike high-level languages, arrays in Assembler have no internal structure, consist of elements of the same length and do not contain any additional information.

There are no restrictions on defining arrays recursively. This means that you can use arrays of arrays of arrays of ... For example, in practice it is often useful to consider the string defined by the directive

```
Years db "1991199219931994"
```

as array of strings defined as

```
Years db "1991", "1992", "1993", "1994"
```

Later on in this chapter, in the Library section, we'll give an example of treating a sequence of bytes as an array of strings.

Declaring an Array

The DB, DW and DD directives are used to declare an array in assembly language. In MASM 6.0 and higher, you can also use the extended directives BYTE, WORD, DWORD, QWORD, SBYTE, SWORD,

SDWORD, REAL4, REAL8, REAL10. For example, the line

```
ArrByte   db 'This is array of bytes'
```

defines an array of bytes which is already known to you as a string. An array of words can be defined as

```
ArrWord   dw 1991,1992,1993
```
or
```
ArrWord2 word  1994,1995,1996
```

To define arrays consisting of equal elements, you can use the DUP operator. For example the directive

```
ManyZeros   dw 100 dup (0)
```

defines an array consisting of 100 words with the initial value 0.

Although any array can be defined using just the DB directive, the DW and DD directives are often more convenient. One reason for using these data definition directives is that they allow you to use the natural representation of data when initializing array elements. For example, the line:

```
YearsB   db 0C7h,07h, 0C8h,07h, 0C9h,07h
```

could be rewritten as

```
YearsW   dw 1991,1992,1993
```

We don't need to point out which of these is preferable, do we! Another reason is that Assembler uses the array definition to determine the size of its element. In the example above, the array YearsW is an array of 3 one word elements, while YearsB consists of 6 elements of one byte each. Both operands in an instruction must be the same size, meaning that the following instructions are valid:

```
......
      mov   ax,YearsW      ; load first element into AX
      mov   dl,YearsB[3]   ; load third element into DL
      mov   Years[1],cx    ; store CX in first element
......
```

while the following instructions are invalid because the operands are not the same size:

```
......
    mov    ax,YearsB[2]
    mov    al,YearsW
......
```

MASM provides specific operators for finding out information about arrays:

SizeOf   - number of bytes occupied by an array
LengthOf   - number of elements in an array
Type   - size of an element in an array

For example, the value of the expression SizeOf YearsB is 6 which is the same as SizeOf YearsW. The expression LengthOf YearsB is 6 (6 one-byte elements) and LengthOf YeardsW equals 3 (3 elements of 1 word or 2 bytes). The Size operator returns the value 1 for YearsB and 2 for YearsW. In short, the following is true for any array:

SizeOf *array* = LengthOf *array* * Type *array*

Providing Additional Information for String Variables

Having covered the process of defining assembler strings, let's look at how to provide the additional information which is often needed, especially for creating modules for use with high-level languages. Here we'll consider two basic techniques, adding special delimiters and calculating the length of a string.

Many DOS and BIOS services need 0-terminated and $-terminated strings, which can be defined in the following way:

```
ASCIIZ_string  DB ' This is a 0-terminated string ',0
Str1           DB ' This is a $-terminated string $'
Str2           DB ' This is a $-terminated string  too','$'
Str3           DB ' This is a $-terminated string  too',24
```

Note that the character "0" in the first string is not a delimiter! Its ASCII code is 30h (48 in decimal system), while the ASCII code of the ASCIIZ-string delimiter is 0. The example we have chosen illustrates one of the practical problems presented by strings; if you try to output one of the variables Str1, Str2 or Str3 using the DOS service "Output character string" (function 09h), you will only get the text "This is a" output on the screen. This is because strings are processed by DOS services from left to right (from the beginning to the end, from lower addresses to the higher ones) and the first matching character is treated as a delimiter. As a result, you cannot include the "$" sign within $-terminated strings.

The second important technique used in string processing is to accompany the string with a variable containing the length of the string. This is useful for counting the bytes of a string as they are processed individually. To calculate the size of the memory allocated for a string, several different techniques can be used. For example, the next fragment of program code uses the basic tools provided by MASM 6.0:

```
......
.data
......
LenDb    db    LenEqu           ; using assembly-time variable
LenDbD   db    NexAdr-StrDef    ; using expression
StrDef   db    ' This string is defined by the DB directive'
NexAdr   equ   $                ; This marks byte that follows string
LenEqu   equ   NexAdr-StrDef    ; defining assembly-time variable
LenFun   db    SizeOf StrDef    ; using assembly-time function
......
```

The comments in each line of code name the feature being used. The line StrDef defines a string in Assembler, meaning of course a sequence of characters. The next line defines an assembly-time variable NexAdr and assigns the current value of the address counter to it. Unlike usual variables, an assembly-time (or, in high-level languages, compile-time) variable is created by Assembler, and can only be changed at compilation time. Such a variable does not correspond to any memory location or register in a program. The "$" character, which represents the current value of the address counter, should in this case be considered as an offset from the beginning of the data segment.

The next two strings labelled LenEqu and LenFun are directives which define a constant equal to the length of the string. The difference between these lines is that the first defines the assembly-time constant used by Assembler during the process of program translation, while the second one defines a constant, usually one byte long, that is available during the run-time. You can use the assembly-time variable LenEqu as an immediate operand in assembler instructions, while the run-time variable LenFun defines the content of a byte located in the memory.

For example, although the following strings use a different form of addressing, they give the same result:

```
        mov   cl,LenEqu
......
        mov   cl,LenFun
```

The first instruction uses an immediate operand while the second one employs the direct memory operand. If the actual value of the string then had to be changed at a certain point in the program, you could use the instructions:

```
......
        inc   LenFun
......
        sub   LenFun,3
......
```

Note that the following instruction would cause an error while compiling the program though because it attempts to change the constant value:

```
    dec   LenEqu
```

Using and Addressing Arrays

Since the principles of strings and arrays are the same, all string processing operations can be used for processing arrays. The instructions that perform these operations can be used in several different forms. For example, the MOVS instruction, intended for copying strings, has several modifications: MOVSB - moves strings byte by byte, MOVSW - moves strings word by word and MOVSD - moves strings double word by double word.

Unlike arithmetic instructions, string processing instructions do not usually have explicit operands. Even when operands are present, they only specify the size of operands actually used, for example

```
......
ByteArr  db    '123456789'
WordArr  dw    1,2,3,4,5,6,7,8
......
        movs  ByteArr  ; this is the same as MOVSB
......
        movs  WordArr  ; this is the same as MOVSW
```

The actual addresses or operands for these instructions must be placed into the correct registers before the operation. The address of the first byte of the source and destination strings must be moved into the DS:SI and ES:DI registers, respectively. Note that some instructions only have one operand. In this case it is treated either as the source, or as the destination operand.

As we have already seen, the value of the CX register and the DF flag can also affect the way string processing instructions are performed. Most instructions which process strings also use the value in the CX register to determine the number of bytes to be processed.

Addressing Modes

The ways of addressing arrays in memory covered in this chapter are usually used in instructions for processing a sequence of memory elements (bytes, words and double words), and are therefore very useful in loops.

First in the line up is the **register indirect mode**. In this mode, one of the operands is written as

```
[BX]
[BP]
[DI]
[SI]
```

for example the instruction

```
mov ah,[bx]
```

uses the AH register as the first operand. The effective address of the source operand used in this instruction consists of thesegment address stored in the DS register and the offset contained in the BX register. If you need to access an operand located within a segment addressed through a segment register other than DS, specify the name of this register in front of the offset as follows:

```
mov ah,cs:[bx]
```

This loads a byte with the segment address contained in the CS register and an offset contained in BX.

Different instructions use different registers for storing the segment part of an effective address. If you don't specify a segment register in an instruction, for example

```
mov    ax,[si]
jmp    [bx]
```

the DS register will usually be used for data processing instructions, and the CS register for flow control instructions. However, remember when you use [BP], it is equivalent to SS:[BP], not to DS:[BP]. This means that the instruction

```
mov    bx,[bp]
```

must be treated as

```
mov    bx,ss:[bp]
```

rather than

```
mov    bx,ds:[bp]
```

When you use this form of addressing, the effective address of a memory location is calculated as

```
SEG:[reg]
```

where SEG means the segment register and [reg] means the content of a register.

The next form of addressing is the **base relative addressing** mode also known as *base indirect addressing with displacement* or *index indirect addressing with displacement*, which allows you to use an operand in the following form:

```
Var [reg]
```

The meaning of var[BX] is common to both Assembler and Pascal (and all other languages based on Pascal such as Ada). Thus in Pascal, the denotation var[BX] means an element of the array VAR located BX elements after the start. In Assembler this denotes a memory element (byte, word or double word, depending on the size of the other operand) which has an effective address

```
SEG:[disp+reg]
```

where SEG means the content of a segment register, disp is an offset of an array processed from the beginning of a segment and reg is the content of a register. For example, the following instructions load the 15h byte of the string StrVar into the AL register:

```
mov    bx,15h
mov    al,StrVar[bx]
```

Next on our list is **Direct index** addressing. This works in the same way as the base relative addressing, but instead of BX and BP, the SI and DI registers are used, giving us instructions like

```
MOV al,TableS[SI]
MOV TableD[DI],al
```

The most intricate form of addressing is **base indexed,** also referred to as *base and index indirect addressing with displacement.* As you can probably guess, this mode uses both the base register (BP or BX) and the index register (SI or DI). This time, a memory operand can be written in one of the following forms:

```
var[BX+SI]
var[BX+DI]
var[bx][si]
var[bx+si]
```

All forms of indirect addressing are based on the same principle. An offset address of an operand consists of two components, one of which corresponds to the initial address of an operand, while the second component is stored in the base or index registers and can change while the program is running. The values stored in the special index registers SI and DI are changed automatically by string processing instructions such as MOVS.

Manipulating Strings and Arrays

The size of the elements in an array depends on the directive used to define it. This definition also determines how instructions for manipulating the array element by element will work. For example, the CMPSB instruction will compare a string byte by byte, while CMPSW will do the same with words. The following code fragment contains two blocks, the first is labelled CmpB and the second CmpW:

```
......
Str1   db     '01234567'
Str2   db     '012345x7'
......
       cld                    ; process strings from left to right
```

```
CmpB: lea    si,Str1    ; DS:SI point to STR1
      lea    di,str2    ; ES:DI point to STR2
      mov    dx,si      ; save offset of STR1
      mov    cx,8       ; length of string in bytes
      repe   cmpsb      ; compare bytes
      sub    si,dx      ; number of unmatching element
......
CmpW: lea    si,Str1    ; DS:SI point to STR1
      lea    di,str2    ; ES:DI point to STR2
      mov    dx,si      ; save offset of STR1
      mov    cx,4       ; length of string in words
      repe   cmpsw      ; compare words
      sub    si,dx      ; number of unmatching element
```

Although both blocks perform the same task, they produce different results. Before discussing the results, let's have a look at how they actually work.

First of all, the program sets the direction in which the strings will be processed. This is determined by the state of the Direction Flag - from beginning to end if the Direction Flag DF is clear, or from the end to the beginning if this flag is set. You can control this by setting the flag with the STD instruction, or clearing it with CLD instruction. As the Direction Flag is clear when the program is loaded, the normal direction for processing strings is from beginning to end, from low addresses to high addresses and from left to right.

Once the CLD instruction has cleared the Direction Flag, specifying that strings will be processed from left to right, the program compares two strings - Str1 and Str2. The two blocks labelled CmpB and CmpW compare these strings byte by byte and word by word, respectively. Since both blocks are organized in the same way, we'll consider them together.

The first two instructions in each block load the SI and DI registers with the addresses of strings to be compared. The value in the SI register is then stored in the DX register in order to calculate the number of the unmatching element. After this, the length of the strings compared is loaded into the CX register. Note that this value is 8 in the first block (the number of **bytes** occupied by a string) and 4 in the second (the number of **words** occupied by a string). The CMPS* instruction with REPE is then used to compare the strings. This instruction places the addresses of the first unmatching elements of arrays into the DS:SI and ES:DI registers. We have used the term "arrays" intentionally because strings are treated in two ways here- as arrays of bytes (as usual) and as arrays of words. The first block uses the CMPSB instruction while the second block uses the CMPSW instruction. After the CMPS* instruction has been performed, the initial value contained in the SI register (offset address of the Str1 variable) is subtracted from the current value in SI. The result returned is the displacement of the unmatching element from the beginning of the string.

When the first block has been performed, the result in SI will be 7, which is the offset from the beginning of the string of the **byte** that follows the unmatched one. After the second block, it will be 8, the offset of the **word** following the unmatched one.

Structures

Most up to date Assemblers offer certain facilities more often associated with high-level languages. For instance, the concept of structures in assembly language is similar to the notion of records in Pascal. You can declare a structure using the STRUCT directive - for example, take the declaration of the Date structure below:

```
Date    STRUCT
Day     DB      2 DUP (?)
Month   DB      3 DUP (?)
Year    DB      4 DUP (?)
Date    ENDS
```

Here Date is coded as day - a string of two numbers, month - a string of three letters and year - a string of four numbers. Of course, this isn't the only way of defining the Date structure; alternatively you could code its fields (day, month, year) as numbers.

Once you have declared the Date structure, you can declare the variable

```
Herbirthday Date {'01','Apr',1973}
```

and refer to its fields

```
lea    bx,HerBirthday.Month
mov    al,[bx]
```

These instructions will send the ASCII code of letter A to the AL register.

The power of the STRUCT directive can only really be seen in large programs working with complex data structures. The example given above can easily be rewritten as

```
......
Day    DB    '01'
Month  DB    'Apr'
Year   DB    '1973'
.......
```

In practice, you will seldom use the STRUCT directive. However, the data definition using the STRUCT directive can help you to make your programs easier to understand. This directive can also be really useful when creating subroutines that process complex data passed from high-level languages.

Unions

The notion of a **union** in assembly language is similar to unions in ALGOL-68, variant records in Pascal, and unions in extended versions of FORTRAN and BASIC. The UNION directive is very similar to the STRUCT directive, the only difference being that all elements of a union refer to the same memory location. For example, below, the directive will define a double word which can also be accessed as two words or four bytes:

```
UniDWB    union
DefDW     dd    ?
DefW      dw    ?,?
DefB      db    ?,?,?,?
UniDWB    ends
```

If you define the UniDWB union as we have above, you can then use the name UniDWB as a new MASM directive for defining new variables, for example:

```
UniVar    UniDWB
```

Now you can refer to different components of the variable UniVar as

```
UniVar.x[i]
```

where x is one of the labels DefDw, DefW or DefB and i is an offset from the beginning of the UniVar. For example, the instruction

```
mov    ax,UniVar.DefW
```

loads the lower word of the variable UniVar into the AX register.

In practice, especially in programs which operate with data that has a relatively simple structure, it is often easier to use the PTR operator for accessing different fields of variables. For example, you can access the high byte of a variable defined as a word, using the BYTE PTR operator as follows:

```
......
VarW    dw    1234h
......
        mov   al,byte ptr VarW[1] ; high byte of VarW into AX
......
```

Defining String Constants

Up to now, we have defined a string as a sequence of characters that can be processed by a program during execution. However certain strings, known as string constants or text macros, can be used by MASM during assembly time.

Strictly speaking, the term "constant" is not an exact description; as you'll see in this chapter, these "constants" can be changed at assembly-time using special MASM directives and functions. A more fitting definition for this kind of data would be "a named sequence of characters used by Assembler at the time of compilation". Surprisingly enough, we'll stick to the commonly used, if slightly inaccurate, term!

We will move on now to consider the basic operations for processing string constants. Remember that these operations are performed during compilation though, unlike operations with string variables which are performed during execution.

Manipulating String Constants

Let's start at the beginning of the life of a constant, with its definition. There are two directives that you can use for this task -the EQU directive or = directive:

```
MyConst1 EQU    <No Changes>
```

or

```
MyConst2 =    <Changes possible>
```

Be careful here, there's a potential trap - don't confuse the name of a variable with the value of the string denoted by this variable. The FLY variable can contain "ELEPHANT" string.

String constants can be manipulated at the assembly stage using the string functions CATSTR, INSTR, SIZESTR, SUBSTR. The CATSTR directive concatenates strings as shown below:

```
Boy      equ      John
Girl     equ      Mary
Couple   CATSTR   Boy, < and >, Girl
```

The value of the constant Couple is the same as that defined by the directive:

```
Couple EQU John and Mary
```

The INSTR directive is used to locate the starting position of a sub-string in a string.

The SUBSTR directive does the opposite and determines a sub-string by its length and starting position.

The SIZESTR directive evaluates the length of the string.

At this point you couldn't be blamed for thinking that these operations do not really add much to your work with constants. Later on though you'll see how they really come into their own with regard to macros.

Tools

Moving Strings - The MOVS* Instructions

This instruction is designed for copying strings (sequences of symbols coded in bytes). It stands for **MOV**e String and has the following format:

```
MOVS
```

This instruction has some modifications which mean that you can deal with memory units other than bytes. These instructions can be used as MOVS*, where * is B - bytes, W - words and D - double words. If the instruction is used without a letter, it processes the memory byte-by-byte.

The source and destination segment addresses must be placed into the segment registers. By default, the value stored in the DS register is used as the segment address of the source operand and the value in the ES register - as the destination address. The offset addresses of the source and destination operands must be placed into the SI and DI registers, respectively. To load the DI and SI registers with source and destination offset addresses, use the LEA instruction as follows:

```
LEA    SI,SourceString
LEA    DI,DestinationString
MOVSB
```

It is assumed that DS and ES registers point at segments containing these variables (source and destination, respectively). MOVSB then copies one byte of SourceString into one byte of DestinationString.

When the operation MOVSB is performed, the values of the SI and DI registers are changed. If the Direction Flag DF is clear then MOVSB increments SI and DI by 1. If DF is set, then MOVSB decrements SI and DI by 1.

You might think that an example as simple as this could be performed equally well with two MOV instructions, which we won't argue with. The real power of the MOVS* instructions only really becomes apparent when it is used together with the REP prefixes which cause the repetition of string instructions.

Comparing Strings - The CMPS* Instructions

The CMPS instruction is designed specifically for performing string comparison operations. This instruction has modifications CMPSB, CMPSW and SMPSD which compare bytes, words and double words, respectively. If you use the CMPS form, Assembler chooses an appropriate instruction automatically, depending on the size of the operand. Note however, that this operand is only used as the length specifier. So, to avoid possible confusion, it is better to use the relevant form of the CMPS instruction explicitly. For example:

```
Bytes1   db    .......
Bytes2   db    .......
Words1   dw    .......
Words2   dw    .......
......
         lea   si,Bytes1
         lea   di,Bytes2
         cmps  Bytes1        ; this is the same as CMPSB
......
         lea   si,Words1
         lea   di,Words2
         cmps  Words1        ; this is the same as CMPSW
```

The rules for using registers by CMPS* instructions are the same as for MOVS* instructions. After performing an instruction, the SI and DI registers are changed depending on the size of the operands and the state of the Direction Flag. The DI and SI registers are increased if the Direction Flag is clear and decreased if it is set. The value of the increment or decrement is defined by the size of the operands and equals 1 for CMPSB instructions, 2 for CMPSW and 4 for CMPSD.

Although this instruction is traditionally called "Compare Strings", it works just as well with arrays. This instruction is usually used with the conditional REP prefixes, considered later in this chapter.

Searching Strings - The SCAS* Instructions

You can search a string for either a sub-string or a character. The family of SCAS* instructions includes the SCASB, SCASW and SCASD instructions which work with bytes, words and double words, respectively. The name SCAS is treated by Assembler differently depending on the size of the operand. The rules for choosing an appropriate encoding are the same as for MOVS and COMS instructions.

This instruction compares an element of the string, the address of which is stored in ES:DI, with the value in the accumulator. SCASB uses the AL register (byte), SCASW - the AX register (word) and SCASD - the EAX register (double word). This instruction changes the value in the DI register according to the size of the element processed and the state of the Direction Flag. The SCAS* instructions are usually used with the conditional repetition prefixes REPE (REPZ) and REPNE(REPNZ).

Processing String Elements - The LODS and STOS Instructions

The string processing instructions considered so far operate with two strings, source and destination. The LODS and STOS instructions can be used for loading data from the string to the accumulator and writing data from the accumulator to the string. The address of the string to be processed must be placed in the DS:SI register for the LODSB instruction and into the ES:DI register for the STOSB instruction. These instructions can process bytes, words or double words (the last of these is only available on 386 and later processors). The accumulator used depends on the size of an element, the instructions use AL when processing bytes, AX when processing words and EAX when processing double words.

Like other instructions for string processing, LODS and MOVS change the value of the index registers (SI and DI, respectively) to correspond to the size of the element being processed and the state of the Direction Flag. You can specify the size of an element being processed using the last letter in the instruction name as follows:

LODSB/STOSB   load/store a byte from/to a string to/from accumulator

LODSW/STOSW   load/store a word from/to a string to/from accumulator

LODSD/STOSD   load/store a double word from/to a string to/from accumulator

If you use the name LODS or STOS, you will need to specify the size of an element loaded or stored explicitly, for example, by using the PTR operator.

```
lodsw word ptr Char_Data
```

increases the SI register by 2 when the Direction Flag is clear and decreases SI by 2 when the flag is set.

Although both instructions can be used with the repetition prefixes, in practice the LODS instruction is very rarely employed like this since there is no sense loading bytes in the register one by one without processing them. The STOS instruction however, can be used to fill the string with a certain value. For example, the next instruction sequence clears the string by storing a blank character into all of its bytes:

```
    cld                    ; process string from left to right
    lea   di,BlankStr      ; address of string to be filled
    mov   al,' '           ; character to be stored
    mov   cx,StrLen        ; CX - length of string
rep stosb                  ; fill string with character in AL
```

This instruction is also useful for giving new values to arrays. The following example shows how to use this instruction for doing something quite unexpected like clearing the video screen. This works because the screen image is defined by the contents of a special memory area - the video buffer. We'll look at the video buffer in more detail in Chapter Eight. At this stage, let's look at an example that will clear a color screen:

```
    mov   ax,0B800h        ; address of video buffer
    mov   es,ax            ; ES points to video buffer segment
    mov   di,0             ; ES:DI - address of video buffer
    mov   ax,20h           ; AX contains "blank"
    mov   cx,4000          ; size of video buffer
rep stosw                  ; code in AX into video buffer
```

The REP Prefix

The REP prefix can only be used with instructions that manipulate strings and has the following format:

REP *string_instruction*

which in practice looks like

REP MOVSB

The REP prefix causes the repetition of the *string_instruction*. The number of repetitions must be put in the CX register, with each repetition decrementing this by 1. The direction in which the addresses in the SI and DI registers are changed depends on the value of the Direction Flag. If this flag is clear, SI and DI are increased by each repetition of the MOVSB instruction. If the flag is set by the STD instruction, then the index registers are decreased.

The following example shows a typical use of the MOVSB instructions for copying a string. We suppose that both source and destination strings are located in the same segment, addressed through the DS register:

```
......
        StrS    db      'This is the source string'
        StrD    db      256 dup (' ') ; space for target string
......
        mov     cx,SizeOf StrS      ; length of source string
        lea     si,StrS             ; effective address of source
        lea     di,StrD             ; effective address of destination
rep     movsb                       ; copy source string to destination
......
```

In this example, one line of code

```
rep movsb
```

replaces the following instruction sequence:

```
RepMovsb:   movsb
            loop    RepMovsb
```

Without the MOVSB instruction, the example of copying strings would look like:

```
......
        StrS    db 'This is the source string'
        StrD    db 256 dup (' ') ; space for target string
......
        mov     cx,SizeOf StrS  ; length of source string
        lea     si,StrS         ; effective address of source
        lea     di,StrD         ; effective address of destination
;===    imitation of the MOVSB instruction with REP prefix
        push    al              ; AL used as intermediate
ImInst: mov     al,[si]         ; take byte from source string
        mov     [di],al         ; put byte into destination
        inc     si              ; advance source index
        inc     di              ; advance destination index
        loop    ImInst          ; repeat process [CX] times
        pop     al              ; restore initial AL
;===    block imitating MOVSB with REP finishes here
......
```

If this fragment does not strike you as being that complex, remember that the MOVSB instruction actually does a bit more than we have shown above. This example will only work properly when the Direction Flag is clear. If it is set, you will need to replace the INC instructions with the relevant DEC instructions and load the addresses of the last bytes of the string processed at the beginning of the fragment.

The REP prefix, which is an unconditional repetition, is the simplest form of repetition prefix. There is also a set of prefixes which perform conditional repetitions: REPE, REPNE, REPNZ, REPZ all of which can only be used with string processing instructions which affect flags - CMPS* and SCAS*. As you have probably already guessed, the last letter of the instruction name defines which memory unit the instruction deals with. Consequently, the CMPSB and SCASB instructions process strings byte by byte, the MOVSW and SCASW - word by word and MOVSD and SCASD - double word by double word.

Specifying Memory Units in Instructions - The PTR Operator

Sometimes, it might be necessary to specify the size of an operand in instructions explicitly. For example, you might need to read a byte from an array of words. In this case you should specify the type of operand explicitly:

```
......
Words dw    20 dup (?)
......
      mov   ax,byte ptr Words[10]
......
```

Similarly, you can read a word or double word from a string:

```
......
StrB  db    'This defines a sequence of bytes'
......
      mov   ax,word ptr StrB[5]
```

the PTR (**PoinTeR**) operator is usually used for accessing different areas of variables.

Labels

The LABEL directive is used to give a name to a memory object and to assign the size qualifier to that object. For example, you can use it to name a pair of objects:

```
Vector   label   dword
SegAddr  dw      ?
OffAddr  dw      ?
```

The practical value of using this directive is that it gives you the choice of referring to the variable Vector as whole, or to its components Segaddr and OffAddr.

The following example illustrates both techniques:

```
......
      call  Vector        ; using Vector as a double word
......
      mov   es,SegAddr     ; load first component of Vector
      mov   bx,OffAddr     ; load second component of Vector
......
```

Library

Copying Strings - RepBios

This program shows how to search a string for a certain character and also how to copy a string located in a different segment.

The program outputs a string containing the creation date of the ROM BIOS installed on your computer. The creation date of ROM BIOS is mainly stored by the manufacturer at the address 0F00:FFF5h, and is represented as an ASCIIZ string "dd/mm/yy" or "mm/dd/yy" (9 characters). The program searches the ROM BIOS data segment starting at this address for the NUL character, and then checks whether this character is located 9 bytes from the address 0F000:0FFF5h.

The full text of the program is stored on your program disk and given in Listing 4.1:

```
 1
 2 .model  small
 3 .stack
 4 .data
 5 TitMsg    byte 'Your computer has ROM BIOS version '
 6 Vers      byte 64 dup (' ')
 7 .code
 8 .startup
 9          mov   DatSeg,ds        ; save DATA segment address
10          mov   es,ROM_BIOS      ; ES points to ROM BIOS
11          mov   di,0FFF5h        ; ES:DI point to BIOS date
12          mov   cx,64            ; 64 character to search
13          mov   al,0             ; AL - character to search
14 repne    scasb                  ; find first match
15          jnz   ExProg           ; NUL not found - exit
16          mov   cx,di            ; DI -> character following NUL
17          sub   cx,0FFF5h        ; CX now contains data length
18          cmp   cx,9             ; date must look like xx/xx/xx
19          jb    ExProg           ; if not 9 characters, exit
20          mov   bx,cx            ; BX contains position of NUL
21          mov   ds,ROM_BIOS      ; DS points to ROM BIOS
22          mov   es,DatSeg        ; ES points DATA segment
23          lea   di,Vers          ; ES:DI point to Vers
24          mov   si,0FFF5h        ; DS:SI point to BIOS date
25 rep      movsb                  ; copy BIOS date to Vers
26          mov   ds,DatSeg        ; DS points to ROM BIOS
27          mov   Vers[bx-1],'$'   ; append EndOf Message
28          lea   dx,TitMsg        ; address of message for output
29          mov   ah,09h           ; func. 09 - output text string
·30          int   21h             ; DOS service call
```

```
31 ExProg: .exit   0
32 ROM_BIOS dw              0F000h
33 Datseg   dw     0
34          end
```

Listing 4.1 Copying Strings - The RepBios Program

The program first sets up the ES:DI register to point to the start of the area to be searched, and then sets CX to the maximum length of this area, here being 64 bytes. Note that the initialized variable ROM_BIOS is used for loading the ES register with the segment address of the ROM BIOS segment. You can use this technique instead of using an intermediate register for loading segment registers. The SCASB instruction with the REPNE prefix (scan for first matching) is used to search for the NUL character. After this instruction has been performed, the program checks the state of the Zero Flag. If it is not set (no matching character), the program finishes. Otherwise, the program subtracts the value 0FFF5h from the DI register, which at this point contains the address of the character following the first NUL character.

The result in DI is the offset of the character at the address 0F000:0FFF5h. If this value is less than 9 it means that the string examined is not a valid date format (dd-mm-yy or mm-dd-yy). In this case the program returns control to DOS, otherwise the string is copied into the internal variable Vers using the MOVSB instruction with the REP prefix. The length of the string to be copied has already been calculated in the CX register. The program then adds the "$" character at the end of the string and outputs the text created onto the screen.

Comparing Strings - CompStr

This program uses the string instruction CMPSB for comparing two strings, one of which is defined in the program, the second is read from the keyboard. For inputting text, the program uses the DOS service 0Ah (buffered input, which we'll consider in detail later on in Chapter Seven). For output the program uses macro commands from the library MACLIB.INC stored on your program disk. The full assembler text of the program is given in Listing 4.2.

```
1
2 .model small
3 .stack
4 .data
5 StrBuf db     80
6 ActLen db     0
```

```
 7 Str1      db        80 dup (' ')
 8 Str2      byte      'ABCDEFGHIJKLMNOPQRSTUVWXYZ'
 9 .code
10           include  maclib.inc
11 .startup
12           push     ds
13           pop      es
14           NewLine
15   Outmsg 'Enter alphabet characters:ABCD.. in capital letters:'
16           NewLine
17           mov      ah,0Ah        ; function 0Ah - input string
18           lea      dx,StrBuf     ; DS:DX - buffer address
19           int      21h           ; DOS service call
20           .IF      ActLen < 1
21           .exit    1
22           .ENDIF
23           lea      di,Str2 ; ES:DI point to string 2 (etalon)
24           lea      si,Str1 ; DS:SI point to string 1 (enterd)
25           mov      ch,0          ; clear high byte of CX
26           mov      cl,ActLen     ; CX contains  length of string
27           .IF      cx > LengthOf Str2
28           mov      cx,LengthOf Str2
29           .ENDIF
30           NewLine
31           OutMsg   'Entered text:   '
32           OutBytes Str1,cx
33           Newline
34           OutMsg   'Compared with:  '
35           OutBytes Str2,LengthOf Str2
36           NewLine
37           cld                    ; process strings from left to right
38 repe      cmpsb                  ; compare strings
39           .IF ZERO?
40                    OutMsg 'Right!'
41           .ELSE
42           mov      al,ActLen
43           cbw
44           sub      ax,cx
45           OutMsg   'Character at position '
46           OutInt   ax
47           OutMsg   ' is: "'
48           OutChar [si-1]
49           OutMsg   '"; must be "'
50           OutChar [di-1]
51           .ENDIF
52           Newline
53 .exit 0
54           end
```

Listing 4.2 Comparing Strings - The Program CompStr

The data that this program uses has quite a complex structure: one-byte constant defining the maximum value of the string to be read from the keyboard, one-byte field for the actual length of the string typed and an 80-byte area for the input string itself. All areas are defined using the DB directive and initial values are assigned to the StrBuf and Str1.

The key parts of the program are two blocks - one from lines 23-39 and the second beginning at line 37.

The first block loads the DS:SI and ES:DI registers with the addresses of the strings to be compared. It then places into the CX register the length of the shorter string out of the string read from the keyboard and the string constant Str2 defined in the program. The size of the string constant Str2 is determined using the LengthOf compile-time function introduced in MASM 6.0. This value can also be calculated using the $ operator. In this case, string definition would be:

```
Str2    byte  'ABCDEFGHIJKLMNOPQRSTUVWXYZ'
LStr2   equ   $ - Str2
```

The instruction for loading the string length into the CX register (in preparation for the string comparing instruction) could be:

```
mov   cx,Lstr2
```

The block also includes the run-time directive .IF to replace CX with the length of Str2 if it is longer than Str1. These directives are very similar to the conditional statements used in high-level languages such as C, Pascal or BASIC.

The second block performs the string comparison using the COMPSB instruction with the REPE prefix. After performing this instruction, the Zero Flag is set if strings are equal, and the CX register contains the number of characters in the rest of the string. Depending on the state of the Zero Flag, the program either outputs the number of non-matching elements in the strings, or reports that the strings are equal.

Sorting Strings - The Program BSort

The subroutine BSort is designed for sorting strings located in memory.
The address of an array to be sorted is passed to the subroutine through
the DS:SI registers. The full text of the subroutine is given in Listing
4.3 and is stored on your program disk as file BSORT.ASM.

```
 1 ;*********************************************************
 2 ;
 3 ; Character arrays sorting. Version 1.4
 4 ;
 5 ; Author: A.I.Sopin, Voronezh University, 16/03/93 1993
 6 ;
 7 ; Using from assembler programs:
 8 ;
 9 ; Call BSORT
10 ;
11 ; Modified bubblesort algorithm is used
12 ;
13 ; Parameters passed
14 ;
15 ; Entry parameters:
16 ; ------------------
17 ;
18 ; DS:SI - address of the array to be sorted
19 ; CX    - the array element length
20 ; DX    - number of elements
21 ;
22 ; Sorting order
23 ;
24 ; AX = 0 - increasing
25 ;      1 - decreasing
26 ;
27 ; Output (error code in the AX register)
28 ; -----------------------------------
29 ; AX = 0 - normal finish
30 ;      1 - elements longer than 48 bytes
31 ;      2 - invalid parameters specified
32 ;
33 ; The source array remains unchanged
34 ;
35 ;*********************************************************
36 .model    large
37 public    bsort
38 MaxLen    equ 48   ; maximum record   length
39 .code
40 BSORT   PROC   FAR pascal uses bx cx dx es si di bp
```

```
41  ;---------------------------------------------
42  ; Check parameters passed
43          cmp   cx,MaxLen    ; array length valid?
44          jng   ChkN         ; less than maximum - continue
45          mov   ax,1          ; indicate "elements too long"
46          jmp   Exit         ; return
47  ChkN:   cmp   dx,0          ; number of elements = 0?
48          jg    Work         ; if not continue
49          mov   ax,2          ; indicate "no elements in array"
50          jmp   Exit         ; return
51  ;---------------------------------------------------
52  Work:   mov   CS:SrtOrd,ax  ; store Sort Order
53          cld                 ; Clear Direct Flag
54          mov   CS:RecLen,cx   ; store Record Length
55          mov   CS:RecNum,dx   ; store Number Of Records
56          mov   CS:AddrArr,si  ; store Array Address
57          push  ds            ; push DARA segment address
58          pop   es            ; ES now points to DATA segment
59  ; External loop (WHILE SWP = 1, i.e while elements moved)
60  ExtLoop: mov  CS:SWP,0      ; indicate "no elements moved"
61          mov   ax,0          ; Normal Return Code
62          dec   CS:RecNum; decrease number of records to process
63          jz    Exit         ; if no more records - exit
64          mov   dx,CS:RecNum  ; of DX - number records left
65          mov   bp,CS:AddrArr ; starting address of array
66          mov   CS:BP0,bp     ; save address of first record
67  ; Nested loop (comparing adjacent records)
68  M1:     mov   si,CS:BP0     ; address of current record
69          mov   di,si         ; address of following record
70          mov   cx,CS:RecLen  ; record length
71          add   di,cx         ; address of next record
72          cmp   CS:SrtOrd,0   ; increasing?
73          jnz   DecrS         ; AX <> 0 - decreasing
74  IncrS:  repe  cmpsb         ; compare adjacent records
75          jbe   Swapped       ; if following < current
76          jmp   short SWAP    ; swap records
77  DecrS:  repe  cmpsb         ; compare adjacent records
78          jae   Swapped       ; if following > current
79    ; Swapping records
80  SWAP:   mov   cx,CS:RecLen  ; CX - record length
81          mov   bp,CS:BP0     ; BP - address of current record
82          mov   bx,bp         ; BX points to current record
83          add   bx,cx         ; now BX points to next record
84  SwBytes: mov  al,DS:[BP]    ; byte from current record to AL
85          xchg  al,[bx]       ; swap bytes in AL and next record
86          mov   DS:[BP],al    ; put byte into next record
87          inc   bp            ; next byte in current record
88          inc   bx            ; next byte in next record
89          loop  SwBytes       ; repeat swapping
90          mov   CS:SWP,1      ; indicate swapping
91  ; advance parameters of external cycle
92  Swapped: mov  ax,CS:RecLen  ; AX - record length
93          add   CS:BP0,ax     ; BP points to next record
```

```
94              dec    dx        ; decrease number of records to process
95              jnz    M1        ; next step of nested cycle
96              cmp    CS:SWP,0  ; have elements been swapped?
97              jnz    ExtLoop   ; yes - repeat process
98              mov    ax,0      ; Normal Return Code
99  ; Restore registers and return (exit code in AX)
100 Exit:       ret
101 BSORT       ENDP
102 ;------------------------------------------------------------
103 ; Data area in CODE segments
104 SrtOrd      DW     0         ;
105 RecLen      DW     0         ;
106 RecNum      DW     0         ;
107 AddrArr     DW     0         ;
108 BP0         DW     0         ; address of current record
109 SWP         DB     0         ; swappings indicator
110             END
```

Listing 4.3 BSort Subroutine for Bubble Sorting

The subroutine processes strings which are not longer than 48 bytes. If you want to change this value, change the definition of the MaxLen constant at the beginning of the program.

This subroutine uses a modified bubble sorting algorithm which compares two adjoining elements and swaps them when necessary. This process is repeated until there are no more elements to be swapped. The criteria for swapping elements are:

▲ First element is greater than second when increasing order is requested.

▲ First element is less than second when decreasing order is requested.

After the first revision of the array, the maximum element becomes the last one in the array. The number of elements to be examined is then decreased by 1 and the process is repeated. The swapping indicator is cleared (set to 0) at the beginning of each iteration. When elements are swapped, this indicator is set to 1. The value of this indicator is checked at the end of each iteration and if it is still equal to 0 the program finishes. If the indicator value is zero once this process has been completed, it means that no swappings were performed, and consequently, that the array has been sorted. You will have realized now why it's called a bubble sort - the largest elements " float " to the top of the array.

The subroutine starts by checking the values of parameters passed. If an invalid value is found, the subroutine sets the corresponding value of the error code in the AX register and passes control to the label Exit which marks the final block of the subroutine. This block restores the registers used and returns control to the caller.

The block labelled ExtLoop clears the swapping indicator and loads the starting address of an array into the variable AddrArr. This is the beginning of the process which performs the revision of an array.

Label M1 starts the block which compares adjacent elements and passes control to the block that swaps elements where necessary. The labels IncrS and DecrS are given to sub-blocks which check for either an increasing or decreasing order, respectively. To compare elements of an array, the CMPSB instruction with the REPE prefix is used. This compares the elements of the strings specified by the addresses in DS:SI and ES:DI registers while they are equal (the Zero Flag is set). After the CMPSB instruction has been performed, control is passed either to the block which swaps two strings (the label Swap) or directly to the end of the swapping block. The next repetition of the cycle (the label Swapped)is then prepared. The conditional jump instruction JBE (Jump if Below or Equal) is used for an increasing sort order, or JAE (Jump if Above or Equal) for a decreasing order. These instructions pass control to the instruction labelled SWAPPED - the end of the block swapping elements.

The label SWAP marks the block which swaps the two strings. The block begins by loading the length of the strings to be sorted into the CX register. Then the addresses of the two adjacent strings are placed in the DS:BX and DS:BP registers. The block then loads one byte from the string specified by the address in the DS:BX registers into the AL register and swaps this byte with the byte of second string, the address of which is stored in the DS:BP registers. The process of swapping bytes (label SwBytes) is repeated for all bytes in the strings, then the swapping indicator is set to 1.

The block labelled Swapped finishes the process of examining strings. This block calculates the addresses of the strings to be examined next and checks whether all strings have been processed. The swapping indicator is then checked and if it is set, the block performs the next iteration. To do this, control is passed to the label ExtLoop, otherwise the block assigns the value 0 to the return code and passes control to the calling program.

An example of the calling program for the BSORT subroutine is shown in Listing 4.4:

```
1  ;***********************************************************
2  ;
3  ; Array sorting: demo program
4  ;
5  ; Author: A.I.Sopin, Voronezh University. 1993
6  ;
7  ;***********************************************************
8         EXTRN BSORT : FAR
9         .MODEL  SMALL
10        .STACK 100h
11 ;-------------------------------
12        .DATA
13 BELL   EQU 07 ;  sound signal
14 LF     EQU 10 ;  Line Feed
15 CR     EQU 13 ;  Carriage Return
16 TEXT0  DB   CR, LF, CR, LF, " String sorting: demo program."
17        DB   " Press any key to continue...", BELL,CR,LF, "$"
18 TEXT1  DB   CR, LF, " Outputting an original sequence: "
19        DB   " Press any key...", BELL, CR, LF, "$"
20 TEXT2  DB   CR, LF
21 ARRAY2 DB   "YYYYYYY EEEEEEE 1234567 ZZZZZZZ 0000000 QQQQQQQ "
22        DB   "$"
23 TEXT3  DB   CR, LF, CR, LF,  " Increasing sequence. "
24        DB   " Press any key...", BELL, CR, LF, "$"
25 TEXT4  DB   CR, LF
26 ARRAY4 DB "YYYYYYY EEEEEEE 1234567 ZZZZZZZ 0000000 QQQQQQQ","$"
27 TEXT5  DB   CR, LF, CR, LF, " Decreasing sequence. "
28        DB   " Press any key...", BELL, CR, LF, "$"
29 ERTXT  DB   CR, LF, CR, LF, " Sorting error. "
30        DB   " Press any key...", BELL, CR, LF, "$"
31 VMODE  DB 0    ; video mode saved
32 ;------------------------------------------------------------
33        .CODE
34 OutMsg macro   Txt
35        lea     dx,Txt     ; address of message
36        mov     ah,09h     ; function 09h - output text string
37        int     21h        ; DOS  service call
38   endm
39
40 WaitKey macro
41        mov     ah,0       ; function 0-wait for key pressed
42        int     16h        ; BIOS keyboard service
43 endm
44
45 ;------------------------------------------------------------
46 .STARTUP
```

```
47 ; Output initial message
48        OutMsg   TEXT0          ;  output initial message
49   WaitKey
50 ;
51        OutMsg   TEXT1          ;  output initial message
52        OutMsg   TEXT2          ;  output initial message
53   WaitKey
54 ; Call subroutine BSORT - sorting array (increasing)
55        mov      ax,0           ;  AX = 0 for increasing sequence
56        mov      cx,8           ;  length of record
57        mov      dx,6           ;  number of records
58        lea      si,ARRAY2      ;  DS:[SI]-address will be sorted
59        Call     BSORT          ;  perform sorting
60        cmp      ax,0           ;  normal return?
61        jnz      ErSort         ;  if not, output error  and exit
62        OutMsg TEXT3            ;  output header
63        OutMsg ARRAY2           ;  output array sorted
64   WaitKey
65 ; Call subroutine BSORT - sorting array (decreasing)
66        mov      ax,1           ;  AX = 1 for decreasing sequence
67        mov      cx,8           ;  length of record
68        mov      dx,6           ;  number of records
69        lea      si,ARRAY4      ;  DS:[SI]-address will be sorted
70        Call     BSORT          ;  perform sorting
71        cmp      ax,0           ;  normal return?
72        jnz      ErSort         ;  if not, output error  and exit
73        OutMsg TEXT5            ;  output header
74        OutMsg ARRAY4           ;  output array sorted
75   WaitKey
76 ;------------------------------------------------------------
77 ; Terminate program and exit to DOS
78 ExProgr:.exit       0
79 ErSort:    OutMsg ERTXT
80   .exit    1
81        END
```

Listing 4.4 DemoSort - The Calling Program for BSort

The program DemoSort performs two calls of the BSort subroutine passing to it addresses of two areas treated as 6 eight-character strings. The sequences of strings are sorted in increasing order and then in decreasing order. Results of both calls are then output onto the screen.

Summary

In this chapter we have seen how the apparently unstructured way in which Assembler handles data puts the onus on the programmer to create his own structures.

We have learnt how practically all data can be defined as a group of bytes, and manipulated accordingly. We have also seen how strings can be defined and processed using a number of built-in string functions.

A final note: while these tools provide almost unlimited flexibility, the price is a greater reliance on the programmer to maintain the integrity of the data, especially when compared to a strongly typed high-level language such as Pascal.

Program Flow
and Design

This chapter describes how an assembly language program can be constructed from separate parts - procedures and macros. We will explain the methods used for controlling program flow when constructing such programs. Finally, as usual we will look at some programs and a small macrolibrary.

Fundamental Knowledge

Procedures in Assembly Language

As we saw in Chapter Three, the contents of the CS (code segment) register and the IP (instruction pointer) register determine the address of the next instruction to be called from memory and executed by the CPU. The CS register contains its segment address and the IP register the offset.

The byte at the specified location contains an operation code (opcode), which informs the processor whether or not other bytes need to be fetched and how their contents are to be processed. When the instruction has been executed, the contents of IP are incremented by the number of bytes that have been fetched.

You can alter this process by using instructions such as JMPs and LOOPs (see Chapter Three), which allow you to in effect change the contents of the IP register.

As a rule, you are most likely to use intrasegment jumps, i.e. jumps within one code segment, which is usually located in one file. When performing intersegment and intermodule jumps, you need to declare labels using directives such as PUBLIC and EXTRN to tell the Assembler that these labels are defined outside the module currently being processed.

You can also use procedures to alter the sequence of program execution. This can be very useful when it comes to structuring a program, as it means that you can write the program in small parts, debug them separately and then combine them into one program. Writing long, spaghetti-like, one module programs is usually not a good idea, even in high-level languages, and in assembly language it is practically impossible. Even if you're convinced that straight-line assembly code makes your program faster, you can bet on spending quite a while debugging it.

An Example of Procedures

The program we will take as an example only has one code segment. This means that all the code is in one physical segment and therefore simplifies the procedure's header. Look at the program shown in Listing 5.1.

```
TITLE   Hello Example Program 4      ; title is not necessary
.MODEL  SMALL                        ; declare memory model
                                     ;
.CODE                                ; declare code segment
Main    PROC                         ; declare main procedure
        MOV AX,@Data                 ; copy address of data
        MOV DS,AX                    ; segment into DS
        LEA DX,Hello
        CALL Display_DX              ; call procedure
        MOV AH,4Ch                   ; define DOS function to exit
        MOV AL,00h                   ; with code zero
        INT 21h                      ; exit to DOS
        ;---------------------!
        ;    Procedure section !
        ;---------------------!
Display_DX PROC                      ; declare procedure Display__DX
        RET                          ; return to MAIN
Display_DX ENDP                      ; end of procedure
        ;-------------------------!
        ;End of procedure section !
        ;-------------------------!
Main    ENDP                         ; end of code section
                                     ;
.DATA                                ; declare data segment
Hello   DB    'Hello!$'              ; define string to display
                                     ;
.STACK                               ; Declare stack segment
        DB    128 DUP (?)            ; reserve 128 bytes for stack
                                     ;
        END Main                     ; end of program
                                     ;
```

Listing 5.1 The Hello Program with Procedures

The code segment in this program is structured in the following way:

```
.CODE
Main              PROC
                  ...
                  CALL Display_DX
       ...
Display_DX        PROC
                  ...
                  RET
Display_DX        ENDP
Main              ENDP
```

The code segment is declared as Main PROC, it finishes with the directive

```
Main     ENDP
```

The procedure Display_DX is placed inside the Main procedure. It starts with the directive

```
Display_DX  PROC
```

for declaring the procedure and finishes with the directive

```
Display_DX  ENDP
```

which marks the end of the procedure. The instruction

```
CALL     Display_DX
```

changes the natural order in which the instructions are executed, passing control to the first instruction of the Display_DX procedure. This means that the execution of the line

```
CALL     Display_DX
```

changes the contents of IP to the offset of the line

```
MOV      AH,09h
```

However, before doing this, the CPU pushes onto the stack the address (offset) of the line following

```
CALL     Display_DX
```

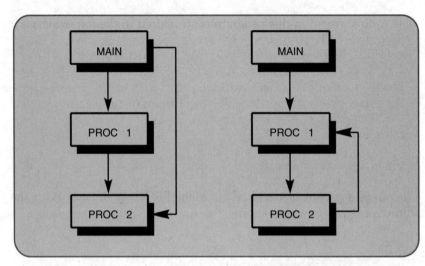

Figure 5.1
**Calling Nested
Procedures**

in the Main procedure. The RET instruction in the Display_DX procedure makes the CPU take the address (offset) from the stack and put it into the IP register, passing control back to the Main procedure.

Note that although you can write as many procedures as necessary, only one of them can gain control when the program is loaded. This means that you have to have only one Main procedure and call other procedures as subroutines. Of course, a particular procedure can be called several times.

You can also include nested calls, where one procedure calls another (see Figure 5.1). Note that although the example on the right is perfectly feasible, it is a little dangerous as the stack pointer will not point to the correct address of the stack. Use these with caution - you don't want to end up like Munchausen who fell into a lake and tried to lift himself out by pulling on his own hair.

Writing a Procedure (SMALL Memory Model)

Before you write your procedure you need to decide what you want it to do - every procedure must have a specific purpose. You then have to estimate the size and complexity of your planned procedure. The ideal size is about a half to a full page of code. The simpler your procedure is, the easier the task of debugging your program. To keep your procedures simple, you can divide larger ones into smaller parts, declare each part as a separate procedure, then use nested calls.

The next step is determining input and output parameters for the procedure and deciding how the arguments will be passed. One option is to use the stack, which is probably the most powerful and flexible way of passing parameters. Another method is to place them into a specific memory area. The quickest way is to place the arguments into the general purpose registers, however this may cause additional work while debugging the program, especially if the program is quite complex.

When you have done all this, you can begin writing your procedure. Start with the comment header describing in detail its purpose, the input and output parameters, the method of passing parameters and any other procedures which are needed to make your main procedure work.

Actually writing the code is the last stage (the last before debugging, that is). A good style to adopt is to start by putting the values of all the registers that you will use in the procedure onto the stack. You should then restore the values of these registers at the end of the procedure.

The last, but by no means least important point is using labels and names of variables in procedures. You must make sure that the names you give these objects do not appear anywhere else in your program. If you can't avoid this, you can get round this problem by using the LOCAL directive, available in MASM 5.1 and above. The next example shows how to define two variables with the same WorkVar in two procedures:

```
......
Proc1    proc  near    ; first procedure starts here
local    WorkVar
......
Proc1    endp
......
Proc2    proc  near    ; second procedure starts here
local    WorkVar
......
Proc2    endp
......
```

In this case the two procedures use two different variables WorkVar, located at different memory addresses.

Passing Parameters

It is not realistic to restrict a procedure to operating on the same set of data every time it is called. As a rule, it is much better to have procedures which will, for example, display or print any string or any icon than to write a special procedure for each individual case. It is for this reason that we use procedures that have parameters, which contain or point at data to be processed.

MASM 6.0 and above have a facility for listing parameters in instructions which call procedures. This is the INVOKE directive which has the following format:

```
invoke procedure-name,parameter-list
```

If you don't have the latest version of MASM, don't worry that we're going to leave it at that. Since many other assemblers do not have an INVOKE type directive, we will continue by discussing how parameters can be passed manually, either through the registers or RAM - starting with registers.

Passing Parameters Through Registers

To pass data through a particular register you simply have to give the necessary value to this register, then execute the CALL instruction, assuming that the relevant procedure operates on the register in a suitable way. The process of returning a parameter from a procedure through a register is very similar: place the value in the register in the procedure, then once the procedure has been executed, you can use the result contained in the register. Naturally, you must also include a comment header in the procedure with a full description of the registers used for passing parameters.

Let's look at the program shown in Listing 5.1 as an example of passing parameters through registers. The address of the data to be processed is passed to the procedure through the DX register.

Sometimes however, there are too few registers and they are too small and too important to program execution for use as parameter storage. In such cases, it would be better to find an alternative for passing the parameters.

Passing Parameters in Memory

There are two ways of passing procedure parameters through RAM; as variables or through the stack. The first method is quite simple. The procedure processes the data located in RAM in the area marked by a variable with a prescribed name. This variable (there can actually be more than one) is usually defined in the data segment. Here is a simple example (Listing 5.2) which is a remake of the program shown in Listing 5.1.

```
TITLE       Hello   Procedure  Example  Program
.MODEL      SMALL
.CODE
MAIN        PROC
Start:
            CALL DISPLAY_Hi
            MOV AX,4C00h
            INT 21h
;--------------------------------
; Procedure section
;--------------------------------
Display_Hi  PROC                        ; procedure displays string at
                                        ; the data segment named Hi
            MOV AX,@data
            MOV DS,AX
            MOV DX,OFFSET Hi
            INT 21h
            RET
Display_Hi  ENDP
;--------------------------------
;   End of procedure section
;--------------------------------
Main        ENDP
.DATA
Hi          DB    "Hello!$"
.STACK
            DB    128 DUP ('STACK128')  ; reserves 1024 bytes for stack
            END Main
```

Listing 5.2 Using Variables for Passing Parameters

Once again, if you use this method for passing parameters through variables you must describe these variables in your comment header. This method gives more flexibility than using the registers; it doesn't restrict the number of parameters, so you can write a procedure where the number of parameters exceeds the number of registers in CPU. However, the work involved in placing data into prescribed variables is quite laborious.

Passing Parameters Using the Stack

The most powerful and flexible method of passing parameters is using the stack. The length of these parameters can either be described beforehand, or passed by other parameters. The parameter addresses are calculated inside the procedure, then data at these addresses is processed by the procedure. To prevent the stack becoming too big, you can remove the parameters once the procedure has finished. This is especially necessary if you use nested calls (when a procedure calls another one). You can do this using the RET n instruction which releases n additional bytes from the stack.

To illustrate this method we'll rewrite the program First, from Chapter One - see Listing 5.3.

```
.Model Small
.CODE
INCLUDE MACLIB.INC
Begin     MOV      BX,0
          InpInt   BX
          MOV      CX,BX
          InpInt   BX
          PUSH     CX          ; place first argument onto stack
          PUSH     BX          ; place second argument onto stack
          CALL     AddShow
Finish:   MOV      AX,4C00h
          INT      21h
;------------------------
;   Procedure section
;------------------------
AddShow   PROC                 ; adds summands and display results
          PUSH     BP          ; Save BP
          MOV      BP,SP       ;
          MOV      CX,[BP+6]
          MOV      BX,[BP+4]
          ADD      BX,CX
          OutInt   BX
          POP      BP
          RET      4
AddShow   ENDP
;--------
;End of Procedure Section
;--------
.DATA
.STACK
          END      Begin       ;  End of the program
```

Listing 5.3 Remake of the Program First From Chapter One

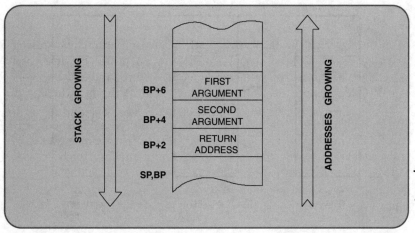

Figure 5.2
**The Contents of
the Stack with
Two Parameters
Passed**

Notice how the arguments are passed to the procedure. They are pushed onto the stack just before the procedure call. Since each argument is the size of a word, the value of SP decrements by 4. (Remember, that the stack "grows" downwards). The current value of BP is then saved in the stack since the BP register is used for accessing parameters pushed onto the stack by the caller, and the stack pointer SP is copied to BP. The offset of the first argument is then determined as BP+6 and the offset of the second argument as BP+4 and the necessary actions are performed. The contents of the stack on entry into the sub-program is shown in Figure 5.2.

You might wonder why we haven't used the POP instruction to get the values of arguments from the stack into the registers. Quite simply, it is not as convenient as the way we have chosen. The POP instruction modifies the stack pointer, then the next PUSH instruction overwrites the parameter value. So, if you need to use a parameter more than once in a procedure, pop it at the start of the subroutine and copy it into a local variable.

You can make a procedure more reliable by protecting the initial values in the registers from being damaged by the procedure. This can be done at the beginning of a procedure by pushing the values of the individual registers used in the procedure onto the stack with the PUSH instruction. Alternatively, you can push the values of all registers using the PUSHA instruction. At the end of the procedure you must pop them from the stack with the POP (or POPA) instruction. Although this technique is valid, it makes it difficult to pop the arguments from the stack. Fortunately, it does not prevent the evaluation of the address (offsets) of all the arguments.

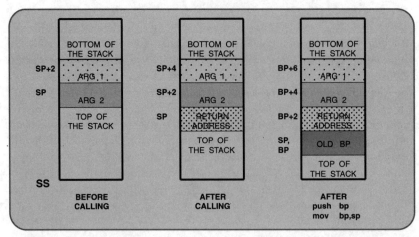

Figure 5.3
Stack Changes Through Time

Look at Figure 5.3, which shows the location of arguments for this example program.

The reason we have used a register other than SP for evaluating addresses is obvious. It means you can save the value of SP at the beginning of a procedure in another register (usually BP). You can then push and pop until you get tired - SP will change but BP remains constant.

Calling Procedures Using INVOKE

We'll now come back to the INVOKE directive in MASM 6.0 that we mentioned earlier, to see how it works in practice. The following example shows the complete Assembler program that uses the internal procedure for outputting a text string:

```
.model    small
.stack
.data
Msg1      db            'Message 1',0Dh,0Ah,'$'
Msg2      db            'Message 2',0Dh,0Ah,'$'
.code
ProcOut   proc          near PASCAL, MsgAddr:ptr byte
          mov           dx,MsgAddr      ; take address of parameter
          mov           ah,09h          ; function 09 - output string
          int           21h             ; DOS service call
          ret                           ; return to caller
ProcOut   endp
.startup
          invoke        ProcOut,addr Msg1
          invoke        ProcOut,addr Msg2
.exit     0
end
```

If you look at the additional parameters in the PROC directive you'll see that the first operand of the directive specifies the call distance and the method for passing parameters. The specifier NEAR tells the Assembler that the procedure is located in the same segment as the caller. The language specification PASCAL defines that parameters will be passed according to PASCAL conventions - pushed onto the stack in direct order from the list, from left to right. The parameter specification which comes next defines the parameter MsgAddr as the address of a variable one byte long (in fact this is the address of the first byte in the array of characters).

The INVOKE directive is used to call the ProcOut procedure twice. The address of each text message is passed as a parameter. If you run this program under CodeView, you'll see that parameters are passed in the same way as we described in the previous section (through the stack). The advantage is that the source code is much shorter and more readable.

NEAR and FAR Procedures

We have already mentioned that it is possible to write programs which have more than one code segment. This may result in the calling procedure, for example the Main one, and the called procedure being called in different code segments. You can deal with this by using the qualifiers FAR and NEAR in procedure definitions to avoid corrupting the contents of the stack.

If a procedure is defined as NEAR, the CALL and RET instructions have to work only with values of the IP register and do not touch the CS register. The CALL instruction for a NEAR procedure is encoded into 3 bytes (1 for operation code and 2 for the distance from the CALL instruction to the start of the procedure). The return address is coded in 2 bytes (one word). If the procedure is defined as FAR, then the values of the CS and IP registers are used in the CALL and RET instructions. The CALL instruction in this case is written in 5 bytes (1 for opcode, 2 for offset and 2 for the segment address of the procedure). Similarly, the return address is coded in 4 bytes (2 words).

The qualifiers NEAR and FAR actually determine how the CALL and RET instructions are performed. CALL and RET must be both FAR or NEAR, otherwise, on return, the subroutine might pass control to the wrong address. At best, this will give you the wrong value of the stack pointer on return from the subroutine. For example, let's assume that you use the far CALL instructions for calling a procedure. The return address of 4 bytes long will be pushed onto the stack. Suppose that the subroutine then uses the RETN (near return) instruction for returning to the caller. The microprocessor will load the IP register with the offset address of the instruction that follows the subroutine call, but the CS register will keep the segment address of the **subroutine** code segment.

Even if you're lucky and the segment address of the subroutine and caller are the same (this might happen if the memory model you are using is relatively small), the top of the stack contains the segment address of the subroutine. The results of the program (if it finishes abnormally due to a corrupted stack) are probably wrong. You will get a much bigger mess if the subroutine called as NEAR uses the RETF instruction. Control will be returned to the address calculated using the correct offset but incorrect segment (the value on the top of the stack). You can probably guess what part of the program will actually gain control!

The Directives PUBLIC and EXTRN

Good use of procedures reduces the amount of program source code and makes it more readable. In addition, they allow you to use certain parts of a program several times for processing different data. The directives PUBLIC and EXTRN let you create an executable program, where procedures originating in one source file are called from procedures which originate in another source file.

These procedures, stored in different source files, can be combined into a library for future use. As we explained in Chapter Two, the precise process depends on which compiler you are using. To refresh your memory of how it works, we'll give a brief outline here of the basic process of compiling and linking modular programs.

Before it can be used from another program, a procedure has to be converted into a intermediate form and then combined with the calling program unit. The most common way of storing a compiled subroutine is as an object module. As you will remember, MASM generates an object module when the parameter /c is specified in the command line while invoking Assembler. These object modules can then be stored in libraries (special files, usually with the extension .LIB). The Assembler directive PUBLIC provides information used by the linker to determine which procedures and variables, located in one object module, can be accessed from other modules.

If a procedure is declared as PUBLIC in one file, and its name is included in the EXTRN directive in the procedure from the second file, then the first procedure can be called from the second one. The compiler will not detect an error and the linker will set up the necessary connections.

This means that you can create large procedure libraries with a long shelf-life. The PUBLIC and EXTRN directives can also be used for labels and variables. If you define them as PUBLIC and then declare them as EXTRN in other procedures you can use them anywhere in your program. The PUBLIC and EXTRN directives describe the connection between objects located in different program units. The following example shows how to make a variable "visible" from another module

```
......
        public   PubVar
......
LocVar  db       0
PubVar  db       1
......
```

The variable PubVar is defined as PUBLIC which means that the object module will contain information for the linker about the address and length of this variable. If we take another module and write the lines

```
......
        extrn    PubVar
......
        mov      ah,LocVar
        mov      al,PubVar
......
```

Assembler will detect an error in the line which refers to the variable LocVar because there is no definition for this variable in this module. The variable PubVar, will still be treated as valid, but its address will be formed later, by the linker rather than Assembler.

An Introduction to Macros

Modular programming is the process of creating complex programs comprised of procedures. Another approach is to use a different kind of separately prepared component - the **macro**, also known as macrocommand or macroinstruction.

Macros are a very simple and appealing concept. A name is given to a piece of code and whenever this name occurs in your program, it is substituted by this piece of code at the very start of the assembly process.

The action of naming a macro is rather grandly called "creating a macro definition" or defining a macro. The action itself is very simple as you can see below:

```
Name_of_Macro     macro                    ; comments
;_____
;...  the sequence of instructions
;_____
                  endm
```

Suppose for example, that you need to save and restore registers several times in program (which is boring to say the least in really large programs). You can combine these instructions giving them the name SaveRegs for saving registers and RestRegs for restoring them. The corresponding macros would be:

```
SaveRegs    macro
            pop     ax
            pop     bx
            pop     cx
            pop     dx
            endm
RestRegs macro
            pop     dx
            pop     cx
            pop     bx
            pop     ax
            endm
```

You can then use these macros as ordinary assembler instructions in your programs - as below:

```
......
        SaveRegs
;................
;       the functional part working with registers
;................
        RestRegs
......
```

You can use macros in basically the same way as procedures - so you can rewrite your programs using macros instead of procedures.

Like procedure calls, a macro may be used several times in a program. The only potential problem here though is how the labels and various names will be treated. MASM starts by generating several copies of each and will report the redefinition of symbols. The correct way to solve this problem is to use the LOCAL directive for declaring names inside the macro.

The following example shows part of the MASM 6.0 listing of the program First, stored on your program disk. MASM includes the text generated from macros when the parameter /Sa (maximize listing) is specified in the command line.

```
                        InpInt  bx          ; Input the first operand
                   1    local   Read , ExitMac , Number
001A 51            1    push    cx
001B 53            1    push    bx
001C BB 0000       1    mov     bx,0
001F B9 0000       1    mov     cx,0
0022 BB 0000       1    mov     bx,0
0025              1  ??0000:
0025 B4 01        1      mov     ah,1      ; Prepare Dos Service Call-function1
0027 CD 21        1      int     21h       ; DOS Service 01-get symbol with echo
0029 8A D0        1      mov     dl,al     ; Save symbol to proceeding
                   1    ;
                   1    ; Check if symbol is a number 0 ... 9
                   1    ;
002B 3C 30        1      cmp     al,'0'    ; Compare symbol in AL and ASCII code "0"
002D 7C 15        1      jl      ??0001    ; If symbol is less than "0" - not a number
002F 3C 39        1      cmp     al,'9'    ; Compare symbol in AL and ASCII code "9"
0031 7F 11        1      jg      ??0001    ; if greater than "9" - not a number
                   1                       ;=== Leave macro
0033              1  ??0002:               ;
0033 B4 00        1      mov     ah,0
0035 2C 30        1      sub     al,48     ; Convert symbol in AL into number
0037 8B C8        1      mov     cx,ax     ; Save this number into CL
0039 B8 000A      1      mov     ax,10     ; Prepare to computing result
003C F7 E3        1      mul     bx        ; AX = BX * 10
003E 03 C1        1      add     ax,cx     ; AX = ( BX * 10 )+ AX
0040 8B D8        1      mov     bx,ax     ; Save the current result
                   1                       ;
0042 EB E1        1      jmp     ??0000    ; Read next symbol
                   1
0044              1  ??0001:
0044 8B C3        1      mov     ax,bx     ; Save result into AX register
0046 5B           1      pop     bx        ; Restore BX ( work register )
0047 59           1      pop     cx        ; Restore CX ( work register )
0048 8B D8        1      mov     bx,ax     ; Put result into target
                                                                           ;
004A 8B CB               mov     cx,bx     ; Save it in CX register
```

Note that some labels begin with the characters "??". These are generated by Assembler to prevent identical labels, even when a macro is used several times in the program.

Macros with Parameters

Macros have a much greater potential than simply being used to duplicate pieces of code. They really come into their own when used with parameters. The definition of such a macro is given below:

```
Name_of_Macro  macro  par1,......,parn  ;        comments
;_____
; text of macro goes here
;_____
;         ENDM
```

The number of parameters is restricted by the length of the line.

Try this out on one of your programs, rewriting it using a macro with a parameter. In the line where the macro is used ("called") each parameter is substituted by an argument which can be immediate data or register or memory data. Obviously, working with parameters is much easier if you write a macro rather than a procedure. Macro parameters are referred to within the macro simply by names, whereas with procedures care must be taken about addressing parameters. To demonstrate, let's compare two examples. The first example shows a short macro with three parameters that adds the first and second parameters and puts the result into the third:

```
Add3   macro    par1, par2, par3
       push     ax
       mov      ax,par1
       add      ax,par2
       mov      par3,ax
       pop      ax
       endm
```

The procedure performing the same task could be as follows:

```
ProcAdd  proc  near
         push  bp          ; save BP
         mov   bp,sp        ; current value of stack pointer
         mov   ax,[bp+8]    ; load first parameter (value) into AX
         add   ax,[bp+6]    ; add second parameter (value)
         mov   bx,[bp+4]    ; load address of third parameter
         mov   [bx],ax      ; return the result
         pop   bp           ; restore original BP
         ret   6            ; return and restore stack
AddShow  ENDP
```

As you see the procedure looks much more complicated.

Macro Libraries

Having written or copied some useful macros, you will probably want to use them in your programs whenever possible. You don't need to copy each macro into your program file - you simply need to write a directive line such as

```
INCLUDE  MACROLIB.INC
```

in your program. In this example, the file MACROLIB.INC. should contain all the macros you need in this program. An example of a macro library is given in the Library section of this chapter. This library is stored on your program disk as the file MACLIB.INC.

Macros vs Procedures

Macros and procedures provide roughly the same service but they just go about it differently. The big question is, how do you choose between the two?

One of the most attractive things about macros is that you can use them to create portable programs. That is, you could write a set of macros which perform instructions for a hypothetical machine. Instructions like ADDINT (add integers), COMPVAL (compare values) and so on will use registers and memory operands in the way most convenient to you. For example, the ADDINT instruction would have 3 operands: two summands and a result. The corresponding macro would look like this:

```
AddInt    macro    Operand1, Operand2, Result
          push     ax              ; save register used
          mov      ax,Operand1     ; take first summand
          add      ax,Operand2     ; perform addition
          mov      Result,ax       ; store result
          pop      ax              ; restore register used
          endm
```

Unlike the machine instruction ADD, this macro can deal with the operands and the result located in the memory. Furthermore, it does not change any registers until its operands have been stored in these registers.

Using an instruction set like this to write a program has distinct advantages. Faced with another microprocessor or Assembler, you simply need to rewrite the macros to generate the appropriate instructions, then recompile your program -giving you an executable module that can work on another platform without changing a line of source program!

This approach can also be used for creating special programming languages by writing macros which can be used as statements in such a language.

It is probably slightly easier to write a macro than a procedure, whereas debugging a program with a procedure is slightly easier than debugging a program with a macro. This is because most debuggers allow you to step through the called procedures. The complication with macros is that it is often quite difficult to determine which machine instructions are generated from which macro.

Since a macro doesn't waste time performing the CALL and RET instructions and does not do any extra work with the registers, programs with macros are slightly faster than similar ones written with procedures.

However, if a macro is used several times in a program, you can end up with an unreasonably large machine code program, in which case, you'd be better off using procedures.

Directives and Operators
Computations and Tests During Program Assembly

Operators are an interesting feature of MASM which allow you to carry out computations or tests while assembling the machine code program i.e. before runtime.

For example, the operators SEG, OFFSET are used for address computation and DUP, PTR are used for working with data while the machine code program is being assembled.

They are also put to more sophisticated use; for example, suppose that you have to create an installation program for an application. You will need several variations of the program to suit each type of processor from the 80x86 family, different sizes of RAM, and different types of device. As a result, your program will be very large and will occupy too much space in RAM. You can get round this problem though by creating a program that writes information about the hardware configuration list and then another program that uses this information

at the time of assembly to avoid assembling any unnecessary parts. This program will contain MASM decision directives such as IF and ELSE. Although this approach forces you to compile and link your program on the target machine, it does have its uses when you're creating special applications in which you want to reduce the amount of memory used.

Tools

Starting With the END!

In this section we will give a brief description of the directives and instructions which are most useful as far as program design is concerned. The syntax is not given in full, but in its clearest and most frequently used form.

We will start with the directive that must be included at the end of every module which contains an assembly language program:

```
END    [label]
```

If a module contains a main procedure, the attribute "label" points to the start of program execution. This attribute is simply omitted if there is no main procedure.

The SEGMENT and ENDS Directives

The SEGMENT and ENDS directives have the following formats:

```
name   SEGMENT
. . . . . . . . . . . . .
. . . . . . . . . . . . .
name   ENDS
```

As you can see, the SEGMENT directive starts a segment and the ENDS directive finishes it. You can give the segments any name you want. There are usually at least three segments in a program - code, data and stack - each of which is declared by its own SEGMENT and ENDS directives.

The .MODEL Directive

In MASM 5.0 and above, you can also declare segments using the .MODEL directive, which is placed at the very beginning of the program. This directive can be written in the following form:

```
.MODEL   MemoryModel
```

where MemoryModel can be SMALL, COMPACT, MEDIUM, or LARGE and also HUGE, TINY or FLAT.

SMALL means that by default all code is placed in one physical segment and likewise all data declared in data segments is also placed in one physical segment. Therefore, by default, all procedures and variables are addressed as NEAR by pointing at offsets only.

COMPACT means that by default all elements of code (procedures) are placed into one physical segment but each element of data can be placed by default into its own physical segment. Consequently, data elements are addressed by pointing both at the segment and offset addresses. Therefore, by default, all code elements (procedures) are addressed as NEAR and data elements (variables) are addressed as FAR.

MEDIUM denotes the opposite: by default, data elements are treated as NEAR and code elements are addressed as FAR.

As you have probably guessed, the LARGE memory model implies that by default both code elements (procedures) and data elements (variables) are addressed as FAR i.e. by pointing at both the segment and offset addresses.

To choose the appropriate memory model for a particular program, you should take into account several factors. The most important of these is the amount of code and data in your program. If you are creating a compact, fast program that operates small quantities of data, use the SMALL or TINY model. These allow you to use up to 64K of memory (one physical segment), but the object code is the fastest since only near references are used in addresses. The only difference between these models is that using the TINY model you will get a -COM module where you cannot use far references. The LARGE model allows you to write programs which have more than one code segment and operate data located in different segments. This model is suitable for creating large, complex programs or programs processing a large amount of data.

We will discuss HUGE, TINY and FLAT memory models in Chapter Twelve.

The Logical Segment Declaration Directives

These directives are used together with the .MODEL directive and include .CODE, .DATA, and .STACK.

The format of the .CODE directive is:

```
.CODE [name]
```

This directive allows you to declare code segments with different (or the same) names. Each procedure in these segments is addressed as NEAR or FAR depending on how it was declared, or by default, according to the memory model declaration. Jumps and calls are performed according to these explicit or implicit declarations.

The .DATA directive creates a NEAR data segment. Other directives that create data segments include: .DATA?, .CONST, .FARDATA, and .FARDATA?. A line with the .STACK [size] directive both starts and finishes the stack segment in a program. You can define the size in bytes - by default its value is 1024.

The ASSUME Directive

This directive informs the assembler of the location of the various segments at assembly time. The syntax is as follows:

```
ASSUME sreg:sloc[,sreg:sloc...]
```

where *sreg* is one of the four segment registers CS,SS,DS and ES while *sloc* is a name of a segment defined by the SEGMENT directive. Here is a typical example:

```
ASSUME cs:OurCode, ds:Ourdata, ss:OurStack
```

The ASSUME directive is usually placed just after the SEGMENT directive of the code segment.

The Procedure Treatment Directives and Instructions

This group includes the PROC, CALL and RET directives. PROC starts the text of a procedure

```
name  PROC  [distance]
```

The "distance" attribute can be NEAR or FAR; this defines the way in which code is generated by RET, and sometimes how the address for the CALL itself is generated. FAR indicates that addressing is performed using the segment address (in the CS register) and the offset address (in the IP register). NEAR means that only the offset address (in IP) is used. By default, the distance is determined by the memory model declared in the .MODEL directive.

The next instruction, CALL, is used to pass execution of the program to the procedure called. Its syntax is

```
CALL operand
```

The operand can be the name of the procedure defined by the PROC directive, or alternatively, a direct or indirect register or memory operand, which contains the procedure address. This means that you can use the following forms of the CALL instruction.

```
CALL    ProcName            ; ProcName has been defined by PROC directive
CALL    ProcAddrs           ; Procedure address has been
                            ; stored into variable ProcAddrs
CALL   WORD PTR ProcTabW[rg] ; procedure address is selected from the
                            ; procedure's addresses located in the
                            ; table ProcTabW, rg - register, usually BX or SI
CALL DWORD PTR ProcTabD[rg] ; procedure address is selected from the
                            ; procedure's addresses located in the table
                            ; ProcTabD, rg - register,usually BX or SI
```

The qualifier "distance" in the procedure definition indicates which type of code (NEAR or FAR) should be used for the CALL instruction. If the address (label) is hidden in a variable, the variable determines the type of call - a NEAR call is generated for a variable defined as a word and a FAR call is generated for a double word variable. Similarly, if you select a procedure from a table, a NEAR call is generated if you refer to the memory with WORD PTR and a FAR call is generated if you use DWORD PTR.

The instruction RET returns control from the procedure when the procedure has been executed. Its syntax is:

```
RET [number]
```

and it precedes the ENDP directive. If you use this instruction in the following form:

```
RET
```

you won't have too many problems. However if you don't mind a bit of arithmetic, you can also use a number with it, for example:

```
RET  4
```

The number is an integer that is added to the SP register after return. This number must be equal to the total length in bytes of all the procedure parameters passed through the stack. You can obtain shorter code by using RET with an operand, since it enables you to combine the actions of the lines with the POP instructions and the RET instruction into one line. The way the operand n is used in the RET instruction depends on how you deal with the parameters. If you use the BP register for addressing parameters, you need to adjust the stack by using the RET n instruction. If you use the POP directive for accessing parameters, you can return from the subroutine without additional actions (of course this assumes that you POP all the parameters and do not POP extra parameters from the stack).

You should note that there are variations of the RET instruction: RETN and RETF, which enable you to explicitly specify a return from a NEAR (RETN) or a FAR (RETF) procedure. Assembler treats the RET instruction as RETN or RETF automatically, depending on the distance specifier in the procedure header. So, you only need to use them explicitly if you actually want to change the type of return.

Indirect JMPs and CALLs

One way of writing the JMP instruction is to point at the label as follows:

```
JMP  Label1
```

Another way is to place the address (offset) of the instruction marked with this label into a register, CX for example, and then to write

```
JMP   CX
```

which is known as indirect jumping. This technique uses an intrasegment jump. You can make both intrasegment and intersegment indirect jumps by using the memory, for example:

```
JMP   WORD PTR[SI]; Intrasegment jump
JMP  DWORD PTR[SI] ; Intersegment jump
```

This form of the JMP instruction is useful if you need to select one of several program flow paths. You can also make indirect calls, for example:

```
CALL  CX
CALL  WORD PTR[SI]    ;  Intrasegment call
CALL  DWORD PTR[SI]   ;  Intersegment call
```

Using the CALL instruction in this way lets you create a table of the addresses of procedures and select a procedure by pointing at the position in the table instead of having to call a procedure by its name.

The PUBLIC, EXTRN and EXTRNDEF Directives

These directives enable a variable, label or procedure declared as PUBLIC in one module to be accessed from other modules, where it is declared as EXTRN. The syntax of PUBLIC is as follows:

```
PUBLIC name1[,name2[........]]
```

The list of names can be continued in more than one line. The syntax of the EXTRN directive is as follows:

```
EXTRN name1:type1[,name2:type2[........]]
```

Here the names can denote variables, labels or procedures. The possible values of the type qualifier are described in Table 5.1.

In Table 5.1 the asterisk indicates types which can be used in MASM 6.0 and later versions.

Type	Type (* - feature available in MASM 6 and later)	
Variable	BYTE	
	SBYTE	*
	WORD	
	SWORD	*
	DWORD	
	SDWORD	*
	FWORD	
	QWORD	
	TBYTE	*
Label, procedure	NEAR	
	FAR	

Table 5.1
Possible Values for Type Qualifier in EXTRN Directive

In MASM 6.0 you can write EXTERN as well as EXTRN. MASM 6.0 enables you to use just one directive - EXTERNDEF - instead of EXTRN and PUBLIC. The syntax of this directive is as follows:

```
EXTERNDEF name1:type1[,name2:type2[......]]
```

where names and types are the same as for the EXTRN directive. This directive is suitable for defining shared data, entry points and external procedures. Assembler treats this directive as PUBLIC or EXTERN depending on whether the name specified in this directive is defined in the current program unit.

Macro Treatment Directives

The MACRO and ENDM directives define the body of a macro. The syntax of the MACRO directive is as follows:

```
name MACRO [parameter1[,parameter2....]]
```

The end of a macro is marked by the ENDM directive which is written as

```
ENDM
```

or

```
name ENDM
```

The INCLUDE Directive

This directive is often used with macro libraries. For example, if you want macros from the "Filename" file to work in your program, you should write

```
INCLUDE Filename
```

for example:

```
INCLUDE maclib.inc
```

The directive inserts the text of the "Filename" file into the text of the current file during assembly. The text is inserted at the position of the directive. It is therefore better to have several small macrolibraries (files containing texts of macros) for different purposes than one large one. This prevents your source code from growing too large. If the "Filename" is not a full pathname, MASM will look for the file in several directories, including the current one.

The LOCAL Directive

This directive is useful for macros and (in MASM 5.1 and later versions) for procedures. A name defined as LOCAL can only be accessed from the procedure or macro where it is defined. If you use a macro more than once in your program, you should use the LOCAL directive to avoid having to redefine labels when the macro is used more than once in a program. The format of the directive is as follows:

```
LOCAL name [[count]:type]
```

where "name" is the name of the local variable or label, "type" is the same as in Table 5.1, and "count" is used when the "name" variable is an array consisting of a "count" number of a given type.

Assembly - Time Conditions

These assembly-time directives allow you to branch while creating machine instruction code. One of these directives is IF with the following syntax:

```
IF          expression1
            statement1
[ELSEIF     expression2
            statement2]
[ELSE
            statement3]
ENDIF
```

The expressions are evaluated during assembly. The assembly of statements depends on whether the corresponding expressions are true (nonzero) or false (zero), as shown in Figure 5.4.

There are a lot of synonyms for ELSEIF, each of which starts with ELSEIF, e.g. ELSEIFDEF. You can also construct loops during assembly by using the directives WHILE, REPEAT and FOR.

The following example illustrates using assembly-time conditions. The program we've written does nothing - but it works in different ways, depending on what Assembler is used.

```
        .model small
        .stack
        .data
        .code
                IF @Version GE 600
        .startup                    ; segment registers initializing (6.0)
                ELSE
                mov    ax,@data     ; address of data segment
                mov    ds,ax        ; DS points to start of the DATA segment
                ENDIF
;......
;       the functional part of the program goes here
;......
                IF @Version GE 600
        .exit   0                   ; return to DOS with the exit code 0
        ELSE
                mov    ax,4C00h     ; function 4Ch - terminate process
                int    21h          ; DOS service call
                ENDIF
                end
```

While compiling this program, Assembler uses the predefined variable @Version to establish the version. It then includes in the source code either the simplified MASM directive for initializing segment registers and exiting the program, or the code used for this in earlier versions of MASM. If you process this program using MASM 6.0, then compare it to one compiled by MASM 5.1, you will see that the object code is different. You can use a similar technique for generating different object codes from the same source program.

Library

A Small Macrolibrary for Input and Output

You will find this macrolibrary on your program disk in the MACROLIB.INC file. The text of this file is given in Listing 5.4. This file includes macros for input and screen output, namely

InpInt	To input an integer
OutInt	To output an integer on the screen
OutStr	To output a string on the screen
NewLine	To start a new line on the screen
UpCase	To convert a letter to upper case
ToFlags	To put a value into the Flag register
GetFlags	To read a value from the Flag register

You should recognize some of these from the first four chapters.

```
 1 .XLIST
 2 ;      M A C R O   D E F I N I T I O N
 3 ; _____
 4 ;
 5 InpInt macro Dest
 6        local Read , ExitMac , Number
 7        push  cx
 8        push  bx
 9        mov   bx,0
10        mov   cx,0
11        mov   Dest,0
12 Read:
13        mov   ah,1     ; Prepare Dos Service Call-function 1
14        int   21h      ; Dos Service 01 - get symbol with echo
15        mov   dl,al    ; Save symbol to proceeding
16 ;
17 ;   Check if symbol is a number 0 ... 9
18 ;
19        cmp   al,'0'   ; Compare symbol in AL and ASCII code "0"
20        jl    ExitMac  ; If symbol is less than "0" it is no number
21        cmp   al,'9'   ; Compare symbol in AL and ASCII code "9"
22        jg    ExitMac; If symbol is greater than "9" it is no number
23                       ;=== Leave macro
24 Number:               ;
25        mov   ah,0
26        sub   al,48    ; Convert symbol in AL into number
27        mov   cx,ax    ; Save this number into CL
28        mov   ax,10    ; Prepare to calculate the result
29        mul   bx       ; AX = BX * 10
30        add   ax,cx    ; AX = ( BX * 10 )+ AX
```

```
31          mov   bx,ax     ; Save the current result
32                          ;
33          jmp   Read      ; Read next symbol
34
35 ExitMac:
36          mov   ax,bx     ; Save result into AX register
37          pop   bx        ; Restore BX ( work register )
38          pop cx          ; Restore CX ( work register )
39          mov   Dest,ax   ; Put result into target
40          endm
41                          ;
42 OutInt macro Src
43          local NexDiv,OutSym
44          push  ax
45          push  bx
46          push  cx
47          push  dx
48          mov   ax,Src   ; Place number to be printed into AX.
49          mov   bx,10    ; Place number '10'(divider) into DI.
50          mov   cx,0
51 NexDiv:
52          mov   dx,0
53          div   bx       ; Divide command. After this result is in
54                         ; AL register and remainder in AH.
55          push  dx       ; Push Remainder into stack.
56          inc   cx       ; Increase counter
57          cmp   ax,0     ; Check if result is zero and
58          jne   NexDiv
59          mov   ax,200h
60 OutSym: pop dx
61          add   dl,30h
62          int   21h
63          loop  OutSym
64          pop   dx
65          pop   cx
66          pop   bx
67          pop   ax
68          endm
69 OutStr macro tpar
70          local locpar,aftcon   ; These label are internal
71 ;;
72 ;;       Attention! That's really wonderful!
73 ;;       If you replace the name "locpar" with the
74 ;;       name "par", MASM 5.0 will put the message
75 ;;       "Error between phases".
76 ;;
77          push  ds       ; Save
78          push  dx       ; the
79          push  ax       ;    registers
80 ;
81 ;        This locates parameter text in memory
82 ;
```

```
83          ifndef  par    ; Check whether parameter
84                         ; is present
85          jmp     aftcon ; Avoid to execute constants
86 locpar db  tpar         ; Text string into memory
87          db      0Dh, 0Ah ; Line fee   d, carriage return
88          db      '$'    ; This is needed for DOS
89 aftcon:
90          endif
91          mov     dx,cs
92          mov     ds,dx
93          mov     dx,offset cs:locpar
94 ;
95          mov     ah,9     ; Service 09 - put symbol
96          int     21h      ; Dos service call
97          pop     ax       ; Restore
98          pop     dx       ; the
99          pop     ds       ; registers
100         endm
101
102 NewLine macro   Num
103         push    ax
104         push    cx
105         push    dx
106         mov     ax,200h
107         mov     dx,0Dh
108         int     21H
109         mov     dx,0Ah
110         int     21h
111         pop     dx
112         pop     cx
113         pop     ax
114         endm
115
116 UpCase macro Letter
117         local UpCase,NotLet
118         cmp     Letter,'a'
119         jl      NotLet
120         cmp     Letter,'z'
121         jg      NotLet
122 UpCase: and al,0DFh    ; Force upper case
123 NotLet:
124         endm
125 ToFlags macro   prm
126         push  prm
127         popf
128         endm
129 GetFlags macro  prm
130         pushf
131         pop   prm
132         endm
133 .List
134 .sall
```

Listing 5.4 An Example of a Macro Library

The Macro InpInt - Input Integers

We'll take a detailed look at the first macro in the library - InpInt. This macro begins by pushing values from BX and CX onto the stack and then clears these registers and the operand Dest. A character is then accepted from the keyboard and tested: if it is not one of the following - 0, 1, 2, 3, 4, 5, 6, 7, 8 or 9, control is passed to exiting the Macro, otherwise it is treated as the next decimal digit of a decimal number. First of all it is converted from a character into a number in AL and is sent to CX. This conversion is based on the fact that the ASCII code of a cypher is equal to its value plus 48. The current value of the number input from BX is then multiplied by 10 and added to the number in CX. This result is then saved in BX and the next character is read. If the next character is not a cypher, the result in BX is copied to the operand Dest and BX and CX are restored. The last character to be input remains in DL.

Figure 5.4 shows the flowchart for the InpInt macro. The other macros from MACLIB.INC are no more difficult than InpInt.

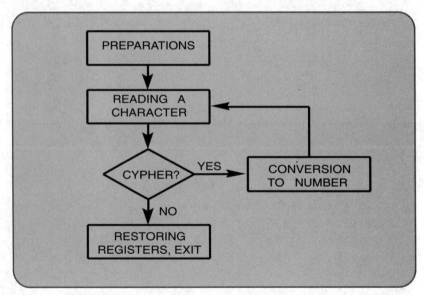

Figure 5.4
The Flowchart of the InpInt Macro

Using Macros - The Program "Calculator"

This program illustrates using macros, the macrolibrary and branching. It performs four arithmetic operations over 16-bit unsigned (positive) integer numbers. Each number, including the result, should be less than 65536. When you run this program, it will display certain instructions asking you to enter a number. The last digit of the number which is being input should be followed by one of four arithmetic operation signs, namely +, -, * or /. Then the second operand should be input, followed by an equals sign = . The program will calculate the result according to the sign which has been input and display the result on the screen. For example, if you input

```
9*10=
```

you will get the following line on the screen.

```
9*10=90
```

The flow-chart for this program is shown in Figure 5.5, the text is given in Listing 5.5, and the program is included on your program disk in the file **CALCUL.ASM**.

```
1
2      Page 55,132
3  .NoListMacro
4  .SALL
5  ;
6  ; This is a sample of Assembler program.  It represents an
7  ; arithmetic  calculator  that  can  proceed with 16-bit
8  ; unsigned integers.  This supercalculator can perform the
9  ; four arithmetic actions:  addition, subtraction,
10 ; multiplication and division.  Each number must be
11 ; less than 65536 (including result).  You should enter the
12 ; first operand, then the sign "+" (plus), "-" (minus), "*"
13 ; (asterisk)  or "/"  (slash), then the second operand and
14 ; finally the sign "=" (equals).  The result will be shown
15 ; immediately!
16 ;
17 .model SMALL          ; This line defines the memory model
18 IF1                   ; On first pass
19 include maclib.inc ; open macro library
20 ENDIF                 ; End of macro including block
21
22 .data                 ; This line defines the DATA segment
```

```
23 fir dw   0
24 sec dw   0
25 res dw   0
26
27 .stack
28
29 .code
30
31 Begin: mov  ax,@data      ; Load segment address for Datasegment
32        mov  ds,ax         ; into DX register
33
34        NewLine
35        OutStr  'Enter number, sign, number, equals sign'
36        OutStr  'To exit press ESC or ENTER'
37        NewLine
38        OutStr  'Example: 1951+41='
39        NewLine 2
40
41 Next:  mov  ax,0          ; Clear AX register
42                           ;
43        InpInt fir         ; Input first operand into AX register
44                           ;
45        cmp  dl,0Dh
46        jne  TstEsc
47 JmpFin: jmp  Finish
48 TstEsc: cmp  dl,1Bh
49        je   JmpFin
50
51        mov  cl,dl         ; Save last symbol accepted
52                           ;
53        InpInt sec         ; Input second operand into AX register
54                           ;
55        mov  ax,fir        ; Load the first operand into
56                           ; accumulator
57        mov  dx,0
58                           ;
59 TesMin: cmp  cl,'-'        ; Check the subtraction operation
60                           ; If last symbol you have entered
61        jne  TesMul        ; is minus subtract operands
62        jmp  Minus
63                           ;
64 TesMul: cmp  cl,'*'        ; Check the multiplication operation
65                           ; If last symbol you have entered
66        jne  TesDiv        ; is asterisk multiply operands
67        jmp  Mult
68                           ;
69 TesDiv: cmpcl,'/'          ; Check the divide operation
70                           ; If last symbol you have entered
71        jne  TesPl         ; is slash divide operands
72        jmp  Divide
73                           ;
74 TesPl: cmp  cl,'+'         ; Check the addition operation
75                           ; If last symbol you have entered
```

```
76            je   Plus          ; is plus, add operands
77                               ;
78 Plus:    add ax,Sec          ; add operands
79            jmp PrtRes          ; to output result
80                               ;
81 Minus:   sub ax,Sec          ; subtract operands
82            jmp PrtRes          ; to output result
83                               ;
84 Mult:    mul Sec             ; multiply operands
85            jmp Prtres          ; to output result
86                               ;
87 Divide: div Sec              ; divide operands
88            jmp PrtRes          ; to output result
89                               ;
90 PrtRes: mov res,ax
91            OutInt res          ; display result on screen
92            NewLine
93
94            jmp Next            ; process next input string
95                               ;
96 Finish: mov ax,4C00h;function 4Ch-terminate process,0-exit code
97            int 21h             ; DOS service call
98
99            end Begin
```

Listing 5.5 The Program "Calculator"

The program "Calculator" uses the macrolibrary for input and output
described at the beginning of the library section. The four diamonds
(rhombi) in the diagram perform selection. Although there is an
alternative selection method which is much shorter, it is considerably
more complicated.

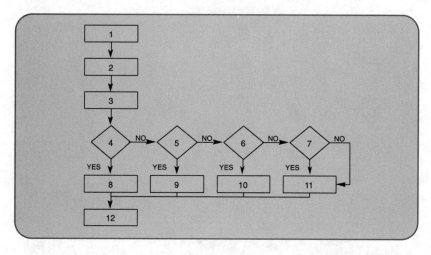

Figure 5.5
**The Flowchart
of the
Calculator
Program**

The main blocks of the program denoted by numbers on Figure 5.5 are:

1 - output of the initial information
2 - input of the first operand and saving of the operation sign
3 - input of the second operand
4 - check for **minus sign**
5 - check for **asterisk**
6 - check for **slash**
7 - check for **plus sign**
8 - performing subtraction
9 - performing multiplication
10 - performing division
11 - performing addition
12 - output of the result

Finally, note that you can control the process of generating a source listing using the following directives:

.NOLISTMACRO	this directive switches off printing macro expansions in listings generated by Assembler
.XLIST	when Assembler meets this directive, it stops generating the source listing
.LIST	switches on source listing generation
.SALL	synonym for the .NOLISTMACRO directive; kept in MASM 6.0 for compatibility with earlier versions

Summary

This chapter has given you an insight into the structure of assembly language programs. This entailed looking at procedures and macros, as well as considering how information can be passed between them by parameters. We finished off by analyzing a program which performs simple arithmetic calculations.

CHAPTER
6

Using BIOS and DOS

This chapter covers the basic notions of MS-DOS and shows how you can use DOS facilities from within programs written in assembly language. We will show you where to look for the most important system information and how this information is represented in the memory. You will also meet the most important tools for using the DOS service - the interrupts. To demonstrate using the DOS facilities we have designed various small programs which you should be able to include in your routine work.

Fundamental Knowledge

What is DOS?

The term "DOS" first appeared along with mainframes. As an abbreviation of "**D**isk **O**perating **S**ystem" it referred to the operating system resident on a magnetic disk. Times and computers have changed and now when we talk about "DOS" we usually mean the operating system for IBM-compatible personal computers - systems like MS-DOS from Microsoft, PC-DOS from IBM, DR-DOS from Digital Research and so on. Since about two-thirds of all the computers in use today are of this type, it's okay just to call them DOS machines. Before we look at the DOS features available to assembler programmers, a bit of historical background on DOS is useful.

The first versions of MS-DOS were quite similar to the well known operating system, CP/M, for the i8080 microprocessor. Before the launch of the 16-bit IBM PC in 1981, CP/M was the leading operating system for 8-bit microcomputers, and it was sensible to make porting existing CP/M applications to MS-DOS as easy as possible. MS-DOS has since been developed considerably and is now the most widely used operating system in the world. MS-DOS compatible operating systems are now sold by many different vendors under license from Microsoft, however from a programmer's point of view these are all essentially the same as the original MS-DOS. They have the same basic user interface, the same utilities set, and can execute any program written for MS-DOS. These systems are often called MS-DOS emulators, a famous example being DR-DOS from Digital Research.

Due to the great success of MS-DOS, most PC operating systems are now DOS-compatible. Likewise, several UNIX-like systems have tools which allow you to run programs originally written for MS-DOS. Multitasking and multiuser systems such as PC-MOS or VM/386 have the same user interface and support MS-DOS programs. Most computers, including mainframes and supercomputers, have software that allows you to transfer data to and from MS-DOS computers.

Levels of DOS Service

As a programmer, you can treat DOS as a set of programs that use the computer's resources to perform specific functions. There are in fact three basic ways in which you can control the computer's resources:

▲ High-level programming languages
▲ DOS and BIOS services
▲ Direct hardware control

Figure 6.1 shows the relationship between these three ways. Each one uses a particular level of the service provided by DOS or the hardware.

The first way is the easiest, and therefore the most common, especially amongst users who are not professional programmers. For most jobs, a high-level language suffices, but sometimes you need to go beyond the features it provides. Most high-level languages include library procedures for calling DOS and BIOS services such as **intr** in Turbo Pascal or **int86** in C. However, it is often more effective to use small assembler procedures, written specifically for a particular purpose. This technique lets you increase the speed of your programs and reduces the amount of memory required.

However, programs which use assembler routines are sometimes less portable than ones written in high-level languages. This is because the

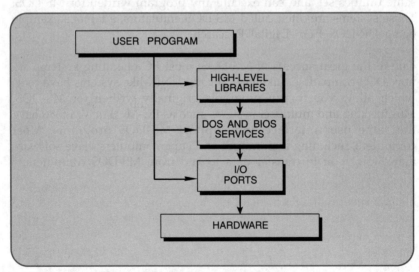

Figure 6.1
Levels of Controlling the PC

interface to Assembler can differ from one compiler to another (Microsoft Pascal, Turbo Pascal or Top Speed Pascal for example), from one operating system to another (DOS, OS/2, XENIX and so on) or even from one version of a compiler to another. So, if you include pieces of assembler code in your programs, be prepared to change these blocks while running your program under other operating systems, other compilers or on other computers.

The second way, using the BIOS and DOS service, is most common among assembler programmers, and allows you to get the most out of your computer and DOS. Suppose you are writing a big application using Turbo Pascal; you can access the disks, the system tables, and write TSR programs and drivers using only Turbo Pascal. However, by replacing relatively small parts of your program with modules written in Assembler, you can make your main program much faster and more concise. You can also use the modules written in assembly language for other projects, simply changing the portions of assembler code which control the interface with high-level languages.

The third way is the most powerful, and inevitably the most difficult. Although it really requires an advanced knowledge of assembly language and computer hardware and is therefore best covered in a more advanced book, we will introduce some aspects of using the hardware directly.

In this and subsequent chapters, we will concentrate on the second level of controlling the hardware- utilizing the DOS and BIOS services available through interrupts using assembly language. If you are using mainly high-level languages such as C or Pascal, you wll learn how to integrate the power of Assembler into your programs. The examples we have included demonstrate the technique commonly used by assembler programmers for programs written in Pascal and C. We will also show you how to add new functions to object module libraries for Clipper.

The Main DOS Components

If you look at the disks distributed with DOS, you will see that they contain several files. Each file has a specific purpose and function, and is itself a program. Most DOS files are optional, and you can customize your system depending on how you use your computer. For example, if you are not working on a network, you don't need to keep the DOS

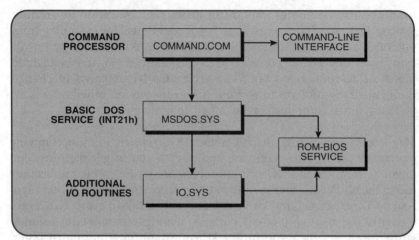

Figure 6.2
**Basic
Components of
MS-DOS**

utilities that support this feature on disk. However, some files are essential and DOS will not work without them. In MS-DOS these are:

```
MSDOS.SYS

IO.SYS

COMMAND.COM
```

These files contain the basic MS-DOS components which are illustrated in Figure 6.2. They support the user interface on one hand, and communicate with the hardware on the other, forming a shell around the machine. These components do not interact with the hardware directly, but do so through code that is built-in to the machine called the BIOS, which is where we start our examination of the components of MS-DOS.

BIOS - Basic Input/Output System

It may seem surprising that one of the basic components of MS-DOS does not belong to MS-DOS at all. The BIOS, or **B**asic **I**nput/**O**utput **S**ystem, is a collection of programs that resides in a special area of the system ROM and whose function is to control the hardware. Practically all software uses the services provided by BIOS - user programs, application systems, operating systems and so on. It is thanks to the existence of this software in ROM that IBM-compatible computers really are compatible. It provides a uniform platform over which DOS can run, and means that you can write a program using BIOS services and then run this program on a 486-computer as well as on an XT with an 8088 processor.

Apart from the IBM ROM BIOS there are several other versions of BIOS for IBM-compatible PC's, either produced under license from IBM, or created and developed by other firms. For example, the most popular third-party version of BIOS is the Phoenix BIOS, which is a completely original design. From the programmer's point of view though, all BIOS versions should be the same, so you may expect your program to work on any IBM-compatible PC. If, however, you have problems using BIOS services, look at the initial screen output after turning the power on. BIOS usually outputs its version, manufacturer's name and date of production when activated. If necessary, you can replace BIOS with a more recent or more powerful version by replacing some of the chips on the computer's motherboard. You will need to do this when upgrading your computer - for example if you decide to turn your AT 286 into the super-AT 386 without buying a new one.

Most operating systems, including DOS, use BIOS routines as the foundation for performing basic input-output operations. However, DOS and BIOS are to an extent similar in that they are both simply a collection of routines that perform frequently needed tasks. Usually, you will not need to know whether the program that performs your task is part of BIOS or DOS, but the whole truth is that some operating systems replace BIOS with their own routines. For example, OS/2 replaces built-in BIOS routines for screen output (video service) with its own programs which work faster. If you don't encounter any problems with your programs, you don't need to worry about these details. However, we will show you how you can find out where the program that performs a particular service is located - in the BIOS or DOS area. Originally, the memory addresses above 0F0000h were reserved for ROM BIOS. Now, since controllers such as VGA/EGA video cards and hard disk controllers use this address range for accessing their own I/O routines, the memory area above 0C0000h is often considered the ROM BIOS area.

The BIOS service is a low-level service. This means you have to explicitly carry out all details of a particular operation using the service. For example, if you want to output a symbol onto the screen, you have to move the cursor to the correct position first, output the symbol, and then move the cursor to the next position. The system does not give you any help on this one, like DOS does, because you're working way below that level. The only way of moving the cursor around is using the corresponding BIOS procedures yourself.

From the functional point of view, BIOS and DOS differ only in the kinds of services they offer. BIOS routines deal with physical devices and character operations, whereas DOS handles mostly files and strings. It's up to you to choose the best tool for the job - employ BIOS if you want to use special hardware features, and DOS if you want to concentrate on the logical features of your task. For example, the best way to write a sophisticated security system is using the BIOS service (or maybe by direct control of the hardware), while the DOS service is more suitable for writing a text processor.

In this chapter we will give a short list of BIOS interrupts, then explain all the BIOS functions available to the assembler programmer in more detail later on when we look at taking control of the components of your system.

Hidden DOS Files

There are two special files on your hard disk which are essential to DOS, IO.SYS and MSDOS.SYS. These files cannot be dealt with in the usual way, i.e., you cannot copy, rename or delete them using standard DOS commands. Moreover, unless you have DOS 5, you cannot even view them using the standard DIR command: these files have a special attribute making them hidden. With DOS 5 the files can be listed using the modified DIR command:

```
DIR C: /A
```

You can also look at these files using any of the many popular DOS shells, such as Norton Commander and Xtree, or using PC Tools utilities.

These hidden DOS files have different names in different systems, but their purpose and functions are all the same. The various names of the hidden system files are shown in Table 6.1.

File IO.SYS is an extension of BIOS. When DOS is loaded, this file resides in the memory and works as a continuation of, and partially as a replacement of, BIOS. IO.SYS contains programs that pass input and output data between DOS and the various peripheral components of your system, such as the keyboard and the display. There are also similar handlers in the BIOS area, but you won't usually notice any difference between using these built-in handlers in BIOS and loadable handlers in IO.SYS.

System	BIOS Extension	DOS Resident
MS-DOS	IO.SYS	MSDOS.SYS
PC-DOS	IBMBIO.COM	IBMDOS.COM
Compaq DOS	IBMBIO.COM	IBMDOS.COM
DR DOS before 6.0	DRBIOS.SYS	DRDOS.SYS
DR DOS 6.0	IBMBIO.COM	IBMDOS.COM

Table 6.1
The Hidden Files for Different Systems

The file MSDOS.SYS is the kernel of MS-DOS, and contains the programs which provide the high-level DOS functions, passing the requests on to IO.SYS. For example MSDOS.SYS contains basic programs for memory management, file system control and so on. The most important and widely used routine included in the MSDOS.SYS file is the handler of interrupt 21h which provides the greater part of the DOS service.

The interface between two components of MS-DOS (IO.SYS and MSDOS.SYS) is always the same, regardless of the peripheral devices connected to the PC. As a result, DOS is hardware-independent, since adding new devices does not effect the MS-DOS kernel. It is for this reason device drivers were used to service high-capacity diskettes under DOS 2 before support for them was included in more recent versions.

The Command Processor

The command processor COMMAND.COM provides the command line interface, and receives and executes your commands. In executing these commands, the operating system runs one or more of the programs that make up the kernel of MS-DOS. If you take a look at the DOS directory, you'll see programs with names which are very similar to familiar DOS commands. For example, program FORMAT.COM corresponds to the command FORMAT and program DISKCOPY.EXE executes the command DISKCOPY. You won't, however, see DIR.COM or DIR.EXE, COPY.COM or COPY.EXE etc. which should correspond to DOS commands DIR or COPY.

This is because DOS commands are divided into internal and external commands. Programs which correspond to external commands are stored separately in your DOS directory, while the programs which carry out internal commands are grouped together and included in the command processor.

In the original MS-DOS, the command processor was called COMMAND.COM. Now, however, there are several programs on the market which you can use instead of, or together with, the standard command processor, for example 4DOS from J.P.Software.

The command processor has two parts - resident and transient. The resident part is loaded into the memory when MS-DOS starts and remains there, usually using 3 - 4 Kbytes of memory depending on the version. The transient part can be unloaded if the user program requires more memory than is available at that moment. Once the program has finished, the transient part of the command processor must be reloaded to enable DOS to continue working.

If you intend writing your own resident programs or using DOS commands from within your programs, you will need to understand the structure and function of the command processor, and how it sits in memory.

When you enter a command at the DOS prompt, the command processor does the following:

Analyzes the command
Searches for the corresponding program
Passes parameters to this program from your command
Runs the program
On completion, restores the transient part if necessary

We'll give some examples of using these functions from within your programs in this and later chapters.

Interrupts

As a programmer, there are a number of ways you can access DOS services. The DOS user types command lines such as DIR, COPY, WP, FLY and so on. Each of these commands calls either a built-in DOS routine, or a program stored on disk as an executable module. High-level language programmers on the other hand use procedures or functions such as "Write" in Pascal, "printf" in C, "PRINT" in BASIC or SAY in Clipper. Last, but naturally by no means least, assembler programmers use special DOS routines called **interrupts**. Strictly speaking, we will be dealing with programs called **interrupt handlers**, but the two terms are often confused.

An interrupt is a situation caused by a particular event, while an interrupt handler is a program designed to process this situation. When you come across a phrase like "interrupt 09h serves the keyboard", in real terms it means "the keyboard is served by the program that is the handler of interrupt 09h which is generated by pressing a key".

The appearance of an interrupt has the following effects:

> Stops the user program
> Saves all the registers and flags
> Passes control to a special program - the interrupt handler
> Performs the interrupt handler
> Restores the registers that were saved
> Continues the user program

Interrupts can be divided into two main groups - hardware interrupts and software interrupts. Hardware interrupts are caused by hardware events, for example by a timer signal or machine error. Pressing a key on the keyboard, also causes a hardware interrupt (namely interrupt 09h). Software interrupts are caused by performing a special INT instruction. The operands of this instruction indicate the number of the interrupt generated, from 0 to 0FFh. Note however that not all numbers in this range are valid as some of them are reserved for a special purpose; for example, number 2 denotes a machine error and 1Fh - a special table used by the video system.

Hardware interrupts can be subdivided into two groups - non-maskable and maskable. The non-maskable interrupts (NMI) can not be disabled, while maskable interrupts can be disabled by the CLI instruction. Sometimes you will need to disable certain interrupts. For example, there is no point in immediately answering a signal from an external modem when DOS is trying to correct a disk error. Non-maskable interrupts such as Parity Check (an error in the computer's memory) cannot be disabled by the programmer.

Software interrupts are numbered from 10h to 0FFh but not all of them actually have handlers. Interrupts 0F1h to 0FFh and 60h to 66h are referred to as user interrupts and initially have dummy handlers - handlers which return control to the caller once they have been called.

Interrupts supported by DOS are known as system interrupts. There is no real difference between these two kinds of interrupts - their handlers both gain control in the same way and can use the same resources. Recent versions of DOS include handlers for all 256 interrupts, but some of these handlers do not actually do anything other than immediately returning control to caller.

As far as the programmer is concerned, interrupt handlers are subroutines intended for performing certain tasks. To emphasize the point we made above, descriptions like "disks are served by interrupt 13h" actually mean "the handler of interrupt 13h is a routine designed for performing disk input/output and controlling functions". We have already mentioned some DOS services, like the DOS function 4Ch (function 4c of interrupt 21h) which returns control to DOS when a program finishes, for example:

```
mov    ah,4Ch    ; function number - processed by INT 21h handler
mov    al,01     ; return code - processed by handler's subroutine
int    21h       ; DOS service call (performing INT 21h handler)
```

The DOS Memory Map

The memory is one of the most significant resources of a computer. In Chapter Three we covered the basic components, size and organization, but just to remind you, a computer's memory is usually 1M bytes or more, 640K of which are directly accessible to DOS and user programs. This memory is known as conventional memory.

In order to execute, each program requires a certain amount of space in the memory, while as we have seen, MS-DOS itself also takes up part of this memory. Figure 6.3 shows the memory layout for a DOS system with a typical memory configuration, showing how the memory is allocated between programs.

The main areas shown in Figure 6.3 are briefly described below. The start and end addresses are given for each area. Addresses which depend on the DOS version and the set of drivers and resident programs installed are denoted by "????" characters. To determine the addresses of these components, you can use the MEM utility which is included in DOS versions since 4.0. Type MEM/? at the command line for help in using this utility.

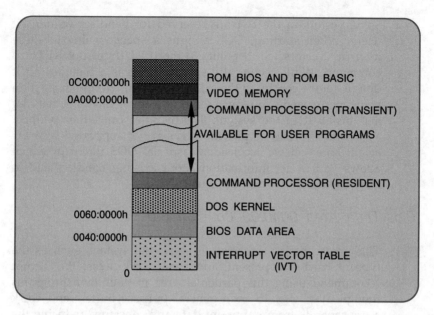

0C000:0000h — ROM BIOS AND ROM BASIC
0A000:0000h — VIDEO MEMORY
— COMMAND PROCESSOR (TRANSIENT)
AVAILABLE FOR USER PROGRAMS
— COMMAND PROCESSOR (RESIDENT)
0060:0000h — DOS KERNEL
0040:0000h — BIOS DATA AREA
0 — INTERRUPT VECTOR TABLE (IVT)

Figure 6.3
Memory Layout in an MS-DOS System

Interrupt Vector Table 0000:0000 - 0030:00FFh

The interrupt vector table is located in the low address area and contains the addresses of interrupt handlers. There can be as many as 256 (100h) interrupts and each address is represented in segment:offset form. Each element in the table takes two words of memory - the first contains the offset and the second contains the segment address for the corresponding handler. In mathematics, the term vector denotes both a magnitude and a direction, so it is usually graphically represented as an arrow. Likewise, IVT elements are also called vectors since they point to the handlers like arrows on a map.

The area for the interrupt vector table is 1024 (400h) bytes long and uses memory in the address range from 0000:0000 to 0030:00FFh. To find the address of a handler, multiply its number by 4 (or shift it to the left by 2 bits). The two words of memory at this location will contain the address we need - the first of them is the offset and the second is the segment address for the interrupt handler. DOS uses these elements to create an effective address for a handler and to pass control to that handler when it's needed. So, as you can see, DOS uses the IVT for accessing the proper handler for each interrupt. In this light, the IVT is the assembler programmer's gateway to BIOS and DOS service.

Some vectors in the IVT are reserved for handlers written by users. When starting, DOS assigns a special value to these interrupt vectors which points to the IRET (Interrupt **RET**urn) command. While technically speaking this is a handler, all it does is return control to the calling program without any action being performed. You can create your own interrupt handler and install it in the system. This handler can either perform additional services or provide services not supported by DOS at all. Later on we'll consider a special DOS interrupt which allows you to get information about existing handlers and to install handlers written by a user.

Bios Data Area 0040:0000h - 0050:00FFh

This area contains information about the system, such as the type of hardware present, and some work areas. We do not recommend using this particular area in your own programs though. It's better to keep general purpose buffers and work areas separate from important data and constants, reducing the probability of overwriting constants and data accidentally. Nevertheless, in this instance, it works and works well. You'll find an example of using data from the BIOS area and a macro for defining field names in this area later in this chapter.

DOS Kernel Area 0060:0000h - ????:????

The DOS kernel area contains programs from IO.SYS and MSDOS.SYS files. Then comes the buffer area for disk input/output operations and the area for file system control tables - FCB's (File Control Block). Resident programs, or drivers, which control the hardware are located at the top of this area. To distinguish them from built-in BIOS drivers they are sometimes called *installable* drivers.

Command Processor ????:???? - ????:????

The next section of memory contains the resident part of the command processor. This DOS component is always stored in RAM and is the last DOS component in the low-addressed memory. The section above this is reserved for your programs.

The initial address of this area depends on which version of DOS you are using. Usually, the more recent the version of DOS, the less space there is for your programs. However, the older the DOS version the less service you get from it!

Free Space ????:???? ????:????

The space above the end of the resident part of the command processor up the 640K boundary (absolute address 9FFFFh) is not occupied by DOS routines and can be used by applications. This area is referred to as user memory and is available for your programs although its high part is usually occupied by routines belonging to the command processor. However, when necessary, this part of the command processor is automatically removed by DOS and restored after an application has finished.

Transient Part of the Command Processor ????:???? - 9000:FFFFh

This part of the command processor contains routines used for processing command lines, finding and loading user programs, interpreting BAT-files and so on. These routines are usually present in memory until a user program is big enough. When this is the case the transient part of the command processor is removed from memory (that's why it's called *transient*) and the memory occupied by this part of the command processor becomes available for user programs. When a program finishes, DOS checks whether the transient part of the command processor is still in memory and isn't corrupted. If so, DOS continues its work, otherwise it looks for the command processor using the environment variable COMSPEC and reloads it.

Video Memory A0000:0000h - B0000:FFFFh

Video memory is used as a screen buffer for output in text and graphics modes. Not all of this part of memory is always in use - different video adapters use different parts of it in different modes.

Additional ROM BIOS C000:0000h - C000:FFFFh

This part is used in different ways on different computers. Most commonly, it contains routines for controlling hard disks and video adapters.

Free for ROM Extensions D000:0000h - E000:FFFFh

This area is most often used by different ROM BIOS extensions which should be installed separately. LIM EMS drivers also use memory located in this range of address space. On some earlier computers this area was reserved for ROM BASIC.

ROM BIOS F000:0000h - F000:FFFFh

ROM BIOS which includes the set of routines controlling the basic hardware and data used by these routines. Applications cannot change data located in this area but reading information from ROM BIOS is possible.

Fortunately, recent versions of DOS such as MS DOS - 5 and DR DOS - 6 can work in only 12-15 Kbytes of conventional memory providing you have at least 1Mbyte of memory. Hence powerful versions of DOS aren't so powerful when they are run on small computers like a PC or PC XT.

Tools

The Instruction INT

Interrupts are the most frequently used tools for accessing DOS services. Although they are numbered from 0 to 255, MS-DOS has more than 256 service functions. This is because almost every interrupt handler uses the information you pass to it to determine a function to be performed. So, each interrupt handler might execute several functions.

The microprocessor has an instruction for passing control to the interrupt handler. The syntax of this instruction is:

```
INT interrupt-number
```

where *interrupt-number* is the number of the interrupt you want to call. This can be a constant or a variable with a value in the range 0 - 255 (0h - 0FFh). When we come to describing the BIOS and DOS interrupts, we'll explain how to pass the parameters to the interrupt handler and how the handler returns the results.

The functions performed by each interrupt handler are usually grouped according to their purpose. For example, interrupt 16 (10h) performs most of the video functions, interrupt 19 (13h) - most disk/diskette functions and so on. Interrupt 21 (15h) performs a number of functions including controlling cassette read\write operations (when was the last time you saw a computer with a cassette recorder?) and extended memory management that are used by multitasking software such as DesqView.

Finally, the DOS interrupt 33(21h), called the DOS service dispatcher is so powerful and flexible it deserves a book of its own to explain it! It has already done great work for us earlier on managing our input and output.

Using the INT Instruction

When writing a complex program which you divide into several modules, one of the most important points to consider is the information interchange between these modules. Interrupt handlers are quite complicated modules and more often than not, they require more information than is specified in the INT instruction. This additional information is usually passed via the registers.

For example, one of the most popular and universal DOS interrupts is our old friend the interrupt 33 (21h in hexadecimal system) through which we can access the function 4Ch. This particular function terminates the current process and passes a return code to DOS or back to the original calling program. The return code can then be used to indicate the result of running a program. For example, return code 0 usually means that your program has finished successfully while non-zero values denote different errors detected while running the program. DOS provides the special function ErrorLevel designed for examining the return code passed from an executed program.

Using the interrupt from Assembler looks like this:

```
MOV    AL,00h       ; Return code into AL
MOV    AH,4Ch       ; Function number into AH
INT    21h          ; Interrupt call
```

Alternatively, the first two lines can be combined and replaced with one statement:

```
MOV    AX,4C00h     ; Function number and return code
                    ;    into AX
INT    21h          ; Interrupt call
```

The advantage of writing them separately is that you can change the return code without repeating the full fragment of code. For example, look at the following extract from an assembler program:

```
           .....
Block1:
           .....
    mov    RetCode,2    ; Return code will be 2
    jmp    ExProg       ; Pass control to exit
           .....
Block2:
           .....
    mov    RetCode,1    ; Return code will be 1
    jmp    Exprog       ; Pass control to exit
           .....
ExProg:
           .....
    mov    al,RetCode   ; Value of return code into AL
    mov    ah,4Ch       ; Function 4Ch - terminate
    int    21h          ; DOS service call
           ......
    RetCode db 0        ; Default value for return code
```

The two blocks labelled Block1 and Block2, both set a new value for the return code and pass control to the final block of the program. The final block returns control to MS-DOS using function 4Ch of DOS interrupt 21h - "terminate process". Note that the value for the return code is copied to the AL register from the variable RetCode. If the variable RetCode does not change during program execution, the default value 0 is used. Later in this chapter we'll give two examples of complete programs which use a similar trick for passing the return code.

How the INT Instruction Works

You now know how to enter an interrupt. At this point you might be wondering why, if the interrupt handler is just another program, we don't just use the CALL instruction to run it, rather than a special INT instruction. Actually, it is possible to use the CALL instruction to invoke interrupt handlers, but it involves some additional work. To understand just what this involves we'll take a closer look at the INT instruction.

The INT instruction starts by pushing the flags and registers CS and IP onto the stack. It then clears the trap and interrupt flags before finally jumping to the interrupt handler. You'll see why this is important later on. This jump means that the next instruction to be performed will be the instruction whose segment:offset address is contained in the interrupt vector which corresponds to *interrupt_num*. Consequently, the INT instruction replaces at least two instructions: PUSHF and CALL.

Since the interrupt handler is usually called in a special way, it follows that there is also a special way for leaving it - the IRET instruction.

The Instruction IRET

If you are writing your own interrupt handlers, it is essential that you start and finish the corresponding program correctly. This means that a process broken by the execution of an interrupt handler should be properly continued once the handler has finished.

In order to do this successfully, some critical information about the program that is being interrupted must be saved before passing control to the interrupt handler. This information must then be restored before execution of the original program can continue. As we saw earlier, the first problem is solved by the INT instruction pushing the information about registers and flags onto the stack. The instruction IRET does the opposite once the interrupt has completed its task. The format of this instruction is:

```
IRET
```

or

```
IRETD
```

The latter can only be used on i80386/i80486 processors. The instruction IRET pops IP, CS and the flags from the stack. Note that the INT instruction puts these values onto the stack in reverse order. This instruction enables interrupts in the same way as the STI instruction. So, IRET successfully returns execution from the interrupt handler. When creating your own interrupt handler it is better to finish with the IRET instruction, otherwise you have to arrange for popping flags and enabling interrupts yourself.

The IRETD Instruction is quite similar to IRET, but it pops the extended 32-bit flag register and IP. Use this command if you are going to write interrupt handlers for the 32-bit mode of i80386/i80486 processors. Note that the instruction INT in this case pushes corresponding 32-bit values automatically, and you can use the INT instruction in both 16-bit or 32-bit mode.

The Interrupt Vector Table

The Interrupt Vector Table, usually called the IVT, is located in the memory at 0000:0000. As we have already explained, it contains the addresses of interrupt handlers. Here we'll discuss some details, which might be useful for work with the IVT.

The IVT consists of elements called vectors. Each vector consists of two words - the first is treated as an offset and the second as a segment address. The process of passing control to the interrupt handler, located in RAM is shown in Figure 6.4.

The interrupt vector usually represents the location of the interrupt handler, so if you come across "the vector 21h", it means "the element of an interrupt vector table that contains an address of a handler for an interrupt 21h". However, some elements of the IVT point to specific areas of memory which contain special tables rather than programs.

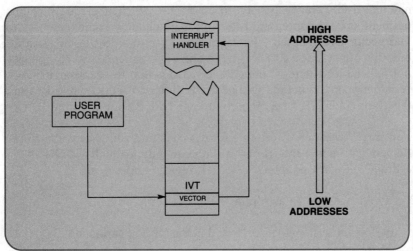

Figure 6.4
Activation of an Interrupt Handler

Some books might try and tell you that "vector 1Fh is **not** a vector". While this is strictly true, we think it's a bit confusing. For this reason, we will always refer to the elements of IVT as **vectors**, saying something like:

"vector 21h points to the handler but vector 1Fh points to the graphic symbols table".

The IVT is one of the most important features of a computer. Although it is one of the memory areas most frequently used by DOS, it is also available for your own programs. Unlike other computers and other operating systems, there is no special protection for IVT in MS-DOS on IBM-compatible PC's. Therefore be especially careful while accessing the IVT from within your programs - there are plenty of nasty things you can do. There are two reasons why you might want to access IVT:

>   To get information from it.
>   To change certain information in it.

The first of these is relatively safe - even if something does go wrong the worst that can happen is you don't get the information you wanted. DOS stays as DOS and continues working. The second can have slightly more dire consequences. Suppose you want to install your own interrupt handler; to do this you need to replace the corresponding vector with the new value that points to your program. Imagine that your program has only replaced the first word of the vector, then precisely at this moment, the corresponding interrupt is invoked by some other event. The vector is corrupted - its segment part points to the old handler but the offset points to the new one. The outcome is completely unpredictable. The most hopeful scenario is that the computer hangs. A rather worse outcome is that it continues to work, while treating the command DIR *.* as the command DEL *.* for example.

You might wonder where this unexpected interrupt has come from? Remember - some interrupts can appear independently, - caused by a timer, network adapters, external devices and so on.

To avoid possible catastrophes - here is some advice:

▲ Use the system tools provided in the form of various DOS services for accessing the IVT.

▲ If you must work directly with the IVT, use the CLI instruction to disable interrupts before accessing the IVT and the STI instruction to enable them after accessing.

▲ Think twice before hooking important hardware interrupts such as NMI - non-maskable interrupt which is caused by the hardware error - memory parity check.

In this chapter we have included two examples of accessing the IVT to determine the address of one of the interrupt handlers: one using the function 35h of interrupt 21h to get information from the IVT and one reading the IVT straightaway. Try to start both programs and compare the results. If they are different, this means you've caught on to an interesting problem.

While reading one word of an IVT element, a hardware interrupt may appear, resulting in the execution of the corresponding handler. There is a small chance that this handler will change the contents of the IVT element currently being processed. When control is then returned to your program, the second word of the IVT element will be read. However, this could be part of the *changed* element! Fortunately, this rarely happens in practice, but it is worth knowing about all the same. It is better to be over cautious than to find your system just crashes one day.

Enabling/Disabling Interrupts - CLI and STI

As we have seen, interrupts are caused by certain events. While this is how PCs usually work, there are times when you will want to protect yourself against their appearance. With this in mind, instructions CLI and STI are designed for disabling and enabling interrupts, respectively.

Neither of these instructions have any parameters. To disable interrupts, use the instruction CLI (**CL**ear Interrupts), to enable them - STI (**SeT** Interrupts). For example, if you were writing a program that dealt with the IVT directly, you would include these instructions as follows:

```
            cli                 ; disable interrupts
    CrytBeg:
    ;......................
    ;           accessing the IVT
    ;......................
    CrytEnd:
            sti                 ; enabling interrupts
```

Virtually no program can break the instructions between the labels CrytBeg and CrytEnd. What do we mean by *"virtually?"* Well, there are programs that can gain control even when the interrupts have been disabled, namely the handlers of non-maskable interrupts (NMI). The group of non-maskable interrupts includes those intended to process critical situations such as machine errors. When an NMI occurs, it usually means that there is something wrong with your computer.

The STI instruction is also frequently used to enable interrupt handlers which have been disabled by the INT instruction. An interrupt handler should enable them as soon as possible after it gains control to allow for BIOS and DOS to process other interrupts.

Inside an Interrupt Handler

We'll now consider what happens when the INT instruction is performed or a particular hardware interrupt is generated.

Control is passed to the program located at the address stored in the corresponding element of the IVT. At this point, interrupts are disabled and the stack contains the value of the flag register. Registers are usually used for passing parameters on entry and returning results on return. Interrupt handlers work in basically the same way as procedures written by a user, but there are some important differences.

The following example shows a skeleton of an interrupt handler:

```
Handler  proc
;........
        Critical part- saving registers, accepting parameters and so on
;        interrupts are disabled!
;........
        sti                      ; enable interrupts
;........
;       main part of the handler
;........
        iret                     ; return from handler
Handler endp
```

Now that you know what an interrupt handler is and how it works, let's look at services provided by BIOS and DOS, in other words, at the basic functions performed by interrupt handlers included in BIOS and DOS.

The BIOS Service

The BIOS service is accessible through interrupts 00h - 1Fh. The corresponding vectors usually point to the ROM BIOS area which starts at 0C800h. In this chapter we'll give you a program that you can use to determine where these vectors really point, and in such a way discover which handler actually processes each interrupt. Don't worry if you discover that in fact some vectors from the range 00h - 1Fh point to the DOS area - i.e. part of the conventional memory. This just means that the corresponding interrupts are hooked up either by DOS programs such as DOSKEY or DRIVER.SYS, or by resident programs like ProKey, SideKick and so on. DOS also intercepts some BIOS interrupts and replaces BIOS routines with its own programs to enhance the power of BIOS and DOS built-in handlers. The function of the various BIOS interrupts is shown in Table 6.2.

Note that vectors 1Dh - 1Fh don't actually point to real interrupt handlers but to the addresses of special tables, containing various data and parameters. For example, the DOS memory-resident utility GRAFTABL changes the vector 1Fh to point to the table of characters used in the graphic display mode on CGA displays. This table is stored in the memory occupied by the GRAFTABL utility.

Int No.	Function
00	Divide error
01	Step-by-step execution
02	Hardware non-maskable interrupt
03	Operation code 0CCh (one-byte)
04	Overflow
05	Print Screen function
06	Bound checking (80186 and above)
07	Math units missed (80286 and above)
08	Timer
09	Keyboard (low level)
0A	EGA video service
0B	Communication port 1
0C	Communication port 2
0D	PC - hard disk, AT and PS-2 - LPT2
0E	Flexible disk
0F	Printer
10	Video service
11	Equipment information
12	Memory size information
13	Disk service
14	Input/Output through serial ports
15	Cassette and miscellaneous - DesqView, TopView etc.
16	Keyboard
17	Printer
18	ROM BASIC
19	System reboot
1A	Clock
1B	Ctrl-Break pressed
1C	Clock (low level - one tick)
1D	Video table for 6845
1E	Diskette parameters
1F	Graphic character set

Table 6.2
*Bios Service
(Interrupts 00h -
1Fh) Functions*

The BIOS Data Area

The BIOS data area contains information on your hardware configuration, and how it is currently being used. This information is vitally important for ensuring the basic functioning of the computer and must never be destroyed by your programs. The section of memory which contains BIOS data starts at the address 400h or 0040h:0000h in segment:offset form, and occupies 256 (100h) bytes. By changing some of this data, you can control your hardware. In this chapter we'll show how you can control the keyboard state by changing *one bit* in this area. Take extra care when changing any information in the BIOS data area - changing certain fields can even result in the loss of data stored on disk!

The DOS Service

As we noted, DOS and BIOS services are essentially the same from the programmer's point of view. The only difference is that programs which provide DOS services are located in the DOS area rather than in ROM BIOS. That's the theory anyway - in practice it's hard to say what is DOS and what is BIOS. For example, interrupt 09h usually belongs to the BIOS service but if you install a special keyboard driver or pop-up program like a calculator, this interrupt will have two handlers - one in the BIOS and one in the DOS area. Moreover, your new handler can work without passing control to the standard BIOS handler. In other words, a user's handler can process before, after or instead of standard ones. You can call a standard handler from within a new one using a sequence of instructions like the following:

```
        pushf                   ; push flags onto stack
        call   OldVect          ; call previous handler
        .......
OldVect dw          ?,?         ; IVT element is stored here
```

The double-word variable OldVect should contain the element of the IVT which corresponds to the standard handler.

Writing Your Own Interrupt Handlers

Now let's have a look at how you can install your own handler to provide additional services. Initially, you can treat interrupts as kinds of procedures in your program. However, unlike procedures, you must install a handler before using it.

We have already noted that it is better, and certainly safer, to use the system features for installing handlers. Function 25h of the DOS interrupt 21h is especially designed for this. To use this function, perform the following actions:

> Put the segment address of the new handler into DS.
> Put the offset address of new handler into DX.
> Put the value 25h into AH.
> Put the number of the interrupt you want to intercept into AL.
> Call the interrupt 21h.

The following example shows the installation of a new handler for interrupt 13h:

```
push     ds                      ; Save DS
mov      ax,seg Handler          ; Segment address of handler into AX
mov      ds,ax                   ;    and copy it into DS
mov      dx,offset Handler       ; Offset address of handler
mov      ah,25h                  ; Function 25h - Set new handler
mov      al,13h                  ; Number of interrupt hooked
int      21h                     ; Dos service call
pop      ds


. . . . . . . . . . . . . . . .

Handler  proc
. . . . . . . . . . . . . . . .
         iret
Handler  endp
```

The label *Handler* marks the beginning of the new handler to replace, which in this example is the DOS dispatcher normally invoked by INT 21h. Note that the handler finishes with the IRET instruction rather than RET.

When writing your own handlers you must restore the original interrupt handler unless you decide to replace the standard handler permanently. In order to restore the standard handler, you must have first saved its vector using the function 35h of interrupt 21h before installing the new handler. Then, before finishing your program, simply re-install the standard handler as in the previous example. To use the function 35h, put the value 35h into AH, the number of the interrupt in AL and call the interrupt 21h. As a result you'll get the segment address of the corresponding handler in ES register and the offset address in

BX. The following example shows a fragment of code which performs the functions we have just described. The new handler for interrupt 1Ch (timer tick) is installed:

```
......
OldOff  dw   ?
OldSeg  dw   ?
......
;===  saving an old interrupt vector
        mov   ah,35h            ; function 35h - get INT  vector
        mov   al,1Ch            ; number of INT
        int   21h              ; DOS service call
        mov   OldOff,bx         ; save original offset
        mov   Oldseg,es         ; save original segment
.....
;===  installing new handler
        mov   es,segment NewHand ; segment address of handler
        mov   bx,offset NewHand  ; offset address of  handler
        mov   ah,25h            ; function 25h-set INT  vector
        mov   al,1Ch            ; number of INT
        int   21h              ; DOS service call
;===
......
;===  reinstalling original handler
        mov   es,OldSeg         ; address of original handler
        mov   bx,OldOff         ; address of original handler
        mov   ah,25h            ; function 25h - set INT  vector
        mov   al,1Ch            ; number of INT
        int   21h              ; DOS service call
......
;===  new handler for interrupt hooked
NewHand  proc
......
        iret
NewHand  endp
......
```

Library

Using DOS Service - Getting the DOS Version

This relatively small and simple program uses the DOS service available through interrupt 21h to get the DOS version. It also shows how to get parameters from the command line. The text of the program is shown in Listing 6.1.

```
1
2  page 55,132
3  ;
4  ;    PROGRAM DosVer
5  ;
6  ;  15 Jan 1992
7  ;
8  ;  This is a sample of DOS service usage.  This program
9  ;  gets the DOS version number and sets the return code
10 ;  equal to this value.  You can use this result in
11 ;  BAT-files with the help of ErrorLevel function.  You
12 ;  can get either the major or minor part of the number.
13 ;  To get the major part of the number, pass the letter
14 ;  H to the program as a parameter by typing the
15 ;  following command line
16 ;
17 ;  DosVer H
18 ;
19 ;  The return code will be equal to the major part  of
20 ;  the  number  of your DOS version (for example if you
21 ;  are using MS-DOS 3.31 the result  will  be 3).
22 ;  Passing  the  parameter L to the program you can get
23 ;  the  minor part  of  your DOS  version  number (for
24 ;  example if you are using MS-DOS 3.31 the result will
25 ;  be 31).
26 ;
27 .model tiny              ; This is needed for COM- files
28 .code                    ; This starts the CODE segment
29        org  100h         ; This is needed for COM- files
30 begin:
31        mov  bx,0                    ; Clear the offset register
32        mov  bl,byte ptr cs:80h      ; Read  parameters length
33        mov  dl,byte ptr cs:[bx]+80h ; Read last symbol
34                                     ;      of parameter string
35        and  dl,0DFh                 ; UpCase the letter in DL
36        mov  ah,30h      ; DOS service 30h - get the DOS version
37        int  21h         ;  AH - minor part, AL - major part
38        cmp  dl,'L'      ; Check if the minor part required
39        jne  finish      ;  If not, leave the major part in AL
40        mov  al,ah       ;  If yes, move the minor part into AL
41 Finish: mov  ah,4Ch     ; DOS service 4Ch - terminate program
42        int  21h         ; AL - the return code
43        end  begin       ; The running starts from label BEGIN
```

Listing 6.1 The Program DosVer - Getting the DOS Version

This program uses the DOS interrupt 21h and gets the information from PSP. This area is taken up by DOS when the program starts. To make it easier to get information from PSP and to decrease the size of an executable module, this program is designed to be a -COM module rather than an -EXE module. You will remember that when DOS loads a -COM module it puts the segment address of the PSP into all segment registers (DS, ES, CS and SS). To create the -COM module you should use the directive

```
.model tiny
```

(line 27) and instruction

```
org 100h
```

(line 29).

The program accepts the parameter from the last symbol of the command line. This means that the program will only treat the last symbol in the command line as a parameter. Thus, the lines

```
DosVer h
```

and

```
DosVer read the version part high
```

have the same effect because they both end with the letter *h*.

The program accepts the last symbol by first loading the length of the parameters from the byte with the offset 80h, known as the command tail count, from the beginning of PSP into the register BX. Note that when DOS initializes the COM- module, the CS register contains the segment address of the PSP. The program then loads one byte of memory from CS:[BX]+80h into the DL register. The locations at offset 081h-0ffh in the PSP always contain the parameters passed at the command line (there is a listing of the contents in the PSP in Chapter One, The Assembler Environment). Because BX contains the length of these parameters, this byte is actually the last byte of the command line. The symbol stored in the DL register is then converted into a capital letter, using the fact that ASCII codes for upper and low case letters differ by one bit. The instruction

```
and    dl,0DFh
```

clears this to create a capital letter.

The next two instructions (lines 36 and 37) are the DOS service call. They execute the function 30h of interrupt 21h - and get the DOS version. As a result, the register AH contains the minor part and register AL - the major part of the version number.

The program then checks whether "L" is the last symbol of the parameters. If this is not the case, the instruction

```
jne    finish
```

in line 39 passes control to the last part of the program. This part consists of lines 41 and 42 which call the function 4Ch of interrupt 21h - the DOS service "terminate process". This function treats the contents of the register AL as a return code. Because this register keeps the value of the major part of the number, the return code will have the same value. If the letter L is the last symbol of the parameters, the instruction

```
mov    al,ah
```

copies the value of the minor part of the number into register AL. The program then proceeds as described before.

You can use this program in your BAT-files to perform actions which depend on the DOS version. For example, in DOS 5 you can use the command **loadhigh** to load resident programs into the high memory. In earlier versions this command is treated as an error. The following fragment of a BAT-file shows how you can use the information about the DOS version in the AUTOEXEC.BAT file:

```
DosVer H
If ErrorLevel 5 GoTo Dos5
FastOpen C:
GoTo EndInst
:Dos5
LoadHigh FastOpen C:
:EndInst
```

This fragment loads the resident DOS utility FASTOPEN into high memory if you have DOS 5 or above and into conventional memory if you are using an earlier version.

Using Bios Service - Output Special Symbols

You can use either BIOS or DOS facilities to output text. The program OutSpec shows the difference between the high-level DOS service and low-level BIOS service. This program outputs the symbol BELL (ASCII code 07) twice by using BIOS through the function 0Ah of interrupt 10h and then using DOS through the function 02 of interrupt 21h. The assembler program text is given in Listing 6.2.

```
 1
 2     page 55,132
 3  ;
 4  ; This  is  an  example  of using two different levels
 5  ; of output procedures - BIOS service and DOS service.
 6  ;
 7  ; Note  that  the  BIOS  procedure  outputs the symbol
 8  ; "BELL" as  visible  symbol  while  the DOS procedure
 9  ; takes the corresponding action - let's look and hear!
10  ;
11  .model    small
12  .code
13      mov  ah,0Ah      ; function 0Ah - output symbol
14      mov  al,07h      ; AL - symbol to be output (BELL)
15      mov  bh,0        ; Video page is supposed to be 0
16      mov  bl,0        ; Used in graphic mode - here not needed
17      mov  cx,1        ; CX - number of symbols
18      int  10h         ; BIOS video service call
19
20      mov  ah,02       ; Function 02h - output symbol
21      mov  dl,al       ; DL - symbol to be output
22      int  21h         ; DOS service call
23
24  .exit
25  end
```

Listing 6.2 OutSpec - Output Symbols Using BIOS and DOS Services

The source code for the program OutSpec is stored on your program disk. You can run this program using the BAT-files from your program disk or any way you like. To use BAT-files, type the following commands:

```
asm outspec
run
```

The first result you'll get is that the symbol • will appear on the screen. This is the graphic representation of the ASCII code 07 - for the symbol BELL. You will then hear a beep which is your hardware's interpretation of the BELL code.

The difference between BIOS and DOS is that DOS routines treat all symbols literally according to their meaning. This means that if you output the symbol CR (**C**arriage **R**eturn) for example, DOS actually moves the cursor to the next line. The BELL symbol really causes a BELL and so on. The BIOS routines, however treat all the symbols symbolically. This means that BIOS only outputs the graphic representation of a symbol and nothing more.

Using BIOS Data Area - Mastering Hardware

The program below uses the BIOS data area to control hardware. This program turns off the keyboard NumLock by changing the corresponding information in the BIOS data area. The full assembler program text is given in Listing 6.3.

```
 1
 2 page 60,132
 3 ;
 4 ;              PROGRAM NumlOff
 5 ;
 6 ;         30 Nov 1991, Voronezh
 7 ;
 8 ; This is a sample of BIOS data usage.This
 9 ; program turns off the NumLock state.  It is known
10 ; that the extended  AT  keyboard  held the NumLock
11 ; state after DOS had finished loading. By executing
12 ; this  program  you  may  turn  the  NumLock  off
13 ; without pressing any  key.  Sometimes it may be
14 ; useful to include the following line in  your
15 ; AUTOEXEC.BAT file:
16 ;
17 ; NumLOff
18 ;
19 ; If you decide  to do this, include the executable
20 ; module of  this  program  (NumlOff.COM   or
21 ; NumlOff.EXE)  in any directory that is available
22 ; during the DOS loading process.
23 ;
24 .model tiny                  ; The TINY memory model
25                              ; is needed to build
26                              ; the COM- program
27
28 BiosData      segment at 40h; BIOS data definition
29         org   17h            ; Keyboard flags from address 0417h
30 KbdSt1 db     ?             ; Keyboard_status byte 1
31 KbdSt2 db     ?             ; Keyboard_status byte 2
32 BiosData      ends           ; End of BIOS data
33
34 .code                        ; CODE segment starts here
35 begin:
```

```
36          assume es:BiosData  ; BIOS data area will be accessed
37                              ; through register ES
38          mov   ax,BiosData   ; Load address of BIOS data segment
39          mov   es,ax         ; into AX and copy it into ES
40          and   KbdSt1,0DFh   ; Clear the NUMLOCK status (bit 5)
41
42          mov   ax,4C00h      ; Set the exit code 0
43          int   21h           ; and return to DOS
44
45          end   begin
```

Listing 6.3 NumLOff - Using BIOS Data Area to Control Hardware

Since you shouldn't have any problem understanding this program, our explanation only covers those aspects that have not come up before.

Note that this program can be transformed into a COM- module as well as into the EXE-module. This is possible because the program does not contain any commands that might be affected by changes to the contents of segment registers CX and DX. There are no jumps or memory operands in this program and the segment register ES is set up directly. This information might help you to write small programs which can be used either as COM- modules or EXE- modules.

To access the BIOS data area we have used the assembler directive SEGMENT with attribute AT. To define the offset within the segment you can use the directive ORG as in line 29 in Listing 6.3. The main instruction in the program is line 40. The hexadecimal code 0DFh can be represented in the binary system as 1101 1111b. So the command

```
and KbdSt1,0DFh
```

only changes bit 5 in the byte at location KbdSt1. This byte stands for NUMLOCK state, and by clearing it, you turn this state off. Note, that changing the data may have unexpected effects. Be careful when accessing the BIOS data area!

Using ROM BIOS Data - Determining the Type of Computer

ROM BIOS is located in addresses above 640K or A000h in the hexadecimal system. You cannot change the information stored here but you can read it into RAM to process. For example, since BIOS contains information about your computer, your program can check which model is being used. The program DetPc uses data from ROM BIOS to get this information. The program text is shown in Listing 6.4.

```
1
2   page 55,132
3   .model large
4
5   HiBios  segment at 0F000h
6           org         0FFFEh
7   PcType  db  ?                  ; Computer identifier
8   HiBios  ends
9
10  .code
11          assume es:HiBios       ; use ES to access ROM BIOS area
12  Begin:  mov ax,@data           ; load  address of DATA segment
13          mov ds,ax              ; DS points to DATA segment
14          mov ax,HiBios          ; load  address or ROM BIOS data
15          mov es,ax              ; ES points to ROM BIOS segment
16          mov cx,Ltable          ; Load length of table to be searched
17          mov dl,PcType          ; Extract the type from BIOS area
18
19  Search:mov bx,cx               ;  Current address of table element
20          cmp dl,TypeTbl[bx-1]   ; Compare type, element of table
21          je  EndSear            ; If found, stop searching
22          loop Search            ; Test next element of table
23
24  EndSear:mov al,cl              ; number element passed as return code
25          mov ah,4Ch             ; DOS service 4H - terminate process
26          int 21h                ; DOS service call
27  .data                         ;
28
29  ;    Table of microprocessors' types
30
31          db   0                 ;  0 - Uknown type
32  TypeTbl db  0F8h               ;  1-IBM PS/2 model 80
33          db   0F9h              ;  2-IBM PC Convertible
34          db   0FAh              ;  3-IBM PS/2 Model 30
35          db   0FBh              ;  4-PC XT Ext keyboard,3.5"drives
36          db   0FCh              ;  5-PC-AT or PS/2 Models 50,60
37          db   0FDh              ;  6-IBM PC-JR
38          db   0FEh              ;  7-PC-XT
39          db   0FFh              ;  8-IBM PC
40          db   09Ah              ;  9-Compaq XT / Compaq Plus
41          db   030h              ; 10-Sperry PC
42          db   02Dh              ; 11-Compaq PC / Compaq Deskpro
43  Ltable equ $-TypeTbl
44          end begin
```

Listing 6.4 DetPc - Using Information from ROM BIOS

This program uses the segment which has a fixed location with attribute AT. The corresponding directives are labelled HiBios (see lines 5-8).The byte labelled PcType is the only relevant byte from this segment for this program. The line 11 tells Assembler that the segment HiBios will be addressed through the segment register ES.

Lines 13-15 load the segment registers DS and ES. Line 16 loads the cycle counter with the length of the table that contains possible computer types. This value is calculated by using the assembler directive EQU. The constant Ltable is defined in line 43 and its value depends solely on the amount of elements in the table, in other words - on the length of table. You can add or delete elements in the table without changing the lines which generate instructions.

Line 17 loads the computer identifier read from PCType into register DL. Lines 19 - 22 are the cycle for searching the table TypeTbl. Each element in the table is compared with the value in register DL.

Line 24 copies the value of the cycle counter into register AL. This value will be used as a return code. Note that if the search was unsuccessful and the PC identifier wasn't found in the table, the cycle counter is equal to 0.

This program can be useful for creating BAT-files working in different ways depending on the which model of computer you have. An example of this kind of BAT-file is given below:

```
@Echo off
Echo.
Echo The BAT-file %0 is intended for determining your computer type
Echo.
detpc
If ErrorLevel 1 GoTo More0
Echo Type 0: Your computer is not recognized
GoTo EndProc
:More0
If ErrorLevel 2 GoTo More1
Echo Type 1: Your computer is IBM PS/2 model 80
GoTo EndProc
:More1
If ErrorLevel 3 GoTo More2
Echo Type 2: Your computer is IBM PC Convertible
GoTo EndProc
:More2
If ErrorLevel 4 GoTo More3
Echo Type 3: Your computer is IBM PS/2 model 30
GoTo EndProc
:More3
If ErrorLevel 5 GoTo More4
Echo Type 4: Your computer is PC XT extended
GoTo EndProc
:More4
```

```
If ErrorLevel 6 GoTo More5
Echo Type 5: Your computer is IBM PC-AT or PS/2 model 50 or 60
GoTo EndProc
:More5
If ErrorLevel 7 GoTo More6
Echo Type 6: Your computer is IBM PC-JR
GoTo EndProc
:More6
If ErrorLevel 8 GoTo More7
Echo Type 7: Your computer is IBM PC-XT
GoTo EndProc
:More7
If ErrorLevel 9 GoTo More8
Echo Type 8: Your computer is IBM PC
GoTo EndProc
:More8
If ErrorLevel 10 GoTo More9
Echo Type 9: Your computer is Compaq XT or Compaq Plus
GoTo EndProc
:More9
If ErrorLevel 11 GoTo More10
Echo Type 10: Your computer is Sperry PC
GoTo EndProc
:More10
If ErrorLevel 12 GoTo More11
Echo Type 11: Your computer is Compaq PC or Compaq Deskpro
GoTo EndProc
:More11
Echo Type 12 or higher: Your computer is not recognized
:EndProc
```

Using ROM BIOS Routines - Restart System

ROM BIOS has a set of routines which can be used by the system software to control the computer. Your programs can also access these routines to perform quite special tasks. The example below demonstrates the routine "Cold Restart". This routine has the same effect as pressing the "RESET" key on the front panel of your computer, or turning the power off and then on again. After each of these actions, the computer starts again from the very beginning - from the power-on self-testing procedure.

```
1
2  page 55,132
3  ;
4  ;    System reload
5  ;    =============
6  ;
7  ; Voronezh, 03 February 1993
8  ;
9  ; Comment: no comment
```

```
10 ;
11 .model    small
12 FarSeg         segment at 0F000h
13       org       0FFF0h
14 ReLd          dw ?
15 FarSeg        ends
16 .code
17        assume ds:FarSeg
18 Begin :
19        jmp     Far ptr Farseg:Reld
20        end     begin
```

Listing 6.5 Reset - Using ROM BIOS Routine - Restart System

This program is similar to the program DetPc described earlier. It uses the same technique to define the data in the ROM BIOS area (lines 12 - 15) and it passes control to the system restart routine located in this area.

Locating Interrupt Handlers - The DOS Service

Here is an example of using a DOS service to get information about the location of interrupt handlers. The full assembler text of the program is given in Listing 6.6.

```
 1
 2 page 59,132
 3 ;
 4 ;        Program IntLoc
 5 ;        _____
 6 ;
 7 ;        Voronezh, 30 January 91
 8 ;        _____
 9 ;
10 ; This is a sample of an assembler program that uses a simple
11 ; DOS service.  It outputs  the  table of interrupts onto the
12 ; system output  device  and reports where the corresponding
13 ; handler is located.  The letter B means BIOS, the  letter
14 ; D - DOS, the letter N - not set (dummy handler).
15 ;
16 .model    small
17 .stack
18 .data
19 tbint     db    16 dup ('xx-X ') , '$'
20 HexSym    db    '0','1','2','3','4','5','6','7'
21           db    '8','9','A','B','C','D','E','F'
22 NumInt    db    0
23 NumIntL   db    0
24 .code
25          movax,@data
```

```
26          movds,ax
27
28          movcx,16        ; Line counter
29  Rows:                   ; Lines cycle starts here
30          push cx         ; Save outward counter
31          mov  di,0        ; Counter within line
32          mov  cx,16       ; Columns counter
33          mov  al,NumInt
34          mov  NumIntL,al
35  Intrs:                  ;
36          mov  al,NumintL  ; Load interrupt number
37          mov  ah,35h      ; Get interrupt vector (DS:BX)
38          int  21h         ; DOS service call
39          mov  dx,es       ; address of interrupt handler
40          cmp  dx,0A000h   ; Compare to BIOS start address
41          ja   InBios      ; If DX is greater- handler is in BIOS
42          mov  tbint[di+3],'D'   ; Set indicator 'DOS'
43          jmp  DoneInd          ; To the end of block
44  InBios:    mov  tbint[di+3],'B'   ; Set indicator 'BIOS'
45  DoneInd:                        ; This is the end of block
46
47          cmp  byte ptr es:[bx],0CFh  ; First instruction IRET?
48          jne  PresHan              ; If not- handler presented
49          mov  tbint[di+3],'N'      ; Set indicator 'Not set'
50  PresHan:                         ;
51          mov  ah,0       ; AL keeps the interrupt number
52          mov  dl,16      ; Prepare to converting AL to symbols
53          div  dl         ; AX / 16
54
55          mov  bx,offset HexSym
56          xlat
57          mov  byte ptr tbint[di],al  ; symbol into output line
58          mov  al,ah
59          xlat
60          mov  byte ptr tbint[di+1],al; symbol into output line
61
62          add  di,5               ; Next position in the line
63          add  NumIntL,16         ; Increase interrupt number
64          loop Intrs              ; Next step - next interrupt
65          pop  cx                 ; Restore cycle counter
66          mov  ah,09              ; Function 09 - output string
67          mov  dx,offset tbint    ; Address of string in DS:DX
68          int  21h                ; Output one string
69          inc  NumInt             ;
70          loop Rows               ; Next step - next string
71          mov  ax,4C00h
72          int  21h
73          end                     ;
```

**Listing 6.6 IntLoc - Getting Information About Interrupt
Handlers Using DOS Service**

This program can help you locate the handlers for all 256 possible interrupts. It outputs a table of 16 lines and 16 columns which contain the interrupt numbers followed by the letters B, D or N. These letters denote the area where the segment address of the interrupt points. The letter **B** stands for BIOS and the letter **D** stands for DOS. The letter **N** means that the interrupt has a dummy handler - a handler which has an IRET instruction as its first instruction. Let's have a look at how this program works.

The data area contains a pattern for the output string, an array of constants and two variables. The pattern for the output string is made up of 16 fields each of which is 5 bytes long. The array HexSym contains 16 text constants which are ASCII representations of 16 hexadecimal numbers. The variable NumInt contains the number of the first interrupt to be output in the line. The variable NumIntL is the number of the interrupt in current column of this line. The initial value for both these variables is 0.

The program begins as usual by loading segment registers in lines 25 and 26. Line 28 puts the value 16 into register CX. This specifies the number of lines to be printed, and register CX will be used as a counter for the corresponding cycle. This cycle starts in line 29 labelled **Rows**.

The first instruction in this cycle saves the cycle counter CX because CX is used in a nested cycle that starts in line 35 labelled **Intrs**. Lines 31 - 34 prepare this cycle by putting the initial value in registers DI and CX. DI is used as an index of the current element in the output string and CX as a cycle counter. Lines 34 and 35 put the number of first interrupt in current line into NumIntl.

Lines 36-38 use the DOS service "Get Interrupt Vector" which is accessible through the function 35h of interrupt 21h. To use this service, put the number of the interrupt you want to locate into register AL. The result will be given in registers ES and BX - ES will contain the segment address of the corresponding interrupt handler and BX will contain its offset address.

Lines 39 and 40 load the segment address into DX and compare it with the value A000h which is the beginning of the BIOS area (see the memory map on Figure 6.1). Lines 41-45 are designed to put the corresponding letter (B or D) in the current field of the output string. Each field is output in one column. The expression **tbint[di+3]** defines the place for this letter. Here, DI contains the offset current field from the beginning of the string - 0 for the first element, 5 for second, 10 for third and, finally, 75 for the last one. Constant offset 3 defines the position of the letter within the current field.

Lines 47 - 49 contain instructions which check whether the first instruction of handler is an IRET instruction. The operation code for this instruction is 0CFh. If this code is found at location es:[bx] (the beginning of the interrupt handler) the corresponding interrupt is marked by the letter N (Not set).

Lines 51 - 53 convert an unsigned integer number of the interrupt in register AL into symbolic representation suitable for output. Because this number is less than 256 it cannot consist of more than two hexadecimal digits. Divide the 8-bit number by 16 to get these digits. The quotient is the first digit of the result and the remainder - the second one. Note that after the DIV command for 8-bit integers, the quotient from the DIV command is stored in register AL and the remainder in register AH.

Lines 55 - 60 transform the 8-bit integers contained in registers AL and AH into ASCII codes and place these codes into the corresponding fields in the output string.

Lines 62 and 63 prepare counters for next step - DI is increased by 5 (the width of one column in a table to be printed) and NumIntL by 16 (the difference between the number of interrupts in adjoining columns). Line 64 repeats the cycle until CX is equal to 0.

Line 65 restores the contents of register CX - the cycle counter, which outputs the current line of the table.

Lines 66 - 68 output the line created by the execution of the nested cycle. The usual way for putting the text string onto the screen is using the function 09h of interrupt 21h. To use this function, place the address of the string into registers DS (segment) and DX (offset).

Line 70 is the end of the cycle that started in line 29.

Lines 72 and 73 are the standard way of finishing a program. The return code will be 0.

A sample of the output created by this program is shown in Figure 6.5. You might get a slightly different picture, depending on what resident programs and installable device drivers you are using.

```
00-D 10-D 20-D 30-D 40-B 50-D 60-D 70-B 80-D 90-D A0-D B0-D C0-D D0-D E0-D F0-B
01-N 11-B 21-D 31-B 41-B 51-B 61-D 71-B 81-D 91-D A1-D B1-D C1-D D1-D E1-D F1-D
02-D 12-B 22-D 32-N 42-B 52-B 62-D 72-D 82-D 92-D A2-D B2-D C2-D D2-D E2-D F2-B
03-N 13-D 23-D 33-N 43-B 53-B 63-D 73-D 83-D 93-D A3-D B3-D C3-D D3-D E3-D F3-D
04-N 14-B 24-D 34-N 44-B 54-B 64-D 74-D 84-D 94-D A4-D B4-D C4-D D4-D E4-D F4-B
05-B 15-D 25-D 35-N 45-B 55-B 65-D 75-B 85-D 95-D A5-D B5-D C5-D D5-D E5-D F5-D
06-B 16-D 26-D 36-N 46-B 56-B 66-D 76-D 86-D 96-D A6-D B6-D C6-D D6-D E6-D F6-D
07-B 17-B 27-D 37-N 47-B 57-B 67-B 77-N 87-D 97-D A7-D B7-D C7-D D7-D E7-D F7-D
08-D 18-B 28-D 38-N 48-B 58-B 68-D 78-D 88-D 98-D A8-D B8-D C8-D D8-D E8-D F8-D
09-D 19-D 29-D 39-N 49-B 59-B 69-B 79-D 89-D 99-D A9-D B9-D C9-D D9-D E9-D F9-D
0A-D 1A-B 2A-N 3A-N 4A-B 5A-B 6A-B 7A-D 8A-D 9A-D AA-D BA-D CA-D DA-D EA-D FA-D
0B-D 1B-D 2B-N 3B-N 4B-B 5B-B 6B-B 7B-D 8B-D 9B-D AB-D BB-D CB-D DB-D EB-B FB-D
0C-N 1C-N 2C-N 3C-N 4C-B 5C-B 6C-B 7C-D 8C-D 9C-D AC-D BC-D CC-D DC-D EC-D FC-B
0D-D 1D-D 2D-N 3D-N 4D-B 5D-B 6D-D 7D-D 8D-D 9D-D AD-D BD-D CD-D DD-D ED-B FD-D
0E-D 1E-D 2E-N 3E-N 4E-B 5E-B 6E-B 7E-D 8E-D 9E-D AE-D BE-D CE-D DE-D EE-D FE-D
0F-N 1F-B 2F-D 3F-N 4F-B 5F-B 6F-D 7F-D 8F-D 9F-D AF-D BF-D CF-D DF-D EF-D FF-D
```

Figure 6.5
A Sample of Output Created by IntLoc

Locating Interrupt Handlers - Direct Access to the IVT

This next program performs the same task, using immediate access to the interrupt vector table. Our explanation only covers those parts of the program that differ from the IntLoc program described in the previous section.

```
1
2  page 59,132
3  ;
4  ;        Program   IntLocD
5  ;        _____
6  ;
7  ;        Voronezh, 30 January 91
8  ;        _____
9  ;
10 ; This is a sample of an assembler program that uses a simple
11 ; DOS service. It outputs the table of interrupts onto the
12 ; system output device and reports where the corresponding
13 ; handler is located. The letter B means BIOS, the letter
14 ; D - DOS, the letter N - not set (dummy handler).
15 ;
16 .model small
17 IntSeg segment at 0
18 IntVec dw     512 dup (?)
19 IntSeg ends
20 .stack
21 .data
22 tbint  db     16 dup ('xx-X ') , '$'
23 HexSym db     '0','1','2','3','4','5','6','7'
```

```
24           db      '8','9','A','B','C','D','E','F'
25 NumInt   db      0
26 NumIntL  db      0
27 .code
28           assume  es:IntSeg
29           mov     ax,@data
30           mov     ds,ax
31
32           mov     ax,IntSeg
33           mov     es,ax
34
35           mov     cx,16           ; Line counter
36 Rows:                             ; Lines cycle starts here
37           push    cx              ; Save outward counter
38           mov     di,0            ; Counter within line
39           mov     cx,16           ; Columns counter
40           mov     al,NumInt
41           mov     NumIntL,al
42 Intrs:            ;
43           mov     bh,0
44           mov     al,NumintL      ; Load interrupt number
45           mov     bl,al
46           shl     bx,1
47           shl     bx,1
48           mov     dx,IntVec[bx+2]
49           cmp     dx,0A000h       ; Compare to BIOS start address
50           ja      InBios          ; If DX is greater- handler is in BIOS
51           mov     tbint[di+3],'D' ; Set indicator 'DOS'
52           jmp     doneind         ; To the end of block
53 InBios: mov       tbint[di+3],'B' ; Set indicator 'BIOS'
54 DoneInd:                  ; This is the end of block
55
56           cmp     byte ptr es:[bx],0CFh ; First instruction IRET?
57           jne     PresHan         ; If not - handler presented
58           mov     tbint[di+3],'N'    ; Set indicator 'Not set'
59 PresHan:          ;
60           mov     ah,0            ; AL keeps the interrupt number
61           mov     dl,16           ; Prepare to convert AL to symbols
62           div     dl              ; AX / 16
63
64           mov     bx,offset HexSym
65           xlat
66           mov     byte ptr tbint[di],al   ; symbol into output line
67           mov     al,ah
68           xlat
69           mov     byte ptr tbint[di+1],al; symbol into output line
70
71           add     di,5                ; Next position in the line
72           add     NumIntL,16          ; Increase interrupt number
73           loop    Intrs               ; Next step - next interrupt
74           pop     cx                  ; Restore cycle counter
75           mov     ah,09               ; Function 09 - output string
76           mov     dx,offset tbint     ; Address of string in DS:DX
```

```
77          int    21h              ; Output one string
78          inc    NumInt           ;
79          loop   Rows             ; Next step - next string
80          mov    ax,4C00h
81          int    21h
82          end                     ;
```

Listing 6.7 IntLocD - A Sample of Direct Access to the Interrupt Vector Table

The segment IntSeg defined in lines 17-19 gives you access to the interrupt vector table. This segment has a special attribute AT which means that the segment starts at a fixed location in the memory.

Lines 43 - 48 get the segment address for the interrupt handler. The number of the interrupt stored in register BX is shifted to the left by 2 bits, which has the same effect as multiplying by 4. In this way, we get the address of the element of the interrupt vector table. Since the segment address of the handler is stored in the second word of the element, the instruction

```
mov    dx,IntVec[bx+2]
```

loads that segment address into register DX. From this point on the program IntLocD works in the same way as the program IntLoc described in the previous section. This example should be useful because it shows you how to use segments with a fixed starting address to access a particular area in the memory.

Your First Interrupt Handler

Now it is time to try to write and install your first interrupt handler. We will use the most universal interrupt, 21h and a relatively simple and safe function of this interrupt - the function Get Dos Version Number (function 30h). This program replaces the value returned by function 30h of interrupt 21h with the value you defined in the program. We have chosen the value 7.1 but you can replace it with any number you like, or add the block to the program that accepts the value from the command line. The program text is given in Listing 6.8.

```
1
2  page 55,132
3  CODE      SEGMENT PARA
4            ASSUME  CS:CODE
5  ToOld:       ;=== Passing control to the old handler
6            db     0EAh ; This is code for JMP FAR
```

```
 7 OldOff     dw      0         ; offset
 8 OldSeg     dw      0         ; segment
 9
10 Handler    label byte        ; Start of new handler for INT 21
11            cmp     ah,30h    ; Check function number
12            jne     ToOld     ; If not a function 30h - to old handler
13            mov     ax,0107h  ; Function 30h-Return the version number
14            iret              ; Return from handler
15
16 INSTALL:                     ; Installation starts here
17            mov     ax,3521h  ; Get handler's address
18            int     21h       ; ES - segment, BX - offset
19            cmp     bx,offset Handler; Vector points to this handler?
20            je      already   ; If so - put message end exit
21            mov     cs:OldOff,bx  ; Save offset of old handler
22            mov     cs:OldSeg,es  ; Save segment of old handler
23            mov     ax,cs     ; Command segment of this program
24            mov     ds,ax     ; into DX (for setting handler)
25
26            mov     dx,offset Handler ; Address of handler
27            mov     ax,2521h      ; Function 25h - Set new handler
28            int     21h           ; Dos service call
29
30            lea     dx,INSTALL
31            add     dx,15
32            mov     cx,4          ; Set counter for shift
33            shr     dx,cl         ; 4 bits to the right- divide by 16
34            add     dx,16         ; Add size of PSP in paragraphs
35            mov     ax,3100h      ; Terminate and
36            int     21h           ; stay resident
37
38 already:
39            push    cs            ; Copy the value of CS
40            pop     ds            ; into the register DS
41            lea     dx,loaded     ; DX := address of message text
42            mov     ax,0900h      ; Function 09 - output string
43            int     21h           ; DOS service call
44            mov     ax,4C01h      ; Function 4Ch-stop (return code 01)
45            int     21h           ; DOS service call
46 loaded     db      'User handler is already loaded!',10,13,'$'
47 CODE       ENDS
48 END        INSTALL
```

Listing 6.8 UserHand - User-Written Interrupt Handler

We'll explain the main part of this program line-by-line because it is our first sample of an interrupt handler written by the user. The program is written using the simplest technique suitable for interrupt handlers, device drivers and TSR programs. First of all, note that the program only contains one segment - the CODE segment. This makes working with segment registers, saving the information when entering handler and restoring this information when returning, much simpler.

The body of the handler starts with the label *Handler* in line 10. The next line is for checking the function number passed in the register AH. Then, if this number differs from 30h, control is passed to the label ToOld. The standard function 30h is replaced with instruction in line 13, which assigns to the register AX the value 0107 that corresponds to the *new* DOS version. If you don't want to see DOS version 7.1, replace the constant in the line 13 with the value you like - for example, your date of birth. Line 14 finishes the handler in the way handlers should be finished - with the IRET instruction (see Using the INT instruction in this chapter).

The lines 5 - 8 have the special purpose - here the command for jumping to the standard handler is formed. These lines generate 5 bytes of code - the first one is the byte filled with the value 0EAh, the next two bytes contain the offset of standard handler and, finally, the last two bytes are the segment of the standard handler. In this way, remembering that the code 0EAh stands for the

```
far JMP
```

instruction, we get the full instruction

```
JMP    OldSeg:OldOff
```

that jumps exactly to the standard handler (if OldSeg and OldOff have the right values).

Lines 17 and 18 use the function 35h of interrupt 21h for getting the address of the corresponding handler. Then, line 19 compares the offset stored in the BX register with the offset for label *Handler* to be sure that this handler hasn't been already installed. There are many ways to perform this task but this is the easiest (maybe, not the best!). If the compared values are equal, then control is passed to the label *already* where the block for error processing starts. This block (lines 38 - 46) outputs the corresponding message and finishes the program with the return code 1.

Lines 21 and 22 form the command for far jumping to the standard handler.

Lines 23 - 28 install the new handler using function 25h of interrupt 21h.

The final block (lines 30 - 36) counts the length of the resident part of the program (in other words, length of your handler) and finishes the program using the function 31h of interrupt 21h. This function is called "Terminate and Stay Resident" and we'll consider this function and programs which use it in later chapters.

Summary

In this chapter we have examined the services and information provided by the system software of the PC. We have seen how BIOS and DOS services interact and how they are invoked via interrupt vectors. Having seen how to use these existing services, we then learnt how to install our own interrupt handlers.

Most of what you have learnt in this chapter is not in itself practically useful. However, having mastered the basic concepts of BIOS and DOS, we are well equipped to move on and take control of all the system resources, starting with the keyboard.

CHAPTER

7

Mastering the Keyboard

This chapter deals with BIOS and DOS interrupts which affect the keyboard.

In Chapter Six we gave you some basic information about the keyboard, and showed how to switch the NumLock on and off using fields in the BIOS data area. Moving on from there, this chapter covers three levels of the keyboard service - the hardware interrupt 09h, the software interrupt 16h and the functions of the universal DOS interrupt 21h which are relevant to the keyboard.

We will also explain more fields of the BIOS data area related to the keyboard. You will learn how to get information about the keyboard and alter its state by reading and changing data in this area.

The assembler programs given in this chapter are designed to be useful for routine work - there's a program to determine scan codes, a set of Clipper functions for controlling the keyboard, and a simple device driver which increases the size of the keyboard buffer.

Fundamental Knowledge

The History of Data Input

If we go back several hundreds of years and look at the origins of the word "computer", it becomes obvious that computers were initially designed for operating specifically with numbers. When fingers no longer sufficed for counting, people started to use small objects such as pebbles, hence the name calculator from the Latin word calculus, which means pebble! As always, though, people wanted more - that is, they wanted their computer to do more than just calculate figures.

The most important functions that computers provide now involve the processing of symbols and logical programming, rather than simply processing numbers. Before these functions can be realized, however, computers need to be able to accept and store symbolic information. Furthermore, these characters have to be presented in a form that computers can understand.

One form of representation is the hexadecimal system, which is accessible to both people and computers. Surprising as it may seem, not that long ago, in order to input text into the computers memory when using a language such as AutoCode, programmers had to record each character as a sequence of hexadecimal (or octal) codes and write them on bits of paper which were then passed to operators who punched them onto special cards. Really keen programmers could read the holes in punchcards and translate them into texts without the help of any electronic devices!

Thankfully, PCs now have an alphanumeric keyboard that translates our text into hexadecimal codes automatically. This job (unfortunately this only applies to the translating, not the typing) is done by a built-in keyboard processor and the keyboard transmits the hexadecimal codes into the PC's main block for every key that you press.

Once the codes generated by pressing a key have been processed by the DOS routines, they are passed to your programs. What you then do with this information depends on the programming language you are using. Most languages have a set of statements or library procedures for reading characters. For example, Pascal has the procedures Read or ReadLn that accept character strings as a whole and the functions

ReadKey and KeyPressed which deal with separate keystrokes. There are four possible levels of accessing the keyboard for assembler programmers:

1. Using the DOS interrupt 21h
2. Using the BIOS interrupt 16h
3. Hooking into the hardware interrupt 09h
4. Using ports related to the keyboard directly

Levels of Keyboard Access

Figure 7.1 shows the interaction between the user program and the chain of keyboard interrupts. Note that the block labelled "The user program" covers the service routines from run-time libraries or other similar tools that your program may use. The diagram also shows that as a programmer, it is possible to break into this chain at a number of points, gaining access to the keyboard at many levels. Which level you choose, and why, depends on what it is you want to do. In this chapter we'll explain the first two levels of accessing the keyboard and give you an introduction to the hardware interrupt 09h and its handler.

Figure 7.2 demonstrates the flow of information when you access the keyboard in the standard way. This is how an application program works, unless you use the instructions IN and OUT to read and write data from and to the hardware ports connected with the keyboard.

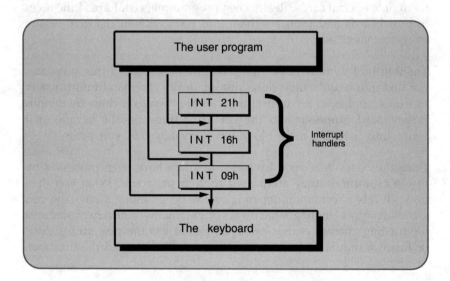

Figure 7.1
Levels of Keyboard Access

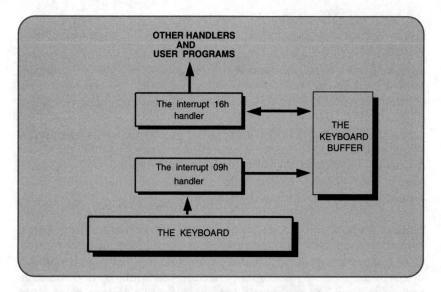

Figure 7.2
**The Standard
Flow of
Character
Information**

The simplest and easiest way to read information from the keyboard is to use the DOS interrupt 21h. It works in a similar way to high-level language functions and allows your programs to perform the same tasks.

The BIOS interrupt 16h provides the most basic level at which you can access the keyboard. It is useful for directly processing special keys such as cursor control keys or functional keys.

The hardware interrupt 09h is not intended for direct use by programmers. This interrupt is generated by the hardware and its handler is called automatically when you press any key on the keyboard. You can add your own handler to the standard one, or even replace it with your own using MS-DOS tools. As this gives maximum control over the keyboard, it is a very popular technique among experienced assembler programmers.

Accessing the keyboard ports directly is the most difficult but the most powerful way. It is how software developers or producers of new operating systems and other special software work.

The best way to understand the keyboard is to examine step-by-step the process of capturing the information from a key press, and turning it into useful information for our programs. In truly logical fashion, we'll start at the very beginning.

ASCII Codes and Scan Codes

We'll start by looking at the different ways of representing characters to make them suitable for processing by a PC. The most widespread form is the hexadecimal system, which is used for the representation of numbers, as well as characters. There are many ways of representing characters hexadecimally, although some of them are not used that often. The most popular code for representing characters in computers is the extended ASCII code which allows you to use 256 different characters. Each character is denoted by a two-digit hexadecimal code from 00h to 0FFh. For example, the letter A corresponds to the ASCII code 41h (65 in the decimal system).

Usually, when you press a letter key, the corresponding letter immediately appears on the screen. So, it would be natural to assume that the computer gets the ASCII code for this letter from the keyboard. In actual fact, the only information that the computer gets is the scan code of the key and its state (a key can have two states - pressed or released). However, the input/output procedures in high-level languages only give you the ASCII codes. This means that you cannot use the dBASE statement GET, or the Pascal statement READ for reading function key codes or controlling the cursor keys since the I/O routines of high-level languages process the key pressed before your program. This allows you to edit input text while typing it, but your program will get only the final version of text typed, without any information about control keys such as Ins, Del, BkSp or cursor control keys. This is the price you pay for having it easy with the high-level functions!

The process of converting the number of the key you pressed into the corresponding ASCII code is done by BIOS.

The number of the key on the keyboard is known as its **scan code** - usually represented as a one-byte integer ranging from 1 up to the number of keys on the keyboard. The meaning of the term "scan code" changed when enhanced keyboards were introduced. Strictly speaking, it no longer refers to "the number of a key" because some keys on an enhanced keyboard give more than one byte of information when pressed. For example, the right Ctrl key generates the sequence E0h 1Dh, while the left Ctrl key has the scan code 1Dh.

For more information on ASCII and scan codes, for both standard and enhanced keyboards, see Appendix B and Appendix C

Keyboard Low Level - Interrupt 09h

Interrupt 09h is called by your hardware and performs three basic functions: it reads data from the keyboard port, decodes it and places the corresponding scan and ASCII codes into the keyboard buffer. This interrupt is also known as IRQ1 - Interrupt Request number 1. The term "interrupt request" indicates that this interrupt is caused externally, without using any instruction from your program. These interrupts, generated automatically, are referred to as **hardware interrupts**, in contrast to software interrupts, generated by the INT instruction.

The hardware interrupt 09h is generated when you press any key. You must not use the instruction in the following way:

```
INT    09h
```

unless you are writing an exceptionally special program (off the top of our heads we can't imagine such a program, but you might have more luck). The only way to use INT 09h relatively safely is to create your own handler for this interrupt and to install it either as device driver or as a Terminate and Stay Resident program (TSR). This is how pop-up programs, keyboard drivers, data security systems and other similar programs are created. The main difference between a device driver and TSR program is how these programs are constructed. In this chapter we will give an example of creating a device driver (Listing 7.7). This is a program which can be installed in a special memory area during the DOS boot process. In Chapter Eleven we'll cover TSRs, many of which hook interrupt 09h.

Getting back to the point of how this interrupt works, the handler of interrupt 09h gets the scan code of the key you pressed or released. These codes differ slightly depending on which keyboard you are using. As you probably know, there are two main types of PC keyboard: the original 83-key XT model with key pad and cursor movement keys combined, and the enhanced AT style keyboard with 101 keys in the US version, and 102 keys in the European version. You can check whether you have an enhanced keyboard by testing the 4th bit of the byte located at 0040:0096h in the BIOS data area. This bit is set if you have an enhanced keyboard actually operating in enhanced mode. Note also that 101/102 keyboards can have two states, usually defined as "XT" and "AT". These states can be set using the switch on the underside of the keyboard. Choose the state appropriate for the type of computer you are using - XT or AT.

Here is a simple example of using DEBUG to determine the type of keyboard in use.

```
DEBUG
-R  DS
250:  0040        ;SET register DS to 0040h
-D  96  97        ;Display contents of 0040:0096h & 0040:0097h
                10  12

-Q
```

Now if we examine address 0040:0096h

```
            7 6 5 4 3 2 1 0  bit number
            8 4 2 1 8 4 2 1  binary weight
            _____
10 hex =    0 0 0 1 0 0 0 0  binary
```

Now we can examine bit number 4 which is logic one, ie a 101/102 keyboard is present.

Generating Scan Codes

Each key on a standard keyboard has a one-byte scan code. When you press a key, control is passed to the handler of interrupt 09h. It reads the scan code from the port 60h which is also known as port B of the PPI (Programming Parallel Interface). We'll look at the PPI in more depth in Chapter Ten, where we will use the IN instruction to access bytes placed at the ports directly.

If you hold a key down, the same scan code is generated until you release the key. This process is called auto-repeating, and is another of the functions performed by the resident keyboard processor. In this chapter we will give an example of a program that you can use to change the speed of auto-repeating.

On an 83-key keyboard, the scan code generated by releasing a key is the same as that generated by pressing the key, except that the 7th bit is set to 1. For example, the scan code for key "A" is 09h when you press it, and 89h when you release it. You can calculate the scan code for releasing a key by adding the value 80h to the value of the scan code for pressing this key.

Things are a little different for 101/102 enhanced keyboards. For example, there are two Ctrl keys, two Alt keys, and the cursor control keys are also duplicated. These additional keys generate special scan codes, consisting of two or even more bytes.

For example, the Ctrl key on an 83-key keyboard has the scan code 1Dh when pressed and 9Dh when released. The left Ctrl key on an enhanced keyboard behaves in exactly the same way, but the right Ctrl key generates the scan code consisting of two bytes. The first of them contains the value 0E0h which is a signal that the next byte (or, in some cases, bytes) is the actual scan code. For example, the full scan code of the right Ctrl key is 0E0h 1Dh when pressed and 0E0h 9Dh when released. Sometimes the sequence of bytes which make up the scan code can be quite complex, for example on some notebooks the cursor control keys generate sequences of 4 bytes when pressed and 4 bytes when released. This is worth remembering when writing programs that deal with the keyboard directly - such as a special keyboard driver that intercepts the hardware keyboard interrupt 09h.

In this chapter we will give you an example of a program that shows the scan codes for keys you have pressed. You can use the program ScanCode to determine which keys on your keyboard have special scan codes. You can also examine how special keys such as Shift or Ctrl work. Appendix C contains a table of scan codes.

Besides the keyboard type flag, there are other fields in the BIOS Data area that we must consider in order to understand how the keyboard passes information to our applications.

Keyboard Fields in the BIOS Data Area

The BIOS Data Area, which is located in the segment at address 0040:0000, contains various fields which reflect the state of the keyboard, and a temporary work area called the keyboard buffer. The main fields in the BIOS Data Area related to the keyboard are listed in Table 7.1

First, we'll look at the various flags in the BIOS data area.

When you press a special key like Shift, Ctrl or NumLock, they do not generate characters for DOS or application programs. Instead, they set or clear the corresponding bit (or several bits) of the BIOS data area. The program responsible for this is the handler of interrupt 09h and the bytes used for reflecting the state of keyboard are usually called the **keyboard flags**.

The main keyboard flags are two bytes at the address 0040:0017h, the definition of each bit of byte 0040:0017h is shown in Table 7.2, and of byte 0040:0018h - in Table 7.3.

There's no problem with accessing these two bytes directly. You can turn the corresponding state of the keyboard on or off by changing the value of the corresponding bit in byte 0040:0017h. This should be familiar ground, as an example of this type of program was given in Chapter Six, where the program NumlOff cleared the 5th bit in byte

Offset in bytes	Length in bytes	Type	Meaning
17h	1	Byte	Keyboard Flag 1 (status)
18h	1	Byte	Keyboard Flag 2 (keys pressed)
19h	1	Byte	Alt input buffer
1Ah	2	Word	Keyboard buffer head pointer
1Ch	2	Word	Keyboard buffer tail pointer
1Eh	32	Word	Default keyboard buffer
80h	2	Word	Offset address of keyboard buffer star
82h	2	Word	Offset address of keyboard buffer end
96h	1	Byte	Keyboard Flag 3 (Extended)
97h	1	Byte	Keyboard Flag 4 (Extended)

Table 7.1
The Main BIOS Data Fields Related to the Keyboard

Bit	Hex	Dec	Meaning
7	80	128	Insert mode locked
6	40	64	CapsLock state locked
5	20	32	NumLock state locked
4	10	16	ScrollLock state licked
3	08	8	Alt momentarily pressed (either key is pressed)
2	04	4	Ctrl momentarily pressed (either key is pressed)
1	02	2	Shift (Left) momentarily pressed
0	01	1	Shift (Right) momentarily pressed

Table 7.2
Keyboard Flag 1 - Byte 0040:0017h (State Active)

0040:0017h which switches the NumLock state off. You can easily write similar programs which switch certain keyboard states on or off, and call them as procedures or functions from programs written in high-level languages.

For example, it might be easier to translate the keyboard input to uppercase letters by switching the CapsLock state on, rather than using another technique such as the XLAT instruction. If you use this instruction you need to keep a table of characters in memory and use each character read from the keyboard as the number of the character in this table. Note that changing the status of keyboard toggles such as NumLock won't change the LED indicators on the XT keyboard.

The byte at location 0040:0019h is used as a work variable when codes are input using the numeric pad and the Alt key. When you press the

Bit	Hex	Dec	Meaning
7	80	128	Insert momentarily pressed
6	40	64	CapsLock momenarily pressed
5	20	32	NumLock momentarily pressed
4	10	16	ScrollLock momentarily pressed
3	08	8	Pause state locked
2	04	4	SysReq momentarily pressed
1	02	2	Left Alt momentarily pressed
0	01	1	Left Ctrl momentarily pressed

Table 7.3
Keyboard Flag 2 - Byte 0040:0018h (Key Pressed)

Alt key, BIOS assigns a zero value to this variable, then forms an integer number 1 - 255 using the same technique for numeric input, as we illustrated in the program NumIO in Chapter Four.

When you press a key on the numeric pad holding the Alt key down, BIOS multiplies the value stored in byte 0040:0019h by 10 and adds to it the number corresponding to the key pressed (the integer number 0 - 9, don't mix up this value with the scan code!). When you release the Alt key, BIOS stops this process and treats the result as the ASCII code of a character. BIOS then appends the scan code 0 to the ASCII code of the "key" pressed and places this pair of bytes into the keyboard buffer. The value of the scan code equal to 0 in this case means that this character was created in a special way and does not correspond to a particular key on the keyboard.

If you try to enter a number greater than 255, BIOS will convert it by subtracting 256 until it falls within the valid range. For example, the number 256 will be treated as 0, 257 - as 1, 514 - as 2 and so on. Note that if the value of byte 0040:0019h is 0, BIOS does not place it in the keyboard buffer. This means that you cannot use this technique for inputting the NUL symbol (the character which corresponds to the ASCII code 0).

Apart from bytes 0040:0017h and 0040:0018hh, there are two other keyboard flags in the BIOS data area at location 0040:0096h and 0040:0097h (see Tables 7.4 and 7.5). These variables contain additional information about the state of the enhanced keyboard and let you perform tasks like determining which of two functionally identical keys such as Ctrl or Alt has been pressed: left or right.

Bit	Hex	Dec	Meaning (* = internal BIOS flags)
7	80	128	Read ID in progress *
6	40	64	Last character is 1st ID character *
5	20	32	Force NumLock if read ID & KBX *
4	10	16	1 if 101/102 key keyboard 0 if 83/84 key keyboard
3	08	8	Right Alt pressed
2	04	4	Right Ctrl
1	02	2	Last code was 00E0h
0	01	1	Last code was 00E1h

Table 7.4
Keyboard Flag Bitmaps 0040:0096h

Bit	Hex	Dec	Meaning
7	80	128	Keyboard transmit error
6	40	64	Mode indicator update
5	20	32	Resend receive flag
4	10	16	Acknowledge received
3	08	8	Reserved but must be 0
2	04	4	CapsLock LED 1 = on
1	02	2	NumLock LED 1 = on
0	01	1	ScrollLock LED 1 = on

Table 7.5
Keyboard Flag
Bitmaps
0040:0097h

The Keyboard Buffer

The keyboard buffer is the part of the memory used for temporarily storing information accepted from the keyboard. When you press a key, the interrupt handler for interrupt 09h places its scan code and corresponding ASCII code into the keyboard buffer.

Figure 7.3 shows the structure of the keyboard buffer and the relevant pointers in the BIOS data area. These are:

Buffer start pointer	0040:0080h
Buffer end pointer	0040:0082h
Buffer head pointer	0040:001Ah
Buffer tail pointer	0040:001Ch

Two of them - the **buffer start** and **buffer end** - define the buffer location in the memory. DOS sets their values while loading and does

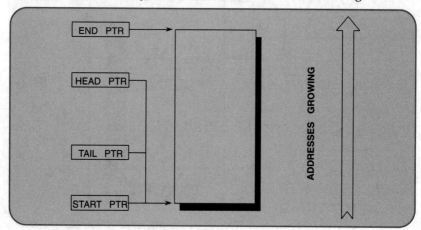

Figure 7.3
An Empty
Keyboard Buffer

not change them during the course of your work. These initial values are 1Eh for the start of the buffer, and 3Dh for the end. The other two - the **buffer head** and **buffer tail** change each time a key is pressed. The **buffer head** points to the first character to be read by the system, while the **buffer tail** points to the last character that was placed into the buffer by INT 09h. Immediately after DOS has been loaded, three pointers have the same initial value - the buffer start, the buffer head and the buffer tail. The state of all four pointers in this case is shown in Figure 7.3.

When you type the first DOS command, for example the simplest command DIR, you press four keys - "D", "I", "R" and the ENTER key. Each time you press a key, a pair of scan and ASCII codes is placed into the keyboard buffer and the buffer tail pointer is increased by two. Table 7.6 shows the contents of the keyboard buffer after this command has been entered. The state of the pointers is represented in Figure 7.4. When you press the ENTER key, the command processor reads the command text from the buffer and interprets it. Normally, a character should be read from the buffer by a program as it is placed into the keyboard buffer. If, however, you type the next character before the current character is read and the buffer tail pointer has been decreased, some characters might be lost.

The command processor clears the keyboard buffer after the command is executed by setting the head and tail pointers to the same value that points to the byte which follows the last character of the command line.

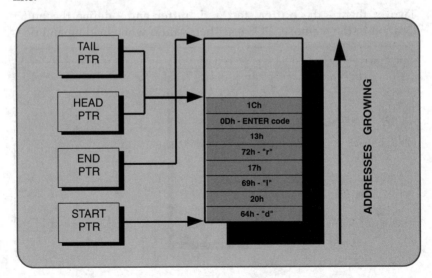

Figure 7.4
The Keyboard Buffer Containing the DIR Command

Buffer address	Code	Meaning
x+0h	64h	ASCII code for "d" key
x+1h	20h	scan code for "d" key
x+2h	69h	ASCII code for "i" key
x+3h	17h	scan code for "i" key
x+4h	72h	ASCII code for "r" key
x+5h	13h	scan code for "r" key
x+6h	0Dh	ASCII code for ENTER key
x+7h	1Ch	scan code for ENTER key

Table 7.6
Contents of Keyboard Buffer for Command "DIR "

As we have said, the default values for these pointers are set by DOS during the process of initialization: 1Eh for the start of the buffer and 3Eh for the end. These values are offsets; the full addresses are 0040:001Eh for start and 0040:003Eh for end. The buffer length is

```
3Eh - 1Eh = 20h
```

or 32 in the decimal system. This is the default location and default size for the keyboard buffer used in MS-DOS and it allows you to store approximately 15 keystrokes. Why only 15, and what's more, why only approximately? Good question!

Firstly, fifteen because two bytes are stored for each key pressed - the **scan** code and the **ASCII** code. Secondly, approximately fifteen because not each keystroke takes exactly two bytes - some keys on the enhanced keyboard generate more bytes and some keys do not produce any information for storing in the buffer. You can find out which keys on your keyboard generate codes and what these codes are, using the program ScanCode which is stored on your program disk and described later in this chapter. For example, you'll see that keys **Caps Lock**, **Num Lock** and so on, do not generate codes to be stored in the keyboard buffer.

How the Keyboard Buffer Works

The keyboard buffer is a special memory area used for storing information read from the keyboard and organized as a cyclic queue. "Queue" refers to the fact that the information is written into the buffer and read from it in FIFO (First In - First Out) order. The term "cyclic" means that when you try to write information into the byte following the last byte of the buffer, this information will in fact be written into the first byte of the buffer, which may cause you to lose some information. It's surprising, but the trouble that can be caused by this was illustrated ages ago in the story about a snake biting its own tail!

As you'll remember, the tail pointer points to the first free byte of the keyboard buffer, which is where INT 09h will place the scan and ASCII codes for the next key stroke. If the last character written to the buffer was placed at the end memory location (default 03Dh), then the tail pointer is updated to point to the start of the buffer (default 01Eh). Of course while all this has been taking place, higher level functions will have been taking characters out of the buffer from the location pointed to by the head pointer, which will be pursuing the tail pointer around the buffer. The structure of the buffer in this instance is shown in Figure 7.5.

You can see that two areas in the buffer are full - shaded in Figure 7.5 - one from the buffer head to the buffer end, the other from the buffer start to the buffer tail.

So far we have concentrated on a filled buffer, and it would be logical to assume that the buffer is empty when both its head and tail point to the start of the buffer. Although this is true, there's more to it than that. The buffer is always empty when its head pointer and its tail pointer have the same value, even when this value differs from the buffer start or buffer end. An example of an empty buffer is shown in Figure 7.6.

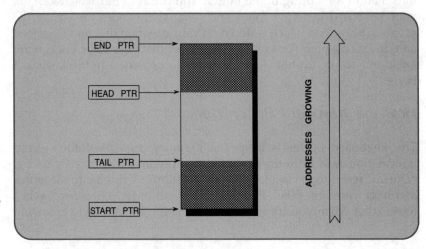

Figure 7.5
The Keyboard Buffer Partially Filled with Codes

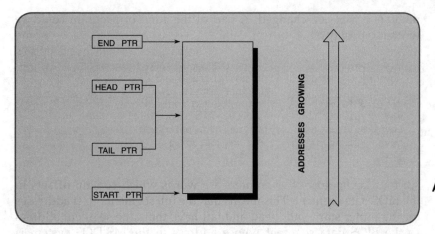

Figure 7.6
**An Example of
an Empty
Buffer**

Changing the Size and Location of the Keyboard Buffer

If there's one characteristic that children and most programmers have in common it's that when faced with something new, two thoughts immediately spring to mind - first, how does it work and second, how can they change it? Since we have satisfied your initial curiosity by explaining the basics of how the keyboard buffer works, we'd better show you how and why you can change it.

There are two important attributes of the keyboard buffer which you can change - its size and its location.

To change the location of the buffer you simply need to change the value of two words in the BIOS DATA area - the buffer start pointer at location 0040:0080h and the buffer end pointer at location 0040:0082h. It's simple, isn't it? However, there are certain rules you have to abide by when working with system resources, particularly with the keyboard buffer.

First of all, it is vital that you prevent any program from accessing the keyboard buffer while you are changing its location. If you don't do this, an application program might read the data from an area which appears to be the keyboard buffer, but in actual fact is not. This could happen if your program changes the buffer start pointer, but the other pointers (head, tail or end) retain their previous values. To prevent this happening, use the CLI instruction before you start to change the pointers and the STI instruction immediately after all the pointers have been changed. A part of this kind of program could be written as follows:

```
mov    ax,NewStart    ; AX contains new START address
mov    bx,NewEnd      ; BX contains new END address
cli                   ; No interrupt allowed
mov    BufStart,ax    ; Set new START address
mov    BufHead,ax     ; Set new HEAD pointer
mov    BufTail,ax     ; Set new TAIL pointer
mov    BufEnd,bx      ; Set new END address
sti                   ; Allow interrupts
```

All four keyboard buffer pointers are words which contain **offsets** in the BIOS data segment. This means that the full segment:offset addresses for the buffer start, end, head and tail have the same segment address as the BIOS data segment whose address in the MS-DOS system is 0040h. This means that the keyboard buffer must be located in the first physical segment of the memory - in the first 64K bytes.

To ensure that any program you write relocates the keyboard buffer correctly, take the following steps:

1. Reserve a space within the program body which will be used as a new keyboard buffer.

2. Design this program as a device driver to force DOS to load this program into the lower memory addresses, since the keyboard buffer has to be located within the first physical segment of memory.

3. Include the corresponding string for this driver in your CONFIG.SYS file.

You must not use the MS-DOS 5 or DR-DOS 6 commands for loading drivers into high memory. Rather, use the command DEVICE= instead of the MS-DOS command DEVICEHIGH or DR-DOS command HIDEVICE. Moreover, to make sure that the program is loaded within the first 64K bytes boundary, place the DEVICE= command for this program in your CONFIG.SYS file **before** the corresponding lines for any other drivers.

In this chapter we'll consider the program KbdBuf which is an example of a device driver designed in the way we have just described.

The size of the keyboard buffer is equivalent to the difference between the start and end values of the buffer. The standard size is 20h bytes (32 in decimal system). You can choose any size you like if the new keyboard buffer is located in first 64K of memory. The advantage of using a keyboard buffer which is bigger than the standard one, is that it allows you to store more keystrokes for the application program before this program actually reads them. This means that you can put long strings into the buffer either typing them ahead or using the corresponding service (for example, the function 05 of interrupt 16h).

To finish with the keyboard buffer, we would like to warn you that not all programs allow you to change the location of the keyboard buffer. If a program assumes that the keyboard buffer always starts at the address 0040:001Eh, then it is incompatible with software that changes the size and location of the keyboard buffer. However, if an application program uses the start and end addresses of the keyboard buffer which are stored in the corresponding pointers, it will always work properly with the keyboard buffer. Programs which use the default values for buffer location may fail while working together with keyboard extenders that change the size or location of the keyboard buffer.

Once the data is in the buffer, there is a choice of services for accessing it.

Altering the Hardware Interrupt 09h

The handler for interrupt 09h is the first program that is activated when you press a key on the keyboard. It accepts the scan codes from the keyboard, determines whether the key is a control key, such as Shift, Ctrl or Alt, takes the corresponding actions and places the ASCII code and scan code into the keyboard queue.

If you want to alter this process you have to write an additional handler for interrupt 09h and install it in DOS. Although interrupt 09h is a hardware interrupt, you are the one who actually causes it, since, as we said earlier, it is generated when you press or release any key on your keyboard. You can write an additional handler for this interrupt, or replace the standard handler with your own in the usual way using the DOS function Get/Set Interrupt Vector. In this chapter there is an example of a program that adds certain actions to the ones performed by a standard handler. You might ask - why would I want to change the way the keyboard functions? Well, there are three main reasons.

The first reason is that one of the best ways of writing a national keyboard driver is to write additional code for the handler of interrupt 09h. You can select a key for switching the keyboard mode (standard or national) then when interrupt 09 is activated, your handler will check whether this selected key has been pressed. If you think this is a pointless exercise, given that there are enough drivers in standard MS-DOS, just consider the millions of Japanese, Russians, Chinese and other nations who have different alphabets.

The second reason is that there are 256 characters in the ASCII character set, while even the most up to date keyboards only have 102 keys. Naturally, it would be quite useful to have characters which allow you to create tables, equations and so forth, on the keyboard. So, writing a special driver for the keyboard enables you to enter all the characters from the extended ASCII table without using the Alt key or sophisticated text processors like T_EX or ChiWriter.

The final reason is that you can activate resident pop-up programs using an additional handler for interrupt 09h to determine whether the key pressed is the hot key for a particular pop-up program.

Tools

Keyboard Basic Level - Interrupt 16h

The basic level of keyboard service is provided by the BIOS interrupt 16h. It allows you to get more information from the keyboard than the DOS interrupt 21h, but demands that you know a bit more about the codes generated by the keyboard.

The function 00h of BIOS interrupt 16h returns two values for each key pressed. One of them is the same character code (ASCII code) that is returned by interrupt 21h and the second one is a special code called a **scan code**, which is the same as the one received from the keyboard by interrupt 09h.

Unlike interrupt 21h, you need only call the BIOS interrupt 16h once, regardless of the codes it returns. You can decide whether the value returned by interrupt 16h was generated by pressing a character key such as "A", "B", "C" or by pressing a control or function key, by analyzing the scan code returned in the AL register. Special keys return a value of 0 or E0h, while character keys return a value from 0 to 127 (7Fh).

Interrupt 16h has three principal functions as well as a few additional ones that are dependant on the hardware. The basic functions are:

- Reading the scan code and ASCII code of a key.
- Checking whether there is data in the keyboard buffer.
- Getting information about special keys like Ctrl, Alt, NumLock, Shift and so on.

To call a function of interrupt 16h, place its number into the AH register and then write an **INT** instruction. The interrupt handler usually uses the same register for returning results, namely the AX register. By way of an example, we'll describe the basic functions of interrupt 16h. For more details see Appendix F.

The Function 00h - Get Character from Buffer

Register AH must contain 00h, the number of the function. When the interrupt handler has finished its work, the AH register contains the scan code and the AL register contains the ASCII code for the key you pressed. This function waits until you press any key. It is mainly used for either putting a pause in your programs, or for getting information about pressing special keys such as ESC, SysReq, ENTER and so on. Note that this function removes the character from the keyboard queue. The following example shows the simplest way of using the basic keyboard service - letting you check whether a particular key has been pressed:

```
......
        mov    ah,00       ; function 00 - read a character
        int    16h         ; BIOS keyboard service
        cmp    ah,01       ; ESC key pressed?
        jne    ContProg    ; if not, continue the program
.exit                      ; finish the program
......
```

The Function 01h - Get Keyboard Status

Register AH must contain 01h. This function checks whether there is a character ready for input. If there is, then the AX content is the same as for function 00h. If there is no character for input, the Zero Flag ZF is set. Unlike function 00h, this function does not make the program wait until a key is pressed. The following example shows a fragment of code which performs a cycle and checks whether the ESC key has just been pressed:

```
NextStep:
;......
;       The cycle body goes here
;......
        mov    ah,01       ; function 01h - check keyboard buffer
        int    16h         ; BIOS keyboard service
        jz     NextStep    ; if no key was pressed, perform next step
        cmp    ah,01       ; ESC key pressed?
        jne    NextStep    ; if not, continue the program
.exit                      ; finish the program
```

The Function 02h - Get Keyboard Flags

Register AH must contain 02h. This function returns the value of the keyboard flag in the AL register, exactly as it is stored in the BIOS data area, at location 0040:0017h. The advantage of this function is that you do not need to worry about accessing the BIOS data area. Furthermore, you will always get the correct keyboard flags values in multi-tasking environments such as the OS/2 compatibility box. Tables 7.2-7.5 give details of the bitmaps for the keyboard flags.

The Function 03h - Set Repeat Rate

This function only works on AT and PS computers. To use it you must place the value 0305h in the AX register. Then store the value for the repeat delay, from 00h to 03h, in BH, and the value for the keyboard repeat rate, from 00 to 1Fh, in BL. The smaller the value in the BH register, the shorter the delay before the code for the key you have pressed is repeated. Similarly, the smaller the value in the BL register, the "faster" your keyboard works, i.e. the higher the frequency for repeating codes of pressed keys. For example, to get the fastest keyboard with the minimum delay time, use the following instructions

```
mov    ax,0305h    ; AH - function, AL - subfunction
mov    bx,0        ; BH - delay, BL - repeat rate
int    16h         ; BIOS keyboard service call
```

Note that you can achieve the same effect using the DOS command MODE if you have MS-DOS 4 or 5, DR DOS 5 or DR DOS 6. To do this type the following command line:

```
mode con rate=32 delay=1
```

In this case the rate can be in the range 1 - 32 and the delay can have values from 1-4. If you have an enhanced keyboard, use the functions 10h, 11h and 12h instead of functions 00, 01, 02 respectively. This allows you to get scan codes for the F11, F12 and additional cursor control keys etc. When you use function 12h, you will get two bytes of extended keyboard flags in the AX register. The meaning of the bits in these flags is given in Tables 7.2 and 7.3.

The Function 05h - Push Character and Scan Code into Buffer

Register AH must contain 05h, register CH - the scan code and register CL - the ASCII code for the character to be pushed. This function allows you to emulate the pressing of keys on the keyboard. Use this function for inserting keystrokes into the input stream for application programs.

Function 05h has another potentially useful asset - it enables DOS to fulfil a command without you having to type this command on the keyboard. If your program pushes certain text followed by the scan code 1Ch and ASCII code 0Dh (this denotes the ENTER key), MS-DOS will treat this text as a command and that command will be performed after finishing your program. The following example shows a procedure for pushing one keystroke onto the keyboard buffer:

```
PushCh  proc  near pascal uses ax cx, Scan:byte, ASCII:byte
        mov   ah,05        ; Function 05h - Push scan/ASCII code
        mov   ch,Scan      ; Scan code for char to be pushed
        mov   cl,ASCII     ; ASCII code for char to be pushed
        int   16h          ; BIOS keyboard service
        ret                ; return to caller
PushCh  endp
```

The only drawback is that the standard keyboard buffer is only 32 bytes long, which is too short for using relatively complex commands in the way described above. Don't despair though, in this chapter we'll give you a program that increases the size of standard BIOS keyboard buffers.

The High-Level Keyboard Service - Interrupt 21h

Interrupt 21h provides the high-level keyboard service, which is also called the logical level service. It performs two main tasks, reading both strings and characters. When you read a string, the memory contains exactly the same image of the string as it appears on the screen. This means that when you're typing a string, you can use the same special keys for line editing as for typing DOS command lines - they will not appear as the relevant ASCII codes.

The DOS interrupt 21h also includes functions for reading keystrokes. These functions allow you to read the information generated by pressing special keys such as function keys, cursor control keys or ENTER. You can also read composite keystrokes - codes created by pressing a character or control key together with a special key such as Shift, Ctrl or Alt.

If you are using high-level languages such as Pascal or C you will be familiar with standard keyboard input procedures. Take the Pascal function ReadKey for example; it returns the ASCII code for a key you press on the keyboard. However, sometimes this code is equal to 0, which means that the key you have pressed is a special key such as a function key, control key or ENTER. In this case you must call the ReadKey function once again, then take the code that it returns as the code for a special key.

For example, if the ReadKey function returns the code 59 this corresponds to the character ";" (semicolon). However, if the first call returns 0 and the second - the code 59, it corresponds to the F1 functional key. This is exactly what one of the functions of interrupt 21h does. In fact, this function calls function 00h of the BIOS interrupt 16h (10h for an enhanced keyboard) and returns the ASCII code of the key pressed. If this code is 0, an internal indicator within the handler of interrupt 21h is set and the next call of the same function will return the scan code of the special key pressed.

An input function like Read or ReadLn in Pascal reads the text string from the keyboard character by character until you press the ENTER key. Note that the string passed to your program does not contain the code for the ENTER key itself. This is another function of interrupt 21h.

You can also use the interrupt 21h function 3Fh which is called "Read File or Device" or "Read with Handles", for reading data from the keyboard. This is the highest keyboard level that DOS provides for users. You can use this function to gain access to any file that can be used for reading data, including the keyboard. Which file is used depends on the value of the handle stored as one 16-bit word. If you want to use the keyboard in particular, you must specify handle 0, which is the pre-defined value for the keyboard.

In order for the function to work even in situations where the standard input stream is redirected, i.e. when the disk file or another device is used instead of the standard console, use it together with function 3Dh of interrupt 21h - the function "Open". You must specify the ASCIIZ-string "CON" as a file name. This can be done with the help of the DB assembler directive as follows:

```
Fname db 'CON' , 0
```

On exit this function returns a value for the handle that can (and should) be passed to the function 3Fh call. Note that functions 3Fh and 3Dh are only available in DOS versions 2.0 and above.

Broadly speaking, the keyboard functions of INT 21h allow your assembler programs to deal with keyboard input like a high-level language. For more detailed information on interrupt 21h, see Appendix G1.

Below, we have given a brief description of the keyboard functions which are supported by the DOS interrupt 21h. To use each of them you must place its number into the AH register (this rule is common to BIOS and DOS services) and then call the interrupt 21h.

The Function 01h - Direct Character Input

On return , the handler puts the character read into AL. If AL contains 0, it means that a special key was pressed and you must call this function once more. This second call will return the scan code for the special key that was pressed. For example, the piece of code for reading the symbol might be as follows:

```
          mov   IndSpec,0    ; Set an indicator "Character Key"
          mov   ah,01h       ; Function 01h - Read the character
  Accept: int   21h          ; DOS service call to get ASCII code
          cmp   al,0          ; Is the key you pressed a special key?
          jne   CharKey       ; If not, continue process
          mov   IndSpec,1    ; Set an indicator "Special Key"
          int   21h          ; Dos service call to get the scam code
  CharKey:                    ; Now character code/scan code is in AL
  ...
  IndSpec db    0            ; Key indicator (1 if special key)
```

This function supports the redirection of input/output, so in fact it not only reads characters from the keyboard, but also from the system input device as well. Similarly, it echoes the character not only to screen, but also to the system output device.

You might find this feature useful for writing programs that will run on any hardware. For example, you can create a file that contains data for the program and redirect input and output so that the program will read the input data from one file and write the results in the other file. Such a program can be run as a background process if your operating system allows this. At the moment these features are present in OS/2 and some DOS extensions (For example in DesqView and Windows).

The function 01h recognizes the special key combinations such as Ctrl-C, Ctrl-Break and Ctrl-Alt-Del and takes the corresponding actions.

The Function 06h - Direct Console I/O

This function can be used to either output or input characters, depending on the value in the DL register. To use the function 06h for input put the value 0FFh into the register DL. The function returns results in the Zero Flag ZF and in the AL register. If ZF is set, it means that the function hasn't received a character , because there are no characters ready for input in the keyboard buffer or on the system input device.

Like the function 01h, the function 06h also supports input/output redirection. If ZF is clear on return from this function, it works exactly as the function 01h. Note that this function does not recognize Ctrl-C and Ctrl-Break key combinations.

The following example uses the DOS function 06h for reading a character from an input device (the keyboard, unless it has been redirected) and then outputting it onto an output device (normally the screen):

```
......
          mov    ah,06       ; function 06 - direct console I/O
          mov    dl,0FFh     ; subfunction 0FFh - read character
          int    21h         ; DOS service call
          jz     NotReady    ; jump if no character ready for input
          cmp    al,0        ; special key pressed?
          jne    ProcSym     ; if not, process character read
          int    21h         ; call INT 21h again to get ASCII code
ProcSym:  mov    dl,al       ; character read into AL
          int    21h         ; output character in DL
......
NotReady:
;      process situation "no character ready for input"
```

The Function 07h - Direct Character Input Without Echo

This function works exactly as the function 01h except that it does not pass the symbol that has just been read to the system output device. While working without the I/O redirection this means that the character corresponding to the key you have pressed on keyboard will not appear on the screen. The Ctrl-C and Ctrl-Break key combinations are not recognized. The following example shows how to use this function for inputting characters:

```
          mov    ah,07     ; function 07 - direct console input
          int    21h       ; DOS service call
;         character read is now in AL
```

The Function 08h - Character Input Without Echo

This works exactly like function 07h except that the CTRL-C and Ctrl-Break combination are recognized and the corresponding actions are taken. This means that if you press the Ctrl-C keys when typing input data, your program will be broken and the handler of interrupt 23h will gain control. Normally, the standard handler aborts the user program and returns control to DOS. However, you can intercept interrupt 23h and perform another action, for example you can ignore the Ctrl-C keystroke and continue your program.

The Function 0Ah - Buffered Input

This function reads a character string from the system input device. On entry, the registers DS:DX must contain the segment:offset address of the buffer. Remember this is nothing to do with the keyboard buffer in the BIOS data area - it is a block of memory reserved by your program to store the input string. The first byte of the buffer must contain the maximum length of string that can be read. On return, the second byte will contain the current length of the string. The bytes from 3 up to the end of the buffer contain the string itself. Figure 7.7 shows the content of the buffer employed for reading data using the DOS service 0Ah.

Note that if you are planning, for example, to deal with strings up to 128 bytes long, you have to reserve 130 bytes for the buffer. This function works like text input procedures in high-level languages, such as READ procedure in Pascal.

Another thing to remember is that the special keys need two bytes in the buffer - the first byte is 0 and the second is the scan code. The following example shows how to read a text string using the DOS service 0Ah:

```
......
ReqInp   db    255
FactInp  db    0
Str1     db    256 dup ('$')
......
;=== Input text string (DOS service)
         mov   ah,0Ah       ; function 0Ah - input text string
         lea   dx,ReqInp    ; DS:DX - address of input buffer
         int   21h          ; DOS service call
......
```

The variable ReqInp contains the maximum length for an input string. Once the function has been performed, DOS places the actual length of the string into the variable FactInp. The label Str1 marks the start of the memory area where the text of the string itself will be placed. All this is made obvious in the Library section, where we have included an example of a program that reads data from the keyboard using both BIOS and DOS services.

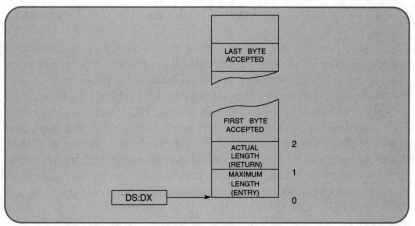

Figure 7.7
**The Buffered
Input - The
Structure of the
Buffer**

The Function 3Fh - Read File or Device

This function reads the portion of data from the destination specified by the file logical number (**handle**) passed through the BX register. On entry, the registers DS:DX must contain the segment:offset of the buffer for data and the CX register must contain the number of bytes to be read. If the function is successful, it returns the actual number of bytes read in the AX register, otherwise AX contains the error code. The Carry Flag CF determines the result of the function call - it is set if there was an error, otherwise it is clear. The next example shows using the DOS function 3Fh for reading data from the standard input device. By default (if not redirected) standard input corresponds to the keyboard.

```
.data
......
StrBuf      db    32767 dup (?) ; Buffer for string to be read
StrBufE     label byte
......
.code
......
    mov    cx,StrBufE-StrBuf ; Max number of symbols to be read
    mov    ah,3Fh            ; Function 3Fh - Read File or Device
    lea    dx,StrBuf         ; DS:DX point to String Buffer
    int    21h               ; DOS service call
```

Using this service makes your programs more flexible because the input performed by function 3Fh can be easily redirected for reading data from any files, without changing the program. You can see this for yourself in the program GetStr.

Using the Hardware Ports for Accessing the Keyboard

The lowest possible level of accessing the keyboard is manipulating
the hardware port directly. Although this is the most powerful way,
it is the most dangerous, too. We have included a program that uses
the hardware ports for reading data from the keyboard, but we'd like
to warn you that it is much safer to use the BIOS and DOS functions
until you are ready to create your own handler for the keyboard
interrupt 09h, using it instead of the standard one. Having said that,
this technique will have an immediate use, albeit limited, for accepting
single keystrokes in resident applications. Later on in the book we'll
give an example of such an application which turns off the screen if
the keyboard is idle for some time, then restores it when you press
any key.

We'll start with a basic guide to using the keyboard ports. The scan
code can be read from port 60h using the IN instruction:

```
in    al,60h            ; read the scan code
```

That's hardly complicated, is it? However, this is only the very
beginning. We must now calculate the ASCII code of the key pressed,
put this code into the keyboard buffer, modify the keyboard buffer
pointer, and, finally, reset the keyboard to allow the next keystrokes
to be accepted and send the signal (End Of Interrupt) to a special chip
called PIC (Programmable Interrupt Controller).

Since this technique is usually only used in applications for detecting
single keystrokes, we'll concentrate on the last two operations. The
task of resetting the keyboard is performed by:

Reading the content of port 20h
Setting the 7th bit of this value to 1
Sending the changed value back to the port
Waiting
Sending the original value to port 20h.

The following example shows the piece of code that performs these steps:

```
in    al,20h    ; read current value of port 20h
or    al,80h    ; set 7th bit to 1
jmp   $+2       ; delay (on fast Pcs can be repeated)
out   al,20h    ; send value with 7th bit set to port 20h
and   al,7Fh    ; clear 7th bit
jmp   $+2       ; delay (on fast PCs can be repeated)
out   al,20h    ; send value with 7th bit clear to port 20h
```

Notice that the instruction

```
jmp   $+2
```

is used, which delays the program. This might be necessary because hardware needs some time to prepare for performing the next I/O operation.

Generating the EOI signal is quite simple - just send the value 20h to port 20h as shown below:

```
mov   al,20h    ; code 20h - End Of Interrupt
out   20h,al    ; send  to port 20h
```

Library

InpStr - Input Text Strings

In this chapter we discussed the BIOS and DOS services intended for reading data from the keyboard. The program InpStr given in Listing 7.1 illustrates using the character-oriented BIOS service (function 00h of interrupt 16h) and the string-oriented DOS service (function 0Ah of interrupt 21h).

```
 1
 2 .model small
 3 .stack
 4 .data
 5 CR       equ  0Dh
 6 LF       equ  0Ah
 7 Msg16    db   CR,LF, 'BIOS service:Type a string and press ENTER:'
 8          db   CR,LF,'$'
 9 Msg21    db   CR,LF, 'DOS service :Type a string and press ENTER:'
10          db   CR,LF,'$'
11 MsgOut   db   'The following text entered: ' ,'$'
12 ReqInp   db   255
13 FactInp  db   0
14 Str1     db   256 dup ('$')
15 .code
16 .startup
17 ;===    Output message about BIOS service
18          mov ah,09          ; function 09 - output text string
19          lea dx,Msg16       ; address of message 'BIOS service'
20          int 21h            ; DOS service call
21 ;===    Creating string from characters (BIOS service)
22          mov bx,0           ; BX - number of current character
23 Next16: mov ah,0            ; function 00h - read character
24          int 16h            ; BIOS keyboard service
25          cmp al,0           ; special key?
26          je  Next16         ; ignore special key and read next
27          mov Str1[bx],al    ; store current character into string
28          inc bx             ; increase counter to store next char
29          cmp al,CR          ; ENTER key pressed(Carriage Return)?
30          jne Next16         ; if not, read next character
31 ;===    Append characters CR and LF to the end of the string
32          mov Str1[bx],LF    ; add Line Feed to the end of string
33          mov Str1[bx+1],'$' ; End Message character
34 ;===    Output header and string entered
35          mov ah,09          ; function 09 - output text string
36          lea dx,MsgOut      ; address of message 'Text entered'
37          int 21h            ; DOS service call
38          lea dx,Str1        ; address of string obtained
39          int 21h            ; DOS service call
40 ;===    Output message about DOS service
41          mov ah,09          ; function 09 - output text string
```

```
42          leadx,Msg21        ; address of message 'BIOS service'
43          int21h             ; DOS service call
44  ;=== Input text string (DOS service)
45          mov  ah,0Ah        ; function 0Ah - input text string
46          lea  dx,ReqInp     ; DS:DX - address of input buffer
47          int  21h           ; DOS service call
48  ;=== Append characters CR and LF to the end of the string
49          mov  bl,FactInp    ; length of string actually read
50          mov  bh,0          ; high byte of length =0(length < 256)
51          mov  Str1[bx],CR   ; Append Carriage Return
52          mov  Str1[bx+1],LF ; Append Line Feed
53          mov  Str1[bx+2],'$' ; Append End of Message
54  ;=== Output header and string entered
55          mov  ah,09         ; function 09 - output text string
56          lea  dx,MsgOut     ; address of message 'Text entered'
57          int  21h           ; DOS service call
58          lea  dx,Str1       ; address of string obtained
59          int  21h           ; DOS service call
60  .exit
61  end
```

Listing 7.1 InpStr - Using BIOS and DOS Services for String Input

The program starts by outputting a message about the service used.

The next block of the program reads the text input from the keyboard, character by character, using the BIOS service - function 0 of interrupt 16. The character returned by this function in the AL register is then checked to determine whether it is 0 (denoting a special key) or the Carriage Return (the Enter key). The program ignores special keys such as cursor control keys or functional keys and treats the Enter key as the end of the string.

If the character accepted is neither a special keystroke nor Enter, it is placed into the memory and the character counter is increased by 1. Note that the DI register is used as the counter for characters that have been accepted. When the Carriage Return symbol is accepted, the DI register contains the length of the string. The program then adds the Line Feed and "$" characters to the end of the string, then outputs it using the corresponding DOS service. Note that when you type a string on the keyboard, the characters do not appear on the screen and the cursor location is not changed.

The next block of the program outputs the message "DOS service" and reads the string using function 0A of interrupt 21h. This string is then output in the same as way the previous block, using the DOS service 09h. Note that in this instance, all characters appear on the screen when you press the corresponding key and you can use the control keys for editing the input string.

This program can also be used for demonstrating another DOS feature - input redirection. Start the program InpStr again and type the redirection symbol "<" and the name of file you wish to use at the command line. This file will then be used instead of the keyboard for inputting data. For example, the following command line will start the program InpStr and redirect its input to the file C:\CONFIG.SYS:

```
InpStr < C:\CONFIG.SYS
```

As you can see, although the input process performed by the BIOS service works exactly as before, the block which uses the DOS service does not wait for the keyboard input. Instead, it reads the first line of your CONFIG.SYS file and outputs it to the screen.

The Program GetStr - Using File-oriented Service for Reading Texts

The program Getstr given in Listing 7.2 shows how to use the file-oriented DOS service (the function 3Fh - Read File with Handle).

```
1
2          page 55,132
3  .model    small
4  .stack
5  .data
6  OutStr  db      0Dh,0Dh,'<<<=== The text read: ===>>>',0Dh,0Ah
7  StrBuf  db      32767 dup (?) ; Buffer for string to be read
8  StrBufE  label byte
9  .code
10 .startup
11 IsOpen: mov    bx,ax          ; Store handle code into BX
12         mov    cx,StrBufE-StrBuf; Max number of symbols to read
13 GetNext:mov    ah,3Fh         ; Function 3Fh - Read File or Device
14         lea    dx,StrBuf      ; DS:DX point to String Buffer
15         int    21h            ; DOS service call
16         jnc    TstStr         ; If NO CARRY - string is read
17         mov    al,ah          ; Set ErrorLevel to Read Error Code
18         jmp    ExProg         ; Exit the program
19 TstStr: cmp    ax,3           ; any characters apart CR,LF?
20         jb     Compl          ; If not, terminates the work
21         mov    di,ax          ; DI points at the end of text read
22         mov    StrBuf[di],'$';Append Message End for service 09h
23         lea    dx,OutStr      ; DS:DX - address of text to be outpu
24         mov    ah,09          ; function 09h - output text string
25         int    21h            ; DOS service call
```

```
26           jmp    GetNext      ; Read next string
27 Compl: mov    al,0         ; Set ErrorLevel to 0
28 ExProg: mov    ah,4Ch       ; Function 4Ch - terminate process
29           int    21h          ; DOS service call
30           end
```

Listing 7.2 GetStr - Using File-Oriented Service for String Input

This program uses the DOS service "Read File with Handle" (the function 3Fh of the interrupt 21h) for reading data. The value of the file handle is 0, which corresponds to the standard input (usually the keyboard). Although this program is not that different from the program InpStr discussed above, we want to draw your attention to certain peculiarities in the service used.

The main difference is that the service 3Fh allows you to read large files consisting of several strings as one portion of data, while the service 0Ah treats the first Carriage Return symbol as the end of data. You can only uncover this difference when the input is redirected, or a non-zero value of the file handle is used. When dealing with the keyboard, both services work in the same way.

ScanCode - Program for Watching Keyboard Scan Codes

The ScanCode program is designed to examine how interrupt 09h works. This program shows you the contents of port A of PIC (the keyboard port) upon entry into the handler of interrupt 09. It also determines and shows the type of keyboard you're using. The full assembler text for ScanCode is given in Listing 7.3. The source code and the executable module for this program are on your program disk as files **scancode.asm** and **scancode.exe**, respectively.

Start the program and press and release any key, for example the key "Q". The codes 10h and 90h will appear on screen. These are the scan codes for pressing and releasing this key respectively. Note that all the codes are given in hexadecimal form although the letter h isn't present. Press the key again and hold it for some time. A sequence of the code 10h will appear on the screen. This represents the scan code for autorepeating. The autorepeating code is usually the same as the scan code for pressing the key. Now release this key and the sequence will finish with the code 90h.

Let's see how the special keys work. We'll start with the cursor control keys. Press and release the key "Up Arrow". If you have an enhanced keyboard, use the key on the numeric pad. You'll see the codes 48 C8 where 48h is the scan code for pressing this key and 0C8h is the scan code for releasing it. If you have an enhanced keyboard, now press and release the key "Up Arrow" located between the keys "Right Shift" and "1" on the numeric pad. If you have a standard keyboard you'll just have to believe us on this one, or ask a friend with an enhanced one. You will see four codes - E0 48 E0 C8. The scan code for pressing this key on an enhanced keyboard is E0h 48h (two bytes) and the scan code for releasing the key is E0h C8h (also two bytes).

In this way you can examine any key on your keyboard except the ESC key. We have reserved this key as a signal for finishing the program so the program only shows the scan code for **pressing** the ESC key and then de-installs the additional handler for interrupt 09h. The following part of the program performs this task:

```
cmp   ah,EscScan    ; Is the ESC key pressed?
jne   NextKey       ; If not - process the next key
```

If you want to treat the ESC key like all the other keys, either replace EscScan with the value you want, for example 10h (the "Q" key) or simply replace these two lines with the following:

```
jmp   NextKey
```

Note that in the last case the only way to exit this program is to perform the RESET operation on your computer.

```
1
2            page 55,132
3  .model  small
4  .stack  512
5  .data
6  CR       equ  0Dh   ; The Carriage return code
7  LF       equ  0Ah   ; The Line feed code
8  TAB      equ  09h   ; The TAB code
9  BELL     equ  07h   ; The BELL code
10 EscScan  equ  01h   ; The Scan code for ESC key
11 KbdPort  equ  60h   ; PPI 9225 port A
12 EndMsg   equ  24h   ; Dollar sign-end of message for DOS service
13 NewHand  dd   NewInt9 ; Reference to the new handler for int 09
14 FuncN    db   0     ; Function number for interrupt 16h
15 BegMsg   db   CR,LF,LF,BELL,TAB, 'SCAN CODES BROWSER'
16          db   '(INT 09h) Version 2.0 19.05.1992'
17          db   CR,LF,TAB
18          db   ' Copyright (C) 1992, V.B.Maljugin, Russia,Voronezh'
```

```
19          db    CR,LF,EndMsg
20 Kbd83    db    CR,LF,TAB,TAB, '83-key keyboard in use',EndMsg
21 Kbd101   db    CR,LF,TAB,TAB,'Enhanced 101/102 keyboard',EndMsg
22 InsMsg   db    CR,LF,CR,LF,TAB
23          db    'Additional handler for int 09h will be called'
24          db    CR,LF,TAB,' through the function '
25 TFuncN   dw    '00'   ; Text representation for FuncN
26          db    'h of BIOS interrupt 16h.'
27          db    CR,LF,TAB,TAB,'Codes above 0F9h ignored.',CR,LF
28          db    CR,LF,TAB,'Press ESC to exit or any other key to '
29          db    'determine its scan code',CR,LF,LF,EndMsg
30 FinMsg   db    CR,LF,LF,BELL,TAB,TAB
31          db    'SCAN CODES BROWSER - End of job.'
32          db    CR,LF,EndMsg
33 .code
34
35 OldDS    dw    ?
36 LinePos  db    0
37 Before9  db    0
38 Con16    db    16
39 OutByte  db    'xx ',EndMsg
40 CrLf     db    CR,LF,EndMsg
41 HexTab   db    '0','1','2','3','4','5','6','7'
42          db    '8','9','A','B','C','D','E','F'
43
44 NewInt9 proc far          ; Additional handler for INT 9
45          push ax
46          push bx
47          push dx
48          push ds
49          in   al,KbdPort   ; Read scan code from keyboard port
50          push ax           ; Push this SCAN CODE for processing
51          pushf             ; This is needed for interrupt call
52          db   9Ah          ; OpCode for FAR CALL
53 Off9     dw   ?            ; Offset address for standard handler
54 Seg9     dw   ?            ; Segment address for standard handler
55          pop  ax           ; AL contains the scan code
56          cli               ; to avoid keyboard buffer overflow
57 ;        in   al,KbdPort   ; Read scan code from keyboard port
58          mov  ah,0         ; AX now in range 0 - 255
59          cmp  al,0FAh
60          jb   ProcScan
61          jmp  NotShow
62 ProcScan:
63          div  Con16        ; AL - first hex digit, AH - second
64          mov  bh,0         ; Clear high part of BX
65          push cs           ; After this CS and DS are equal to
66          pop  ds           ;   address internal area of handler
67          mov  bl,al        ; Take the first hex digit
68          mov  al,HexTab[bx] ; Take the corresponding character
69          mov  OutByte[0],al ; Place it into output string
70          mov  bl,ah        ; Take the second hex digit
71          mov  al,HexTab[bx] ; Take the corresponding character
72          mov  OutByte[1],al ; Place it into output string
```

```
 73        lea  dx,cs:OutByte   ; Address of scan code text into DX
 74        mov  ah,09           ; Function 09h - output text string
 75        int  21h             ; Dos service call
 76        inc  LinePos         ; Increase counter of bytes output
 77        cmp  LinePos,24      ; 24 code per line are valid
 78        jb   NotSkip         ; If less than 24, don't skip line
 79        mov  LinePos,0       ; Clear counter of codes in line
 80        lea  dx,CrLf         ; Address of LineFeed code into DX
 81        int  21h             ; Dos service call
 82 NotSkip:
 83 NotShow:
 84        pop  ds
 85        pop  dx
 86        pop  bx
 87        pop  ax
 88        iret
 89 NewInt9 endp
 90 .startup
 91
 92        mov  OldDS,ds
 93        lea  dx,BegMsg       ; Address of start message into DX
 94        mov  ah,09           ; Function 09h - output text string
 95        int  21h             ; Dos service call
 96
 97        mov  ax,40h          ; 40h - segment address for BIOS area
 98        mov  es,ax           ; Place this address into ES
 99        test byte ptr es:[96h],10h; Bit 4 for 101/102 keys
100        jnz  Pres101         ; If enhanced keyboard is present
101        lea  dx,Kbd83        ; Address of message into DX
102        mov  ah,09           ; Function 09h - output text string
103        int  21h             ; Dos service call
104        jmp  PrtInstr        ; To print the initial message
105
106 Pres101:
107        lea  dx,Kbd101       ; Address of start message into DX
108        mov  ah,09           ; Function 09h - output text string
109        int  21h             ; Dos service call
110        mov  FuncN,10h       ; 10h - Read From Enhanced Keyboard
111        mov  TFuncN,'01'     ; Text '01' because TFuncN is a word!
112
113 PrtInstr:
114        lea  dx,InsMsg       ; Address of message into DX
115        mov  ah,09           ; Function 09h - output text string
116        int  21h             ; Dos service call
117
118        mov  ah,35h          ; Function 35h - Get interrupt vector
119        mov  al,09h          ; Interrupt number is 09h
120        int  21h             ; DOS service call
121        mov  Off9,bx         ; Save offset address of old handler
122        mov  Seg9,es         ; Save segment address of old handler
123        lds  dx,NewHand      ; DS:DX - full address of new handler
124        mov  ah,25h          ; Function 25h - set interrupt vector
125        int  21h             ; DOS service call
126        mov  ds,OldDS
```

```
127
128 NextKey:
129     mov ah,0            ; Function 00h - read character
130     int 16h             ; BIOS keyboard service
131     cmp ah,EscScan       ; Is the ESC key pressed?
132     jne NextKey          ; If not - process the next key
133
134 Finis:
135     mov dx,Off9          ; Offset address for old handler
136     mov ds,Seg9          ; Segment address for old handler
137     mov ax,2509h         ; Set interrupt vector for INT 9
138     int 21h             ; DOS service call
139
140     mov ah,0Ch           ; Function 0Ch - clear keyboard buffer
141     int 21h             ; Dos service call
142
143     mov ds,OldDS
144     lea dx,FinMsg        ; Address of message into DX
145     mov ah,09            ; Function 09h - output text string
146     int 21h             ; Dos service call
147
148     mov ax,4C00h         ; Function 4Ch - terminate process
149     int 21h             ; DOS service call
150
151     end
```

Listing 7.3 Program ScanCode - Examining the Scan Codes

After loading, ScanCode determines the type of keyboard installed, using information from the BIOS data area, then outputs a message. It then sets a new handler for the keyboard interrupt 09h and reads data from the keyboard using the BIOS interrupt 16h. The new handler of interrupt 09h reads the scan code from port 60h, outputs it to the screen and passes control to the standard handler. When the scan code corresponding to the ESC key is detected, the program stops work.

Keyboard Control - Set Repeat Rate and Delay

The program SetKbd uses function 03h of the BIOS interrupt 16h to set new values for the repeat rate and delay time. This function only works on AT and PS computers and has the same effect as the DOS command

```
MODE CON RATE=x DELAY=Y
```

in MS-DOS versions 4.x and 5.x and DR-DOS versions 5 and 6. You can use this program to make your keyboard "faster" if you have an AT-compatible or PS computer and DOS version earlier than 4.0.

```
 1
 2 .model tiny
 3 .code
 4   mov   ax,0305h      ; AH - function 03, AL - subfunction 05
 5   mov   bx,0          ; BH - delay (0 - 3 , 0 for smallest)
 6                       ; BL - rate (0 - 1Fh , 0 for fastest)
 7   int   16h           ; BIOS interrupt - keyboard service
 8   mov   ax,4C00h      ; 4C - terminate process, 00 - return code
 9   int   21h           ; DOS service call
10   end
```

Listing 7.4 SetKbd - Set Keyboard Repeat Rate and Delay Time

You can use this technique to change the keyboard parameters from within your application programs. For example, it might be useful to "slow down" the keyboard when your program demands important information like a password or a request to delete the master file of a database and "speed up" processing for ordinary text input.

The speed of autorepeating, and the value of the delay before starting to generate autorepeat codes, depends on the value that is sent to the BX register. In program texts, the values for the speed of autorepeating and the delay before starting the autorepeat are given as "speed" and "rate", respectively.

PushKbd - Push Key Codes onto Keyboard Buffer

Function 05h of interrupt 16h - "Push scan/ASCII code" is used to imitate keystrokes from within application programs. A sample of this type of program is given in Listing 7.5. It represents a simple program that pushes the text of the DOS command DIR onto the keyboard buffer.

DOS automatically interprets the command line contained in the keyboard buffer after the program has finished. Note that the codes that the program pushes onto the keyboard buffer last are codes for the ENTER key since DOS commands must be finished by pressing the ENTER key.

```
 1
 2 page 55,132
 3 .model  small
 4 .stack
 5 .data
 6 .code
 7 .startup
```

```
 8    mov  cx,10
 9 Lp:
10    push cx
11    mov  ah,05    ; Function 05h - Push scan/ASCII code
12    mov  ch,20h   ; Scan code for key "D"
13    mov  cl,'d'   ; ASCII code for key "D"
14    int  16h      ; BIOS keyboard service
15
16    mov  ah,05    ; Function 05h - Push scan/ASCII code
17    mov  ch,17h   ; Scan code for key "I"
18    mov  cl,'i'   ; ASCII code for key "I"
19    int  16h      ; BIOS keyboard service
20
21    mov  ah,05    ; Function 05h - Push scan/ASCII code
22    mov  ch,13h   ; Scan code for key "R"
23    mov  cl,'r'   ; ASCII code for key "R"
24    int  16h      ; BIOS keyboard service
25
26    mov  ah,05    ; Function 05h - Push scan/ASCII code
27    mov  ch,1Ch   ; Scan code for ENTER key
28    mov  cl,13    ; ASCII code for ENTER key
29    int  16h      ; BIOS keyboard service
30    pop  cx
31    loop lp
32
33 Finish:
34    mov  ax,4C00h ; Function 4Ch - terminate process
35    int  21h      ; DOS service call
36    end
```

Listing 7.5 PushKbd - Pushing Keystrokes into Keyboard Buffer

This facility is particularly useful for executing DOS commands from within user programs. For example, take a program that deals with data files. It seems easier to call the DOS command BACKUP or other programs for saving data, using the Push Codes function, than to organize an interface for such a program using the standard tools included in the program language you are using. After all, not all languages have standard tools for this purpose! However, when using this feature in your programs, it is important to remember that DOS reads and interprets the content of the keyboard buffer only after your program has finished.

Unfortunately, the design of standard keyboard buffers only allows you to store 15 keystrokes. This is another good reason for using keyboard buffer extenders.

An Example of Clipper Functions for Controlling the Keyboard

We have already shown how you can control the keyboard state, for example the NumLock state. The program KeybServ is a set of UDF (User Defined Functions) intended for accessing the keyboard and can be used in programs written in Clipper. We have chosen this compiler for two reasons - firstly, it is a favorite tool among programmers and secondly, the standard Clipper library does not contain functions for controlling the hardware.

The full assembler text of KeybServ is given in Listing 7.6. Note that these functions use the macro library EXTENDA.INC that comes with Clipper Summer 87 and is especially designed for MASM 5.0 so you can not use it with MASM 6.0. (It may seem strange, but even the option M510 that makes MASM 6.0 compatible with MASM 5.0, won't help you out here!) However, Appendix H shows you how to make macros stored in the EXTENDA.INC file work with MASM versions 6.0 and higher.

The function IsKbdEnh is designed as a Clipper function that returns the logical value TRUE if your keyboard is an 101/102 enhanced keyboard and FALSE if you have the standard 83-keys keyboard. This function checks bit 4 of the byte at location 0040:0096 by comparing that byte with the hexadecimal constant 10h. Remember, this bit denotes an enhanced keyboard.

The function GNumLock returns the current NumLock state as a logical value. The value returned by the GNumLock function is equal to TRUE if the NumLock state is turned on otherwise this value is equal to FALSE. This function has no parameters so you can call it from a Clipper program as follows:

```
IndState = False

. . .

IndState = GNumLock()
```

where IndState is a logical variable. Note that the first line in this example is in fact a definition of the variable IndState because Clipper does not have tools for explicitly defining variables.

The function SNumLock turns the NumLock either on or off, depending on the parameter. This parameter must be an integer constant or variable. If the parameter is equal to 1, the function SnumLock will turn the NumLock state on, otherwise the NumLock state will be switched off. The value returned by the function SnumLock corresponds to the state of the NumLock flag once it has been switched by this function. The following example shows how to turn the NumLock state on:

```
SNumLock(1)
```

The functions GCapsLock and SCapsLock work in the same way as the functions GNumLock and SNumLock but they deal with the CapsLock state. For example, to get the current status of the CapsLock state you can use the following Clipper statement:

```
IndState = GCapslock
```

The following statement turns the CapsLock off:

```
SCapsLock(0)
```

Note that on standard 83-key keyboards and on enhanced keyboards connected to a PC or PC/XT, the functions SNumLock and SCapsLock do not affect the corresponding light indicators.

There are two ways you can include KeybServ in your Clipper programs, either by adding a corresponding object module while linking the program, or by creating an additional library which contains this object module. Your program disk contains the library ClippAdd.lib and object module KeybServ.Obj. You can run the demo program ClipDemo.prg from your program disk in either of these ways.

```
 1
 2          page 55,132
 3          NAME KeybServ
 4          INCLUDE EXTENDA.INC
 5  BiosDat segment at 40h
 6          org     17h
 7  KbdFl1  db      ?
 8  KbdFl2  db      ?
 9          org     96h
10  KbdFl3  db      ?
11  BiosDat ends
12
13          CODESEG KeybServ
14          DATASEG
15
16  CLpublic <IsKbdEnh, GnumLock, Gcapslock, Snumlock, Scapslock>
17  CLstatic
```

```
18
19 $define FALSE 0000h
20 $define TRUE  0001h
21 KbdRDF   db    00h     ; Read Character function number
22 KbdGSF   db    01h     ; Get Status function number
23 KbdGFF   db    02h     ; Get Flag function number
24 IndEnh   db    0
25 CNumL    equ   20h
26 CCapL    equ   40h
27
28 WORKFUNCS
29
30 ChecKbd  proc near
31 ;
32 ; This procedure checks if an enhanced keyboard is being used.
33 ; All registers are preserved after returning from the procedure.
34 ; Result: The variable IndEnh (byte) is non-zero.
35 ;
36       push    es              ; Save the segment register
37       push    ax              ; Save the accumulator register
38       mov     ax,BiosDat      ; Address of BIOS data segment
39       mov     es,ax           ; Now ES points to the BIOS data
40       mov     al,es:KbdFl3    ; Take the KEYBOARD FLAG 3([0496h])
41       mov     IndEnh,al       ; Store it into the memory
42       and     IndEnh,10h      ; Bit 5 - sign of enhanced keyboard
43       pop     ax              ; Restore the accumulator
44       pop     es              ; Restore the segment register
45       ret                     ; Return to the caller
46 ChecKbd endp
47
48 GetFl12 proc near
49 ;
50 ; This procedure extracts the keyboard flags 1 and 2
51 ; (bytes 0040:0017h and 0040:0018hh) from the BIOS data area and
52 ; puts them into AX register (AH - flag 1 , AL - flag 2).
53 ; All registers except  AX register are preserved after returning
54 ; from the procedure.
55 ;
56       push es            ; Save the segment register
57       mov ax,BiosDat     ; Address of BIOS data segment
58       mov es,ax          ; Now ES points to the BIOS data
59       mov ah,es:KbdFl1   ; Take  KEYBOARD FLAG 1 ([00040:0017h])
60       mov al,es:KbdFl2   ; Take KEYBOARD FLAG 2 ([00040:0018hh])
61       pop es             ; Restore the segment register
62       ret                ; Return to the caller
63 GetFl12 endp
64
65 PutFl12 proc near
66 ;
67 ; This procedure writes the values from the AX register
68 ; (AH - flag 1, AL - flag 2) into the keyboard flags 1 and 2
69 ; ( bytes 0040:0017h and 0040:0018hh) in the BIOS data area.
70 ; All registers preserved after returning from this procedure.
71 ;
72       push es                 ; Save the segment register
```

```
73            push   ax              ; Save the work register
74            mov    ax,BiosDat      ; Address of BIOS data segment
75            mov    es,ax           ; Now ES points to the BIOS data
76            pop    ax              ; Restore the work register
77            mov    es:KbdFl1,ah    ; Put KEYBOARD FLAG 1 ([0040:0017h])
78            mov    es:KbdFl2,al    ; Put KEYBOARD FLAG 2([0040:0018hh])
79            pop    es              ; Restore the segment register
80            ret                    ; Return to the caller
81   PutFl12 endp
82
83            ENDWORK
84
85            CLfunc log IsKbdEnh
86            CLcode
87            mov    ax,FALSE        ; Set the keyboard type to STANDARD
88            call   ChecKbd
89            cmp    IndEnh,0        ; Is enhanced keyboard present?
90            je     IsKbdEnhR       ; If not - return
91            mov    ax,TRUE         ; Set the keyboard type to ENHANCED
92   IsKbdEnhR:
93            CLret  ax              ; AX contains the value to be returned
94
95            Clfunc log Gnumlock
96            Clcode
97            mov    dx,FALSE        ; Set the NumLock indicator to OFF
98            call   GetFl12         ; Get the Keyboard Flags
99            test   ah,Cnuml        ; Is the NumLock state on? (bit 5)
100           jz     GNumLockR       ; If not - return
101           mov    dx,TRUE         ; Set the NumLock indicator to ON
102  Gnumlockr:
103           Clret  dx              ; DX contains the value to be returned
104
105           Clfunc log Gcapslock
106           Clcode
107           mov    dx,FALSE        ; Set the CapsLock indicator to OFF
108           call   GetFl12         ; Get the Keyboard Flags
109           test   ah,Ccapl        ; Is the CapsLock state on?  (bit 6)
110           jz     GCapsLockR      ; If not - return
111           mov    dx,TRUE         ; Set the CapsLock indicator to ON
112  Gcapslockr:
113           Clret  dx              ; DX contains the value to be returned
114
115           Clfunc log Snumlock <int SnlP>
116           Clcode
117
118           call   GetFl12         ; Get the Keyboard Flags
119           and    ah,not Cnuml    ; Clear the NumLock state (bit 5)
120           mov    dx,SnlP         ; Copy the parameter to returned value
121           cmp    dx,1            ; Is it request for setting?
122           jne    SNumLockR       ; If not - return
123           or     ah,Cnuml        ; Set the NumLock state (bit 5)
124  Snumlockr:
125           call   PutFl12         ; Write the Keyboard Flags
126           Clret  dx              ; DX contains the value to be returned
127
```

```
128        Clfunc  log Scapslock <int SCplP>
129        Clcode
130        call    GetFl12      ; Get the Keyboard Flags
131        and     ah,not Ccapl ; Clear the CapsLock state (bit 6)
132        mov     dx,Scplp     ; Copy the parameter to returned value
133        cmp     dx,1         ; Is it request for setting?
134        jne     SCapsLockR   ; If not - return
135        or      ah,Ccapl     ; Set the CapsLock state (bit 6)
136 Scapslockr:
137        call    PutFl12      ; Write the Keyboard Flags
138        Clret dx             ; DX contains the value to be returned
139
140    END
```

**Listing 7.6 ClipDemo - A Set of Clipper Functions for
Controlling the Keyboard**

Apart from the functions described above, the complex KeybServ
contains some auxiliary functions which we think are worthwhile
explaining as it will give you a better understanding of how it works.
According to the rules of the Clipper-Assembler interface (note that
we are talking about Clipper Summer 87 and its macro library
EXTENDA.INC) the auxiliary functions between macro call
WORKFUNC and ENDWORKS (see Listing 7.6) are:

>   CheckKbd   - determines the keyboard type,
>   GetFL12   - loads the AX register with the keyboard flags,
>   PutFl12   - writes the contents of the AX register into the
>   keyboard flags.

Remember that keyboard flag 1 and flag 2 are stored in the BIOS data
area at location 0040h:0017h and 0040h:0018h, respectively.

The functions which can be called from Clipper programs follow the
ENDWORK statement. Each function must start with the Clfunc
statement and finish with the Clret statement. Note that we are referring
to the lines "Clfunc" and "Clret" as statements although in fact they
are macro calls. Our justification is that they perform the same task
as statements in high-level languages.

The statement Clfunc defines the function name and type. For example,
line 85 of Listing 7.6 defines the function IsKbdEnh as a logical function.
The statement Clret returns control to the calling program in the same
way as the Clipper statement RETURN does. The interface between
Clipper and assembler programs will be explained in greater detail in
the chapter called "Interfacing to High-level Languages".

Now pick any function you like and look at the code. You'll notice that all functions have the same structure: they get information from the keyboard flags, analyze that information and, probably, change the contents of the keyboard flags.

You can use the functions given here to control the keyboard state from within your program - for example, you can turn on the NumLock state before inputting numeric data. It might also be easier to turn the CapsLock state on before inputting text that needs to be in capital letters than to process the text after input.

We hope that you'll be able to use the simple library we've just described for routine work. At least, treat it as a guide for creating your own libraries to increase the power of your programs.

KbdBuf - An Example of a Device Driver

This program increases the size of the keyboard buffer. Designed as a device driver, it is a special program loaded during the process of DOS initialization, which will then be treated as a part of the DOS kernel.

Its full assembler text is given in Listing 7.7 and its binary code is stored on your program disk as the file KbdBuf.sys. If you want to use it, copy the file KbdBuf.sys in the root directory of the boot device and include the following command line in the CONFIG.SYS file located on this device:

```
DEVICE=KbdBuf.sys 256
```

This installs the program KbdBuf during the boot process and specifies the new size of the keyboard buffer allocated by this program. To avoid possible problems which may happen if the driver KbdBuf.sys interferes with other software you are using, we advise you to take the following measures:

▲ Make a new bootable diskette.

▲ Copy system file command.com onto it.

▲ Copy driver KbdBuf.sys on it.

▲ Create the corresponding config.sys file on that diskette.

▲ Reboot DOS from that diskette.

▲ Try to perform DOS commands or run your favorite software.

When performing this process you should get the following:

```
C>format a: /s /u /f:360
Insert new diskette for drive A:
and press ENTER when ready...

Formatting 360K
Format complete.
System transferred

Volume label (11 characters, ENTER for none)?

362496 bytes total disk space
 81920 bytes used by system
280576 bytes available on disk

      1024 bytes in each allocation unit.
       274 allocation units available on disk.

Volume Serial Number is 2232-14F3

Format another (Y/N)?n

C>copy command.com a:
      1 file(s) copied

C>copy kbdbuf.sys a:
      1 file(s) copied

C>copy con a:config.sys
device=kbdbuf.sys
^Z
      1 file(s) copied
```

Now, when you load DOS from the disk you have just created, besides the usual messages you should see on the screen the following initial message of the KbdBuf.sys driver:

```
Keyboard buffer extender is successfully installed

A>
```

Let's have a close look at how the KbdBuf driver works. For now, don't worry about the instructions which make this program into a device driver. We have already explained that the keyboard buffer must be located in the first physical segment of memory, i.e., in the first 64K. Because the program KbdBuf establishes the new keyboard buffer within its body, it must also be loaded in memory area below the 64K bytes boundary.

The easiest way to ensure that a program will always be loaded in this area is to design this program as a device driver. In a later chapter we'll explain the structure of a device driver and give you a pattern of device driver's shell. At the moment we'll concentrate on parts of this program which are related to our subject - the keyboard data fields, the keyboard buffer in particular.

```
 1
 2            page 55,132
 3 ;
 4 ;            Device request header
 5 ;
 6 ReqHeader       segment   at 0
 7 HeaderLen       db        ?
 8 UnitCode        db        ?
 9 CommandCode     db        ?
10 Status          dw        ?
11 Reserved        db        8 dup (?)
12 Units           db        ?          ; Number of units
13 EndOffset       dw        ?          ; Segment:Offset address of
14 EndSegment      dw        ?          ; the end of resident part
15 ArgOffset       dw        ?          ; Segment:Offset address of
16 ArgSegment      dw        ?          ; the parameter string
17 ReqHeader       ends
18 ;
19 ;            BIOS data segment
20 ;
21 BiosData        segment   at 40h
22                 org       1Ah
23 BufHead         dw        ?          ; Buffer head ptr
24 BufTail         dw        ?          ; Buffer tail ptr
25                 org       80h
26 BufStart        dw        ?          ; Points to the buffer start
27 BufEnd          dw        ?          ; Points to the buffer end
28 BiosDat a ends
29
30 CR              equ       0Dh        ; Carriage return code
31 LF              equ       0Ah        ; Line feed code
32 EndMsg          equ       24h        ; Dollar sign code
33 Space           equ       20h        ; Blank code
34 InitCommand     equ       0          ; Command "INIT driver"
35 DoneRep         equ       0100h      ; Code "Device ready'
36 FailRep         equ       8003h      ; Code "Error-unknown command"
37 BufferDef       equ       80         ; Buffer default length
38 BufferMin       equ       16         ; Buffer minimal length
39 BufferMax       equ       512        ; Buffer maximal length
40
41 _TEXT           segment public 'CODE'
42                 assume  cs:TEXT,ds:_TEXT,es:ReqHeader,ss:_TEXT
43                 org       0
44 ;
45 ;            Header
```

```
46 ;
47 NextDev      dd      0FFFFFFFFh ; Pointer to the next driver
48 DevAttr      dw      8000h      ; Character device
49 Dev_Strat    dw      Strategy   ; Offset of STRATEGY proc
50 Dev_int      dw      Interrupt  ; Offset of INTERRUPT proc
51 Dev_name     db      'KbdBuf '  ; Driver name ( 8 characters)
52
53 ReqOffset    dw      ?
54 ReqSegment   dw      ?
55 StackSeg     dw      ?
56 StackPtr     dw      ?
57 ThisSeg      dw      ?
58 ThisOff      dw      ?
59 ParamVal     dw      0
60 Ten          db      10
61 Sixteen      dw      16
62 BufLen       dw      0
63 StatusWord dw        DoneRep
64
65 Strategy proc far
66 ;
67 ;   The procedure STRATEGY is called while installing the driver.
68 ;   This procedure is a dummy procedure because the driver
69 ;   doesn't control any real device.
70 ;
71           mov     ThisSeg,cs          ; Save the current segment
72           mov     ThisOff,offset NextDev; Save offset of beginning
73           mov     ReqSegment,es       ; Save the segment of REQUEST
74           mov     ReqOffset,bx        ; Save the offset of REQUEST
75           push    ax
76           push    dx
77           push    ds
78           mov     ah,09
79           mov     ds,ThisSeg
80           mov     dx,offset HeadMsg
81           int     21h
82           pop     ds
83           pop     dx
84           pop     ax
85           ret
86 HeadMsg db       'Keyboard buffer extender ',EndMsg
87 Strategy endp
88
89 Interrupt proc far
90           push    ax
91           push    bx
92           push    cx
93           push    dx
94           push    ds
95           pushf
96           mov     al,CommandCode[bx]    ; Get the command code
97           mov     MsgAddr,offset InstMsg
98           cmp     al,INITcommand        ; Is it the INIT command?
99           je      ProcessCommand        ; If so, continue the work
```

```
100         mov     StatusWord,FailRep; If not, report the error
101         mov     MsgAddr,offset FailMsg
102         jmp     ReturnToDOS       ;  and exit the driver
103
104 ProcessCommand:
105
106         mov     StatusWord,DoneRep; Report "DONE" to DOS
107         mov     EndSegment[bx],cs ; Return address of the end
108         mov     EndOffset[bx],offset DriverEnd
109
110         mov     cs:StackSeg,ss    ; Save the stack segment
111         mov     cs:StackPtr,sp    ; Save the stack pointer
112         mov     ax,cs             ; Get the current segment
113
114         cli                       ; No interrupts allowed while
115                                   ;changing stack registers
116         mov     ss,ax             ; Stack is in current segment
117         mov     sp,0FFFEh         ; Stack is at the top of seg
118         sti                       ; Interrupts are now allowed
119
120         push    es                ;
121         push    si                ;
122         push    bp                ;
123
124         call    ReadParm          ; Read parameter string
125
126         call    CountEnding       ; Address of buffer end
127
128         jc      NotInstall        ; If Carry Flag is set driver
129                                   ; is not located in first 64K
130
131 ; Following two lines put SEGMENT:OFFSET address of the driver's
132 ; resident part into the DATA field for INIT command
133
134         mov     es,ReqSegment
135         mov     bx,ReqOffset
136         mov     ax,ParamVal       ; Buffer length into AX
137         add     EndOffset[bx],ax  ; Offset address of buffer end
138
139         push    es
140         mov     ax,EndSegment[bx] ; Segment address of buffer end
141         mul     Sixteen           ; Right shift by 1 hex digit
142         add     ax,EndOffset[bx]  ; Effective address
143         sub     ax,400h           ; Subtract start address of
144                                   ;   BIOS data area
145         assume  es:BiosData
146         mov     dx,BIOSdata
147         mov     es,dx             ; ES points to BIOS data seg
148         cli                       ; No interrupts allowed!
149         mov     es:BufEnd,ax      ; New BUFFER END PTR
150         sub     ax,ParamVal       ; Subtract length of buffer
151         mov     es:BufStart,ax    ; New BUFFER START PTR
152         mov     es:BufHead,ax     ; New BUFFER HEAD PTR
153         mov     es:BufTail,ax     ; NEW BUFFER TAIL PTR
```

```
154        sti                       ; Pointers are set - allow INT
155        pop     es
156        assume  es:ReqHeader
157 NotInstall:
158        pop     bp
159        pop     si
160        pop     es
161
162        cli
163        mov     ss,cs:StackSeg ; Restore the stack segment
164        mov     sp,cs:StackPtr ; Restore the stack pointer
165        sti
166
167 ReturnToDOS:
168        push    cs
169        pop     ds
170        mov     ah,09          ; Function 09 - output string
171        mov     dx,MsgAddr     ; DX- Address of initial message
172        int     21h            ; DOS service call
173        mov     es,ReqSegment  ; ES:BX point to the request
174        mov     bx,ReqOffset   ;   header area
175        mov     ax,StatusWord  ; Remember the status word
176        mov     Status[bx],ax  ; and return it to the DOS
177
178        popf
179        pop     ds
180        pop     dx
181        pop     cx
182        pop     bx
183        pop     ax
184
185        ret
186 InstMsg db 'is successfully installed',Cr,LF,EndMsg
187 FailMsg db 'failed - not in the first 64K of memory',CR,LF,EndMsg
188 MsgAddr dw ?
189 Interrupt endp
190
191 DriverEnd label dword          ; This marks the END of driver
192
193 ReadParm proc near
194        mov     es,ReqSegment  ; ES:BX point to the request
195        mov     bx,ReqOffset   ;   data field
196        mov     si,es:ArgOffset[bx] ; ES:SI - offset of arguments
197        mov     es,es:ArgSegment[bx]
198        mov     BlankId,0
199        mov     bx,0
200 CopyParm: mov al,es:[si+bx]
201        cmp     al,CR
202        je      EndParm
203        cmp     al,LF
204        je      EndParm
205        cmp     al,0
206        je      EndParm
207        cmp     al,'0'
```

```
208                 jl        NonDigit
209                 cmp       al,'9'
210                 ja        NonDigit
211                 push      ax
212                 sub       al,'0'       ; Character to number
213                 mov       ah,0             ; Clear high part of AX
214                 mov       CurNum,ax    ; Store current cypher
215                 mov       ax,ParamVal
216                 mul       Ten
217                 add       ax,CurNum
218                 mov       ParamVal,ax
219                 pop       ax
220  NonDigit:      inc       bx
221                 cmp       BlankId,0
222                 jne       EndParm
223                 jmp       CopyParm
224  EndParm:       cmp       ParamVal,0      ; Is parameter set?
225                 jne PresentParm          ; If so, process its value
226                 mov ParamVal,BufferDef  ; Else set default value
227  PresentParm: cmp  ParamVal,BufferMin  ; Compare to minimal value
228                 ja        GreaterMin         ; Continue if it is bigger
229                 mov  ParamVal,BufferMin   ; Else set minimal value
230  GreaterMin: cmp  ParamVal,BufferMax  ; Compare to maximal value
231                 jb        EndAccParm         ; If less-accept the value
232  TooBig:        mov  ParamVal,BufferMax  ; Else set maximal value
233  EndAccParm:
234                 ret
235  BlankId        db        ?
236  CurNum         dw        ?
237  ReadParm endp
238
239  CountEnding proc near
240                 push      es
241                 push      bx
242                 mov       es,ReqSegment
243                 mov       bx,ReqOffset
244                 mov       ax,EndSegment[bx]
245                 mul       Sixteen
246                 jc        EscapeProc
247                 add       ax,EndOffset[bx]
248                 jc        EscapeProc
249                 add       ax,ParamVal
250  EscapeProc: pop         bx
251                 pop       es
252                 ret                         ; AX now contains the effective
253                                             ; address of buffer end
254  CountEnding endp
255
256  TxtParm db     (64) ('$') , CR, LF, EndMsg
257
258  _TEXT          ends
259                 end
```

Listing 7.7 KbdBuf - The Keyboard Buffer Extender - Installable Driver

As a device driver the program KbdBuf includes two main procedures called Strategy and Interrupt.

The task of the Strategy procedure is to prepare the driver for processing requests from the operating system, or a device when possible. An active device can generate requests using hardware interrupts. For example, a modem attached to a communication port is an active device. On the other hand, a disk drive cannot generate a hardware interrupt and the device driver must check its state to decide whether a particular action should be taken. In this case, the procedure Strategy only saves the current values of CS:IP and the segment:offset address of the block of request. After this it outputs the initial message and finishes its work.

The Interrupt procedure is intended to process commands passed from the operating system. The command is specified by the command code passed in a special area of memory. In our example, this is the area that starts at the label ReqHeader. The Interrupt procedure processes only one type of request from the operating system - "initialize the driver". To do this it completes the following main steps:

Checks whether the request code is a valid code,
Reads the parameter string,
Calculates new values for buffer start and buffer end,
Changes the keyboard buffer pointer in the BIOS data area.

The procedure Interrupt calls two auxiliary procedures: ReadParm and CountEnding. The procedure ReadParms reads the tail of the string DEVICE= from the config.sys file and converts the value of the buffer size (if it is specified) into an integer stored in a word. The procedure CountEnding calculates the value of the new buffer end address and sets the Carry Flag if that value exceeds 64K. Then the Interrupt procedure writes the new value into four keyboard buffer pointers - Buffer Start, Buffer End, Buffer Head and Buffer Tail. Note that the Buffer Head and Buffer Tail pointers have the same value, which means that the keyboard buffer is empty.

Summary

This chapter has given you information about one of the computer's main devices - the keyboard. You can now write a program for accessing the keyboard using BIOS and DOS interrupts. Following on from this, we also covered direct usage of the hardware ports related to the keyboard.

To round everything neatly off, we'll finish by outlining how the different methods of accessing the keyboard can be used. We discussed three possible techniques - using the low-level hardware, using the BIOS services (the basic level) and using the DOS services (the logical service). Each of these has its advantages, depending on the task in hand.

The low-level gives you the greatest power, but is inevitably the most difficult and means that you really do need to know your way around the hardware. The result of using this technique also depends on which operating system is used. For example, it's not that hard to imagine a multi-user multi-tasking system (current versions of UNIX and OS/2 are not far off) that prevents user programs from dealing directly with the hardware at all. Our advice is, only use this technique when you really have to - for example for creating special software such as national keyboard drivers, terminal emulators or security systems.

Using the BIOS service makes your programs more adaptable. Since it uses the ROM BIOS routines, it can be used under any operating system that allows user applications to deal with ROM BIOS. This technique gives you access to most keyboard features, such as determining the keyboard state, reading scan codes or organizing parallel input when your program processes one portion of data while reading the next one. The only slightly negative point is that you need to process special keystrokes such as cursor control keys, INS and DEL keys or functional keys for editing an input string.

As is to be expected, the DOS service is the most flexible. It means that you can concentrate on processing data, rather than on data input. When you redirect input, you can use your program for processing data stored in files, without making any changes to the program. Furthermore using the DOS service means you can make your program

hardware-independent because DOS takes care of all interfaces with
ROM BIOS and the hardware. It is also reasonable to expect that
programs which use the DOS services will work under any operating
systems which support DOS applications.

CHAPTER
8

Using Video

In this chapter we will introduce the basic principles of the PC video system and explain how the programmer can exploit its features.

We will once again examine the three levels of control available to the programmer - DOS, BIOS, and the direct hardware level - and discuss the pros and cons of each technique in relation to the video system.

For many programmers, better control of the video system is a primary reason for using assembly language. The speed gains that can be realized from direct manipulation of hardware mean that we shall focus on that area rather more than in other chapters, but not before a full examination of the services available in DOS and BIOS.

Fundamental Knowledge

Monitor and Video Adapter Card

The video system of a personal computer consists of two main parts: a display monitor and a video adapter card.

The display monitor (often referred to as a *monitor*, a *video display* or simply a *display)* is the unit that is used to represent text and graphic information in a readable form. This unit looks like an ordinary TV-set and performs some similar functions. Actually, it is not uncommon for people with very basic personal computers to use a TV-set as their display monitor.

The term "adapter" generally stands for a device that is designed to accept one kind of signal and convert them into other signals. For example, the arm that held the needle in your grandmother's gramophone was called an adapter, and converted signals from the tracks in the vinyl into the latest dance sounds. A video adapter is slightly more sophisticated - it converts digital signals, operated by the microprocessor of a PC, into video signals for controlling the display monitor.

Sometimes the video adapter is referred to as a video card, graphic card or just simply an adapter. The video adapter card is literally a card which is installed in the system block. This isn't always the case, as the video adapter is often located on the motherboard or combined with other adapters, for example the printer adapter. Regardless of its name or location, this unit comprises the following main parts or, at least, it behaves as if all these parts were actually present:

- ▲ CRT controller (microprocessor Motorola 6845 or similar).
- ▲ Control registers accessible through the I/O ports (CRT controller registers).
- ▲ ROM of the character generator for storing the fonts.
- ▲ Video memory (16Kbytes for old adapters, 256Kbytes and more for VGA and modern cards).
- ▲ A controller for the monitor electron-beam tube (signal controller).

The connection between these main parts of the video card is shown in Figure 8.1.

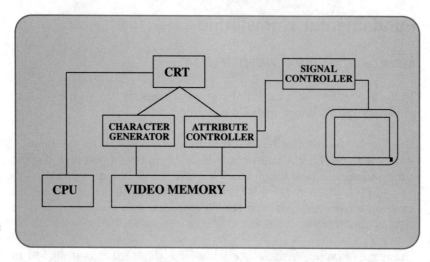

Figure 8.1
Structure of a Video Card

Unless you aspire to being a hardware developer, you don't really need to know much about the microprocessor or CRT controller. Furthermore, we do not intend to give a full description of programming the video adapter's control registers in this book. To cover all the possible features of today's video systems needs a book in itself, and most programmers are able to get by without the more arcane, and hardware specific, techniques.

The Video Buffer

The image you get on your monitor's screen appears as a result of writing information into a special part of the memory known as the **video memory**, or the **video buffer**. This is a special kind of memory which supplements the conventional memory and can be directly used under MS-DOS. This memory starts at the segment address 0A000h and can be accessed directly by the 6845 microprocessor as well as the CPU. When a piece of information is placed into the video memory by the CPU, the 6845 reads it and displays it on the screen. This commonality is called **memory-mapping**, and exploiting it is the key to a lot of video effects. It also means that you don't have to keep a record of what is on the screen, as your programs can look at it directly. This is how a games programmer keeps track of his animated sprites, or a spell-checker looks at what's on the screen.

Although conventional memory is 640K bytes, the address bus is 20 bits wide for 8088 microprocessors and 32 bits for i80486, which means that these microprocessors can operate with at least 20^{10} = 1024K or

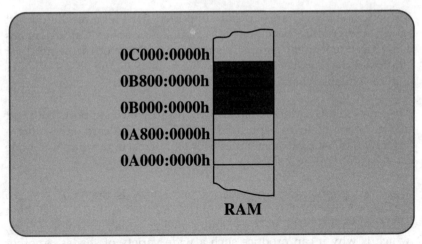

0C000:0000h
0B800:0000h
0B000:0000h
0A800:0000h
0A000:0000h

RAM

Figure 8.2
**Address Space
used by Video
Cards**

1M bytes. This leaves at least 384K of memory which can be used by i80x86 microprocessors, in addition to the 640K available for DOS programs.

Memory from 0A0000h to 0FFFFFh is not located in RAM chips on the motherboard, but is included in the address space of the microprocessor. Video cards use the address space between 0A0000h and 0BFFFFh as shown in Figure 8.2. The amount of video memory that is actually used and its start address (the number of the paragraph) depends on the type of video adapter and current mode.

Video Cards

There are a variety of video adapter cards which can be used with IBM and compatible PCs. The oldest one, the MDA - **M**onochrome **D**isplay **A**dapter was developed by the IBM corporation in 1981. This card is a bit limited however, in that it only supports a text mode of 80x25 i.e., it only displays characters in 80 columns and 25 lines.

Another popular card which is no longer produced is the CGA - **C**olor **G**raphics **A**dapter. The CGA card allows you to work with 4 main colors (Red, Green, Blue, Black) and to use the text modes 80x25 and 40x25 as well as the graphics mode. In the graphics mode it displays 640 pixels (points) in a row horizontally and 200 in a column vertically. Consequently the resolution of CGA is given as 640x200. Although you cannot buy this adapter new now, it is still used on many PC and PC XT systems.

The next adapter to appear that supported both high-resolution text modes and graphics was the HGC - **H**ercules **G**raphics **C**ard. Hercules were an independent peripherals company who spotted the need for improved displays before IBM did. Later, in 1985, the HGC+ adapter with a loadable character generator was released.

The **E**nhanced **G**raphics **A**dapter (EGA) card which supports both text and graphics mode also appeared in 1985. The EGA card offers a high-resolution of 640x350 (sometimes 640x480) pixels in the graphics mode and a palette of 16 colors.

The most popular type of video adapter now is the VGA - **V**ideo **G**raphics **A**rray card. It supports up to 256 colors and has a resolution of 640x480 pixels. The VGA generates analog signals for color control, which is why it can produce such a wide variety of shades. Another big bonus is that the VGA card can emulate the work of all the video cards mentioned above. The only drawback of VGA cards is that, unlike the EGA, there is no accepted standard, hence cards from different manufacturers are often slightly incompatible with each other. Fortunately the differences are only really significant when dealing with advanced hardware manipulation.

There are a number of new video adapters available now: Super VGA, MCGA, VESA. The development of video adapters and a comparison of the most efficient types are shown in Figure 8.3.

The two branches shown in Figure 8.3 are more closely connected than you may think. The adapters in each branch are downward compatible, for example the EGA adapter accepts all the commands of the CGA adapter and can emulate its work. The VGA adapter can emulate the work of both EGA and CGA adapters. Moreover, the VGA adapter can emulate the work of the HGC adapter and the Hercules InColor Card supports all the features of CGA, EGA and VGA adapters.

Finally, all video adapters have one feature in common - their output signals control (or at any rate can be used for controlling) a video monitor.

Display Monitors

The display monitor is the most popular device for outputting information. It looks like an ordinary television set and is connected to the video card.

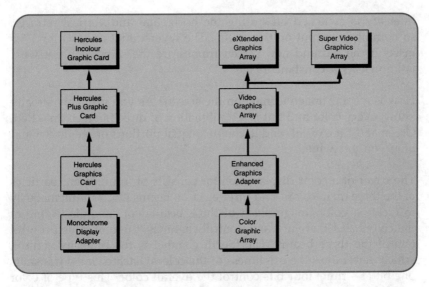

Figure 8.3
Different Types of Video Adapters

Let's have a look at the main principles involved in creating a screen image, as it will help you to understand the process which transforms a sequence of bits into a color picture. The video signal for the electron scanning beam is formed in the video adapter. The electron beam scans the screen rows starting at the upper left corner of the screen. When the beam hits a luminescent cover on the screen it produces a luminescent point - a pixel. This process is shown in Figure 8.4.

The brightness of a pixel depends on the intensity of the video signal. The electron beam forms 640 pixels (this is more for some monitors) in a row then moves to the start of the row immediately below (horizontal retrace) until it reaches the lower right corner. To create the next frame this beam then returns to the upper left corner of the screen. This reverse motion of the beam is known as vertical retrace.

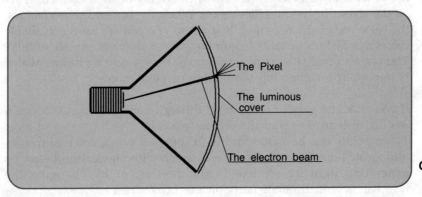

Figure 8.4
Process of Creating a Pixel on the Screen

Intensity is switched off during the horizontal and vertical retraces, so nothing is output on the screen. The reverse motion lasts for 1-1.5 msec. If the old and new screen frames are the same, you get what is known as a constant image.

How is a color image formed on the screen? As you probably already know, every color and tint is a combination of three main colors - Red, Green and Blue (RGB) and if you mix equal portions of red, green and blue you get white.

The cover of a color display monitor consists of luminescent particles of the three main colors, and three electron beams work simultaneously to create a color image. Each of these beams corresponds to one of the colors and there are four control channels, three of which control one of the three beams. The fourth channel is for Intensity control, which determines the brightness of the colors. Each channel transmits one bit at a time; four bits control the overall color. This type of color control system is called an IRGB palette. Let's have a look at the 4-bit color code:

Blue	0001b = 1
Green	0010b = 2
Red	0100b = 4
Intensity	1000b = 8

When the highest bit is set to one, the color becomes more intense (bright). To get different tints, you simply need to combine the numeric codes, for example blue (1) + green (2) gives cyan (3). The IBM color coding is given in Table 8.1.

The programs PG0802 - PG0804 from your program disk demonstrate the process of color creation. These programs draw a colored "net" on the screen in the graphics mode. When the screen frame changes, the color code is incremented by one, so you can see all the available colors detailed in the table (assuming your monitor is capable of this). You can also evaluate the focus of two or three scanning beams, which is important for checking the quality of your monitor.

If you look at a grey or white pixel through a magnifying glass you'll see that it is made up of three points of color - red, green and blue. These points can be made visible in different ways, for example by hitting the luminescent cover of the screen with an electron beam, by generating light by semiconductor devices, or by changing the transparency of different parts on the LCD screen.

I R G B	Value	Color
I = 0 - The intensity bit is switched off		
0 0 0 0	0	Black
0 0 0 1	1	Blue
0 0 1 0	2	Green
0 0 1 1	3	Cyan
0 1 0 0	4	Red
0 1 0 1	5	Magenta
0 1 1 0	6	Brown
0 1 1 1	7	Grey
I = 1 - The intensity bit is switched on (bright colors)		
1 0 0 0	8	Dark grey
1 0 0 1	9	Light blue
1 0 1 0	10	Light green
1 0 1 1	11	Light cyan
1 1 0 0	12	Light red
1 1 0 1	13	Light magenta
1 1 1 0	14	Light yellow
1 1 1 1	15	White

Table 8.1
An IBM Color Code Table

The characteristics of a pixel define the characteristics of the monitor as a whole. Generally speaking, the smaller the pixels are, the less distance there is between them and consequently the brighter the picture they produce. Now we'll consider the main characteristics of the monitor which determine the quality of the image you see on the screen.

Palette and Resolution

The most important features of a display monitor are the **palette** and **resolution**. The palette can be defined as the number of colors which can be reproduced on the screen at one time. The term "resolution" describes the number of pixels on the screen.

A palette can have 2 (for monochrome displays), 4, 16, 64, 256 or more colors. The color of a monochrome display depends on the luminous cover of the screen: usually grey, orange or green. Although monochrome monitors are less tiring on your eyes, color images are a lot more attractive, which accounts for their great popularity.

Since every screen image is made up of separate points (pixels), the resolution of a monitor is defined by the number of pixels in a row and in a column. The higher the resolution, the better the quality of the image on the screen and, consequently, the better the monitor. The most commonly used monitors have a resolution of 640x350 (640 pixels in a row and 350 pixels in a column), 640x480 or 800x600. The monitors used on old PCs with CGA adapters have a resolution of 640x200 but the best monitors used on the most-up-to date PCs and workstations offer 1024x768 and 1280x1024.

The resolution and characteristics of a monitor can differ depending on the regime in which the monitor is working. Usually, the better the monitor - the wider the range of features.

Video Modes

All adapters (except MDA) can support two modes - text and graphic, which you can switch between by changing the video adapter control registers.

We mentioned the basic principles of graphics mode (constructing an image using pixels) above. The main difference between text and graphics modes is that text mode only lets you output characters from a predefined set, while graphics mode allows you to create your own characters, use different fonts at the same time, draw impressive pictures and diagrams and even re-produce full motion video.

This is because graphics mode lets you address each pixel on the screen individually. The end result you get is a bit like the difference between pre-fab houses and skilled brick masonry - the former go up very quickly, giving you a standard model; the latter gives you your "dream home", but takes a lot more effort.

Although using graphics mode is beyond the scope of this book, we will use it in a few programs to demonstrate certain effects. From now on though, our discussion of the video system will be largely restricted to the text mode.

Character Display in Text Mode

While working in text mode, the screen is divided into rows (usually 25, 43, or 50) and columns (usually 40 or 80). Each character has two coordinates - X and Y, where X is the number of the column and Y is the number of the row. The rows and columns on the screen are numbered from 0 up to the maximum number. The most frequently used values for the maximum number of rows and columns are 24 and 79 which makes the total amount of rows and columns on the screen 25 and 80, respectively. The way rows and columns are numbered on the screen is shown in Figure 8.5.

As there are up to 640x400 pixels on the screen, each of these character locations has enough pixels in it to represent adequately all the necessary symbols. Since there are 80x25 characters on the screen, each character is placed within a square area known as a character cell or pointwise matrix. The size of a character cell in a pixel can be evaluated as $(X_{pixels}/X_{characters}) \times (Y_{pixels}/Y_{characters})$. To demonstrate this, we'll calculate the size of the character cell for an EGA monitor (640 x 350 pixels) working in the text video mode 3 (80 x 25 characters). In this case, the size of X is 640/80 = 8 and Y - 350/25 = 14. This confirms what you might have known anyway - the size of the character cell for EGA screens is 8x14 pixels. This value varies, depending on the video adapter, for example - 8x8 (CGA), 9x14 (Hercules), 8x16 (VGA). Since 8 bits represent one byte, information about a character on a CGA, EGA and VGA screen can be stored in 8, 14 or 16 bytes respectively. Each byte is responsible for setting the points of one row, starting at the top. If a bit is set, the corresponding point is lit on the screen.

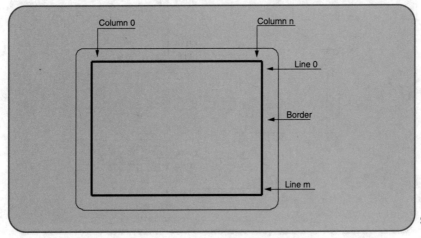

Figure 8.5
**Text Mode
Screen Mapping**

A group of character images (matrices), is called a font. To explain what this means in practical terms, let's have a look at matrix 8x16 for the character "F", shown in Table 8.2. The bits which are set are marked by an asterisk.

The images of the matrices are placed into a part of the video memory known as a character generator. With early video cards, (MDA and CGA) the character generator was stored in ROM which meant that in order to change the fonts you had to manipulate the hardware. Modern video adapters allow you to load any user created fonts, including national alphabets, specials symbols and so on into the adapter's RAM. Now there are even font editors, which are programs that let you create elaborate fonts. The ability to swap fonts is critical for those whose native language is not the same as the inventors of the PC.

The Attribute Byte

There are two things you need to decide on before you start creating a character image on the screen: what character you want to output, and how you want it to look on the screen. The first condition is defined by a hexadecimal character code which determines the image in the font table. The second condition is defined by a special byte associated with this code, the **attribute byte**, which is transmitted to the video memory. This byte defines such characteristics as color, brightness and blinking of a character (foreground) or of the background. The format of an attribute byte is shown in Table 8.3.

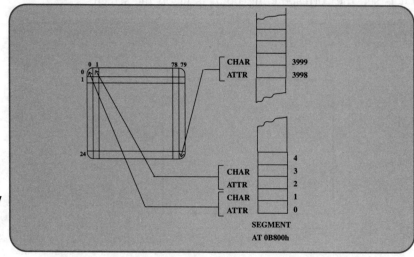

Figure 8.6
Screen Memory Showing Character and Attribute Bytes

Row	Image of Matrix 8 x 16								Hex Representation of the Byte
0	.	.	.	.	.	.	.	.	00h <==== Beginning
1	.	.	.	.	.	.	.	.	00h of matrix
2	*	*	*	*	*	*	*	.	0FEh
3	.	*	*	.	.	*	*	.	66h
4	.	*	*	.	.	.	*	.	62h
5	.	*	*	.	*	.	.	.	68h
6	.	*	*	*	*	.	.	.	78h
7	.	*	*	.	*	.	.	.	68h
8	.	*	*	.	.	.	.	.	60h
9	.	*	*	.	.	.	.	.	60h
10	.	*	*	.	.	.	.	.	60h
11	*	*	*	*	.	.	.	.	0F0h
12	.	.	.	.	.	.	.	.	00h
13	.	.	.	.	.	.	.	.	00h
14	.	.	.	.	.	.	.	.	00h
15	.	.	.	.	.	.	.	.	00h <==== End of matrix

Table 8.2
The Character Matrix for the Letter "F"

An attribute determines four characteristics:

1. Background color (i.e., the color of the area in which the character appears).
2. Background characteristics (character blinking or highlighted background).
3. Color of the character (the foreground).
4. Intensity of the character (dark or light color).

As an example we'll display the following text on the screen:"ABCDE" with a color scheme of light-yellow characters on a blue background.

Bits	7	6	5	4	3	2	1	0	Meaning
	1	.	.	.	.	.	.	.	Blinking/intensity of background
	.	1	.	.	.	.	.	.	Red background component
	.	.	1	.	.	.	.	.	Green background component
	.	.	.	1	.	.	.	.	Blue background component
	.	.	.	.	1	.	.	.	High intensity of foreground
	.	.	.	.	.	1	.	.	Red foreground component
	.	.	.	.	.	.	1	.	Green foreground component
	.	.	.	.	.	.	.	1	Blue foreground component

Table 8.3
Format of an Attribute Byte

The line in the data segment should be as follows:

```
STRING    DB  "A", 1Eh, "B", 1Eh, "C", 1Eh, "D", 1Eh, "E", 1Eh
```

The following code will send this sequence to the video memory:

```
mov   ax,0B800h   ; 0B800h - address of video buffer (color)
mov   es,ax       ; ES points to video buffer
mov   di,0        ; ES:DI - effective address of video buffer start
lea   si,string   ; DS:SI - effective address of text to be output
mov   cx,10       ; total length of string
rep   movsb       ; send string to video memory
```

For the purposes of our example, we have assumed that video page 0 is active. If this is not the case, you must place the corresponding value into the DI register - 800h (4096) for page 1, 2000 (8192) for page 2 and so on.

You can experiment with the video memory using the DEBUG utility included in your DOS. Simply run DEBUG, then when its prompt (the "-" character) appears on the screen, execute the command for filling the memory with a particular value. For example, the command

```
f b800:0 9f 01 1e
```

outputs 80 yellow "☻" characters on a blue background in the first line on the screen.

If you specify the same color for the background and foreground, the characters will be "invisible". This is a useful tip to bear in mind when creating password systems.

The Structure of the Video Buffer

In the 80x25 text mode, the screen buffer requires 2x80x25 = 4000 bytes for the character and attribute. The simplest graphics mode operates as 320x200=64000 pixels, in 4 colors. Since information about each pixel takes up two bits (four pixels in one byte), the amount of memory required for the video buffer is 320x200/4=16000 bytes. It follows that the more colors you use, the more video memory you need. The most up-to-date adapters, able to display up to 1024x768 pixels, usually have 512K (or even as much as 1M bytes) of memory on the video card.

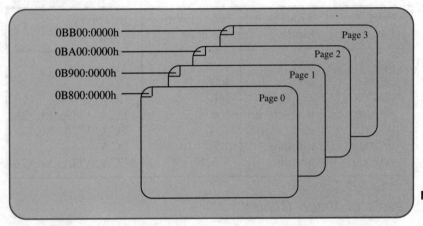

Figure 8.7
Using Video Memory in Text Modes

As far as the text mode is concerned, all available video memory is divided into sections called pages. Each page contains an image of one full screen. The size of each page is 4K (4096 = 1000h) bytes. Video pages are numbered from 0 up to the maximum number determined by the current video mode and the amount of memory installed. For example, if the current mode is 40x25, you have eight video pages, in 80x25 - four pages. Information to be output on the screen may be stored in different video pages and your program can quickly change an image on the screen by referring to the corresponding page. The video page most often used is 0.

Similar divisions are used in the graphics mode. The size and quantity of pages in the graphics mode depend on the size of the video adapter's RAM and on the number of colors used. Most adapters working in the graphics mode only allow you to use video page 0.

As we have already pointed out, the video memory starts at address 0A0000h, so the segment address is 0A000h. However, the start address of the video buffer depends on the type of adapter, the current mode (text or graphic), and the size of the video adapter's RAM. The information contained in Table 8.4 will come in useful when we create video images by writing directly into the video memory. It also illustrates the importance of your program knowing which adapter is present, particularly for working at the hardware level.

Table 8.4
Start Paragraphs of Video Buffer Memory for Different Video Adapters and Modes

Start Paragraph	Video Mode	Size of Video Memory	Adapter Type
0B000h	text	4000	MDA
0B800h	text	4000	CGA
0B800h	graphic	16K	CGA
0B800h	text (color)	4000	EGA, VGA, MCGA
0B000h	text (mono)	4000	EGA, VGA, MCGA
0A000h	graphic	32K	EGA
0A000h	graphic	> 32K	EGA, VGA, MCGA

Levels of Video Control

Earlier on, we looked at the three levels for controlling the keyboard. Similarly, the video system can be controlled on 3 levels which mean there are three ways of handling the screen display:

▲ Using the MS-DOS service
▲ Using the BIOS service
▲ Directly controlling the hardware

When considering a particular aspect of the video system we will look at the different methods involved for each level.

MS-DOS Video Service

The services provided by MS-DOS consist of several routines of the DOS interrupt 21h and the ANSI.SYS installable device driver. The functions of interrupt 21h are used to output separate characters in lines on the screen. The ANSI.SYS driver lets you control the screen and cursor by outputting special text strings called ESC-sequences. Note that the MS-DOS service routines are relatively limited and the tools provided do not allow you to deal with the screen very effectively. The exception to this is function 09h of interrupt 21h for outputting a line which ends with the $ character.

The following example puts the text "this is my string" onto the screen at the current cursor position.

```
DATA    SEGMENT
TEXT    DB    "this is my string", CR, LF, "$"
DATA    ENDS
CR      EQU   13          ; carriage return
LF      EQU   10          ; line feed ASCII codes

; Code segment
        push  ds          ; save segment register
        mov   ax,DATA     ; address of data segment
        mov   ds,ax       ; set DS to start of data segment
        mov   ah,9        ; function 09h - output text string
        lea   dx,TEXT     ; DS:DX point to text string
        int   21h         ; DOS service call
        pop   ds          ; restore segment register
; After this the cursor will be placed at the beginning
; of the next line on the screen (CR and LF will be processed)
```

The BIOS Video Service

In BIOS several functions for video system control are combined into the interrupt 10h handler. The functions of interrupt 10h are given in detail in Appendix F. In this chapter we'll discuss the functions of interrupt 10h designed to perform such operations as outputting characters, moving the cursor, getting/setting video modes and so on. For example, the following code uses the BIOS video service to move the cursor to line 12, column 28. The coordinates of the upper left-hand corner of the screen are (0.0).

```
mov   ah,2        ; AH = 2 - function number
xor   bx,bx       ; BX = 0 - number of video page
mov   dh,12       ; DH = 12 - line  (0 - 24)
mov   dl,28       ; DL = 28 - position (0 - 79)
int   10h         ; BIOS service call
```

Video Information in the BIOS Data Area

We have already discussed the most important fields of the BIOS data area related to video access. They occupy 30 bytes in the BIOS data area from address 0040h:0049h up 0040h:0066h. An example of using DEBUG for looking at these fields is shown in Figure 8.8.

The following list details the fields of the BIOS data area which you are most likely to use in your programs:

0040:0049h	1 byte	**Current video mode** (from 0 to 0Fh).
0040:0044Ah	2 bytes	**Screen width** (number of columns 20,40,80)
0040:0044Ch	2 bytes	number of bytes used for a video page (one screen). Usually 1000h.
0040:0044Eh	2 bytes	**Current video page offset address**. Dividing the offset by the length of the video page, gives the number of the active video page.
0040:0050h	16 bytes	**Cursor position** for 8 separate video pages. The lower byte of each word is the column (counting from (0,0)) and the higher byte is the row in which the cursor is located.
00040:0046h	2 bytes	**Cursor size** coded in scanning line numbers. The lower byte is the final line, the higher byte is the starting line for scanning.
0040:00462h	1 byte	**Current video page number**.
0040:00463h	2 bytes	**Video controller 6845 port address**. Equals 3B4h for a monochrome mode, 3D4h - for color.
0040:0065h	1 byte	**Display mode setting**.
0040:0066h	1 byte	**CGA palette registers settings**.
0040:0087h	1 byte	**EGA/VGA status bit**. The value 0 corresponds to MCGA. Otherwise check the value of bit 3: xxxx ?xxx. If it equals 1, then neither EGA nor VGA is active. Bits 5 and 6 describe the video adapter memory: the value 00 denotes 64K bytes, 01 - 128K, 10 - 192K and 11 - 256K bytes.

Controlling the Video Hardware

The third way of handling screen display, using the hardware directly, is more difficult and demands a thorough understanding of the features of your hardware. It does mean, though, that your programs will be

```
c:\>debug
-d 40:49
0040:0040                            03 50 00 00 10 00 00          .P.....
0040:0050  00 18 00 00 00 00 00 00-00 00 00 00 00 00 00 00   ...............
0040:0060  07 06 00 D4 03 29 30 88-05 87 90 00 42 4B 0E 00   .....)0.....BK..
0040:0070  00 00 00 00 00 00 01 00-14 14 14 14 01 01 01 01   ...............
0040:0080  1E 00 3E 00 18 0E 00 60-F9 00 00 45 58 00 00 37   ..>....'...EX..7
0040:0090  74 07 00 00 3A 00 10 10-00 00 00 00 00 00 00 00   t...:..........
0040:00A0  00 09 00 00 00 00 00 00-C8 04 00 C0 00 00 00 00   ...............
0040:00B0  00 00 00 00 00 00 00 00-00 00 00 00 00 00 00 00   ...............
0040:00C0  00 00 00 00 00 00 00 00-00                        ........
-q

c:\>_
```

Figure 8.8
The BIOS
Video Data
Area Listed by
DEBUG

faster, because there are no intermediate routines adding to the
performance time. For screen output, you only need to write data into
the video buffer (using the MOV, STOS and MOVS instructions) making
use of the fact that it can map directly onto the display. This is illustrated
in the following example which shows how to clear the screen and
paint it with a given color by outputting a blank character with the
corresponding attributes.

```
......
BlnkStr db   80 dup (' ',17h) ; Blank string (white on blue-17h)
......
        mov   ax,0B800h    ; 0B800h - address of video buffer (color)
        mov   es,ax        ; ES points to video buffer
        mov   cx,25        ; repeat 25 times for whole screen
RepOut:mov   di,0   ; ES:DI, effective address of video buffer start
        lea   si,BlnkStr; DS:SI, effective address of text to output
        Con10 dw,10
        push  cx           ; save strings counter
        mov   cx,80        ; total length of string
rep     mov   sb           ; send string to video memory
        pop   cx           ; restore strings counter
        add   es,Con10     ; increase effective address by 160
        loop  RepOut
......
```

This task can also be performed using the BIOS service (function 09h)
of interrupt 10h):

```
        mov   ah,09h   ; function 09h - output character and attribute
        mov   bh,0     ; video page 0 will be used
        mov   cx,2000  ; 2000 characters (80*25)
```

```
mov    al,' '    ; character to be output
mov    bl,17h    ; attribute (white on blue)
int    10h       ; BIOS Video service
```

Although the second example may seem more appealing as it looks simpler, it is unfortunately a lot slower.

Reading data from the screen on the low-level involves an additional process, in that you have to receive data from the video buffer. Although this sounds quite simple, in practice it is not. When low-level programming the screen, besides reading from and writing to the buffer you also have to deal with the video adapter registers (via their input/ output ports). Furthermore, you need to understand how the BIOS data area works with video functions. However, although the low-level technique isn't easy to use, it is often preferable for writing programs. This method works equally well for text and graphics modes and the speed of data interchange is several times faster than using BIOS functions or slow MS-DOS functions.

You can check this by running two demo programs: PG0800 and PG0801 from your program disk. Both programs perform the same action; they fill the screen in the text mode with a given character. The program PG0800 uses interrupt 10h (BIOS service) for screen output and PG0801 writes the image directly into the video buffer. Experimenting with PG0803 is even more impressive! These programs draw a colored net in graphics mode at incredible speed.

Choosing the Right Level

In deciding how to approach video programming, the first point to bear in mind is that using the standard video services (BIOS, MS-DOS) takes less effort, makes your programs more portable and provides compatibility with the most recent versions of MS-DOS and its clones.

Low-level programming however, is incredibly fast and offers much greater opportunities for screen input/output, which are often inaccessible by other means. If you are creating graphics programs, there are really no alternatives to low-level techniques.

The most effective way of working is to combine these three methods and to select one depending on the particular task in hand. For example, it is easier to move the cursor using the functions of BIOS interrupt 10h, whereas writing directly into the video buffer is much more convenient for outputting text strings.

Tools

Getting the Current Video Mode

A program that works with the screen, especially in the low-level, has to begin by reading and saving the current screen mode. The simplest way of doing this is to use function 0Fh of the BIOS interrupt 10h.

```
mov    ah,0Fh      ; function 0Fh - get video mode
int    10h         ; BIOS video service call
mov    VMODE,al    ; save video mode
```

The possible screen mode values are given in Table 8.5.

Mode	Resolution	Colors	Text/Graphics	Videoadapter
00h	40x25	Mono (16)	text	CGA, EGA, MCGA, VGA
01h	40x25	16	text	CGA, EGA, MCGA, VGA
02h	80x25	Mono (16)	text	CGA, EGA, MCGA, VGA
03h	80x25	16	text	CGA, EGA, MCGA, VGA
04h	320x200	4	graphics	CGA, EGA, MCGA, VGA
05h	320x200	Mono (4)	graphics	CGA, EGA, MCGA, VGA
06h	640x200	2	graphics	CGA, EGA, MCGA, VGA
07h	80x25	Mono (2)	text	MDA, EGA, VGA
08h	160x200	16	graphics	PCjr only
09h	320x200	16	graphics	PCjr only
0Ah	640x200	4	graphics	PCjr only
0Bh	reserved			
0Ch	reserved			
0Dh	320x200	16	graphics	EGA, VGA
0Eh	640x200	16	graphics	EGA, VGA
0Fh	640x350	Mono (2)	graphics	EGA, VGA
10h	640x350	4	graphics	EGA, VGA (64 KB)
10h	640x350	16	graphics	EGA, VGA (128 KB)
11h	640x480	2	graphics	MCGA, VGA
12h	640x480	16	graphics	VGA
13h	320x200	256	graphics	MCGA, VGA

Table 8.5
Possible Video Modes for Different Adapters

This task can also be performed using the low-level technique by reading one byte from the BIOS data area at the address 0040h:0049h. This byte always contains the current video mode. The following portion of code shows how you can do this.

```
    mov    ax,40h        ;  start of BIOS data area
    mov    es,ax         ;  ES points to BIOS data
    mov    al,es:[49h]   ;  AL - current video mode
```

If you want to change the video mode you have to reset it by performing the Setting Video Mode operation, discussed below.

Setting the Video Mode

To set a video mode use function 0 of interrupt 10h. Before you call the interrupt, place the code of the video mode you require into the AL register:

```
; set graphics mode (640x350, 16 color, EGA or VGA)
    mov    ax,0010h      ;  video mode = 10h
    int    10h           ;  set video mode
```

Note that changing the value at location 040h:49h (the video mode byte in the BIOS data area) does not change the video mode. While setting the video mode the BIOS routines perform a sequence of actions such as clearing the screen, setting up the correct registers for the video adapter and reprogramming the character generator.

You can change the video mode manually using the input/output instructions but it is rather a complicated approach. For this reason it's better to use the standard BIOS function when you are writing programs that use different video modes. It is possible to disable the screen clear on the EGA and VGA by setting bit 7 of AL to 1. In this case the contents of the video memory will not change, so you'll see the same picture on the screen that you saw before the video mode was changed.

Once MS-DOS has been loaded, it sets the video to mode 3, text mode 80x25, and fills all the attribute bytes of the screen with 07h (grey on black).

To ensure that the programs you create work reliably, even when the video mode changes, there are a few basic steps you should follow:

Read the current screen mode
Save it in the memory
Perform the necessary actions
Restore the screen mode
Exit the program

Here is an example of a program created in this way (we have only given the key parts of the code).

```
; save preceding video mode
begin:  mov   ah,0Fh      ; get video mode
        int   10h         ; call BIOS service
        mov   VMODE,al    ; save video mode
......
; main part of program
......
; exiting program and returning to DOS
ExProg:
        mov   al,VMODE    ; preceding video mode
        xor   ah,ah       ; AH =0 -set video mode
        int   10h         ; call BIOS service
        mov   ax,4C00h    ; return code =00
        int   21h         ; exit to MS-DOS
```

If you follow these guidelines, you shouldn't have any problems when using the video system.

You can set the screen mode using a built-in MS-DOS tool - the ANSI.SYS driver. This driver controls the display monitor according to special control character strings called ESC-sequences. To use these strings, start by forming a control sequence, then output it onto the screen as ordinary text:

```
DATA  SEGMENT
VMODE DB    1Bh          ; code of ESC character
      DB    '[='         ; operation code
      DB    07h          ; video mode required
      DB    '$'          ; end of string
DATA  ENDS
```
```
; set monochrome video mode
begin:mov   ax,DATA      ; address of DATA segment
      mov   ds,ax        ; set segment register
      mov   ah,9         ; function 09h - output text string
      lea   dx,VMODE     ; DS:DX - address of string
      int   21h          ; DOS service call
```

Determining the Video Adapter Type

If you are writing directly into the video buffer, you will often need to know which type of video adapter is being used, particularly when working in graphics mode. Determining the type of video adapter is much more difficult than determining the video mode. There are several ways of going about this, but we will just look at the two most typical.

The first way which we will consider involves reading the byte at the address 0040h:0087h from the BIOS data area, which contains information about the status of an EGA display. If this byte equals 0, it means that the adapter is neither EGA nor VGA. If this is not the case, you need to test its third bit: xxxx ?xxx. This time, a value of 1 indicates that an EGA or VGA are either not active, or not present at all. The next step is to test for MDA. If the adapter is monochrome, then bits 4 and 5 of the lower byte of the hardware list will be set. You can get the hardware list using BIOS interrupt 11h or directly from the BIOS data area at the address 0040h:0010h. Finally, if neither VGA, EGA nor MDA are discovered, you can assume that the system is using a CGA card. Below we have given part of a program which returns the code for a video adapter in the AL register: 0 - MDA, 1 - CGA, 2 - EGA or VGA.

```
        push   es                      ; save segment register
        mov    ax,40h                  ; segment of BIOS data
        mov    es,ax                   ; ES points to BIOS data
; Looking for EGA/VGA adapters
EGAVGA:
        test   byte ptr es:[87h],0     ; EGA or VGA not installed ?
        jz     MDA                     ; test MDA
        test   byte ptr es:[87h],08h   ; is EGA or VGA active ?
        jnz    MDA                     ; test MDA
        mov    al,2                    ; EGA or VGA is present
        jmp    short Exit              ; return
; Looking for an MDA adapter
MDA:    mov    ax,es:[10h]             ; get equipment list
        and    al,30h                  ; mask bits
        cmp    al,30h                  ; is MDA present ?
        jne    CGA                     ; test CGA
        xor    al,al                   ; AL =0 -MDA
        jmp    short Exit              ; return
CGA:    mov    al,1                    ; AL =1 -CGA
exit:   pop    es                      ; restore segment register
```

This algorithm is sufficient in most cases, since you will probably only need to know whether you have a color or monochrome monitor. If you need more detailed information, such as the amount of memory installed on the video card, use the BIOS service interrupt 10h, function 1Ah provided on VGA adapters.

Start by calling function 1Ah of interrupt 10h by placing 1A00h into the AX register and then executing interrupt 10h. Now examine the contents of the AL register. If AL = 1Ah you can then analyze the contents of the BL register using Table 8.6 and determine the active display. A similar code for the inactive display can be read from the BH register, should another adapter be present.

If the AL register is not equal to 1Ah, it means that the adapter is neither VGA nor MCGA (1Ah means a VGA BIOS is present). In this case, the content of the BX register does not change. To determine the presence of an EGA adapter, use subfunction 10h of function 12h - the BIOS service "getting information on the EGA/VGA configuration":

```
; checking whether an EGA adapter is installed
CHCKEGA: mov   ah,12h      ; function 12h -
         mov   bl,10h; subfunction 10h-get EGA/VGA configuration
         int   10h         ; call BIOS video service
```

Codes (BL)	Video Type
00h	not defined
01h	MDA
02h	CGA
03h	reserved
04h	EGA
05h	EGA
06h	PGA
07h	VGA (monochrome)
08h	VGA (color)
09h	reserved
0Ah	MCGA (color digital)
0Bh	MCGA (monochrome analogous)
0Ch	MCGA (color analogous)

Table 8.6
The Meaning of the BL Register Contents (INT20h)

The result will be returned in the BX and CX registers as follows:

```
BH   = 0 - Color Display
BH   = 1 - Monochrome Display
BL   = memory installed on EGA board:
BL   = 0 -  64 KB
BL   = 1 - 128 KB
BL   = 2 - 192 KB
BL   = 3 - 256 KB
CH   = feature bits
CL   = switch setting
```

If the CX register is equal to 0 it means that the video adapter is not an EGA and you need to check for an MDA or CGA. You can also use this function to test quickly for the presence of an EGA or VGA by placing a known value in BX other than 0,1,2,3. If this value is still present after the function call, then the display adapter is neither EGA nor VGA. Note that if a monochrome monitor is connected to either EGA, VGA or MCGA cards, then the segment address of the video buffer is 0B000h as for an MDA card.

The methods we have looked at let you get information with varying amounts of detail. If you just want basic, initial information, you can use a small program like the one given at the beginning of this section. If you have determined that your adapter is at least EGA, but still need more information, use the BIOS service (subfunction 10h of function 12h of interrupt 10h). At the other end of the scale, you can get the most detailed information available on VGA/MCGA adapters and monitors with the help of function 1Ah of the BIOS video service (interrupt 10h).

The algorithm we have discussed forms the basis for three subroutines which are designed to be called from Assembler, Microsoft QUICK BASIC (also suitable for Microsoft FORTRAN and Microsoft Pascal) and C programs. The texts of these subroutines are given on your program disk in files VIDTYP.ASM, FVIDEO.ASM and CVIDEO.C.

The example below will determine the video adapter type in an assembly language program:

```
; Check whether EGA / VGA adapter installed
     Call   VIDTYP       ; call subroutine for determining adapter
     cmp    al,3         ; EGA or higher?
     jnl    Graph        ; OK - continue
     lea    dx,TEXT1     ; DX - address of message
```

```
mov     ah,9        ; function 09h - output text string
int     21h         ; DOS service call
xor     ah,ah       ; function 0 - read a key
int     16h         ; BIOS keyboard service
jmp     ExProg      ; to finish program
```

Fragments similar to the one just shown are used in the demo programs PG0800 - PG0808 stored on your program disk. This fragment checks the type of the video adapter that is returned in the AL register by the VidTyp subroutine. Then, depending on this value, the program either continues working or outputs a message "EGA/VGA not installed" and passes control to the final block of the program.

The program VidTyp returns the type of the video adapter in the AL register and the segment address of the video buffer in the DX register. The contents of the BX and CX registers are the same as the values returned by subfunction 10h of function 12h of interrupt 10h. The value in the DX register is 0B000 for MDA or HGC video adapters and 0B800 for color adapters, the meaning of the AL register is as follows:

AL = 0 - MDA
AL = 1 - CGA
AL = 2 - MCGA
AL = 3 - EGA
AL = 4 - VGA

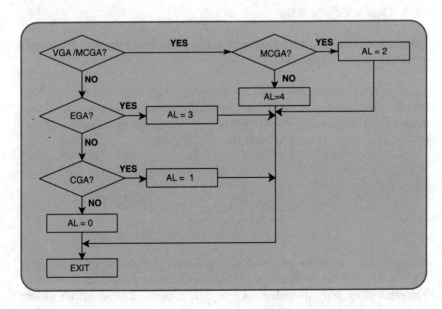

Figure 8.9
Flow Chart for the VidTyp Program

Selecting the Active Video Page

Although all video cards, except the MDA, have at least 16K bytes of memory, only 4000 bytes are used to create the screen image in text modes. You can use these free parts of video memory to prepare the contents of several whole screens "in advance" and then swiftly change the screen image by switching between these parts.

The area of the memory intended for storing the screen contents is divided into sections of 4096 bytes, called video pages. These are numbered from 0 up to the maximum number, which is determined by the total amount of video memory installed. For example, if your PC uses 16K bytes of memory for the video buffer, you can use 4 video pages: 0, 1, 2 and 3. The video page currently displayed on the screen, is called the active page. The active video page number is frequently used in calling BIOS video services.

If you use the functions of interrupt 10h (BIOS video service), the number of the active video page will usually be placed into the BH register. As a rule, BH = 0 in the graphics mode.

To write text into, or read it from the video buffer directly, you need to calculate the displacement of the active video page from the start of the video buffer. You can do this using the following formula:

$$Disp = Page \times 4096$$

where *Disp* is the value of displacement in bytes and *Page* is the number of video pages required.

You can select the active page by using function 05h of interrupt 10h (BIOS video service). The following example shows how to select the active video page using the BIOS service. Note that the number of the new active page is placed into the AL register.

```
; Selection of the active video page
    mov    ah,5      ; Function 05h - Select Video Page
    mov    al,2      ; Number of page selected
    int    10h       ; BIOS video service
```

As far as low level programming is concerned, it is better to use the BIOS data area for determining the current video page and access the corresponding part of video memory. The offset of the active video page is stored as one word, located at the address 0040h:004Eh. To get the number of the active video page you simply need to divide this value by 4096. Note that the same value (the number of the active video page) is stored in the BIOS data area in one byte at the address 0040h:0062h. You can switch the active video page by changing the offset at the address 0040h:004Eh. Have a look at the example below:

```
; Selection of the active video page
     mov    ax,40h      ; Segment of BIOS data area
     mov    es,ax       ; ES points to start of BIOS data
     mov    al,2        ; Number of active video page
     cbw                ;  AX -Page Number
     mov    cl,12       ; Number of bits for shift into CL
     shl    ax,cl       ; Shift to left: Page * 4096
     mov    es:[4Eh],ax ; Set new active video page
```

The 8 words placed at the address 0040h:0050h determine the location of the cursor for each of the 8 video pages. The first byte of a word determines a column, the second - a row.

Program PG0807.ASM on your program disk demonstrates managing video pages. It forms 4 screen images, each of which is written in its own video page. The video pages 0 - 3 are selected consecutively, which means that the screen image changes very quickly. As you can see, this technique is very useful for creating applications which need fast graphics, such as animation.

Controlling the Cursor

One of the most important features of the video system is the cursor. It is only present in text modes and is used to indicate the current active position on the screen.

Screen output performed by the BIOS and DOS video services usually begins from the current position of the hardware cursor. Note that in graphics modes, text operations such as the output of text are actually performed from the current position of the cursor, even though it isn't shown on the screen. If you are operating at a low-level (writing into the video buffer), output is performed independently of the cursor. In fact, you can actually switch off the hardware cursor and create your own. Furthermore, if you have several windows on the screen, you can create a cursor for each window.

If several video pages are used, each of them has its own cursor. The position of the cursor is described using the standard text mode co-ordinates, with the columns ranging from 39 to 79 and the rows from 24 to 49.

The cursor is usually generated by the 6845 microprocessor (the hardware cursor) and appears as a short line which blinks. You can easily change the location and size of the cursor using the BIOS service, or directly by changing the contents of certain special registers of the video cards. Changing the frequency at which the cursor blinks is a little more complicated.

To control the cursor you can use the BIOS video service (functions of interrupt 10h), MS-DOS tools including ESC-sequences available through the ANSI.SYS driver and various low level techniques (programming the registers of the video controller). In this chapter we'll describe the basic methods available for controlling the cursor using the BIOS and DOS services. The tasks which you are most likely to need this information for are:

- Reading the current position of the cursor.
- Changing the position of the cursor.
- Determining and changing the size of the cursor.
- Switching the cursor on and off.

Reading the Position of the Cursor

Function 03 of the BIOS interrupt 10h lets you read the position of the cursor. Just place the video page number into the BH register and then call interrupt 10h:

```
; Reading the current location of the cursor on the video page 0
      xor    bh,bh        ; Page Number = 0
      mov    ah,3         ; Function 03 - Get cursor parameters
      int    10h          ; BIOS video Service
```

As a result, the cursor coordinates will be returned in the DX register:

DH - row (Y coordinate)
DL - column (X coordinate)

The width of the cursor can be derived from the CX register:

> CH - starting line of the cursor in the video matrix
> CL - finishing line of the cursor in the video matrix

As an example we'll take the video matrix 8x14

N of row	Video matrix 8x14
0	. . . .
1	. . . .
2	. . . .
3	. . . .
4	. . . .
5	. . . .
6	. . . .
7	. . . .
8	. . . .
9	. . . .
10	* * * * * * * . CH = 10-Starting Line of Cursor
11	* * * * * * *
12	* * * * * * * . L = 12-Ending Line of Cursor
13	. . . .

For low-level cursor control, you can use the 8 words in the BIOS data area at locations 0040h:0050h - 0040:005E. Each of these words contains the cursor coordinates: the column is given in the low byte, the row in the high byte.

The word at the address 0040h:0060h contains the size of the cursor - the low byte contains the ending line of the cursor, and the high byte contains the starting line in the video matrix. Here is an example of reading the position of the cursor for page 0:

```
; Reading the characteristics of the cursor for video page 0
        xor   ax,ax          ;
        mov   es,ax          ;
        mov   dx,es:[44Eh]   ; DL -Column, DH -Row
        mov   cx,es:[460h]   ; CL -Ending Line
                             ; CH -Starting Line
```

Positioning the Cursor

Function 02h of the BIOS interrupt 10h lets you position the cursor. First place the parameters into the BH and DX registers in the following way:

> BH - number of the video page
> DH - row for cursor position
> DL - column for cursor position

Then place the number of the function (02h) into the AH register and call interrupt 10h.

```
; Positioning the cursor for video page 0
; into position (11, 19)
        xor     bh,bh           ; clear page number  (page 0)
        mov     dh,11           ; row  (X)
        mov     dl,19           ; column (Y)
        mov     ah,2h           ; function 02 - position cursor
        int     10h             ; BIOS video service
```

You can do the same thing using the ANSI.SYS driver that comes with MS-DOS. To do this, send the text of the corresponding ESC-sequence to the screen.

```
; The DATA segment
DATA SEGMENT
POS     DB      1Bh, '['  ; beginning of ESC sequence
        DB      '[11;19'  ; 11 row, 19 - column
        DB      'H'       ; operation "position cursor"
        DB      '$'       ; end of string
DATA ENDS
; The CODE segment
; Positioning the cursor into (11, 19)
        mov     ax,DATA   ; address of DATA segment
        mov     ds,ax     ; access DATA through DS register
        lea     dx,POS    ; DS:DX point to ESC sequence
        mov     ah,9      ; function 09h - output text string
        int     21h       ; MS-DOS service call
```

Note that the MS-DOS service only works for the active video page.

Low-level cursor control again involves programming the video card registers, which is quite a complicated task. So, for simplicity's sake, we advise you to use the BIOS video service.

Changing the Size of the Cursor

As we explained earlier, the hardware cursor is made up of a few short scanning lines. The size of the cursor is determined by the number of these lines and you can get this information through function 3 of the BIOS video service. This function returns the size in the CX register in the following way:

> CH - Starting Line for Cursor
> CL - Ending Line for Cursor

The size of the cursor is stored as one word in the BIOS data area at the address 0040h:0060h.

Function 01h of interrupt 10h sets the values for the starting and ending lines of the cursor. Parameters are passed through the CX register.

```
; Changing the size of the cursor
      mov   ah,1     ;  function
      mov   ch,3     ;  CH - starting line for cursor
      mov   cl,13    ;  CL - ending line for cursor
      int   10h      ;  BIOS service
```

Executing this program gives you an upright rectangular cursor. Note that when you are changing the size of the cursor you do not need to specify the number of the video page, because the size of the cursor is made standard for all video pages.

Low-level programming again involves working with the video cursor registers, which we do not intend to cover.

You can see a working example of all these processes by executing the demo program PG0808. Another example of controlling the cursor size is the resident program CursKeep stored on your program disk. This can be used for avoiding the "disappearing" cursor syndrome in DR-DOS 6 which can happen when working on some versions of EGA BIOS.

Switching the Cursor On/Off

Sometimes it is useful to remove the hardware cursor from the screen, for example if you want to use your own program cursor. Unfortunately there is no BIOS video service function which lets you do this directly. What you can do though is position the cursor outside the screen borders using function 02 of interrupt 10h:

```
; Switching the cursor off by positioning it outside the screen
     xor    bh,bh      ; page number 0
     mov    dh,25      ; row = 25
     mov    dl,80      ; column = 80
     mov    ah,2       ; function 02 - position cursor
     int    10h        ; BIOS video service
```

Although this is the simplest way, it does have its disadvantages. The most significant one being that if you then output text onto the screen, this text must start from the current cursor position, which is actually outside the screen. Another way to switch the cursor off is to set a size that cannot be displayed, which we will demonstrate in the "Library" section.

Text Input and Output

The BIOS and MS-DOS services for text input and output both work very slowly and have very poor facilities for managing color images. Moreover, they output characters or lines from the hardware cursor position, which is not very convenient. A further disadvantage with MS-DOS is that the functions can only use the active page.

Directly writing to/reading from the video buffer is by far the better option. It lets you create high-quality, color images without using the hardware cursor. It is also a relatively simple method to grasp as it only involves common data transfer instructions: **MOV**, **STOS** and **LODS**.

Although most programs and program packages use method 3, direct access to the video memory, we will actually look at each way in detail.

Outputting Text Using BIOS

The BIOS video service offers three functions for outputting characters onto the screen and one function for writing a string of characters, which is available on PCs with an EGA or more recent adapter. The services are as follows.

The Function 09h - Write a Character and Attribute at the Cursor

This function outputs a character with the specified attribute at the current position of the cursor. Note that this function doesn't change the cursor's position. The character to be output must be placed into the AL register and the attribute - into the BL register. The CX register must contain the number of repetitions for writing the character and the attribute.

The Function 0Ah - Write a Character at the Cursor

This function works in the same way as the function 09h. The only difference is that the function 0Ah does not change the attribute of the current position on the screen so the BL register isn't used by this function. Likewise, the position of the cursor isn't changed by the function call.

The Function 0Eh - Output a Character in Teletype Mode

This function uses the attribute which already exists in the video memory. The rules for passing parameters are the same as for the function 0Ah. After writing a character the cursor moves to the next position on the right. When the cursor reaches the end of a row it automatically moves to the start of the next row. You might find this function useful for writing a string of characters, like the example below, which writes an ASCIIZ-string onto the screen starting at row 2, column 0.

```
..............................................................
STR    DB    'Hello World!' ; text string
       DB    0              ; end of string
..............................................................
;  code segment
;  output of characters in teletype mode
       lea   si,STR         ; DS:SI - address of string
       xor   bh,bh          ; video page = 0
cycle:lodsb                 ; AL - symbol of string
       and   al,al          ; end of string ?
       jz    ExProc         ; yes
       mov   ah,0Eh         ; function 0Eh - write character
       int   10h            ; call BIOS service
       jmp   short cycle    ; repeat
ExProc:
..............................................................
```

The Function 13h - Write a String in Teletype Mode

The process for calling this function is quite complicated. To call it, place the number of the function into the AH register, as usual. The AL register contains the number of the subfunction, i.e. its contents define the output mode. The valid subfunction numbers are 0,1,2 and 3. The meaning of the value in the AL register is as follows:

> 0 - The characters are written ignoring the attributes stored in the video memory, the attribute in BL is used instead and the cursor doesn't move;
>
> 1 - The characters are written ignoring the attributes stored in the video memory, the attribute in BL is used, the cursor moves.
>
> 2 - The characters are written ignoring attributes, the cursor doesn't move;
>
> 3 - The characters are written ignoring attributes, the cursor moves.

The value in the CX register is the full length of the string. The DX register contains the coordinates of the string's beginning on the screen: Y coordinate (Row) in DH and X coordinate (Column) in DL. The address of the string is passed in the ES:BP registers. The following example shows how to use this service for outputting a very familiar string:

```
. . . . . . . . . . . . . . . . . . . . . . . . . . . . . . . . . . . . . . . . . . . . . . . . . . . . . . . . . . . .
STR   DB 'Hello World!' ; text string
. . . . . . . . . . . . . . . . . . . . . . . . . . . . . . . . . . . . . . . . . . . . . . . . . . . . . . . . . . . .
; code      segment
; output of string in teletype mode
      push  ds              ; address of DATA segment onto stack
      pop   es              ; ES now points to DATA segment
      lea   bp,STR          ; ES:BP - address of string
      xor   bh,bh           ; video page = 0
      mov   bl,71h          ; attribute (blue on white)
      mov   al,1            ; move cursor, attribute in BL
      mov   cx,12           ; length of string
      int   10h            ; BIOS video service
ExProc:
. . . . . . . . . . . . . . . . . . . . . . . . . . . . . . . . . . . . . . . . . . . . . . . . . . . . . . . . . . . .
```

Outputting Text Using DOS

MS-DOS offers two ways of outputting characters, INT 21h, INT 29h. Each of these functions writes a white character on a black background (attribute equals 07h) using the video page 0 only. The cursor moves to the next position on the right and jumps to the next row after reaching the end of the current one or on detecting control symbols like CR = 0Dh - Carriage Return and LF = 0Ah - line feed.

Interrupt 21h has three functions for outputting texts. Note that the function number must be placed into the AL register before calling interrupt 21h. The first function is 02h which is designed for character output. Two functions, 09h and 40h, can be used to write a string on the screen. Both these functions write a string with black and white characters onto the active video page from the cursor position. Let's look at how they work.

The Function 02h - Output Character at Cursor Position

This function recognizes the Ctrl+Break symbol and processes it. To use the function 02h, place the character to be output into the DL register, place the number of the function into the AH register and call the interrupt 21h. Here is an example:

```
; Code segment
; Output of black-and-white character "B" (function 02h):
    mov    dl,"B"    ; output symbol
    mov    ah,02h    ; function
    int    21h       ; MS-DOS service
```

The Interrupt 29h - Fast Character Output

To use interrupt 29h, Fast Putchar, start by placing the code of the character into the AL register, then call interrupt 29h. This interrupt uses the teletype mode (function 0Eh of the interrupt int 10h).

The Function 09h - String Output

This function writes a string of characters, ending with the $ sign. The address of the string is passed in the DS:DX registers.

After the string has been written, the cursor automatically moves to the next position after the end of the string. This function does not move the cursor to the start of the next row on the screen. To do this you have to use the control codes CR (Carriage Return) and LF (Line Feed).

To write a string, place the function number into the AH register and the start address of the string into DS:DX, then call interrupt 21h.

```
CR      EQU     0Dh                     ; CR
LF      EQU     0Ah                     ; LF
; Data segment
DATA    SEGMENT
STR     DB      'This is my Text !!!'   ; text string
        DB      CR, LF                  ; CR & LF
        DB      "$"                     ; end of string
DATA    ENDS
```

```
; code segment
; output string from cursor position
        mov     ax,DATA                 ; segment address of DATA
        mov     ds,ax                   ;
        lea     dx,STR                  ; DS:DX - address of string
        mov     ah,9                    ; function
        int     21h                     ; call MS-DOS service
```

It's good, isn't it? It's easy to see why this function is so popular for outputting messages and so on.

Int 21h Function 40h - Write File with Handle

Although this function can be used for outputting characters onto the screen, in practice it is rarely used for this purpose. It was originally designed for file processing but we have included it here because it might be useful for creating device-independent programs.

To use this function place the address of the string into the DS:DX registers, the value of the file handle into the BX register and the length of the string - into the CX register. Then call the DOS service - interrupt 21h.

The following example shows how to use function 40h for outputting a character string on the screen. The example given is the complete program that outputs the text "Hello World!" onto the screen.

```
.model small
.stack
.data
TextStr db 'Hello World!'
.code
.startup
        mov     ah,40h          ; function 40h - write file with handle
```

```
        movbx,1            ; 1 - value of handle for screen
        movcx,11           ; length of string for output into CX
        leadx,TextStr      ; DS:DX - address of string to be output
        int    21h         ; DOS service call

        mov    ax,4C00h    ; function 4Ch - terminate process
        int    21h         ; DOS service call
        end
```

Outputting Text Using Low Level Access

We'll now move on to the low level, which involves writing characters and attributes directly into the video buffer. We have already explained that the text for screen output is transferred onto the screen from the buffer in the video memory by the video controller, and that the CPU has direct access to this memory. As you already know, the video memory is located in the video adapter card and its size depends on the type of video adapter; its starting segment address is 0A000h, just after the 640K mark, and it ends at the segment address 0C800h (see Figure 8.1). Only part of this memory is used in text mode.

The starting segment address of the video buffer is 0B000h for a monochrome display (with adapters MDA, MCGA, EGA, VGA), and 0B800h for all color displays (with adapters CGA, MCGA, EGA, VGA). Note that the starting segment address for CGA is always 0B800h.

Before starting to write directly into video memory you need to determine the type of video adapter and display present. This information allows you to select the right value of the starting address of the video buffer from the two possible values (0B000h or 0B800h).

Your program disk contains the subroutine VidTyp which uses information located in the BIOS data area and returns the type of video adapter as well as the segment address for the beginning of the video buffer (in the DX register). To call this subroutine, follow the standard procedure:

```
CALL VIDTYP
```

No input parameters are required. Note that this subroutine is used in all demo programs (in this chapter at least).

The example given here will fill the first row of the screen with the character "E", giving you a blue background, with a light yellow foreground. The video adapter type is CGA (color display) or EGA/

VGA in color mode.

```
; Output of "E" characters in first row.
mov    ax,0B800h        ; video buffer segment address
mov    es,ax            ; ES points to video buffer
xor    di,di            ; output from beginning of screen
mov    ah,1Eh           ; attribute (yellow on blue)
mov    al,"E"           ; character to be written
mov    cx,80            ; quantity of repetitions
cld                     ; direction - forward !!!
repstosw                ; ES:[DI] -output character
```

Preventing Snow on the CGA

The procedure described above in fact works perfectly with all video adapter types except the CGA. With this adapter, short white lines and spots will appear on the screen during output. This is what is known as "snow" and unfortunately, it even falls in summer!

This phenomenon is an unfortunate feature of the CGA card and is caused by interference. It happens because both the microprocessor of the videocard (while forming an image) and the CPU (while reading from or writing to the video buffer) have access to the video memory. "Snow" starts falling when they both use the video memory at the same time, for example when reading or writing is performed using the video buffer. There are two ways of weather proofing yourself against snow:

▲ Switch off the screen while the video buffer is being filled.

▲ Only access the video buffer during the retrace of an electron beam (the beam is switched off during this process, so there is no interference on the screen).

Both of these methods use registers of the 6845 microprocessor, namely the Mode Select Register and the Input Status Register. These registers are accessible through the I/O ports 3D8h and 3DAh using the IN and OUT instructions. In the course of your life as a programmer, you will undoubtedly come across expressions like "the video register 3D5h". Although we all understand what this means, don't forget that there is a clear difference between the I/O port and the register which belongs to hardware. On the whole you can treat the I/O ports as the microprocessor's door to the outside world. For example, one port can be used for accessing several registers even if they belong to different

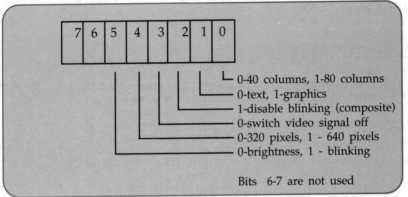

Figure 8.10
The Meaning of the Mode Select Register Bits

chips. Having said that though, remember that one register of a controller can be accessed through more than one I/O port. So, when you say something like "the video register 3D8h" it pays to bear in mind that you actually mean "a register of the video controller currently accessible through the I/O port 3D8h".

Getting back to where we were, note that the 3D8h register is only used for writing and 3DAh - for reading. Figures 8.10 and 8.11 describe the bitwise fields of the registers. The current value of the Mode Select Register is stored at the address 0040h:0065h.

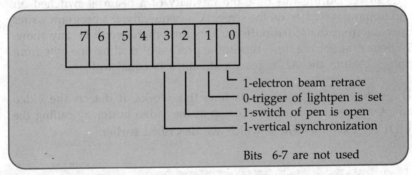

Figure 8.11
The Meaning of the Input Status Register Bits

The following example demonstrates clearing the snow by switching off the screen.

```
; switching CGA-screen off before writing into video buffer
; current mode value locates at address 0:[465h]
    xor   ax,ax          ; segment address of BIOS data area
    mov   es,ax          ; ES becomes 0
    mov   al,es:[465h]   ; current mode value
    mov   bl,al          ; saving current mode value
```

```
        mov    dx,3D8h          ; mode register
        and    al,0F7h          ; switch video signal off
        out    dx,al            ; switch display off
; outputting "E" symbols from start of screen
        mov    ax,0B800h        ; video buffer segment address
        mov    es,ax            ; ES points to video buffer
        xor    di,di            ; output from start of screen
        mov    ah,1Eh           ; attribute (yellow on blue)
        mov    al,"E"           ; symbol to output
        mov    cx,80            ; quantity of symbols to output
        cld                     ; direction - forward !!!
        rep    stosw            ; ES:[DI] -output character
; switching on screen after writing into video buffer
        mov    dx,3D8h          ; mode register
        mov    al,bl            ; switch video signal on
        out    dx,al            ; switch display on
```

This method completely eliminates the snow but slows down the interchange with the screen. You will find another example of this method on your program disk. The program COLOR.ASM fills the screen with a prescribed color, switching the screen off in the CGA mode.

The method of using the period of electron beam retrace is more effective. The horizontal retrace is performed when bit 0 of the 3DAh register equals 1. As you'll remember, the horizontal retrace lasts for 1-1.5 msec. During this time the intensity of a beam is switched off and nothing is written on the screen. Consequently, if a program writes or reads from the video buffer at this time there won't be any snow. To detect the retrace time, repeat the process of reading one byte from port 3DA into the AL register until bit 0 is equal to 0.

The following program shows how this works. It detects the video adapter type and segment address of the video buffer by calling the VIDTYP.ASM subroutine which we described earlier.

```
; outputting "E" characters into first row
        call   VIDTYP           ; DX - segment address of video buffer
        mov    bl,al            ; AL = 1 - CGA video adapter
        mov    es,dx            ; ES points to target segment
        xor    di,di            ; output from start of screen
        mov    cx,80            ; quantity of symbols
        cld                     ; direction - forward !!!
; outer loop for sending 80 symbols to first row
; testing type of video adapter, is it CGA ?
cycle0:
        cmp    bl,1             ; is it CGA ?
        jne    WrChar           ; no, it's safe to write
        mov    dx,3DAh          ; status register
```

```
;  waiting for completion of current retrace
cycle1:
      in    al,dx          ;  reading status register
      test  al,1           ;  is retrace being executed now ?
      jnz   cycle1         ;  yes, wait for end
;  testing , is writing without snow possible ?
cycle2:
      in    al,dx          ;  read status register
      test  al,1           ;  is retrace being executed now ?
      jz    cycle2         ;  no, continue testing
;  writing character and it's attribute into video buffer
WrChar:
      mov   ah,1Eh         ;  attribute (yellow on blue)
      mov   al,"E"         ;  character to output
      stosw                ;  ES:[DI] -output character
      loop  cycle0         ;  come to start of loop
```

Although CGA cards are rarely used now, any program that works directly with a video buffer should detect the type of video adapter and, if necessary, eliminate snow.

Most demo programs from your program disk that work with the screen use direct access to the video buffer and suppress snow.

The programs PG0800 and PG0801 from your program disk fill the screen with the character "E". Program PG0800 uses the BIOS video service (function 0Eh, interrupt 10h) to do this whereas PG0801 works in low level and writes directly into the video buffer. When you run this, you will see how much faster a program works when you use direct access.

Reading a Character or a String From the Screen

The standard BIOS video service (interrupt 10h) only provides one function for this purpose. Function 8h reads a character and an attribute from the current cursor position on the video page specified by the number stored in the BH register. The result is returned in the AX register: AL contains the character which has been read and AH - the attribute of this character.

As far as working with the video buffer (in low level) is concerned, the reading operation is quite similar to writing. The obvious distinction is that instead of sending data, you must take it from the buffer.

Let's consider the following example which illustrates low-level access; it reads a character and an attribute from row 12, column 50, video page 2 (naturally, we start counting from 0).

This program is quite similar to the previous one which wrote characters into a string. Since we are using a video page with a non-zero number, its offset has to be evaluated from the beginning of the video buffer (for video page 2 the offset equals 1000h).

Next you have to determine the address of the character in the video page. Remember that each character in a video buffer occupies two bytes: one for the character and one for its attribute.

```
; determining offset of character in video buffer
        call  VIDTYP      ; DX - segment address of video buffer
        mov   bl,al       ; store adapter type in BL
        mov   ds,dx       ; DS points to video buffer
        mov   si,1000h    ; offset of videopage 2
        mov   ax,12       ; row number (0 - 25)
        mov   bh,80*2     ; multiplier - length of one row
        mul   bh          ; AX - offset of row 12
        add   ax,50*2     ; offset caused by position
        add   si,ax       ; offset in video buffer
; testing video adapter  (CGA ?)
cycle0: cmp   bl,1        ; is it CGA?
        jne   RdChar      ; no, it's safe to read
        mov   dx,3DAh     ; status register
; waiting for completion of current retrace
cycle1: in    al,dx       ; read status register
        test  al,1        ; is retrace being executed now?
        jnz   cycle1      ; yes, wait for completion
; testing, if reading without snow is possible
cycle2: in    al,dx       ; reading status register
        test  al,1        ; is retrace executed now, may we read?
        jz    cycle2      ; no, go on testing
; reading character and attribute from video buffer ( DS:[SI])
RdChar: mov   ax,[si]     ; AH - attribute; AL -character
```

If you need to read more than one character, you will have to organize a loop.

Clearing the Screen and Filling it with a Prescribed Color

The simplest way of clearing the screen is to set a video mode using function 0 of interrupt 10h (BIOS video service). The screen is filled with blanks and all attributes are set to 07 which will give you grey letters on a black background. This is most often used at the start of programs, when a specific video mode is going to be set anyway. The screen will be black once you have cleared it.

Another way of clearing the screen is to write characters and attributes into all screen positions using function 9h of interrupt 10h (BIOS video service). This method lets you set colors for both the foreground (characters) and background.

In the following example, the whole screen will be filled with blue and the characters will be yellow.

```
; clearing screen by writing blanks with attributes
mov   ah,02      ; function 02h - positioned cursor
mov   bh,0       ; video page 0 is used
mov   dx,0       ; cursor to position 0,0 - left top corner
int   10h        ; BIOS video service  call
mov   ah,9       ; function  number
mov   cx,2000    ; number of characters for output
mov   bl,1Eh     ; attribute - yellow on blue
mov   al,' '     ; character to fill screen - blank
int   10h        ; BIOS video service  call
```

Both of the methods we have looked at clear the whole screen. If necessary though, you can clear just part of the screen (a window) by using functions 6h and 7h of interrupt 10h (BIOS video service). These functions shift the screen rows either up or down. Note that rows can only be shifted in the prescribed window. If the number of shifts is defined as 0, then the window will be cleared. Take some time to look at this as using these functions is not as easy as it seems.

As an example, we will clear a window with coordinates: (2, 10) - (16, 56), using the red-characters-on-grey-background attribute.

```
; clearing part of screen by shifting rows
    mov   ah,6       ; function number
    xor   al,al      ; clearing, as number of shifts = 0
    mov   bh,74h     ; red on grey attribute
    mov   ch,2       ; Y - coordinate of left upper corner
    mov   cl,10      ; X - coordinate of left upper corner
    mov   dh,16      ; Y - coordinate of right lower corner
    mov   dl,56      ; X - coordinate of right lower corner
    int   10h        ; BIOS Service
```

All three ways we have mentioned so far use the BIOS video service (interrupt 10h). If you are using the MS-DOS service you can clear the screen using the ESC-sequences through the ANSI.SYS driver. This lets you clear all the screen or part of a row, from the current cursor position to the end of the row.

The example below shows how this process works for clearing the whole screen.

```
; Data segment
  DATA  SEGMENT
  CLS   DB      1Bh          ; Esc
        DB      '[2J'        ; clearing all screen
        DB      '$'          ; end of string
  DATA  ENDS
; code segment
        mov    ax,DATA       ; address of data segment
        mov    ds,ax         ;
        lea    dx,CLS        ; DS:DX -Esc string
        mov    ah,9          ; function
        int    21h           ; MS-DOS service
```

The last way that we'll consider involves using the low level which entails writing blanks and attributes into the video buffer.

This example will give you a green screen with black characters. To simplify things we have assumed that you are using a color video adapter other than CGA.

```
; clearing all the screen by writing into video buffer
        mov    ax,0B800h     ; segment address of video buffer
        mov    es,ax         ; ES points to output segment
        xor    di,di         ; output from beginning of screen
        mov    ah,20h        ; attribute (black on green)
        mov    al," "        ; character to fill - blank
        mov    cx,2000       ; quantity of characters to output
        cld                  ; direction - forward !!!
        repstosw             ; ES:[DI] -output character
```

The subroutine COLOR.ASM will let you fill the screen with a prescribed color. Start by placing the input parameters in the following registers:

AH   - attribute (background and foreground colors)
CH   - start row for clearing (counting from 1)
DH   - end row for clearing (counting from 1)

You can clear the whole screen by specifying: CH =1, DH =25.

This program writes blanks directly into the video buffer. We have used the method of switching the screen off while filling the video buffer to avoid snow. After running this program you will have a blue screen, with white characters.

```
EXTRN COLOR : FAR

; clearing all the screen using subroutine  COLOR.ASM
     mov    ah,1Fh        ; attribute
     mov    ch,1          ; start row
     mov    dh,25         ; end row
     call   COLOR         ; clear screen
```

Controlling the Blinking/Intensity of a Color

We have already described the structure of an attribute byte. Now look closely at the seventh bit which controls the blinking-intensity. Which attribute do you need to output black characters on a yellow background? If you look at Table 8.1 you should come up with the answer 0E0h.

The demo program creates and outputs two yellow windows on the screen. The first window WIND1 has a dark yellow background (06h) and black characters (attribute byte = 60h).

The attribute byte for the next window, WIND2 is equal to 0E0h which gives black characters on a light yellow background. When you run this program you'll see black blinking characters on a dark yellow background in the WIND2 window. To get the result you want, you need to use a special setting for the seventh bit.

Function 10h of interrupt 10h (BIOS video service) allows you to manipulate the seventh bit to determine blinking or background intensity. To select the blinking-intensity mode place the constant 03h into the AL register. The value you place into the BL register will determine the working mode:

BL = 0   - intensity
BL = 1   - blinking.

Now call the interrupt 10h.

After the following fragment is performed, the program will output black characters on a light-yellow background.

```
; toggle blink/intensity bit (for EGA, VGA...)
      mov    ah,10h        ;  function
      mov    al,3h         ;  subfunction
      xor    bl,bl         ;  intensity toggle
      int    10h           ;  call BIOS service
```

If you want to do the same thing for a CGA card you need to write the program on the video card registers level. This is possible via 3D8h port (see above). The mode is defined by the setting of the fifth bit: 0 - intensity, 1 - blinking. Remember that the current screen mode is located in one byte of the BIOS video data area at address 0:[465].

```
; toggle blink/intensity bit (for CGA only)
  CGA:     xor    ax,ax          ;
           mov    es,ax          ;
           mov    al,es:[465h]   ;  preceding mode
           or     al,10h         ;  blink (bit 5 =1)
           cmp    ch,1     .      ;  blinking ?
           je     Out3D8         ;
           and    al,0EFh        ;  intensity (bit 5 =0)
  Out3D8:  mov    dx,3D8h        ;  working mode port address
           out    dx,al          ;  blinking mode change
```

In the case of the CGA, we are forced to manipulate the video registers directly, as the BIOS function 10h of Int 10h is an extension on EGA VGA systems only. This function has a number of other subfunctions that allow direct control of the color palette registers in the video adapter, see Appendix F. If you have a monochrome display you should use an attribute byte for controlling the blinking-intensity mode (see Table 8.1).

Another way of controlling blinking-intensity is to use the BLINK.ASM subroutine. To select this mode, set the value in the AL register:

AL = 0 - intensity, AL = 1 - blinking.

Then call BLINK.

Note that the default mode is blinking. So if your program has been working in the intensity mode, don't forget to return to the blinking mode before exiting the program.

Screen Control Using ANSI.SYS ESC-Sequences

As we said earlier, screen control in MS-DOS is performed by means of ESC-sequences through the ANSI.SYS driver. An ESC-sequence is a special string which begins with an ESC-character (ASCII code 1Bh) and an open square bracket "[", followed by other codes and closed with the "$" symbol. To use this facility, write your ESC-sequence in the data segment and output it on the screen, using function 9 of interrupt 21h.

This example will clear one row from the current cursor position:

```
DATA  SEGMENT
CLS   DB      1Bh           ; Esc
      DB      '[K'          ; clearing to end of row
      DB      '$'           ; end of string
DATA  ENDS
```

```
; Code segment
      mov     ax,DATA       ; base address of data segment
      mov     ds,ax         ;
      lea     dx,CLS        ; DS:DX -Esc string
      mov     ah,9          ; function
      int     21h           ; MS-DOS service
```

We will finish off by giving a description of the control codes for ESC-sequences. For ESC you must write 27 or 1Bh. Character # denotes a decimal number. Upper and lower case letters must be written as shown - they are not interchangeable.

Esc [#A	moving the cursor up for # rows
Esc [#B	moving the cursor down for # rows
Esc [#C	moving the cursor to the right for # columns
Esc [#D	moving the cursor to the left for # columns
Esc [#;#H	moving the cursor to a given position: row;column
Esc [s	saving the current cursor position
Esc [u	restoring the current cursor position (after the execution of the previous function Esc [s).
Esc [2J	clearing the screen
Esc [K	clearing the row from the cursor position

Outputting a Pixel - BIOS Service

Having discussed screen input/output operations in text mode, it would be unreasonable simply to keep silent about graphic operations and pretend they weren't important. However, a detailed discussion about manipulating graphic images could be the subject for a whole book. So, as a compromise, we have included some demo programs for graphic modes on your program disk. In this section we'll consider in detail a procedure for outputting a pixel onto the screen which is used in demo program PG0802 to draw a colored grid on the screen:

```
HORLINE   PROC   NEAR
          xor    cx,cx         ;  X - starting column for output (0)
HOR1:     mov    ah,0Ch        ;  function 0Ch - output pixel
          mov    al,Col        ;  put pixel color into AL
          mov    dx,Nstr       ;  Y - line for output
          mov    bh,0          ;  video page 0 is used
          int    10h           ;  BIOS video service
          inc    cx            ;  increase column counter
          cmp    cx,H_Leng     ;  end of string?
          jl     HOR1          ;  if not, output next pixel
          RETN                 ;  return to caller
HORLINE   ENDP
```

This procedure draws a horizontal line using the BIOS video service 0Ch (draw pixel). The Y coordinate of the line is stored as a word in the variable Nstr, the start column (on the left) is 0 and the end column (on the right) is stored in the variable H_Leng also as a word. The color of the pixel is stored in the one-byte variable Col. The function 0Ch of the BIOS video service used in this procedure, outputs a pixel of the color specified by the value in the AL register in the column X and row Y. The value of X and Y must be placed into the CX and DX registers, respectively. Note that the maximum values of the row and column on the screen depend on the current graphic mode and video adapter type. A more detailed description of this function and related services is given in Appendix F.

Library

CursOff and CursOn - Controlling the Cursor

The program CursOff is an example of a small utility that can be used from BAT-files or from the command line.

This program (see Listing 8.1 for the full assembler text) makes the cursor invisible by setting bits 4 and 5 of the CH registers to 1, then performing function 01 of interrupt 10h. This defines a cursor which starts in line 30h (48). Since this value exceeds the limits of the character cell, the cursor cannot be displayed and, consequently, disappears from the screen.

```
1
2       page 55,132
3  .model  small
4  .code
5          org100h
6  begin:
7  ;=== read number of active video page from BIOS data area
8          mov  ax,0        ; clear AX
9          mov  es,ax       ; prepare ES for accessing BIOS data area
10         mov  bh,es:[462h]; active video page into BH for next calls
11 ;=== get parameters of cursor on active video page
12         mov  ah,03h      ; function 03h - get cursor parameters
13         int  10h         ; BIOS video service
14 ;=== turn off cursor on active video page
15         mov  ah,01h      ; function 01h - set cursor parameters
16         or   ch,30h      ; set bits 4 and 5 of CH register to 1
17         int  10h         ; BIOS video service call
18 ;=== exit program
19         mov  ax,4C00h; function 4Ch-terminate process; exit code-0
20         int  21h         ; DOS service call
21         end  begin
```

Listing 8.1 The Program CursOff - Switching the Cursor Off

If you don't get the result you expected after running this program, look more carefully at the software you are using. Some program products restore the video mode whenever they wait for user input. For example, popular shells such as Norton Commander and Xtree Gold, and the command shells 4DOS and NDOS behave like this.

Don't worry though, you can still control the cursor. You simply need to create a BAT-file for performing your task and you'll be able to switch the cursor on and off any time control is still within the BAT-file. An example of such a BAT-file is given in Listing 8.2.

```
@Echo off
CursOff
Echo  Cursor is now invisible
Pause
CursOn
Echo  Cursor is now visible
Pause
```

Listing 8.2 The Demo BAT-File for Switching the Cursor On/Off

In practice, you will need to replace the PAUSE commands with commands relevant to the task in hand. This technique can also be employed for writing small subroutines to be used from high-level languages which have no built-in tools for controlling the cursor. For example, it would be useful to remove the cursor when the program displays tables or other text which you don't intend the user to edit. Consequently, when the cursor appears on the screen, the user can take it as a sign to input data.

The program CursOn given in Listing 8.3 makes the cursor visible by setting the right size and location.

```
1
2           page 55,132
3  .model small
4  .code
5         org    100h          ; this is needed for COM-files
6  ;=== block 1: get equipment information
7  begin:                      ; program starts here
8         int    11h           ; BIOS service-get equipment information
9         and    al,30h        ; emphasize bits 4,5 - display mode
10        cmp    al,30h        ; bits 4 and 5 are set - monochrome
11        je  mono             ; process monochrome display
12 ;=== block 2: enable CGA cursor emulation
13        mov    ah,11h        ; function 11h - character set service
14        mov    al,0          ; allow cursor emulation
15        mov    bl,34h        ; subfunction 34h - cursor emulation
16        int    10h           ; BIOS video service
17        mov    cx,0607h      ; CGA cursor locates within lines 6 -7
18        jmp    SetCur
19 ;=== block 3: set cursor parameters - monochrome mode
20        mono: mov cx,0B0Dh   ; MDA/HGC cursor: lines 13-14
21 ;     block 4: set cursor parameters - color mode
22 SetCur: mov ax,40h          ; segment address of BIOS data area
```

```
23          mov  es,ax      ; ES will point to the BIOS data area
24          mov  al,es:49h  ; AL-current video mode for some BIOS
25          mov  bh,es:62h  ; BH contains number of active video page
26          mov  ah,01h     ; function 01 - set cursor type
27          int  10h        ; BIOS video service call
28 ;=== block 5: exit program
29 ExProg:mov   ax,4C00h  ;function 4Ch-terminate process exit code 0
30          int  21h        ; DOS service call
31          end  begin
```

Listing 8.3 The Program CursOn - Force the Cursor On

This program can be used from the AUTOEXEC.BAT file, or any time you are working in the text mode, for restoring the cursor if it has been switched off by the CursOff program.

Another reason for using this program is that some software does not work efficiently on certain video adapters. For example, on some PCs, DR DOS 6 loses the cursor after performing the MODE command to switch the codepage on the video display. Unfortunately, this is not an isolated example; many operations that change the video mode have the same effect on these computers.

Furthermore, some software packages set the wrong value for the cursor's start and end lines on MDA and HGC adapters. The reason for this is that these adapters are not able to emulate the CGA cursor which is located within a cell of 8x8 dots. This means that if you set the standard values 6 and 7 for the start and end lines of the cursor, the cursor will appear in the middle of the string because the character height on this display is 14 dots.

Let's consider how this program works. It starts by determining the type of video adapter installed on your computer. To do this it uses the BIOS service "Get Equipment Information" available through interrupt 11h. This interrupt returns the information about the current video mode in bits 4 and 5 of the AX register. If both these bits are set, it means that the monochrome adapter is active, or that the universal video adapter is currently working in the monochrome mode. Note that the constant 30h, which is stored as a word, corresponds to bits 4 and 5. For this particular task it is enough to distinguish the monochrome video adapter from all the rest. How the program then continues depends on what type of video adapter is detected.

If a monochrome adapter is found, the program sets the values 11 and 13 for the start and end lines of the cursor, respectively. For all other adapters, the program performs the operation "Enable CGA cursor emulation" (interrupt 10h, function 11h, subfunction 34h).

Program GotoXY - Cursor Movement

The program GoToXY moves the cursor to a specified position. It accepts parameters from the command line and then uses the BIOS interrupt to move the cursor. Data which is output after the program will then be placed on the screen at the new cursor position. You can use this program in batch files for organizing menus or outputting messages. The full assembler text of this program is given in Listing 8.4 and the text of the demo BAT-file, in Listing 8.5.

```
 1
 2          page 55,132
 3  ;
 4  ;        cursor moving program     version 1.2 26.05.1992
 5  ;        copyright (C) V.B.Maljugin 1992 Voronezh,  Russia
 6  ;
 7  .model   SMALL               ; this defines memory model
 8  .stack
 9  .data                        ; this starts DATA segment
10  factor  dw     0             ;
11  ten     dw     10            ;
12  X       db     0             ; number of ROW on screen
13  Y       db     0             ; number of COLUMN on screen
14  .code                        ; this starts CODE segment
15  ;=== block0 - start the program
16  .startup
17  ;=== block 1 - prepare to work
18          mov    cx,0          ; clear cycle counter
19          mov    cl,es:80h     ; set counter to parameter string length
20          inc    cl            ; CX points to first character
21          mov    ax,es         ; we can't process ES content directly
22          add    ax,8h         ; ES now points to parameter string
23          mov    es,ax         ; set new ES content
24          mov    bx,0          ; BX points to start of parameter string
25  ;=== block 2 - read an X coordinate from parameter string
26          call   SkipBlank     ; skip blank characters
27          call   ReadNext      ; read next number
28          mov    X,al          ; store ROW number (X)
29  ;=== block 3 - read a Y coordinate from parameter string
30          call   SkipBlank     ; skip blank characters
31          call   ReadNext      ; read next number
32          mov    Y,al          ; store COLUMN number (Y)
33  ;=== block 4 - check whether coordinates are non-zero
34          add    al,X          ; add X and Y coordinates
35          cmp    al,0          ; sum X+Y is 0 when both X and Y are 0
36          je     Finish        ; if X and Y are 0 - exit
37  ;=== block 5 - move cursor into a new position
```

```
38              mov     ax,40h          ; segment address of BIOS data area
39              mov     es,ax           ; ES points to BIOS data area
40              mov     bh,es:62h       ; [462] - active video page number
41              mov     dh,X            ; DH - ROW on screen
42              mov     dl,Y            ; DL - COLUMN on screen
43              mov     ah,2            ; function 02h - move cursor
44              int     10h             ; BIOS video service
45      ;=== block 6 - exit program
46      Finish:                         ;
47              mov     ax,4C00h        ; function 4Ch - terminate process
48              int     21h             ; Dos service call
49      ;
50      ; ============= work procedures  =================
51      ;
52      SkipBlank   proc  near
53      ;this procedure scans parameter string and skips blank characters
54      ;
55      ; parameters on entry:
56      ; BX - offset of current character
57      ;  DL-a first digit character (if any) or last character of string
58      ;
59      GetS:   inc     bx              ; BX will point to next character
60              mov     dl,es:[bx]      ; get current character into DL
61              cmp     cx,bx           ; is that end of parameter string?
62              jl      AllParm         ; if so - process the accepted values
63              cmp     dl,30h          ; current character less than 0?
64              jl      GetS            ; if so - get next character
65              cmp     dl,39h          ; current character greater than 9?
66              ja      GetS            ; if so - get next character
67      AllParm:
68              ret
69      SkipBlank   endp
70
71      ReadNext        proc  near
72      ;
73      ; this procedure reads a parameter from command line
74      ; and transfers it to numeric form
75      ;
76      ; parameters on entry:
77      ; DL - current character
78      ; BX - offset of current character from beginning of string
79      ; CX - maximum number of characters in string (length of string)
80      ; ES - segment address of parameter string in PSP ( Seg PSP + 8 )
81      ;
82      ; result will be returned in AL
83      ;
84              mov     ax,0
85      ProcSym:
86              cmp     dl,30h   ; current character less than 0?
87              jl      EndNext  ; if so - stop the process
88              cmp     dl,39h   ; current character greater than 9?
89              ja      EndNext  ; if so - stop process
90              sub     dl,30h   ;transform character into 8-bit integer
91              mov     Factor,dx ; store that integer
92              mul     ten      ; multiply AX by 10
```

```
93              add     ax,Factor       ; add current character (as integer)
94              mov     dx,0            ; prepare DX to process next character
95              inc     bx              ; increase character's counter
96              mov     dl,es:[bx]      ; read next character into DL
97              cmp     bx,cx           ; is that end of parameter string?
98              jl      ProcSym         ; if not - process current character
99   EndNext:
100             ret
101  ReadNext        endp
102             end
```

Listing 8.4 GoToXY - The Program for Moving Cursor

There are two basic parts to the program - the main body and two work procedures, considered later on in this section. The main body is divided into 7 functional blocks numbered from 0 to 6.

Blocks 0 and 6 are intended to start and finish the program in the usual way - there is nothing new to you in these blocks.

Block 1 sets the ES:BX register so that it points to the start of the parameter string. Remember that on loading the program, DOS creates the PSP and puts its starting segment address into the ES register. This string, which forms the rest of the command line, follows the program or internal command name. For example, if you type the command line - **fc file1.ext file2.ext** - the text "file1.ext file2.ext" will be treated as a parameter string. MS-DOS stores the parameter string in the PSP at offset 80h.

To simplify your work with the parameter string, we'll set the initial value of the BX register to 0 which corresponds to the beginning of the parameter string. In actual fact, the BX register points to the current character in the parameter string. This little trick is made possible because the parameter string is located in the memory at the paragraph boundary i.e., the last hexadecimal cypher in its full address is 0.

Blocks 2 and 3 are designed to read the value of the parameters from the command line. They work almost identically, only differing in one line - block 2 reads the X coordinate of the new cursor location and block 3 reads the Y-coordinate. To do this, both blocks call the work procedure SkipBlank. This procedure determines the position of the first digit character following the current one or the position of the end of the string - whichever is found first. The result is returned in the BX register. This is followed by the call for the ReadNext procedure which returns the value of the parameter in the AL register. If this procedure doesn't find a text that can be treated as a valid parameter, it returns 0.

Block 4 checks whether there are any parameters. Since the value of the missing parameter is 0 it only needs to compare the sum of the parameters with the value 0. If the sum is 0, this block passes control to block 6 which finishes the program, leaving the cursor at its current location.

Block 5 simply loads the new values for the coordinates of the cursor as required by the BIOS video service and then performs function 02 of interrupt 10h - the BIOS service "Set New Cursor Location". Note that the program gets the number of the current video page from the BIOS data area at location 0040h:0062h.

Now let's have a more detailed look at the work of the subroutine ReadNext which performs the task of converting the character string to an integer. It involves the following steps:

▲ Puts the value 0 into the result.

▲ Checks whether the current character comes before "0" in the ASCII Table.

▲ If so, stops the process and exits the subroutine.

▲ Checks whether the current character comes before "9" in the ASCII Table.

▲ If not, stops the process and exits the subroutine (non-digit character found).

▲ Converts the character to a binary integer by subtracting the value 30h.

▲ Multiplies the result by 10 (shifts 1 decimal place to the left) and adds the current digit.

▲ Increases the character counter so that it points to the next character .

▲ Checks for the end of the string (the character counter is equal to the length of the string).

▲ If this is not the end of the string, repeats the process from the second step (checking whether the character is within the range "0" - "9").

An example of using the GoToXY program in the BAT-file is given in Listing 8.5.

```
@Echo off
Cls
GoToXY 3 27
Echo The demo BAT-file %0
GoToXY 5 12
Echo this is an example of using cursor movement program GoToXY
GoToXY 8 22
Echo Version 1.1  23.04.92 Voronezh, Russia
GoToXY 12 12
Echo Use this program to organize screen output from BAT-files
GoToXY 14 12
Echo in a following way:
GoToXY 16 0
Echo ...
Echo GoToXY 15 10
Echo This text will be output starting at column 10 on row 15
Echo ...
GoToXY 23 1
```

Listing 8.5 The BAT-file for Cursor Movement Demonstration

This BAT-file simply puts a few messages onto the screen starting at different locations. The program GoToXY moves the cursor at the requested position and then outputs a message starting from the current cursor location using the internal DOS command Echo.

The most recent versions of high-level programming languages are provided with either built-in or library functions for cursor control. For example, we could remind you of the Clipper statements SET CURSOR ON and SET CURSOR OFF or the Pascal procedure GoToXY which prompted us to write a similar program to be used directly from your DOS BAT-files.

ScrTbl - Displaying an ASCII Table

The program ScrTbl considered below uses BIOS and DOS Video services to show the whole character set which can be displayed on your screen. This program can be used in either the graphics or text screen modes and gives the screen representation for all characters in the range 00 - 0FFh including control symbols such as CR (Carriage Return), LF (Line Feed), Bell and so on. The program ScrTbl might be useful for creating your own screen font or a new national character set. The full assembler text of the program ScrTbl is shown in Listing 8.6 and an example of its screen output - in Listing 8.7.

This program demonstrates the majority of the techniques discussed in this chapter and employs the most widely used BIOS and DOS video services.

```
1
2       page 55,132
3  ;
4  ; this program outputs ASCII character table onto screen
5  ; character set currently loaded will be shown
6  ;
7  .model  small
8  .stack
9  .data
10 CR       equ  00Dh       ; carriage return code
11 LF       equ  00Ah       ; line feed code
12 Con16    db   16         ; integer constant 16
13 EndMsg   equ  024h       ; "dollar" sign - end of message
14 StMsg    db   CR,LF,LF
15          db   'screen font show utility  14 Jun 92  version 1.2',CR,LF
16          db   'copyright (C) 1992  V.B.Maljugin, Voronezh, CIS',CR,LF
17 CrLf     db   CR, LF, EndMsg
18 Pattern  db   'xx-' , EndMsg
19 HexSym   db   '0','1','2','3','4','5','6','7'
20          db   '8','9','A','B','C','D','E','F'
21 CodSymdb     0
22
23 .code                    ; CODE segment starts here
24 .startup                 ; standard prologue (MASM 6)
25          mov ax,40h      ; segment address of BIOS data area
26          mov es,ax       ; ES will point to BIOS data
27          lea dx,StMsg    ; address of message into DX
28          mov ah,09       ; function 09h - output text string
29          int 21h         ; DOS service call
30          mov cx,16       ; number of lines in table
31 ;=== enclosing cycle starts here
32 PrtTable:
33          push cx         ; save enclosing cycle counter
34 ;=== nested cycle - output 16 columns in current row
35          mov  cx,16      ; set counter for nested cycle
36 rows:
37 .        push cx         ; save outward counter
38          mov al,CodSym
39 ;=== convert code of current character code into two hex digits
40 ToHex:                   ;
41          mov ah,0        ; character code (0-0FFh) in AX
42          div Con16       ; low digit into AL, high - into AH
43          mov bx,offset HexSym       ; offset of hex symbols table
44          xlat                       ; convert AL to character
45          mov  byte ptr Pattern,al ; and place it into output line
46          mov  al,ah                 ; place high digit into AL
47          xlat                       ; convert AL to character
48          mov byte ptr Pattern[1],al ; and place it into output line
49 ;=== Output hexadecimal representation of character (DOS service)
```

```
50              mov   ah,09         ; function 09 - output string
51              lea   dx,Pattern    ; address of text to be output
52              int   21h           ; DOS service call
53  ;=== output symbolic representation of character (BIOS service)
54              mov   bh,es:[62h]    ; number of active video page
55              mov   bl,0           ; color in some graphics modes
56              mov   ah,0Ah         ; function 0Ah - output symbol
57              mov   al,CodSym       ; AL - symbol to be output
58              mov   cx,1            ; CX - repeat counter
59              int   10h            ; BIOS video service
60  ;=== prepare for output next column
61              mov   ah,03          ; function 03h- get cursor location
62              int   10h            ; BIOS video service
63              mov   ah,02          ; function 02h - set cursor location
64              add   dl,2           ; new location - 2 places to right
65              int   10h            ; BIOS video service
66              pop   cx             ; restore counter of nested cycle
67              add   CodSym,16      ; code for character in next column
68              loop  Rows           ;=== end of nested cycle body
69  ;=== enclosed cycle continues from here
70              lea   dx,CrLf        ; address of message into DX
71              mov   ah,09h         ; function 09h - output text string
72              int   21h            ; DOS service call
73              pop   cx             ; restore counter of enclosed cycle
74              inc   CodSym         ; code for first character in next line
75  EndMain:loop PrtTable           ; print next line
76  ;=== finish program. return code = 0
77              mov   ax,4C00h       ; function 4Ch - terminate process
78              int   21h            ; DOS service call
79              end
```

Listing 8.6 ScrTbl - Character Set Demonstration

The table created by ScrTbl contains 16 lines, each of which contains hexadecimal and graphic representations for 16 characters in the range x0h - xFh where x is a hexadecimal number from 0 up to F. This means that this program shows you the full character set currently loaded into the character generator of your PC's video adapter. Now let's have a look at how the ScrTbl program performs this task.

The program starts by putting the segment address of the BIOS data area into the ES register. This allows for future accessing of the objects located in that area. The next step is to output an initial message about the version of the program using the DOS service "Output text string" (function 09h of interrupt 21h). This is followed by the body of the main cycle which starts in the line labelled PrtTable and ends in the line labelled EndMain.

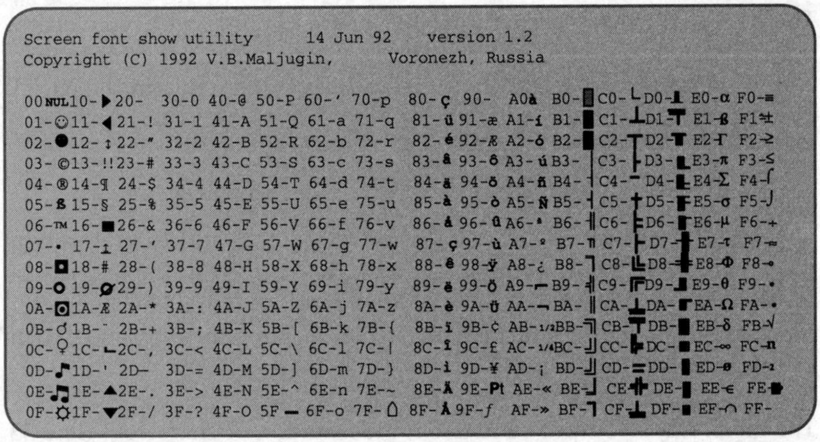

```
Screen font show utility     14 Jun 92    version 1.2
Copyright (C) 1992 V.B.Maljugin,       Voronezh, Russia

00 NUL 10-▶ 20-  30-0 40-@ 50-P 60-` 70-p  80-ç 90-  A0▲ B0-▒ C0-└ D0-┴ E0-α F0-≡
01-☺ 11-◀ 21-! 31-1 41-A 51-Q 61-a 71-q  81-ü 91-æ A1-í B1-▒ C1-┴ D1-┬ E1-ß F1-±
02-☻ 12-↕ 22-" 32-2 42-B 52-R 62-b 72-r  82-é 92-Æ A2-ó B2-▓ C2-┬ D2-╥ E2-Γ F2-≥
03-♥ 13-‼ 23-# 33-3 43-C 53-S 63-c 73-s  83-â 93-ô A3-ú B3-│ C3-├ D3-╙ E3-π F3-≤
04-♦ 14-¶ 24-$ 34-4 44-D 54-T 64-d 74-t  84-ä 94-ö A4-ñ B4-┤ C4-─ D4-╘ E4-Σ F4-⌠
05-♣ 15-§ 25-% 35-5 45-E 55-U 65-e 75-u  85-à 95-ò A5-Ñ B5-╡ C5-┼ D5-╒ E5-σ F5-⌡
06-™ 16-▬ 26-& 36-6 46-F 56-V 66-f 76-v  86-å 96-û A6-ª B6-╢ C6-╞ D6-╓ E6-µ F6-÷
07-• 17-↨ 27-' 37-7 47-G 57-W 67-g 77-w  87-ç 97-ù A7-º B7-╖ C7-╟ D7-╫ E7-τ F7-≈
08-◘ 18-↑ 28-( 38-8 48-H 58-X 68-h 78-x  88-ê 98-ÿ A8-¿ B8-╕ C8-╚ D8-╪ E8-Φ F8-°
09-○ 19-↓ 29-) 39-9 49-I 59-Y 69-i 79-y  89-ë 99-Ö A9-⌐ B9-╣ C9-╔ D9-┘ E9-Θ F9-∙
0A-◙ 1A-→ 2A-* 3A-: 4A-J 5A-Z 6A-j 7A-z  8A-è 9A-Ü AA-¬ BA-║ CA-╩ DA-┌ EA-Ω FA-·
0B-♂ 1B-← 2B-+ 3B-; 4B-K 5B-[ 6B-k 7B-{  8B-ï 9B-¢ AB-½ BB-╗ CB-╦ DB-█ EB-δ FB-√
0C-♀ 1C-∟ 2C-, 3C-< 4C-L 5C-\ 6C-l 7C-|  8C-î 9C-£ AC-¼ BC-╝ CC-╠ DC-▄ EC-∞ FC-ⁿ
0D-♪ 1D-↔ 2D-- 3D-= 4D-M 5D-] 6D-m 7D-}  8D-ì 9D-¥ AD-¡ BD-╜ CD-═ DD-▌ ED-ø FD-²
0E-♫ 1E-▲ 2E-. 3E-> 4E-N 5E-^ 6E-n 7E-~  8E-Ä 9E-Pt AE-« BE-╛ CE-╬ DE-▐ EE-∈ FE-■
0F-☼ 1F-▼ 2F-/ 3F-? 4F-O 5F-_ 6F-o 7F-⌂  8F-Å 9F-ƒ AF-» BF-┐ CF-╧ DF-▀ EF-∩ FF-
```

Figure 8.12
The Output Screen of the ScrTbl Program

While the program is running this block is performed 16 times, each time outputting one line of the table shown in Figure 8.12. The main cycle contains a nested cycle that includes the lines between labels Columns and EndNest. Each execution of this cycle produces a part of the table that corresponds to one ASCII character. For example the part for character "A" is 41-A

Each performance of the main cycle involves 16 executions of the nested cycle so the body of the nested cycle is performed 256 times, which corresponds to the full set of ASCII characters from 0 to 0FFh.

The block titled "Convert code of current character into two hex digits" (line 40 in Listing 8.6) prepares the symbolic representation of the hexadecimal code for printing. The hexadecimal code 0 - 0FFh stored in the AX register is divided by 16. This operation places the high digit (the result) into the AL register and the low digit (the remainder) into the AL register and the low digit (the remainder) into the AH register. The XLAT instruction is then used to convert each digit to character representation. This instruction is designed to convert characters from one code system to another using the look-up table. The character to be converted is treated as the number of an element in the table which can contain up to 256 bytes. Before using the XLAT instruction, you need to place the offset address of the converting table into the BX register, and the character to be converted into the AL register. The segment address of the table is assumed to be stored in the DS register unless another register is explicitly specified. The instruction puts the result into the AL register overwriting the character to be converted.

The XLAT instruction usually has no operands unless the converting table is located in the segment address through a register other than DS. In this case you can specify the address of the table in the XLAT instruction, as follows

```
XLAT ES:FarTable
```

which tells the Assembler that the array FarTable is addressed through the ES register. In the program ScrTbl, the converting table used in the XLAT instruction is 16 bytes long and contains the character representation of hexadecimal digits 0h - 0Fh (lines 19 and 20 in Listing 8.6).

The block titled "output symbolic representation of character" (line 53 in Listing 8.6) uses the BIOS service "Output character" (function 0Ah of interrupt 10h). Note that this block uses the number of the active video page which is stored in the BIOS data area at the location 0040:0062h.

The next block, "prepare for output next column", uses the BIOS video services "Get cursor location" and "Set cursor location" for moving the cursor after output.

Once the whole line of the table has been output, the program uses the DOS service "Output text string" for starting a new line on the screen. A combination of the Carriage Return and Line Feed characters is output for this purpose.

Demo Programs Included on Your Program Disk

Your program disk contains the set of demo programs mentioned in this chapter. We have not given their full text in the book since it is written on the program disk as files with the extension .ASM. The executable modules are written as files with the extension .EXE. Here we will give a brief description of the demo programs used in this chapter.

Programs PG0800 and PG0801 fill the screen with the character "E". Program PG0800 uses the BIOS video service "write a character in teletype mode" - function 0Eh of interrupt 10h, and program PG0801.ASM writes the characters directly into the video memory. If you compare the results of these programs you will see that writing directly into the video memory is much faster than the standard BIOS video service.

Programs PG0802, PG0803, PG0804 demonstrate the process of drawing the color grid on the screen. These programs all work in the graphics mode but they use different methods and, consequently, the speed of their work is different. All three programs work in the same way - they draw the grid in a certain color and wait for a keystroke. If you press the ESC key the program finishes, if you press any other key it changes the color and draws the grid again. Program PG0802 uses the BIOS video service "write a pixel" - function 0Ch of the interrupt 10h. Program PG0803 uses the low-level technique - it accesses the video registers directly. Program PG0804 uses the advanced low-level technique which allows 8 pixels to be output simultaneously. This method allows you to draw a horizontal line on the EGA screen using 80 output operations, whereas the standard technique requires one output operation for each pixel - which means 640 operations per line on the EGA screen.

The program demonstrates the features of the blinking/intensity control. It draws two windows colored in with brown. The highest bit of the attribute in the second window is set, which makes the image blink. Then the program changes the function of the blinking/intensity bit so the image becomes bright.

The program PG0806 shows the process of changing the configuration of the character on the screen. This program loads the new image for the character "E", an inverted "E", into the character generator of the EGA or VGA adapter. The image is shown on the screen and then the original configuration of the character is restored. To load the character generator the BIOS video service (interrupt 10h, function 11h, subfunction 00h) is used.

The program PG0807 deals with the video pages in the text mode. It forms 4 pages, each of which is filled with the character that denotes its number (for example, the page 0 is filled with the character "0", the page 1 - with the character "1" and so on) and then switches these pages using function 05h of interrupt 10h. The process of switching pages causes the screen image to change instantaneously.

The program PG0808 performs functions similar to the program CursCon described in this chapter but uses the low-level technique for all video adapters except EGA. On the EGA adapters function 01h of the interrupt 10h (Set Cursor) is used.

The Auxiliary Video Library

While creating the demo programs included on your program disk additional routines were used. You have this library on your program disk and can use the modules included in it to create your own programs. The full assembler text of these routines is written on your program disk as files with the extension .ASM, the object modules - as files with the extension .OBJ. The object modules are also grouped into the library stored on the program disk in the file OBJECT.LIB.

To help you understand the material better, we will give a brief formal description of the modules used in this chapter. This includes the name and purpose of the program, the parameters required and the results returned. The short comments are included in case some information about the subroutine is not included in the formal description.

VidTyp

Function: Determines the type of video adapter installed.
Input: None
Output: AL - the video adapter type
        0 - MDA
        1 - CGA
        2 - MCGA
        3 - EGA
        4 - VGA
        DX - the segment address of the video buffer
Comments: The DX register contains the segment address of the video buffer - 0B000h for a monochrome adapter or an adapter in the monochrome mode (note that such adapters as VGA or SVGA can emulate MDA or HGC adapters). For the EGA adapter the contents of the BX and CX registers are the same as returned by function 12h, subfunction 10h of interrupt 10h.

Color

Function: Clears the screen and paints it with the color requested
Input: AH - required background color
        AL - required foreground color
        CH - the number of start line to be cleared
        DH - the number of last line to be cleared
Output: None

Blink

Function: Switches the blink/intensity bit meaning
Input: AL - the value defining the meaning of the bit 7 in the attribute byte
                 0 - intensity mode (highlighted background)
                 1 - blinking (DOS default)
Output: None
Comments: The VidTyp program is required.

WrChar

Function: Writes a character into the video memory
Input: AH - the attribute of the character to be output
                 AL - the character to be output
                 BH - the number of the current video page
                 BL - the type of video adapter as returned by VidTyp
                 CX - the number of output repetitions
                 DH - the number of the start row on the screen for output
                 DL - the number of the start column on the screen for output
                 ES - the segment address of the video buffer must point to the video buffer. The DX register is used for storing the coordinates of the output position on the screen - DH and DL for the row and column respectively.
Output: None
Comments: Call the VidTyp program before using WrChar to put the appropriate values in the BL and ES registers.

RdChar

Function: Reads a character from the video memory
Input: BH - the number of the current video page
                 BL - the type of video adapter as returned by VidTyp
                 DH - the number of the row on the screen
                 DL - the number of the column on the screen
                 ES - the segment address of the video buffer must point to the video buffer. The DX register is used for storing the coordinates of the output position on the screen - DH and DL for the row and column respectively.
Output: AH - the attribute of the character to be output
                 AL - the character to be output
Comments: Call the VidTyp program before using RdChar to put the appropriate values in the BL and ES registers.

PutStr

Function: Outputs ASCIIZ-string onto the screen
Input: AH register must contain the attribute of all characters output
            CX - the maximum length of the string (from 1 to 80 bytes)
            DH - the number of the start row on the screen for output
            DL - the number of the start column on the screen for output
            DS:SI - the address of the string to be output
Output: None
Comments: The end of the string is recognized when the zero byte is found or when the number of the current position is equal to the value stored in the CX register. The VidTyp and WrChar programs are used.

All the routines accept parameters from the registers and likewise return results (if any) through the registers. To use these routines in your assembler programs you can use the assembler instruction CALL; for example, to call the VidTyp routine you only need to write the following statement:

```
CALL VidTyp
```

Fview - The File Browsing Program

The program FView lets you look through the contents of a file. The executable module of the program, the file FVIEW.EXE, is stored on your program disk and is used in the BAT-files, described in Chapter One, for viewing listings created by Assembler. When you run the program, you must specify the name of the file you want in the command line. You can move through the text using the following cursor control keys:

PgDn	scroll one screen down
PgUp	scroll one screen up
Home	display the first 23 lines of the file
End	display the last 23 lines of the file
↓	scroll one line down
↑	scroll one line up
→	scroll one position to the right
←	scroll one position to the left

| Ctrl+Home | scroll contents displayed to the left, placing the first character in each line in the first left-hand column of the screen. |
| Esc | finish working and return to MS-DOS |

If necessary, you can recompile the program or print its source text. To use the program, copy its executable module FVIEW.ASM into the directory where you store frequently used utilities, or specify the name of the directory where the program FVIEW is located, in the PATH command in your AUTOEXEC.BAT file. You can then call the program by typing the command line:

```
[path]FVIEW [path-to-file]file
```

where path is the full path to the file FVIEW.EXE, when the directory containing this file is not included in the current PATH command, path-to-file is the path to the file you wish to browse and file is the name of that file. For example, to view your AUTOEXEC.BAT file, type

```
FVIEW c:\autoexec.bat
```

To finish the program, press the ESC key.

The program outputs two lines of information which cannot be scrolled: the full path to the file being processed (at the top of the screen) and a list of control keys (at the bottom of the screen). Only 23 lines of the file can be displayed at a time. The program FVIEW reads blocks of 32768 bytes and places them in RAM. After the program has been loaded, it uses all the memory made available by DOS as work space. A low-level technique (writing directly into the video buffer) is used to output text on the screen and to perform horizontal and vertical scrolling. The Carriage Return and Line Feed symbols are used to break the contents of the file onto separate lines. All other special characters such as BackSpace, Bell, Esc or EndOfFile are treated as ordinary characters, so how they are displayed depends on the character set currently loaded.

The FVIEW program consists of several blocks, the main ones being:

▲ Allocating the work space in RAM (starts at the line labelled START)

▲ Determining and saving the current video mode (the label NORM)

▲ Accepting the name of the file to be processed from the command line (label GetPath)

▲ Opening that file and determining its size (label OPEN)

▲ Outputting information lines at the top and bottom of the screen (label ClrStr)

▲ Reading a block up to 32768 bytes long (label READ)

▲ Analyzing the block read and determining the number of lines it contains using the CR and LF codes as End-Of-Line symbols (label PutScr)

▲ Outputting the screen buffer (initially the first 23 lines) onto the screen and waiting until a key is pressed (label GetKey)

▲ Analyzing the code of the key pressed and performing the corresponding subroutine for scrolling the screen, or exiting the program if the ESC key has been pressed (label ESC0)

▲ Restoring the original video mode and returning control to DOS (label EXIT).

The following piece of code illustrates how FVIEW scrolls one line down:

```
; Screen scrolling downwards by one line
        mov   si,3678    ; source offset (end of line 22)
        mov   di,3838    ; target offset (end of line 23)
        mov   ES,VIDSEG  ; target segment (video buffer)
        mov   DS,VIDSEG  ; source segment (video buffer)
        mov   cx,22*80   ; number of words to be scrolled (22 lines)
        std              ; scroll down
        Call  SCROLL     ; functional subroutine call
        cld              ; Clear Direction Flag
```

The parameters for the subroutine SCROLL are prepared, then the subroutine call is performed. The SI and DI registers are loaded with the addresses of the characters in the video buffer which correspond to the last characters in lines 22 and 23 respectively. DS and ES both point to the video buffer segment (0B800 for color adapters). The text of the subroutine SCROLL is given below:

```
;*****************************************************************
;
;   The procedure for screen scrolling
;
```

```
;  DS:[SI] - address of string to be output
;
;  ES:[DI] - address of the string in the video buffer
;
;  CX      - number of words to be scrolled
;
;  The Direction Flag is used to define the scrolling direction
;
;  CLD     - scroll upwards
;
;  STD     - scroll downwards
;
;****************************************************************
SCROLL   PROC   NEAR
         mov    bl,CGA        ; take CGA indicator
         cmp    bl,1          ; CGA card?
         jne    Cycle7        ; no, don't check for retrace
;  Wait for retrace
Cycle4:  mov    dx,3DAh       ; video state register (CGA)
Cycle5:  in     al,dx         ; read state register
         test   al,1          ; retrace?
         jnz    Cycle5        ; yes, wait for finishing
;  Check whether it is possible to write into video buffer
Cycle6:  in     al,dx         ; read state register
         test   al,1          ; retrace (writing allowed)?
         jz     Cycle6        ; no, check again
         lodsw                ; take character and attribute
         stosw                ; output character and attribute
         loop   Cycle4        ; next step of outward cycle
         RETN                 ; return to caller
;  Non-CGA video card - direct writing always allowed
Cycle7:  rep    movsw         ; output character and attribute
         RETN                 ; return to caller
SCROLL   ENDP
```

The content of the video buffer is copied, so that the characters which correspond to the second line on the screen are moved to the third line, the characters from the third line - to the 4th line and so on. As a result, lines 2 - 22 become lines 3-23 (remember that lines are numbered from 0 to 24). If you look at the text of the SCROLL procedure you can see that on an EGA/VGA card all this is actually done by one instruction MOVSW with the REP prefix (label Cycle7). This is slightly more complicated on a CGA; since we can only write to the video memory safely during the retrace period, the sequence of the LODSW and STOSW instructions is used in the cycle which starts at the line labelled Cycle4.

At last, we have fulfilled the promise we made in Chapter Four and shown how string processing instructions can be used in a utility for controlling the video system.

Summary

In this chapter we have covered the basic methods of accessing video systems. The video services described include the following groups:

Low level - controlling the video memory and registers directly
Basic level - using BIOS video service (interrupt 10h)
High level - using DOS service (interrupts 21h and 29h) and the ANSI.SYS device driver

Each group is advantageous for certain purposes and therefore the choice of group depends on the purpose of the program.

The MS-DOS video service provides maximum portability of your programs. The functions of the MS-DOS service are supported by software such as the OS/2 compatibility box and DOS emulators. This means that you can run your program without any changes under OS/2, PC-MOS, VM/386 or even under UNIX-like systems. In addition, it allows you to redirect the output in the file, so it is the simplest way of using video for hardware-independent text output.

The BIOS video service is closely connected to hardware so it brings flexibility to your programs. Although this method provides the basic set of functions for outputting texts and graphics, it is relatively slow and requires more knowledge from programmers.

Direct access to the video register is the most powerful technique, especially for creating complex graphic applications. However, this is also the most complicated method, it requires a thorough understanding of hardware features and can therefore only be recommended to rather advanced programmers. However, we hope that the examples and explanations given in this chapter will help you to master this technique, and that the library included on your program disk will be useful for further work.

CHAPTER

9

Using Disks

This chapter deals with disk functions, covering the BIOS and DOS disk services which are accessible through BIOS interrupt 13h and DOS interrupts 21h, 25h and 26h. We will also look at some important disk tables, including those contained in the BIOS data area and accessible through the IVT.

We will not be covering low-level disk programming since it is a relatively complicated and risky technique that is only rarely used in practice anyway.

Our description of the BIOS disk service covers the basic functions of interrupt 13h which allow you to perform operations such as reading and writing physical sectors, seeking disk heads and formatting disks and separate tracks. We have also described the basic fields of the BIOS data area which are related to these disk functions.

The DOS service covered in this chapter includes reading and writing logical disks (interrupts 25h and 26h) and basic file operations - functions of interrupt 21h. You should find that the DOS disk service is easier to use than the BIOS one for dealing with the sectors of logical disks. The file functions are good for creating, deleting, renaming, finding, reading and writing files. We have also explained the hierarchical structure of directories and the DOS functions which allow you to manage them.

Your program disk includes a set of disk utilities (executable modules and full assembler texts) based on the BIOS and DOS functions described in this chapter.

Fundamental Knowledge

Floppy Disks

Floppy disks (or **diskettes**) were the first external memory devices widely used with PCs. Diskettes were already being used with mini computers, so PC manufacturers simply adapted the 5.25" disks. Initially, these diskettes had a capacity of just 160K bytes. Since then, several types of floppy disk, varying in size and capacity have been developed. The best ones available now are 3.5" with a capacity of 2.88M bytes. Hardware manufacturers are currently promising an even better diskette, smaller than the 3.5" and with increased capacity.

We'll start by looking at the two most commonly used types of diskette 5.25" and 3.5".

There are two main parts:

- A plastic disk covered by a magnetic substance.
- A protective envelope.

The magnetic covering is used to store information which is read from and written to the diskette by the read/write heads installed in the disk driver.

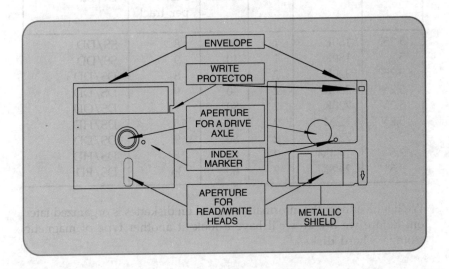

Figure 9.1
Diskettes

There are four apertures in the envelope:

1. For the read/write heads.
2. For a disk drive axle.
3. An index marker.
4. For write protection.

The construction of a 3.5" is similar but some aspects have been improved. For example, the envelope is made from stiff plastic, the aperture for the read/write heads is usually covered by a metal shield and the envelope has a special latch for write protection.

Table 9.1 details the most commonly used diskettes.

The abbreviations we have used are standard:

SS - Single Side
DS - Double Side
SD - Single Density
DD - Double Density
QD - Quad Density
HD - High Density
ED - Extra High Density

Table 9.1
Characteristics of Floppy Disks

Size	Capacity	Sides	Tracks	Sectors per track	Denote
5.25"	160K	1	40	8	SS/DD
5.25"	180K	1	40	9	SS/DD
5.25"	320K	2	40	8	DS/DD
5.25"	360K	2	40	9	DS/DD
5.25"	720K	2	80	9	DS/QD
5.25"	1.2M	2	80	15	DS/HD
3.5"	720K	2	80	9	DS/DD
3.5"	1.44M	2	80	18	DS/HD
3.5"	2.88M	2	80	36	DS/ED

We'll look at how the information stored on diskettes is organized later on. Before we do so, we'll have a look at another type of magnetic storage - **hard disks**.

Hard Disks

Hard disks really are hard! They are made of a special alloy which is covered with a magnetic substance. The main difference between hard disks and diskettes is that hard disks actually contain several disks, which are individually known as platters. So, when we refer to the hard disk, we actually mean several platters grouped together in a hermetically-sealed cover making one device.

Another important characteristic is that hard disks are stationary devices. Unlike diskettes, which you can change easily, hard disks are permanently installed in the main block of your PC by the manufacturer. Strictly speaking, you can get changeable hard disks but they are generally more expensive and less effective than stationary ones.

The first hard disks had a capacity of 5M bytes. This has been substantially increased to a standard 120M or 200M. Currently, the largest hard disks have a capacity of over 1G bytes (1G stands for 1 gigabyte, i.e. 1024M kilobytes or 1024x1024K bytes or 1024x1024x1024 bytes which is equal to 1,073,741,824 bytes!). On average, one page of text contains 400 words, or 2000 characters, which means that these disks can store more than 500,000 pages of information.

Disks at the Physical Level

We can view the organization of data on the disk at a physical or logical level; the physical level being what actually exists on the disk in reality, while the logical level is how that structure is represented by the operating system. As we access the disks at a progressively higher level, so the logical structure becomes more sophisticated and more powerful. We will start by looking at the physical organization of the disk, which from the programmer's point of view is very similar for both hard and floppy disks.

The disk surface is broken down into concentric circles called *tracks*, each track containing several *sectors*. If a disk contains more than one working surface, then the set of tracks on different sides with the same diameter is called a *cylinder*. All the tracks and cylinders are numbered starting from the edge of the disk. All the sectors on each track are

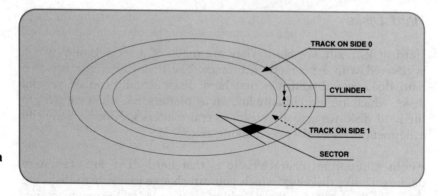

Figure 9.2
Structure of a Floppy Disk

also numbered. Figure 9.2 shows the structure of a floppy disk. The structure of hard disks is very similar, but a cylinder consists of more than two tracks. A hard disk has several platters, so a cylinder on a hard disk actually covers all the same-numbered tracks on each platter. Figure 9.3 shows the structure of a hard disk.

MS-DOS uses contiguous parts of 512 bytes called sectors as the standard units for storing information on disks. BIOS, however, can deal with sectors of various lengths - 128, 256, 512 or 1024 bytes. This feature is useful for reading disks prepared on other operating systems such as CP/M.

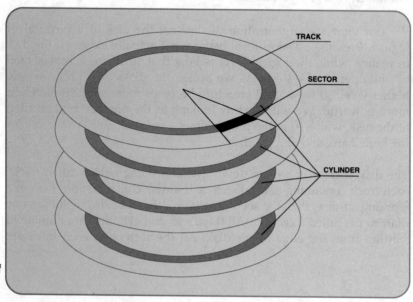

Figure 9.3
The Structure of a Hard Disk

Before you use a new diskette, it must be formatted using the DOS utility FORMAT. This utility performs two tasks: physical, or low-level formatting and logical formatting. In a low-level format, the utility writes onto the disk sectors which are filled with a specific code. This code is especially selected as being the most likely to cause writing errors. The utility then reads the contents of the sector and compares it to the original code that was written. If the information read from a sector isn't exactly the same as what was written, the utility marks that sector as "bad", meaning it will not be used by DOS until the disk is reformatted. In a logical format, the utility writes special system data on the disk to inform DOS that it is ready to use.

There is a variety of software, such as PC Tools, which does this task but we'll concentrate on standard MS-DOS. New hard disks also need to be formatted and must be prepared first by the DOS utility FDISK or something similar. Sometimes it's necessary to perform a low-level or physical format, or preformat. This operation writes system data such as sector numbers on the disk, and is best left to highly-qualified specialists.

Disks at the Logical Level

The logical structure of stored data is usually different for hard and floppy disks. A hard disk can contain areas called *partitions*, belonging to different operating systems. For example MS-DOS, OS/2 and Xenix can share your hard disk, although only one system can be active at a time.

These partitions can then be divided further into separate parts. In MS-DOS, these are called *logical disks* and are denoted by the letters C, D, E and so on. The first logical disk, or active partition of the hard disk, is denoted by the letter C since the letters A and B are reserved for floppy disks. The active partition (active logical disk or simply active disk) is where the operating system is loaded from when you switch your machine on. You can create, delete or reallocate logical disks, and change or switch the active partition using the DOS utility FDISK. The maximum size of a logical disk is 32Mbytes in DOS 3.3 and up to 512Mbytes in later versions. MS-DOS versions earlier than 3.3 do not support logical disks at all, so to use hard disks greater than 32Mbytes with these versions you need to install additional software such as Disk Manager.

Once you have created the logical disk, you need to format it as we have said with the DOS utility FORMAT. This command will let you give the disk a name (often called a *label* or *Volume ID*) which you can change at any time using the LABEL command. Later on in this chapter we will show you how you can read and write the disk label in assembly language.

The DOS File System

The basic logical component of disk organization is the file, which is simply a set of data that has a name and is stored on a device. Note that a file always has a name, even if it says "unnamed". This just means that the name has been created by the operating system or an application program - for example 130692.$$$ or something even more strange! Sometimes you will not actually be able to read the name - for example if it contains special characters which can not be typed on the keyboard.

A file name is made up of two parts: the name itself and its extension. The name can be 1 to 8 characters, while the optional extension can be up to 3 characters long. The file name and extension must be separated by a period ".", for example in the file COMMAND.COM, COMMAND is the name and COM the extension.

The characteristics of the file - such as its name, extension, location on disk, date and time of creation, and size, are stored in the directory. Each file allocated on disk has a directory entry of 32 bytes.

Directories are in turn stored on the disk as files. Let's think about this for a minute - the information about files is stored in directories which are files themselves! This circular problem is overcome by having a **main directory** or **root directory**. Once the disk is available (the hard disk is always available and floppy disks are available when inserted in the disk drive), MS-DOS looks for this root directory. All the other files and directories can then be located using the information it contains.

Some entries in a directory might correspond to another directory rather than to a file. This is known as a nested directory or **subdirectory**. Figure 9.4 shows the relationship between files and directories in this hierarchical structure.

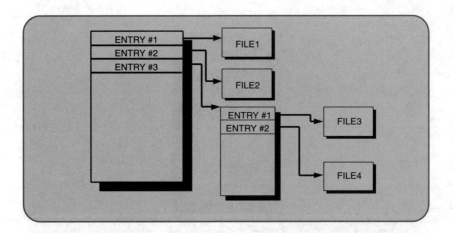

Figure 9.4
**Nested
Directories**

There is no significant difference between directories and subdirectories, since each directory can be defined as a subdirectory of the root directory. The earliest versions of MS-DOS supported only one directory on each disk. It was only later that the hierarchical system of nested directories, borrowed from UNIX-like systems, was introduced in MS-DOS, allowing users to group related files together.

Although information is physically stored on disks in sectors, MS-DOS operates with an allocation unit called a **cluster**. A cluster is a group of sequentially located sectors which MS-DOS considers as a whole. The size of a cluster varies depending on the type of disk - on 360K diskettes it occupies 2 sectors and on 20M hard disks - 4 sectors.

All the clusters allocated to a particular file form a chain, with the individual clusters distributed almost randomly over the physical disk. When you create a file, the first cluster is marked as occupied and its number is placed into the directory entry which corresponds to the created file. If a file occupies more than one cluster, the reference to the following cluster is given in the previous one. Consequently a chain is created whereby the first cluster points to the second, the second to the third, and the last one contains a special pointer that points nowhere. A special part of the disk called FAT - File Allocation Table (considered later in this chapter) contains information describing how clusters are united in chains.

Besides data files, each disk has special areas which contain information which describe its layout and contents. We will now look at where these special areas are and the type of information they contain.

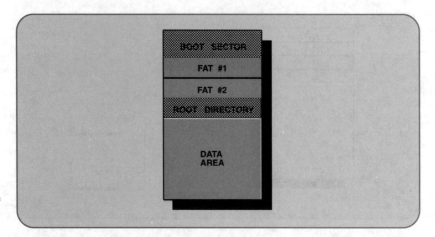

Figure 9.5
**Distribution of
Disk Space**

System Data on Disks

The allocation of system data on disk is shown in Figure 9.5.

The disk starts with the boot sector, which is sometimes confusingly referred to as the boot record. The boot record is actually part of the boot sector. Another common confusion occurs because hard disks can contain many logical disks, each of which also has a first sector. In this situation, the first sector of the physical disk is called the Master Boot Sector.

The next system area is taken up by two copies of the FAT - File Allocation Table. The reason there are two copies is simply for security - if one copy is accidentally destroyed, you can restore the information on disk using the second one. These copies of FAT must be identical. If they are not, it means that you have a problem with your disk and must repair it using Norton Disk Doctor, Diskfix from Central Point Software or something similar. Carrying out repairs is not as easy as it may sound, as you need to understand the disk structure. The DOS utility CHKDSK compares these two versions of the FAT as a test for disk integrity.

The second copy of the FAT is followed by the root directory. This area contains information about the first level of the hierarchical file structure on the disk. If there are no subdirectories on this disk, then the root directory contains information about all the files on the disk.

The Structure of the Boot Sector

The boot sector contains the program for loading the MS-DOS system (IPL - Initial Program Loader) and technical information about the disk. The layout of the disk boot sector is given in Table 9.2.

The fields marked by an asterisk (*) are not present in versions earlier than DOS 3.31.

The first instruction in this sector performs the jump to the boot program. The boot sector always contains the boot program, even when there is no operating system on the disk. The contents of the boot sector depend on which operating system was in use when this disk was formatted. Thus, the boot sector of a disk formatted under MS-DOS differs slightly from the boot sector of a disk prepared by PC-DOS or DR-DOS.

Offset	Size	Meaning
0	3	Instruction for jumping to IPL
3	8	The manufacturer identifier
0Bh	2	The length of sector in bytes
0Dh	1	The number of sectors per cluster
0Eh	2	The number of sectors preceding FAT#1
10h	1	The number of FAT copies
11h	2	The number of entries in the root directory
13h	2	The total number of sectors (partition <= 32M) if 0 see the value at offset 20h
15h	1	The media descriptor
16h	2	The number of sectors in one copy of FAT
18h	2	The number of sectors per track
1Ah	2	The number of surfaces or heads
1Ch	2	The number of hidden sectors (low word)
1Eh *	2	The number of hidden sectors (high word)
20h *	4	The total number of sectors (partitions > 32M)
24h *	1	The drive number (80h-hard, 0 - floppy)
25h *	1	Reserved
26h *	1	Extended boot record signature that is 29h
27h *	4	The volume serial number
2Bh *	0Bh	The volume label
36h *	8	The FAT type (FAT12 or FAT16)
3Eh		... Start of boot program and data ...

Table 9.2

The Layout of the Disk Boot Sector

```
Reading-modifying a sector of hard disk.     A.I.Sopin, Voronezh, 1992

Disk drive= A
     1                          Sector= 0000000
Displacement----------------Hex codes---------------- ASCII value
    0000(0000)  EB 3C 90 4D 53 44 4F 53 35 2E 30 00 02 01 01 00   _<_MSDOS5.0
    0016(0010)  02 E0 00 60 09 F9 07 00 0F 00 02 00 00 00 00 00   _ ' _
    0032(0020)  00 00 00 00 00 00 29 D5 15 5E 46 4E 4F 20 4E 41      )_ ^FNO NA
    0048(0030)  4D 45 20 20 20 20 46 41 54 31 32 20 20 20 FA 33   ME    FAT12 _3
    0064(0040)  C0 8E D0 BC 00 7C 16 07 BB 78 00 36 C5 37 1E 56   ____ |  _x 6_7V
    0080(0050)  16 53 BF 3E 7C B9 0B 00 FC F3 A4 06 1F C6 45 FE   S_>|_  ____ _E•
    0096(0060)  0F 8B 0E 18 7C 88 4D F9 89 47 02 C7 07 3E 7C FB   _  |_M__G _ >|_
    0112(0070)  CD 13 72 79 33 C0 39 06 13 7C 74 08 8B 0E 13 7C   _ ry3_9 |t _  |
    0128(0080)  89 0E 20 7C A0 10 7C F7 26 16 7C 03 06 1C 7C 13   _ |_ |_& | |
    0144(0090)  16 1E 7C 03 06 0E 7C 83 D2 00 A3 50 7C 89 16 52   | |__ _P|_ R
    0160(00A0)  7C A3 49 7C 89 16 4B 7C B8 20 00 F7 26 11 7C 8B   |_I|_ K|_ _& |_
    0176(00B0)  1E 0B 7C 03 C3 48 F7 F3 01 06 49 7C 83 16 4B 7C   | _H__ I|_K|
    0192(00C0)  00 BB 00 05 8B 16 52 7C A1 50 7C E8 92 00 72 1D   _ _ R|_P|__ r
    0208(00D0)  B0 01 E8 AC 00 72 16 8B FB B9 0B 00 BE E6 7D F3   _ __ r ____ __}_
    0224(00E0)  A6 75 0A 8D 7F 20 B9 0B 00 F3 A6 74 18 BE 9E 7D   _u __ _ __t __}
    0240(00F0)  E8 5F 00 33 C0 CD 16 5E 1F 8F 04 8F 44 02 CD 19   __ 3__ ^__D _

PgDn -forward, PgUp -back, Esc -exit, F3 -edit, F1 -change panel
```

Figure 9.6
The Bootsector of a Floppy Disk (First 256 Bytes)

Figures 9.6 and 9.7 show the contents of the boot sector of a floppy disk formatted by the MS-DOS 5.0 FORMAT command. They are both created by the program DSERV7 stored on your program disk. This program is designed for reading and possibly changing the content of disk sectors. Look at the text constants IO.SYS and MSDOS.SYS at the end of the boot sector. These are the names of the hidden system

```
Reading-modifying a sector of hard disk.     A.I.Sopin, Voronezh, 1992

Disk drive= A
     2                          Sector= 0000000
Displacement ----------------Hex codes---------------- ASCII value
    0256(0100)  58 58 58 EB E8 8B 47 1A 48 48 8A 1E 0D 7C 32 FF   XXX___G HH_ |2
    0272(0110)  F7 E3 03 06 49 7C 13 16 4B 7C BB 00 07 B9 03 00   __ I| K|_ _
    0288(0120)  50 52 51 E8 3A 00 72 D8 B0 01 E8 54 00 59 5A 58   PRQ_: r___T YZX
    0304(0130)  72 BB 05 01 00 83 D2 00 03 1E 0B 7C E2 E2 8A 2E   r_ __ |___.
    0320(0140)  15 7C 8A 16 24 7C 8B 1E 49 7C A1 4B 7C EA 00 00   |_ $|_I|_K|_
    0336(0150)  70 00 AC 0A C0 74 29 B4 0E BB 07 00 CD 10 EB F2   p __t)__ __ __
    0352(0160)  3B 16 18 7C 73 19 F7 36 18 7C FE C2 88 16 4F 7C   ; |s _6 |•__ O|
    0368(0170)  33 D2 F7 36 1A 7C 88 16 25 7C A3 4D 7C F8 C3 F9   3__6 |_ %|_M|___
    0384(0180)  C3 B4 02 8B 16 4D 7C B1 06 D2 E6 0A 36 4F 7C 8B   __ _ M|__ 6O|_
    0400(0190)  CA 86 E9 8A 16 24 7C 8A 16 25 7C CD 13 C3 0D 0A   ____ $|_6%|__
    0416(01A0)  4E 6F 6E 2D 53 79 73 74 65 6D 20 64 69 73 6B 20   Non-System disk
    0432(01B0)  6F 72 20 64 69 73 6B 20 65 72 72 6F 72 0D 0A 52   or disk error  R
    0448(01C0)  65 70 6C 61 63 65 20 61 6E 64 20 70 72 65 73 73   eplace and press
    0464(01D0)  20 61 6E 79 20 6B 65 79 20 77 68 65 6E 20 72 65    any key when re
    0480(01E0)  61 64 79 0D 0A 00 49 4F 20 20 20 20 20 20 53 59   ady  IO      SY
    0496(01F0)  53 4D 53 44 4F 53 20 20 20 53 59 53 00 00 55 AA   SMSDOS   SYS U_

PgDn -forward, PgUp -back, Esc -exit, F3  -edit, F1 -change panel
```

Figure 9.7
The Bootsector of a Floppy Disk (Last 256 Bytes)

files, needed to make the disk "bootable" or "system". As we said earlier, the names of these hidden files are different for different operating systems.

The hidden DOS files cannot be placed on disk in the usual way - using the DOS command COPY or XCOPY. They must be stored on disk either by selecting the relevant functions of the FORMAT command when a new disk is being formatted or, in DOS 3.0 and above, by the SYS command.

The last 66 bytes of the boot sector of a hard disk contain the *partition table*. This table consists of 4 elements, each of which is 16 bytes long. These elements describe parts of the hard disk - how long they are, which operating system they belong to and which are marked as bootable. The last two bytes of the partition table contain the constant 055AAh which is the partition table signature.

The File Allocation Table - FAT

As you can guess from its name, the File Allocation Table describes how disk space is allocated to files. It consists of elements defining the status of each disk cluster and additionally includes some system information describing the disk and the FAT itself. There are two types of FAT: 12-bit and 16-bit. The 12-bit FAT is still used to allow for compatibility with the earlier versions of DOS. Each element of 16-bit FAT takes 2 bytes and two elements of 12-bit FAT take 3 bytes.

The first byte of the FAT defines the disk type. The next two or three bytes (depending on the type of the FAT) define a dummy cluster. This element of the FAT is only used for alignment and does not correspond to any real cluster. Each element of the FAT can contain either the number of the next cluster in an allocation chain (if it has been allocated), or a special code that describes the cluster state. Table 9.3 shows the possible values for the FAT elements.

12-bit FAT	16-bit FAT	Meaning
0	0	A free cluster
0FF0h - 0FF7h	0FFF0h - 0FFF7h	A reserved cluster
0FF7h	0FFF7h	A bad cluster
0FF8h - 0FFFh	0FFF8h - 0FFFFh	The last cluster in a chain
0002h - 0FEFh	00002h - 0FFEFh	The next cluster's number

Table 9.3
The Values of a FAT element

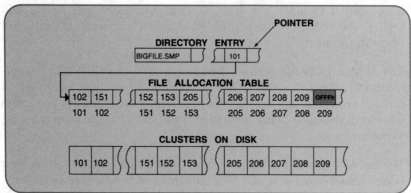

Figure 9.8
The Distribution of Cluster Belonging to a File

As it is unlikely that you will need to deal with clusters, we won't give a full explanation of the techniques for using the FAT. However, you might find it useful to know the basics of what it is and how it works. Figure 9.8 shows an example of the cluster chain for a short file. We will assume that:

The name of the file is BIGFILE.SMP
This file occupies clusters 101, 102, 103, 152, 153, 206, 207, 208, 209

The number of the first cluster that belongs to the file is given in its directory entry at the offset 1Ah. In our example, this is the number 101. The element of the FAT that corresponds to this cluster contains the number of the second cluster, then the second cluster points to the third one and so on. This sequence of clusters is called an allocation chain. Note that the element of the FAT that corresponds to the last cluster in a chain, contains a special value which indicates that it is the **last** cluster. This value contains the hexadecimal value 0Fh all in nibbles except the last one, which can vary from 8h up to 0Fh (see Table 9.3).

The MS-DOS file system uses the FAT for any access to a file. The FAT is DOS's road-map to data on the disk.

The Structure of a Directory Entry

Basic information about a file is kept in its directory entry. This entry occupies 32 bytes and contains various fields that we'll now look at by first considering Table 9.4 which shows the structure of a directory entry.

Offset	Size	Meaning
0	8	The name of file (up to 8 characters)
8	3	The extension (up to 3 characters)
0Bh	1	The file attribute
0Ch	10	Reserved
16h	2	The time of last updating
18h	2	The date of last updating
1Ah	2	The number of first cluster in a chain
1Ch	4	The size of file in bytes

Table 9.4
The Structure of a Directory Entry

The meaning of most fields in this table is quite clear. We have already explained what the name, extension and first cluster are. The date and time of the last update refer to when you most recently edited the file (note that reading information does not affect these values). The size of the file is its length in bytes. The actual space occupied by a file is usually greater than this, as the unit for space allocation is a cluster. Hence a file of only 1 byte requires 1024 bytes on a 360k diskette, so most files leave some part of the last cluster unused.

We will look at the file attribute in more detail, as we will need to use it when we consider file access. Table 9.5 shows the meanings of the file attribute.

To work out the value of the file attribute, you need to calculate the sum of the components. Thus the value of the attribute byte for a file with attributes Read-Only and Hidden will be equal to 3 because 01 + 02 = 03.

Bit No 7 6 5 4 3 2 1 0	Value	Meaning
. . . . 1	01h	Read-only
. . . . . . 1 .	02h	Hidden
. . . . . 1 . .	04h	System
. . . . 1 . . .	08h	Volume label
. . . 1	10h	Directory
. . 1	20h	Archive
. 1	40h	Not used
1	80h	Not used

Table 9.5
The Meaning of the File Attribute

Different Levels of Disk Control

There are three levels of disk control, as there are for the video system:

> Logical level - using the DOS service (interrupts 25h, 26h and
> functions of universal DOS service interrupt 21h)
>
> Basic level   - using the BIOS service - interrupt 13h
>
> Low-level   - direct hardware control.

The relationship between these levels is shown in Figure 9.9. This also shows well which component of software or hardware performs which level of service, and which object on disk is affected as a result.

Again, each of the three levels has its pros and cons, but compared with video programming, the pros are weighted towards higher level access using DOS services. The pros of low-level access, ie. control and speed, are far outweighed by its cons. You should approach low-level disk programming with great caution. One error in your program can mean that you lose all the information on your hard disk. Furthermore, it is really the logical features of disks, ie. directories, files etc., that make them useful. These are constructs of DOS, and to a lesser extent BIOS, and to access the disk sensibly at a low-level requires practically rewriting functions that already exist at the higher level. We will therefore confine ourselves to DOS and BIOS services only.

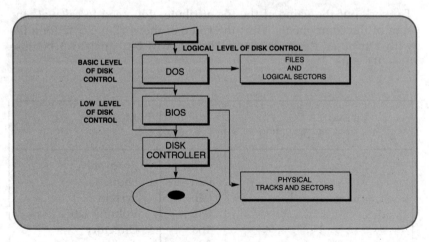

Figure 9.9
Levels of Disk Service

The BIOS Disk Service - Interrupt 13h

The BIOS Disk (Diskette) Service - Interrupt 13h, provides the low-level service for disk drives. Its handler contains programs which perform input-output operations on the physical level, i.e. dealing with the data sector-by-sector on the disk. In fact, any request for disk input/output from a higher level eventually leads to the instruction INT 13h.

The exceptions are a few extremely sophisticated programs like Disk Manager or Disk Repairer which operate disks directly using the disk controller commands. Each disk controller has its own characteristics, making it very hard to incorporate direct manipulation into programs, and although there has recently been some standardization, it is nowhere near the level found for video adapters.

Note that interrupt 13h uses the physical address of the data on the disk. This physical address includes the cylinder number, the head number (or the side number, which in effect, is the same since each head always corresponds to the side of disk), and the sector number. As we have said before, BIOS knows nothing about files or directories.

The following example shows how you can get information about the disk using function 08 of interrupt 13h:

```
    mov     dl,80h      ; DL contains drive number
    mov     ah,08h      ; function 08h -get drive parameter
    int     13h         ; call  BIOS disk service
    jc      Error       ; go to error processing if carry flag =1

; process output parameters: (if  CF = 0)
;
; DL - number of disks attached
; DH - number of read/write heads
; CL - maximum number of sectors
; CH - maximum number of tracks
.....................................................................
error:
;   process error code contained in AH register
```

If you run this for your hard disk, you will probably get an odd number of sides. This is because on some recent disks one side is reserved for addressing information.

The BIOS service also provides format/read/write operations for sectors of non-standard length, which means that you can process disks written under systems other than MS-DOS. Although DOS uses only 512-bytes sectors, BIOS supports sectors of 128, 256, 512 or 1024 bytes long, so you are able to read disks from other computers such as Apple Mac or VAX. Note, however, that in this case you must take care about disk logical structure which can significantly differ from the structure used in DOS.

Besides the regular BIOS services, you might also want information available through three elements of the IVT - the vectors 1Eh, 41h and 46h. They point to the tables of parameters for the floppy disk, first hard disk and second hard disk of your computer. The addresses of these vectors are 0000:0078h for INT 1Eh, 0000:0104h for INT 41h and 0000:0118h for INT 46h.

The example below demonstrates how you can get the address of a floppy disk parameter table:

```
    xor    ax,ax        ;
    mov    es,ax        ; segment address for  IVT
    les    bx,es:[78h]  ; ES:BX - address for floppy disk parameters
```

The contents of the tables mentioned here are described later in this chapter.

The MS-DOS Disk Service

A higher level of disk service is that provided by MS-DOS. The functions it provides are very similar to the ones provided by BIOS, except that MS-DOS processes logical disks while BIOS deals with physical devices.

Unlike its video services, the disk service that MS-DOS offers is rather powerful. There are two elementary ways you can access disks:

Absolute reading of the logical disk - interrupt 25h
Absolute writing of the logical disk - interrupt 26h

MS-DOS uses the logical address to access data on the disk. This address has only one component - the logical number of the sector. In other words, MS-DOS treats the disk as a continuous sequence of numbered sectors, each of which has a unique number in a range from 0 up to the maximum number. The number 0 corresponds to the first sector of the outward track on side 0. For example, take a 360K bytes diskette that has 2 sides containing 40 tracks of 9 sectors each. As far as MS-DOS is concerned, track 0 contains sectors from 0 to 8, track 1 - sectors from 9 to 17, track 2 - from 18 to 26 and so on up to the last track (track 39 on side 1) - which contains sectors from 711 up to 719.

However, the real picture of locating sectors on a track is usually not so simple. Imagine we are going to read three sequential sectors from the disk - sectors 1, 2 and 3. After sector 1 is read, the controller is busy for a while, transferring data into the memory, but the disk is still spinning. When the controller is ready to read sector 2, the read/write head is already at the middle of this sector or even farther. So the controller needs to wait until the required sector is in a position for reading again. The same thing will happen to sector 3 and so on. In this way we can read only one sector in one turnover of the disk.

To make the process of reading/writing data on disks faster, a technique called **interleaving** is used. It assumes that sectors on a track are numbered with a constant offset called the **interleaving factor**. For example, if the track consists of 9 sectors and the interleaving factor is equal to 5, the sectors are located in the following order: 1, 6, 2, 7, 3, 8, 4, 9, 5.

As you can see, if the sectors to be read have sequentially increasing numbers, the controller can complete the process of passing data to, or accepting it from, memory before the next sector is ready for processing. Note, however, that choosing the optimum value for the interleaving factor is not that simple. There are several utilities specifically designed to do this, which you can use to help you. Moreover, some PCs have built-in BIOS routines for determining and setting the optimum interleaving factor.

If you have one of the later versions of MS-DOS, you can divide the hard disk into parts and treat them as separate disks. For example, you can use disk C for the operating system, disk D for software you use regularly and disk E for your programs and data. You can still do this even if your PC only has one physical hard disk. DOS uses the logical addresses for sectors of each logical disk independently, i.e. it addresses each logical disk from the sector number 0. Put more simply - DOS deals with logical sectors, while BIOS uses the physical addresses of sectors.

To enable BIOS to use the logical addresses of sectors they need to be converted into "sector-side-track" form first. The mathematical notation for these formulae is quite frightening and rarely used. However, below is the basic process of converting a disk address from the logical form used by DOS into the BIOS form:

SectorBIOS := 1 + LogicalSectorNumber MOD SectorsPerTrack

SideBIOS := (LogicalSectorNumber DIV SectorsPerTrack) MOD SidesPerDisk

TrackBIOS := LogicalSectorNumber DIV (SectorsPerTrack * SidesPerDisk)

Finally, there are two important points to remember about the MS-DOS disk service:

- If a disk contains several logical disks, the MS-DOS disk service numbers their sectors independently. This means that the first sector of each logical disk is number 0.

- All MS-DOS disk service functions only use 512 bytes sectors, which means that you cannot process non-DOS disks using the MS-DOS disk service.

Reading and Writing Logical Sectors Using MS-DOS

Interrupts 25h and 26h provide the basic level of disk service for logical disks. This service allows you to read and write groups of sectors without taking the logical disk structure into account. This enables you to change the directory structure, to create and to change disk labels, and to edit the files of any structure - to name but a few possibilities. However, if you're unlucky this service can also end up destroying the structure of the disk, meaning that you lose all the data stored on it. You should think at least twice before using these functions and, if you do decide to go ahead with them, save any vital information first!

To use the MS-DOS service, place the parameters into the registers and reserve the buffer for the information which will be transferred. The result of the operation is passed through the Carry Flag CF. If the operation fails, the Carry Flag is set; if it's successful, then it's clear.

Note that interrupts 25h and 26h use the stack to preserve the flag register, so you need to ajust the stack using the POP instruction. Alternatively you can adjust the stack directly, as shown below:

```
add   sp,2
```

Here is an example of reading sectors using interrupt 25h of the DOS disk service:

```
DATA    SEGMENT
BUFSEC  DB 6*512 DB (0)

DATA    ENDS

CODE    SEGMENT
        mov   ax,DATA      ; base address
        mov   ds,ax        ; of data segment
        lea   bx,BUFSEC    ; DS:BX -input buffer
        mov   cx,6         ; number of sectors
        mov   dx,18        ; initial sector
        mov   al,4         ; logical drive E will be used
        int   25h          ; call MS-DOS disk service
        pop   cx           ; stack alignment
        jc    error        ; error if carry flag =1
```

Processing Disk Files

So far we have only dealt with data stored on the disk, as if the sectors were just an array of storage bins. To access anything on the disk requires knowing its exact location, which limits its usefulness. A more powerful method is using the MS-DOS file structure, which can be accessed in two different ways:

▲ Using File Control Blocks (FCB)
▲ Using File Handles

The first method is virtually obsolete. It was used in DOS 1.0, having been inherited from CP/M, and is virtually forgotten. This technique works for files in the current directory and does not support the hierarchical structure provided by recent versions of DOS. We don't advise using this method and will not describe it in this book.

The second method was introduced in DOS 2.0 and is still used in current versions of DOS. It is based on the notion of the **file handle** which specifies the file and its processing methods. The file handle

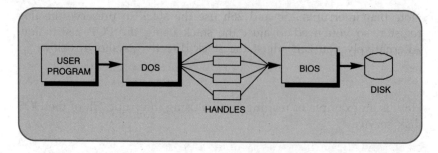

Figure 9.10
**Using File
Handles by
DOS**

for a particular file is created when the File Open procedure runs. For practical purposes, just treat the file handle as a logical number of a file, which is used to identify that particular file in subsequent operations.

Figure 9.10 shows the interaction between a user program, the DOS file system and BIOS. As you can see, DOS uses file handles as channels for passing information that actually deals with the information on physical level to and from BIOS. Each channel can be identified by its number, and this number is all you need to know for performing I/O operations on a file.

When DOS starts a program, it automatically opens 5 standard files. The names and values of the file handles for these files are as shown in Table 9.6.

Other files need to be opened explicitly. The maximum number of files which can be opened at one time is defined by the FILES= parameter in the CONFIG.SYS file.

Table 9.6
*Names and
Values of File
Handles*

Handle	File Name	Meaning
0	CON	Standard input (usually a keyboard)
1	CON	Standard output (usually a screen)
2	CON	Standard output for error messages
3	AUX	Standard communication device
4	PRN	Standard printer (usually either LPT1: or PRN:)

Creating and Deleting Files

Most real programs need more than 5 standard DOS files. Certain files needed for a program might not exist before that program starts and others become superfluous once the program finishes. Of course, you could always create files using DOS commands, such as COPY then delete them using DEL, but there is a more convenient way. To cut down on the number of operations you have to perform, DOS lets you create and delete files from within your program.

To create a file, you simply need to inform DOS of its characteristics: the file name and the full path to that file. Next, call the corresponding DOS service through interrupt 21h. When creating a file, you can also specify its attributes, for example you can create Read-Only or Hidden files.

DOS creates a file by putting the new entry in the corresponding directory. The most important fields in the directory entry are the name of the file and the number of its first cluster. DOS also corrects the element of the FAT which corresponds to the first cluster of the file being created, so that it denotes the last cluster in the chain. The resulting file has the following characteristics:

▲ File contains one cluster only
▲ File is 0 bytes long
▲ The file pointer is set at the start (the first byte of the file is available for recording)

This technique produces an interesting result. When creating a file, DOS does not check whether this file already exists. So if you try to "re-create" a file, you'll lose data stored in that file because DOS changes its current length to 0.

Although errors are rare, there are two main reasons for them - no room in the directory for storing a new entry, or insufficient disk space. Another reason for abnormal termination is that the disk cannot be written onto, either because of physical damage to the surface or errors in the system areas such as the FAT or boot sector.

Deleting files is even simpler. DOS simply changes the first character of the file name to code 0E5h ("X" in symbolic representation") and marks all clusters belonging to that file as free ones. You can try and restore the deleted file by changing the first character of the corresponding directory entry back to a valid letter, then marking clusters of the corresponding chain as they are used. This is exactly how utilities such as PC Tools, Norton Utilities, UnDelete work. Note however, that this procedure only works until its clusters are allocated to another file. Furthermore, any operation which packs the directories removes the entries which correspond to the deleted files.

Opening and Closing Files

Given the original meaning of the word "file", it's hardly surprising that we need to *open* a file before using information stored in it. In the same vein, you'd expect to close it when you've finished.

The procedure which opens a file fills special system tables with values which relate to the actual file. DOS also returns the value of the file handle which you will use for working with that file. In fact, you can treat file opening as a process which creates the handle for a file.

Closing a file is just the same - in reverse. While performing this operation, DOS writes all the data from the file buffers to the file, then clears the internal system tables related to that file. This means that DOS disconnects the file handle from the file being closed. To use this handle again, you need to open another file (or reopen the file that was just closed).

Note that in assembler programs you must perform file opening and closing operations explicitly. Generally speaking, DOS does not carry out these operations automatically. So, if a programming language does let you use files without opening/closing them, it usually means that the compiler simply inserts the code for these operations in the object module of your program.

Like most of the file services, the open/close procedures in MS-DOS are part of the DOS service and are available through the DOS interrupt 21h.

Reading and Writing Disk Files

You can read data from and write it to disk files using the service provided by DOS through interrupt 21h. With early versions of DOS, employing the FCB technique meant using a special area called DTA - **Disk Transfer Area** (which is 128 bytes long) for I/O operations. Although the FCB method is now seen as archaic and is not used, the DTA is worth spending some time on as it is still used for functions such as FindFirst and FindNext.

Before performing reading/writing operations, you need to reserve a buffer long enough to keep the largest portion of data transferred. You must then pass the value of the file handle, the address of the buffer and the number of bytes to be processed (the length of the data portion) to DOS. These parameters tell DOS three important things:

- Which file you want to process
- The location of the data for transfer (or where this data should be placed)
- The amount of data

All I/O operations which read or write data start at the current position in the file, which is marked by a special value called a **file pointer**. When the file is open, DOS automatically sets the file pointer to 0 which means that subsequent I/O operations will start at the beginning of the file.

The File Pointer

While reading/writing files, you need to know which part of the file is currently in use. The file pointer can simply be treated as an offset value from the beginning of the file. When dealing with ordinary sequential files, you do not need to worry about this file pointer, as DOS modifies it automatically. As you read bytes of data from the file, DOS increases the file pointer by the number of bytes read. The same thing happens when you write data to the file. An example will illustrate how useful the file pointer can be.

Suppose you have a file containing information about a telephone directory. All the lines in this file are the same length and each line has a unique number, ranging from 1 to the maximum. In other words, the lines have numbers 1, 2, 3,... (without missing out any numbers). In this case, the line number defines the distance from the beginning of the file. By changing the value of the file pointer, you can process the part of file you need. For example, to get information about person number n you simply need to set the file pointer to this value

```
l x (n - 1)
```

where l is the length of the line. So, if you want information about person number 10 and each line is 100 bytes long, you must set the value of the file pointer to 100 x (10 - 1) = 900.

You can also use the file pointer to organize your data stored on disks as direct-access files. DOS provides the Move File Pointer operation which lets you give the file pointer a new value. Later in this chapter we'll explain how you can use this function to set a new value and get the current value of the file pointer.

Handling Errors

Like anything in life, I/O operations can finish successfully or otherwise! There are two types of errors: ones that allow the program to continue and ones that require the user to do something. An example of the first type of error is "file not found". In this instance, DOS returns an error code to the program and continues working. An error like "drive not ready" means that you will have to perform a manual operation, such as closing the door of the disk drive. These errors are called **critical errors** and are processed in a special way.

The main reason that critical errors are given special treatment is that DOS is a friendly system! Imagine what would happen if an error caused the immediate termination of the program (do you remember MVS?). You've just spent hours working on some text that you decide to save on a diskette and the text processor terminates because your diskette is write protected or there isn't sufficient space to store your file!

When a critical error occurs in MS-DOS, DOS automatically calls interrupt 24h. The default handler of this interrupt is a program that outputs a message describing what has happened and waits for your reaction.

You can create your own handler for critical errors. To do this you need to write the corresponding procedure, then set vector 24h so that it points to this procedure.

Tools

Basic Functions of the BIOS Disk Service

As we have seen, the BIOS service provides the foundation for all disk operations. Here we will give a brief, non-formal description of certain functions of the BIOS interrupt 13h which are used most often in application programs. For more detailed information about the BIOS disk service, see Appendix F.

The number of the function must always be given in the AH register, and the information about the disk in the DL register. Values 00h - 7Fh denote floppy disks and values 80h - 0FFh, hard disks. The result of the operation is passed through the Carry Flag CF. If CF is set, it means that the operation failed and AH contains the disk status when an error occurs. The value in AH is also often referred to as an error code. If the operation is successful, CF is clear and AH usually contains 0. If we come across a function that passes parameters or results differently, we'll draw your attention to it.

The Function 00h - Reset Disk System

This function resets the disk controller and recalibrates the drives attached to it. Use this function to prepare the disk and the controller for I/O operations and after any input/output error before the program retries an operation that has failed. If you specify the hard disk in the DL register, the floppy disk controller will also be reset. A disk drive, like all mechanical devices, is prone to inexplicable failure sometimes, in which case it's a good idea to reset the drive and try again at least three times.

The Function 01h - Get Disk Status

This function returns the status of the last disk I/O operation. When the result is returned, AH contains 0 and AL contains a one-byte status code. This function is useful for determining whether the disk is write-protected.

The Function 02h - Read Sector

This function reads one or more sectors from a disk (diskette). AL must contain the number of the sector, DH the number of the head. Register CX contains the number of the cylinder and the number of the sector, placing low bits of the cylinder number into the CH register, the number of the sector into bits 0 - 5 of the CL register and the high bits of the cylinder number into bits 6 - 7 of the CL register. For example, suppose you want to read 5 sectors from cylinder 950 starting at sector 10. To do this, you would have to write the following sequence of instructions:

```
mov     ah,02       ; function 02 - read sector(s)
mov     al,05       ; 5 sectors to be read
mov     dh,1        ; number of head
mov     dl,80h      ; hard disk drive 0
mov     cl,0CAh     ; number of sector and high part of cyl. no.
mov     ch,0B6h     ; low part of cylinder number
int     10h         ; BIOS disk service call
```

Note that 950 = 3B6h, which is greater than 0FFh, so this value can not be stored in one byte. Therefore two extra bits of the cylinder number are stored in the bits 6 and 7 of the CL register. The value in the CL register is therefore 1100 0000b = 0C0h. Finally, if we add the number of the sector that is equal to 10 = 0Ah to this value we get the value 0CAh. Consequently, the total content of the CX register must be 0B6CAh. Figure 9.11 shows the content of the CX register for this example.

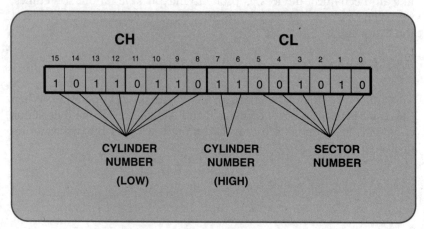

Figure 9.11
Storing the Sector Number in the Register

In finishing with the Read Sector function, make sure that the pair of registers ES:BX contain the buffer address in segment:offset form. After the function has been completed, the data will have been placed into the buffer area ready for further processing.

If the operation is successful, the Carry Flag is clear, AH is zero and AL contains the number of sectors read. If the operation failed, the Carry Flag is set and AH contains the disk status as usual.

Note that this function can only access devices which have less than 1025 cylinders, because the number of a cylinder can only take up 10 bits (8 bits of CH plus two high bits of CL).

If you request a multi-sector operation (that is, you want to read more than one sector), and you get errors while reading, the operation will be terminated after the sector in which the error occurred.

The Function 03h - Write Sector(s)

This function writes one or more sectors onto your hard disk or a diskette. The rules for passing parameters are exactly the same as for function 02h (read sector) except that the operation works in the opposite way - it writes data from the buffer onto the disk. To use this function, place the address of the buffer that contains the data to be written into the ES:BX registers.

The Function 04h - Verify Sector(s)

This function checks whether the data on your disk is readable. The parameters are the same as for function 02h (read sector).

The Function 08h - Get Drive Parameters

This function returns the hard disk parameters on all types of PCs and the floppy disk parameters on AT and PS. We looked at this function while introducing interrupt 13h in the last section.

The Function 0Dh - Reset Fixed Disk System

This is very similar to function 00h but it only resets the hard disk controller.

The Function 0Eh - Read Sector Buffer

This function is used on XT machines for reading the data from the adapter's internal buffer into the memory area at an address contained in the ES:BX registers. No real input/output operations are performed using the physical disk.

The Function 0Fh - Write Sector Buffer

This function is the opposite of function 0Eh - it writes data into the adapter's internal buffer.

The Function 10h - Get Drive Status

This only works for hard disk drives. If the disk isn't operational, it returns the status of the drive in AH. Otherwise, it returns 0 in AH and clears the Carry Flag. Use this function to ensure that the disk is OK before performing important I/O operations such as formatting or reorganizing.

The DOS Disk Service - Interrupts 25h and 26h

The functions performed by interrupts 25h and 26h are very similar to those performed by the BIOS disk service 13h - they read and write disk sectors. You can use these interrupts to perform special tasks such as analyzing and editing disk areas not accessible through the file system, for example the boot sector or root directory. Interrupts 25h and 26h deal with the logical sectors, numbered from 0 up to the maximum number (which is determined by the disk capacity). In DOS 3.31 and above, interrupts 25h and 26h can process logical disks that exceed 32M bytes. There are two ways of specifying parameters for these interrupts, depending on the disk size. We'll start with the "old-fashioned" form used for disks smaller than 32M bytes.

To use interrupts 25h and 26h, put the drive number into the AL register (0 denotes drive A, 1 - B, etc), the number of sectors to be processed into CX and the number of the first logical sector used into the DX register. The pair of registers DS:BX must contain the address of the buffer area. The interrupt 25h reads data from the disk and puts them into this area, interrupt 26h takes the data from the buffer and writes it onto disk.

Offset	Size (bytes)	Meaning
00h	4	First logical sector number
04h	2	Number of sectors to process
06h	4	Address of the buffer

Table 9.7
Structure of the Read/Write Packet

Interrupts 25h and 26h have more recently been developed to use the concept of a **read/write packet**. The address of the read packet (for interrupt 25h) or the write packet (for interrupt 26h) is passed in the DS:DX registers. CX contains the value -1 (0FFFFh). The stucture of the Read/Write packet is shown in Table 9.7.

If the operation performed by interrupt 25h or 26h fails, the AX register contains an error code. The value in AL is the extended error code, issued to INT 24h - the critical error handler. The code in AH describes the error that occurred:

01h - unknown or bad command
02h - address mark bad or missing
03h - disk is write-protected (INT 26 only)
04h - requested sector not found
08h - DMA failure
10h - error while transferring data (bad CRC)
20h - controller error
40h - seek operation error
80h - attachment failed to respond

If the operation is successful, the Carry Flag CF is clear and the Al register contains the value 00h.

Note that interrupts 25h and 26h push the flag register onto the stack, so you must either pop it, or directly adjust the value of SP by increasing it by 2. This will leave anything else you pushed onto the stack at the top, where you would expect to find it. In MS-DOS versions 3.1 to 3.3, these interrupts have a bug - they set the word at location ES:[BP+1Eh] to FFFFh if AL contains an invalid drive number on entry.

Since the DOS disk service available through interrupts 25h and 26h is easier to use than the corresponding BIOS service, we advise you to use these interrupts when dealing with the disk as a whole. Your program disk contains the program DSERV7 which uses the DOS disk service for reading and modifying sectors of logical disks. The boot sector dump, shown earlier in this chapter, was obtained using this program. You can experiment with this program, but tread cautiously when modifying important disk data such as the root directory or FAT.

Floppy Disk Parameters - Vector 1Eh

When working with disks, you may need to know some important parameters such as sector size or number of sectors per track. This information is accessible through the element of IVT which corresponds to interrupt 1Eh. Note that this vector points to a table rather than an interrupt handler, so don't use instructions like

```
INT    1Eh
```

Instead, get access to the BIOS data area and read the corresponding information as shown below:

```
mov    ax,0h       ; segment address of IVT
mov    es,ax       ; ES points to the IVT segment
mov    bx,es:78h   ; take offset for vector 1Eh (78h=4*1Eh)
mov    ax,es:7Ah   ; take segment address for vector 1Eh
mov    es,ax       ; ES:BX now point to Floppy Disk Parameter Table
```

There is a table for floppy disk parameters stored in ROM-BIOS which occupies 11 bytes. By default, the vector 1Eh points to this table until you change its value to point to your own table. Some commercial programs do this to change the characteristics of diskettes, for example to store 10 sectors per track instead of 9. The format of the diskette parameters block is shown in Table 9.8.

Offset (hex)	Length (bytes)	Contents
00	1	Bits 4-7: step rate, 0-3: head unload time
01	1	Bits 0-6: head load time, 7: DMA flag
02	1	Motor off time
03	1	Sector size in bytes (MS-DOS standard - 02)
04	1	Last sector on track
05	1	Size of gap between sectors on read/write
06	1	Length of data transfer (standard - 255)
07	1	Size of gap between sectors on format
08	1	Byte for sector filling on format
09	1	Head-settle time in ms
0A	1	Motor start-up time

Table 9.8
The Floppy Disk
Parameter Block

Hard Disk Parameters - Vectors 41h and 46h

There is a similar table for hard disk parameters, which you can use to get information such as the number of cylinders and heads. The address of this table is stored in the IVT as vector 41h. You must remember that there are no handlers for this vector and that it points to a special block in the memory area.

You can access hard disk parameters using function 35h (Get Interrupt Vector) of the DOS interrupt 21h. We mentioned this service briefly in Chapter Six and it will be described in detail in Chapter Eleven. Tables 9.9 and 9.10 show the structure and purpose of the hard disk parameters block for PC/PC XT and AT/PS, respectively.

Offset (hex)	Length (bytes)	Type	Contents
00	2	word	Maximum number of cylinders (from 0)
02	1	byte	Maximum number of heads
03	2	word	Starting cylinder for reduced writing
05	2	word	Starting cylinder for precompensation
07	1	byte	Maximum ECC burst length
08	1	byte	Drive options
09	1	byte	Standard value for time-out
0A	1	byte	Time-out value for format drive
0B	1	byte	Time-out value for check drive
0C	4	byte	Reserved

Table 9.9
Disk Parameter Block for PC/XT

Offset (hex)	Length (bytes)	Type	Contents
00	2	word	Maximum number of cylinders (from 0)
02	1	byte	Maximum number of heads
03	2	word	Reserved
05	2	word	Starting cylinder for precompensation
07	1	byte	Maximum ECC burst length
08	1	byte	Drive options
09	3	byte	Reserved
0C	2	word	Cylinder for landing zone
0E	1	byte	Sectors per track
0F	1	byte	Reserved

Table 9.10
Disk Parameter Block for AT/PS

The meaning of the byte with offset 08h - the "drive option" byte is different for PC/XT and AT/PS. The description of this byte for the PC and XT is as follows:

> bit 7 is set if disable disk-access retries
> bit 6 is set if disable ECC retries
> bits 3 - 5 are equal to 0
> bits 0 - 2 - drive option

On the AT and PS this byte can be encoded as follows:

> bits 6 - 7 are nonzero if disable access retries
> bit 5 is set if the defect map is stored by the manufacturer on the maximum cylinder plus 1
> bit 3 is set if disk has more than 8 heads

Other bits are not used.

If you have two hard disks, vector 46h points to the parameter block for the second hard disk. The structure and the meaning of its fields are the same as for the block that corresponds to vector 41h.

In this chapter we have given an example of using the BIOS disk service - a utility for hard disk parking. This utility finds out the maximum number of cylinders, increases it by 2 and positions the heads at the calculated cylinder. An earlier version of this program used information from the areas defined by vectors 41h and 46h which led to an interesting discovery. At least one of the computers that we tried the utility Parking on contained decidedly strange information in the area where vector 41h pointed, which meant that it couldn't be treated as a disk parameter block. Our guess is that some computers that are not fully compatible might use vectors 41h and 46h in a non-standard way, so be careful while using this information in your programs.

The DOS File Service - Get/Set Current Drive

So far we have accessed disk data without the full benefit of the DOS file services. As we discussed earlier, the most powerful method of accessing these DOS functions is using file handles, for which you have to be able to specify the complete path to the file you want to process. Since the path must include the name of the disk and the directory which contains the file, it is important that we master the DOS services for controlling disks and directories. We'll start by looking at the beginning of the path string - the disk identifier.

The Function 19h - Get Current Disk

This function allows you to determine the current logical disk, as shown in the following example:

```
    mov  ah,19h     ; function 19h -get drive number
    int  21h        ; call MS-DOS disk service
    .......         ; error if carry flag = 1
```

To find out the current drive, first check the Carry Flag CF. If it is set it means there has been an error, otherwise the current drive identifier is returned in the AL register. The value 0 in AL stands for drive A, 1 - for drive B, 2 - for C and so on. Note that this function deals with the *logical* disks, so a partitioned hard drive will have more than one identifier (C,D,E...).

The Function 0Eh - Set Current Disk

This function is designed to let you change the current drive. To use it place the value for the disk you want to make current into the DL register.

The parameters are the same as for function 19h. The following example shows how to make disk D current:

```
;   logical disk D will be current
    mov   dl,3            ; constant 3 denotes disk D
    mov   ah,0Eh          ; function 19h -set drive number
    int   21h            ; call MS-DOS disk service
```

You can determine that the operation was performed successfully by checking the Carry Flag. If it is clear, the current disk has been changed, otherwise there has been an error.

The DOS File Service - Working with Directories

MS-DOS provides four functions for dealing with directories:

- Create a directory - function 39h
- Remove a directory - function 3Ah
- Set current directory - function 3Bh
- Get current directory - function 47h

To use the first three functions place the appropriate number into the AH register, and place the address of the ASCIIZ string with the full path to the required directory into the registers DS:DX. Remember - an ASCIIZ string is a sequence of ASCII characters that finishes with the 0 character - Zero. Next, perform the INT instruction to call the DOS service - interrupt 21h.

To use the last function to get the current directory name, place the address of the buffer for the path into the DS:SI registers and the number of the disk you want to search into the DL register. Note that the convention for denoting the disk is different from the functions mentioned earlier - 0 stands for the current disk, 1 for disk A, 2 for B and so on. Then place the function code 47h in AH and call interrupt 21h. If the Carry Flag is clear on return, the buffer will contain the path to the current directory on the drive requested, but without the name of the disk itself (e.g. masm\exam). The maximum length of the string returned is 64 bytes.

To create the full path to the current directory you should add three characters (the drive letter, colon and backslash) to the beginning of an ASCIIZ-string returned by function 47h. To determine the name of the current drive, use function 19h of interrupt 21h.

Note that the maximum length of a string returned by function 47h is 64 bytes. Make sure that the buffer, the address of which is passed in the DS:SI registers, is not shorter than 64 bytes - otherwise you might destroy data. That's the theory - now let's see how it works in practice!

The Function 39h - Creating a Directory

Suppose you want to create a new directory called NEWDIR as a subdirectory of the directory DIRECT1 that already exists on disk D. The following code will perform this task:

```
. . . . . . . . . . . . . . . . . . . . . . . . . . . . . . . . . . . . . . . . . . . . . . . . . . . . . . . . . . . . . . . .
DATA  SEGMENT
PATH  DB    "D:\DIRECT1\NEWDIR", 0  ; ASCIIZ string for path
      . . . . . . . .
DATA  ENDS
. . . . . . . . . . . . . . . . . . . . . . . . . . . . . . . . . . . . . . . . . . . . . . . . . . . . . . . . . . . . . . . .
CODE  SEGMENT
      mov   ax,DATA     ;  base address
      mov   ds,ax       ;  of data segment
      lea   dx,PATH     ;  DS:DX - address of full path
```

```
        mov   ah,39h      ; function 39h -create subdirectory
        int   21h         ; call MS-DOS service
        jc    error       ; error, if carry flag = 1
        ........
        ........
CODE    ENDS
```

The Function 3Ah - Removing the Directory

The next example will remove the directory you created above.

```
DATA    SEGMENT
PATH    DB    "D:\DIRECT1\NEWDIR", 0   ; ASCIIZ string for path
        ........
DATA    ENDS

CODE    SEGMENT
        mov   ax,DATA     ; base address
        mov   ds,ax       ; of data segment
        lea   dx,PATH     ; DS:DX - address of the path string
        mov   ah,3Ah      ; function 3Ah -delete subdirectory
        int   21h         ; call MS-DOS service
        jc    error       ; error, if carry flag = 1
        ........
CODE    ENDS
```

Note that you can only remove empty directories, i.e. a directory that does not contain any files.

The Function 3Bh - Set the Current Directory

This function will make the directory D:\DIRECT1\NEWDIR the current directory:

```
DATA    SEGMENT
PATH    DB    "D:\DIRECT1\NEWDIR", 0   ; ASCIIZ string for path
        ........
DATA    ENDS

CODE    SEGMENT
        mov   ax,DATA     ; base address
        mov   ds,ax       ; of data segment
        lea   dx,PATH     ; DS:DX - pointer to path name
        mov   ah,3Bh      ; function 3Bh -set subdirectory
        int   21h         ; call MS-DOS service
```

```
        jc    error        ; error, if carry flag = 1
        ........
   CODE  ENDS
```

The Function 47h - Get Current Directory

This is an example of getting information about the current directory using the MS-DOS service. Note that it is designed to get the full directory name, including the disk name.

```
   DATA    SEGMENT
   PATH    DB    68 dup (0)     ; buffer for path name
           ........
   DATA    ENDS

   CODE  SEGMENT
         mov   ax,DATA      ; base address
         mov   ds,ax        ; of data segment
   ; first 3 positions reserved for disk name and separator
         mov   word ptr PATH+1,'\:' ; place separator into buffer
         lea   si,PATH+3     ; DS:SI - address of buffer
         mov   ah,47h        ; function 47h - get current directory
         int   21h           ; call MS-DOS service
         jc    error         ; error, if carry flag = 1
   ; get the current disk name
         mov   ah,19h         ; function 19h - get drive number
         int   21h           ; call MS-DOS disk service
         add   al,41h         ; 41h is ASCII code for "A"
         mov   PATH,al        ; full path is formed!
         ........
   CODE  ENDS
```

There are a few tricks in this example which you might want to add to your repertoire, so we'll consider it in more detail. The buffer for function 47h is actually located at the address PATH+3 rather than PATH. This is because function 47h doesn't return the disk name so we have to form it manually - which is why we reserved the first three bytes of the memory area labelled PATH. We placed the characters ':\' in the second and third bytes of the buffer which separates the disk name and the directory name. Finally we used function 19h to get the disk name (in fact the disk number) and then converted the value returned into a character by adding it to the constant 41h which corresponds to the letter A. So the numeric constant 0 becomes the character constant "A", 1 - "B" and so on. By placing this character into the first byte of the area labelled PATH we get the full name of

Offset	Length in bytes	Meaning	Method of Creation
0	1	Drive letter	Returned by function 19h
1	2	Colon symbol and backslash	Placed manually by instruction MOV
3	64	Current path	Returned by function 47h

Table 9.11
Using Buffer for Creating the Full Path to the Directory

the current directory including the drive name, colon ":" and backslash "\". Table 9.11 illustrates how the buffer area is used in the example we have just considered.

You can use a routine like this to protect against switching to another directory. For example, if your program needs to work with files located in different directories, it would determine the current directory, save the path in the memory, change the current directory to work with the files and finally return to the directory that was current when the program started.

The DOS File Service - Find A File

Before you can do anything to a file, you need to get access to it. As we have already shown, MS-DOS provides functions for finding, creating/deleting, opening/closing, and reading/writing files. We'll start our consideration of the Find File operations with the Set DTA function. To find specific files we need an auxiliary tool, the DTA - Disk Transfer Area which was extensively used in the FCB technique. Although the DTA is only used in a few operations, such as FindFirst or FindNext, it is invaluable to file processing, so we'll start with the function which sets the DTA.

The Function 1Ah - Set DTA

This function sets the DTA. You can treat this operation as the initialization of the corresponding area of memory. To perform this function, place the address of the DTA buffer (usually 128 bytes long) into the DS:DX registers and call the MS-DOS service dispatcher - interrupt 21h.

Offset	Size in bytes	Meaning
0	21	Reserved
21	1	File attribute
22	2	Time of last modification
24	2	Date of last modification
26	4	Size of file in bytes
30	13	ASCIIZ string containing name of file

Table 9.12
The Meaning of the DTA Fields (FindFirst)

The meaning of the relevant DTA fields is given in Table 9.12.

The Function 4Eh - Find First

This function is used for finding a file in a specified directory. If you haven't defined the complete filename, the function searches the current directory.

Before using this function you should set the DTA using function 1Ah. Put the address of the file name mask into the DS:DX registers. Next put the file attribute mask into the CX register. Then call interrupt 21h. If an appropriate file is found, the Carry Flag CF is clear otherwise it's set. As we haven't come across file name and file attribute masks before, we'll have a look at them now in greater detail.

The file name mask is an ASCIIZ string that contains a file name including wildcards, as used in DOS commands (for example in command DIR). The mask C:COMMAND.COM defines only one file - the file COMMAND.COM on disk C. The mask C:COMMAND?.COM corresponds to files COMMAND.COM, COMMAND1.COM, COMMANDS.COM and other files on disk C which have 8-character names beginning with COMMAND. The mask COM*.* corresponds to all files of any legal length beginning with COM and with any extension. Finally, the mask c:*.* describes all the files in the current directory on disk C.

The attribute mask occupies one byte and represents the sum of all the file attributes you are interested in (see Table 9.5). For example, if you want to find a volume label only, the file mask must be 10h. The mask 03h denotes all files with Read-Only and Hidden attributes (01 + 02), the mask 37h - all files except volume labels. Mask 3Fh describes all files.

If the operation is successful, the characteristics of the file found are returned in the DTA buffer.

The Function 4Fh - Find Next

This function lets you search for a group of files. You can use this function after the function Find First (4Eh) to find the next file which corresponds to the masks. Function 4Fh uses the same DTA buffer as the last operation 4Eh. Find First and Find Next are usually employed in the following way:

▲ The DTA buffer is initialized using function 1Ah.
▲ The Find First operation is performed.
▲ The Find next operation is called until the Carry Flag CX is set.

The following example demonstrates searching for all files with the extension .ASM except volume labels and directories. The corresponding attribute mask is 07h.

```
.............................................................
DATA    SEGMENT
PATH    DB      "D:\DIRECT1\*.asm", 0 ; file name mask
DTA     DB     128 dup (0)      ; DTA buffer
        ........
DATA    ENDS
.............................................................
CODE    SEGMENT
; Step 0 - prepare system registers
        mov    ax,DATA      ; base address
        mov    ds,ax        ; of data segment
; Step 1 - "set DTA" operation
        lea    dx,DTA       ; DS:DX - address of DTA
        mov    ah,1Ah       ; set DTA
        int    21h          ; call MS-DOS service
; Step 2 - find first file
        mov    cx,07h       ; attribute mask
        lea    dx,PATH      ; DS:DX - address of ASCCIZ mask
        mov    ah,4Eh       ; function 4Eh - FindFirst
        int    21h          ; call MS-DOS service
        jc     error        ; error, if carry flag = 1
; Step 3 - find next files until CF is clear
Cycle: lea    dx,PATH      ; DS:DX - address of file name mask
        mov    ah,4Fh       ; function 4Fh - FindNext
        int    21h          ; call MS-DOS service
        jc     exit         ; exit, if carry flag = 1
;=== process the file found ===
        ........
        jmp    Cycle        ; continue searching
Exit:  ........
CODE    ENDS
.............................................................
```

The technique used here is shown in detail in the program FindF included in the Library section with the full assembler text and flow chart. Here is a brief explanation of the program flow - in English!

step 0:   load segment registers for proper addressing
step 1:   set DTA to be used as a buffer for functions 4Eh and 4Fh (FindFirst and Findnext)
step 2:   find the first file that matches the file mask; if no file is found, proceed to the block processing error situation
step 3:   find the next matching file; if no file is found, exit the program, otherwise process the file
step 4:   repeat step 3.

The DOS File Service - Creating/Deleting/Renaming Files

MS-DOS provides functions 3Ch and 41h, for creating and deleting files, respectively. To use these functions, place the address of the ASCIIZ-string that contains the path to the file into the DS:DX registers. Note that if you don't specify the full path of the file you want to process, MS-DOS will look for this file in the current directory of the current disk.

The Function 3Ch - Create a File

The example below creates the file NEWFILE in the current directory of the current disk.

```
DATA    SEGMENT
PATH    DB    "NEWFILE", 0   ; name of file to be created
HANDLE  DW    0              ; handle of file created
        ........
DATA    ENDS

CODE    SEGMENT
    mov    ax,DATA           ; base address
    mov    ds,ax             ; of data segment
    lea    dx,PATH           ; DS:DX -address of file name
    mov    ah,3Ch            ; function 3Ch - create a file
    xor    cx,cx             ; CX =0 -ordinary file
    int    21h               ; call MS-DOS service
    jc     Error             ; error, if carry flag = 1
    mov    HANDLE,ax         ; save value of file handle
    ........
CODE    ENDS
```

The value of the file handle is returned in the AX register, which you must keep for further work with this file. In future operations on the file you can just use this handle, rather than worrying about drives, directories and filenames. The type of file created is defined by the value of the file attribute passed in the CX register. You can create an ordinary file (CX = 0), read-only file (bit 0 of CX is set), hidden file (bit 1 of CX is set) and so on. The meaning of the file attribute bits is detailed in this chapter in Table 9.5.

An important point to remember is that if you try to create a file that already exists, you'll get a file 0 bytes long. As a result, you will lose all the information stored in that file. It makes sense therefore to check whether the file you want to create already exists on the disk.

The Function 41h - Delete a File

This function is designed to delete files which already exist. The following example shows how to delete a file located in the current directory.

```
. . . . . . . . . . . . . . . . . . . . . . . . . . . . . . . . . . . . . . . . . . . . . . . . . . . . . . . . . . . . . . . . . .
DATA   SEGMENT
PATH   DB    "OLDFILE", 0   ; file name
       . . . . . . . .
DATA   ENDS
. . . . . . . . . . . . . . . . . . . . . . . . . . . . . . . . . . . . . . . . . . . . . . . . . . . . . . . . . . . . . . . . . .
CODE   SEGMENT
       mov    ax,DATA      ;  base address
       mov    ds,ax        ;  of data segment
       lea    dx,PATH      ;  DS:DX - address of file name
       mov    ah,41h       ;  function 41h -UNLINK
       int    21h          ;  call MS-DOS service
       jc     error'       ;  error, if carry flag = 1
       . . . . .
CODE   ENDS
. . . . . . . . . . . . . . . . . . . . . . . . . . . . . . . . . . . . . . . . . . . . . . . . . . . . . . . . . . . . . . . . . .
```

This function will let you delete both open and closed files. This means that you do not need to open a file before deleting it. Note, however, that if you delete a file while processing it you may get unpredictable results - the least drastic thing that can happen is the immediate termination of your program.

If you accidentally delete a file, don't worry, you can recover it. DOS doesn't destroy data stored in your file. All it does when it deletes a file is change the first character of the file name with the code 0E5h and mark the clusters that belong to this file as free. As long as these clusters have not been allocated to another file, you can simply change the code 0E5h in the file name back to the original character. This is another point in favor of using programs that can edit disk sectors. System utilities such as Undelete in MS-DOS 5 and DR-DOS 6 can also perform this task for you.

The Function 56h - Rename a File

This function is similar to the function Delete File, but it needs an additional parameter - the new name of the file. This parameter must be an ASCIIZ string and its address must be placed in the ES:SI registers. The following example shows how to rename the file OLDFILE, located in the directory DIRECT1 on the logical disk D, as NEWFILE:

```
. . . . . . . . . . . . . . . . . . . . . . . . . . . . . . . . . . . . . . . . . . . . . . . .
DATA   SEGMENT
PATH1  DB     "D:\DIRECT1\OLDFILE", 0   ;  old file name
PATH2  DB     "D:\DIRECT1\NEWFILE", 0   ;  new file name
     . . . . . . . .
DATA   ENDS
. . . . . . . . . . . . . . . . . . . . . . . . . . . . . . . . . . . . . . . . . . . . . . . .
CODE   SEGMENT
       mov    ax,DATA         ;  base address
       mov    ds,ax           ;  of data segment
       mov    es,ax           ;
       lea    dx,PATH1        ;  DS:DX - old name
       lea    di,PATH2        ;  ES:DI - new name
       mov    ah,56h          ;  function 56h -RENAME
       int    21h             ;  call MS-DOS service
       jc     error           ;  error, if carry flag = 1
       . . . . . . . .
    CODE ENDS
. . . . . . . . . . . . . . . . . . . . . . . . . . . . . . . . . . . . . . . . . . . . . . . .
```

The DOS File Service - Open/Close a File

One way of opening a file is to create an ASCIIZ string containing its full name and place the address of that string into the DS:DX registers. The file handle is returned in AX. Put the value of the **access mode** into the AL register. The bits of these values determine different modes for accessing the file (see Table 9.13).

The Close File operation is much simpler: put the value of the file handle into the BX register and call interrupt 21h. Now let's look at some examples.

Bit	Value	Meaning
0	01h	read only
1	02h	write only
2	04h	read/write
3	08h	reserved, must be 0
4	10h	... used
5	20h	... in sharing
6	40h	... mode
7	80h	inheritance flag

Table 9.13
*The Meaning
of the Access
Mode Bits*

The Function 3Dh - Open a File

This example will open the file OLDFILE, located in the directory
DIRECT1 on logical drive D. The value of the file handle returned by
function 3Dh will be written in the variable HANDLE as one word.

```
DATA       SEGMENT
PATH       DB    "D:\DIRECT1\OLDFILE", 0  ; file name
HANDLE     DW    ?              ; file handle
........
DATA       ENDS

CODE       SEGMENT
           mov   ax,DATA        ; base address
           mov   ds,ax          ; of data segment
           lea   dx,PATH        ; DS:DX - address of file name
           mov   al,2           ; access mode - read & write
           mov   ah,3Dh         ; function 3Dh - open file
           int   21h            ; call MS-DOS service
           jc    error          ; error, if carry flag = 1
           mov   HANDLE,ax       ; store file handle for future usage
........
CODE       ENDS
```

The Function 3Eh - Close a File

The next example will close the file opened in the previous example.

```
DATA  SEGMENT
HANDLE DW   ?           ; file handle
........
DATA   ENDS

CODE   SEGMENT
```

```
        mov    ax,DATA       ;  base address
        mov    ds,ax         ;  of data segment
        mov    bx,HANDLE     ;  put file handle into BX
        mov    ah,3Eh        ;  function 3Dh -close file
        int    21h           ;  call MS-DOS service
        jc     error         ;  error, if carry flag = 1
        ........
CODE    ENDS
```

Always perform the Close File operation before exiting the program. This ensures that all data has been transferred and that none has been left in the buffers.

The DOS File Service - Read/Write a File

Before you can read from and write to a file, you need to open it using function 3Dh. Similarly, when you have finished working with a file, you must close it using function 3Eh. To perform read/write operations you need to reserve a buffer long enough to hold the largest part of data to be transferred. Put the value of the file handle into the BX register and the number of bytes transferred into the CX register. Note that while opening the file you must specify an appropriate access mode value - read only or read/write for the Read File operation and write only or read/write for the Write File operation.

Both functions return results in the Carry Flag CF and the AX register. If the Carry Flag is set, there has been an error. If CF is clear, the AX register contains the number of bytes actually transferred. It is better to compare this value with the value of the transfer request passed to the CX register on entry. If both values are the same, it means that the operation was successful. The implications of different values depend on the operation that was performed. If you call the Read File function and get less data than expected, it means that the file is smaller than it should be. This situation is usually called the "unexpected end of the file". If CF is clear and AX equals 0 it means that the end of the file was reached as soon the operation started. If you get a value in AX indicating that you have written less bytes than requested, the most likely reason is a shortage of space on the target disk.

The Function 3Fh - Read a File

This is an example of reading data from an open file. 4096 bytes are transferred.

```
DATA      SEGMENT
HANDLE    DW    ?                   ; file handle
BUF       DB    4096 dup (0)        ; I/O buffer
          ........
DATA      ENDS

CODE      SEGMENT
    mov   ax,DATA                   ; base address
    mov   ds,ax                     ; of data segment
    lea   dx,BUF                    ; DS:DX - address of buffer
    mov   bx,HANDLE                 ; file handle into BX
    mov   cx,4096                   ; number of bytes to be read
    mov   ah,3Fh                    ; function 3Fh - read file
    int   21h                       ; call MS-DOS service
    jc    error                     ; error, if carry flag = 1
          ........
CODE   ENDS
```

The Function 40h - Write a File

This sample demonstrates writing information. The amount of information is the same as in the previous example.

```
DATA      SEGMENT
HANDLE    DW    0                   ; file handle for opened file
BUF       DB    4096 dup (0)        ; buffer for data to be written
          ........
DATA      ENDS

CODE      SEGMENT
          mov   ax,DATA             ; base address
          mov   ds,ax               ; of data segment
          lea   dx,BUF              ; DS:DX - address of buffer
          mov   bx,HANDLE           ; file handle for file processed
          mov   cx,4096             ; number of bytes written
          mov   ah,40h              ; function 40h -write file
          int   21h                 ; call MS-DOS service
          jc    error               ; error, if carry flag = 1
          cmp   ax,cx               ; is all the data written?
          jne   error               ; if not - process an error
          ........
CODE      ENDS
```

The Function 42h - Move the File Pointer

This function sets the file pointer to a new position and defines how the pointer will be counted. To perform this function, place the value of the file handler into the BX register and the value of the file pointer into the register pair CX:DX (the high part in DX). The value of AL determines one of 3 possible methods used for counting:

00 means that the pointer is presented as the offset from the beginning of the file.
01 corresponds to the offset from the present location.
02 means that the pointer is the offset from the end of the file.

The function returns the new absolute offset (in bytes) from the beginning of the file in registers DX:AX.

You can use this function for processing direct-access files or adding information to an existing file. For example, if you move the file pointer to the end of the file (method 02 and the offset 0 in CX:DX), all further write operations will add information to the file.

Library

Finding Files

This program demonstrates how to find files using the DOS services FindFirst and FindNext (functions 4Eh and 4Fh). The program lists all the files which match the pattern you type in the command line, including hidden and system files, directories and volume labels. For example, to get a list of all the files with an extension .BAK and starting with the character L, type:

```
findf l*.bak
```

The program performs the following actions:

- ▲ Accepts the pattern from the command line.
- ▲ Sets the DTA for use as a buffer for information about files.
- ▲ Finds the first file that matches the pattern.
- ▲ Prints the name of the file found.
- ▲ Finds the next matching file and prints its name; if there is no such file, the program finishes.

The flow chart of the program is shown in Figure 9.12, the full assembler text is given in Listing 9.1.

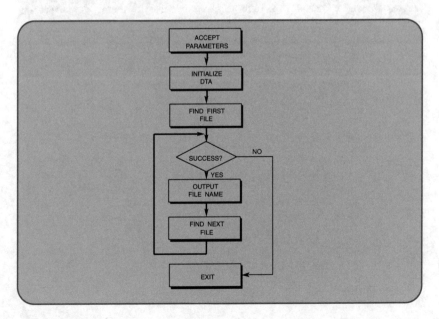

Figure 9.12
Flow Chart of the Program FindF

```
1
2 page 55,132
3 .model  small
4 .stack
5 .data
6 DTA    db   21 dup (?)  ; first 21 byte reserved
7 Attrib db   ?           ;======== File Attributes:
8                         ; 01 - Read Only
9                         ; 02 - Hidden
10                        ; 04 - System
11                        ; 08 - Volume Id
12                        ; 10 - Directory
13                        ; 20 - Archive
14 Time  dw   ?           ; time of last modification
15 Date  dw   ?           ; date of last modification
16 Fsize dd   ?           ; size of file in bytes
17 NameF db   13 dup (' ') ; name of file
18       db   85 dup (?)  ; not used but defined (up to 12 bytes)
19 FName db   80 dup(0)   ; file name mask (ASCIZ string)
20
21 .code
22 .startup
23 ;=== Accepting parameters (file mask)
24       mov ah,51h        ; function 51h - get PSP segment
25       int 21h           ; DOS service call
26       mov es,bx         ; ES points to PSP
27       mov bx,0          ; BX will be used as index
28       mov cl,es:[80h]   ; length of parameter string into CX
29       mov ch,0          ; high part of parameter length = 0
30       cmp cl,3          ; parameter must be longer than 3chars
31       jb ExProg         ; if parameter shorter, exit
32 GetParm:mov  al,es:[bx+82h] ; get current character of parameter
33       cmp al,0Dh        ; Carriage Return?
34       jne TestCR        ; if not - check for CR
35       mov al,0          ; replace Carriage Return with NUL
36       jmp CopChar       ; add current character to string
37 TestLF:cmp al,0Ah       ; Line Feed?
38       jne CopChar       ; if not, add current character
39       mov al,0          ; replace Line Feed with NUL
40 CopChar: mov FName[bx],al; and copy it into data segment
41       inc bx            ; increase characters counter
42       loop GetParm      ; get next character
43 ;=== Set DTA for subsequent usage as a disk buffer
44       lea dx,DTA        ; DS:DX contain address of DTA buffer
45       mov ah,1Ah        ; function 1Ah - set DTA
46       int 21h           ; DOS service call
47 ;=== Find first matching file
48       lea dx,FName      ; file name mask
49       mov cx,3Fh        ; file attribute mask 3Fh - any file
50       mov ah,4Eh        ; function 4Eh - Find First
51       int 21h           ; DOS service call
52 ;===If search failed, exit from the program
53 Next: jc ExProg         ; file not found - exit
54 ;===Output file name onto the screen
```

```
55        mov byte ptr NameF[12],0Dh   ; add LF symbol to file name
56        mov byte ptr NameF[13],0Ah   ; add CR symbol to file name
57        mov byte ptr NameF[14],'$'    ; add EndOfString symbol to file
                                          name
58        mov dx,offset NameF      ; address of file name for outputting
59        mov ah,09                ; function 09 - output string
60        int 21h                  ; DOS service call
61 ;- clear the string containing the file name (preparing next step)
62        push cx                  ; save CX content (file mask)
63        mov cx,12                ; set cycle counter to file name length
64        mov bx,0                 ; prepare index
65 Clear: mov NameF[bx],' '        ; clear next character
66        inc bx                   ; increase index (go to next character)
67        loop Clear               ; perform cycle
68 ;===Find next matching file
69        pop cx                   ; restore file mask for DOS service (CX)
70        mov ah,4Fh               ; function 4Fh - Find First
71        int 21h                  ; DOS service call
72 ;===Jump to checking whether the searching was successful
73        jmp Next                 ; process next file
74 ;===Final block: leave the program with the return code 0
75 ExProg: mov ax,4C00h            ; function 4Ch - terminate process
76        int 21h                  ; DOS service call
77        end
```

Listing 9.1 The Program FindF - Searching For Files

Note that all the parameters of the file pattern must be included in the command line. FindF is not like the DOS command DIR, which lets you specify the pattern C:*.* simply as C:.

The program uses the DOS services described in the Tools section, so you can easily recognize the pieces of code given as examples earlier. The comments lines, which begin with "===" mark the blocks shown on the flow chart (see Figure 9.12). The only blocks which we have not already looked at are those marked "Accepting parameters" (line 23 in Listing 9.1) and "Output file name onto the screen" (line 54), which we will do now.

The program reads parameters from the PSP which contains the tail of the command line (after the name of the program) at the offset 81h. The byte at the offset 80h contains the length of the command line's tail and the byte at the offset 81h - the first character of this tail, namely the character of the command line which immediately follows the name of the program. This means that the parameter itself is stored in the PSP starting at the offset 82h. For example, if the command line is specified as

```
FindF C:\*.*
```

the byte at the offset 80h of the PSP contains 07h - the length of the command line's tail, the byte at the offset 81h - the blank character (20h), the bytes at the offset 82h - 87h - the text "C:*.*"and the byte at the offset 88h - the Line Feed character (0Ah). The program copies characters starting from the offset 82h into the data field labelled FName and replaces the Line Feed and Carriage Return characters with the value 0 to convert the parameter string into the ASCIIZ form required by the DOS service FinfFirst.

The block for outputting the file name to the screen starts by converting the file name returned by the DOS services FindFirst and FindNext into the form required by the DOS service Output Text String. To do this, the program puts the symbols Line Feed (0Ah), Carriage Return (0Dh) and '$' at the end of the string that contains the file name and outputs the result string using function 09 of interrupt 21h. The program then fills the file name with the code 0h to prepare it for the next FindNext function call.

The next block performs the FindNext operation and passes control either to the block for printing the file name or to the final block, depending on the state of the Carry Flag. If the Carry Flag is set (file not found) the program finishes its work, otherwise it outputs the file name and repeats the FindNext operation.

Hard Disk Control - Parking Heads

This program is a utility for parking hard disk heads. It is an example of using the BIOS disk service - interrupt 13h. You can use this utility to park your hard disk before turning the power off. This might help prolong the life of your hard disk - at any rate, it won't shorten it!

The program Parking determines the maximum cylinder number of the hard disk and moves the heads to be situated after the last cylinder as shown in Figure 9.13. If the heads land on the disk surface in the landing zone, they will not damage the disk area that contains important data. Of course, you might say - "My computer parks the heads automatically when I turn it off!" You are quite right in assuming this, but you should also be able to see the sense in performing one extra action which ensures that you don't come to your machine one day to find all your data has been destroyed.

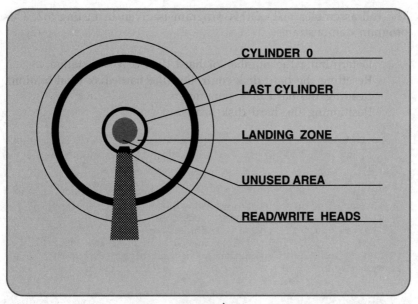

CYLINDER 0

LAST CYLINDER

LANDING ZONE

UNUSED AREA

READ/WRITE HEADS

Figure 9.13
**The
Distribution of
the Hard Disk
Surface**

When you run this program, it outputs a message, telling you how many hard disks it has found and where it moves the heads of each disk. The program waits until a key is pressed and ignores all keystrokes except ESC. When you press the ESC key, the program finishes its work and returns control to DOS. Figure 9.14 shows an example of the screen output of the program Parking.

```
The Hard Disk Parking utility   06.04.1992    Version 1.4
Copyright (C) 1992 V.B.Maljugin,    Voronezh, Russia

1 hard disk drive(s) found

Heads of the hard disk drive 0 have been positioned at the cylinder
1023

Turn off the power or press the ESC key to return to DOS
```

Figure 9.14
**Screen Output
of the Program**
Parking

The full assembler text of this program is given in Listing 9.2. This program demonstrates:

Determining the number of hard disk drives installed,
Resetting the hard disk controller (the hard disk recalibration),
Reading the hard disk parameters,
Positioning the hard disk heads.

```
1
2      page 55,132
3   .model tiny
4   .stack
5   .data
6  CR equ        00Dh   ; Carriage return code
7  LF equ        00Ah   ; Line feed code
8  EscScan equ 001h     ; Scan code for ESC key
9  EndMsg equ 024h      ; Dollar sign-end of message for DOSservice
10 Ten      db  10      ; Constant to convert binary to string
11 StMsg    db  CR,LF,LF,'The Hard Disk Parking utility 06.04.1992'
12          db  ' Version 1.4', CR , LF
13          db  'Copyright(C)1992 V.B.Maljugin,Voronezh, CR,LF,LF'
14 Ndrives db  '0'
15          db  ' hard disk drive(s) found', CR, LF, EndMsg
16 PrkMsg   db  CR,LF,'Heads of the hard disk drive '
17 DrNum1   db  '/'
18          db  ' have been positioned at the cylinder ',EndMsg
19 FinMsg   db  CR,LF,LF
20          db  'Turn off power or press ESC key to return to DOS'
21          db  CR,LF,LF,EndMsg
22 LandZone     dw   0
23 Drive    db  7Fh
24 HexTab db  '0' , '1' , '2', '3', '4' , '5', '6' , '7'
25          db  '8' , '9' , 'A', 'B', 'C', 'D', 'E' , 'F'
26
27 .code                     ; The CODE segment stars here
28 .startup                  ; This is a standard prologue
29       org 100h
30 ;=== Getting the number of drives installed
31       mov cx,0            ; Clear CX
32       mov es,cx           ; ES points to 0:0
33       mov cl,es:[475h]    ; Get number of drives from BIOS area
34       add Ndrives,cl      ; Form text for number of drives
35 ;=== Outputting the initial message
36       lea dx,StMsg        ; Address of message into DX
37       mov ah,09           ; Function 09h - output text string
38       int 21h             ; Dos service call
39 ;=== Checking whether there are drives to be processed
40 ToNext:
41       add DrNum1,1        ; Text for message about parking
42       add Drive,01h       ; Take the next disk drive 1
43       mov al,DrNum1       ; Load current drive number (char)
44       cmp al,Ndrives      ; Compare it with the number of drives
```

```
45            jb   ProcDrives  ; If not all the drives - continue
46            jmp  Finish      ; Otherwise proceed to the exiting
47 ProcDrives:;== Processing the current drive starts from here ==
48    ;=== Recalibrate the current drive
49            mov  ah,11h      ; Function 11h - recalibrate drive
50            mov  dl,Drive    ; DL - drive number (80h for drive 1)
51            int  13h         ; BIOS disk service call
52            jnc  DriveOK     ; If recalibration successful-continue
53            jmp  ToNext      ; If failed, proceed to the next drive
54 ;=== Getting the maximum number of cylinders
55 DriveOK:
56            mov  ah,08       ; Function 08 - Get drive parameter
57            int  13h         ; BIOS disk service
58            mov  al,ch       ; Low part of maximum cylinder number
59            shl  cx,1        ; Bit 7 of CL into bit 0 of CH
60            shl  cx,1        ; Bits 6,7 of CL into bits 0,1 of CH
61            and  ch,3        ; Bits 0,1 of CH will be used
62            mov  ah,ch       ; Form maximum number of cylinder
63            add  ax,2        ; One cylinder farther maximum
64            cmp  ax,1023     ; Is it above 1023?
65            jle  le1023      ; If not - process this number
66 ;=== Replace the number of cylinders greater than 1023 with 1023
67            mov  ax,1023     ; If it is so - replace it with 1023
68 ;=== Prepare input parameters for positioning the heads
69 le1023:                    ;
70            mov  LandZone,ax ; Store Landzone to be output
71            mov  ch,ah       ; CH - low byte of cylinder number,
72            shr  cx,1        ; Shift bits 0 and 1 of CH into
73            shr  cx,1        ; bits 6 and 7 of CL (high bits)
74            mov  ch,al       ; Low bits of LandZone
75 ;=== Positioning the heads
76            mov  ah,0Ch      ; Function 0Ch - heads positioning
77            mov  dh,0        ; Head number = 0
78            mov  dl,Drive    ; Drive number (80h for drive 0)
79            int  13h         ; BIOS disk service call
80 ;=== Outputting the message "parked at ..."
81            lea  dx,PrkMsg   ; Address of message "parked" into DX
82            mov  ah,09       ; Function 09h - output text string
83            int  21h         ; Dos service call
84 ;=== Convert the number of landing cylinder into text fo printing
85            mov  ax,LandZone ; Place number to be printed into AX.
86            mov  cx,0        ; Initial value for counter of digits
87 NexDiv:
88            div  byte ptr Ten ; Division the number by 10. Result in
89                             ; AL register and remainder in AH.
90            push ax          ; Push Remainder into stack.
91            mov  ah,0
92            inc  cx          ; Increase counter
93            cmp  al,0        ; Check if result is zero
94            jne  NexDiv      ; If not, get the next digit
95 ;===  Outputting the number of landing zone
96            mov  ah,02h      ; Function 02h - output symbol
97 OutSym: pop  dx             ; Pop next digit of result
```

```
98          mov  dl,dh        ; Cypher into DL for output
99          add  dl,30h       ; Convert it to character
100         int  21h          ; Output it using DOS service
101         loop OutSym       ; Proceed to the nextdigit
102
103         jmp  ToNext       ; Proceed to the next drive processing
104
105 Finish:
106         lea  dx,FinMsg    ; Address of message into DX
107         mov  ah,09        ; Function 09h - output text string
108         int  21h          ; Dos service call
109 ;===Waiting for a key pressed
110 WaitKey:
111         mov  ax,0      ; Function 00h-read character from keyboard
112         int  16h          ; BIOS keyboard service call
113         cmp  ah,EscScan   ; Is the ESC key pressed?
114         jne  WaitKey      ; If not - Wait for next key pressing
115 ;===    Exit to DOS if necessary
116         mov  ax,4C00h     ; Function 4Ch - terminate process
117         int  21h          ; DOS service call
118         end
```

Listing 9.2 Parking - Hard Disk Parking Utility

This program is designed to be a COM-module. If you would like to use it as an EXE-module, remove the lines **.model tiny** and **org 100h** from its source text and re-compile it. In the listing, each block of program has a header which briefly explains the task performed by that block.

Since the program uses important BIOS disk service functions we'll look at each action individually.

The program starts by determining the number of drives installed. This information is stored in the BIOS data area at location 0040h:0047h. The program reads this information, converts it into a character string and writes it into the variable **Ndrives**. The initial message that contains information about the version of the program is then output.

Next, the program checks whether all the drives have been processed. It does this by increasing the number of drives to be processed, and comparing it with the total number of drives found. If this figure is less than the total number of drives, the program continues, otherwise it passes control to the final block. This blocks starts, logically enough, at the line labelled **Finish**. We'll explain what this final block does a bit later.

The main part of the program Parking starts at the line labelled **ProcDrives**. The first block of the main part performs function 11h of the BIOS interrupt 13h - Recalibrate Drive. This function resets the hard disk controller and returns the result in the Carry Flag CF. If recalibration is performed successfully, the Carry Flag is clear. If the recalibration process for the current hard disk drive fails, the program proceeds to the next drive by passing control to the line labelled **ToNext**.

The block that starts at the line labelled DriveOK gets the hard disk parameters using function 08h of interrupt 13h. The information needed here is the highest number of the cylinder that is passed through the CX registers. The program places the full number of the cylinder (in the range 0 - 1023) in the AX register. This process is needed because of the strange way in which the information returned by function 08 of interrupt 13h is presented - the low part of the maximum cylinder number is stored in the CH register and the high part - in the CL register. The block finishes its work by writing the landing cylinder number into the AX register. The number of the landing cylinder is calculated by adding 2 to the maximum number of cylinders returned by interrupt 13h. Even if the number obtained is greater than 1023 it will be recorded as 1023. This is because most disk controllers cannot deal with cylinder numbers greater than 1023.

The label **Le1023** opens the block that prepares the operations for the positioning heads. To do this the program converts the integer number of the landing cylinder kept in the AX register into a form suitable for interrupt 13h (that is the high part in the CL register and low part in CH). Note that the same number is stored in the variable LandZone.

Function 0Ch of the BIOS interrupt 13h is used to position the drive heads. Note that the number of the current drive to be parked is stored in the variable Drive. The program then outputs the message "Hard disk drive X heads have been positioned at the cylinder", where X is the number of the hard disk drive parked.

The next block converts the number of the landing cylinder into a character string and outputs it on the screen. This block finishes by passing control to the process that handles the next disk drive.

The program finishes by outputting the final message and reading a character from the keyboard using function 0 of interrupt 16h. If the key pressed is the ESC key, the program completes its work and returns control to DOS.

Your program disk contains the source code for the program described in the file **parking.asm** and the executable module in the file **parking.com**. You can use this program after every session on your computer to protect your hard disk. Even if your computer has a built-in automatic disk parker it is better to perform a thousand extra calls to the parking utility than to discover that you've lost important data because of an accident with the automatic parker!

FileServ - A Set of Clipper UDF

The following program is an example of using DOS file services from programs written in Clipper. Appendix H shows how to alter your EXTENDA.INC file so that the macros stored in it will run with MASM 6.0 and higher. The program below contains two functions which can be used as Clipper UDF - User Defined Functions. The function FileSize takes the name of the file that is passed to the function as a text string and returns the size of the file. The function FileAttr works in the same way but returns the attributes of the file. The meaning of the attributes is given in Table 9.5.

These functions are examples of using the DOS file services for getting information about files from the directory entry. They also can be used in real Clipper programs as extension of the standard Clipper library. Thus, it might be useful to compare the dates of main database and archive files to avoid using the out-of-date versions. It can be also useful to check whether the diskette has enough room for storing a file. It may seem surprising, but the standard Clipper library contains the function for determining the free space on diskette and no functions for determining the size of file!

The value returned by the FileAttr function is the sum of the attributes. For example, if the file has attributes Read-Only (1), Hidden(2) and Archive(32), the value returned will be 35 because

```
1 + 2 + 32 = 35
```

These functions are combined in the module called FileServ, and the full text is given in Listing 9.3. An example of a calling program written in Clipper is given in Listing 9.4. The demo program calls the functions FileSize and FileAttr using three file names: **c:config.sys**, **c:msdos.sys** and **c:ibmdos.sys**. The hard disk usually contains only one operating system so MS-DOS and PC-DOS hidden file names are used to show what happens if the necessary file is not found. In this case the function FileSize returns the value -1 and the function FileAttr - the value 0.

```
1
2              page 55,132
3              NAME FileServ
4              INCLUDE EXTENDA.INC
5
6              CODESEG FileServ
7              DATASEG
8
9              CLpublic <FileSize, FileAttr, CurDisk>
10
11             CLstatic <long FileLen, long Fattr, long Fdate >
12
13  DTA     db    21 dup  (?)
14  Attrib  db    ?    ;=========== ; 01 - Read Only
15                                  ; 02 - Hidden
16                                  ; 04 - System
17                                  ; 08 - Volume Id
18                                  ; 10h - Directory
19                                  ; 20h - Archive
20  Time    dw    ?
21  Date    dw    ?
22  SizeF   dd    1951
23  NameF   db    13 dup (' ')
24          db    90 dup (0)
25          db    0
26  AttribF db    2
27  SrcFile db    76 dup (0)
28
29          WORKFUNCS
30
31  FindF proc near
32  AccPrm:                         ;
33          mov   al,es:[si+bx]     ; Take one byte from file name
34          cmp   al,' '            ; Is it blank?
35          jne   NotBlank          ; If not - proceed the next byte
36          mov   al,0              ; Else replace it with 0
37  NotBlank:              ;
38          mov   SrcFile[bx],al    ; Copy the byte into work area
39          inc   bx                ; Increase the counter
40          loop  AccPrm            ; Next byte
41                                  ;
42          lea   dx,DTA            ; Load address of DTA into DS:DX
43          mov   ah,1Ah            ; Function 1Ah -
44          int   21h              ; DOS service call
45                                  ;
46          lea   dx,SrcFile   ; Address of ASCIIZ file name into DS:DX
47          mov   cx,3Fh            ; Attribute 3Fh - any file
48          mov   ah,4Eh            ; Function 4Eh - FindFirst
49          int   21h              ; Dos service call
50          ret
```

```
51  FindF    endp
52
53           ENDWORK
54
55           CLfunc  long FileSize <char fname>
56           CLcode
57
58           mov   bx,0               ;
59           mov   cx,80              ; Maximal length of file name
60           les   si,fname           ; File name address into ES:SI
61
62           call  FindF
63
64           jnc   Success            ;If CARRY flag isn't set - successful
65           mov   word ptr SizeF,-1     ; else set return value to -1
66           mov   word ptr SizeF[2],-1 ; to signal that file not found
67
68  Success:
69
70           mov   ax,word ptr SizeF   ; Place length of file into DX:AX
71           mov   dx,word ptr Sizef[2] ; to return as FORTRAN function
72           mov   word ptr FILELEN[0],ax
73           mov   word ptr FILELEN[2],dx
74
75           CLretFILELEN
76
77           CLfunc  long FileAttr <char fname>
78           CLcode
79
80           mov   bx,0               ;
81           mov   cx,80              ; Maximal length of file name
82           les   si,fname           ; File name address into ES:SI
83
84           mov   word ptr FATTR[0],0
85           mov   word ptr FATTR[2],0
86           Call  FindF
87
88           jc    RetFlen            ; If CARRY flag isn't set-successful
89           mov   ah,0
90           mov   al,byte ptr Attrib ; Place length of file into DX:AX
91           mov   word ptr FATTR[0],ax
92  RetFlen:
93           CLret FATTR
94           CLfunc  long CurDisk<>
95           CLcode
96           push  ds
97           mov   ah,32h             ; function 32h - get drive parameters
98           mov   dl,0               ; 0 - current drive
99           int   21h
100          mov   al,ds:[bx]
101          pop   ds
102          mov   word ptr NDisk[2],0
103          mov   ah,0
```

```
104         mov  word ptr NDisk[0],ax
105 RetNDisk:
106         CLret NDisk
107             END
```

Listing 9.3 FileServ - The Set of Clipper Functions for Getting the File Information

You have already come across the macrocommands for interfacing Clipper-Assembler, so we will just give you a brief reminder of their purpose. The directive INCLUDE tells MASM that it must compile the file specified as an operand of this macro together with your program. The CODESEG macro defines the name of the result object module. The DATASEG macro specifies the data segment in the module. The ClPublic and ClStatic macros define entry points and global variables, respectively. The descriptions of the internal procedures used in the module are located between the macros WorkFunc and EndWork. Each function that can be called from the Clipper program begins with the macros ClFunc, specifying the name and parameters of the function and ClCode (in that order). The ClRet macro finishes the function's body and specifies the value returned by the function.

An example of a calling program written in Clipper Summer 87 is given in Listing 9.4.

```
Clear

Fn = 'c:config.sys'
Lf = FileSize(Fn)
La = FileAttr(Fn)
 ? 'File: ', Fn, ' Length: ' , Lf, ' Attribute: ', La

Fn = 'c:MsDos.sys'
Lf = FileSize(Fn)
La = FileAttr(Fn)
 ? 'File: ' , Fn, ' Length: ' , Lf, ' Attribute: ', La

Fn = 'c:IBMDos.com'
Lf = FileSize(Fn)
La = FileAttr(Fn)
 ? 'File: ' , Fn, ' Length: ' , Lf, ' Attribute: ', La
```

Listing 9.4 ClfServ - The Calling Program for FileSize and FileAttr Functions

A Set of Utilities for Processing Disks

You can use the methods described in this chapter for creating real disk processing programs. We have included a set of disk utilities which we hope will come in useful. We have also given their full assembler texts so that you can use them as models for creating your own programs to perform similar tasks. These utilities are:

DSERV2 - A program for reading/writing the physical sectors of floppy disks. This program uses the BIOS disk service - interrupt 13h and can process disks written under operating systems other than MS-DOS.

DSERV7 - A program for reading/writing logical disks. This program uses the DOS service - interrupts 25h and 26h.

VOLUME - A program for creating or changing volume labels. Unlike the standard DOS command LABEL, this program can create labels which can contain any characters, including lowercase letters. The program uses the DOS disk service - interrupts 21h, 25h and 26h.

COPYA - A program for file copying. This program copies files from any logical disk to another logical disk. The program works faster than the standard DOS command COPY and reports the length of the files and the time required for copying.

To use these programs, copy the corresponding executable files (files with the extension .EXE) onto your hard disk and include the name of the directory in which they are stored in the command PATH in your AUTOEXEC.BAT file.

Summary

In this chapter we have dealt with the basic methods of accessing disks. The functions described can be broken down into 4 principle groups:

> Managing physical disks - the BIOS disk service (interrupt 13h)
> Managing logical disks - the DOS service (interrupt 25h and 26h)
> Managing directories   - the DOS service (interrupt 21h)
> Managing files   - the DOS service (interrupt 21h)

We have not included the FCB (File Control Block) because it is not often used. Moreover, we advise you not to use the FCB technique in your programs unless you are planning to run them under DOS versions earlier than 2.0.

Although you will naturally develop your own way of working with the BIOS and DOS functions described in this chapter, you might like to keep these guidelines in mind:

▲ Use the BIOS service (INT 13h) to access disks directly; it is very efficient and allows you great flexibility but you must be careful how you handle the structure of the disk.

▲ The DOS disk service is the best for accessing logical disks; it is easier to use than BIOS, especially when you are dealing with hard disks which have more than one logical disk.

▲ When you are dealing with high-level languages, it is best to use the DOS functions for managing directories and files; these functions are particularly useful for writing modules to be called from programs written in high-level languages.

As we have already mentioned, low-level disk programming is extremely complex and risky. It's probably best to avoid using this method unless you are creating special software such as disk managers, data security systems or test systems for disks and disk controllers. If you do decide to employ low-level techniques, we advise you to save the contents of your hard disk before running these programs.

CHAPTER 10

Controlling the Hardware

This chapter rounds off our discussion of controlling the peripheral devices of a PC. The keyboard, video and disks were considered in Chapters Seven, Eight and Nine, respectively. This chapter covers the printer, the communication ports and the mouse.

As usual, we have divided our explanation into three levels - the MS-DOS service, the BIOS service and direct control. Wherever possible, we have included examples of these methods for each hardware component in the Library section.

The description of the printer covers the MS-DOS service available through the functions of interrupt 21h, the special BIOS printer service - interrupt 17h and direct access to the printer control registers.

We will also look at the ground rules for programming the serial ports, describing the registers, and the basic service provided by the BIOS interrupt 17h.

Finally, we will spend some time looking at incorporating mouse input into assembly language programs, using various functions of the mouse device driver accessed through interrupt 33h.

Fundamental Knowledge

Peripheral Devices - Communication with the External World

Having got to this point in the book, you will understand the most important peripheral devices of a PC such as the video system, keyboard and disk system. While these are integral components of a working system, for a computer engineer they are actually peripheral devices connected to the PC's heart - the microprocessor.

As we explained previously, all the components of a computer are connected through buses. Although there are several types of bus, each with different functions (even within one computer), all of them can be defined as a unit able to transfer information between two or more terminal devices. A good analogy would be a phone network, which is like a bus, with the telephones connected to it acting as terminal devices.

Having said that there are several kinds of buses, there are actually two basic types used in computers - one intended for connecting no more than two devices (a direct connection) and the other for connecting three or more devices. As you can see in Figure 10.1, when a bus connects only two devices, each of them can only send information to one other device. In contrast to this, when a bus connects several devices the whole set up becomes more complicated. We need to know

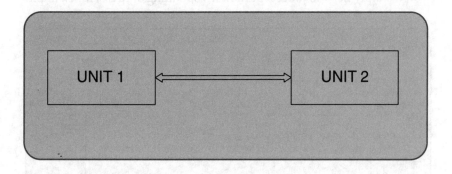

UNIT 1   UNIT 2

Figure 10.1
**Direct
Connection**

which signal comes from which device and which signal is addressed to which device. Figure 10.2 shows a set of devices connected by a common bus.

The first type of bus is mainly used for connecting high-speed units such as the CPU and cache memory, and cannot be controlled by ordinary applications. This means that a dedicated bus has relatively limited use on a PC, so we will concentrate on using peripheral devices connected through a common bus.

Ports - Gates to External Devices

The picture given in Figure 10.2 is only an outline of the real structure of a computer. In actual fact, more than one bus is involved in connecting the different units - remember the data bus, the address bus and the control bus. However, in the present context, we will represent all the buses connecting different units as one line, as in Figure 10.2. We must ensure that any byte of data that is sent will reach the correct device, and vice versa - when receiving data, we must know where it has come from. This means that any device connected to the common bus must have a unique identifier.

There are different ways of identifying devices connected to the bus. For example, one option is to reserve a particular range of addresses for passing data to, and receiving it from, peripheral devices. This allows you to use data copying instructions for performing input-output operations. So, if you wanted to output a character to the printer, you would simply need to place it at the corresponding address, for example

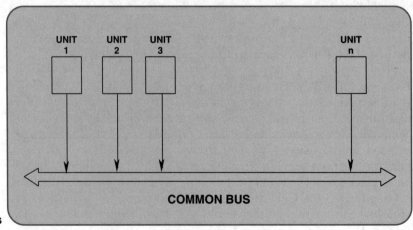

Figure 10.2
A Bus
Connecting
Several Devices

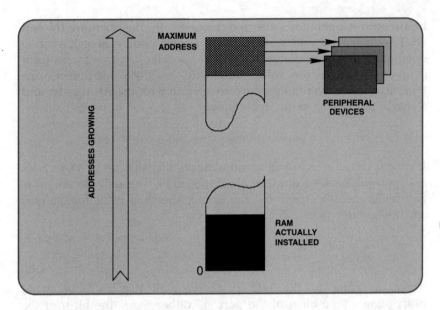

Figure 10.3
Addressing
Peripherals
Using Memory
Addresses

0FFFFF0h. Then, you could use the next address to send control signals to the printer, which would then read that character. An example of this is given in Figure 10.3.

The simplicity of this method makes it seem quite an attractive option; however it does have some disadvantages, namely a lack of control over what is actually output. For example, imagine the situation known as "index out of range", when a program tries to change the value of an array element located outside that array. If the compiler you are using checks the values of indexes when operating with arrays - you're OK. Also, if your computer can recognize when a program tries to change memory which was not actually allocated to this program, an error will be detected. If none of these safety nets apply though, the program will write data onto an external device (for example, onto the boot sector of the hard disk).

IBM-compatible PCs use **ports** for addressing peripheral devices. Just as we explained that a specific range of address space can be used for addressing peripheral devices, ports can be treated as special areas of memory which have another form of addressing, which cannot be accessed in the usual way. The process of writing data into these memory locations actually transfers that data to an external device, while placing data from the external devices into this area allows it to be read into the CPU or transferred into memory. In short, ports work like gates between the external world and the internal hardware of your PC.

Input/output operations are performed by the instructions **IN** and **OUT**, which read and write directly to the ports. These have two operands - an accumulator and a port specified by an address from 0 up to the maximum value. Originally, on i8086 microprocessors, I/O instructions were introduced to operate with the AL register and a maximum of 255 ports, for example:

```
in al,61h      ; read 8-bit scan code from keyboard port
```

It is now possible to use an accumulator of any size - AL, AX or EAX and port addresses from 0 to 65535 (0FFFFh). The only limitation is that for immediate operands, you cannot specify a value for the port address greater than 255.

```
mov    dx,3D8h  ; port number into DX
out    al,dx    ; send byte contained in AL to port 3D8h
```

When referring to the I/O ports we will use an abbreviated description - "the bit n of the port m" rather than "the bit n of the byte read from or written to the port m".

As a rule, certain ports are intended for communication with particular devices, for example ports 3B0h - 3BBh are allocated to the display adapter, and are used by the MDA adapter, or by EGA/VGA adapters working in monochrome mode. Table 10.1 shows a port map for an IBM-compatible PC.

Port Address	Device Connected
020h - 023h	Programmable interrupt controller 8259
030h - 03Fh	Interrupt controller 1 (AT and PS/2)
040h - 043h	Timer
060h - 06Fh	PPI on PC and XT, keyboard on AT and PS/2
1F0h - 1F8h	Fixed disk controller (AT)
278h - 27Fh	Parallel printer (LPT2)
2E8h - 2EFh	Serial port 4
2F8h - 2FFh	Serial port 2
3B0h - 3BBh	MDA or VGA mono video adapter
3BCh - 3BFh	Parallel printer (LPT1)
3C0h - 3CFh	EGA/VGA video adapter
3D0h - 3DFh	CGA/VGA video adapter
3E8h - 3EFh	Serial port 3
3F0h - 3F7h	Floppy disk controller
3F8h - 3FFh	Serial port 1

Table 10.1
I/O Port Map for an IBM-Compatible PC

This table only covers the most frequently used ports. For a full description of all the ports and related devices you should refer to the technical manual for your machine.

The Basics of Controlling the Peripherals

Earlier on in the book, we discussed the three levels of controlling the most commonly used hardware (the keyboard, the video system and the disk system) - i.e. using the DOS and BIOS services and directly operating I/O ports and system data areas. In this section we will concentrate on low-level access to further peripheral devices. As examples we'll take the printer, the mouse, the serial (communications) ports and some internal chips such as the timer and the PPI, used for sound generation.

I/O ports are physically located in different chips belonging either to the motherboard (for example, timer), or to other cards (disk or video controllers). Basic hardware control is performed by writing certain values to relevant ports, then reading the results using the IN and OUT instructions, respectively. The chips most frequently used are the:

Peripheral interface	- Intel 8255
Interrupt controller	- Intel 8259
Timer	- Intel 8253
Parallel ports (used for printers)	
Serial port	- UART 8250

I/O ports which belong to these chips or their functional equivalents are often referred to as interface registers. Although the way they are used is fairly standard, certain details may vary from one PC to another. For example, there is no Intel 8255 chip in the IBM AT computer, but its work is fully simulated by other chips (the same input/output ports are used). Furthermore, the IBM AT computer uses the real time clock chip Motorola MC146818 which has its own I/O ports, different from those in other IBM models.

In order to gain full access to your hardware, you might need to determine the type of computer before you start programming the chips. Your program disk contains the program DetPC from Chapter Six which reads the PC type flag from the BIOS data area and generates the corresponding return code. This program can be included in your BAT-files.

Methods of Controlling Hardware

In Chapter Six we looked at two kinds of interrupt - hardware and software. Keeping in line with this, there are two ways of performing input/output operations - polling and event-driven methods. To understand exactly what this means, we'll run through the two ways of working with the keyboard again, as a typical example of a device that can be accessed in both ways.

There are two BIOS interrupts for dealing with the keyboard - the hardware interrupt 09h and the software interrupt 16h. The main difference between them is that the handler of interrupt 09h is activated as a result of a hardware event - a key stroke, while the handler of interrupt 16h must be called explicitly by the INT instruction.

The handlers for interrupts 09h and 16h are perfect examples of programs which use two different approaches to the input/output operation. The handler of interrupt 16h is typical of the technique known as polling, and entails actively checking whether a certain event has happened. In contrast, the handler of interrupt 09 can gain control at any time, regardless of the current state of the system. This approach is referred to as event-driven or interrupt-driven input/output.

The main difference between these two methods is that a program using polling must periodically (or in some cases, constantly) check the state of a certain indicator. For example, the following block of the program Sound (given in full in this chapter) constantly checks the contents of the timer counter located in the BIOS data area:

```
......
Delay:cmp    es:[6Eh],dx ; has high part of time counter changed?
      jne    IsTime       ; suppose that time has gone
      cmp    es:[6Ch],bx ; has time gone
      jb     Delay        ; if not, continue to wait
IsTime:
......
```

This fragment uses the DX and BX registers for storing the high and low words of the 32-bit time counter value. Note that the program does not do anything else while this block is active, which reduces the overall speed of program performance. However, it makes creating and debugging programs easier, as you know for sure that no other program will try to break your program and change its data. Many popular commercial software packages use polling as a basic technique for performing input/output operations. For example, if you run the popular Norton Commander in a multitasking environment you will probably notice that no other tasks can start while this program is active. So, although polling is the simplest way of dealing with certain hardware (and sometimes the only way of working with a device) it is not really suitable for programs intended primarily for performing I/O operations such as device drivers.

The approach to I/O operations is to use hardware interrupts. If you remember, back in Chapter Seven we looked at the program ScanCode that is only active when you press a key. While you could get this result using a polling technique, the program ScanCode actually works by intercepting interrupts 00h - 0Fh. These are invoked by hardware events, and any program intercepting them will also be activated as a result of that event, such as a keystroke. Programs which employ this technique are called event- or interrupt-driven.

Your program disk contains an example of a complete interrupt-driven program ScanCodd which is a remake of the program ScanCode. The difference is that ScanCodd completely replaces the interrupt 09h handler for the duration of the program, and therefore shows you the exact scan codes as they are generated by the keyboard processor. Interrupt-driven programs are usually designed as TSRs (this type of program is explained fully in the next chapter) or as device drivers. In practice, these two kinds of programs are not dissimilar, the main difference being in how they are installed.

These methods are rarely used as they stand on their own. A program will usually intercept a hardware interrupt (most often the keyboard interrupt 09h), hardware timer interrupt 08h, or user timer interrupt 1Ch. When the program gains control as a result of a hardware interrupt, it can check the state of a device which does not generate hardware interrupts, such as a printer. For example, many programs wait for a few seconds before outputting a message that your printer isn't ready. Your TSR, having gained control as a result of the timer interrupt (normally, 18.2 times per second) will check the printer state and inform you immediately. Later on, in Chapter Eleven, we'll demonstrate the technique of using the timer and keyboard interrupts to activate a program.

We'll start our explanation of the PC's hardware with the most frequently used device connected through I/O ports - the printer.

Parallel Ports LPT1-LPT3 (Printer Output)

Before discussing access to the hardware through I/O ports, we would like to warn you about a common confusion. If a description like "ports 378h - 3F7h are related to the parallel port LPT2" has you scratching your head blankly - don't worry! It actually makes perfect sense, at least from a programmer's point of view.

The word "port" has been around a lot longer than any computer. Basically, it denotes an area intended for supporting the process of sending and receiving something. So, the phrase given above simply explains the different levels of interfacing between the printer and the microprocessor: the term "parallel port LPT1" means "the physical interface connecting the first printer to the PC's system block" while "I/O ports" means components of that interface, also referred to as parallel port registers.

The operating system maintains three parallel ports which can be used for connecting printers: LPT1, LPT2, LPT3. The maximum number of parallel ports depends on the configuration of the computer.

Every parallel port has its own adapter, which is controlled by three registers, available through the corresponding I/O ports. I/O ports belonging to a parallel port have sequentially increasing addresses, the first of which is referred to as the base address of a corresponding parallel port.

The base addresses of parallel ports LPT1 - LPT3 are stored in the BIOS data area at location 0040h:0008h, 0040h:000Ah and 0040:000Ch, respectively. PCs other than the PS/2 can also support the LPT4 printer, the base address of which is stored at location 00Eh.

If the value of a base address is zero, the corresponding parallel port is not installed. Alternatively, to determine the number of parallel ports your PC has, you can examine bits 15-14 of the word at location 0040:0010h which contains configuration information. The meaning of each of the bits in this word is detailed in Table 10.2.

Bits	Meaning
15 - 14	number of parallel ports installed
13	if set, an internal modem present (PC convertible)
11 - 9	number of serial ports installed
7 - 6	number of floppy disk drives (0-1 drive, 11-4 drives)
5 - 4	initial video mode:
	00 EGA or VGA
	01 color 40x25
	10 color 80x25
	11 mono 80x25
1	if set, math co-processor installed
0	if set, the floppy disk is available for system boot

Table 10.2
Configuration Word 0040:0010h

Bits 3, 8 and 12 are reserved. Bit 2 on a PS/2 indicates that the pointing device (a mouse or something similar) is installed. On other PCs this bit is reserved.

Now let's look at the purpose of the three parallel port registers:

Output Data Register
    Receives the byte which is being printed. The address of this register for LPT1 is stored in the word 0040h:0008h.

Status Register
    Describes the most recent I/O operation. To get the address of the port connected to this register, simply add 1 to the base address, eg. for LPT1 it is 0040h:0009h. Table 10.3 shows the meanings of the status register bits.

Bit	Meaning if set
0	Timeout
1-2	Not used
3	I/O error
4	Printer is On-Line
5	Out of paper
6	Acknowledge (if zero - normal setting)
7	Printer is not busy

Table 10.3
The Printer Status Register

Bit	Meaning if set
0	sending byte
1	CR treated as CR+LF
2	normal setting (reset printer when 0)
3	select printer
4	enable printer IRQ (IRQ 7 for LPT1)
5-7	not used

Table 10.4
The Printer
Control Register

Control Register

Initializes the adapter and controls the output of data to the printer. Its address is equal to the address of the output data register (base address) +2, eg. for LPT1 it is 0040h:000Ah. The meanings of the bits are given in Table 10.4.

Levels of Access to the Printer

Earlier on, we said that there are three levels of mastering the hardware. Similarly, the printer has three corresponding levels:

▲ Logical level - MS-DOS service available though functions of interrupt 21h.
▲ Basic level - BIOS service available through interrupt 17h.
▲ Low level - Controlling the printer ports directly.

Let's have a look at these three levels.

The logical level allows you to print character strings onto the printer, in a similar way to using the corresponding statements of high-level languages. In fact many of the built-in procedures of high-level languages actually use these functions. For example, when you call the Pascal procedure Write, you are in fact using the MS-DOS function "Write File with Handle".

The basic level uses the BIOS interrupt 17h, which allows you to initialize the printer, check its state and print a character. This level lets you check the printer state manually and then take the actions you want, instead of the standard DOS ones.

As usual, the low-level technique is the most powerful and most difficult way, although the difference between this level and the basic level is not as significant as it is for the video system. In fact, the only real advantage of using the low-level technique is that it slightly increases the speed of programs that deal with the printer.

Mouse Input

When you use a mouse, moving it around and pressing its buttons generates signals. These are accepted by the mouse driver and are used for controlling a special screen pointer called the mouse cursor. The mouse driver can also pass information about which buttons have been pressed, to the user program. Later in this chapter we'll give an example of using the mouse for selecting an item from a menu.

Programs which support the mouse must be capable of receiving and interpreting the signals it generates. There are several ways of connecting the mouse to a computer and passing signals to programs. When they first came out, there were special mouse controllers, which amounted to a separate card which you had to install into an expansion slot. Currently, things are a bit more sophisticated and there are two standard ways of connecting a mouse to a PC; the bus interface (where the mouse uses a special physical interface) and serial interface (where the mouse is connected to the standard communication port, installed on most PCs).

Although in practice, all the signals generated by the mouse could be processed directly in a user program, very few applications actually do this. The majority of programs use the service functions provided by the mouse driver - a special program which either comes with the mouse or can be purchased separately. A well known example of a mouse driver is the Microsoft Mouse driver included in all Microsoft programming systems (including MASM 6.0) and most Microsoft program products such as Windows.

The Mouse Driver

All mouse drivers currently available perform a standard set of mouse service functions, combined into the handler of interrupt 33h, known as the mouse interrupt or mouse service. The complete set of functions that are supported can vary from one driver to another, so before you start writing your own mouse-oriented programs, you should look through the manual which comes with your mouse driver. However, it's generally not a good idea to use functions that are specific to your driver, as it can make things difficult if you want to run your program on other computers.

Note that there is no mouse driver in standard DOS. Moreover, in earlier versions of DOS, the vector of interrupt 33h points to the address 0000:0000, instead of to the IRET instruction, so performing the instruction

```
int     33
```

might cause problems. To avoid possible difficulties, your program must first of all check whether the vector of interrupt 33h is nonzero and points to an instruction other than IRET, i.e. if a driver is present.

Mouse Programming

An application program that uses a mouse gets information about its state and location, and performs a relevant action in response. One of the most common uses of the mouse in applications is for selecting an item from the menu, illustrated in the demo program PMOUSE2 given in this chapter. This process involves the following basic steps:

1. Output the corresponding text (usually a list of numbered strings) onto the screen.

2. Check the mouse state - has a button been pressed? If not, repeat this step.

3. Get the coordinates of the mouse pointer; if it is located within the area corresponding to a menu item, then perform the relevant function.

The mouse cursor is generated by the mouse driver that changes its location when you move the mouse. When it is moved, the mouse generates short impulses called *mickeys* - (christened by Bill Gates). The number of mickeys generated by moving the mouse 1 inch varies from one mouse to another; the average is about 200, but high-resolution mice can generate 320, 400 or more mickeys per inch. Usually, the driver moves the cursor by 1 pixel per mickey horizontally, and 2 pixels per mickey vertically, but these values can be changed by a special function of interrupt 33h.

Once the program has got the cursor coordinates, it can check whether the mouse cursor is located within an area that corresponds to a particular menu item (i.e whether it points to a certain character on the screen) and perform the relevant action.

The Mouse and the Screen

The first thing that you will notice, faced with a mouse-oriented program, is the mouse cursor. In order to display the mouse cursor properly, the mouse driver intercepts the BIOS video service (interrupt 10h) and provides the additional service needed for controlling the appearance and location of the mouse cursor on the screen. You can choose from three different types of mouse cursor: the hardware cursor, or two kinds of software cursor - text and graphic. Note that only one of these can be used at a time.

The hardware cursor is the same as the one that we looked at in Chapter Eight, and appears on the screen as a blinking square rectangle. You can specify the start and end lines of the cursor within the character cell. If the start and end lines are the same, the cursor appears as a blinking line.

The software cursor is defined using the corresponding functions of the mouse interrupt 33h. There are two kinds of software cursor - text software cursor and graphic software cursor. Which of these is currently used obviously depends on the current screen mode.

The text software cursor can be used in all text modes and is controlled by the mouse driver. To make the text software cursor visible, the mouse driver changes the video attributes of the character at the current location of the mouse cursor using special masks specified by the programmer. Your program disk contains demo programs which show how to define the software mouse cursor in text modes.

The graphic mouse cursor is a user-defined icon, with a size of 16x16 pixels. The mouse driver provides a special function for defining and controlling the graphic cursor. You can choose any form you like, then change it while the program is running. For example, the mouse cursor can start off as a pointing hand when the program is waiting for the user to select a menu item, then change to a clock when the program is performing an internal task.

The Serial Ports - COMx

So far we have only looked at the parallel printer ports LPT1 - LPT3. They are termed "parallel" because a whole byte of data can be transferred at a time, i.e. every bit is transferred through its "own" line.

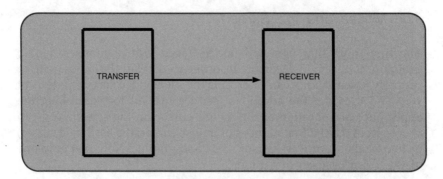

Figure 10.4
Serial Data
Transfer

This is not the only approach to data transfer, though. There is another method known as asynchronous or serial data transfer. According to this method, all the bits of the byte being output are transferred sequentially, one by one, through one line. Figure 10.4 illustrates this process.

Information that is input or output using this method is either transferred in a special form or "serialized" by the hardware port. Let's look at this process more closely.

Sending or receiving one byte of data through the serial channel actually involves transferring the following sequence of bits:

> Header (one start bit)
> Information bits (bits 8,7,6,5,4 depending on the work mode)
> Parity bit (optional)
> Stop bits (one or two)

The speed at which these bits are transferred is measured in bauds (bits per second). The lowest rate is 110 baud, the highest is 115K baud.

A special chip, Intel UART 8250 (**U**niversal **A**synchronous **R**eceiver Transmitter) was designed to support serial data transfer. Access to this chip is gained through the communication ports.

MS - DOS operating systems support two basic communication ports - COM1 and COM2. Their base addresses are stored in the BIOS data area at location 0040:0000h (COM1) and 0040:0002 (COM2). The base address of port COM1 is usually 3F8h and for COM2 - 2F8h, but it does vary depending on the model. For example, 2F8 for COM1 and 3F8 for COM2 are also common addresses. For this reason, to get the exact address you should always read the information in the BIOS data area.

Port	MODE value	DLAB	Meaning
3F8h	OUT	0	Transmitter holding register
3F8h	IN	0	Receiver buffer register
3F8h	OUT	1	Divisor latch (low byte)
3F9h	OUT	1	Divisor latch (high byte)
3F9h	OUT	0	Interrupt enable register
3FAh	IN		Interrupt identification register
3FBh	OUT		Line control register
3FCh	OUT		Modem control register
3FDh	IN		Line status register
3FEh	IN		Modem status register

Table 10.5
The Asynchronous Adapter Registers

Since the majority of computers have serial ports, asynchronous communication is widely used in local area networks, not least in order to make cabling cheap. It allows you to interconnect two computers for data exchange without any additional hardware such as net adapters and modems. Other hardware devices such as a mouse, printers, plotters and modems, can also be attached to the serial ports.

The 8250 chip is programmed by 10 one-byte registers, available through the corresponding I/O ports. Some registers are write-only, some are read-only and the remainder can be both read and write. The addresses of these registers are 3F8h - 3EFh for COM1 and 2F8h - 2FEh for COM2.

Although this range covers only 7 addresses, you can increase the number of registers actually available to 10 by setting the 7th bit of the line control register (3FBh). This bit is called DLAB - **D**ivisor **L**atch **A**ccess **B**it). Table 10.5 gives the complete list of registers.

Levels of Access to the Serial Ports

As with all hardware components, there are 3 ways of controlling the serial ports:

1. Using the MS-DOS service
2. Using the BIOS service
3. Direct control

The MS-DOS service provides function 40h (Write File with Handle) of interrupt 21h. This method treats the communication port as a standard file named AUX with a logical number (descriptor) equal to 3. Only one of the ports is available - COM1. The input/output parameters are as follows: I/O velocity is 2400 baud, there is no parity control, one stop bit and 8 bits per symbol are used.

This method is rarely used since the restrictions are fairly limiting.

The most common way of programming the serial ports is through the BIOS service (interrupt 14h). The functions of interrupt 14h allow you to initialize the port and set parameters for transferring data such as the number of stop bits, the type of parity control and the speed of transfer. Although managing the communication ports using the BIOS service is relatively simple, it only allows you to use the I/O speed up to 9600 baud even if your hardware is much faster.

Low-level programming lets you use all the UART 8250 chip facilities, including working with the transfer speed up to 115K baud and over, but requires the hardware interrupt related to communication ports to be processed by your program. Due to the complexity of this technique, we are not going to explain it in this book.

Peripheral Interface - PPI

The Programmable Peripheral Interface (PPI) was originally based on the 8255A chip, and is used for controlling the keyboard, the internal sound generator and for getting information about the system configuration. This chip provides the standard way of accessing hardware components. Note that not all PCs actually have an 8255A chip, but since all IBM-compatible PCs emulate its work, as far as programmers are concerned, it is always present.

In this chapter we'll give an example of using the PPI ports for controlling the keyboard using an adaptation of the program ScanCode from Chapter Seven. This program uses the PPI ports for reading the scan codes directly from the keyboard and controlling the keyboard state. We will also show you how to use the PPI with the programmable timer for sound generation.

The 8255A chip (or one which emulates its work) is controlled through the ports that are attached to it. Although the number of PPI ports

Denotation	Address	Type	Purpose
Port A	60h	R/W	Keyboard input
Port B	61h	R/W	Configuration info, speaker and keyboard control
Port C	62h	R	Getting system information
	63h	R	Mode control for ports A-C
	64h	R	Keyboard status (AT or PS/2)

Table 10.6
The Programmable Peripheral Interface - PPI

Bit	Meaning
0	Timer 2 gate (speaker)
1	Timer 2 data
2	Must be 0
3	1 = read high switches; 0 = read low switches
4	0 = enable RAM parity checking; 1 = disable
5	0 = enable I/O channel check
6	0 = hold keyboard clock low
7	0 = enable keyboard; 1 = disable keyboard

Table 10.7
Port B of PPI - the Port 61h

varies for different computers (the maximum possible is 16), we will limit our discussion to the four ports on IBM-compatible PCs, and the keyboard status port present on AT and PS/2 machines. The denotations, addresses and purpose of the PPI ports are given in Table 10.6.

To give you an idea of what the PPI ports do, we'll now give a brief description of some of the most common ways of using them.

The byte sent to port B (61h) defines the reading mode for ports A (60h) and C (62h). The meaning of the bits of port B are given in Table 10.7. If the high bit of port B is clear (equal to 0) bits 0-7 of port A

Bit	Contents
0	0 - no floppy disk drives
1	Not used
2-3	The number of memory banks on the system board
4-5	Display mode = 11 - monochrome
	10 - color 80x25
	01 - color 40x25
6-7	PC: the number of floppy disk drives

Table 10.8
*The Contents of
the PPI Port A
(Bit 7 of Port B
is Set)*

Bit	Meaning
0	Values of DIP switches as in Equipment List
1	"
2	"
3	"
4	Must be 0
5	If set - Timer channel 2 out
6	If set - I/O channel check
7	If set - RAM parity check error occurred

Table 10.9
*The Contents of
Port C (Bit 2/3
of Port B is
Set)*

contain the 8-bit keyboard scan codes. If this is not the case, then port A contains information about the hardware as shown in Table 10.8.

Port C is a read-only port which contains information about the hardware as given in Table 10.9.

The following example illustrates the process of reading keyboard scancodes and testing for the "hot" key F6 (its scan code is 40h).

```
        cli               ; disable interrupts
        push  ax          ; save AX contents
        in al,60h         ; get the scan-code (port A)
        jmp   $+2         ; a short delay for fast PCs
        cmp   al,40h      ; is it a "hot" key?
        jne   Exit        ; no, exit
        in    al,61h      ; keyboard state (Port B)
        or    al,80h      ; enable keyboard accessing
        out   61h,al      ; sent confirmation bit (set)
        and   al,7Fh      ; clear confirmation bit
```

```
; this program fragment contains the processing of the "hot" key .
; finish the work and exit:
Exit: pop ax                    ; restore AX contents
      sti                       ; enable interrupts
```

As we stated earlier on, although there is no Intel 8255 chip in the IBM AT model, the same ports are used to control the work of the keyboard and timer.

The Interrupt Controller - Intel 8259

This chip is also known as the PIC (Programmable Interrupt Controller). It ensures that hardware interrupts are processed according to their priorities. The interrupt signal is generated by the hardware and sent to the microprocessor to inform it that the hardware state has changed and that certain operations need to be performed.

Since there can be more than one interrupt request at any time, there are several interrupt priority levels. The IBM PC and IBM XT have 8 interrupt priority levels (it takes one 8259 chip to implement them). The IBM AT has two 8259 controllers, which means that up to 15 interrupt priority levels can be processed. If only one 8259 controller is used the interrupt priority levels are denoted as IRQ0 - IRQ7 (Interrupt Requests). If there are two 8259 controllers (in IBM AT) the priority levels are IRQ0-IRQ7 and IRQ8-IRQ15 respectively.

The highest priority level corresponds to the hardware interrupt 0 (IRQ0) which is caused by the system timer. The next level, IRQ1, corresponds to the keyboard interrupt. As a rule, every interrupt request is maintained by a matching BIOS vector. For example, 8h corresponds to IRQ0, 9h to IRQ1(keyboard) etc.

Priority levels IRQ8 - IRQ15 (for IBM AT) are located between IRQ2 and IRQ3 and use the interrupt vectors INT 70h - INT 77h. There are 3 one-byte registers in the 8259 chip, available through the ports 20h (Interrupt Service Register - ISR), 21h (Interrupt Mask Register - IMR) and 22h (Interrupt Request Register IRR). Registers 20h and 21h are the most frequently used.

The examples given later in this chapter show how you can disable and enable all, or some of the interrupts. If you want to disable all the hardware interrupts, use the assembler instruction CLI (Clear Interrupt) and to enable them all - STI (Set Interrupt). Note however that you cannot disable interrupt 02, aptly called the NMI - Non Maskable Interrupt.

The Interrupt Mask Register (IMR) gives you individual control over the different levels of interrupts. The least significant bit of this mask corresponds to IRQ0. If it is equal to 1, the corresponding interrupt is disabled, otherwise it is enabled. This register is available through port 21h (or the levels IRQ0 - IRQ7). Information can be both read from and sent to it.

If you have installed a second 8259 controller, the following I/O ports are used: 0A0h (ISR), 0A1h (IMR), 0A2h (IRR). These addresses differ from the corresponding addresses for the first controller in one bit, namely bit 3. Table 10.10 details all the interrupt levels.

In order to disable an interrupt on one of these levels, you need to read the information from the IMR register (ports 21h or 0A1h) and then set the corresponding bit to 0 as shown in the table. Once you have done this you can send the byte to the necessary port.

Level	Vector	Mask Enable	Disable	Meaning
IRQ0	08h	XXXX XXX0	XXXX XXX1	Timer
IRQ1	09h	XXXX XX0X	XXXX XX1X	Keyboard
IRQ2	0Ah	XXXX X0XX	XXXX X1XX	I/O channel
The IRQ8 - IRQ15 levels are used on AT only				
IRQ8	70h	XXXX XXX0	XXXX XXX1	Real-time Clock
IRQ9	71h	XXXX XX0X	XXXX XX1X	Translated into IRQ2
IRQ10	72h	XXXX X0XX	XXXX X1XX	Reserved
IRQ11	73h	XXXX 0XXX	XXXX 1XXX	Reserved
IRQ12	74h	XXX0 XXXX	XXX1 XXXX	Reserved
IRQ13	75h	XX0X XXXX	XX1X XXXX	Math co-processor
IRQ14	76h	X0XX XXXX	X1XX XXXX	HDD controller
IRQ15	77h	0XXX XXXX	1XXX XXXX	Reserved
IRQ3	0Bh	XXXX 0XXX	XXXX 1XXX	COM2 (AT), COM1 (XT)
IRQ4	0Ch	XXX0 XXXX	XXX1 XXXX	COM1 (AT), COM2 (XT)
IRQ5	0Dh	XX0X XXXX	XX1X XXXX	HDD (LPT2 for AT)
IRQ6	0Eh	X0XX XXXX	X1XX XXXX	FDD controller
IRQ7	0Fh	0XXX XXXX	1XXX XXXX	LPT1

Table 10.10
The Hardware Interrrupts

You might come across manuals which tell you that the IMR register is write only - this is not true. It can be read to change the necessary bit of the mask. Once the interrupt has been processed, you must send the code 20h to the Interrupt Service Register (ISR, ports 20h or 0A0h) before executing the IRET instruction. This action sets up the interrupt controller 8259.

The following example shows how to exit the interrupt handler.

```
; exit interrupt handler
      push  ax           ; save register
      mov   al,20h        ; EOI - End Of Interrupt code
      out   20h,al        ; interrupt processed
      pop   ax            ; restore register
      IRET                ; exit interrupt handler
```

Remembering the EOI procedure shouldn't take much effort - send the value 20h to port 20h! This connection is purely coincidental - it has no special significance!

We'll put all this theory to some use now with a few practical examples of enabling and disabling interrupts.

To disable the hardware keyboard interrupt, set bit 1 of the interrupt mask to 1:

```
      in    al,21h        ; read interrupt mask(IMR)
      jmp   $+2           ; delay for fast PCs
      or    al,02h        ; disable keyboard interrupt
      out   21h,al        ; write mask obtained
; after this keyboard is locked
```

To enable the hardware keyboard interrupt, set bit 1 of the interrupt mask to 0:

```
      in    al,21h        ; read interrupt mask(IMR)
      jmp   $+2           ; delay for fast PCs
      or    al,not 02h    ; disable keyboard interrupt
      out   21h,al        ; write mask obtained
; after this keyboard is unlocked
```

These two examples are the same except for one line - the program which enables the keyboard uses the value 0FDh which is represented here as not 02h.

You can get or change the value of the ports described above manually, for example using the DOS utility DEBUG. Start DEBUG and enter the command:

```
I 21
```

which reads the contents of port 21h (the Interrupt Mask Register IMR). The value you are most likely to get is 0B8h. If you want to lock the keyboard, set bit 1 to 1; the corresponding interrupt mask is 0BAh. Send this mask to port 21h with the command

```
O 21 0BAh
```

This will lock the keyboard which means that you will have to "cold" start your computer. This example illustrates the dangers of directly managing the hardware - certain operations can destroy the information on disk and even damage devices such as the monitor.

The Programmable Timer - Intel 8253

This is a universal counter-timer that has 3 channels. Although the IBM AT computer uses an 8254 chip instead of 8253, they are programmed in exactly the same way. They are processor independent and operate at a frequency of 1.193Mhz under the control of the 8284A generator.

The three channels: 0, 1 and 2 are available through ports 40h, 41h and 42h, and the command register is available through port 43h. The command register controls the mode for sending values to the channel and chooses the necessary channel. Let's consider the purpose of the channels and the command register more closely.

Channel 0 is used by the system clock to calculate the time of day. While DOS is loading, BIOS programs this channel so that it issues 18.2 pulses per second. These pulses are often referred to as **ticks**. A counter for these timer pulses (4 bytes) is stored in the BIOS data area at location 0040h:006Ch. Every pulse initiates the timer interrupt INT 8h (IRQ0), after which the value of the counter is renewed. This counter is also used to synchronize disk operations. Since programming this channel can result in damaging the process of disk reading and writing, it's best left well alone!

EVERY INT 8H DOES AN INT 1CH.
USE INT 1CH FOR TIMER.

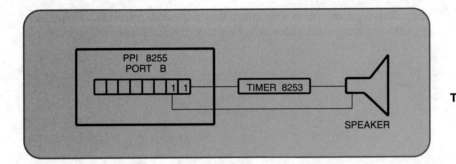

Figure 10.5
The Interrupt Controller, Timer and Speaker Interface

Channel 1 is responsible for refreshing RAM and counts the pulses during disk operations, so that it can reset the timer counter upon completion of an operation. It is highly unlikely that you will need to program this channel as it is only used by a few sophisticated programs. In practice you can use it to make your computer run a bit faster by changing the intervals at which the memory is refreshed. Approach this with caution though, it is quite a complex procedure which can have unexpected consequences such as loss of data while working with disks.

Channel 2 (port 42h) of the 8253 chip is connected to the computer's speaker and issues square-wave pulses which are used to make sounds. You can use this channel to change the sound frequency. Note that the 8255 chip, (PPI), is also involved in generating sound and that bits 0 and 1 of port B (61h) also control the speaker. Figure 10.5 shows the interface for these chips.

The command register (port 43h) indicates the number of the channel to be programmed and the mode for outputting data to this channel. The meanings of the bits of this register are given in Table 10.11.

Bit	Meaning
0	0 - binary data, 1 - BCD
1-3	Number of mode used (000 - 101)
4-5	Operation type:
	00 - send the value of counter
	01 - read/write high byte
	10 - read/write low byte
	11 - read/write both high and low bytes
6-7	Number of channel to be programmed

Table 10.11
The Programmable Timer Command Register

The following example is a program that generates sound at a frequency of 1000 Hz and terminates it when any key is pressed.

```
.............................................................
; Permission of channel 2, Port B  (8255) is programmed for this
purpose
       in    al,61h       ; read current setting of Port B
       jmp   $+2          ; short delay
       or    al,03h       ; set necessary bits
       out   61h,al       ; permission of speaker
; Setting registers of channel 2 (8253)
       mov   al,0B6h      ; necessary mode
       out   43h,al       ; write into command register
; Evaluation of necessary delay, frequency for this is  1.193 Mhz
; is divided by the necessary frequency  1000 hz. Result = 1193
       mov   ax,1193      ; evaluated delay
       out   42h,al       ; write lower byte
       mov   al,ah        ; value of higher byte
       out   42h,al       ; write higher byte
; Speaker generates sound of 1000 hertz until key pressed
       xor   ah,ah        ; wait for pressing of any key
       int   16h          ; Call BIOS Service
; Switching sound off,  bits 0, 1 of Port B are cleared for this
purpose
       in    al,61h       ; read current setting of  Port B
       jmp   $+2          ; short delay
       and   al,0FDh      ; clear necessary bits
       out   61h,al       ; switch speaker off
.............................................................
```

Later on in this chapter we'll describe the sub-program SOUND which generates sound at a given frequency and for a specific duration. You can call this sub-program from your programs using the assembler instruction CALL as shown below:

```
Call SOUND
```

Tools

MS-DOS Printer Services

Interrupt 21h has two functions which can be used for printer output: function 05h and function 40h.

The Function 05h - Print a Character

Function 05h of interrupt 21h only outputs one character to the printer. This character must be placed into the DL register and the function number should be in the AH register as usual. The following example demonstrates the process of printing a string using the MS-DOS service (function 05h of interrupt 21h):

```
; data segment
  DATA    SEGMENT
  CR      EQU    13
  LF      EQU    10
  String  DB "This is my String for the Printer (INT 21h)", CR, LF
  Lstr    EQU    $-String
  DATA    ENDS

; code   segment

          mov    ax,DATA      ; address of data segment
          mov    ds,ax        ; DS - points to data segment
          mov    cx,Lstr      ; length of string in counter
          lea    bx,String    ; DS:BX - address of string
          mov    ah,05h       ; function 05h - character print
  PrtStr: mov    dl,[bx]      ; take character to print
          int    21h          ; MS-DOS service call
          inc    bx           ; advance counter
          loop   PrtStr       ; to print next character
```

The Function 40h - Write File with Handle

We explained this function earlier while looking at the file system. To recap, it outputs to a file with a given descriptor (file handle). The standard file name for the printer is PRN and its logical number (file handle value or descriptor) is 4. This file is opened when the program starts and is always available for output.

There are a few preparatory steps you need to perform before using this function:

- ▲ Place the function number 40h in the AH register.
- ▲ Place the value of the file handle (4) in the BX register.
- ▲ Place the number of bytes to be output in the CX register.
- ▲ Place the address of the output data in the register pair DS:DX.

This function returns the result through the Carry Flag CF. If CF is set, it means that there is an error code in the AX register.

The following example shows how to output a text string to the printer using the MS-DOS service (function 40h of interrupt 21h):

```
; Data segment
    DATA    SEGMENT
    CR      EQU     13
    LF      EQU     10
    String  DB      "This is my String for Printer (INT 21h)", CR, LF
    Lstr    EQU     $-String
    DATA    ENDS
; Code segment
            mov    ax,DATA     ; segment address of data
            mov    ds,ax       ; DS points to data segment
            mov    cx,Lstr     ; length of string
            mov    bx,4        ; file handle for PRN
            lea    dx,String   ; DS:DX - address of string
            mov    ah,40h      ; function 40h - write file
            int    21h         ; DOS service call
            jnc    Exit        ; if CF is clear - exit
; The code for error processing goes here
    Error:
            ........
; Finish processing and exit
    Exit:
```

Note that regardless of the method of printer output used, each line must finish with the carriage return symbol (its code is 0Dh).

BIOS Printer Services - Interrupt 17h

The BIOS service lets you use all of the parallel ports - LPT1, LPT2 and LPT3. To use this printer service, place the function number into the AH register and the code of the parallel port into the DX register. Value 0 stands for LPT1, 1 - for LPT2 and 2 - for LPT3. The BIOS printer service comprises three functions:

> Initialize printer port - function 01h.
> Get printer status - function 02h.
> Output a character - function 00h.

which work in the following ways:

The Function 01h - Initialize Printer Port

Once you have turned your printer on, you have to initialize the printer port before outputting information. The exception to this is if the printer is already connected up to your computer when you switch the whole system on. In this case, the printer would be initialized by DOS automatically. To do this manually, put the value 01h into the AH register, the printer code into the DX register and then call interrupt 17h. A code for the printer status will then be returned in the AH register (see function 01h). The following example demonstrates initializing LPT1.

```
; code segment
......................................................................
    mov    ah,1     ; function 01 - initialize printer port
    xor    dx,dx    ; DX = 0 means LPT1
    int    17h      ; BIOS printer service call
......................................................................
```

The Function 02h - Get Printer Status

This function returns the printer status code just as function 00h does. Use this function before you start outputting any text to ensure that the printer is OK, i.e. there is enough paper and no error occurred during previous operations. The status codes are given in Table 10.12.

Bit	Significance (if set)
0	Printer timed-out
1	Unused
2	Unused
3	I/O error
4	Printer selected
5	Out of paper
6	Printer acknowledge
7	Printer not busy

Table 10.12
Codes for the Status of the Printer

The Function 00h - Print a Character

This function takes one byte from the AL register and outputs it to the printer connected to the port specified in the DX register. If you want to output a string of characters, you will need to organize a program cycle. When output has been completed, the AH register contains the printer status. It is important that you check this value to make sure that there have not been any errors. The following example illustrates printer output to LPT1.

```
; data segment
 .data
 CR       EQU   13
 LF       EQU   10
 String   DB    "This is my String for Printer (INT 17h)", CR, LF
 Lstr     EQU   $-String

; code segment

 .code
 .startup
   mov   cx,Lstr       ; length of string
   xor   dx,dx         ; DX = 0 stands for LPT1
   lea   si,String     ; DS:SI - address of string
; Cycle to output one character
 Cycle: lodsb          ; next character into AL
   mov   ah,00h        ; function 00 - print character
   int   17h           ; BIOS printer service call
   loop  Cycle         ; next repetition of cycle
   test  ah,8          ; I/O Error ?
   jz    Exit          ; if not - exit
; The code for error processing goes here
 Error:
 ........
; Complete work and exit
 Exit:
```

Low-Level Printer Techniques

Low-level control of the printer is more difficult as it involves dealing with the structure of the control and status registers. The process of printing involves three mains steps - initializing the printer port, transferring data and determining the result of the operation.

You must initialize the printer port before you start to send data to the printer. To set up the initialization mode, clear bit 2 of the printer control register. For ordinary data transfer, this bit equals 1.

To initialize the printer port you have to take the following steps:

1. Set bits 2 and 3 of the printer control register to the ordinary setting so that the value of the byte sent to the control port is 0Ch.

2. Wait about 0.05 sec.

3. Set bit 2 of the control register to 0 (initialization), bit 3 to 1 (ordinary setting); the corresponding value of this byte is 80h.

The example below shows how these steps work in practice. To provide the delay the program uses the LOOP instruction, which is the simplest technique. The number of repetitions used in this example is equal to 3000 and is enough to produce a delay of about 0.05 seconds, on an average 286 computer (16 MHz). Note that if you have a very fast computer you might need to increase the number of empty cycles used for the delay.

```
;— code segment
;— printer port initialization
        mov    ax,DATA         ; address of data segment
        mov    DS,ax           ; DS points to data segment
        mov    ax,40h          ; segment address of BIOS data area
        mov    ES,ax           ; ES points to BIOS data area
        mov    dx,ES:[8]       ; base address of LPT1 port
;— beginning of printer port initialization
        inc    dx              ;
        inc    dx              ; address of control register
        mov    al,0Ch          ; 0Ch - command code of initialization
        out    dx,al           ; initialize port
        mov    cx,3000         ; number of empty cycles
        loop   $               ; empty cycle (delay)
        mov    al,08h          ; 08h - command code of initialization
                               ;   complete
        out    dx,al           ; complete initialization
```

The process of transferring data to the printer is more complicated. The data byte must be sent to the data register through the base printer port. Once you have done this you must send a strobe signal to the control register - set bit 0 of this register to 1.

```
        DATA   SEGMENT
        CR     EQU    13
        LF     EQU    10
        LPT1   DW     0
String         DB     "This is my String for Printer (Low Level)", CR, LF
```

```
Lstr      EQU   $-String
. . . . . . . . . . . . . . . . . . . . . . . . . . . . . . . . . . . . . . . . . . . . . . . . . . . . . . . .
;  code segment
;- send ASCII - string onto printer
          mov   ax,DATA      ; address of data segment
          mov   DS,ax        ; DS points to data segment
          mov   ax,40h       ; address of BIOS data area
          mov   ES,ax        ; ES points to BIOS data area
          mov   dx,ES:[8]    ; base address of printer port
          mov   LPT1,dx      ; save base address
          mov   cx,Lstr      ; length of string to be printed
          lea   si,String    ; DS:SI - address of string
          cld                ; direction - forward
; send a character onto printer
Next:     lodsb              ; send character int AL accumulator
          mov   dx,LPT1      ; LPT1 will be used
          out   dx,al        ; send character to printer
          inc   dx           ;
          inc   dx           ; address of control register
          mov   al,0Dh       ; value of strobe impulse
          out   dx,al        ; send strobe impulse
          dec   al           ; restore normal state of register
          out   dx,al        ; disable strobe
; check whether operation is complete
          dec   dx           ; address of status register
          in al,dx           ; read status register
          test  al,08h       ; is there error on printer?
          jz Error           ; if so, output error message
; wait until printer is free
Wait0:    in    al,dx        ; read status register
          test  al,80h       ; is printer busy?
          jz    Wait0        ; if so, continue wait
          loop  Next         ; repeat cycle
          jmp   Exit         ; end of job
; the code for error processing goes here
Error:
. . . . . . . .
; complete work and exit
Exit:
. . . . . . . . . . . . . . . . . . . . . . . . . . . . . . . . . . . . . . . . . . . . . . . . . . . . . . . .
```

The demo program PRINLOW, which is given in the Library section in this chapter, uses the low-level technique to print a string. If you take this text and compare it with the PRINDOS program text you'll see straight away why we said that the low-level technique is complicated. As a rule, unlike the video system, which is often more effective when the low-level technique is used, the best way of printing texts is using the MS-DOS service.

Programming the Mouse with Interrupt 33h

The mouse differs from other devices considered in this book in that there is no mouse support in DOS and BIOS. Furthermore, we do not recommend using low-level techniques for controlling the mouse. The only way of accessing the mouse that we'll consider is the mouse interrupt 33h.

Since there is no handler for the mouse interrupt in standard BIOS and DOS, the mouse driver must be installed separately as a device driver (usually called MOUSE.SYS) or TSR program (usually called MOUSE.COM). The first operation that a mouse-oriented program must perform is to check whether the system has a mouse driver. This is done by examining interrupt vector 33h. First of all the program must determine whether it points to address 0000:0000, then it checks for the dummy handler - the IRET instruction. The following example illustrates this in an assembler program:

```
    mov    ax,3533h        ; function 35h - get interrupt vector
    int    21h             ; DOS service call
    mov    ax,ES           ; segment address of mouse handler to AX
    or     ax,bx           ; both segment and offset zero?
    jz     NoINT33         ; no handler present - exit
    cmp    byte ptr es:[bx],0CFh   ; first instruction IRET?
    je     NoINT33         ; dummy handler - exit
;......
;          continue program
;......
.......................
NoINT33:                           ; no mouse found - error !
.......................
```

Since the functions provided by the Microsoft Mouse driver are considered as a de facto standard, we'll follow the conventions used for Microsoft-compatible mice.

From the programmer's point of view, the most important feature of interrupt 33h is that decimal numbers are used for describing its functions. Now let's look at the basic functions of interrupt 33h.

The Function 00h - Reset Driver and Read Status

This function must be used first in a mouse-oriented program. It initializes the internal variables of the mouse driver and returns the value 0 in the AX register if no driver has been installed, or no hardware support is available. If the driver has been initialized successfully, the value in the AX register is -1 (0FFFFh). This function also returns the number of mouse buttons in BX: 2 or 3, denoting 2 or 3 buttons, respectively; 1 if your mouse has less than 2 or more than 3 buttons. This function assigns the initial value -1 to the internal Mouse Cursor Flag which corresponds to the hidden cursor. This means that initially there is no mouse cursor on the screen. The following example shows how to use the function 0 of the mouse interrupt for initializing the mouse driver:

```
      . . . . . .
        xor    ax,ax          ; function 0 - initialize mouse
        int    33h            ; mouse service call
        cmp    ax,0           ; is driver installed?
        jnz    Working:       ; if so, continue
        jmp    NoMouse        ; if not, exit program
Working:
      . . . . . .
```

The Function 01h - Make the Mouse Cursor Visible

This function increases the current value of the internal Mouse Cursor Flag (or counter) by 1. If the result obtained is zero, the cursor appears on the screen. If the value is already 0, the mouse driver does not perform any actions. This function has no input parameters and does not return any value.

The Function 02h - Hide the Mouse Cursor

This function makes the mouse cursor invisible and decreases the value of the internal Mouse Cursor Flag. No input parameters are required and no result is returned. This function decreases the mouses cursor Flag each time it is called, so you should take care to restore the mouse cursor when necessary. Note that any time the video mode is changed, this function is performed by the mouse driver automatically. It is useful to perform this function before changing the screen image at the cursor location, especially in graphic modes. It is also recommended that this function is performed at the end of any program using a mouse.

The Function 03h - Get Cursor Location and Button State

This function is used for determining the current location of the mouse cursor on the screen and the state of the mouse buttons. The function has no input parameters and places the results into the BX, CX and DX registers. The CX and DX registers contain the coordinates of the current cursor location on the screen - the X coordinate (the column) in CX and the Y coordinate (the row) in DX. Note that coordinates are given in pixels even for text video mode. To obtain the coordinates of a character at the mouse cursor location in text modes, you should divide the values returned by the mouse driver by 8 (the width of the character cell). On return from this function, the BX register contains the current state of the mouse buttons: bit 0 is set when the left button is pressed, bit 1 corresponds to the right button and bit 2 is set when the middle button is pressed. The following example shows how to use the function 03 for getting the mouse state:

```
Mchck:  mov   ax,3        ; get button status and location
        int   33h         ; mouse service call
        mov   CX0,cx       ; save X coordinate (column)
        mov   DX0,dx       ; save Y coordinate (row)
        and   bx,1         ; left button pressed?
        jnz   LeftP        ; process left button pressed
        and   bx,2         ; left button pressed?
        jnz   RightP       ; process right button pressed
        jmp   Mcheck       ; no button pressed - check again
......
LeftP:                     ;
......
RightP:
```

The Function 04h - Set Cursor Position

This function moves the mouse cursor to the position on the screen defined by the value in the CX and DX registers. No result is returned. The following example moves the mouse cursor to the center of the EGA screen (640x350 pixels):

```
mov   ax,4      ; function 4 - set cursor position
mov   cx,320    ; X coordinate - column
mov   dx,175    ; Y coordinate - row
int   33h       ; mouse service call
```

The Function 07h - Set the Horizontal Cursor Movement Range

The function sets the left and right boundaries of the screen area which is available for moving the mouse cursor. If the current cursor location is out of range at the moment when function 07 is performed, the mouse driver moves the cursor to the corresponding boundary. For example, to allow the cursor to be moved within the screen area with coordinates 10 - 50, simply call the function 07 as shown below:

```
mov    ax,7      ; set cursor movement limits
mov    cx,10     ; left boundary
mov    dx,50     ; right boundary
int    33h       ; mouse service call
```

This function always treats the minimum value of 2 stored in the CX and DX registers as the left boundary.

The Function 08h - Set the Vertical Cursor Movement Range

This sets the vertical range of the mouse cursor movement exactly in the same way as function 07 does for the horizontal range. The values in the CX and DX registers define the upper and lower boundaries of the area available for cursor movement. The minimum of these two values is treated as the upper boundary.

The Function 09h - Define the Graphic Mouse Cursor

This function defines the color and appearance of the mouse cursor in graphic modes. The graphic cursor is defined as a rectangle of 16x16, 8x16 or 4x16 pixels depending on the video adapter type and current video mode. One of the pixels which made up the graphic mouse cursor is referred to as the "cursor hot spot". The mouse driver functions which determine the cursor position return the coordinates of this pixel. The graphic mouse cursor in a program is represented as two arrays of 16, 8 or 4 words depending on the current screen resolution. On EGA and VGA adapters the mouse cursor has the size 16x16 pixels. One of the arrays defining the mouse cursor is called the screen mask and defines the appearance of the cursor on the screen, the second one is referred to as the cursor mask and describes the cursor color. The mouse driver performs the operations described in the Table 10.13 on each bit in a pixel description within the graphic cursor area. The logical OR operation is performed with this bit and the corresponding

Bit in pixel description	Screen mask	Cursor mask	Result
0	0	0	0
0	0	1	1
0	1	0	0 (not changed)
0	1	1	1 (inverted)
1	0	0	0
1	0	1	1
1	1	0	1 (not changed)
1	1	1	0 (inverted)

Table 10.13
Defining the Mouse Cursor with the Screen and Cursor Masks

bit of the screen mask and then the exclusive OR operation is performed on the result and the corresponding bit of the cursor mask.

The X and Y coordinates of the hot spot for the graphic mouse cursor can be in the range 0 - 15. The default value for both coordinates is 0 which corresponds to the upper left-hand corner of the cursor rectangle.

Before calling this function you should specify the input parameters: the X and Y coordinates of the cursor hot spot in the BX and CX registers, respectively. ES:DX must contain the addresses of two arrays defining the screen and cursor masks (in that order). The following example demonstrates the definition of the mouse cursor image "pointing hand":

```
;   Screen mask for pointing hand
PtrHand  LABEL WORD
DW 0E1FFh, 0E1FFh, 0E1FFh, 0E1FFh, 0E1FFh, 0, 0, 0
DW 0, 0, 0, 0, 0, 0, 0, 0,
:
;   Cursor mask for pointing hand
DW 1E00h,   1200h,    1200h,    1200h
DW 1200h,   13FFh,    1249h,    1249h
DW 0F249h,  9001h,    9001h,    9001h
DW 8001h,   8001h,    8001h,    0FFFFh
......
mov      ax,09          ; function 09 - Define Graphics Cursor
mov      bx,0           ; column of cursor hot spot in bitmap
mov      cx,0           ; row of cursor hot spot in bitmap
push     ds             ;
pop      es             ; ES now points to Data Segment
lea      dx,PtrHand     ; ES:DX - address of cursor bitmap
int      33h            ; mouse service call
.........
```

The Function 10h - Define Text Mouse Cursor

This function defines what kind of text cursor will be used and specifies its characteristics. The cursor type is defined by the value in the BX register: 0 means the software cursor, 1 - the hardware cursor. For the hardware cursor the contents of the CX and DX registers specify the first (top) and last (bottom) lines in the character cell, respectively. For the software cursor the CX register contains the screen mask and the DX register contains the cursor mask. In text modes, the mouse driver works with the screen and cursor masks in the same way as in graphic modes - the same operations AND and XOR are executed. The driver takes the attribute byte and ASCII character located in video memory at the address corresponding to the mouse cursor location, and performs the AND and XOR operations as described for the graphics cursor. Let's look at an example which defines the software cursor:

```
mov     ax,10           ;  define text cursor
xor     bx,bx           ;  software cursor is used
mov     cx,0FFFFh       ;  screen Mask
mov     dx,4700h        ;  cursor Mask
int     33h             ;  mouse service call
```

The screen mask in this example has all bits set. After performing the AND operation the values of the character and attribute at the cursor location will not change since 1 AND 1 gives 1, and 0 AND 1 gives 0. The XOR operation is then performed on the result of the previous operation. The value of the ASCII code will not change since the corresponding part of the cursor mask is 0, and the value of the attribute is obtained as the result of the XOR operation. For practical purposes it would be enough to specify the value of the cursor mask as 8000h. Only bit 15 of this value is set, so the blink/intensity bit of the character at the cursor location will be inverted. This makes normal characters blink and vice versa.

Access to Communication Ports - The BIOS Service

The routines provided by BIOS are combined in the handler of interrupt 14h. You can use both communication ports - COM1 and COM2. Place the function number into the AH register, the number of the port to be used into the DX register (0 denotes COM1, 1 - COM2), additional parameters into the relevant registers and call interrupt 14h. When the interrupt handler has finished processing, the AH register usually contains the port status. If bit 7 of the AH register is set, it means that there has been an error. We'll continue by looking at the most frequently used functions of interrupt 14h.

The Function 00h - Initialize the Communication Port

The communication ports must be initialized for the selected I/O mode before the input/output process begins. To do this, place the function number and the port number into the AH and DX registers, place the initial value into the AL register and call interrupt 14h. The meanings of the initial values are given in Table 10.14. The value which describes the state of the serial port is returned in the AH register.

Let's take an example. Suppose you want to use the following parameters for the communication port COM1:

word length	= 7 bits
I/O speed	= 4800 baud
number of stop bits	= 1
no parity control	

Bit	Meaning
0-1	Length of data portion (10 - 7 bits, 11 - 8 bits)
2	Number of stop bits (0 - 1 stop bit, 1 -2 stop bit)
3-4	The type of the parity control:
	01 - odd
	11 - even
	00 - no parity control
	10 - no parity control
5-7	The transfer velocity in baud
	000 = 110 baud
	001 = 150 baud
	010 = 300 baud
	011 = 600 baud
	100 = 1200 baud
	101 = 2400 baud
	110 = 4800 baud
	111 = 9600 baud

Table 10.14
The Values for Initializing the Serial Ports

If you work out this value using Table 10.14 you should get the result 11000010B (0C2h). The program below shows how to initialize the serial port using the value we've just obtained:

```
; The initialization of the COM1 communication port

    mov   al,0C2h    ; initializing value
    xor   dx,dx      ; DX = 0 stands for COM1
    xor   ah,ah      ; function 00h - initialize serial port
    INT   14h        ; Call BIOS Service
```

The Function 01h - Send a Character to the Communication Port

This function sends a character contained in the AL register to the communication port. When the function has finished, it returns the current state of the communication port in the AH register and the AL register does not change. The following example shows how to send one byte from the memory to the port COM1. The character to be sent is defined by the DB directive labelled SYMBOL.

```
; transferring character into the communication port
    xor   dx,dx       ; DX = 0 - port COM1 is used
    mov   ah,1        ; function 01 - send character to COMx
    mov   al,SYMBOL   ; AL - character to be sent
    INT   14h         ; Call BIOS Service
```

To determine whether the function was completed successfully, check bit 7 of the AH register. If it is set, it means that a time-out error has occurred. If it is clear, bits 0-6 describe the port state as shown in Table 10.15.

Bit	Meaning if set
0	Data ready
1	Overrun error. The previous byte is lost
2	Parity error
3	Framing bits error. Bad stop bit(s)
4	Connection broken
5	Transmitter holding register empty. Data transferred
6	Transmitter empty. No data sent

Table 10.15
The Status of the Communication Port

The Function 02h - Read Character from the Communication Port

This function reads one character from the communication port. The character accepted is returned in the AL register, the port status in the AH register. The meaning of the status bits is the same as for function 01h but only bits 0-4 are used. The following example illustrates the process of reading one byte of data from the port COM2.

```
.........................................................
;  read a character from the port COM2
      xor   dx,dx     ; DX = 1 means COM2
      mov   ah,2      ; function 02 - read byte from COMx
      INT   14h       ; Call BIOS Service
;  now the character read is in the AL register
.........................................................
```

The Function 03h - Get the Communication Port Status

This function simply returns the current state of the communication port. This can be useful for checking that no errors have occurred in the communication line since the last operation. The meanings of the status bytes are the same as those given in the previous table (10.15).

Library

Printing Using DOS

The demo program PrinDos outputs a text string to the printer. It uses the BIOS service to determine the status of the printer and the DOS service for printing. The full assembler text of the program is given in Listing 10.1.

```
 1
 2   ;************************************************************
 3   ;
 4   ;   The program for outputting text string onto the printer
 5   ;
 6   ;   Author: A.I.Sopin, Voronezh, Russia,  1991
 7   ;
 8   ;   The MS-DOS service (INT 21h, function 40h) is used
 9   ;
10   ;************************************************************
11
12   ;--------------------------------------------
13   DATA  SEGMENT
14   CR     EQU  13
15   LF     EQU  10
16   MSG1 DB ' Output a string onto the printer(MS-DOS,INT 21h,
             AH=40h) '
17        DB   CR, LF
18   LMSG1 EQU $-MSG1
19   MSG2 DB 13,10,'Error while outputting the string !',13,10,'$'
20   MSG3 DB 13,10,'Printer not ready !',13,10,'$'
21   MSG4 DB 13,10,'Error during printer initialization!',13,10,'$'
22   DATA ENDS
23   ;--------------------------------------------
24
25   CODE   SEGMENT 'CODE'
26        ASSUME CS:CODE, DS:DATA
27   ;=== Check whether printer is ready
28   Begin: mov  ax,DATA ;
29          mov  DS,ax         ;  DS points to data segment
30          mov  ah,02h        ;  function 02h - get printer status byte
31          xor  dx,dx         ;  DX=0 corresponds to LPT1
32          int  17h           ;  BIOS printer service
33          cmp  ah,90h        ;  check bits 7 and 4 of status byte
34          je Print           ;  if printer is OK - print
35          lea  dx,MSG3       ;  address of message "not ready"
36          jmp  Text          ;  output message and exit
37   ;--------------------------------------------
38   ;=== Output ASCII string onto the printer
39   Print: mov  cx,LMSG1 ;  length of string to be output
40          lea  dx,MSG1       ;  DS:DX - address of beginning of string
41          mov  bx,4          ;  4 is value of file handle for LPT1
42          mov  ah,40h        ;  function 40h - write file with handle
```

```
43              int  21h        ;  DOS service call
44              jnc  Exit       ;  if Carry Flag is clear, exit
45  Error: lea  dx,MSG2        ;  else output error message
46  ;────────────────────────────
47  ;=== This is the final block
48  Text:  mov  ah,9          ;  function 09h - output text string
49              int  21h        ;  DOS service call
50  Exit:  mov  ax,4C00h      ;  Function 4Ch - terminate process
51              int  21h        ;  Return to  MS-DOS
52  CODE    ENDS
53          END  Begin
```

Listing 10.1 PrinDos - Printing Text - The DOS Service

This program uses the DOS service "Write File With Handle" - function 40h of interrupt 21h. The name of the printer file is PRN and the value of the file handle is 4. You don't need to worry about opening this file as it is done automatically when the program starts. Note that this technique only works if the printer is attached to the LPT1 port. If you intend to use another printer (for example LPT2 or a printer connected to the serial port) you must define the text string containing the file name, open the file using the DOS service and use the value of the file handle for future operations.

The technique used in this program requires very little effort as far as programming is concerned and makes your program portable. Most high-level languages use this MS-DOS function for text output operations.

The program contains three main blocks.

Block 1 checks whether the program can really print, using the BIOS function "Get Printer State" (function 02 of interrupt 17h). The printer is considered ready to print when bits 4 and 7 are set (that is, the value of the status register is 90h) which denotes "selected" and "not busy". Some printers do not generate the signal "selected" when they are not active. In this case the value of the status byte is 80h. If the demo-programs in this chapter do not work with your printer, replace the constant 90h with 80h (line 33 in Listing 10.1 and line 29 in Listing 10.2). Also, the constant 10h in line 37 of 10.1 should be replaced with the constant 0. The most important thing, as far as printing text is concerned, is to know whether the printer can accept the next character. If the value of the status register is not 90h, you can check the other bits to determine why the printer isn't ready. If the printer is ready, control is passed to the block which performs the print operation, otherwise the address of the message "Printer is not ready" is placed in the DS:DX registers and control is passed to exit the program.

Block 2 uses the DOS service "Write File With Handle" for printing the text in the usual way. The rules for using this function were described briefly in Chapter Nine "Using Disks" and details are given in Appendix G.

Block 3 simply exits the program in the standard way using the DOS service "Terminate Process" - function 4Ch of interrupt 21h.

Printing Using BIOS

The demo program PRINBIOS demonstrates how to use the BIOS service (interrupt 17h) for printing texts. Its full assembler text is given in Listing 10.2:

```
1
2    ;*************************************************************
3    ;
4    ;   The program for outputting text string onto the printer
5    ;
6    ;   Author: A.I.Sopin, Voronezh, Russia, 1991
7    ;
8    ;   The BIOS service (INT 17h, function 00h) is used
9    ;
10   ;*************************************************************
11   .MODEL SMALL
12   .STACK
13   .DATA
14   ;─────────────────────────────────────────────────
15   CR     EQU    13    ;  Carriage Return
16   LF     EQU    10    ;  Line Feed
17   MSG1 DB      ' Output a string to the printer (BIOS, INT 17h) '
18        DB    CR, LF
19   LMSG1 EQU   $-MSG1
20   MSG2 DB 13,10, 'Error while outputting the string!',13,10,'$'
21   MSG3 DB 13,10, 'Printer not ready!',13,10,'$'
22   MSG4 DB 13,10, 'Error during printer initialization!',13,10,'$'
23   ;─────────────────────────────────────────────────
24   .CODE
25   .startup
26        mov   ah,02h    ;  function 02h - get printer status byte
27        xor   dx,dx     ;  DX=0 corresponds to LPT1
28        int   17h       ;  BIOS printer service
29        cmp   ah,90h    ;  check bits 7 and 4 of status byte
30        jz    Init      ;  if printer is OK - initialize it
31        lea   dx,MSG3   ;  address of message "not ready"
32        jmp   Text      ;  output message and exit
33   ;─ Initialize the printer
34   Init: mov   ah,1      ;  Function 01h - initialize printer
35        xor   dx,dx     ;  DX=0 denotes LPT1
36        int   17h       ;  BIOS printer service
```

```
37      cmp   ah,00h    ;  check printer status
38      jz    Print     ;
39      lea   dx,MSG4   ;  address of message "Printer is not ready"
40      jmp   Text      ;  output message and exit
41  ;────────────────────────────
42  ;— Send ASCII-string onto the printer
43  Print: mov cx,LMSG1 ;  length of string into CX
44         lea si,MSG1  ;  DS:SI - address of string
45         cld          ;  direction - forward!
46         xor dx,dx    ;  DX=0 stands for LPT1
47  Next:  xor ah,ah    ;  clear AH (function 0 - print character)
48         lodsb        ;  send current character into AL
49         int 17h      ;  BIOS printer service
50         test ah,08h  ;  was there an error?
51         jnz Error    ;  if so - put message and exit
52         loop Next    ;  print next character
53         jmp Exit     ;  exit program (normal exit)
54  Error: lea dx,MSG2  ;  DS:DX - address of error message
55  ;────────────────────────────
56  ;— Exit the program (normal or error)
57  Text:  mov ah,9     ;  function 09h - output text string
58         int 21h      ;  DOS service call
59  Exit:  mov ax,4C00h ;  Return Code =0
60         int 21h      ;  Return to MS-DOS
61         END
```

Listing 10.2 PrinBios - Printing Text Using the BIOS Service

This program is very similar to the PrinDos program that we discussed earlier. The difference lies in the actual printing operation. As you will have noticed, this program contains two printing blocks (one for printer initialization and one for output) compared with one in PrinDos.

Printer initialization is performed by the BIOS printer service (function 01 of interrupt 17h). If initialization fails, a message to this effect will be output on the screen. The text of the message is stored in the line labelled MSG4 in the data segment.

The text string is output to the printer by function 00h of the BIOS interrupt 17h. As you'll remember, this function is designed to output only one character, so we organized a cycle for processing all the characters in the string. The body of the cycle begins by loading the number of the function into the AH register (line 47 in Listing 10.2) and finishes in the standard way (the LOOP instruction in line 52). The characters are then loaded one by one into the AL register and the BIOS printer service is called. Note that the program checks the error indicator after each character has been printed.

If you compare this program with the previous program (PrinDos) you'll see that the BIOS service is not as easy to use as the DOS service.

Printing Using Low-Level Techniques

The program PrinLow uses direct control of the LPT registers. The full assembler text of this program is given in Listing 10.3:

```
1
2  ;****************************************************************
3  ;
4  ;  The program for outputting a text string to the printer
5  ;
6  ;  Author: A.I.Sopin, Voronezh, Russia,  1991
7  ;
8  ;  The LPT registers programming is used
9  ;
10 ;****************************************************************
11 ;------------------------------------
12 .MODEL SMALL
13 .STACK
14 .DATA
15 CR    EQU 13 ; Carriage Return
16 LF    EQU 10 ; Line  Feed
17 LPT1  DW 0
18 MSG1  DB ' Output string onto the printer (low-level technique) '
19       DB CR, LF
20 LMSG1 EQU $-MSG1
21 MSG2  DB 13,10,'Error while outputting the string!',13,10,'$'
22 MSG3  DB 13,10,'Printer not ready!',13,10,'$'
23 MSG4  DB 13,10,'Error during printer initialization!',13,10,'$'
24 ;------------------------------------
25 .CODE
26 .startup
27 ;- Check the printer status register
28       mov    ax,40h     ;  segment address of BIOS data area
29       mov    ES,ax      ;  ES points to BIOS data area
30       mov    dx,ES:[8]  ;  address of LPT1 port into DX
31       mov    LPT1,dx    ;  store LPT1 address into memory
32       inc    dx       ;  address of printer status register into DX
33       in     al,dx      ;  get printer status
34       jmp    $+2        ;  this is needed for fast PC's
35       test   al,80h
36       jnz    Init       ;
37       lea    dx,MSG3    ;  address of error message into DS:DX
38       jmp    Text       ;  output error message and exit
39 ;- Initialize the printer port
40 Init: mov    dx,LPT1    ;  address of LPT1 port into DX
41       add    dx,2       ;  address of control register
42       mov    al,0Ch     ;  value 0Ch is initial code
43       out    dx,al      ;  initialization
44       mov    cx,3000    ;  number of dummy cycles for delay
```

```
45        loop  $              ; empty cycle (delay)
46        mov   al,08h         ; value for initialization completion
47        out   dx,al          ; complete initialization
48 ;--------------------------------
49 ;- Send the ASCII - string onto the printer
50 Print: mov  cx,LMSG1        ; length of string to be output
51        lea   si,MSG1        ; DS:SI - address of string
52        cld                  ; direction - forward!
53 ; send a character onto printer
54 Next:  lodsb                ; load character into AL
55        mov   dx,LPT1        ; address of LPT1 port into DX
56        out   dx,al          ; send one character onto printer
57        inc   dx             ;
58        inc   dx             ; address of control register
59        mov   al,0Dh         ; value for strobe impulse
60        out   dx,al          ; send strobe
61        dec   al             ; normal state of register
62        out   dx,al          ; switch strobe off
63 ; Testing result of the operation
64        dec   dx             ; state register address
65        in    al,dx          ; read state register
66        test  al,08h         ; printer error ?
67        jz Error             ; output error message
68 ; Waiting for release of printer
69 Wait0: in    al,dx          ; read status register
70        test  al,80h         ; is printer busy?
71        jz    Wait0          ; if so, wait
72        loop  Next           ; if not, process next character
73        jmp   Exit           ; exit program
74 Error: lea  dx,MSG2 ; address of error message into DS:DX
75 ;--------------------------------
76 ;- Exit at successful finish of printing or at error
77 Text:  mov   ah,9           ; function 09h - output text string
78        int   21h            ; DOS service call
79 Exit:  mov   ax,4C00h       ; Return Code = 0
80        int   21h            ; Return to MS-DOS
81 END
```

Listing 10.3   PrinLow - Printing Texts Using the Low-Level Technique

Since this program deals with the printer using neither the BIOS nor the DOS service, we'll take a closer look at it.

The program starts by determining the base address of the LPT1 port. As you know, this is kept in the BIOS data area at the location 0040h:0008h. It then reads the status byte and checks whether the printer is ready.

The next stage is the initialization of the printer. This block starts in the line labelled Init. Note that once bits 2 and 3 of the control register have been set (line 43), an empty cycle containing one instruction

```
loop $
```

is performed to create a delay. On very fast computers this delay might not be long enough to allow for initialization. If you are fortunate enough to have one of these PCs, simply increase the value in line 44.

The process of printing the string is similar to the PrinBios program. Note, however, that this program writes the characters directly to the base printer port rather than writing them into the register. It then sets the printing operation going by sending the relevant value to the printer control register instead of calling the BIOS service. Similarly, the program gets the printer state directly from the printer status register instead of using the corresponding BIOS functions.

Compared with the other two programs, the low-level technique seems a relatively difficult way of controlling the printer.

The Mouse Demo Program - Selecting From a Menu

The program Pmouse2 shown in Listing 10.4 demonstrates the most commonly used mouse functions such as initializing the mouse driver, determining the location of the mouse cursor location and the state of the mouse buttons.

```
 1 ; ***************************************************************
 2 ;
 3 ; The demo program for mouse (the menu selection, Text Mode)
 4 ;
 5 ; Author: A.I.Sopin, Voronezh University. 1993
 6 ;
 7 ; The interrupt 33h (mouse service) is used
 8 ;
 9 ; Mouse driver must be installed
10 ;
11 ; ***************************************************************
12 NAME PMOUSE2
13   .DOSSEG
14   .MODEL  SMALL
15   .STACK  100h
16 ;─────────────────────────────────────────────
17      .DATA
18 BELL EQU     07 ; sound signal
```

```
19 LF       EQU    10 ; Line Feed
20 CR       EQU    13 ; Carriage Return
21 TEXT0    DB     " The MOUSE demo program (INT 33h). "
22          DB     " Press any key to continue...", BELL, CR, LF, "$"
23 TEXT1    DB     " The mouse driver is not installed !!!."
24          DB     " Press any key...", BELL, CR, LF, "$"
25 TEXT2    DB     " An active mouse driver found."
26          DB     " Press any key...", BELL, CR, LF, "$"
27 TEXT3    DB'The menu command selection using the mouse(text
                  mode).'
28 Ltxt3    EQU    $-TEXT3
29 TEXT8    DB     "Select Command and press Left Button:"
30 Ltxt8    EQU    $-TEXT8
31
32 TEXT10   DB     "1 - Command one  "
33 Ltxt10   EQU    $-TEXT10
34 TEXT11   DB     "2 - Command two  "
35 Ltxt11   EQU    $-TEXT11
36 TEXT12   DB     "3 - Command three"
37 Ltxt12   EQU    $-TEXT12
38 TEXT13   DB     "4 - Command four "
39 Ltxt13   EQU    $-TEXT13
40 TEXT14   DB     "5 - Command five "
41 Ltxt14   EQU    $-TEXT14
42 TEXT15   DB     "6 - Exit "
43 Ltxt15   EQU    $-TEXT15
44
45 TXT3L    DB     "Left button pressed.  Command "
46 NumSel   DB     20h
47          DB     " selected."
48          DB     BELL, "$"
49
50 VMODE    DB     0              ; video mode saved
51 ATTR     DB     0              ;
52 ROW0     DB     0
53 COL0     DB     0
54 CX0      DW     0
55 DX0      DW     0
56 ;-----------------------------
57 .CODE
58 OutMsg macro   Txt    ;======= output text message
59          lea    dx,Txt    ; address of message
60          mov    ah,09h    ; function 09h-output text string
61          int    21h       ; DOS service call
62          endm
63
64 WaitKey macro        ;======= Wait for a key pressed
65          xor    ah,ah     ; function 0 - wait for key pressed
66          int    16h       ; BIOS keyboard service
67 endm
68
69 SetCurs MACRO   Row,Column  ;======= Move the cursor
70          mov    ah,2      ; function 02h - set cursor position
71          xor    bh,bh     ; video page 0 is used
```

```
72              mov     dh,&Row         ;  cursor row
73              mov     dl,&Column      ;  cursor column
74              int     10h             ;  BIOS video service call
75  ENDM
76
77  PutStr  MACRO Row,Column,Text,Leng,Attrib
78              Local M0
79              push    si
80              mov     cx,Leng         ;  string length
81              lea     si,Text         ;  DS:SI - address of text string
82              mov     dl,Column       ;  initial position (column)
83              cld                     ;  process strings from left to right
84  ;  Outputting one character
85              M0:     SetCurs Row,dl;
86              lodsb                   ;  AL - character to be output
87·             mov     bl,Attrib       ;  BL - attribute
88              mov     ah,9            ;  function 09 - output char+attr
89              xor     bh,bh           ;  video page 0 is used
90              push    cx              ;  save cycle counter
91              mov     cx,1            ;  number of characters output
92              int     10h             ;  BIOS video service call
93              pop     cx              ;  restore cycle counter
94              inc     dl              ;  next position for output
95              loop    M0              ;  next cycle step
96              pop     si              ;
97              ENDM
98
99  ;------------------------------------------
100 .STARTUP
101             mov     ah,0Fh          ;  function 0Fh - get video mode
102             int     10h             ;  BIOS video service call
103             mov     VMODE,al        ;  save current video mode
104             mov     ah,0            ;  function 0 - set video mode
105             mov     al,3            ;  80x25  Text
106             int     10h             ;  BIOS video service call
107 ;  Output initial message
108             OutMsg TEXT0            ;  output initial message
109             WaitKey
110 ;  check for mouse driver present
111             mov     ax, 03533h       ;  function 35h - get interrupt vector
112             int     21h             ;  DOS service call
113             mov     ax,es           ;  segment address of handler
114             or      ax,bx           ;  AX - segment .OR. offset of int 33
115             jz      Nomouse         ;  if full address is 0 - no mouse
116             mov     bl,es:[bx]      ;  get first instruction of handler
117             cmp     bl,0CFh         ;  is this IRET instruction?
118             jne     Begin           ;  if not - driver installed
119 Nomouse:
120         OutMsg TEXT1                ;  output message "driver not found"
121         WaitKey                     ;  wait for key to be pressed
122             jmp     Exit            ;  Exit program
123 ;------------------------------------------
124 Begin:  OutMsg TEXT2                ;  output message "driver installed"
125             WaitKey                 ;  wait for key to be pressed
```

```
126 ;------------------------------------------
127 ;  Initialize mouse and report status (function 0 of INT 33h)
128 Func0:
129     xor    ax,ax      ; Initialize mouse
130     int    33h        ; mouse service call
131     cmp    ax,0       ; is mouse installed?
132     jnz    Clear25    ; if so, pass to function 10
133     jmp    Exit       ; if not, exit program
134 ; Fill the screen (yellow character on blue background)
135 Clear25:SetCurs 0,0   ; cursor to left upper corner
136     mov    ah,9       ; function 09h - output char+attr
137     xor    bh,bh      ; video page  0 is used
138     mov    al,20h     ; character to be output
139     mov    bl,1Eh     ; attribute - yellow on blue
140     mov    cx,2000    ; number of characters to be output
141     int    10h        ; BIOS video service call
142 ;------------------------------------------
143 ;  Output the header and the menu text onto the screen
144     PutStr  2,16,TEXT3,Ltxt3,1Eh
145     PutStr  8,20,TEXT8,Ltxt8,1Eh
146     PutStr  10,20,TEXT10,Ltxt10,1Fh
147     PutStr  11,20,TEXT11,Ltxt11,1Fh
148     PutStr  12,20,TEXT12,Ltxt12,1Fh
149     PutStr  13,20,TEXT13,Ltxt13,1Fh
150     PutStr  14,20,TEXT14,Ltxt14,1Fh
151     PutStr  15,20,TEXT15,Ltxt15,1Fh
152 SetCurs 25,80   ; move cursor out of screen
153 ;------------------------------------------
154 ;  Function 10 - define text cursor
155 Func10: mov    ax,10      ; define text cursor
156         xor    bx,bx      ; software cursor is used
157         mov    cx,0FFFFh  ; screen Mask
158         mov    dx,4700h   ; cursor Mask
159         int    33h        ; mouse service call
160 ;------------------------------------------
161 ;  Function 1 - show the mouse cursor
162 Func1:  mov    ax,1       ; function 01 - show mouse cursor
163         int    33h        ; mouse service call
164 ;------------------------------------------
165 ;  Determining mouse keys pressed
166 Func3:  mov    ah,1       ; function 01h - check keyboard buffer
167         int    16h        ; BIOS keyboard service
168         jz     ContF3     ; if no key pressed, continue
169         jmp    Exit       ; exit if key pressed
170 ContF3: mov    ax,3       ; func. 03 - button status and location
171         int    33h        ; mouse service call
172         mov    CX0,cx     ; save  X coordinate (column)
173         mov    DX0,dx     ; save  Y coordinate (row)
174         test   bx,1       ; left button pressed?
175         jnz    X_Range    ; OK !
176         jmp    short Func3   ; no button pressed - check again
177 ;  Check horizontal cursor location
178 X_Range:mov    ax,CX0     ; X coordinate (Column)
179         mov    cl,3       ; number bits to shift
```

```
180          shr    ax,cl        ;  shift by 3 - divide by 8
181          cmp    ax,20        ;  cursor on the left ?
182          jb     Func3        ;  not - continue check
183          cmp    ax,36        ;  cursor on the right?
184          ja     Func3        ;  not - continue check
185  ; Check vertical cursor location
186  Y_Range:mov    ax,DX0       ;  X coordinate (Column)
187          mov    cl,3         ;  number bits to shift
188          shr    ax,cl        ;  shift by 3 - divide by 8
189          cmp    ax,10        ;  cursor on the top ?
190          jb     Func3        ;  not - continue check
191          cmp    ax,15        ;  cursor on the bottom?
192          ja     Func3        ;  not - continue check
193  ; report the number of the command selected
194          mov    ax,DX0       ;  Y coordinate (Row)
195          mov    cl,3         ;  number bits to shift
196          shr    ax,cl        ;  shift by 3 - divide by 8
197          cmp    ax,15        ;  line 15 (Exit) ?
198          je     Exit         ;  if so - finish
199          sub    ax,9         ;  number of command selected
200          or     al,30h       ;  convert to ASCII character
201          mov    NumSel,al    ;  put number to output message
202          SetCurs 17,20       ;  move cursor
203          OutMsg TXT3L        ;  output message "command selected"
204          jmp    short Func3  ;  check again
205  ;------------------------------------------------
206  ; Terminate program and exit to DOS
207  Exit:   mov    al,VMODE     ;  remember video mode on entry
208          mov    ah,0         ;  function 0 - set video mode
209          int    10h          ;  BIOS video service
210          Call   CLRKEY       ;  clear keyboard buffer
211          mov    ax,4C00h     ;  function 4Ch - terminate process
212          int    21h          ;  DOS service call
213  ;------------------------------------------------
214  ;
215  ;   This procedure clears the keyboard buffer
216  ;
217  ;------------------------------------------------
218  CLRKEY PROC   NEAR uses ax es
219          mov    ax,40h       ;  address of BIOS data segment
220          mov    ES,ax        ;  ES points to BIOS data
221          cli                 ; no interrupts - system data modified
222          mov    ax,ES:[1Ah]  ;  buffer head printer
223          mov    ES:[1Ch],ax  ;  clear buffer (head ptr = tail ptr)
224          sti                 ;  buffer cleared - allow interrupts
225          ret
226  CLRKEY ENDP
227          END
```

Listing 10.4 PMouse2 - Working with the Mouse in Text Mode

The program starts by determining the current video mode and saving it in the variable VMODE. The text video mode 3 (80 columns and

25 rows) is then set. Next the program checks whether the mouse driver is present. This is done using the technique described earlier in this chapter - interrupt 33h vector is examined. If both the segment and offset components of the vector are zero, the program finishes its work. Otherwise, the program examines the first byte of the handler of interrupt 33h. If this byte differs from 0CFh (the IRET instruction) the program passes control to the block labelled BEGIN which starts the main part of the program.

The first action performed by the program is function 0h, which checks for the driver. If this function returns the result -1, it confirms that the handler of interrupt 33h is the correct mouse driver and the program can continue.

The block labelled Func10 defines the text mouse cursor. The screen mask is 0FFFFh which tells us that all bits of the attribute and character are used for creating the software mouse cursor. The cursor mask is 4700h which affects the attribute byte only.

The cursor is then made visible by using the mouse function 01 (show cursor).

After this, the program outputs the menu text onto the screen and checks whether a key on the keyboard has been pressed (function 01 of BIOS interrupt 16h). The length of the menu strings is needed for text output and for determining whether the mouse cursor is located within the menu area. This length is calculated as the distance between the first byte of a message and the byte following its last byte. This technique allows you to change the menu text without making significant changes to the source program. You only need to edit the menu text and re-compile the program.

If no key has been pressed, the program assumes that you are working with a mouse and determines the current location of the mouse cursor and the state of the mouse buttons. If the left mouse button has been pressed, the program checks whether the mouse cursor is located within the menu area. To do this, the program first converts the cursor coordinates from pixels to columns and lines on the screen by dividing the value returned by the mouse driver by 8. If the cursor is located in a menu string, a corresponding message is output and the program checks the keyboard again. If no key on the keyboard has been pressed, this block repeats the same process, starting by determining the location and state of the mouse. To finish the program, you just need to press a key on the keyboard.

A Sound Generation Subroutine for Assembler Programs

The sub-program Sound is designed to be called from an assembler program to produce sound effects. This subroutine generates sounds at different frequencies for a set duration using the 8253 chip. The full assembler text of this program is given in Listing 10.5:

```
1  ;*********************************************************
2  ;
3  ;  Program for outputting a sound of prescribed tone
4  ;
5  ;  Author: A.I.Sopin   Voronezh, Russia   1990 - 1992
6  ;  ——
7  ;
8  ;  Call from Assembler programs:
9  ;
10 ;    Call SOUND
11 ;
12 ;  Parameters passed through the registers:
13 ;
14 ;  Frequency- DI register (from   21  to  65535  hertz)
15 ;
16 ;  Duration -BX register (in hundredth of second)
17 ;
18 ;  Registers  AX, CX, DX, DS, ES, SI  are retained by the program
19 ;
20 ;
21 ;
22 ;*********************************************************
23 PUBLIC SOUND
24 CODE    SEGMENT
25      ASSUME   CS:CODE
26 SOUND  PROC  FAR
27      push   ax
28      push   c
29      push   dx
30      push   ds
31      push   es
32      push   si
33 ;————————————————————————————————————
34      in     al,61h        ; Read current port mode B (8255)
35      mov    cl,al         ; Save current mode
36      or     al,3          ; Switch on speaker and timer
37      out    61h,al        ;
38      mov    al,0B6h       ; set for channel 2 (8253)
39      out    43h,al        ; command register  8253
40      mov    dx,14h        ;
41      mov    ax,4F38h      ; frequency divisor
42      div    di            ;
43      out    42h,al        ; lower byte of frequency
44      mov    al,ah         ;
```

```
45        out      42h,al         ; higher byte of frequency
46 ; Generation of sound delay
47        mov      ax,91          ; multiplier - AX register !
48        mul      bx             ; AX =BX*91 (result in  DX:AX)
49        mov      bx,500         ; divisor, dividend in  DX:AX
50        div      bx             ; result in AX, remainder in  DX !
51        mov      bx,ax          ; save result
52        mov      ah,0           ; read time
53        int      1Ah            ;
54        add      dx,bx          ;
55        mov      bx,dx          ;
56 Cycle: int      1Ah            ;
57        cmp      dx,bx          ; Has time gone ?
58        jne      Cycle          ;
59        in       al,61h         ; Read mode of port B (8255)
60        mov      al,cl          ; Previous mode
61        and      al,0FCh        ;
62        out      61h,al         ; Restore mode
63 ;--------------------------------------
64 ; Restoring registers and exit
65 Exit: pop      si             ;
66        pop      es             ;
67        pop      ds             ;
68        pop      dx             ;
69        pop      cx             ;
70        pop      ax             ;
71        RETF                    ; exit from subroutine
72 SOUND ENDP
73 CODE  ENDS
74        END
```

Listing 10.5 Sound - Controlling the Speaker

This subroutine starts by reading the content of the port B of the PPI (port 61h) and saves it to be restored at the end of the program. This ensures that the actual state of the PPI will not be changed after the program finishes. It then turns the speaker on by setting the two lowest bits of port 61h. The next task is to obtain the frequency divisor and to send it to channel 2 of the timer (port 42h). This value is the number of oscillations generated by the 8284A chip (or its equivalent) before the next signal is sent to the speaker. The less this value is, the higher the frequency of the sound generated. To calculate the value of the frequency divider, the program divides the value of the frequency generated by the 8284A chip (1.93MHz or 144F38h) by the value passed in the DI register and sends the result to port 42h. Note that the value of the signal frequency is passed through DX.

The next block from lines 46-62 delays the program for the length of time defined by the value of the sound duration. The value of the delay is passed through the BX register. The program then converts this value into timer ticks (18.2 ticks per second), adds it to the current value of the ticks counter (interrupt 1Ah) and saves the result. The current value of the ticks counter (which is constantly updated) is then read and checked to determine whether it's time to switch the speaker off. The last operation, turning the speaker off, is performed by restoring the original contents of port 61h.

An example of a main assembler program is given in Listing 10.6. This program produces 7 signals at different frequencies which make up the C-major scale. Since this program is relatively small and hopefully quite clear, we do not intend to go into it in detail.

```
1
2  .model small
3  EXTRN   sound : far     ; external sub-program SOUND will be used
4  .stack
5  .data
6  freq  dw   0,988,880,784,699,659,587,523
7  .code
8  .startup
9        mov    cx,7        ; number of signals produced
10
11 prod: mov    bx,cx       ; number of current signal
12       shl    bx,1        ; multiply number by 2 to obtain offset
13       mov    di,word ptr freq[bx] ; get frequency of current signal
14       mov    bx,50       ; duration - 25 hundredths of second
15       call   sound       ; this produces sound
16       loop   prod        ; next signal
17
18       mov ax,4C00h        ; function 4C - terminate process
19       int 21h             ; DOS service call
20 end
```

Listing 10.6 TSound - The Calling Program for the Subroutine Sound

Summary

In this chapter we have described the most common ways of using hardware components such as the printer, serial ports and speaker. We'll conclude this by giving you a few recommendations as to which service to use for each of the hardware components we have described.

MS-DOS is the most convenient for printing text. You can make your programs even more flexible though by combining it with the BIOS service in the following way:

▲ Use the BIOS service to initialize the printer when you switch it on for the first time.
▲ Use the MS-DOS service for printing.
▲ Use the BIOS service to determine the printer state before continuing to print if there has been an interval since you started printing.

Controlling the printer registers directly is only really necessary for creating special software that works with non-standard printers. However, if the potential difficulties don't put you off, it can be useful for increasing the speed of your programs.

As far as the serial ports are concerned, you will not usually need to program them manually. There are a great variety of communication packages available for transferring data through the serial ports. Nevertheless, if you do actually need to program these ports (for example, for writing your own LAN, intercomputer communication or E-mail system) the best way is to use the low-level technique as it allows you to use all the hardware features. Unfortunately this means that you'll probably have to get yourself a more advanced book.

Which method is most effective for controlling the speaker depends on the task in hand. If you simply want to generate an alarm signal, just write the special Bell character (ASCII code 07) onto the console using the MS-DOS service. This will give you a sound signal at a frequency of 440Hz for about 1 sec. This is usually enough for most people. If your plans are bigger though, and you want to literally sing about it, you will have to use the low-level technique.

TSR Programming

In this chapter we will concentrate on a particular type of program - Resident or Terminate and Stay Resident (TSR-programs). A TSR is a program that remains in the memory even when it is not executing, and can be run from "inside" another program.

The most widely used TSRs are pop-up programs such as Sidekick. They allow the user to interrupt the current environment, perform a simple task, and return safely to the job in hand. Another kind of TSR is the MS-DOS utility PRINT which gives the impression of printing away in the background while you run another program.

Because the TSR is resident in the memory even when it is not executing, it takes up some of the valuable 640K of memory that DOS has for all applications. To keep this overhead to a minimum, TSRs are best written in assembly language.

There are two views on TSRs. Some programmers believe that they are one of the most useful features of DOS, allowing them to increase its power and utility. While this is perfectly true, others believe that TSRs just provide an easy way of including a lot of errors in DOS routines. Unfortunately this is also true! However, since a book covering assembly language and DOS programming would not be complete without mentioning TSRs, we will include them - and let you make up your own mind.

We will explain in detail what a TSR-program is, take a look at its main parts and explain what these parts do. We will also look at the basic MS-DOS tools for creating TSR-programs.

To demonstrate TSRs, we'll consider an example of a TSR program in detail - the program ScrBlank which blanks your monitor screen when the keyboard is inactive for some time. We will take two other examples in less detail - the program FSecret, which prevents writing onto floppy disks and a full version of ScrBlank which supports the most commonly used video adapters.

This chapter also covers installing, running and deinstalling TSR programs. The relevant DOS interrupts, including those not covered in standard documentation, are also explained.

Fundamental Knowledge

TSR - Leaving in Order to Stay

So far we have been working on the assumption that the basic process for running programs under MS-DOS involves three main stages - starting, executing and finishing. The programs that we will cover now differ in that they start, run, finish and... continue to run. Strictly speaking, these programs don't actually finish - they return control to DOS as usual, but stay in the memory like internal DOS routines. This is what is known as a TSR program - **T**erminate and **S**tay **R**esident.

The most distinctive feature of a resident program is this fact that part of it remains in the memory after the program has returned control to the operating system (hence the name TSR). This part of the program can then be activated again at any time.

TSR programs fall naturally into two parts - an **Installation part** and a **Resident part**. When a TSR is loaded, both parts are located in the memory and the installation part gains control. Once the installation part has performed certain initial tasks (described later in this chapter) it returns control to DOS in a way that allows the resident part to be activated following an event such as an interrupt. The resident part is also known as the implementation or functional part, since it is actually responsible for performing the main functions of the TSR. This clear distinction between tasks means that the installation code is similar for most TSRs, while the resident part is unique to each application.

When a TSR returns control to DOS, the memory area occupied by its resident part is not made available for re-allocation to other programs and as such, cannot be overwritten. Consequently, each TSR installed reduces the amount of free memory available for other applications. Figure 11.1 shows the memory allocation for two TSR programs. Once the functional part of the TSR program has been installed you can call it instantly without reloading. By swapping very quickly between the two installed applications, it is possible to implement very limited multitasking in an MS-DOS environment.

The use of TSR programs is widespread: calculators, reference books, notebooks, etc. A well known example is Borland's Sidekick. Anti-virus TSR-programs are also very popular now. Most of these monitor disk write operations and ask the user for confirmation before allowing modification of executable files. More sophisticated anti-virus programs can control a program as it starts, checking it for viruses.

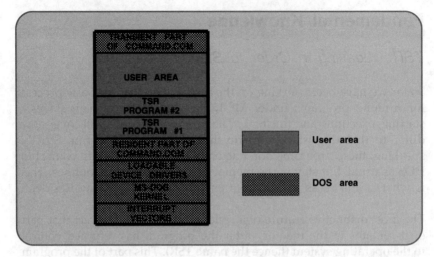

Figure 11.1
**Memory
Layout - Two
TSRs are
Loaded**

One of the first commercial TSR programs was the MS-DOS utility
PRINT which sends output to the printer while another program is
running. It allows you to start outputting a file from a disk to the
printer and then start another program. This is a very simple example
of multitasking.

Two Kinds of TSR Programs - Active and Passive

Let's jump the gun a bit and suppose that you have written a TSR
program and started it. The resident part of the program is placed in
memory and will remain there until you switch off the computer or
delete it from memory. The initialization process is complete and DOS
is ready to execute other programs. At this point it would not be
unreasonable to ask how to make the resident part of the TSR program
work. There are two ways of passing control to a resident TSR program:

▲ Use a specific instruction such us JMP or CALL.
▲ Connect the resident part of the TSR to a particular event, usually
an interrupt.

TSR programs which are designed to be called directly by an instruction
are known as **passive TSRs** (note that any TSR can be called explicitly
but passive TSRs can *only* be called explicitly). The advantage of passive
TSRs is that they can be called by any program at any time, and do
not affect the system resources by hooking onto interrupts and such
like. To call a passive TSR though, you need to know the exact address
of its entry point, which can present problems. Passive TSRs are
therefore usually used only for storing shared data or subroutines. The

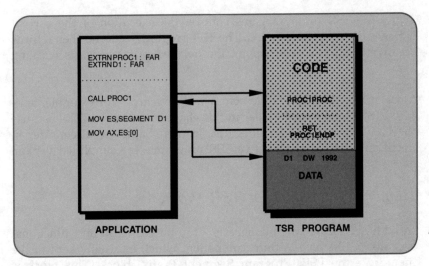

Figure 11.2
**Interaction
Between User
Application and
Passive TSR**

interface between user applications and passive TSRs is shown in Figure
11.2.

Control is passed to an active TSR by invoking an existing interrupt
to which the resident part of the TSR has been attached. By intercepting
the appropriate interrupts, a TSR can be activated by any pre-
determined event such as a keystroke or timer interrupt. To connect
a TSR program with one or more interrupts you must change the IVT
(Interrupt Vector Table) so that the vectors of the selected interrupts
point to the TSR program, instead of to the standard interrupt handler.
We mentioned this technique earlier in Chapter Six and will look at
it more closely later in this chapter. Figure 11.3 shows the interface
between active TSRs and user programs.

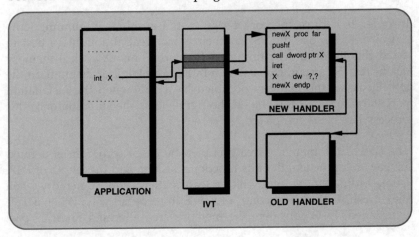

Figure 11.3
**Active TSRs
and User
Applications**

When the TSR program gains control, the execution of the current active program is suspended. The TSR program runs and then returns control to DOS, at which point the delayed program starts working again.

Most of the TSRs you come across will be active. For example, anti-virus TSRs, mentioned earlier in this chapter, are active TSRs because they are activated by an interrupt. In this chapter we'll consider in detail an example of an active TSR program - the simplified version of a resident screen blanker.

Memory Distribution for TSR Programs

In addition to the two main parts - the initialization and functional sections - TSRs have a third component which is usually kept in the memory - the PSP (**P**rogram **S**egment **P**refix) block. This block is separate from the functional section and is created when the program starts. For example, the DOS service "Execute program" (function 4Bh of the interrupt 21h) starts by building the PSP block.

The PSP block occupies 256 bytes of memory starting at the paragraph boundary, i.e. its start address is divisible by 16. It includes several fields which are used by MS-DOS to control program execution. You may remember from when we looked at the PSP in Chapters One and Six, that the tail of the command line is stored in the PSP block at offset 81h. The byte at offset 80h contains the length of this string. The memory area occupied by the PSP is also used as a disk I/O buffer during program execution (this is the disk I/O area DTA mentioned in Chapter Nine).

In order to reduce memory usage to the absolute minimum, some advanced TSRs use the PSP as their work area, although it's best to avoid this if you are writing your first programs. A typical memory layout for TSR programs is shown in Figure 11.4. The diagram on the left illustrates the memory occupied by a TSR when the installation part starts to work; the one on the right shows the situation once this process has been completed.

The size of the memory area occupied by a TSR program is defined as the sum of the length of its functional section and the length of PSP. Unlike ordinary programs, which release all the occupied memory when they finish, TSRs return control to DOS in a special way. When a TSR is installed, DOS considers the memory area allocated for it as part

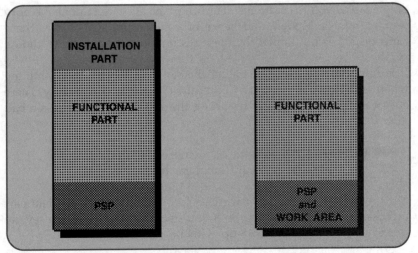

Figure 11.4
**Memory Layout
of a TSR
Program Before
and After
Installation**

of DOS memory and does not reallocate that area to another program. Although this reduces the amount of free memory available for executing user programs, it prevents the TSR program from being over-written in the memory.

Installing TSR Programs

The process of installing a TSR program involves three main stages:

- Checking whether the program is already installed.
- Calculating the size of the resident part of the program.
- Returning control to DOS, leaving the resident part in memory.

This process is performed by the installation part of the TSR.

We'll start with the simplest of the three stages - the last one. There are two MS-DOS functions you can use to 'terminate and stay resident':

Function 31h of interrupt 21h
Interrupt 27h

Both of these replace the usual "exit to DOS" service (interrupt 20h or function 4Ch of interrupt 21h), and do not release the TSR's memory block.

We will consider these functions in detail in the Tools section, but for the time being we will just point out that interrupt 27h is obsolete and only enables you to create resident programs allocated in one memory segment (TINY Model), and hence of a maximum size of 64K. Since function 31h is not limited by these restrictions, it is the better choice.

It is important to avoid installing the same TSR twice by examining whether the resident part of a TSR is already present in memory. There are two main reasons why restarting the installation process is a bad idea:

1 It increases the amount of memory required.
2 It disturbs the interrupt handler chain.

The first reason is straightforward: each copy of the TSR's resident part occupies an area in memory. So if you start the same program several times, you'll eventually end up with no free memory.

The second (and most important) reason is more complex. Suppose your TSR program intercepts an interrupt and returns the old handler of this interrupt at the end of the program. Remember that we gave an example of this type of program in Chapter Seven (the program ScanCode). If the interrupt is then called, your TSR will be executed first, followed by the original handler. Suppose that you then install a second copy of this TSR, which attaches itself to the self-same interrupt but in front of the old version of our TSR, forming a chain. When the corresponding interrupt occurs, this last-installed copy of your TSR program will be called. It will then perform the necessary action before returning control to the old interrupt handler - and what is that old handler? - it is none other than the first copy of your TSR!

You can work out for yourself what is likely to happen in this case. Some actions can be performed twice quite safely, but others can end up destroying information. For example, clearing the screen twice, won't do any harm. However, suppose you want to delete the most recent file, believing it to be a temporary database. If you do this twice, you'll delete *two* files without being sure what the second file contains!

Checking for the Presence of a TSR

There are various ways of checking whether a TSR has already been installed. We will look at two of the simplest ways first, which do not use any system tools. We will then take one which uses a special interrupt, the Multiplex, which is especially designed for TSR support.

The easiest way is to give each TSR a unique code that sits in a known memory location, usually just before the entry point of the functional part of the program. Once the TSR is installed, the interrupt vector it has hooked itself onto will contain the address of this starting point, enabling us to calculate the exact location of its ID code as an offset from this address. Before this TSR comes to install itself again, it finds this location via the designated interrupt and is thus able to check the code of the installed TSR against its own. The question is answered!

You can choose any ID code you like, the only restriction is that it must be unique. This special code is often referred to as the *signature* and must be written at the beginning of the functional section. When the resident TSR program is started, it tests whether the signature is present. If it is, then the TSR has already been loaded and a warning message is usually output and the program terminates. If the signature is not found, initial installation is performed.

Unfortunately however, things are not always this simple. Remember that the interrupt vector always points to the active interrupt handler i.e. the handler which was loaded last. This is fine if the interrupt only has one handler, but handlers can also be organized as a chain. For example, TSRs often intercept interrupt 09. Figure 11.5 illustrates a possible chain of handlers.

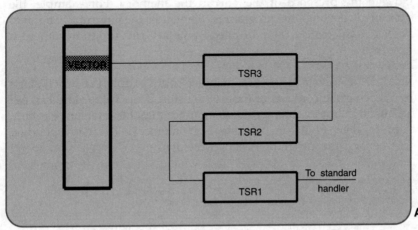

Figure 11.5
A Handler Chain

By getting the address of the interrupt handler from the IVT you gain access to the handler that corresponds to the program TSR3. If you start the program TSR2 again, it will get the address of the resident part of TSR3. It will then look in the body of TSR3 for the signature of TSR2. This search will most probably fail and TSR2 will be reinstalled. We have already considered the possible outcome of this.

The second way of making sure that you don't re-install TSRs is to add a new function to your handler. By passing a certain parameter to your new handler when calling to check its presence, the main function of the handler will not be executed, and instead a return code will be passed back to the caller that indicates the handler is already installed. This code is therefore in effect the signature of your TSR. To determine whether your TSR is installed you can perform the following steps:

▲ Call the new function of the corresponding interrupt.
▲ Check the result.
▲ If the correct signature is returned, the TSR is installed, otherwise you need to install it.

This technique does not have any of the restrictions which limit the first one we looked at. In this chapter we'll look at a TSR program that adds a special function to the interrupt and uses this function to indicate the presence of the TSR in the memory. For example, the simplified version of the program ScrBlank uses the interrupt 1Ch (timer tick) to gain control and to check whether the program has been installed.

This program installs the new handler of interrupt 1Ch which starts by checking the contents of the AH register. If the value stored in AH is equal to NewFunc, the program assumes that this interrupt has been used to check that the program is in memory. The corresponding fragment of the program is shown below:

```
......
Handler proc   near           ; additional handler for interrupt 1Ch
        cmp    ah,NewFunc      ; additional function of INT 1Ch?
        je     Addf            ; new handler for that function
        cmp    ActInd,Act      ; is activity indicator set?
        je     Process         ; if so, continue work
        jmp    ToOld1C         ; if not, pass control to old handler
......
```

The label Addf marks the blocks which process an additional function of interrupt 1Ch. The normal call of interrupt 1Ch is processed by the block labelled Process and the label ToOld1C marks instructions which pass control to the standard handler. The constants NewFunc, CheckIn, Act and Inact are defined with the EQU directive:

```
NewFunc  equ  0E0h        ; additional function for INT 1Ch
CheckIn  equ  0           ; subfunction "check installation"
InAct    equ  0           ; this value indicates "INACTIVE"
Act      equ  1Ch         ; this value indicates "ACTIVE"
```

The functional part of the program starts by calling interrupt 1Ch, as shown below:

```
;=== check whether the program is already installed
        mov   ah,NewFunc     ; new function of INT 10h
        mov   al,CheckIn     ; AL - installation check
        int   1Ch            ; call interrupt 1Ch - timer tick
        cmp   ah,Checkin     ; does AH contain function number?
```

It then checks the contents of the AH register. If this is equal to CheckIn, the program finishes its work, otherwise it installs the functional part of the program.

DOS versions later than 2.0 provide a tool for checking whether a TSR program is in the memory - the **Multiplex interrupt** - interrupt 2Fh, which we'll consider in detail in the Tools section. This interrupt was originally designed to serve the first TSR program which came with DOS - the resident print spooler PRINT.COM. In more recent versions, this interrupt can be shared by TSR programs and allows information to be passed between them. As you'll see later, a TSR which uses the Multiplex must contain the handler for interrupt 2Fh and process the calls of this interrupt.

Unfortunately, installing a TSR isn't the end of it - there's more work to do before it can actually be run.

Preparing to Activate TSR Programs

We said earlier that TSR programs gain control as a result of a particular event - an interrupt (active TSRs) or a direct call from another program (passive TSRs). It all seems quite simple really - the INT instruction is performed, control is passed to the corresponding handler and the TSR starts to work! However, it shouldn't come as a great surprise to learn that there's actually more to it than that.

It's probably fairly clear to you by now that the most important point about installing TSR programs is that you must only install them when they *may* be installed. Well, the same applies to how they work - they must only work when they *may* work! This means that when a TSR program gains control, it must check the state of the hardware, the operating system and other resident programs to determine whether it can work safely. A TSR program therefore may only be activated if it satisfies the following requirements:

- ▲ MS-DOS is not active at the present moment.
- ▲ The critical error handler isn't being performed.
- ▲ The program does not use the stack.
- ▲ The program cannot be interrupted.
- ▲ The program does not call any DOS services.

You might be wondering whether it is really possible to write useful programs bearing in mind these considerable restrictions. The truth is, it is - but not always! In the following sections we'll consider how to go about safely activating a TSR program, by checking to see whether all the conditions of entry are satisfied. We'll also show you how to get the most out of TSRs, without breaking the rules.

Re-Entrancy

It is not always safe to activate a TSR. For example, a TSR which performs disk operations (especially disk writing) should not be activated when another program is using the disk system. This means that before using the DOS or BIOS services, a TSR must know the current state of DOS. Of course, you can easily write a TSR program which only deals with the screen and uses neither BIOS nor MS-DOS interrupts, in which case there is no need to monitor the status of DOS or BIOS. However, if your application needs to use these services, then you must tread carefully.

Let's look at an example. If a TSR program tries to call the video service when video output is being executed, the data area used by the first copy of the video service handler can be overwritten. This might have different consequences. The screen might blink for a few milliseconds or, more likely, you will simply get incorrect information appearing on the screen.

Some services can be used repeatedly, which means that you can call this service before the previous call has been completed. This feature is called re-entrancy and is available when the following requirements are satisfied:

▲ All the registers used are saved on entry and restored on return.
▲ The program does not modify any internal objects. For example, changing the value of a variable located within the program's body makes this program non-reentrant.
▲ All work areas must be allocated outside the program's body.
▲ The program must not override any external resources such as DOS stacks and DOS and BIOS data areas.

Unfortunately, MS-DOS is not a re-entrant system. The main reason for this is that DOS was initially designed as a single-user, single-task operating system intended for running only one program at a time. Although limited multitasking was introduced in DOS 2.0 and developed in subsequent versions, some DOS functions remain non-reentrant. This means that the results of performing a DOS function depend on the current DOS state.

In loose terms, MS-DOS is a *partially re-entrant* system, so only some of the MS-DOS service functions can be used in the body of an interrupt handler (the actual set of functions depends on the system version). For example, line output to the screen (AH = 09h) can be used inside an interrupt handler. File functions (OPEN, CLOSE, READ, WRITE, EXEC) will also work inside a TSR program.

However, you need to take care that you save all the important data of the interrupted program (such as the address of the PSP of an active program) and restore it when the TSR returns control to the caller. In any case, it is always dangerous to work with disk files which are currently in use. Direct writing to the videobuffer (the low level) is the most effective and safe method of screen output in a non-multitasking environment.

TSRs and DOS Flags

MS-DOS has indicators which you can check to determine the current state of MS-DOS and your system's hardware. Similar to those which inform you of the state of the CPU, these indicators are called *flags*. The most important flags you need to know about are:

InDos Flag
Critical Error Flag

The InDos Flag, also referred to as the Critical Section Flag, is set (nonzero) when any code within DOS is being executed. The Critical Error Flag is set when the Critical Error handler (interrupt 24h) is being executed. You can use the DOS service quite safely when both these flags are clear (zero). If however the InDOS Flag is set, it is still possible to run a TSR by waiting until DOS is idle. This is best seen by considering a real example.

We'll start by looking at a typical TSR program activated by "hot" keys. The resident program intercepts the keyboard hardware interrupt 09h and examines all the keys that are pressed until a "hot" key is pressed. When this occurs the interrupt 09h handler *does not* activate the TSR. Instead, it sets a special flag called the **Request Flag** and immediately returns control to the standard handler.

MS-DOS provides a special tool that allows you to catch the right moment for activating a TSR program - interrupt 28h. Interrupt 28h is called the "DOS idle" or "Safety" interrupt. DOS repeatedly calls this interrupt when no DOS routines are being performed and it is safe to activate a TSR program. This interrupt is the real gateway to TSR programming because its handler checks the Request Flag and activates the TSR program when it is set, thereby only passing control to the TSR when it is safe to do so.

TSRs must also monitor certain interrupts working with the hardware such as disk I/O activity and video activity. This is important because the corresponding BIOS routines are non-reentrant, so the TSR program cannot use one while another is being performed.

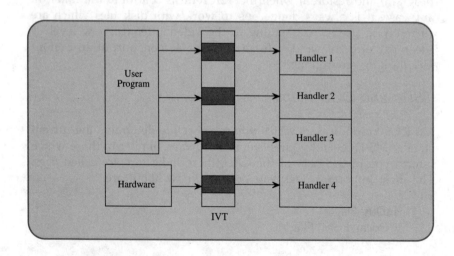

Figure 11.6
TSR with Hooks to Various Interrupts

Since there is no such thing as an InBIOS Flag, and DOS does not provide built-in tools for monitoring interrupts, the TSRs must perform this task by themselves. To do this it's best to intercept the corresponding BIOS interrupts (10h for video and 13h for disks) and to set a corresponding flag. The flag can either be located within the body of a passive resident program accessible to other TSRs, or can be passed to other TSRs using the Multiplex interrupt - interrupt 2Fh. The multiplex is in effect a dead interrupt that has by convention become used as a universal hook for TSRs. We will show how useful this can be in the Tools section.

Activating TSR Programs

Once you have checked that all parts of the system are safe to start, control can be passed to the functional part of the TSR.

Before we give a detailed explanation of activating TSRs, we'll look at some of the basic components that need to be considered. First of all the program may have to intercept the following interrupts:

- **For its activation** - the keyboard interrupt 09h or the timer interrupts 08h (hardware) or 1Ch (user timer interrupt).
- **For avoiding possible conflicts with other programs** - the video interrupt 10h and the disk interrupt 13h.
- **For avoiding conflicts with DOS** - the "safety interrupt" 28h.

You will not always need to intercept all of these interrupts. For example, if your program does not perform video operations, there is no need to monitor interrupt 10h. Similarly, passive TSRs do not need to intercept keyboard or timer interrupts.

Let's consider the tasks performed by the additional handlers for these interrupts:

- The handler of interrupt 09h or 1Ch waits for a signal to activate the program - a "hot" key or a particular pre-set time. When it receives this, it sets the Request Flag and returns control to the standard handler. The TSR is waiting to run.

- The handlers of interrupts 10h and 13h set the corresponding flags (VideoActiveFlag or DiskActiveFlag, respectively), call the standard handler, clear the flag and return control to the calling program via the IRET instruction. For more information about how to call the standard handler you can refer to the program

CursKeep given in the Library section of this chapter. For now, remember that since the INT instruction pushes the Flag Register before passing control to the interrupt handler, you must use a sequence of PUSHF and CALL instructions to call the interrupt handler, for example:

```
......
OldHandler  label Dword ; original vector will be saved here
OldOff      dw          ; offset address of original handler
OldSeg      dw          ; segment address of original handler
......
            pushf       ; push original flags onto stack
            call  OldHandler  ; call original handler
```

The interrupt 28h handler actually activates the TSR. When this handler gains control, it must first check whether the TSR is already active. This can be done by checking the special **Activity Flag** located within the resident part and set to 0 during TSR installation. If this flag is set (nonzero), it means that the TSR is already active and the interrupt 28h handler must return control to DOS. If the Activity Flag is clear and the Request Flag is set, the handler must then check the following flags:

> Video Activity Flag
> Disk Activity Flag
> Critical Error Flag
> InDos Flag

The TSR program can be activated safely if all of them are clear. The process of activating a TSR is illustrated in Figure 11.7.

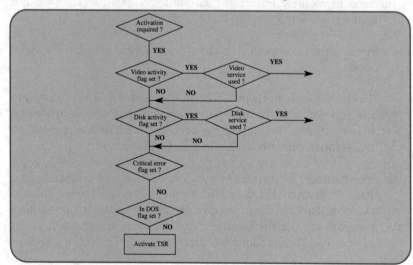

Figure 11.7
Activating a TSR Program

However, not all of these steps are always obligatory. For example, if your TSR does not affect video systems, it can be activated when the interrupt 10h handler is active. Similarly, you can interrupt disk functions if your program does not perform disk operations itself. Theoretically, there is a small possibility that your TSR can cause a program performing low-level operations with the hardware to crash. Fortunately, most such programs disable interrupts before performing critical parts. When the Critical Error Flag is set, your TSR shouldn't be activated. If, however, you need this, note that DOS services with numbers higher than 0Ch must not be performed when the Critical Error Flag is set.

Finally, to avoid running the resident program twice, the first thing that a TSR program must do when it is activated is set the Activity Flag; likewise the last thing that a TSR program must do before exiting, is clear this flag.

Using System Services in TSR Programs

It would be very surprising to find an Assembler program that used neither BIOS nor DOS services, and although TSR programs are no exception, there are some peculiarities which you should be aware of. Firstly, not all BIOS and DOS routines can be used in TSR programs and secondly, even though certain routines are available, they cannot necessarily all be used at the same time.

As we explained before, MS-DOS is not a re-entrant operating system. One of the most significant reasons for this is that most DOS routines set up their own stack. There are three internal stacks in DOS versions later than 2.0:

An I/O stack
A disk stack
An auxiliary stack

The stack is one of the most important DOS resources. Practically every program uses the stack for storing temporary values, passing parameters between procedures, and processing strings - to name but a few purposes. The stack is a completely passive data structure - it is up to the programmer to remember what the data on it represents. If a program uses its own stack incorrectly, it usually leads to a program error and abnormal termination, though this doesn't damage system data and DOS will still work.

If the internal system stack is being used when the TSR program gains control, any modification of the stack registers and pointers (SS, SP and BP) can cause the system to crash. DOS will have been expecting to use data in exactly the same order as it was pushed onto the stack, and any deviation can have serious results. Up to now we have circumvented these problems by not using any DOS services in our TSRs, and by ensuring that DOS is in a safe condition when they are activated.

Which stack a DOS function uses depends on the function number and state of the Critical Error Flag. Table 11.1 details the stack's usage in DOS versions later than 2.0. In addition to the information given in Table 11.1, note that the DOS disk interrupts 25h and 26h use the Disk stack.

Information about how different DOS functions use the DOS stacks can help you to decide whether it is safe to call a particular function. If the stack used by a function is currently in use, calling this function can cause the system to crash.

Function Number	Critical Error Flag	DOS Version 2.x	3.0	Recent
01h-0Ch	Set	Aux	Aux	Aux
	Clear	I/O	I/O	I/O
33Ch	Set	Disk	Disk	Caller
	Clear	Disk	Disk	Caller
50h-51h	Set	Aux	Caller	Caller
	Clear	I/O	Caller	Caller
59h	Set		Aux	Disk
	Clear		I/O	Disk
5D0Ah	Set			Disk
	Clear			Disk
62h	Set		Caller	Caller
	Clear		Caller	Caller
Others	Set	Disk	Disk	Disk
	Clear	Disk	Disk	Disk

Table 11.1
Use of Internal DOS Stacks for DOS Functions

De-Installing TSR Programs

So far you have grasped the basics of writing a TSR program, what it consists of and how it works. Now it's time to consider what you can do with the TSR program once it's installed. Okay, you might say, we want to *de-install* it! This is no joke - it's a very important point.

For example, although an anti-virus program is useful when trying new software, it's better to free the memory occupied by the anti-virus guard for normal work. One option is to reboot the computer, but it would be more helpful if you could install and deinstall the resident program any time you wanted, without rebooting.

As you know, the most important functions performed by the installation part of a TSR program are:

> Fixing the resident part of the program in the memory.
> Changing the corresponding vectors in the IVT.

To deinstall the TSR program you simply have to do the reverse. First of all restore the handler's chain that existed before the TSR was installed. If no TSRs intercept the same interrupts you won't have any problems, you just need to restore the values of the corresponding interrupt vectors which are stored in the body of the resident part. If this is not the case however, the process is considerably more complicated.

The memory occupied by the resident part of a TSR program can be freed using the DOS function "Release Memory Block" - function 49h of interrupt 21h. In order to do this correctly you must know the exact address of the TSR program's PSP. The ES register usually contains this address at the start of the program. For confirmation, you can use the DOS service "Get PSP address" - function 51h of interrupt 21h. This address must be saved in the body of the resident part when you install the TSR. For an example of a TSR that performs de-installation, look at the program FSecret stored on your program disk and briefly described later in this chapter.

There is actually a third step that is sometimes necessary to de-install TSRs - removing the environment block from the memory. When DOS starts a program, it allocates the block of memory containing the copy of the current environment block and places the address of this block into the PSP at offset 2Ch. You can release this block while either installing or deinstalling a TSR. We'd advise you to follow the first option unless your program uses information from the environment block while working. Releasing the environment block while installing the TSR means you can decrease the amount of memory used. The program FSecret, mentioned above, is an example of a TSR program that releases the memory occupied by the environment block while installing the program.

A really good TSR should have a built-in feature for de-installation. If your TSR does not have this facility, you can de-install it manually. The most common way of doing this, which is actually used in certain commercial software packages, is as follows:

- Save the contents of the IVT (or at least the vectors which correspond to the interrupts intercepted by the TSR) before starting a TSR.
- When necessary, restore the original vectors intercepted by the TSR being disabled.
- Release the memory occupied by the TSR.

Strictly speaking, the TSR is disabled after the second step, because it can no longer gain control. The third step is necessary to make all the memory that was occupied by the TSR accessible to user programs.

Tools

MS-DOS Service - Get/Set Interrupt Vectors

The process of installing a TSR program usually involves reading the current value of the interrupt vector used by this program and storing it in a double word. Only then is the address of the new interrupt handler moved to the corresponding vector. Program control is passed to the new interrupt handler as soon as the interrupt signal is generated (or the INT instruction is executed).

On the whole, the interrupt handler is a separate procedure, called by the INT instruction. The IRET instruction in the body of the procedure returns control to the caller.

As we stated earlier, TSR programs are usually activated by hardware interrupts. It is for this reason that the starting section of the TSR program sets its own interrupt handlers by changing the corresponding interrupt vector. MS-DOS provides two functions for this purpose - Get Vector (function 25h of interrupt 21h) and Set Vector (function 35h of interrupt 21h). You will probably use them sequentially - for saving the interrupt vector of the standard interrupt handler and then for setting up the interrupt vector for your handler.

Function 35h - Get Interrupt Vector

This function only has one parameter - the number of the interrupt to be read - which must be placed in the AL register. The result of the function is the corresponding interrupt handler address which is returned in the ES:BX registers. This is usually saved in the body of the resident part and used to pass control to the standard handler. If the functions performed by the TSR program include de-installation, this address is used for restoring the interrupt vector of the standard handler. The following example shows how this function is used in the program Fsecret given in this chapter:

```
......
OldOff   dw    0              ; the original offset will be here
OldSeg   dw    0              ; the original segment will be here
......
         mov   ax,3513h       ; function 35h - Get Interrupt Vector
         int   21h            ; DOS service call
         mov   OldOff,bx      ; save offset of old handler for 13h
         mov   OldSeg,es      ; save segment of old handler for 13h
......
```

Function 25h - Set Interrupt Vector

The parameters for this function are passed through the AL and DS:DX registers.

AL must be equal to the number of the interrupt being set; DS:DX must be equal to the value of the new interrupt handler segment and offset. When these conditions have been met, interrupt 21h is called. The following example shows the installation of the new interrupt handler for interrupt 13h. Note that the offset address of the new handler is saved in the variable ResOff, located in the resident part. This value will be used to restore the original interrupt vector during the deinstallation process. The value in the DS register is equal to that stored in the CS register because, like most TSRs, this program is designed as a -COM module.

```
......
    mov    ResOff,offset Handler    ; save offset of resident part
    mov    ResSeg,ds                ; save segment of resident part
......
    mov    dx,ResOff                ; address of handler
    mov    ax,2513h                 ; function 25h - set new handler
    int    21h                      ; DOS service call
......
```

Obtaining the Size of the Resident Part

In order to allocate sufficient memory to your TSR at the installation stage, DOS needs to know the size of the resident part. The following method lets you define the length of the functional section of a TSR program if the installation part of the program immediately follows its resident part. We'll assume that the resident part immediately follows the PSP block (which is always the case for -COM modules and usually for -EXE modules).

Assign a label (e.g. INSTALL) to the first byte of the installation part. Then load the offset of this label into a register, for example using the LEA instruction for loading the effective address:

```
LEA DX, INSTALL
```

After this command is executed, the DX register will contain the length of the resident part measured in bytes from the entry-point of the resident part. The program size must be measured in paragraphs (one paragraph is 16 bytes) to be used by the 31h function. For this reason, you need to divide the DX contents by 16 (the contents of the register are usually shifted to the right by 4). Once you have done this, you must add the size of PSP (16 paragraphs). A small tip here - most programmers add at least 1 to the result of this calculation, to avoid possible rounding errors. The end result is that the contents of the DX register will be equal to the total size of the memory area occupied by the functional section of the program.

We'll now look at the demo program TSR00.ASM, stored on your program disk. This program is activated by the following keystrokes:

Shift(right)+ number key (1 -9)

When the program has been activated, the following text will be output on the screen:

"Shift + X keystroke has been pressed!!!"

where X is the number key (1-9). After 1.5 seconds the text is erased and the screen contents are restored.

The following example shows how to calculate the size of the functional (resident) section of the program. The structure of the starting section is given below.

```
...............................................................
PRES DW  1234   ; program presence signature
; The functional section code
...............................................................
;
; Program of Initial Loading of the TSR00 Functional Section
;
; Test if TSR00 has been loaded already:
INSTALL:
        mov    ax,3509h       ; get current handler address
        int    21h            ; ES:BX - address of current handler
        mov    ax,cs          ;
        mov    ds,ax          ; data segment is in code segment
        mov    ax,ES:[bx-2]   ; ax = program signature
        cmp    ax,CS:PRES     ; is program in memory?
        jne    Modvec         ; no, modify vector, and install TSR
; Output the message that the program has been loaded and terminate:
        lea    dx,LOAD1       ; address of text message
        mov    ah,9           ; text output function code
        int    21h            ; output message
        mov    ax,4C01h       ; return Code
        int    21h            ; return to MS-DOS
;----------------------------------------------------------------
```

```
; Keyboard interrupt INT 09H vector modification:
;  The necessary program code
      Modvec:


.........

; Functional Section Loading:
      lea    dx,LOAD0      ; address of text message
      mov    ah,9          ; function 09h - output text
      int    21h           ; output message that program is loaded
      lea    dx,INSTALL    ; length of functional section (in bytes)
      mov    cl,4          ; 4 shifts to right (dividing by 16)
      shr    dx,cl         ; length of functional section (paragraphs)
      add    dx,20         ; 16 paragraphs for PSP + 4
      mov    ax,3100h      ; terminate and stay resident
      int    21h           ; KEEP
;-----------------------------------------
;  The Texts of the Necessary Messages are in the Code Segment
.LOAD0 DB    10,13,'Program  *** TSR00 ***  is loaded',13,10,'$'
LOAD1 DB    10,13,'Program  *** TSR00 *** already loaded',13,10 ,'$'
CODE   ENDS
       END    INSTALL
```

When you execute the program for the first time, the INSTALL label
next to the END directive causes the program to begin execution at
INSTALL.

One of the first things this program section does, is to test whether
the TSR program has already been loaded. If it has, a suitable message
is output and the program is terminated. If not, the corresponding
interrupt vectors are set, the program size is calculated and function
31h (KEEP) is executed. The TSR program is ready for action!

Terminate and Stay Resident - Interrupt 27h

Interrupt 27h is obsolete and only allows you to create resident programs
allocated in one memory segment (TINY Model). Although we advise
you not to use it, we will describe it so that you will understand older
versions of programs which you might come across.

Interrupt 27h has only one real parameter - the offset of the byte
following the last byte of the program (i.e. the first byte that does not
belong to the resident part of the program). The second parameter is

passed through the CS register and represents the current command segment. An example of interrupt 27h might look as follows:

```
....................
;     resident part of the program goes here
    .......
....................
INSTALL:
;     installation part starts here
    ........
    lea   dx,INSTALL
    int   27h
....................
```

Unlike DOS function 31h, considered below, interrupt 27h can only be used in -COM programs and does not return an exit code which can be used by the calling process.

Terminate and Stay Resident - DOS Function 31h

Function 31h of the DOS interrupt 21h is not limited by these restrictions, and is therefore the best option. Its parameters are passed through the registers in the usual way. The AH register must contain the function number - 31h; AL defines the exit code in the same way as function 4Ch (terminate process). The contents of the DX register must be equal to the size of the functional part of the TSR program in paragraphs. The following example shows how to finish the installation part with the exit code 0:

```
mov   ah,31h      ; function 31h - Terminate but Stay Resident
mov   al,0        ; exit code will be 0
mov   dx,Size     ; size of resident part into DX
int   21h         ; DOS service call
```

The value of the exit code returned by this function has the same meaning as that returned by the DOS service 4Ch discussed earlier and can be used to pass information to a calling process. For example, the code given above would exit the TSR after the installation of the resident part, while the code below would signal that the TSR has already been installed:

```
mov   ah,4Ch      ; function 4Ch - Terminate Process
mov   al,1        ; return code 1 - signal error
int   21h         ; DOS service call
```

DOS Safety Service - Interrupt 28h

The System Critical Section Flag is set when keyboard input is performed, though many MS-DOS service functions (except keyboard input itself) can still be used at this time. When DOS is idle it calls interrupt 28h which signals that the TSR program can work. This interrupt is consequently called the "safety" or "idle" interrupt.

Interrupt 28h is issued by MS-DOS when the service functions can be used, even though the System Critical Section Flag is set. Initially, before a TSR program sets the vector of interrupt 28h to its own handler, it points to the IRET instruction (dummy handler). The TSR program must set this vector to its own handler, which then activates the functional section of the TSR program.

The TSR program can also use interrupt 28h to signal to other TSRs that it is idle and can be interrupted. Use this interrupt, for example, when your program is waiting for keyboard input in a way shown below:

```
          mov   ah,1        ; function 01 - read a character
  ChkKbd: int   16h         ; BIOS keyboard service call
          jnz   Pressed     ; key has been pressed - process
          int   28h         ; signal "I'm idle..."
          jmp   ChkKbd      ; check keyboard again
```

Getting DOS Flags

If a TSR program actively uses MS-DOS functions, you need to be able to determine whether these functions are available at any given moment. This service is provided by the System Critical Section Flag (InDos Flag), which is stored in the memory. If this flag is set, the MS-DOS system code is being executed. If it is clear, it indicates that MS-DOS functions can be used.

The address of the Critical Section Flag can be obtained using the DOS service Return Critical Flag Pointer - function 34h of interrupt 21h. This function returns the address of the InDos Flag in the ES:BX register. If the byte at this address is non zero, it means that the InDos Flag is set.

The value of the Critical Error Flag is stored in the byte following the Critical Section Flag in DOS 2.x, and in the byte preceding the Critical Section Flag in DOS 3.x and higher.

DOS Multiplex Service - Interrupt 2Fh

We have already described one process which allows you to check whether the resident part of a TSR program has been installed. In addition, DOS provides a tool designed specifically for this purpose which can also be used for communication between TSRs - the DOS interrupt 2Fh known as the **Multiplex Handler**. The most interesting thing about interrupt 2Fh is that in its initial state there is *no* interrupt 2Fh handler, only an IRET instruction. So before you can use interrupt 2Fh, you need to write the corresponding handler and include it in the resident part of your TSR program. You would however, be quite justified in asking: "why should I use a handler that I have to write first?"

The multiplex handler is a general purpose resource for TSR programmers. The only predefined feature is that it uses numeric identifiers (or simply numbers) for each process being executed under DOS according to the following conventions:

- Each process has its own number from 0 to 0FFh.
- Numbers 0 - 191 (0BFh) are reserved for internal DOS usage (assigned to DOS processes).
- Numbers from 192 (0C0h) are free and can be used for identifying user processes (TSRs).
- The multiplex handler is called by interrupt 2Fh.
- The multiplex handler accepts the process number from the AH register.
- The multiplex handler accepts the number of the function to be performed from the AL register.
- Function 00h of interrupt 2Fh is reserved for the installation check.
- Code 0FFh returned in the AL register means that the handler of interrupt 2Fh has been installed.

Any handler of interrupt 2Fh must return the information necessary to identify the TSR. For example it can pass the address of the area that contains the character string - the title of the program, the date of creation and the author's name. It's highly unlikely that this information will be the same for two different programs.

The next example shows a complete multiplex handler which can be used for checking whether a TSR has already been installed.

```
MultH proc
        cmp     ah,193     ; is process 193 requested?
        jne     ExHand     ; if not, exit from handler
        cmp     al,0       ; function 0 - installation check?
        jne     ExHand     ; if not, exit from handler
        mov     ah,0FFh    ; AH = 0FFh - indicator of presence
ExHand:mov      al,0FFh    ; signal to caller that handler is installed
        iret               ; return from handler
MultH endp
```

This handler works as follows:

▲ Checks the process identifier (in this example number 193); if the process number doesn't match, the handler finishes its work

▲ Checks the number of the function requested; if a function other than 0 (presence check) is requested, the handler skips the next step

▲ Reports to the caller that the TSR for user process 193 is installed (in this example - by putting the value 0FFh into the AH register)

▲ Puts the value 0FFh into AL and returns from handler.

The handler just given can be called as follows:

```
        mov     ah,193     ; process 193 is requested
        mov     al,00      ; function 00 - check installation
        int     2Fh        ; multiplex handler call
        cmp     al,0FFh    ; multiplex handler active?
        jne     InstMul    ; no multiplex handler found - install
        cmp     ah,0FFh    ; TSR signature returned?
        jne     InstTSR    ; TSR not installed - perform installation
        mov     ax,4C01h   ; terminate process; 1 - exit code
        int     21h        ; DOS service call
......
InstMul:                   ; multiplex handler installation
......
InstTSR:                   ; install functional part of TSR
......
```

Another useful thing that interrupt 2Fh lets you do is pass information to, and accept it from, the TSR program. For example, you can change parameters or get the current program state.

Before finishing with the Multiplex Handler, let's look at how you can choose the identification number for the TSR. There are three main approaches:

1. By direct assignment (the process ID is defined in the program as a constant).
2. By passing it to the TSR as a parameter in the command line.
3. By choosing it automatically when installing the TSR.

The first way is the simplest but the most unreliable because your number can be used by other programmers. The least harmful consequence of this would be that the TSR would not be installed because the installation part finds the resident part (of another TSR) already present in the memory. However, you can use this method if you provide additional information to be returned by your TSR. For example you can assign the same number to all your TSRs and then distinguish between them by using additional information returned by the handler of interrupt 2Fh.

The second method is very similar but has one difference - the number is accepted from the command line by the installation part and stored in the data area of the resident part. The command line for running the TSR in this case could be

```
MyTSR /ID=195
```

The parameter can also be read from the configuration file if it contains a line like

```
ID=195
```

or if it is accepted as an environment variable defined by the DOS command SET, for example:

```
Set MyTSR_ID=195
```

Although this seems like a good option, note that when working with shells like Norton Commander, XTree, DosShell or ViewMax, you'll have problems with the SET command because these programs call the second copy of the command processor to execute DOS commands. Consequently, the environment variable will be lost after returning from the second command shell.

The third way is the most sophisticated and probably the most reliable. It involves the following steps:

- Putting the value 192 (the number of the first user process) into the AH register and the value 0 (installation check) into the AL register.
- Calling interrupt 2Fh.
- Checking whether the AL register is set to 0FFh.
- If AL differs from 0FFh, a free number is found, otherwise the number in the AH register is increased by 1 and the process is repeated.
- If AL equals 0FFh, checking a specific signature of the resident part of this program to ensure that it hasn't been installed before; if this fails, installing the TSR.

The following example illustrates the technique described:

```
......
ProcId   db 192                   ; first number for user proc
SpecSig  dw 2605
......
TryId:   mov   ah,ProcId          ; process id into AH
         mov   al,0               ; function 0 - check installation
         int   2Fh                ; multiplex handler call
         cmp   al,0FFh            ; 2Fh handler answers?
         jne   FoundId            ; Yes - number found!
         cmp   bx,SpecSig         ; check specific signature
         je    Already            ; this TSR already installed
         inc   ProcId             ; next process id
         jmp   TryId              ; try next identifier
FoundId:             ;=== install TSR
......
Already:             ;=== TSR has already been installed
```

In this example we chose decimal code 2605 as the program signature. Of course, in a real program this signature can be as complicated as you want in order to ensure that it is actually returned by this program.

Returning Control to the Original Handler

Having looked at installing a TSR program and explained how it gains control, it's time to consider the fate of the original handler of an interrupt, intercepted by your program. There are three ways your handler can work with the standard one: before, after or instead of it. The third way is the simplest since there is no need to return control to the standard handler. Your program performs all the tasks required for processing an interrupt and finally returns control using the IRET instruction. In other words, your program completely replaces the standard handler.

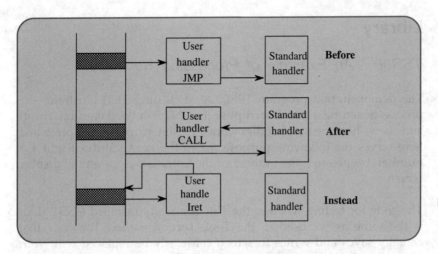

Figure 11.9
**Interaction
Between User
and Standard
Handlers**

You can pass control to the standard handler using either the CALL or JMP instructions, depending on whether control must be returned to your handler. Since the INT instruction pushes the original flags before passing control to the standard handler, both these instructions must be preceded by the PUSHF instruction. The most common protocol for calling the interrupt handler as a subroutine is:

▲ Read the interrupt vector of the interrupt you want to intercept
▲ Save this vector in the memory area within the functional part of the TSR.
▲ Set the interrupt vector so that it points to your handler.
▲ Install the TSR.
▲ Where relevant, pass control to the standard handler using the value of the original interrupt vector as the operand of JMP or CALL instruction.

The following example illustrates using the JMP instruction for passing control to the original handler:

```
......
StdVect    label dword
StdOff     dw    0          ; offset address of standard handler
StdSeg     dw    0          ; segment address of standard handler
......
           pushf            ; this is needed to imitate INT!
           jmp   StdVect     ; jump to standard handler
......
```

If you want to call the standard handler as a subroutine and then return to your program, you simply need to replace the JMP instruction with the CALL instruction.

Library

TSR00 - An Example of Processing Hot Keys

The demonstration program TSR00.ASM (Listing 11.1) illustrates the process of setting a new interrupt vector INT 09h (keyboard interrupt) and shows how the new handler works. The interrupt handler presented here serves the following purpose: when the keys **<Shift> Right + a number** are pressed, the number of the latter is output on the display screen.

The code for testing whether the TSR is already installed (INSTALL:) is the same as we used in the Tools section earlier. The code that actually saves and writes to screen can easily be replaced with your own procedures.

```
;───────────────────────────────────
; All the necessary data is in the code segment
CODE     SEGMENT
OLD09H   LABEL   DWORD ;  address of old handler
OFF09H   DW      0     ;  old INT 09h handler offset
SEG09H   DW      0     ;  old INT 09h handler segment address
. . . . . . . .
PRES     DW      1234  ;  signature indicating presence of program
;───────────────────────────────────
;
;   The new handler of the interrupt 09h:
;
;Processing keystrokes of the type Shift (R) + 1 - 9
;
;───────────────────────────────────
INT09H   PROC  FAR          ;  new INT 09h handler code
         cli                ;  disable interrupts
         PUSHR              ;  macro for pushing all register  used
         mov   ax,40h       ;  segment address of BIOS data area
         mov   ES,ax        ;  ES points to BIOS data segment
         mov   ch,ES:[17h] ;  get keyboard flag 1
         in    al,60h       ;  get scan code
; Test if a "hot" key has been pressed (keys Shift + 1 - 9)
         and   ch,01h       ;  clear all bits  except Right ;
;                              Shift
         cmp   ch,01h       ;  previous  Right Shift ?
         jne   RET09        ;  if not, exit
         sub   al,1         ;  scan code into number
         jng   RET09        ;  exit if key value < 1
         cmp   al,9         ;  digital key ?
         jg    RET09        ;  > 9, exit
; A "hot" key has been pressed (keys Shift + 1 - 9)
```

```
; Necessary processing is done here

        . . . . . . . .

; Restore Registers and Exit
RET09:   pushf                  ; flag register for IRET
         Call   CS:OLD09H       ; call old interrupt handler INT 09H
         POPR                   ; macro call to restore registers
         IRET                   ; exit interrupt handler
INT09H   ENDP
.............................................................
;─────────────────────────────────
;
; Initial loading of TSR00 Functional Section
;
;─────────────────────────────────

INSTALL:
; Test if TSR00 driver has been loaded already.
. . . . . . . . .
;─────────────────────────────────
; Modify the keyboard interrupt (INT 09h) vector
Modvec:
      cli                      ; disable interrupts for modification
                                 period
      mov   ax,3509h           ; get current vector INT0 9h
      int   21h                ;  address ES:BX= old interrupt vector
      mov   CS:OFF09H,bx       ; store old vector offset
      mov   CS:SEG09H,es       ; store old vector segment address
      lea   dx,INT09H          ; DS:DX - new vector address
      mov   ax,2509h           ; set new vector INT 09h
      int   21h                ; DOS service call
      sti                      ; enable interrupts
..........................................
; Program Installation is continued
.............................................................
```

Listing 11.1　TSR00 - Example of Processing Hot Keys

Once the TSR program has been installed the new interrupt handler waits for a keyboard interrupt. When this occurs, the program tests whether the **Right <Shift>** key has been pressed. If it hasn't, the Flag Register is pushed onto the stack and control is passed to the old INT 09h handler by the Call FAR instruction.

If the Right Shift key (the "hot" key) *has* been pressed, the screen contents can be saved in a special buffer. The text is then output at the cursor location and the screen contents can be restored after a delay of about 1.5 seconds.

Control is then passed to the old INT 09h handler and the IRET instruction exits the program.

The program TSR00.ASM illustrates another common technique used in TSR programs; it examines the contents of the BIOS time counter directly (located at 0040:[006Ch]). This counter, which is incremented by one, 18.2 times per second, is used for delaying a program in the DELAY procedure listed below:

```
DELAY PROC  NEAR
      push  es
      push  dx
      push  ax
      mov   ax,40h         ; segment address of BIOS area
      mov   ES,ax          ; ES points to BIOS data segment
      sti                  ; enable interrupts
T0:   mov   dx,ES:[6Ch]    ; initial time (in ticks )
T1:   cmp   dx,ES:[6Ch]    ; has time passed ?
      je    T1             ; no !!!
      loop  T0             ;
      pop   ax
      pop   dx
      pop   es
      RETN
DELAY ENDP
```

By attaching itself to this interrupt instead of the keyboard 09h vector, our program could be activated at regular intervals, rather than in response to a key being pressed. The MS-DOS utility PRINT uses this interrupt to transfer control between itself and the foreground process very quickly, giving the appearance of simultaneous operation.

The program TSR00.ASM is one of the simplest examples of its kind and forms a basic shell for building simple TSRs.

CursKeep - Monitoring BIOS Interrupts

The program CursKeep is an example of a TSR program that intercepts the BIOS video interrupt to perform some additional actions. Its purpose is to correctly set the cursor size for some EGA adapters. DR-DOS 6.0, for example, "loses" the cursor after some video operations such as switching the codepage, loading the character generator or changing the video mode. The reason for this is that when the CGA cursor emulation mode is turned on, the BIOS routines do not convert the values 0Ch - for the cursor's start line - and 0Dh - for the cursor's end line - to the corresponding CGA values (06 and 07 respectively). If you have a computer with this kind of BIOS, you might find the program CursKeep useful not only as a theoretical example but also as a utility that makes your work easier.

The full assembler text of the program CursKeep is given in Listing 11.2

```
1
2          page 55,132
3  NewFunc equ        0E0h
4  CheckIn equ        51h     ; subfunction "check installation"
5
6  _Text     segment para public 'CODE'
7            assume  cs:_Text
8  ;==================== Resident data =======================
9  NumFun  db     ?          ; number of interrupt 10h function
10 SaveAX  dw     ?          ; register AX will be saved here
11 SaveBX  dw     ?          ; register BX will be saved here
12 SaveCX  dw     ?          ; register CX will be saved here
13 SaveDX  dw     ?          ; register DX will be saved here
14 ;==================== Resident code =======================
15 Handler proc   near       ; additional handler for interrupt 10h
16         cmp    ah,NewFunc ; additional function of INT 10h?
17         je     Addf       ; new handler for that function
18 Process: pushf            ; new handler for INT 10h starts here
19         mov    NumFun,ah  ; save number of function called
20         cmp    ah,1       ; is it function "Set Cursor Type"?
21         jne    VidCall    ; if not call standard handler
22         cmp    cl,8       ; is cursor end line greater than 7
23         jb     VidCall    ; if not, call standard handler
24         mov    cl,7       ; otherwise replace cursor end line with 7
25         shr    ch,1       ; divide value of start line by2
26 VidCall:call   dword ptr OldHand ; call BIOS video interrupt
27         cmp    NumFun,0          ; function 0 - Set Video Mode?
28         je     ModCurs           ; if so, reprogram cursor
29         cmp    NumFun,11h; was it function 11 - Character Set?
30         je     ModCurs    ; if so, reprogram cursor
31         iret              ; return from interrupt handler
32 ModCurs:pushf             ; original flags on return from 10h
33         mov    SaveAX,ax  ; save AX in memory, without using stack
34         mov    SaveBX,bx  ; save BX in memory, without using stack
35         mov    SaveCX,cx  ; save CX in memory, without using stack
36         mov    SaveDX,dx  ; save DX in memory, without using stack
37         mov    ah,03h     ; function 03 - get cursor position
38         mov    bx,0              ; video page 0
39         pushf                    ; imitate interrupt
40         call   dword ptr OldHand ; call BIOS video interrupt
41         mov    ah,ch      ; cursor start line into AH
42         and    ah,1Fh     ; bits 0 - 4 are significant
43         cmp    ah,6       ; is start line greater than 6!
44         jb     ModCL      ; if not, modify end line
45         and    ch,07h     ; 4 low bits (value 0 - 15)
46         or     ch,06h     ; divide start line by 2
47 ModCL:  mov    cl,07h     ; end line will always be 7
48         mov    ah,01h            ; function 01-get cursor position
49         pushf                    ; imitate interrupt
```

```
50          call    dword ptr OldHand    ; call BIOS video interrupt
51          mov     dx,SaveDX            ; restore DX from memory
52          mov     cx,SaveCX            ; restore CX from memory
53          mov     bx,SaveBX            ; restore BX from memory
54          mov     ax,SaveAX            ; restore AX from memory
55          popf                         ; restore original flags
56 NoMod:  iret                          ; return from interrupt handler
57 ;=== Pass the control to the standard handler of interrupt 10h
58 ToOld10:jmp     dword ptr OldHand    ; jump to old handler
59 OldHand dw      ?,?                   ; this points to old handler
60 OldOff  equ     OldHand[+0]
61 OldSeg  equ     OldHand[+2]
62 ;=== Process additional function of interrupt 10h
63 Addf:   cmp     al,CheckIn           ; is installation check required?
64         jne     ToOld10              ; if not, jump to old handler
65 Inst:   xchg    ah,al                ; value to be returned into AX
66         iret                         ; return from handler
67 Handler endp
68
69 ;=== Installation part of the program
70 ComSeg  dw      ?
71 PSPAddr dw      ?
72 Start:  mov     PSPAddr,es  ; save address of PSP
73         mov     sp,0F000h   ; set stack
74 ;=== Free the environment memory block
75         mov     es,es:[2Ch]; address of environment block into ES
76         mov     ah,49h      ; function 49h - free memory block
77         int     21h         ; DOS service call
78 ;===
79         mov     es,PspAddr  ; set ES to point to PSP
80         mov     ComSeg,cs   ; save current command segment
81         mov     ds,ComSeg   ; DS = CS - data and code are the same
82 ;=== check whether the program is already installed
83         mov     ah,NewFunc  ; new function of INT 10h
84         mov     al,CheckIn  ; AL - installation check
85         int     1Ch         ; call interrupt 1Ch - timer tick
86         cmp     ah,Checkin  ; does AH contain function number?
87         je      Already     ; if YES, handler is already installed
88 ;=== modifying IVT
89         mov     ax,3510h    ; function 35h - get interrupt vector
90         int     21h         ; DOS service call
91         mov     OldOff,bx   ; save offset of old handler for 10h
92         mov     OldSeg,es   ; save segment of old handler for 10h
93         mov     dx,offset Handler; address of handler
94         mov     ax,2510h    ; function 25h - set new handler
95         int     21h         ; DOS service call
96 ;=== output the message "program is installed"
97         lea     dx,BegMsg   ; DX - address of message
98         mov     ah,09h      ; function 09 - output string
99         int     21h         ; DOS service call
100 ;=== calculate the size of the resident part
101         lea     dx,BegInst
102         add     dx,110h     ; PSP length plus 16 bytes (reserve)
```

```
103          mov     cx,4            ; set counter for shift
104          shr     dx,cl           ; 4 bits to right - (dividing by 16)
105          mov     ax,3100h        ; 31h - terminate and stay resident
106          int     21h             ; DOS service call
107   ;===   Normal exit from program (return code 0)
108   NormEx: mov    al,0            ; return code into AL
109   FullEx: mov    ah,4Ch          ; function 4Ch - terminate process
110          int     21h             ; DOS service call
111   ;===   Process situation "Resident part is already installed"
112   Already:mov    ah,09h          ; function 09 - output text string
113          lea     dx,AlrMsg
114          int     21h             ; DOS service call
115          mov     al,1
116          jmp     FullEx
117   ;===   Data for non-resident part of the program
118   CR     equ     0Ah
119   LF     equ     0Dh
120   EndMsg equ     24h
121   BegMsg db      CR,LF,  ' resident CGA-compatible cursor keeper. '
122          db      CR,LF,'Copyright (C) 1992 V.B.Maljugin,Voronezh'
123   CRLF   db      CR,LF,EndMsg
124   AlrMsg db      CR,LF,'Program has been installed!',CR,LF,EndMsg
125   _text  ends
126          end     Start
```

Listing 11.2 Program CursKeep - Additional Handling of Interrupt 10h

This program intercepts the BIOS video service - interrupt 10h. The program CursKeep doesn't use any system resources so there is no need to monitor system flags; the resident part of the program is activated when interrupt 10h is called.

Instead of setting its own stack, the CursKeep program saves the registers used in - and restores them from - the memory area located within its resident part.

To check whether the program is already present in the memory, the technique of adding a new function, in this case to int 10h, is used. The constant 0E0h is chosen as the additional function number and the constant 51h (CheckIn) as the number of the subfunction "check installation". This constant is placed in AL and the function 0E0h of interrupt 10h is called. If the new handler is already installed, it returns its number (0E0h) in the AL register and the subfunction number (CheckIn) - in AH. By testing the contents of AH, the installation procedure ensures that the additional function really is performed by this TSR, which must therefore have already been installed.

The program supports three functions of the BIOS video service: 00h - Set Video Mode, 01h - Set Cursor Type and 11h - Reprogram Character Generator. With function 01h, the parameters are checked, the cursor size is modified if necessary and then control is passed to the standard BIOS handler. With the other two functions, the standard handler is called as an external procedure and is then used to modify the cursor parameters. When an interrupt handler calls another handler for the same interrupt, the process is known as a handler chaining. Note that this technique is actually used for monitoring the Video Activity Flag: the interrupt 10h handler sets this flag on entry, calls the standard handler and clears the flag on exit.

Let's take a more detailed look at the main blocks of the program and functions performed by these blocks. The block which starts at the label Process determines which function of the interrupt 10h has been requested. The number of the function is saved in the internal variable NumFun. If the function 01h (Set Cursor Type) is requested, the cursor parameters in the CX register are modified and control is passed to the standard handler.

The instruction labelled VidCall calls the standard BIOS video service (interrupt 10h.) Next, the program checks whether either function 0 (Set Video Mode) or function 11h (Character Generator) have been requested. If the function number is neither 0 nor 11h, the handler finishes its work, otherwise it reads the current cursor position and parameters and corrects the cursor size if necessary.

The block labelled Addf processes additional functions of interrupt 10h. This version of the program only processes function 0E0h (installation check). If your video card uses this number for its own purposes, change the definition of the function number (line 3 in Listing 11.2).

The installation part starts at the line labelled Start. It begins by getting the segment address of the PSP block and saving it in the memory. The program then releases the memory occupied by the environment block to reduce the amount of memory required for the resident part of the program. The block that follows checks for the resident part of the program. If the result of the interrupt 10h call indicates that the new handler has already been installed, control is passed to the final block of the program labelled Already.

The block that starts at the line labelled Install performs the installation of the program using the techniques considered in this chapter.

ScrBlank - The Resident Screen Blanker

The program ScrBlank is an example of using the BIOS interrupt 1Ch - the Timer Tick - to activate a TSR program. The full version, which can be used in everyday work, is stored on your program disk. Here we'll consider a small demo version of this program which only serves the VGA adapter. The full Assembler text of this demo version is given in Listing 11.3.

```
1
2          page   55,132
3  NewFunc equ   0E0h
4  CheckIn equ   0        ; subfunction "check installation"
5  InAct   equ   0        ; this value indicates "INACTIVE"
6  Act     equ   1Ch      ; this value indicates "ACTIVE"
7
8  _Text   segment para public 'CODE'
9          assume  cs:_Text
10   ;==================== Resident data =====================
11 ActInd  db   Act        ; activity indicator; if 0 - inactive
12 NumTick dw   0          ; number of timer ticks since last key
13 MaxTick equ  5460       ; 5460 ticks = 5 minutes
14 BlankId db   0          ; screen blank indicator; 0 - not blanked
15 Blanked equ  13h        ; signature "screen is  blanked"
16 ;==================== Resident code ======================
17 NewInt9 proc near        ; additional handler for interrupt 09h
18         mov   NumTick,0 ; key pressed - clear ticks counter
19         cmp   BlankId,Blanked   ; is screen blanked?
20         jne   ToOld9             ; if not - nothing to do
21         mov   BlankId,0          ; clear blank indicator
22 ;===    Save register used
23         mov  SaveAX9,ax
24         mov  SaveBX9,bx
25 ;—      Restore VGA screen
26         mov  ax,1200h ; function 12h - set alternate function
27         mov  bl,36h   ; subfunction 32h - enable/disable refresh
28         int  10h      ; BIOS video service call
29 ;===    Restore registers
30         mov  bx,SaveBX9
31         mov  bx,SaveBX9
32 ;===    Pass control to the standard handler of interrupt 09h
33 ToOld9:
34         db   0EAh     ; this is code for JMP FAR
35 OldOff9 dw   0        ; offset will be here
36 OldSeg9 dw   0        ; segment will be here
37 SaveAX9 dw   ?
38 SaveBX9 dw   ?
39 NewInt9 endp
40 ;===
41 Handler proc near        ; additional handler for interrupt 1Ch
42         cmp  ah,NewFunc ; additional function of INT 1Ch?
```

```
43              je      Addf         ; new handler for that function
44              cmp     ActInd,Act   ; is activity indicator set?
45              je      Process      ; if so, continue work
46              jmp     ToOld1C      ; if not, pass control to old handler
47 ;===     Check whether the screen is already blanked
48 Process:cmp     BlankId,Blanked    ; is screen blanked?
49              je      ToOld1C            ; if so - nothing to do
50 ;===     Has the time gone?
51              inc     NumTick            ; increase ticks counter
52              cmp     NumTick,MaxTick    ; is it time to blank screen?
53              jl      ToOld1C      ; if not, proceed to standard handler
54 ;===     Blank the screen
55              mov     BlankId,Blanked    ; set blank indicator
56              mov     NumTick,0          ; clear ticks counter
57 ;—       save registers
58              mov     SaveAXC,ax
59              mov     SaveBXC,bx
60 ;—       Blank VGA screen
61              mov     ax,1201h   ; function 12h - set alternate function
62              mov     bl,36h     ; subfunction 32h - enable/disable refresh
63              int     10h        ; BIOS video service call
64 ;—       Restore registers
65              mov     bx,SaveBXC
66              mov     ax,SaveAXC
67 ;===     Pass control to the standard handler of interrupt 1Ch
68 ToOld1C:
69              db      0EAh               ; this is code for JMP FAR
70 OldOffC dw   0                  ; offset will be here
71 OldSegC dw   0                  ; segment will be here
72 ;===     Process additional function of interrupt 1Ch
73 Addf:   mov     ah,CheckIn   ; value to be returned into AH
74              mov     al,NewFunc
75              iret                       ; return from handler
76 SaveAXC dw   ?
77 SaveBXC dw   ?
78
79 Handler endp
80 ;===     Installation part of the program
81 Start:  push    cs
82              pop     ds           ; DS = CS - data and code are the same
83 ;===     check whether the program is already installed
84              mov     ah,NewFunc   ; new function of INT 1Ch
85              mov     al,CheckIn   ; AL - installation check
86              int     1Ch          ; call interrupt 1Ch - timer tick
87              cmp     ah,Checkin   ; does AH contain function number?
88              je      Already      ; if YES, handler is already installed
89 ;===     installation part
90 Install:mov     ax,351Ch     ; function 35h - Get Interrupt Vector
91              int     21h          ; DOS service call
92              mov     cs:OldOffC,bx; save offset of old handler for 1Ch
93              mov     cs:OldSegC,es; save segment of old handler for 1Ch
94              mov     al,09h       ; AL - interrupt number, AH keeps 35h
95              int     21h          ; DOS service call
```

```
96            mov    cs:OldOff9,bx  ; save offset of old handler for 09h
97            mov    cs:OldSeg9,es  ; save segment of old handler for 09h
98            cli                   ; caution! critical part of program
99            mov    dx,offset Handler ; address of handler
100           mov    ax,251Ch          ; function 25h - set new handler
101           int    21h               ; DOS service call
102           mov    dx,offset NewInt9 ; address of new INT 09 handler
103           mov    al,09h            ; AL - interrupt number, AH keeps 25h
104           int    21h               ; DOS service call
105           sti                      ; critical part finishes here
106    ;=== output the message "program is installed"
107           mov    ActInd,Act     ; set activity indicator (TSR "ON")
108           lea    dx,BegMsg      ; DX - address of message
109           mov    ah,09h         ; function 09 - output string
110           int    21h            ; DOS service call
111    ;=== calculate the size of the resident part
112           lea    dx,INSTALL
113           add    dx,110h        ; PSP length plus 16 bytes (reserve)
114           mov    cx,4           ; set counter for shift
115           shr    dx,cl          ; 4 bits to right - (dividing by 16)
116           mov    ax,3100h       ; 31h - terminate and stay resident
117           int    21h            ; DOS service call
118    ;=== Process situation "Resident part is already installed"
119 Already:mov    ah,09h            ; function 09 - output text string
120           lea    dx,AlrMsg      ; DS:DX - address of initial message
121           int    21h            ; DOS service call
122    ;=== Exit program
123           mov    ax,4C01h       ; function 4Ch - terminate process
124           int    21h            ; DOS service call
125    ;=== Data for non-resident part of the program
126 CR        equ    0Ah
127 LF        equ    0Dh
128 EndMsg equ    24h
129 BegMsg db     CR,LF,'Resident screen blanker - demo version '
130 CRLF   db     CR,LF,EndMsg
131 AlrMsg db     CR,LF,'Error-program is already
                      installed',CR,LF,EndMsg
132 _text   ends
133         end  Start
```

Listing 11.3 ScrBlank - Using the Timer Tick - Interrupt 1Ch

This program intercepts two interrupts - the hardware keyboard interrupt 09h and the timer tick interrupt 1Ch. The handler for each interrupt is formed as a separate procedure.

The program ScrBlank uses the same technique as the program CursKeep to check installation. Note, however that the new function is only added to one interrupt - interrupt 1Ch.

To blank the screen, this program uses the BIOS service "Enable/Disable Screen Refresh" which is only available on VGA-compatible video adapters. The full version of this program supports the most commonly used video adapters; its source code is stored on your program disk as the file ScrBlank.asm. The demo version is stored in the ScrDemo.asm file.

When the program is activated for the first time, it assumes that the screen isn't blanked and sets the flag "Blanked" to 0. When the handler of interrupt 1Ch gains control, it increases the ticks counter by 1 and compares the result with the maximum value. If the value of the counter is greater than the maximum value it means that the period of time defined by this value is finished. The handler switches off the screen and sets the flag "blanked" to non-zero.

The value of the ticks counter is set to 0 by the handler of the additional interrupt 09h. Therefore the handler of interrupt 1Ch always measures the time from the moment when the last key was pressed. The interrupt 09 handler then tests whether the screen is blank. If it is not blank, control is passed to the previous handler, if it is, the screen is switched on.

The full version of the program ScrBlank stored on your program disk performs some additional tasks. It supports CGA, MDA, HGC, EGA, MCGA, and VGA adapters and monitors both keyboard and mouse activity. If the keyboard or mouse remain inactive for longer than 5 minutes, the screen is blanked. Pressing a key or moving the mouse (if the current program supports the mouse) restores the screen.

The program ScrBlank is an example of a program that uses both the timer and keyboard interrupts (the full version uses the mouse interrupt 33h as well) for activating a TSR program.

FSecret - The Self-De-Installable Disk Guard

The program FSecret is an example of monitoring the disk service. It intercepts the BIOS interrupt 13h (Disk Service) and replaces the Write operations with the Verify operations for floppy disks. This prevents the unauthorized copying of information stored on the hard disk, by making it appear to the user that data has been successfully written to the disk, when it has in fact only got as far as the buffer. This program is an example of one which controls the resident part of a

TSR by its installation part. It can also be used as an example of a deinstallable TSR. Listing 11.4 gives the full assembler text of the program FSecret.

```
1
2       page 55,132
3   ;
4   ;  This program installs additional handlers for interrupt 13h
5   ;
6   ;  New function 0EFh of interrupt 13h has been added.
7   ;  This function has 3 subfunctions:
8   ;  00 - installation check
9   ;  01 - activates the driver
10  ; 02 - deactivates the driver
11  ; 03 -report the driver state;returns the state in AH(1-on,2-off)
12  ; To call new function put its number into the AH register,
13  ; the subfunction number into AL and call interrupt 13h
14  ;
15  NewFunc equ    0E0h
16  CheckIn equ    0        ; subfunction "check installation"
17  IdSwOn  equ    1        ; subfunction "turn program on"
18  IdSwOff equ    2        ; subfunction "turn program off"
19  RepSt   equ    3        ; subfunction "report status"
20  IdUnIn  equ    4        ; subfunction "get resident PSP address"
21  InAct   equ    0        ; this value indicates "INACTIVE"
22  Act     equ    13h      ; this value indicates "ACTIVE"
23
24  _Text    segment para public 'CODE'
25           assume  cs:_Text
26  ;==================== Resident data ========================
27  ActInd db     Act      ; activity indicator; if 0 - inactive
28  ResPSP dw     ?        ; address of resident PSP
29  ResOff dw     ?        ; offset of resident part
30  ResSeg dw     ?        ; segment of resident part
31  ;==================== Resident code ========================
32  Handler proc  near     ; additional handler for interrupt 13h
33          pushf
34          cmp    ah,NewFunc    ; additional function of INT 13h?
35          je     Addf          ; new handler for that function
36          cmp    ActInd,Act    ; is activity indicator set?
37          jne    ToOld13       ; if so, continue work
38  ;===   Check whether the screen is already blanked
39  Process:cmp    dl,79h        ; is floppy disk requested?
40          ja     ToOld13       ; if not, jump to old handler
41          cmp    ah,03h        ; function 03 - write sector
42          je     RepCod        ; new handler for function 03
43          cmp    ah,0Bh        ; function 0B - write long sector
44          je     RepCod        ; new handler for function 0Bh
45          jmp    ToOld13       ; others processed by old handler
46  ;===   Process write commands
47  RepCod:cmp     ActInd,Act    ; is active mode set?
48          jne    ToOld13       ; if not, jump to old handler
49          mov    ah,04h        ; function 04h - verify sector
```

```
50 ;===    Pass control to the standard handler of interrupt 13h
51 ToOld13:
52         db     0EAh          ; this is code for JMP FAR
53 OldOff dw     0             ; offset will be here
54 OldSeg dw     0             ; segment will be here
55 ;===    Process additional function of interrupt 13h
56 Addf:   cmp    al,CheckIn    ; is installation check required?
57         je     Inst
58         cmp    al,IdSwOn     ; turn driver ON?
59         je     SwOn
60         cmp    al,IdSwOff    ; turn driver OFF?
61         je     SwOff
62         cmp    al,RepSt      ; report status?
63         je     Report
64         cmp    al,IdUnIn
65         je     RetPSP
66         jmp    ToOld13       ; unknown command-pass to old handler
67 Inst:   mov    ah,CheckIn    ; value to be returned into AH
68         jmp    ExHand        ; exit handler
69 SwOn:   mov    ActInd,Act    ; set indicator to ACTIVE (ON)
70         mov    ah,IdSwOn     ; value to be returned into AH
71         jmp    ExHand        ; exit handler
72 SwOff:  mov    ActInd,InAct  ; set indicator to INACTIVE (OFF)
73         mov    ah,IdSwOff    ; value to be returned into AH
74         jmp    ExHand        ; exit handler
75 RetPSP: mov    ah,IdUnIn     ; value to be returned into AX
76         mov    dx,ResPsp
77         mov    es:[bx+0],dx  ; segment address of resident PSP
78         mov    dx,OldOff
79         mov    es:[bx+2],dx  ; offset address of old handler
80         mov    dx,OldSeg
81         mov    es:[bx+4],dx  ; segment address of old handler
82         mov    dx,Resoff
83         mov    es:[bx+6],dx  ; offset address of this handler
84         mov    dx,ResSeg
85         mov    es:[bx+8],dx  ; segment address of this handler
86         jmp    ExHand        ; exit handler
87 Report: mov    ah,IdSwOff    ; prepare "InActive" code for returning
88         cmp    ActInd,Act    ; is activity indicator set?
89         jne    ExHand        ; if not, exit handler
90         mov    ah,IdSwOn     ; return "Active" code
91 ExHand: mov    al,NewFunc    ; return additional signature in AL
92         popf
93         iret                 ; return from handler
94 Handler endp
95 ;===    Installation part of the program
96 BegInst label byte
97 ParmInd db     0
98 PspAddr dw     ?
99 ComSeg  dw     ?
100 ResArea dw     5 dup (?)     ; buffer subfunction "return PSP"
101 RetCode db     0
102 Start:  mov    PspAddr,es    ; save address of PSP
103         mov    sp,0F000h     ; set stack at end of program's area
104 ;===    Free the environment memory block
105         mov es,es:[2Ch]      ; address of environment block into ES
```

```
106          mov  ah,49h         ; function 49h - free memory block
107          int  21h            ; DOS service call
108 ;===
109          mov  es,PspAddr      ; set ES to point to PSP
110          mov  ComSeg,cs       ; save current command segment
111          mov  ds,ComSeg       ; DS = CS - data and code are the same
112 ;===     check whether the program is already installed
113          mov  ah,NewFunc      ; new function of INT 13h
114          mov  al,CheckIn      ; AL - installation check
115          int  13h            ; call interrupt 13h - timer tick
116          cmp  ah,Checkin      ; does AH contain function number?
117          je   Already    ; if YES, handler is already installed
118 ;===     installation part
119 Install:mov  ah,09           ; function 09 - text string output
120          lea  dx,BegMsg       ; DX - address of message
121          int  21h            ; DOS service call
122          mov  ResPSP,es       ; save PSP of resident part
123          mov  ax,3513h        ; function 35h - Get Interrupt Vector
124          int  21h            ; DOS service call
125          mov  OldOff,bx       ; save offset of old handler for 13h
126          mov  OldSeg,es       ; save segment of old handler for 13h
127          mov  ResOff,offset Handler  ; offset of resident part
128          mov  ResSeg,ds       ; save segment of resident part
129          cli                 ; caution! critical part of program
130          mov  dx,ResOff       ; address of handler
131          mov  ax,2513h        ; function 25h - set new handler
132          int  21h            ; DOS service call
133          sti                 ; critical part finishes here
134 ;===     output the message "program is installed"
135          mov  ActInd,Act      ; set activity indicator (TSR "ON")
136          lea  dx,Loaded       ; DX - address of message
137          mov  ah,09h          ; function 09 - output string
138          int  21h            ; DOS service call
139 ;===     calculate the size of the resident part
140          lea  dx,INSTALL
141          add  dx,110h         ; PSP length plus 16 bytes (reserve)
142          mov  cx,4            ; set counter for shift
143          shr  dx,cl           ; 4 bits to right (dividing by 16)
144          mov  ax,3100h        ; 31h - terminate and stay resident
145          int  21h            ; DOS service call
146 ;===     Normal exit from program (return code 0)
147 NormEx: mov  ds,ComSeg       ; restore DS (can be destroyed)
148          mov  ah,09h          ; function 09 - output string
149          int  21h            ; DOS service call
150          mov  ah,4Ch          ; function 4Ch - terminate process
151          mov  RetCode,al      ; return code into AL
152          int  21h            ; DOS service call
153 ;===     Process situation "Resident part is already installed"
154 Already:mov  es,PspAddr           ; address of PSP into ES
155          cmp  byte ptr es:[80h],1 ; are there parameters?
156          jle  NoParm          ; if not, set the indicator "NoParm"
157          mov  bx,82h          ; BX - beginning of parameter string
158          cmp  byte ptr es:[bx],'/'; parameters begin with "/"?
159          jne  CheckS              ; if not, check for "-"
160 SkipSep:inc  bx              ; increase counter (skip separator)
```

```
161        jmp  ChkLtr              ; to check character after separator
162 CheckS:cmp byte ptr es:[bx],'-'   ; parameters begin with "/"?
163        je   SkipSep             ; to skipping separator
164 ChkLtr:cmp byte ptr es:[bx],'?'   ; parameters begin with "?"?
165        je   Help       ; if so, "Help" function requested
166        and  byte ptr es:[bx],0DFh ; first letter into uppercase
167        cmp  byte ptr es:[bx],'H'  ; is first letter 'H'?
168        je   Help                ; if so, process "HELP"
169        cmp  byte ptr es:[bx],'D'  ; is first letter 'D'?
170        je   UnInst              ; if so, process "DEINSTALL"
171      cmp  byte ptr es:[bx],'O'  ; is first letter 'O'?
172        jne  InvParm             ; if not - missing or invalid
173        and  byte ptr es:[bx+1],0DFh;second letter into uppercase
174        cmp  byte ptr es:[bx+1],'N' ; is second letter 'N'?
175        je   TurnOn              ; if so, process "ON"
176        cmp  byte ptr es:[bx+1],'F' ; is second letter 'F'?
177        jne  InvParm             ; if not - invalid parameter
178        and  byte ptr es:[bx+2],0DFh; third letter into uppercase
179        cmp  byte ptr es:[bx+2],'F' ; is third letter 'F'?
180        jne  InvParm       ; if not, process "INVALID PARMS"
181        mov  al,IdSwOff      ; code for subfunction "OFF" into AL
182        jmp  Switch         ; switch program state
183 ;=== deinstall new handler
184 UnInst: mov ah,NewFunc    ; AH - code for additional function
185 ;- get information about the resident part (PSP,segment,offset)
186        mov  al,IdUnIn      ; AL - subfunction "deinstallation"
187        mov  es,ComSeg         ; ES points to current segment
188        mov  bx,offset ResArea  ; ES:BX - buffer for "return PSP"
189 ;-     get information about current handler of interrupt 13
190        int  13h           ; call new handler of interrupt 13h
191        mov  ax,3513h       ; function 35h - get interrupt vector
192        int  21h           ; DOS service call
193 ;- is the resident part of this program last handler of INT 13h?
194        mov  ax,es         ; AX - segment of current handler
195        cmp  ax,ResArea[8] ; segment of resident part
196        jne  Over          ; if not equal - res. part overridden
197        cmp  bx,ResArea[6] ; compare offsets
198        jne  Over          ; if not equal - res. part overridden
199 ;- free memory occupied by the resident part of TSR
200        mov  es,ResArea[0] ; address of resident PSP into ES
201        mov  ah,49h        ; function 49h - free memory block
202        int  21h           ; DOS service call
203 ;- make previous handler of interrupt 13 current
204        mov  ds,ResArea[4] ; DS - segment of old handler
205        mov  dx,ResArea[2] ; dx - offset of old handler
206        mov  ax,2513h      ; function 25h - set interrupt vector
207        int  21h           ; DOS service call
208        mov  ds,ComSeg     ; restore data segment register
209 ;- leave program
210        lea  dx,UnInMsg   ; DS:DX - point to message "deinstalled"
211        jmp  NormEx        ; leave program
212 ;- process situation "TSR overridden"
213 Over: lea  dx,OverMsg   ; DS:DX - point to message "overridden"
214        jmp  NormEx        ; leave program
215 ;=== Turn the program ON
```

```
216 TurnOn: mov  al,IdSwOn  ; subfunction "Turn ON"
217 ;=== This block switches program state
218 Switch: mov  ah,NewFunc  ; AH - code for additional function
219         int  13h         ; call new handler of interrupt 13h
220 ;=== Process the situation "no parameter"
221 NoParm: mov  ah,NewFunc  ; AH - code for additional function
222         mov  al,RepSt     ; AL - subfunction "report status"
223         int  13h         ; call new handler of interrupt 13h
224         lea  dx,MakeOff   ; DS:DX - message "turned OFF"
225         cmp  ah,IdSwOn    ; is code "turned ON" returned?
226         jne  FinTst       ; if not, exit; "OFF" will be output
227         lea  dx,MakeOn    ; DS:DX - message "turned ON"
228 FinTst: jmp  NormEx       ; to print message and exit
229 ;=== Output help message
230 Help:   lea  dx,BegMsg    ; DS:DX - address of initial message
231 Help2:  mov  ah,09h       ; function 09 - output text string
232         int  21h         ; DOS service call
233         lea  dx,ParmTxt   ; DS:DX - address of HELP message
234         jmp  NormEx       ; to print message and exit
235 ;=== Process the situation "INVALID PARAMETERS"
236 InvParm:lea dx,Invalid    ; DS:DX address of message "invalid"
237         mov  RetCode,1    ; return code = 1
238         jmp  Help2        ; to print message and exit
239 ;=== Data for non-resident part of the program
240 CR      equ  0Ah
241 LF      equ  0Dh
242 EndMsg  equ  24h
243 Invalid db   CR,LF,'Cannot interpret parameters specified.'
244         db   CR,LF,' Command line is:',CR,LF,EndMsg
245 BegMsg  db   CR,LF,'The disk security system  2.5   29.07.92'
246         db   CR,LF,' Voronezh Russia',
247 CRLF    db   CR,LF,EndMsg
248 Loaded  db   CR,LF,'Program  installed ',CR,LF,EndMsg
249 MakeOn  db   CR,LF,' Disk guard is now ACTIVE',CR,LF,EndMsg
250 MakeOff db   CR,LF,' Disk guard is now INACTIVE',CR,LF,EndMsg
251 HelpTxt db   CR,LF,CR,LF, 'Call: '
252 ParmTxt db   CR,LF,'FSecret [on |off| u |/? | /h |-?|-h] ',CR,LF
253         db   CR,LF,'Parameters:                       '
254         db   CR,LF,'on - make the floppy disk guard active  '
255         db   CR,LF,'off-make the floppy disk guard inactive '
256         db   CR,LF,'d - deinstall the disk guard; it must be'
257         db   CR,LF,'the last handler for interrupt 13h'
258         db   CR,LF,'rest of list - output this text.',CR,LF
259         db   CR,LF,'First call  always means installation.'
260         db   CR,LF,'Call  without parameters to determine  '
261         db   'Current state.', CR,LF,EndMsg
262 OverMsg db   CR,LF,'FSecret is not last handler of INT 13h.'
263         db   CR,LF,'Self - deinstalling impossible'
264         db   CR,LF,EndMsg
265 UnInMsg db   CR,LF,'Program FSecret deinstalled.',EndMsg
266 _text   ends
267         end  Start
```

Listing 11.4 FSecret - A De-Installable TSR

The program FSecret is based on the technique of adding an extra function to an interrupt intercepted by this program. The new handler of interrupt 13h, installed by this program, passes control to the standard handler if the function number passed in the AH register is other than 0E0h. Otherwise, the handler treats the value passed in the AL register as a subfunction number and performs one of the following actions depending on the value in the AL register:

0 - Checks handler installation.
1 - Turns program ON (TSR monitors the interrupt 13h calls).
2 - Turns program OFF (control is always passed to the standard handler).
3 - Returns the current status of the handler in AL (0 denotes inactive).
4 - Returns information about the resident part which is then used for de-installation; these characteristics are stored in a special buffer 5 words long that contains the segment address of the PSP block for the resident part and interrupt vectors for previous and current handlers, respectively; the address of the buffer must be specified in the ES:BX registers.

Before we consider the internal organization of the program FSecret, let's have a look at what it can do and try a few experiments.

Start the executable module of this program which is stored on your program disk. The initial message, telling you that the program is installed, will appear on the screen. Start the program again. You'll now see a message showing the current state of the program. Start the program once more and type the parameter ? or H (Help) in the command line. The program will output a help screen.

Now let's try to determine where this program is located by looking at the memory distribution. First, start any program which can show the programs currently loaded, for example the MS-DOS command MEM included in MS-DOS version 4.0 and later and in DR-DOS. Note that the program FSecret has no environment block.

We have discussed how to release the memory occupied by this block and all the programs included in this chapter will do this. Now start the program FSecret and pass parameter D to it before examining the memory again. You shouldn't be able to find the program FSecret because it treats parameter D as **D**einstall.

Finally, start the program FSecret again and make sure that it is installed. Take a diskette and try to copy any file from the hard disk onto the diskette (small ASCII files such as CONFIG.SYS are preferable). It appears that the operation is being performed: the disk drive is working and DOS reports that the file has been copied. Now perform the DOS command DIR. The information given at this point depends on the type of your floppy disk drive. If you have an old double-density drive (360K 5.25 inch or 720K 3.5 inch) you'll see immediately that no files have been copied. This is because the BIOS disk handler has performed the Verify Sector(s) operation instead of the Write Sector(s) operation. Note, however that almost all DOS disk services call the BIOS interrupt 13h to perform a disk operation. Therefore if you want to write something on a floppy disk without using BIOS you must employ the floppy disk controller commands which is an extremely complex and dangerous process.

If you have a modern high-capacity disk drive however, the command DIR will show you that the file has been copied. You can even look through this file using the DOS command TYPE. However, remove the diskette from the disk drive, insert it again and type DIR. Your file has now disappeared! This occurs because your disk drive signals to BIOS when the diskette in it has been replaced. When the interrupt 13h handler reports to DOS that the disk operation has been successfully completed DOS will use the information from the diskette buffer without re-reading it, until the diskette is replaced.

Now start the program FSecret with the parameter OFF in the command line and repeat the procedure of copying the file. It will copy as usual because the program FSecret is switched off.

We will now look at the internal organisation of the program. Let's start with the resident part which only contains one procedure - the handler of interrupt 13h.

When this handler gains control it checks the function number in the AH register. If this number equals 0E0h (the additional function), the handler performs an action corresponding to the subfunction number passed in the AL register. Otherwise, the handler checks whether it is switched on. If the indicator "switched" is not set, control is passed to the standard handler, otherwise the number of the function requested is checked.

If the function is 03h (Write Sector) or 0Bh (Write Sector Long), the program replaces the contents of the AH register with the value 04h (Verify Sector) and passes control to the old handler. What you will see looks absolutely normal - the disk drive is spinning, the disk heads are moving, the light indicators are on. However, no data is actually being written onto the diskette - the controller *reads* the contents of the sectors being processed instead of writing data.

The block that processes the additional functions first analyzes the number of the subfunction. The program recognizes the following subfunctions:

- ▲ Installation check.
- ▲ Turn the program on.
- ▲ Turn the program off.
- ▲ Report the current status of the program.
- ▲ Return the address of the resident PSP block.

The first function is performed in the same way considered earlier in this chapter, by using a dummy function to return a known value. The next two functions simply set or clear the corresponding indicators (IdSwOn/IdSwOff), which are then tested at the start of the resident code. If there are no parameters, the function "report status" returns the current value of the on/off indicator, while the last function returns the interrupt vectors for the old handler of interrupt 13h, the handler contained in the resident part and the address of the PSP block saved during the installation process.

The installation part of the program works almost in the way described above but contains some additional blocks for passing parameters, installing and deinstalling the resident part.

Deinstallation is performed in 6 steps:

- ① Call the additional function "Return Resident PSP".
- ② Get the current vector for interrupt 13h.
- ③ Compare the vectors for the current handler and FSecret.
- ④ If the vectors don't match (which means that interrupt 13h is currently processed by a handler other than the one installed by the program Fsecret), output a message and exit.
- ⑤ Release the memory occupied by the resident part of FSecret.
- ⑥ Restore the vector for interrupt 13h to make the previous handler current.

TSRPGM - The Step to Task Switching

This program allows you to interrupt any active program and start another program (task switching) and is activated by pressing Alt (Left) + a "hot" key. The path to the program to be started and the value of the "hot" key are passed to the TSR during installation through the command line. The screen save and restore mode can also be set. Since the program is very long we have only included a brief description of how this program works and how to use it. The full assembler text of the program is stored on your program disk.

The program TSRPGM was initially designed for working on XTs under earlier versions of DOS. Although this program can cause problems when working on fast machines in a multitasking environment like Windows or DeskView, it can be considered as an example of limited multitasking. It means that programmers don't have to wait such a long time even when working on slow machines.

The following interrupt handlers are used by the program:

> The hardware timer - interrupt 08h
> The hardware keyboard - interrupt 09h
> The BIOS disk service - interrupt 13h
> The MS-DOS "safety" - interrupt 28h

After the program that was activated by pressing the "hot" key has finished, control is passed to the interrupted program which then continues its work.

The command string for TSRPGM is as follows:

```
/PATH [/PARM /S /K=40]
```

where

> PATH   is the path to the program to be started;
> PARM   is the parameters list (optional);
> S   saves the screen to restore it later on;
> K=XX   is the "hot" key hexadecimal SCAN code. If it is omitted, k=40 is accepted (F6 SCAN code).

Suppose, for example, we want to start the TSRPGM program with the following parameters:

>   The name of the program to be started - DSERV7.EXE
>   The path to that program - D:/SYSTO
>   The "hot" keys - Alt + F1

the screen contents must be saved before the program is started and restored when it is finished.

The following command line starts TSRPGM and passes these parameters to it:

```
TSRPGM /D:\SYSTO\DSERV.EXE  /S  /K=3B
```

TSRPGM is deactivated by pressing Alt (Right) + Shift (Right). All the interrupt vectors are restored and the program is deleted from the memory (program deinstallation takes place).

You can perform several experiments with this program. For example, call TSRPGM, and start some lengthy process (e.g. some Pascal or C compilation). When it starts, activate the resident program. The program specified in the command line PATH, will be started. When it finishes, the compilation will be resumed.

You can improve the program TSRPGM by adding a list of "hot" keys, each of them corresponding to a certain program. TSRPGM will then be able to start more than one program. As a result, you'll get a "task switcher" - software for advanced users written by advanced programmers.

Summary

In this chapter we have covered the basics of TSR programming: the purpose, structure and functions of TSRs and the relevant DOS tools.

A TSR program consists of two main parts - an installation part and a resident or functional part. The main task of the installation part is to check whether the resident part has already been installed. If it has not, it prepares it for work and installs it. We have described the methods which are suitable for this purpose:

▲ Directly examining the area of memory where the corresponding interrupt vector points; this is the easiest but the least reliable way of checking whether the TSR program is in the memory.

▲ Adding a function to the interrupt which has been intercepted by a TSR; this is often the best way of avoiding re-installation of TSRs; the only disadvantage is that it's quite difficult to choose a number for the new function which has not already been used. If you use this technique you must take care to provide the additional information for the TSR signature.

▲ Using the DOS multiplex handler (interrupt 2Fh); this is the most flexible tool for checking installation. It can also be used to pass parameters to the resident part of TSR. The method is fairly complex however, and should only be used by advanced programmers.

The most important task of the resident part of the TSR is to choose the correct moment for activation. This can be done by using the "DOS idle" service (interrupt 28h) and monitoring the system flags. The addresses of the System Critical Section Flag and the Critical Error Flag can be obtained by function 34h of interrupt 21h while TSR is being installed. Other flags such as the Request Flag, Activity Flag, Disk Active Flag and Video Active Flag are not provided by DOS and the TSR program must locate them within the body of its resident part and monitor them by itself.

To sum up, we'll list the interrupt vectors that are most commonly used by TSR programs:

Keyboard interrupt (09h or 16h).
Timer interrupt (08h or 1Ch).
BIOS DOS and video service (interrupts 13h and 10h, respectively).
MS-DOS "idle" interrupt (28h).
MS-DOS Multiplex handler (interrupt 2Fh).

CHAPTER

12

Interfacing with High-Level Languages

In this chapter we will look at the process of interfacing programs written in high-level languages with sub-programs and functions written in assembly language, improving both the speed and efficiency of your high-level programs.

Our intention is to show how you can interface assembler sub-programs with programs written in some of the most commonly used high-level languages such as C/C++, Pascal, BASIC and FORTRAN. We will also review the basic concepts of modular program design by studying how an assembler main program can call assembler sub-programs.

You will find out how to accept parameters passed from the main program as values and as references. We will also consider the new features of MASM 6.0 and higher - the directive PROTO and the additional operands of the directive PROC - which make writing assembler sub-programs much easier.

As you will see, parameters are usually passed onto the stack. We will look at the structure of the stack and consider how different calling conventions affect this process.

The way in which parameters are passed depends on the distribution of the memory occupied by the program. This chapter describes the various memory models which are used to define the memory layout for a program. To show how these memory models are employed, we will cover all six models used in the Microsoft C compiler.

The examples given in this chapter illustrate the two main types of calling conventions used in high-level language compilers - the first is mainly used in C and C++, the second in BASIC, Pascal and FORTRAN. Note that some compilers, such as Turbo C++ and Borland C++, can generate modules using both types of interface depending on the parameters specified.

Fundamental Knowledge

Assembler and Mixed-Language Programming

The majority of programs around now are written in high-level languages - Basic, Pascal, C, xBASE, FORTRAN and so on. The advantage of assembly language compared to these is that it gives you shorter and more effective program code, as well as allowing you to use hardware features which cannot be accessed by programs written in high-level languages.

As a result, assembly language is often used in conjunction with another language for creating program systems. The main part of the software is written in a high-level language and the separate functional sub-programs are written in Assembler, compiled and stored in the object module library. Since programs written in Assembler are usually much faster, using assembler sub-programs ensures maximum efficiency of the main programs.

The sub-programs, stored in object libraries, are combined with the main program using the linker. These sub-programs are then invoked using CALL while the executable module is running. Object module libraries can be specified when linking programs and sub-programs, which means that you can use different object libraries with the same main program and the same object library with different main programs. This allows you to adapt your software to different system configurations, or use the same object library for creating and developing different software.

In this chapter we'll discuss the interface between programs written in high-level languages and assembler subroutines. In practice, you will not usually need to write a calling program in Assembler then call a sub-program written in a high-level language. The only practical reason for doing this would be to organize an interface between two high-level languages which use different calling conventions or different data types. In this case an assembler subroutine would accept the parameters from the calling program then pass them (having converted them where necessary) to another subroutine.

The Assembler - Assembler Interface

As we have just seen, when a high-level language program is compiled it becomes in effect an assembly language program (albeit at the machine code level). The components of the compiled program therefore interact in basically the same way as the components of the programs we have learnt to write in Assembler. So, as a prelude to studying the detail of interfacing to high-level languages, we'll review the mechanics of interfacing assembly language sub-programs to each other.

There is no standard method for calling assembler sub-programs from an assembler main program. The way in which control and parameters are passed is defined by the individual programmer.

The sub-program to be called, and all of its entry points, must be declared explicitly in the calling program by the EXTRN statement, for example:

```
extrn ExSubr      ; ExSubr is defined in another module
```

The name of the called sub-program and all of its entry points must be specified in the body of the sub-program by the PUBLIC statement:

```
public  ExSubr   ; other modules can refer to label ExSubr.
```

These statements generate information which is used by the link editor to combine several object modules into one executable module. The statement

```
Call <the name of sub-program called>
```

is used in the calling program for passing control to a subroutine through its main or additional entry point. Additional entry points can be used to reduce the amount of memory occupied by subroutines. For example, a subroutine designed for performing arithmetic operations on numbers represented in different ways, could be organized in the following way:

```
......
public       ArBin,ArChar
Arith proc
......
ArChar:      ; entry point for processing characters
;.....
```

```
;   accepting character parameters
;.....
;   converting character strings into numbers
;.....
jmp   ProcBin  ; processing binary numbers
ArBin:         ; entry point for processing Binary numbers
;.....
;   accepting binary parameters
;.....
ProcBin:       ; block processing binary numbers starts here
;.....
ret            ; return to calling program
Arith endp
```

Note that if we wrote two separate procedures for processing strings and numbers, we would have to include the block for processing binary numbers in both these procedures.

Both of the following instructions can be used for calling the subroutine Arith:

```
......
call  ArChar  ; this processes character strings
......
call  ArBin   ; this processes binary numbers
......
```

Sub-programs usually have both input and output parameters. The input parameters contain information which is passed to the sub-program by the main program; the output parameters contain the results of the execution of the sub-program. There are two basic methods for passing parameters:

▲ By value - when an actual value of the parameter is passed to a sub-program; this way is usually used for passing numbers, single characters and logical values.

▲ By reference - when a subroutine accesses parameters using addresses passed to it; this is mostly used for passing parameters which occupy large memory areas (strings and arrays in most high-level languages) or have a relatively complex arrangement (structures in Assembler, C or FORTRAN or records in Pascal).

Correspondingly, there are three means by which these parameters are passed:

▲ Through registers - the values or individual addresses of the parameters are passed through the processor registers; this is a popular and relatively simple method, but the number of parameters you can pass is limited by the number of processor registers.

2. Through the stack - the stack is used to store and pass the parameters; this method is commonly used for interfacing with programs written in high-level languages.

3. Through the memory - the address of the parameter list is passed to the sub-program; the list is formed in the calling program and its address is passed to the sub-program through a register or through the stack. This technique was used on mainframes and is now obsolete.

Most of the demonstration programs given in the previous chapters process a limited number of parameters and so use the first method (i.e. parameters are passed through the common registers).

The program PG0801.ASM, which outputs text onto the screen using the low-level technique considered in Chapter Eight "Using Video" calls the functional sub-programs VIDTYP, PUTSTR and WRCHAR, stored in the object modules library OBJLIB.LIB. These sub-programs are denoted by the EXTRN assembler statement that is written at the beginning of the main program and prepares information for the link editor.

For example, once the parameters have been placed in the registers, the sub-program PUTSTR is called by the following statement:

```
Call PUTSTR
```

The corresponding part of PG0801.ASM code is listed below:

```
.................................................................
;────────────────────────────────────────────────────
;   The external sub-programs used are defined here:
EXTRN VIDTYP : FAR, PUTSTR : FAR, WRCHAR : FAR
;────────────────────────────────────────────────────
DATA      SEGMENT
TEXT0     DB ' Output to Screen (Low Level).  Press any key...', 0
          .........
DATA      ENDS
;────────────────────────────────────────────────────
CODE      SEGMENT
          ASSUME   CS:CODE, DS:DATA
Start:    mov      ax,DATA  ;  data segment
```

```
            mov     ds,ax    ; basing
            ........
;─────────────────────────────────────────────────
;   The external sub-program PUTSTR is called here
;   The necessary parameters are passed through the common
registers.
            lea     si,TEXT0 ; DS:SI - address of beginning of text
            mov     ah,07h   ; attribute
            mov     cx,80    ; maximum length of string
            xor     dx,dx    ; beginning of screen output
            xor     bh,bh    ; video page number 0
            Call    PUTSTR   ; text string output
            xor     ah,ah    ; wait for a key to be pressed
            int     16h      ; read ASCII character into AL
            ........
;─────────────────────────────────────────────────
;   Finish the work and exit to MS DOS.
Exit:       mov     ax,4C00h ; return Code = 0
int         21h              ; exit to  MS-DOS
;──────────────────────────────────
CODE        ENDS
            END  Start
```

Now let's consider how the called sub-program must be shaped:

```
.MODEL   SMALL              ; SMALL memory model is used
.CODE
            PUBLIC  PUTSTR  ; entry point from caller
PUTSTR   PROC    FAR        ; PUTSTR is a FAR procedure
;─          save parameters passed through registers
            push    bx      ; save video page number
            push    cx      ; save length of string
            push    dx      ; save output address
            push    si      ;
            push    bp      ;
            push    es      ;
    ; The functional part of the subroutine goes here
            ........
;   Restoring registers and exit
Exit:       pop     es      ;
            pop     bp      ;
            pop     si      ;
            pop     dx      ; restore output address
            pop     cx      ; restore length of string
            pop     bx      ; restore address of string
            RETF            ; Return FAR
PUTSTR   ENDP
            END
```

This sub-program calls the functional sub-programs denoted by the

EXTRN statement. The sub-program contains one procedure which is defined as a FAR procedure (PROC FAR). When the sub-program gains control it saves the registers used in the stack.

The parameters are placed in the common registers: the address of the string - in DS:SI, the attribute of characters to be written - in AH, the video page number - in BH, the start position of the string on the screen - in DX (row number in DH and column number in DL). The maximum length of the string is placed in the CX register.

When the main part of the sub-program has been executed, the contents of the registers are restored and the RET operation is used to exit the sub-program.

Creating and Managing Object Libraries

An object library is a collection of object modules combined into a file where each module can be accessed separately. For example, rather than storing a number of individual program modules that perform various different kinds of screen output, you can include them all in an object library called VIDLIB.LIB. You can then pass the name of this library to a linker, which can then access all the modules contained in the library for resolving external references. This will be home ground to C, Pascal and FORTRAN programmers as it works according to the same principles as object libraries in these high-level languages.

We'll now remind you how to place PUTSTR into an object module library and how to edit the program PG0801 that uses this library.

First of all, the program must be compiled by your assembler:

```
MASM PUTSTR.ASM
```

If you are using MASM version 6.0 or 6.1, the name of the compiler should be ML instead of MASM. For Borland Turbo Assembler, the compiler's name is TASM. If the assembly process is successful, the object module PUTSTR.OBJ will appear in the current directory.

The new module can then be placed in the object module library (e.g., OBJLIB.LIB) by the special library server (LIB for MASM and TLIB for TASM):

```
LIB OBJLIB.LIB -+ PUTSTR.OBJ ;
```

The commands + allow you to delete an existing module with the same name from the library and add a new one.

The next step is to compile the main program PG0801.ASM and to start the link editor LINK (or TLINK if you are using Turbo Assembler). The name of the object module library OBJLIB.LIB is specified in the command line to tell the linker where to look for the entry points which correspond to the external subroutines used in the CALL instructions. The process of putting together objects located in different modules is known as resolving external references. The command line

```
LINK PG0801.OBJ ,,, OBJLIB.LIB ;
```

starts the linker and passes to it the names of the main module PG0801.OBJ and the object library OBJECT.LIB.

You will then obtain the executable file PG0801.EXE, where all the external references are resolved. You can start this program with the following command:

```
PG0801.EXE
```

Using the BAT-files from your program disk, explained in Chapter One, this process can be performed as follows:

1 Select the Assembler to be used (optional, not required if you have already used these BAT-files since DOS has been loaded):

```
AsmSw 6
```

2 Assemble the sub-program PutStr:

```
asm PutStr,PutStr
```

3 Put the object module of the sub-program into the object library (the directory containing the LIB utility must be included in the PATH list, otherwise you need to specify the full path to this utility in the command line):

```
LIB OBJLIB.LIB -+ PUTSTR.OBJ ;
```

4 Set up the environment variable to tell the linker where to look for the private object library:

```
set prlib=objlib.lib
```

5 Compile the main program:

```
asm pg0801
```

6. Link the object module of the main program with the subroutine included in the object library and run the executable module created:

```
run
```

Common Rules for Calling Assembler Sub-programs

The rules which apply to high-level program interfacing depend to a large extent on the high-level language used. The structure of assembler sub-programs and the method of accepting and returning parameters is specific to each language.

Sub-programs which neither accept nor return parameters from the main program can be called without any problem. You just need to make sure that your sub-program restores all the system resources used, most importantly the common registers - especially segment registers. Assembler sub-programs that do not have parameters can be used to perform certain tasks which do not require information from the main program while running, e.g:

1. Initializing non-standard devices such as modems, plotters or sound processors.

2. Performing certain pre-specified I/O operations such as generating a sound signal of fixed frequency and duration, outputting an initial picture onto the screen or locking the keyboard.

3. Performing a sequence of instructions using data located in fixed memory addresses.

Later in this chapter we'll consider how to call assembler sub-programs from programs written in BASIC, Pascal, FORTRAN and C/C++, but first we'll explain how to pass parameters and other information to the assembler sub-program. We'll concentrate on the method of passing information generally used in high-level languages - using the stack.

Passing Information From the Main Program

The information passed to a subroutine from a calling program is used to control how this subroutine functions and to provide initial data. This information usually consists of:

▲ The return address - where control must be returned to when the program finishes.

▲ The number of parameters - how many parameters are passed.

▲ The type of parameters - what these parameters are and how they are presented in the memory (e.g. WORD, BYTE etc.).

▲ The parameters themselves (passing by value) or their addresses (passing by reference).

There are a number of different techniques that can be used for passing parameters to a subroutine, but most high-level compilers use the stack. In practice, not all of the above components are always passed. Some of them are optional and can be used for debugging or for generating more effective code. For example, if the parameter passed is a character string, you can use the length of the string for creating more effective code. We'll illustrate this by taking two examples. The first is intended for processing ASCIIZ strings which are not accompanied by information about their length.

```
......
          mov    bx,0       ; BX-number of characters being processed
   TakeCh: mov    al,CharStr[bx]; load current character into AL
          cmp    al,0       ; zero character found?
          je     ContPgm    ; to next block of the program
          and    al,0DFh    ; convert character to uppercase
          inc    bx         ; increase counter - to next character
          jmp    TakeCh     ; process next character
   ContPgm:
......
```

We have assumed that the address of the string has already been accepted and placed into the CharStr variable before this part of the subroutine gains control.

Now let's look at how this task could be performed if the first byte of a string contained its actual length (this technique is used in some Pascal compilers):

```
      . . . . . .
        mov    bx,1      ; BX - number of character being processed
        mov    cl,byte ptr CharStr; actual length of string into CL
        mov    ch,0      ; clear high byte of CX (length < 256)
TakeCh:mov     al,CharStr[bx] ; load current character into AL
        and    al,0DFh   ; convert character to uppercase
        inc    bx        ; increase counter - to next character
        loop   TakeCh    ; process next character
ContPgm:
      . . . . . .
```

Note that the cycle which starts in the line labelled TakeCh contains only 4 instructions in the second example, while the first one included 6 instructions.

Another good reason for passing information about parameters is that the subroutine can use this information for switching between different parts of the sub-program. This technique allows you to perform such actions as using the same subroutine to process data represented in different forms, for example, as binary numbers and ASCII strings.

We'll now consider the elements of information passed to a sub-program.

The Components of the Parameter List

The return address is always stored on the stack and is used by the RET instruction to pass control to the instruction following the CALL instruction in the main program. This address, the next value of CS:IP, takes one or two words depending on how the sub-program is called - NEAR or FAR. The value is pushed automatically by the code in the calling instruction.

The number of parameters can be passed to check that all parameters really have been passed and that there are no extra ones in the CALL statement - the compiler's debugging features will detect errors, such as a run-time error if the number of parameters passed is incorrect. For example, many compilers can pass the actual length of an array to sub-programs then check whether the current value of an index is within the valid range. Processing additional information which is passed to a sub-program involves including further instructions in the calling program as well as in the subroutines which use this information. Although this makes programs significantly more reliable, it demands more space in the memory and it can considerably reduce the program speed. For this reason, this feature is optional in many compilers.

Parameter type information is also optional. However, if the high-level language compiler does pass this information, you can use it to detect an error if an unmatched parameter is passed. This happens more often than you might expect, since in most languages, values of different types, such as 2, 2.0 and '2', are represented in the memory in different ways and must be processed by different machine instructions. In some languages, for example Pascal, even constants '2' and '2.0' have different types - the first one is Char and the second one - String.

If your compiler passes this information, it also means you can check the type of parameter and choose the best way of processing it.

The addresses or values of parameters are passed every time parameters are presented in the high-level language statement CALL or its functional equivalent (some languages such as Pascal, Ada or Modula do not have a specific CALL statement). Parameters can be passed by their values - when the values of parameters are pushed onto the stack and by reference - when addresses of parameters (FAR or NEAR depending on the memory model used) are passed onto the stack.

Types of Sub-programs

There are many types of sub-programs in high-level languages, including subroutines, procedures, functions and modules. From the assembler programmer's point of view, the main difference between them is the way they accept and return parameters. We will now consider two main types of sub-program - procedures which do not return a value and functions which do.

High-level languages usually have a special statement for calling procedures. This is generally termed the CALL statement but some languages do not use a special denotation. For example in Pascal you can just write the name of the procedure to be called as a separate statement.

Functions are used in the same way as variables in expressions - you simply write the name of the function without using any special denotation. The value returned by the function is then used to calculate an expression. For example, the following string is a valid Pascal statement:

```
SUBR ( X, SIN(X) ) ;
```

This translates as: call the subroutine SUBR and pass two parameters to it, the first being the variable X and the second is - result returned by the function SIN called by parameter X. The following line represents the same statement, split into two separate statements:

```
Y = SIN(X) ; SUBR(X,Y) ;
```

The corresponding statement in BASIC is

```
CALL SUBR ( X, SIN(X))
```

Note that these statements give us no information about the type of variable X. It can be treated by the subroutine as a simple variable (such as an integer number), an array or even an external function without parameters. To avoid possible confusion, the variables used as parameters should have been defined explicitly in the calling program and subroutines.

As far as passing parameters is concerned, there is no difference between procedures and functions. They do differ however in the way they return control to the calling program. Functions perform one more action than procedures - they return a value. As an assembler programmer, you can simply treat this value as an additional output parameter which is returned in a special way. How this value is returned again depends on which high-level language is used and on the type of the value. For example, an integer number can be returned in a common purpose register (usually in AX) and the address of an array in a register or register pair depending on the memory model used.

Using the Stack to Pass Parameters in C and Pascal

As we said earlier, high-level language compilers pass parameters through the stack. We'll now concentrate on the structure of the stack when the sub-program gains control.

When a sub-program is called, the calling program performs the following sequence of actions:

Pushes the parameters
Pushes additional information such as the number of parameters
Pushes the return address
Passes control to the sub-program
Restores the stack once the program has finished

Note that the first two steps are optional. For example, there might not be any parameters in the CALL statement and a compiler might not provide any additional information for sub-programs called. The last step can be performed by either the calling program (like C/C++ compilers) or the subroutine (BASIC, Pascal and FORTRAN compilers). For example, the sequence of assembler instructions for calling an external procedure with 3 parameters A, B and C generated by the BASIC compiler would look like

```
push  A        ; push first parameter
push  B        ; push second parameter
push  C        ; push third parameter
call  ExtProc  ; external procedure call
```

while C compilers usually perform the same action in reverse:

```
push  C        ; push third parameter
push  B        ; push second parameter
push  A        ; push first parameter
call  ExtProc  ; external procedure call
;- 3 following instructions restore the stack pointer
pop   A
pop   B
pop   C
```

Note that the last three instructions perform two tasks. First, they restore the stack pointer so that its value is the same as before the procedure call. Second, they accept the value of the parameters which have been changed by the subroutine. If the subroutine does not return any values, these instructions can be replaced with one line:

```
add   sp,6
```

which simply restores the stack pointer without actually popping values from the stack. This technique is typical of C programs. Pascal and BASIC programs on the other hand require that sub-programs restore the stack pointer themselves. This means that if you are writing a subroutine "manually", you need to use the following instruction for returning to the calling program

```
ret   n
```

where n is the number of bytes additionally popped from the stack (i.e. simply the integer number to be added to the value in the SP register when returning from the subroutine). MASM 6.0 performs this task automatically when you use the extended form of the PROC directive.

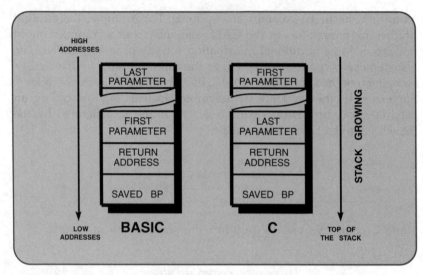

Figure 12.1
Passing Parameters Through the Stack - BASIC and C Conventions

In all these examples we have assumed that the parameters are passed by value and are no longer than one word. Figure 12.1 gives the typical stack contents on entry to the sub-program.

The return address can be a 16-bit address (an offset only) or a 32-bit address (both offset and segment). The addresses of the parameters can also take one or two words (NEAR or FAR addressing respectively). If the calling program provides any additional information, it can also be placed onto the stack.

The Stack Frame

We'll now take a closer look at what happens to the stack when pushing parameters. Figure 12.1 shows the contents of the stack after three parameters and the return address have been pushed. To make things as simple as possible we have assumed that the subroutine was called by the CALL NEAR instruction and that all parameters are one word long and that they are passed by value.

You can see that as soon as the CALL instruction has been performed, the return address is stored at memory location SS:[SP], the first parameter - at location SS:[SP+2], the second - SS:[SP+4] and the third - at location SS:[SP+6]. From now on, we can access them using these addresses. Note however that the value of the SP register changes when any values are pushed onto or popped from the stack. As a result, the offset of a parameter from the top of the stack will differ, depending on the number of PUSH and POP instructions performed.

The simplest way of solving this problem is to pop all the parameters and the return address from the stack, then store them in the memory area located within the subroutine for further use. Note that the return address is also popped, so the JMP instruction must be used instead of RET for returning from the program. Take the example below:

```
......
ExtProc  proc
......
         pop    RetAddr       ; extract and save return address
         pop    ParC          ; extract and save third parameter
         pop    ParB          ; extract and save second parameter
         pop    ParA          ; extract and save first parameter
......
;  procedure body goes here
......
         jmp    word ptr RetAddr; return to caller
......
ParA     dw     ?
ParB     dw     ?
ParC     dw     ?
RetAddr  dw     ?
......
ExtProc  endp
```

Although that is the simplest way, most high-level languages actually use a different method. The part of the stack that contains the parameters and the return address is considered as a separate area called the stack frame and is treated in a special way.

If you look at the assembler listing of a subroutine generated by a high-level compiler, you'll probably find that the two first instructions performed on entry to the subroutine are intended for saving the value of the BP register and copying the current value of SP into BP. For example, the description of the C procedure

```
Void Subr (int M, int L, int N) ;
```

is translated into the following assembler fragment:

```
_Subr    proc   far
         push   bp
         mov    bp,sp
```

After this operation, the stack frame contains (starting at the top, i.e. from higher to lower addresses):

▲ Parameters (or often, information about parameters - their values, addresses and any additional information).

▲ The return address (one or two words depending on the call type (NEAR or FAR).

▲ The saved BP value.

Objects located in the stack frame are then addressed through the SS:BP registers. If we apply this to the example we have just looked at, the third parameter can be denoted as [BP+4].

Note that the BP value is at the top of the stack frame. We will always assume that this value has already been pushed when the functional part of the sub-program starts. When the sub-program is compiled, high-level compilers generate the corresponding instructions automatically. Recent versions of Assembler actually have tools designed specifically for this purpose (the directives PROC and PROTO) which will be considered later in this chapter. If you are writing your assembler sub-program literally "by hand", i.e. without using any auxiliary tools, you should include instructions for saving the BP value at the beginning of the sub-program.

The size of memory required for storing the parameters depends on the memory model used. If you are using the LARGE memory model, the return address will take two words - one for the offset and one for the segment address. The parameter addresses also occupy doublewords. On SMALL or TINY memory models though, only offsets are passed, so each address only takes one word.

Note that the size of the stack frame can be changed manually. For example, if you decrease the value of the SP register immediately on entry to the procedure, the stack frame will be enlarged. Take the following example which shows how to allocate 10 extra bytes to the stack frame:

```
ExtProcL proc
         push  bp        ; save current BP value
         mov   bp,sp     ; address of stack frame
         sub   sp,10     ; move stack pointer to 10 bytes further
;              ten bytes starting at [bp-2] can be now used for internal
               variables
......
```

The extra space added can be used for the allocation of internal variables. In MASM 6.0 you can use the LOCAL directive for defining such variables.

Stack Frames in C and Pascal

Now let's have a closer look at the organization of the stack frame. As we have already explained, parameters can be pushed onto the stack in the same order as listed in the calling statement or in reverse order. When creating assembler subroutines, you need to know which of these methods are currently being used. Using MASM 6.0, you can define the calling conventions used in assembler procedures in MODEL and PROC directives. For example, the following directive

```
.model   small, C
```

tells the assembler that all the logical segments (DATA, CODE and STACK) are located within one physical segment and the C calling conventions will be used as default ones. You can change the default definition by specifying the calling conventions in the PROC directive, for example the directive

```
ProcPas   proc   far Pascal, A: byte, B: byte
```

states that the ProcPas procedure has two parameters and uses the Pascal calling conventions even if the MODEL directive defines another setting.

C and C++ compilers push parameters onto the stack in reverse order and generate instructions for restoring the stack pointer in the calling program. This allows you to vary the number of parameters from one procedure call to another. For example, the following calls of ExtProc, defined as a procedure with 3 parameters are valid.

```
......
ExtProg ;
......
Extprog (Par1) ;
......
Extprog (Par1, Par2) ;
......
Extprog (Par1, Par2, Par3) ;
......
```

Parameters in this case are usually addressed as [BP+displacement] where displacement depends on the memory model used. In this example, the parameter Par1 can be represented as [BP+4], Par2 - as

[BP+6] and Par3 - as [BP+8]. This means that the parameters that come first in the parameter list are always available for subroutines which follow the C/C++ calling conventions. Note that with Pascal, things are different since the offset of the first parameter from the top of the stack depends on the number of the parameters. In the example considered above, the first parameter would be represented as [BP+8], Par2 - as [BP+6] and Par3 - as [BP+4]. When only two parameters are passed, they would be addressed as [BP+6] (the parameter Par1) and [BP+4] (Par2).

Since the stack pointer in C programs is restored by the caller, the correct adjustment will always be made. The caller always "knows", how many parameters are actually passed, so it also knows the value to be added to the stack pointer after the CALL instruction has been performed. The only problem is how the called subroutine actually determines the number of parameters passed. One way this can be achieved is by analyzing the value of the first parameter.

Later on in the chapter we'll consider how the stack frame is organized for different memory models used by C compilers.

Returning Parameters to the Calling Program

As you might have expected, just as there are different ways in which sub-programs can accept parameters, there are also several techniques for returning them. Like input parameters, output parameters can be returned either by value, when the actual values of parameters are stored in registers, or memory or reference, when only the addresses are returned. All of these methods return parameters in one of the following ways:

▲ Through registers.

▲ Through the memory, which involves changing the memory area available to both the subroutine and the calling program.

▲ Through the stack - the most common way, which is also the technique used in high-level languages.

We'll now go over these methods in detail. Although returning parameters through registers might seem very limiting, it is widely used for creating Assembler - Assembler interfaces. This is because the performance of the subroutine is faster and it conveniently takes the least effort. Another important point about this method concerns writing the functions to be called from programs written in high-level languages. The function usually returns a value in a common purpose register (mostly in AX or the AX:DX pair if the value is 32-bit wide).

The next example shows the complete assembler text of the function TestAlt, to be used in Turbo Pascal programs for determining the state of the Alt key. This function returns 1 if this key is pressed or 0 if it has been released.

```
CODE      segment  word public
          assume   CS:CODE
          public   TestAlt  ; entry TestAlt is accessible from
                                other modules
TestAlt   Proc     far
          mov      ah,02h   ; function 02h - get keyboard flag
          int      16h      ; BIOS keyboard service
          and      al,8     ; allot bit 3
          mov      cl,3     ; shift to the right by 3 -
          shr      al,cl    ; bit 3 becomes bit 0
          ret               ; return to calling program
TestAlt   endp
CODE      ends
```

Later on in this chapter we'll consider a Turbo Pascal program which uses this subroutine. For now, simply note that the result is returned in the AX register.

The second way, returning parameters through the memory, has no special characteristics when it comes to accepting parameters. This concept is known as shared data.

The third way, using the stack, is used in programs written in high-level languages. MASM generates the corresponding instructions when you use an extended form of the MASM directive PROC for defining procedures with parameters and the INVOKE directive for calling procedures. Basically, parameters are addressed explicitly by the BP register or, when you use the MASM directives PROC, as a variable. Assembler will replace the addresses of these parameters with the corresponding expressions, for example [BP+4].

Using MASM 6.0 and 6.1 Tools for Interfacing

The most important aspect of interfacing modules written in different languages is ensuring that parameters are passed properly. Most high-level languages have built-in tools for interfacing with other languages, and assembler compilers also include such tools now. The assembler substitutes these directives for blocks of code that perform the routine operations common to all subroutines, such as setting up the stack and capturing the parameters.

When declaring a procedure with the assembler statement PROC you can specify additional information about the procedure, including

▲ Distance (NEAR or FAR) - this defines the call type.

▲ Visibility - this defines the area of the program the procedure can be called from; procedures that you intend to call from other modules must be declared PUBLIC (PUBLIC is the default value).

▲ List of registers used - if specified, an assembler program automatically generates instructions for saving the registers listed on entry to and restoring them on exit from the procedure.

▲ List of parameters - if specified, an assembler program allocates memory for parameters and generates instructions for extracting them so that you can use parameters as ordinary variables.

A single PROC statement can easily replace ten lines of source code.

Another useful feature of MASM 6.0 and higher is the directive PROTO. This can pass information to the assembler about the procedures before they are called, so that it can check the procedure calls for non-matching parameters.

The syntax of the PROC and PROTO directives is the same. The directive PROTO must be placed before segment directives and must precede the directive PROC for a corresponding procedure. It may be helpful to consider it as similar to a function declaration in C.

MASM 6.0 and higher also offers the INVOKE directive that performs the sub-program CALL. It looks like a CALL statement in high-level languages and contains the name of the procedure to be called and its parameter list. For example, to call the procedure SUBR with parameters A, B and C you would write:

```
INVOKE subr A, B, C
```

A possible form of the header for the procedure SUBR is:

```
subr  PROC  uses ax bx cx dx, A:dword, B:word, C:byte
```

In this case the assembler takes care of pushing and popping the appropriate values, leaving your sub-program free to treat the parameters as named variables. It is interesting to note the increasing number of high-level constructions that Microsoft have incorporated in later releases of MASM, of which INVOKE and the expanded PROC directive are some of the most useful.

Note that TASM supports the PROC directive but not the PROTO directive. There is an example of using the PROC directive for accepting parameters later in this chapter.

Data Types

Now that we have explained how to pass parameters to assembler programs, the next step is to consider how to process these parameters once they have been passed.

When processing data passed from high-level language programs, the most important thing you need to know is the correspondence between the data types of different languages. The type of parameters that are handed to the sub-program must be compatible with their declaration in that sub-program. The same assembler data type is treated in different ways not only by different languages, but also by different compilers for the same language. Table 12.1 shows the correspondence between data types in Assembler and Pascal for the three most common Pascal compilers.

MASM	Pascal (MS)	Pascal (Quick)	Pascal (Turbo)
BYTE	byte, char, boolean	Char, Boolean	Byte, Char Boolean
SBYTE		Byte,ShortInt	ShortInt
WORD	word	Word	Word
SWORD	integer2	Integer	Integer
REAL4	real, real4	Single	Single
SDWORD	integer4	LongInt	LongInt
FWORD	Real	Real	
REAL8	real8	Comp, Double	Double
REAL10	Extended	Extended	

Table 12.1
Correspondence Between Data Types (MASM - PASCAL)

As you can see, the types even differ slightly for different dialects of Pascal. Other languages, such as FORTRAN, use the same representation of data in different dialects. Table 12.2 shows the correspondence between data types for Assembler, C, FORTRAN and BASIC.

MASM	MS C/C++	MS FORTRAN	QuickBASIC
BYTE	unsigned char	CHARACTER*1, LOGICAL*1	
SBYTE	char	INTEGER*1	SINGLE*1
WORD	unsigned short, unsigned int		
SWORD	int, short	INTEGER*2	INTEGER(x %)
DWORD	unsigned long		
REAL4	float	REAL*4	SINGLE(x !)
SDWORD	long	INTEGER*4	LONG(x &)
FWORD			
REAL8	real8	REAL*8, DOUBLE PRECISION	DOUBLE(x #)
REAL10	long double		

Table 12.2
Correspondence Between Data Types (MASM - C/BASIC/ FORTRAN)

Tools

Passing Parameters From Microsoft BASIC and Pascal

All high level languages use a stack to pass information between the calling program and the assembler sub-program.

BASIC and Pascal push parameters (passed by value) or their addresses (passed by reference) onto the stack in the order listed by the sub-program CALL. For example, the following statement from a QuickBASIC program

```
QSOUND freq, durat
```

calls the external procedure QSOUND and passes to it two parameters which are defined by the statement

```
DECLARE SUB QSOUND (fr AS INTEGER, dur AS INTEGER)
```

as an integer variable one word long. The equivalent sequence of assembler directives and instructions would be:

```
......
     EXTRN      QSOUND
......
     push       freq
     push       durat
     call       far qsound
```

As a rule, QuickBASIC passes parameters by reference. The sub-program is called as a FAR procedure, which is why two words (segment and offset) are pushed onto the stack.

The following code shows an example of a main BASIC program COL which calls the assembler sub-program BCOLOR. This sub-program fills the screen with a specified color.

```
DECLARE SUB BColor (M AS INTEGER, N AS INTEGER, C AS INTEGER)

DEFINT A - Z

LineW  = 10
NumL   = 15
ColorW = 7

Call BColor (LineW, NumL, ColorW)

END
```

All high level languages form the stack contents and the sequence of machine instructions for calling the sub-programs automatically. Quick BASIC and MS-Pascal compilers perform this task in the following way:

- The FAR addresses of the parameters are pushed onto the stack in the order listed in the CALL statement.
- The address of the main program statement that follows the CALL statement is pushed onto the stack.
- The assembler sub-program is called by the CALL FAR instruction.

The sub-program BCOLOR is called from the main QuickBASIC program by the statement

```
Call BCOLOR (LineW, NumW, ColorW)
```

Its parameters (given in brackets) are :

- LineW - the number of the first string to be filled with the specified color.
- NumW - the number of the last string to be filled with the specified color.
- ColorW - the attribute of the background and character which the screen is to be filled with.

Figure 12.2, which shows the structure of the stack, should help you understand how parameters are passed.

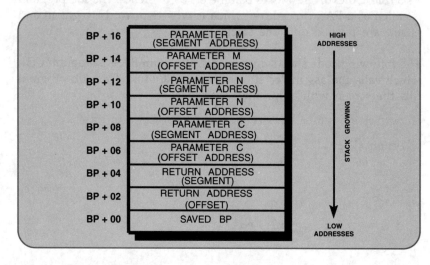

Figure 12.2
The Stack Structure for Pascal/Basic Calling Conventions

Accepting Parameters From QuickBASIC and Pascal

To understand the process of passing parameters according to Pascal conventions, lets look at an example of a subroutine which can be called from programs written in BASIC, Pascal or FORTRAN.

The text of the assembler sub-program BCOLOR is listed below:

```
 1 ;  ********************************************************
 2 ;  The PC screen input/output library Version 1.0
 3 ;  Subroutine for clearing the display screen
 4 ; (filling it with a specified color)
 5 ; Copyright (c): A.I.Sopin, Voronezh, Russia 1990 - 1991
 6 ;
 7 ;  This subroutine can be called from programs written
 8 ;  in MS QuickBASIC
 9 ;
10 ;  Type of parameters: Integer
11 ;
12 ;  Parameters:
13 ;
14 ;  M - first line to be cleared
15 ;  N - last line to be cleared
16 ;  Co - background and character attributes
17 ;
18 ; All parameters are passed by reference, through the stack
19 ;
20 ;  The FAR calls are used
21 ;  ********************************************************
22 ;
23 .model  medium
24   extrn color: far
25   public  bcolor
26 .code
27 bcolor proc  far basic uses ax bx cx dx,
28               M: word, N: word, Co: word
29        mov   bx,Co          ; address of Co into BX
30        mov   AX,[bx]        ; value of Co into AX
31        mov   ah,al          ; convert word into byte (<255)
32        mov   bx,M           ; address of M into BX
33        mov   CX,[bx]        ; value of M into CX
34        mov   ch,cl          ; convert word into byte (<255)
35        mov   bx,N           ; address of N into BX
36        mov   DX,[bx]        ; value of N into DX
37        mov   dh,dl          ; convert word into byte (<255)
38        Call  COLOR          ; call functional subroutine
39        RET                  ; return to caller
40 BCOLOR ENDP
41        END
```

The assembler procedure is defined as a FAR procedure (PROC FAR). Therefore the external procedure COLOR must also be declared FAR in the EXTRN statement. The assembler statement

```
PUBLIC BCOLOR
```

is used to tell the link editor that the procedure can be called from other modules. The registers used by the sub-program are saved on its entry and the base register BP is set at the top of the stack to access the parameters passed by the main program.

The instruction

```
mov    BX,Co
```

moves the address of the Co parameter into the BX register (see Figure 12.2). The operation

```
MOV    AX,[BX]
```

then loads AX with the value of the parameter. The other parameters are received in a similar way. The assembler sub-program COLOR, which clears the screen, is then called.

The stack contents must be restored when you return from the sub-program BCOLOR. If you use an extended form of the MASM PROC directive for passing parameters, Assembler generates the corresponding instruction automatically. You can then use the return instruction in its most simple form:

```
RET
```

A characteristic of BASIC and Pascal is that the called procedure restores the stack. This means that you must use the same number of parameters each time you call the sub-program.

Interfacing Conventions for Microsoft C/C++

You can also use assembler sub-programs with C, declaring them as external functions. The rules which apply to the C compiler for using the stack to pass parameters were considered earlier in this chapter. We do not intend to repeat them all here, but will give a brief list of the basic features of the C-Assembler interface:

▲ **1** The parameters passed to the called sub-program are pushed onto the stack, starting from the end of the parameters list. The first parameter is therefore on the top of the stack. This means you can use a variable number of parameters for the sub-program.

▲ **2** The stack contents are restored by the C program when the assembler sub-program returns control to it.

▲ **3** The C sub-programs are regarded as functions which may either return the function value or not (in which case they are declared void). If the function value is returned, it is moved to either the AX register or the register pair DX:AX.

▲ **4** The names of the assembler procedures and their entry points must begin with the underline symbol (_) because the C compiler puts this symbol before every external name. As with a lot of the other more tedious bits of house-keeping, MASM has directives to take care of this automatically.

▲ **5** Upper and lower case letters must be used carefully because the C compiler is case sensitive.

▲ **6** The names of the assembler program segments must be the same as those used by the C compiler. The easiest way to do this is to use the simplified MASM directive MODEL with the C option.

▲ **7** The size of the stack frame depends on the memory model used since addresses of parameters and the return address can occupy one or two words (NEAR or FAR references).

Modules created by Microsoft C++ use slightly different conventions for passing parameters. Since MASM supports C calling conventions in the PROC, INVOKE and PROTO directives, the easiest way to provide a C++/MASM interface in your programs is to specify "C" for assembler subroutines in C++ modules. You can use the standard C specifier in assembler modules. For example, an assembler subroutine specified in C as

```
extern int DOSCOM (char *Comand);
```

should be defined as follows in C/C++

```
extern "C" int DOSCOM (char *Comand);
```

The interface rules for Turbo C and Turbo C++ are the same as for Borland C and Borland C++. Fortunately, these rules are the same as for Microsoft C. However, if you create an object library, make sure that it only contains assembler modules. If you include an object module generated by a C/C++ compiler in your library, you will only be able to use this library with this particular compiler. This is because the C/C++ compiler inserts instructions for calling auxiliary modules from compiler libraries in the object modules. Furthermore, even if you are only using one compiler, you need to have several object libraries for different memory models since there are different rules for passing parameters. The difference is that addresses of parameters can be either 2-bytes (near addressing, where only the offset address is passed) or 4-bytes (FAR addressing, where both the segment and offset addresses of a parameter are passed). In this chapter we'll consider memory models used by C/C++ compilers. Note that the notion of memory models is used in several high-level languages and always has the same meaning. For example, in all languages the LARGE memory model includes several CODE and DATA segments.

The Microsoft C Memory Models

C/C++ has rapidly become the dominant language for applications development and, recognizing this, Microsoft have added a lot of features to MASM to make interfacing to C code easier. One characteristic feature of C and other high-level compilers that is now extensively supported by MASM is its use of memory models.

By specifying a particular memory model when compiling a program, you can control memory distribution for logical segments in a program (CODE, DATA and STACK) and the type of variables used for addressing (NEAR or FAR). The concept of memory models however is only applicable to computers with segment memory organization or those working under segment-oriented operating systems such as DOS. Operating systems able to use the entire available address space on 386/486 processors, for example OS/2 or UNIX, do not use the segment organization.

We have already noted that the segment size is 64 Kb and the memory address consists of two components: the segment and offset addresses. Direct addressing is only possible in one segment.

The C programming system has six standard memory models: TINY, SMALL, MEDIUM, COMPACT, LARGE and HUGE. There is one additional model for 32-bit unsegmented memory space - FLAT. The

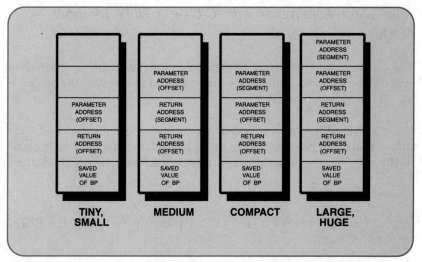

Figure 12.3
The Stack Structure for Different Memory Models (C/C++)

most significant differences in the main structure of C memory models are shown in the way data is passed onto the stack in Figure 12.3. It assumes that only one parameter is passed. This diagram will be useful for learning other high-level languages because the denotation of memory model is frequently used in programming languages for IBM-compatible computers.

The simplified assembler directives .MODEL, .CODE, .DATA and .STACK should be used when interfacing assembler programs. These directives are implemented in the MASM from version 5.0 and in all TASM versions to simplify the process of organizing the memory distribution in assembler programs. Using the wrong memory model in an assembler subroutine called from a high-level program can make the system crash.

For example, suppose that an assembler procedure that uses the memory model LARGE, is called from a C program using the memory model SMALL. In this case the return address, pushed onto the stack by the caller, is 2 bytes long (NEAR call, only the offset address is passed to the subroutine). The assembler procedure, however, will use the RETF instruction for returning to the caller. The FAR 4-byte address will be calculated using the two words at the top of the stack, the first of which is the offset component of the return address passed from the caller. However, the second one can have any meaning except the segment component of the return address, which is unfortunately the one we need. This particular case of bad luck is often referred to as "loss of control".

Interfacing Assembler with C/C++ - TINY Memory Model

The characteristic feature of this model is that both the program data and code are placed in the same segment, and as a result, the program size is no larger than 64 Kb.

Only NEAR addresses are used to access the program's data and code items. When the parameters are being passed, the stack frame is equal to [BP+4]. The assembler procedure is defined as a NEAR procedure:

```
PROC NEAR
```

You can return control to the calling program by using the RETN instruction.

Interfacing Assembler with C/C++ - SMALL Memory Model

This model is widely used in C programs. Two memory segments are used; one of them for program data and the other for code. The total program size must not be larger than 128 Kb. Only NEAR addresses are used to access the program's data and code items. The stack frame, the procedure type (NEAR), and the method of returning control are the same as for the TINY memory model.

The following example is a C program that calls the screen clear assembler sub-program (we looked at a similar QuickBASIC program earlier on)

The C program fragment is as follows:

```
...................................................................
extern void CCOLOR (int  M, int  N, int  C);
void main ()
{
static int   M = 1, N = 25, C = 0x07;
CCOLOR (M, N, C);   /*  set color and clear screen  */
return;
}
...................................................................
```

The assembler sub-program CCOLOR is given below:

```
;    ***************************************************************
;    The dialog system for PC screen input/output Version 1.0
;    Subroutine for clearing the display screen
;    (filling it with a specified color)
;    Copyright (c): A.I.Sopin,   Voronezh, Russia  1990 - 1991
;
;    This subroutine can be called from programs in C/C++
;    by the statement:
;
;    CALL CCOLOR (M,N,C)
;
;    Parameters must be defined in C program: int M, N, C
;
;    Parameters:
;
;    M  - first line to be cleared
;    N  - last line to be cleared
;    C  - background and character attributes
;
;    Parameters are passed  through the stack
;
;    ***************************************************************
          .MODEL    SMALL
EXTRN     COLOR : FAR
          .CODE
          PUBLIC   _CCOLOR
_CCOLOR   PROC   NEAR
          push   bp
          mov    bp,sp             ; address of top of stack
          push   ax                ; save
          push   bx                ; registers
          push   cx                ; used
          push   dx                ;
;─────────────────────────────────────
;  accept parameters passed
          mov    CH,[bp+4]         ; number of first line M
          mov    DH,[bp+6]         ; number of last line N
          mov    AH,[bp+8]         ; color+attribute  C
Call  COLOR       ; function subroutine call
;  restore registers and exit
          pop    dx
          pop    cx
          pop    bx
          pop    ax
          mov    sp,bp
          pop    bp
          RETN                     ; return (NEAR)
_CCOLOR   ENDP
          END
```

Table 12.3
The Stack Frame For C Calling Conventions (SMALL Model)

Address	Value
BP + 00	Saved BP value
BP + 02	Return address (offset)
BP + 04	The value of parameter M
BP + 06	The value of parameter N
BP + 08	The value of parameter C

The sub-program begins with a memory model that describes the directive:

```
.MODEL SMALL.
```

The next string defines the functional sub-program COLOR as external (EXTRN COLOR). The .CODE statement describes the next segment as a code segment.

The structure of the stack for this model is illustrated in Table 12.3.

The parameters' values are pushed onto the stack. As CCOLOR is a NEAR procedure, the return address consists of only one component - the offset. The stack frame begins with the address [BP+4]. You can exit the assembler sub-program by using the RETN command and the contents of the stack will be restored by the calling C program.

Note that although the procedure name (the name of the entry point) begins with the underline character:

```
_CCOLOR PROC NEAR
```

this character is not used in the C program statement that calls CCOLOR since it is added by the C compiler automatically.

It is important to be able to push parameter addresses as well as values on to the stack. As we have already said, this technique is known as passing parameters by reference. If addresses are pushed, the corresponding parameters must be defined as pointers in the function prototype.

The following example shows how the sub-program DOSCOM is called from a C program. DOSCOM processes an MS - DOS command that is passed as a character string by the C program. If the work is completed as normal, DOSCOM returns 0 in the AX register; if not, AX is equal to -1. The interrupt 2Eh is used to perform the command.

```
......
extern int  DOSCOM (char *Comand);
......
static char  COMSTR [81];
......
DOSCOM (COMSTR+1);        /* enter and process an MS-DOS command */
```

The first line in this example declares the sub-program DOSCOM as an external procedure with one parameter - an ASCIIZ string. The second line defines the C variable which will be used when calling the DOSCOM procedure. The last line is a C statement which calls the external procedure DOSCOM and passes to it the address of the second byte of the C string stored in the variable CONSTR.

Interfacing Assembler with C/C++ - MEDIUM Memory Model

When this model is used, the program code is placed in several segments. Since one segment (64 Kb of memory) is allocated for program data, program code can occupy up to 1 Mb of memory. The programs of this memory model therefore use FAR addresses to address code and NEAR addresses to address data.

The assembler procedure is defined as PROC FAR and uses the directive .MODEL MEDIUM. You can exit the procedure using the RETF instruction. The stack frame is equal to [BP+6].

Table 12.4 shows the structure of the stack:

Address	Value
BP + 00	Saved BP value
BP + 02	Return address (offset)
BP + 04	Return address (segment)
BP + 06	The value of parameter M
BP + 08	The value of parameter N
BP + 10	The value of parameter C

Table 12.4
*The Stack Frame
For C Calling
Conventions
(MEDIIUM Model)*

Address	Value
BP + 00	Saved BP value
BP + 02	Return address (offset)
BP + 04	The value of parameter M
BP + 06	The value of parameter N
BP + 08	The value of parameter C

Table 12.5
The Stack Frame For C Calling Conventions (COMPACT Model)

Interfacing Assembler with C/C++ - COMPACT Memory Model

This model works the opposite way round from the previous one: only one segment is allocated for program code, while program data occupies several segments (but no more than 1Mb of memory). NEAR addresses are used for code, and FAR ones for data. The assembler procedure is defined as PROC FAR and uses the directive .MODEL COMPACT. To exit it, use the RETN instruction. The stack frame is equal to [BP+4] and the structure of the stack is shown in Table 12.5.

This memory model is often used for creating programs that operate with large amounts of data, for example a simple text editor that must process large text files quickly.

Interfacing Assembler with C/C++ - LARGE Memory Model

This model is used for C programs that have a large amount of code and data. Several segments are used for both. The program data and code can each occupy up to 1 Mb of memory (in total up to 2 Mb) but no data item (e.g. an array) can be larger than 1 segment. Only FAR addresses are used. The assembler procedure is defined as PROC FAR and uses the .MODEL LARGE directive. To exit it, use the RETF instruction. The stack frame is equal to [BP+6] and the structure of the stack is shown in Table 12.6:

Address	Value
BP + 00	Saved BP value
BP + 02	Return address (offset)
BP + 04	Return address (segment)
BP + 06	The value of parameter M
BP + 08	The value of parameter N
BP + 10	The value of parameter C

Table 12.6
The Stack Frame For C Calling Conventions (LARGE Model)

Interfacing Assembler with C/C++ - HUGE Memory Model

This model is also used for writing C programs that have a large amount of code and data. It is similar to the LARGE model, except that there are no restrictions on the size of an array. Any data item that is larger than one segment is defined by a reserved word .HUGE. Only FAR addresses are used to address code and data. The assembler procedure is defined as PROC FAR and uses the directive .MODEL LARGE. To exit it use the RETF instruction. The stack frame is equal to [BP+6] and the structure of the stack is the same as for the LARGE model.

Using Built-in Assembler - C and Pascal Compilers

Possibly the way of employing an assembler routine in a high-level language program is to include assembler code in your program directly. For example, the most recent C and C++ compilers (Turbo C, Borland C, Microsoft C) allow you to include assembler instructions inside a C program using the key words asm (Turbo C) or asm (Microsoft C).

If more than one assembler command is used, the group of commands must be placed in brackets:

```
_asm {
assembler instructions
}
```

This technique works well when you only need to perform a few instructions (for example, for reading or changing one bit in the BIOS data area). However, it is not suitable for including hundreds of assembler instructions in your program.

Library

An Example of a QuickBASIC-Assembler Interface

Now let's consider a program which uses MASM tools for high-level interfacing. As you know, the MASM directives PROTO and PROC can make creating assembler sub-programs easier by automatically generating a sequence of saving/restoring registers and by accepting parameters. The sub-program QSound, which is designed to create sound effects in programs written in QuickBASIC, demonstrates how to use the MASM directives for interfacing. The full assembler text of the sub-program QSound is given in Listing 12.1, the text of the QuickBASIC calling program - in Listing 12.2.

```
 1
 2    page 55,132
 3  .model  medium,BASIC
 4  ;=== This generates the statement PROTO for MASM 6.0 or PUBLIC
    for others
 5  IFDEF ?? VERSION
 6  public   QSound
 7           ELSEIF @version EQ 600
 8   QSound  PROTO BASIC freq: PTR WORD, durat: PTR WORD
 9           ELSE
10   public  QSound
11           ENDIF
12  ;===     Data segments
13  .data
14  Nticks   dw  0                ; number of ticks for delaying
15  ;===     Code segment
16  .code
17  QSound   PROC BASIC uses ax bx cx dx es di, freq: PTR WORD,
18                  durat: PTR WORD
19  ;===     accept the parameter DURAT (sound duration)
20           mov ax,5000 ; default value for DURAT is 5 seconds
21           mov bx,durat      ; address of DURAT into ES:BX
22           mov bx,[bx]       ; value of DURAT into BX register
23           cmp bx,0          ; compare DURAT to 0
24           je  Accept        ; skip illegal value of DURAT
25           cmp ax,5000       ; compare DURAT to 5000
26           jg  Accept        ; skip illegal value of DURAT
27           mov ax,bx         ; load DURAT into AX
28  ;=== convert DURAT value into timer ticks ( Tics = Msecs * 91 /
        5000)
29  Accept:  mov Nticks,ax     ; save value of DURAT in memory
30  ;=== modify the latch of the timer channel 0 (10 times faster)
31           mov al,00110110b
32           out 43h,al
33           mov ax,1193       ; latch value-1/10 of generator freq.
34           out 40h,al        ; send low byte of latch value
35           mov al,ah         ; prepare for sending high byte
```

```
36              out .40h,al           ; send high byte of latch value
37  ;=== accept the parameter FREQ (sound frequency)
38              mov bx,freq           ; address of frequency into ES:BX
39              mov di,[bx]           ; value of frequency into DI
40              cmp di,0              ; is zero frequency requested?
41              jg  Sound            ; if not, generate sound
42  ;=== zero frequency - disable sound
43              in  al,61h            ; read speaker port content
44              and al, not 00000011b; set bits 0 and 1 of port 61h to 1
45              out 61h,al            ; turn speaker off
46              jmp ToTicks           ; wait for time defined by DURAT
47  ;=== program channel 2 of Programmable Timer for sound generation
48  Sound: mov al,10110110b           ; channel 2, write lsb/msb,
49              out 43h,al            ; operation mode 3, binary
50              mov dx,12h            ; store 12 34DCh (1 193 180) into
51              mov ax,34dch          ; DX:AX for DIV command (divident)
52              div di                ; obtain frequency divisor
53              out 42h,al            ; send low byte of divisor
54              mov al,ah             ; prepare for sending high byte
55              out 42h,al            ; send high byte of divisor
56  ;=== turn the sound on
57              in  al,61h            ; read speaker port content
58              or  al,00000011b      ; set bits 0 and 1 of port 61h to 1
59              out 61h,al            ; turn speaker on
60  ;=== get current time (the number of ticks since midnight)
61  ToTicks:mov ax,40h        ; address of BIOS data segment into AX
62              mov es,ax         ; ES will point to BIOS data segment
63  ;=== calculate when the sound is turned off
64              mov bx,es:[6Ch]       ; low part of ticks number into BX
65              add bx,Nticks         ; add DURAT to that low part value
66              mov dx,es:[6Eh]       ; save high part of ticks number
67  ;=== wait for the obtained number of ticks defined by the DURAT
               parameter
68  Delay: cmp es:[6Eh],dx; has high part of time counter changed?
69              jne IsTime            ; if so, assume that time has gone
70              cmp es:[6Ch],bx       ; has time gone?
71              jb  Delay             ; if not, continue to wait
72  ;== turn the speaker off
73  IsTime: in  al,61h               ; read speaker port contents
74              and al, not 00000011b ; set bits 0 and 1 of port 61h to 1
75              out 61h,al            ; turn speaker off
76  ;==restore the latch of timer channel 0 (default value is 0FFFFh)
77              mov al,00110110b
78              out 43h,al
79              mov al,0FFh    ; this is low byte of value 65535
80              out 40h,al     ; send low byte of latch value (65535)
81              out 40h,al     ; send high byte of latch value (65535)
82  ;=== return to caller
83              ret
84  QSound endp
85              end
```

Listing 12.1 QSound - An Example of a Sub-program for QuickBASIC Programs

```
1
2 DECLARE SUB QSound (fr AS INTEGER, dur AS INTEGER)
3
4 DEFINT A - Z
5
6 FOR i = 1 TO 26
7      durat = 500
8      IF (i < 7) OR (i > 7 AND i < 10) OR (i > 10 AND i < 13) THEN
       durat = 250
9      IF i > 13 THEN durat = 250
10     IF i = 26 THEN durat = 1000
11     READ freq
12     Call QSound (freq, durat)
13 NEXT i
14 STOP
15
16 DATA 330, 294, 262, 294, 330, 330, 330, 294, 294, 294
17 DATA 330, 392, 392, 330, 294, 262, 294, 330, 330, 330, 330
18 DATA 294, 294, 330, 294, 262
19 END
```

Listing 12.2 Mary - Calling an Assembler Program from QuickBASIC

The calling QuickBASIC program defines arrays which contain the frequency for a sequence of sounds. It calls the sub-program QSound 26 times so that it generates a sequence of 26 sounds. The frequency of each sound is defined by the corresponding element of the DATA block. Recognize the tune? It's the same one that Edison used for testing his first phonograph - "Mary had a little lamb".

Note that the sub-program QSound does not contain instructions for saving and restoring registers. Also, it uses actual names for parameters rather than constructions such as dword ptr [BP+4]. The parameter values are obtained using the following technique:

▲ The parameter's offset address is placed into the BX register.
▲ The instruction mov bx,[bx] loads the parameter value into BX (you can use any available register for this purpose).

The main part of the sub-program QSound is a variation on the subject considered in Chapter Ten "Controlling The Hardware". Note that the value of the sound signal's duration is passed to the sub-program as a number of milliseconds. The sub-program reprograms channel 0 of the timer to generate 1000 timer ticks per second instead of the standard 18.2 ticks per second. In some cases this can have unexpected effects (unfortunately not only sound effects). For example, suppose that you have written a TSR program that intercepts the timer interrupt 1Ch (we gave an example of such a program in Chapter Eleven); when the timer has been reprogrammed, the interrupt 1Ch will be generated 1000 times per second. This might cause a problem on very slow machines, in which case you will have to add a special block to the sub-program QSound. This will intercept the interrupt 1Ch on entry to the sub-program and restore the original interrupt vector on exit. The new handler of the interrupt 1Ch will calculate how many times it has been called; for 9 calls it will do nothing (i.e. it performs the instruction IRET) but after the 9th call it will clear the counter and pass control to the previous handler. Another possible problem with the timer is that some operating systems (e.g. Windows), do not allow the user to reprogram the timer so don't be surprised if this program does not work properly under Windows.

AltState - Keyboard Access From Pascal Using Assembler

Although Turbo Pascal allows programmers to use several machine resources directly from Pascal programs (including I/O ports and absolute memory locations), there are still some very good reasons for using assembler subroutines in Pascal programs.

Firstly, most Pascal compilers such as Turbo Pascal, Quick Pascal, Top Speed Pascal and so on use the same Pascal language (or, at least most of them use the standard Pascal) but their extended features may be different. Some Pascal compilers allow you to include assembler statements directly. However if you try to run your program under another compiler, you should not be surprised to learn that it does not work.

The second reason is that C/C++, Pascal, BASIC, and FORTRAN programs make extensive use of assembler subroutines. To use these libraries in Pascal programs, it is much easier to write a small module to accept parameters from a Pascal program, pass them to an assembler subroutine and then call that assembler subroutine rather than rewrite all assembler modules for direct use in Pascal programs.

The third reason, which is often considered the primary one, is probably obvious. That is, using assembler subroutines lets you economize on memory and time, meaning that some programs can run as much as ten times faster.

Having covered the theory, lets see how it all falls into place in practice by taking an example of a Turbo-Pascal - Assembler interface. Our example includes a simple Pascal program which calls an external function, written in Assembler, which checks and reports on the state of the Alt key on the keyboard. Since the rules for using assembler subroutines in Pascal programs are slightly different from those used in C compilers, let's look at the example given in more detail. The full Pascal text of the calling program is given in Listing 12.3.

```
Program PTstAlt ;
Uses Crt, AsmLink ;
Begin
Writeln ; Writeln
('The demo program showing the link between Turbo Pascal and
Assembler' ) ;
Writeln ( 'V.B.Maljugin, 1992, Voronezh, Russia' ) ;
Writeln ; Writeln ('Determining the state of the ALT key on the
keyboard' ) ;
If TestAlt Then Writeln ('The Alt key is DOWN')
Else Writeln ('Alt key is UP') ;
Writeln ('Press the ALT key and hold it for not less than 5 seconds') ;
Delay (5000) ;
If TestAlt Then Writeln ('The Alt key is DOWN')
Else Writeln ('Alt key is UP') ;
Writeln ('Release the ALT key and press ENTER to finish the
program');
Readln;
End.
```

Listing 12.3 PTstAlt - Turbo Pascal Assembler: The Main Program

This program performs a relatively simple task.The only peculiarity is that it employs the USES statement to declare the external library containing the function TestAlt written in Assembler. Note that the USES statement contains the declaration of a special interface unit rather than the function TestAlt itself. The text of this interface unit is given in Listing 12.4.

```
Unit AsmLink ;
interface
Function TestAlt: Boolean;
Implementation
{$L TestAlt}
Function TestAlt; external;
End.
```

Listing 12.4 AsmLink -Turbo Pascal Assembler: The Interface Unit

As we mentioned in Chapter Two, compilers usually generate an intermediate form of machine code (an object module) for a procedure that has been translated separately. Unlike most compilers, Turbo Pascal stores such modules as files with an extension .TPU (Turbo Pascal Unit). The first line of text in Listing 12.4 tells the compiler that this program is a program unit rather than a main program and hence cannot be run directly.

The next line marks the beginning of the INTERFACE section of the program unit. This section describes the procedures and functions included in this unit and specifies their parameters. In our example, the program unit contains only one function which is specified in the line following the INTERFACE directive. As a rule, the functions and procedures listed in the INTERFACE section of a program unit must be specified exactly as they are in the actual Pascal program. In practice this simply means that you must specify the headers of functions and procedures included in this unit.

The directive IMPLEMENTATION begins the part of the program unit that contains the text of all procedures and functions included. The statement

```
{$L TestAlt}
```

includes the object module Testalt.obj as a part of the code generated by the Turbo Pascal compiler. The next statement

```
Function TestAlt; external;
```

specifies the function TestAlt as external which means that the compiler must search for the corresponding object module and include it in the generated code. Note that if you want to use the object code of the program unit (the .TPU file) at a later date, you can save it using the Turbo Pascal compiler (the TPC.EXE program) or by switching the DESTINATION option in the COMPILE menu to DISK.

We can now move on to considering the text of the assembler function that will be called from the Pascal program.

```
CODE      segment word public
          assume  CS:CODE
          public  TestAlt   ; entry TestAlt is accessible
                            ; from other modules
TestAlt   Proc far
          mov ah,02h    ; function 02h - get keyboard flag
```

```
            int  16h       ; BIOS keyboard service
            and  al,8      ; only bit 3 (ALT pressed) is needed
            mov  cl,3      ; shift to the right by 3 - bit 3 becomes bit 0
            shr  al,cl     ; bit 3 becomes bit 0
            ret            ; return to calling program
TestAlt  endp
CODE     ends
         end
```

Listing 12.5   TestAlt - Turbo Pascal Assembler: The Assembler Function

First of all, the assembler directive ENTRY defines the entry point TestAlt, which is followed by the text of the procedure itself. Since this procedure is designed to be called from a Turbo Pascal program, it must return the result in the AX register. The TestAlt procedure uses the BIOS keyboard service "Get Keyboard Status" (function 02h of interrupt 16h) for reading the Keyboard State Flag into the AL register. The procedure then selects bit 3 of this flag (which corresponds to the status of the Alt key) and shifts the content of AL to the right by 3 bits. The resulting value can be now returned to the calling Pascal program as a value of type Logical.

GetScan - Turbo Pascal Function Returning Parameters

This example shows the technique of passing parameters to, and returning them from, assembler subroutines called from Turbo Pascal programs. The Pascal text of the main program is given in Listing 12.6.

```
Program AsmT ;
Uses Crt, Pasasm ;
Var Rdkey: Byte ; IndSpec: Boolean ;
Begin
Writeln ('Turbo Pascal - MASM interfacing') ;
Writeln ; Writeln ('Press ESC key to exit or other to continue ') ;
Writeln ;
Repeat
    Writeln ; Write ( 'Enter character ' );
    RdKey := GetScan(':', IndSpec) ;
    Write (' (', RdKey, '), the indicator of a special key is "',
        IndSpec, '".' );
Until RdKey = 27 ;
End.
```

Listing 12.6   AsmT - Returning Parameters to Turbo Pascal - The Main Program

The program shown reads a key using the DOS keyboard service and sets the indicator when a special key such as a function key or cursor control key is pressed. The character ">" is passed to the procedure by value and parameter IndSpec is returned from the procedure by reference. The sequence of instructions which correspond to the Pascal statement

```
RdKey := GetScan('>', IndSpec) ;
```

is given as follows:

```
mov   al,offset ':'        ; prompt character into AL
push  ax                   ; push value of first parameter
mov   di,Offset IndSpec    ; offset of second parameter
push  ds                   ; push segment of second parameter
push  di                   ; push offset of second parameter
call  far GETSCAN          ; call external subroutine
mov   RdKey,al             ; take result of function
```

This is the assembler equivalent of the Pascal function call.

The Pascal text of the program unit which defines the interface to the external procedure GetScan is given in Listing 12.7.

```
Unit PasAsm ;
interface
Function GetScan (TextPrompt:Char; Var SpecInd:Boolean): Byte ;
Implementation
{$L GetScan}
Function GetScan; external;
End.
```

Listing 12.7 PasAsm - Returning Parameters to Turbo Pascal - The External Unit

Since this program unit is the same as that described in the previous section, let's move straight on to the assembler code of the procedure GetScan.

```
1
2 code segment word public
3 public GetScan
4 assume    cs:code
5 GetScan Proc far pascal, Prompt: byte, SpInd: far ptr byte
6     mov   ah,02
7     mov   dl,Prompt
8     int   21h
9     les   bx,SpInd       ; effective address of SpInd into ES:BX
```

```
10      mov    byte ptr es:[bx],0 ; SpInd := False
11      mov    ah,01h       ; function 01h - accept character
12      int    21h          ; DOS service call
13      cmp    al,0         ; special key pressed?
14      jne    ExSubr       ; if not, return to caller
15      mov    byte ptr es:[bx],1 ; SpInd := True
16      int    21h          ; DOS service call
17 ExSubr: ret              ; return to calling program
18 GetScan endp
19 code    ends
20      end
```

**Listing 12.8   GetScan - Returning Parameters to Turbo Pascal -
The Assembler Subroutine**

The procedure uses simplified MASM directives for generating start
and finish code.

The input parameter Prompt can be read directly from the stack. Its
offset from the beginning of the stack frame is 10 and this parameter
can be addressed using the technique considered in this chapter as
[BP+10]. Note that the parameter SpInd is defined as a FAR reference
in accordance with the rules for passing parameters in Turbo Pascal.

DosCom - Using Assembler for Calling DOS

The program CComm passes the command line entered by the user
to the main copy of the command processor. We are looking at this
program here as an example of passing parameters to an assembler
sub-program in accordance with C conventions. The text of the main
C program CComm is given in Listing 12.10.

```
 1
 2 /************************************************************
 3 *
 4 *  Issuing an MS-DOS command from within a C program
 5 *
 6 *  Author: A.I.Sopin, Voronezh University, Voronezh, Russia  1992
 7 *
 8 *  External functions used (the C60S.LIB library):
 9 *
10 *  DIAM04,  CCOLOR, WINC07, DOSCOM
11 *
12 ************************************************************/
13
14 #include <stdio.h>
15 #include <dos.h>
```

```
16
17 extern void CCOLOR (int  M, int  N, int  C);
18 extern void DIAM04 (int OP, int M, int N, char *Tp, int L, int U,
                       int V,
19                     int *Qp, int *Sp, unsigned char *Wp, char *Ip);
20 extern void DIAM24 (unsigned char *Wp);
21 extern int  DOSCOM (char *Comand);
22 extern void WINC07 (int M, char *T, int L, int V, int *Q, int *S,
                       char *W,
23                     char *I, int RL, int RR);
24
25 union  REGS  regs;
26
27 void main ()
28
29 {
30 static int  Q, S, j;
31 static unsigned  char W[4];
32 static char TEXT23[]={"Enter command line or press ESC to exit"};
33 static char  TEXT1 [ ] ={  "Input and process an MS-DOS command  "
34                      " Author: A.I.Sopin,  Voronezh, 1992  " };
35 static char  COMSTR [81];
36 /*---------------------------------------------------------*/
37 /*  Input a command line                                   */
38
39    *(W+1) = 0;               /* clear the code of the key pressed */
40    while (1)                 /* permanent cycle (wait for key)    */
41    {
42    CCOLOR (1, 25, 0x07);     /* clear screen and set up color */
43    DIAM04 (1, 1, 1, TEXT1, 80, 0, 0, &Q, &S, W, 0);
44    DIAM04 (1, 23, -23, TEXT23, 80, 24, 2, &Q, &S, W, 0); .
45    for (j = 1; j <= 79; j++).*(COMSTR + j) = ' ';/* clear command
46                                               line buffer */
47
48    *COMSTR = '>';                /* output command prompt        */
49    WINC07 (24, COMSTR, 80, 2, &Q, &S, W, 0, 2, 80);
50    if (*(W+1) == 1)  break;  /* Esc - end of program's work    */
51 /*---------------------------------------------------------*/
52 /* Processing the command entered  (ESC - exit)            */
53    DOSCOM (COMSTR+1);/* enter and process an MS-DOS command    */
54    DIAM04 (1, 25, -25, "Press any Key (Esc -Exit)",
55    80, 0, 0, &Q, &S, W, 0);
56    DIAM24 (W);                 /* waiting for a key to be pressed*/
57    if (*(W+1) == 1)  break;  /* Esc - exit program            */
58    } /* End  while (*(W+1) != 1) */
59 /*---------------------------------------------------------*/
60 /* Completion of the work (after pressing Esc)             */
61     exit (0);
62 } /* End  main */
63
```

Listing 12.9 CComm - The Main C Program

The main C program calls the sub-program DosCom defined in the statement

```
extern int  DOSCOM (char *Comand);
```

and passes to it an address of the character string containing the DOS command to be executed. This has the same effect as if you typed that command on the keyboard at the DOS prompt. The assembler subroutine DOSCOM passes this text to the main copy of the command processor using the undocumented DOS service "execute command" available through interrupt 2Eh. This can also be done with the help of the standard C procedure for executing a program, but this program uses the primary copy of the command processor and the master copy of the system environment.

```
 1
 2 ;   **********************************************************
 3 ;
 4 ;   Screen input/output interactive system for PC.  Version 1.4
 5 ;
 6 ;   Input MS DOS command processing
 7 ;
 8 ;   Author:  I.A.Sopin  Voronezh, 1991.
 9 ;
10 ;   Specified in C program as
11 ;
12 ; int near  DOSCOM (char near *Comand)
13 ;
14 ;   Parameter:
15 ;
16 ;   char near  *Comand  - ASCIIZ string containing the DOS command
17 ;
18 ;   Parameters are passed by reference through the stack.
19 ;
20 ;
21 ;
22 ;
23 ;   **********************************************************
24    .MODEL   SMALL, C
25    PUBLIC   DOSCOM
26    .CODE
27
28 DOSCOM  PROC  NEAR C uses BX CX DX SI DI DS ES, AddrStr: word
29 ;
30 ;----------------------------------------
31 ;  Receive parameters from the PARM list:
32        mov  si,AddrStr
33 ;----------------------------------------
34 ;  Define the command length and pass its text contents
35        xor   bx,bx              ; clear length counter
```

```
36       mov    ax,cs          ;
37       mov    es,ax          ;
38       lea    di,COMAND+1    ; output buffer address
39       mov    cx,129         ; loop counter
40 M0:   lodsb                 ;
41       and    al,al          ; end of MS DOS command text?
42       jz     M1             ; execute the command
43       stosb                 ; move DS:SI -> ES:DI
44       inc    bx             ; process the next character;
45       loop   M0             ; goto the beginning of the loop
46       mov    ax,-1          ; error code
47       jmp    Exit           ; exit on error
48 ;-----------------------------------------------------------
49 ; MS DOS command execution (int 2Eh)
50 M1:   mov    byte ptr ES:[di],0dh ; move CR code to buffer
51       mov    CS:COMAND,bl   ; store command length
52       mov    CS:SSKEEP,SS   ; save SS register
53       mov    CS:SPKEEP,SP   ; save SP register
54       mov    ax,cs          ;
55       mov    ds,ax          ; path segment address
56       lea    si,COMAND      ; SI - path string offset
57       int    2eh            ; command execution
58       mov    SS,CS:SSKEEP   ; restore SS contents
59       mov    SP,CS:SPKEEP   ; restore SP contents
60       xor    ax,ax          ;
61 ;-----------------------------------------------------------
62 ; Pop registers and exit
63 Exit: RET
64 ;-----------------------------------------------------------
65 ; Data in the code segment
66 SSKEEP DW   0              ;  Stack segment contents
67 SPKEEP DW   0              ;  SP contents
68 COMAND DB   0              ;  the command length
69        DB   128 dup (?)    ;  the command text
70 DOSCOM ENDP
71        END
```

Listing 12.10 DosCom - An Assembler Sub-program Receiving Parameters by Reference

This subroutine can be called from programs written in Microsoft C/ C++, Turbo C/C++ and Borland C++. However, you need to use different object libraries in each case. For this reason, your program disk contains the following versions of object libraries:

C60S.LIB - Microsoft C/C++ (Model SMALL)
BCS.LIB - Turbo C/C++ and Borland C/C++

Summary

This chapter explained how to use assembler sub-programs while creating complex programs in high-level languages. We have concentrated on the calling conventions used in Microsoft C and Pascal because the conventions used in other high-level languages are usually similar to one or the other.

The most important thing you must do when programming in more than one language is ensure that you pass data and control between program units correctly. We discussed the main ways of passing parameters to an assembler sub-program and showed that using assembler tools such as the directives PROC, PROTO and INVOKE is probably the most effective method.

Assembler sub-programs can significantly increase the power and flexibility of your programs. This is because Assembler performs the following actions:

▲ Increases the overall speed by creating fast sub-programs for the critical parts of the program; this feature is often used in maths intensive programs

▲ Controls peripherals in a non-standard way; this allows you to create exciting graphic images and sound effects which are not possible using the BIOS and DOS services or high-level language libraries

▲ Accesses hardware that either has no DOS device drivers at all or has DOS device drivers which are not completely satisfactory.

You can also use assembler programming techniques without using Assembler itself. Most high-level language compilers such as C and Pascal allow you to include machine instructions directly in the program text. By using this feature, you can create mixed-language programs without separating them into more than one module.

Now that you've got to the end of this book, we hope that you will continue in the exciting world of assembler programming and benefit from the power it offers to all those who learn an assembly language - the native language of computers.

APPENDIX A

Number Systems

This appendix is designed to give you a short introduction to binary and hexadecimal numbers.

Decimal as a Positional Number System

Most readers are probably familiar with the binary system as well as the decimal one, in which case you can pass straight on to the hexadecimal system. If you're not entirely sure of the binary system however - read on.

As you know, the decimal number 1993 is made up of one thousand, nine hundreds, nine tens and three ones which can be written as follows

1000's	100's	10's	1's	Adding
1	9	9	3	Columns
1000	900	90	3	1993

For a negative number -15 we have :

1000's	100's	10's	1's	Adding
0	0	-1	-5	Columns
0	0	-10	-5	-15

As you can see, in the number 1993, the first and second digits are both equal to 9, but the first means nine hundreds and the second - nine tens. So the meaning of every decimal digit in a decimal number is determined not only by its value, but also by its position. That's why the decimal system is called **positional,** and has a counting base of ten.

The Binary System

Although people can work quite happily with the decimal system, it's not that well suited to electronic equipment. As a rule, the elements of such machinery can only have two states: "on" or "off". It follows that another system is needed for the internal representation of numbers in electronic devices. This system has to possess two numerals, one of which can be represented by "0" and the other by "1".

Like decimal, binary is a positional number system that follows the same simple arithmetic rules.

In binary, 10 does not mean *ten*, but *two*, because it is equal to 1x2 + 0x2. The binary number 1001 is thus:

8's	4's	2's	1's	In
1	0	0	1	Decimal
8	0	0	1	9

While 11001101 is:

128's	64's	32's	16's	8's	4's	2's	1's	Equal
1	1	0	0	1	1	0	1	To
128	64	0	0	8	4	0	1	205
2^7	2^6	2^5	2^4	2^3	2^2	2^1	2^0	

The new line at the bottom of this table shows how all the number positions are calculated from powers of 2, but with the power always being one less that of the column number. This is the reason why in programming the first bit is bit 0 not, 1.

It should now be easy for our new binary experts to add the numbers after 11 to the following table:

Decimal	Binary	Decimal	Binary
0	0	6	110
1	1	7	111
2	10	8	1000
3	11	9	1001
4	100	10	1010
5	101	11	1011

Table A : Binary and Decimal Representation of the First 12 Non-negative Numbers

| 0 + 0 = 0 | 1 + 0 = 1 | 0 x 0 = 0 | 1 x 0 = 0 |
| 0 + = 1 | 1 + 1 = 10 | 0 x 1 = 0 | 1 x 1 = 1 |

Table B : Binary Addition and Multiplication Tables

Binary arithmetic is extremely simple; the addition and multiplication tables are especially good news.

With binary numbers, the counting base used is not usually indicated. Faced with a fairly long number consisting of ones and zeros, you should guess that it's binary! When it is necessary to draw attention to the fact that a counting base of 2 is being used, the binary number is followed by the letter **b**. For example, the number 5 can be represented as 101b or 101B. To avoid any confusion, we will usually indicate which counting system is being used (except when it is decimal).

Carrying in addition, and borrowing in subtraction, operate the same way as in decimal.

Converting Binary to Decimal and Vice Versa

The easiest way to convert binary to decimal is to divide the number up into its respective columns as we did in the tables above, multiply it out, and add up the result. There are several ways of doing the reverse though. The most straightforward is to divide the integer by two and take the remainder as the first digit of the corresponding binary number. Now divide the quotient by 2, and take the remainder as the next digit. You then repeat this process until the quotient equals 0.

Converting decimal 20 to binary is shown in Table C. So, writing down the remainders, reading from right to left you get 10100b.

Dividend	20	10	5	2	1
Divisor	2	2	2	2	2
Quotient	10	5	2	1	0
Remainder	0	0	1	0	1

Table C : Converting Decimal to Binary

Hexadecimal System

The binary system is used for the internal representation of numbers in computers. When we want to represent these binary numbers outside the computer, the most convenient form is hexadecimal. The main advantage of the hexadecimal system is how easily it translates from binary, and its similarity to decimal, making it more intuitive for those of us who grew up with base ten. Unfortunately it is only similar, and not identical to decimal, and does require some learning. As you will also see, another great advantage of the hexadecimal system is its economy relative to binary - it is a shorthand binary. The hexadecimal system and numbers are often referred to as simply "hex", so, in keeping with popular trends, we'll do the same.

The **hexadecimal system** deals with powers of 16 (sixteen) and consequently must have 16 numerals denoting numbers from zero to fifteen. These numerals are represented by the numbers 0, 1, 2, 3, 4, 5, 6, 7, 8, 9 and letters A, B, C, D, E, F (see Table D).

Decimal Numbers	0 1 2 3 4 5 6 7 8 9 10 11 12 13 14 15
Hexadecimal Numbers	0 1 2 3 4 5 6 7 8 9 A B C D E F

Table D : Hexadecimal Numerals

Hence, 10 in the hexadecimal system means not *ten*, but *sixteen*, and BBC is not the *British Broadcasting Corporation*, but *three thousand and four*. Let's look at how the hex number 0BBCh is converted into the decimal system:

256	16	1	Adding
B	B	C	Columns
256x11	16x11	12x1	3004
16^2	16^1	16^0	

The symbol h is usually written after a hexadecimal number so as not to confuse it with a decimal one. Thus, 10h=16, 11h=17, 1Ah=26, 1Ch=28, 1Fh=31 and so on.

If the highest digit of a hexadecimal number is A, B, C, D, E, or F, then the symbol "0" usually appears before it to show that it is a number rather than a variable: 0F2h, 0A0h and so on. The rules of arithmetic are essentially the same for any positional system, so you don't need to re-learn them for the hexadecimal system. A useful exercise is to create addition and multiplication tables from 0h+0h to 0Fh+0Fh and from 1hx1h to 0Fhx0Fh, and check the results using the decimal and binary systems. By the time you've finished, both binary and hex will be second nature to you.

Converting Hexadecimal into Decimal and Vice Versa

The rules for converting decimal into hexadecimal are quite similar to those for converting decimal into binary. Just divide by 16 and take the remainder. For example, converting decimal 43969 to hexadecimal is shown in Table E .

So, writing down the remainders in a hexadecimal form reading from the right to the left we get ABC1, and by writing 0 at the beginning (before A) and **h** at the end we obtain 0ABC1h.

Dividend	43969	2748	171	10
Divisor	16	16	16	16
Quotient	2748	171	10	0
Remainder in decimal form	1	12	11	10
Remainder in hexadecimal form	1	C	B	A

Table E : Converting Decimal to Hexadecimal

The Connection Between Binary and Hexadecimal

As promised, we will now explain the connection between the binary and hexadecimal systems.

Every hexadecimal numeral can be represented in binary by a 4-digit number and vice-versa. Obviously, this property is due to the fact that $16=2^4$. See Table F

To go from hex to binary, just replace each hexadecimal digit, one by one, with the corresponding group of four binary digits. To go from binary to hex, first place a few zeros at the beginning of the binary number so that it is made up of one or more complete sections of four digits, then replace each group of 4 binary digits with the corresponding hexadecimal numeral. Easy!

So, the contents of every nibble of computer memory can be represented by one hexadecimal digit or by four binary digits. Having mastered this, we can move on to looking at how the information stored in a computer is represented.

Hexadecimal numeral	Binary number	Decimal number
0	0000	0
1	0001	1
2	0010	2
3	0011	3
4	0100	4
5	0101	5
6	0110	6
7	0111	7
8	1000	8
9	1001	9
A	1010	10
B	1011	11
C	1100	12
D	1101	13
E	1110	14
F	1111	15

Table F : The Correspondence Between Hexadecimal, Binary and Decimal Systems

The Representation of Information in a Computer

As we said earlier, a computer stores information in bits. This means that information is represented internally in binary format, in other words as a sequence of ones and zeros.

The bits are grouped together in sets of 8 known as a byte and every byte consists of 2 nibbles. Since every nibble can be represented by one hexadecimal digit, the hexadecimal format is the simplest form for the external representation of information stored in a computer.

The same group of bits can have several meanings for a computer and can be treated in different ways - either as a command , or as different types of data. How the computer deals with the bits depends on where in the group they are located, on instructions being performed, and on information contained in other parts of the computer's memory. The simplest and most commonly used data are integer numbers. We will now look at how these are represented in computers.

Representation of Integers

There are three main ways integers can be represented on IBM and compatible PCs: as unsigned integers of different sizes, signed integers of different sizes, and binary-coded decimal(BCD) integers of packed and unpacked formats. Table G shows the various types.

Representation of Binary Integers

Unsigned integer representation is shown in the first part of Table G Figure A.1 shows how the eight bits of the unsigned integer are allocated in one byte.

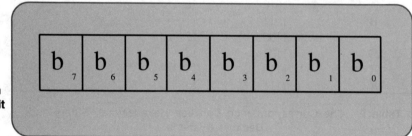

Figure A.1
Allocation of an Unsigned 8 - Bit Integer in One Byte

Type	Size in bits	Supported by							Range of values
		8086	8087	80286	80287	80386	80387	80486	
unsigned integer:									
byte	8	+		+		+		+	$0 - 2^8-1=255$
word	16	+		+		+		+	$0 - 2^{16}-1=64K-1=65535$
double word	32	+		+		+		+	$0 - 2^{32}-1=4M-1$
far word	48	*		*		*		*	$0 - 2^{48}-1$
quad word	64		+		+		+	+	$0 - 2^{64}-1$
tbyte	80		+		+		+	+	$0 - 2^{80}-1$
signed integer:									
byte	8	+		+		+		+	$-128 - 127$
word	16	+		+		+		+	$-2^{15} - 2^{15}-1$
double word	32					+		+	$-2^{31} - 2^{31}-1$
quad word	64						+	+	$-2^{63} - 2^{63}-1$
BCD integer:									
unpacked	8	+		+		+		+	$0 - 99$
packed	8	+		+		+		+	$0 - 99$
packed tbyte	64	+		+		+		+	$-9..9-9..9(18digits)$

Table G : Integer Representation on IBM and Compatible PCs

To convert a number stored in one byte to the decimal system, you need to multiply the value of each bit from 0 to 7 by two to the corresponding power and then add the results.

For example, let's convert the binary number 1100 0101b into the decimal system, as we did in the previous section.

b_7	b_6	b_5	b_4	b_3	b_2	b_1	b_0	
1	1	0	0	0	1	0	1	
128	64				4		1	197

Figure A.2 shows the order for a 16-bit integer.

Figure A.2
The Allocation of an 16 - Bit Unsigned Integer in Two Bytes

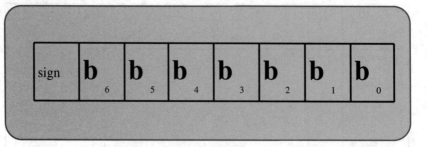

The value of a 16-bit unsigned integer can be obtained in the same way as for an 8-bit but you need to use 16 summands rather than 8.

Signed integers are used for representing both positive and negative numbers. The highest bit of a signed integer is used to represent a sign, which is 0 for positive numbers and 1 for negative. A signed 8-bit integer is allocated in one byte as shown in Figure A.3.

Here "+" is coded as "0" and "-" is coded as "1". The meaning of the digits $b_6...b_0$ is NOT the same as it is for unsigned integers. If *sign=0* (i.e., the number is non-negative), then the value of the integer stored can be calculated in exactly the same way as for an unsigned integer except that you only use the bits from 0 to 6.

If *sign=1* (i.e., the number is negative) you calculate the value of an integer stored in the same way as for positive numbers but you then need to subtract 128 (2^7) for 8-bit signed integers or 32768(2^{15}) for 16-bit numbers.

For example, 0000 0001 (01h) stands for 1 because the sign bit is zero, 1000 0000 (80h) stands for -128 (0 - 128 = -128). The byte with all bits set at 1 stores the value 0FFh which can be treated either as the unsigned integer 255 (127+64+32+16+8+4+2+1) or as -1 (64+32+16+8+4+2+1-128).

This is known as a two's complement notation, and is particularly useful for computer representation of arithmetic operations. For example, 3-2=3+(-2) can be evaluated as follows:

```
  0000 0011
+
  1111 1110
  ─────────
  0000 0001
```

(ignoring the carry) and equals 1. Similarly, 2-3=2+(-3) can be evaluated as

```
 0000 0010
+
 1111 1101

 1111 1111
```

and equals (-1) as it should be. Again ignoring the carry for (-2) + (-3), we get

```
 1111 1110
+
 1111 1101

 1111 1011
```

Thus (-2) + (-3) is equal to (-5). It's great, isn't it?

Have a go at calculating the results for 2+3. If you get 5 (which is the correct answer!) go on and see if you can get the right answer with signed numbers consisting of 16 or more digits. To obtain the value of the two's complement representation of a negative number written in 16, 32 or 64 bits you should subtract the value 2^{15}, 2^{31} or 2^{63} from the value of 15-, 31- or 63-bit positive values, respectively.

There is another, much simpler way of getting the two's complement of an n-digit negative number. You simply replace each binary digit of a negative number with its opposite (i.e., 0 to 1, 1 to 0) and then add 1 to this. If we take 8-bit signed integers, the example -000 0010 first gives (taking the complement) -111 1101, then by adding 1 and writing down "1" for the sign "-" you get 1111 1110, which is what it should be. You can experiment with this and perhaps even try to prove the equivalence of the two ways of getting the two's complement.

This just leaves BCD integer representation, then we've completed Table G.

Binary Coded Decimal (BCD) Representation of Integers

BCD representation was introduced in earlier computers and was widely used in business applications. It is quite a strange combination of human and machine approaches: numbers are represented in the decimal system which is easier for people to understand, but all the arithmetic operations are performed using binary representation for each decimal digit. The use of BCD representation is still limited on PCs in some languages (for example, in COBOL) and spreadsheets so we'll only give a brief description of it here.

The binary representation of decimal digits in BCD format is given in Table H.

There are two reasons why the BCD coding cannot be considered the most economical way of storing numbers in computers. Firstly, as you see in Table I, the binary numbers 1010, 1011, 1100, 1101, 1110 and 1111 are left without a job. The second reason is that the whole byte is used for storing a single digit. However, the advantage of this system is that BCD numbers can be converted into character strings very easily. You simply add the hexadecimal constant 30h to each byte of a BCD number.

If both nibbles of a byte are used to code decimal cyphers, we obtain what is termed a packed BCD integer. In this representation, the decimal numbers from 0 to 99 can be written on one byte. Table I shows a section of packed BCD representation for 1 byte.

So, in packed BCD integer representation, each nibble of a byte is used to code a decimal cypher.

For both packed and unpacked BCD integer representation, the microprocessor's i8086 instructions can only be manipulated using single byte numbers. If you want to use longer BCD integers with i8086 (and

Decimal Cypher	0	1	2	3	4	5	6	7	8	9
BCD Code	0000	0001	0010	0011	0100	0101	0110	0111	1000	1001

Table H : BCD Code For Decimal Cyphers

Decimal number	BCD code	Decimal number	BCD code	Decimal number	BCD code
0	0000 0000	10	0001 0000	90	1001 0000
1	0000 0001	11	0001 0001	91	1001 0001
2	0000 0010	.	.	92	1001 0010
3	0000 0011	.	.	93	1001 0011
4	0000 0100	.	.	94	1001 0100
5	0000 0101	.	.	95	1001 0101
6	0000 0110	.	.	96	1001 0110
7	0000 0111	.	.	97	1001 0111
8	0000 1000	88	1000 1000	98	1001 1000
9	0000 1001	89	1000 1001	99	1001 1001

Table I : BCD Integer Representation For One Byte (Part)

i80286), you have to organize the way the program processes the numbers yourself. In i8087/i80287 coprocessors and i80386/i80486 processors however, signed BCD packed integers consisting of 18 or fewer digits can be treated directly.

A Note on Arithmetic

Rounding off our discussion about the various ways of representing integer numbers, we'd like to make the following points about arithmetic. When two integers are added together, each of them being stored in its own byte, the integer result obtained is stored in a byte again. In the unlikely event that there is not enough room for the result in a byte, the remaining figures are registered as carry or overflow. However, when multiplying two integers, each of which is stored in a single byte, the result obtained is stored in two bytes.

Appendix A

ASCII TABLE

	0	1	2	3	4	5	6	7	8	9	A	B	C	D	E	F
00	NUL 0	☺ 1	● 2	♥ 3	♦ 4	♣ 5	♠ 6	• 7	◘ 8	○ 9	◎ 10	♂ 11	♀ 12	♪ 13	♫ 14	☼ 15
10	▶ 16	◀ 17	↕ 18	‼ 19	¶ 20	§ 21	▬ 22	↨ 23	↑ 24	↓ 25	→ 26	← 27	∟ 28	◆ 29	▲ 30	▼ 31
20	 32	! 33	" 34	# 35	$ 36	% 37	& 38	' 39	(40	) 41	* 42	+ 43	, 44	- 45	. 46	/ 47
30	0 48	1 49	2 50	3 51	4 52	5 53	6 54	7 55	8 56	9 57	: 58	; 59	< 60	= 61	> 62	? 63
40	@ 64	A 65	B 66	C 67	D 68	E 69	F 70	G 71	H 72	I 73	J 74	K 75	L 76	M 77	N 78	O 79
50	P 80	Q 81	R 82	S 83	T 84	U 85	V 86	W 87	X 88	Y 89	Z 90	[91	\ 92	] 93	^ 94	_ 95
60	` 96	a 97	b 98	c 99	d 100	e 101	f 102	g 103	h 104	i 105	j 106	k 107	l 108	m 109	n 110	o 111
70	p 112	q 113	r 114	s 115	t 116	u 117	v 118	w 119	x 120	y 121	z 122	{ 123	| 124	} 125	~ 126	△ 127

Continued Over Page

	0	1	2	3	4	5	6	7	8	9	A	B	C	D	E	F
80	Ç	ü	é	â	ä	à	å	ç	ê	ë	è	ï	î	ì	Ä	Å
	128	129	130	131	132	133	134	135	136	137	138	139	140	141	142	143
90	É	æ	Æ	ô	ö	ò	û	ù	ÿ	Ö	Ü	¢	£	¥	P$_t$	ƒ
	144	145	146	147	148	149	150	151	152	153	154	155	156	157	158	159
A0	á	í	ó	ú	ñ	Ñ	ª	º	¿	⌐	¬	1/2	1/4	¡	«	»
	160	161	162	163	164	165	166	167	168	169	170	171	172	173	174	175
B0	▒	▒	█	│	┤	╡	╢	╖	╕	╣	║	╗	╝	╜	╛	┐
	176	177	178	179	180	181	182	183	184	185	186	187	188	189	190	191
C0	└	┴	┬	├	─	┼	╞	╟	╚	╔	╩	╦	╠	═	╬	╧
	192	193	194	195	196	197	198	199	200	201	202	203	204	205	206	207
D0	╨	╤	╥	╙	╘	╒	╓	╫	╪	┘	┌	█	▄	▌	▐	▀
	208	209	210	211	212	213	214	215	216	217	218	219	220	221	222	223
E0	α	ß	Γ	π	Σ	σ	µ	τ	Φ	θ	Ω	δ	∞	ø	∈	∩
	224	225	226	227	228	229	230	231	232	233	234	235	236	237	238	239
F0	≡	±	≥	≤	⌠	⌡	÷	≈	°	·	·	√	n	²	■	
	240	241	242	243	244	245	246	247	248	249	250	251	252	253	254	255

KEY SCAN CODES

Code Hex	Dec	Character Norm	Shift	Code Hex	Dec	Character Norm	Shift
01h	1	Esc		30h	48	B	
02h	2	1	!	31h	49	N	
03h	3	2	@	32h	50	M	
04h	4	3	#	33h	51	,	<
05h	5	4	$	34h	52	.	>
06h	6	5	%	35h	53	/	?
07h	7	6	^	36h	54	Shift(R)	
08h	8	7	&	37h	55	*	PrtSc
09h	9	8	*	38h	56	Alt	
0Ah	10	9	(	39h	57	SpaceBar	
0Bh	11	0	)	3Ah	58	CapsLock	
0Bh	12	-	_	3Bh	59	F1	
0Dh	13	+	=	3Ch	60	F2	
0Eh	14	BackSpace		3Dh	61	F3	
0Eh	15	Tab		3Eh	62	F4	
10h	16	Q		3Fh	63	F5	
11h	17	W		40h	64	F6	
12h	18	E		41h	65	F7	
13h	19	R		42h	66	F8	
14h	20	T		43h	67	F9	
15h	21	Y		44h	68	F10	
16h	22	U		45h	69	NumLock	
17h	23	I		46h	70	ScrollLock	
18h	24	O		47h	71	Home	[7]
19h	25	P		48h	72	↑	[8]
1Ah	26	[	{	49h	73	PgUp	[9]
1Bh	27	]	}	4Ah	74	Grey	+
1Ch	28	Enter		4Bh	75	←	[4]
1Dh	29	Ctrl		4Ch	76		[5
1Eh	30	A		4Dh	77	→	[6]

1Fh	31	S		4Eh	78	Grey	+
20h	32	D		4Fh	79	End	[1]
21h	33	F		50h	80	↓	[2]
22h	34	G		51h	81	PgDn	[3
23h	35	H		52h	82	Ins	[0]
24h	36	J		53h	83	Del	[.]
25h	37	K		54h	84	SysReq	
26h	38	L					
27h	39	;		:			
28h	40	'		"			
29h	41	`		~			
2Ah	42	Shift		(L)			
2Bh	43	\		|			
2Ch	44	Z					
2Dh	45	X					
2Eh	46	C					
2Fh	47	V					

Additional keys on 101/102 keyboard

Key	Scan code
F11	57h
F12	58h
Right Alt	0E0h 38h
Right Ctrl	0E0h 1Dh
PrintScreen	0E0h 2Ah 0E0h 37h
Shift-PrintScreen (SysReq)	0E0h 37h
Pause	0E1h 1Dh 45h 0E1h 9Dh 0C5h
Ctrl-Pause (Break)	0E0h 46h 0E0h 0C6h
Grey Insert	0E0h 53h
Grey Delete	0E0h 53h
Grey Home	0E0h 47h
Grey End	0E0h 4Fh
Grey ↑	0E0h 48h
Grey ↓	0E0h 50h
Grey →	0E0h 4Dh
Grey ←	0E0h 4Bh
Grey PageUp	0E0h 49h
Grey PageDn	0E0h 51h

Instruction Set Reference

How to Use the Instruction Set Reference

This section explains how the Instruction Set Reference is laid out and what the various abbreviations mean.

The commands are in alphabetical order according to their mnemonics.

The **Header** contains the mnemonic of the instruction, its full name and a list of processors which can perform the instruction.

In the **Syntax** section we give the possible variants of the instruction's syntax corresponding to various addressing modes. The following denotations are used for operands:

acc	any of the following accumulator registers: AX, AL, AH, also EAX on the 80386/486
destination	a destination operand
immed	an immediate constant
label	a labelled memory location
mem	a direct or indirect memory operand
reg	any general purpose register
segreg	a segment register (DS,ES,SS,CS, also FS and GS on the 80386/486)
source	a source memory operand

A numerical suffix on the operand denotation indicates the size of the operand. No suffix means that any admissible size is possible. For example, **reg** means any 8-bit, 16-bit or 32-bit (for the 80386/486) general purpose register, while **reg8** means that in this syntax the operand must be an 8-bit general purpose register.

In the **Function** section the result of performing the command is shown in algorithmic form. The algorithm is written in C-like pseudo-code. The IF-THEN-ELSE construction means the same as it does in C. When necessary, normal language is used.

The **Flags** section consists of a table giving a two-letter abbreviation for the flag name and an indication of how the instruction affects flags. The following denotations are used:

1	the flag is set
0	the flag is cleared
	the flag is not changed
?	the result is unpredictable
*	the flag is changed according to the rules for this flag.

The **Description**, **Comments** and **See Also** sections should not cause you any problems.

The **Timing and Encoding** section has a slightly more complicated structure. It consists of a table containing five columns:

The first column is **Format**. It contains the variants of the instruction or of its operands, which differ in machine code or in time of execution.

The second column is **Encoding**. It shows the machine code of the corresponding variant using binary and hex representations. However, to reduce the number of variants, the following abbreviations are used:

d   direction bit, equals 0, if the reg operand is a source, equals 1, if the reg operand is a destination.

w   word/byte bit; equals 1 for 16 and 32- bit operands, equals. **0** for 8-bit operand.

s   sign bit; equals 1 for extension with a sign of an 8-bit constant to 16 or 32 bits and of a 16-bit constant to 32 bits.

reg   a 3-bit field for coding a general purpose register (see the following table):

reg field register	w=1 16/32-bit	w=0 8-bit register
000	AX/EAX	AL
001	CX/ECX	CL
010	DX/EDX	DL
011	BX/EBpX	BL
100	SP/ESP	AH
101	BP/EBP	CH
110	SI/ESI	DH
111	DI/EDI	BH

sreg a 3-bit field for coding a segment register (see the following table):

sreg	register
000	ES
001	CS
010	SS
011	DS
100	FS
101	GS

data a field consisting of several bytes containing a constant. The possible number of bytes (up to 4) is written in brackets.

r/m a 3-bit field specifying a register or a memory operand. A register operand is specified using the table for the reg field when the mod field (see below) is equal to 11. A memory operand is specified with the other mod field values (see the following table):

r/m		
000	DS:	[BX+SI+disp]
001	DS:	[BX+DI+disp]
010	SS:	[BP+SI+disp]
011	SS:	[BP+DI+disp]
100	DS:	[SI+disp]
101	DS:	[DI+disp]
110	SS:	[BP+disp] *
111	DS:	[BX+disp]

* - r/m = 110 with mod = 00 is a special case

mod a 2-bit field which defines the addressing mode. The list of possible values and their meanings is as follows

> 00 for direct memory operand if r/m equals 110, for indirect memory operand if r/m is not equal to 110

> 01 for indirect memory operand with 8-bit displacement

> 10 for indirect memory operand with 16-bit displacement

> 11 both operands are registers

disp a field of several bytes for displacement of a memory operand, the number of bytes is written in brackets or equals 4 for a 32-bit address.

The segment override in the operand is encoded in machine code as a prefix according to the following table:

Segment register	Prefix in binary form	Prefix in hex form
CS	0010 1110	02Eh
DS	0011 1110	03Eh
ES	0010 0110	26h
SS	0011 0110	36h
FS	0110 0100	64h
GS	0110 0101	65h

The encoding of the 80386/486 instructions may also have some additional prefix bytes, namely Scaled Index Base (SIB) byte, address size byte and operand size byte.

AAA ASCII Adjust After Addition   86,186,286,386,486

Syntax

```
AAA
```

Function

```
If ((AL & 0Fh>9) OR AF = 1) then
    AL = AL + 6, AH = AH + 1
    flags AF and CF are set
else
    AL = (AL & 0Fh)
    flags AF and CF are cleared
```

Flags

OF	DF	IF	TF	SF	ZF	AF	PF	CF
?				?	?	*	?	*

Description

The AAA instruction corrects the binary result of a previous addition instruction in AL to one decimal digit (an unpacked BCD with the high-order nibble zeroed) and increments AH if the result of the previous addition instruction is greater than 9.

The OF, AF, and CF flags are left undefined. If the result of the previous addition is greater than 9, the Carry Flag (CF) and the Auxiliary Carry Flag (AF) are set. If not, the CF and AF Flags are cleared.

Comments

The AAA instruction can be used to add unpacked BCD numbers (one BCD digit per byte). After using the ADD instruction to place the sum in AL, you should use the AAA instruction to correct the sum to a proper BCD digit. You can convert a BCD digit in AL into ASCII code for printing by using AAA and then the instruction:

```
OR AL,30h
```

See Also

AAS	To adjust result in AL after subtraction
AAD	To convert BCD digits in AH and AL into a binary value in AX
AAM	To convert a number (less than 99) in AL into two BCD digits in AH and AL (least significant digit in AL)
ADD	To add two operands
DAA	To adjust the result of adding two packed BCD numbers

Timing and Encoding

Format	Encoding	Examples	Bytes	Clocks	
AAA	0011 0111	aaa	1	8086/88	8
				80286	3
				80386	4
				80486	3

AAD Adjust After Division   86,186,286,386,486

Syntax

```
AAD
```

Function

```
AL = AH * 10 + AL
AH = 0
```

Flags

OF	DF	IF	TF	SF	ZF	AF	PF	CF
?				*	*	?	*	?

Description

The AAD instruction converts a two-digit unpacked BCD number contained in AX (the most significant digit in AH and the least significant digit in AL) into a binary number in AX. It does this by multiplying the contents of AH by 10 and adding the result to AL. The instruction then sets AH to zero. The OF, AF, and CF flags are left undefined; SF is set or cleared depending on the 7-th bit of AL.

Comments

This instruction is often used before dividing a two-digit unpacked BCD value by a single BCD digit.

See Also

AAS To adjust result in AL after subtraction
AAM To convert a number (less than 99) in AL into two BCD
          digits in AH and AL (least significant digit in AL)
DIV To divide one unsigned operand by another

Timing and Encoding

Format	Encoding	Examples	Bytes	Clocks	
AAD	1101 0101	aad	2	8086/88	60
	0000 1010			80286	14
				80386	19
				80486	14

AAM ASCII Adjust AX After Multiplication   86,186,286,386,486

Syntax

    AAM

Function

    AH = AL / 10
    AL = AL mod 10

Flags

OF	DF	IF	TF	SF	ZF	AF	PF	CF
?				*	*	?	*	?

Description

The AAM instruction converts an 8-bit binary value of less than 100, stored in AL, into a two-digit unpacked BCD number in AX. The most significant digit is placed in AH and the least significant digit in AL.

Flags OF, AF and CF are undefined. Flags PF, ZF and SF are set according to the contents of AL; however, SF is always set to 0 as the sign bit of AL is always 0.

Comments

The AAM instruction is often used after multiplying two unpacked BCD digits in AX using the MUL instruction. The MUL instruction stores the result in AL; the AAM instruction divides AL by 10 and stores the quotient in AH and the remainder in AL.

See Also

> AAD To convert BCD digits in AH and AL into a binary value in AX

Timing and Encoding

Format	Encoding	Examples	Bytes	Clocks	
AAM	1101 0111	aam	2	8086/88	83
	0000 1010			80286	16
	(D4 0A)			80386	17
				80486	15

AAS ASCII Adjust AL After Subtraction   86,186,286,386,486

Syntax

```
AAS
```

Function

```
If ((AL & 0Ah) OR AF = 1) then
    AL = AL - 6, AH = AH - 1
    flags CF and AF are set to 1
else
    AL & 0Fh
    flags CF, AF are cleared
```

Flags

OF	DF	IF	TF	SF	ZF	AF	PF	CF
?				*	*	?	*	?

Description

When one unpacked BCD number is subtracted from another, the AAS instruction is used to correct the result to a decimal digit (an unpacked BCD) from 0 to 9 and place it in AL. If the low-order nibble of the result is greater than 9 or if the Auxiliary Flag (AF) is set, 6 is subtracted from AL and AH is decremented. AAS then sets the high-order nibble of AL to 0.

Comments

Note that if the result of the subtraction is less than 9, then the Auxiliary Flag and the Carry Flag are cleared. If the result of the subtraction is greater than 9, both flags are set.

See Also

AAA To adjust result in AL after adding two BCD digits
AAD To convert BCD digits in AH and AL into a binary value in AX
AAM To convert a number (less than 99) in AL into two BCD digits
DAS To correct the result of subtracting one packed BCD number from another
SUB To subtract one operand from another

Timing and Encoding

Format	Encoding	Examples	Bytes	Clocks	
AAS	0011 1111	aas	1	8086/88	8
				80286	3
				80386	4
				80486	3

ADC Arithmetic Add With Carry   86,186,286,386,486

Syntax

```
ADC destination,source
```

Function

```
Destination = destination + source + CF
```

Flags

OF	DF	IF	TF	SF	ZF	AF	PF	CF
*				*	*	*	*	*

Description

The ADC instruction adds the destination operand and the source operand to the value of the Carry Flag and places the result in the destination operand. If the result does not fit, then the Carry Flag (CF) is set.

Comments

If you want to add two 32-bit integers, use ADC with ADD. When using the ADC instruction, the operands cannot both be segment registers or memory operands.

See Also

ADD	To add two unsigned integers
SUB	To subtract two unsigned integers
SBB	To subtract two unsigned integers with borrow

Timing and Encoding

Format	Encoding	Examples	Bytes	Clocks	
ADC reg,reg	0001 00dw mod,rg,r/m disp(0 or 2)	adc al,bl	2-4	8086/88 80286 80386 80486	3 3 2 2
ADC mem,reg	0001 00dw mod,rg,r/m disp(0 or 2)	adc [bx],ch	2-4	8086/88 80286 80386 80486	16+EA 24+EA(w) 7 7 3
ADC reg,mem	0001 00dw mod,rg,r/m disp(0 or 2)	adc dl,[bx+si]	2-4	8086/88 80286 80386 80486	9+EA 23+EA(w) 7 6 2
ADC mem,immed	1000 00sw mod,010,r/m disp(0 or 2) data(1 or 2)	adc ?	3-6	8086/88 80286 80386 80486	3 7 7 3

Appendix D

ADC reg,immed	1000 00sw	adc dx,10	3-8	8086/88	4
	mod,010,r/m			80286	3
	disp(0 or 2)			80386	2
	data(1 or 2)			80486	1
ADC accum,immed	0001 010w	adc ah,4	2-3	8086/88	4
	data(1 or 2)			80286	3
				80386	2
				80486	1

ADD Arithmetic Addition (Unsigned)   86,186,286,386,486

Syntax

```
ADD destination,source
```

Function

```
destination = destination + source
```

Flags

OF	DF	IF	TF	SF	ZF	AF	PF	CF
*				*	*	*	*	*

Description

The ADD instruction adds the source and destination operands and places the
sum in the destination operand. Both operands must be unsigned integers.

Comments

If the result does not fit into the destination operand, the Carry Flag is set.

See Also

ADC To add with carry
SUB To subtract one integer from another
SBB To subtract an integer using the borrow

Timing and Encoding

Format	Encoding	Examples	Bytes	Clocks	
ADD reg,reg	0000 10dw	add ax,bx	2-4	8086/88	2
	mod,reg,r/m			80286	3
	disp(0 or 2)			80386	2
				80486	1
ADD mem,reg	0000 00dw	add sum,cx	2-4	8086/88	16+EA 24+EA (w)
	mod,reg,r/m			80286	7
	disp(0 or 2)			80386	7
	data(1 or 2)			80486	3
ADD reg,mem	0000 00dw	add cx,total	2-4	8086/88	9+EA 13+EA (w)
	mod,reg,r/m			80286	7
	disp(0 or 2)			80386	6
				80486	

ADD mem,immed	1100 00dw	add total,7	3-6	8086/88	17+EA 23+EA (w)
	mod,000,r/m			80286	7
	disp(0 or 2)			80386	7
	data(1 or 2)			80486	3
ADD reg,immed	1000 00dw	add dx,10	3-4	8086/88	4
	mod,000,r/x			80286	3
	disp(0 or 2)			80386	2
	data(1 or 2)			80486	1
ADD accum,immed	0001 010w	add ax,3	2-3	8086/88	4
	data(1 or 2)			80286	3
				80386	2
				80486	1

AND Bitwise Logical AND   86,186,286,386,486

Syntax

```
AND destination,source
```

Function

```
destination = destination AND source
CF = 0, OF = 0
```

Flags

OF	DF	IF	TF	SF	ZF	AF	PF	CF
0				*	*	?	*	0

Description

The AND instruction performs a bitwise logical AND of the destination and source operands and places the result in the destination operand. The Carry Flag (CF) and Overflow Flag (OF) are cleared; all other affected flags are set according to the result of the operation.

Comments

The bitwise AND operation means that if the corresponding bits in each operand are set to 1, the corresponding bit of the result is also set to 1. If not, the corresponding bit of the result is set to 0. Note that after using AND the Auxiliary Flag (AF) is undefined.

See Also

NOT To perform a bitwise NOT of two operands
OR   To perform a bitwise OR of two operands
XOR To perform a bitwise XOR of two operands

Timing and Encoding

Format	Encoding	Examples	Bytes	Clocks	
AND reg,reg	0010 10dw mod,reg,r/m disp(0 or 2)	and dx,bx	2	8086/88 80286 80386 80486	3 2 2 1
AND mem,reg	0010 10dw mod,reg,r/m disp(0 or 2)	and mask,bx	2-4	8086/88 80286 80386 80486	16+EA 24+EA (w) 7 7 3
AND reg,mem	0010 00dw mod,reg,r/m disp(0 or 2)	and cx,total	2-4	8086/88 80286 80386 80486	9+EA 13+EA (w) 7 6 2
AND reg,immed	1100 00sw mod,100,r/m disp(0 or 2) data(1 or 2)	and dx,07h	3-4	8086/88 80286 80386 80486	4 3 2 1
AND mem,immed	1100 00yw mod,100,r/x disp(0 or 2) data(1 or 2)	and mask,FFh	3-6	8086/88 80286 80386 80486	17+EA 23+EA (w) 7 7 3
AND accum,immed	0010 010w data(1 or 2)	and ax,0Fh	2-3	8086/88 80286 80386 80486	4 3 2 1

BSF Bit Scan Forward   386,486

Syntax

```
BSF destination,source
```

Function

```
if (source == 0 ) then
ZF = 1
destination = ???
else
ZF = 0
index = 0
while (bit(source,index) = 0)
index = index + 1
destination = index
endif
```

Flags

OF	DF	IF	TF	SF	ZF	AF	PF	CF
?				?	*	?	?	?

Description

The BSF instruction scans the source operand beginning with bit 0 to find the first bit which is set. If the source operand is 0, then the Zero Flag is set. If the set bit is found, then the instruction writes the bit position to the destination operand and clears ZF. In this case the value of the destination operand is in an undefined state.

Comments

Both operands must be words or doublewords.

BT,BTC,BTR,BTS   To test bit by copying to the Carry Flag
BSR   To scan for a set bit

Timing and Encoding

Format	Encoding	Bytes	Clocks	
BSF reg16,reg16	00001111	2-6	8086/88	--
	10111100		80286	--
	mod,reg,r/m		80386	10+3n*,6
	disp(0,1,2,or 4)		80486	6-42
BSF reg32,reg32	00001111	2-6	8086/88	--
	10111100		80286	--
	mod,reg,r/m		80386	10+3n*,6
	disp(0,1,2,or 4)		80486	6-42
BSF reg16,mem16	00001111	2-6	8086/88	--
BSF reg32,mem32	10111100		80286	--
	mod,reg,r/m		80386	10+3n*,6
	disp(0,1,2,or 4)		80486	6-42

n* - position of set bit from 0 to 31
   if source = 0 then clock = 6

Example

```
       SUB   CX,CX              ; Index set to 0
M1:    BSF   AX,TABLE[CX*4]     ; Scans word
       JNZ   FOUND_ONE          ; any bit is set
       INC   CX                 ; Go to next word
       .
       .
       .
       JL    M1                 ; Scan next entry
       .
FOUND_ONE:
```

BSR Bit Scan Reverse   386,486

Syntax

```
BSR destination_reg,source
```

Function

```
if (destination_reg in [AX,BX,CX,DX,SI,DI,BP,SP]) then
    start = 15
else
    start = 31
endif
if (source == 0) then
    ZF=1
    destination = ???
else
    ZF = 0
    index = 0
    while (bit(source,index) = 0)
        index = index - 1
    destination = index
endif
```

Flags

OF	DF	IF	TF	SF	ZF	AF	PF	CF
?				?	*	?	?	?

Description

The BSR instruction scans the bits of the source operand in the reverse direction, beginning with the most significant bit to bit 0 to find the first bit which is set. If the source operand is 0, then the ZF flag is set and the first operand is in an undefined state. If the source operand is not 0 and any bit is set, then the ZF flag is cleared and the index of the first set bit is placed in the destination register.

Comments

Both operands must be a words or doublewords.

BT,BTC,BTR,BTS	To test bit by copying to the Carry Flag
BSR	To scan for a set bit

Timing and Encoding

Format	Encoding	Bytes	Clocks	
BSR reg16,reg16	00001111	2-7	8086/88	- -
reg32,reg32	10111101		80286	- -
	mod,reg,r/m		80386	10+3n*,6
	disp(0,1,2,or 4)		80486	103-3n#
BSF reg16,mem16	00001111	2-7	8086/88	- -
BSF reg32,mem32	10111101		80286	- -
	mod,reg,r/m		80386	10+3n*,6
	disp(0,1,2,or 4)		80486	104-3n#

n* - position of set bit from 0 to 31
    if source = 0 then clock = 6
n# - bit position from 0 to 31
    clocs=7 if second operand equals 0

Example

```
        MOV  CX,INDEX-1      ; Index of last entry in table
M1:     BSR  AX,TABLE[CX*4]  ; Scan for non-zero bits
        JNZ  find            ; Index is valid
        LOOP M1              ; Loop back

bad:                         ; The table is zero
```

BSWAP Byte Swap   86,186,286,386,486

Syntax

```
BSWAP destination_reg
```

Function

```
temp=destination_reg
destination_reg[ 0.. 7]=temp[24..31]
destination_reg[ 8..15]=temp[16..23]
destination_reg[16..23]=temp[ 8..15]
destination_reg[24..31]=temp[ 0.. 7]
```

Flags

OF	DF	IF	TF	SF	ZF	AF	PF	CF

Description

The BSWAP instruction changes the order of the four bytes of the 32-bit destination register. It exchanges the fourth byte with the first byte, and the second byte with the third.

Comments

This instruction may be useful for exchanging data quickly between 8086/i80x86 processors and other processors.

Timing and Encoding

Format	Encoding	Bytes	Clocks	
BSWAP reg32	0000 1111	2	8086/88	--
	1100 1reg		80286	--
			80386	--
			80486	--

Example

```
BSWAP       ECX
```

CALL Far Procedure Call   86,186,286,386,486

Syntax

```
CALL destination
CALL FAR PTR destination
CALL DWORD PTR address
```

Function

```
push(CS)
push(EIP)
CS:EIP=destination
```

Flags

OF	DF	IF	TF	SF	ZF	AF	PF	CF

Description

The CALL instruction transfers control to the address specified by the destination operand inside the same segment (for a NEAR procedure call). This instruction saves the current CS and address of the next instruction (EIP) on the stack so that an RET instruction can return control to the instruction that follows the CALL instruction.

Comments

The destination operand may be a label that specifies an address in a separate segment, the address of a 32-bit or a 48-bit FAR pointer in the memory, or the contents of a register.

See Also

JMP   To jump unconditionally

RET   To return from a CALL instruction

J*   To jump under certain conditions

Timing and Encoding

Format	Encoding	Bytes	Clocks	
CALL label	1001 1010	5	8086/88	28
	disp(4)		80286	13+m
			80386	17+m
			80486	18
CALL mem32	1111 1111	2	8086/88	37+EA
CALL mem48	mod,011,r/m		80286	16+m
			80386	22+m
			80486	17

Example

```
CALL far_loc
CALL FAR PTR label
CALL far_tab[di]
CALL DWORD PTR [001Ah]
```

CALL Near Procedure Call   86,186,286,386,486

Syntax

```
CALL destination
CALL reg_or_mem
CALL WORD PTR mem
```

Function

```
push(EIP)
EIP=destination
```

Flags

OF	DF	IF	TF	SF	ZF	AF	PF	CF

Description

The CALL instruction transfers control to the address specified by the destination operand inside the same segment (for a NEAR procedure call). This instruction saves the current CS and address of the next instruction (EIP) on the stack so that a RET instruction can return control to the instruction that follows the CALL instruction.

Comments

The destination operand may be a label that specifies an address within the current segment or the contents of a register or memory location.

See Also

JMP	To jump unconditionally to a new place
RET	To return from a CALL instruction
J*	To jump under certain conditions

Timing and Encoding

Format	Encoding	Bytes	Clocks	
CALL label	1110 1000	3	8086/88	19
	disp(2)		80286	7+m
			80386	7+m
			80486	3
CALL mem16	1111 1111	2	8086/88	21+EA
CALL mem32	mod,010,r/m		80286	11+m
			80386	10+m
			80486	5
CALL reg	1111 1111	2	8086/88	16
CALL mem32	mod,010,r/m		80286	7+m
			80386	7+m
			80486	5

Example

```
CALL trans

CALL [BX+AX*4]
```

CBW Convert Byte To Word   86,186,286,386,486

Syntax

```
CBW
```

Function

```
if (bit(AL,7)) then
    AH = 0FFh
else
    AH = 0
endif
```

Flags

OF	DF	IF	TF	SF	ZF	AF	PF	CF

Description

The CBW instruction converts a signed byte stored in the AL register into a signed word in the AX register by copying the sign bit of AL into all bit positions of AH.

See Also

CWD To convert word into a doubleword
IDIV To divide one signed integer by another

Timing and Encoding

Format	Encoding	Bytes	Clocks	
CBW	1001 1000	1	8086/88	2
			80286	2
			80386	3
			80486	3

Example

```
MOV  AL,num     ; num is a one-byte variable
CBW             ; convert value in AL into 16-bit
                ; signed integer
```

CLC Clear Carry Flag   86,186,286,386,486

Syntax

CLC

Function

CF=0

Flags

OF	DF	IF	TF	SF	ZF	AF	PF	CF
								0

Description

The CLC instruction clears the Carry Flag.

See Also

CTC To set the Carry Flag
CMC To reverse the current state of the Carry Flag
CLD To clear the Direction Flag
CLI To set the Interrupt Flag
STI To clear the Interrupt Flag
STD To set the Direction Flag

Timing and Encoding

Format	Encoding	Bytes	Clocks	
CLC	1111 1000	1	8086/88	2
			80286	2
			80386	2
			80486	2

Example

```
SUCCESS:
        CLC             ; Clear CF
        RET             ; Successful return from procedure
```

CLD Clear Direction Flag   86,186,286,386,486

Syntax

```
CLD
```

Function

```
DF = 0
```

Flags

OF	DF	IF	TF	SF	ZF	AF	PF	CF
	0							

Description

The CLD instruction clears the Direction Flag (DF). Other flags are not affected.

Comments

If the Direction Flag is cleared, all subsequent string instructions (CMPS, LODS, MOVS, SCAS, STOS) increment the pointer registers (SI and/or DI) when the instruction has been executed. If the Direction Flag is set, all subsequent string instructions decrement the pointer registers by 1 or 2. In other words, string instructions process up the string in a forward direction from low addresses to high addresses.

See Also

STD   To set Direction Flag to 1

Timing and Encoding

Format	Encoding	Examples	Bytes	Clocks	
CLD	1111 1100	cld	1	8086/88	2
				80286	2
				80386	2
				80486	2

CLI Clear Interrupt Flag   86,186,286,386,486

Syntax

CLI

Function

IF = 0

Flags

OF	DF	IF	TF	SF	ZF	AF	PF	CF
		0						

Description

The CLI instruction clears the Interrupt Flag (IF). Other flags are not affected.

Comments

When the IF flag is clear, the maskable hardware interrupts (IRQ0 through IRQ7 on PC and XT and through IRQ15 on AT and PS) are ignored until the Interrupt Flag is set with the STI instruction. In the protected mode, if the current task's privilege level is less than or equal to the value of the IOPL Flag, then CLI sets the flag to 0.

See Also

STI   To set Interrupt Flag to 1

Timing and Encoding

Format	Encoding	Examples	Bytes	Clocks	
CLI	1111 1010	cli	1	8086/88	2
				80286	3
				80386	3
				80486	5

CMC Complement Carry Flag   86,186,286,386,486

Syntax

```
CMC
```

Function

```
If CF = 0 then
    CF = 1
else
    CF = 0
```

Flags

OF	DF	IF	TF	SF	ZF	AF	PF	CF
								*

Description

The CMC instruction toggles the state of the Carry Flag.

Comments

This instruction is often used for toggling the Carry Flag when CF is used as an error indicator.

See Also

CLC   To clear the Carry Flag
STC   To set the Carry Flag to 1

Timing and Encoding

Format	Encoding	Examples	Bytes	Clocks	
CMC	1111 0101	cmc	1	8086/88	2
				80286	2
				80386	2
				80486	2

CMP Compare Two Operands   86,186,286,386,486

Syntax

```
CMP destination,source
```

Function

```
destination - source
```

Flags

OF	DF	IF	TF	SF	ZF	AF	PF	CF
*				*	*	*	*	*

Description

The CMP instruction subtracts the source operand from the destination operand and sets the flags according to the result. The following table illustrates how the flags are set:

	if signed compare	if unsigned compare
destination>source	ZF=0 and SF=OF	CF=0 and ZF=0
destination>=source	SF=OF	CF=0
destination=source	ZF=1	ZF=1
destination<=source	ZF=1 and SF!=OF	CF=1 or ZF=1
destination<source	SF=OF	CF=1

This instruction does not return the result and both operands remain unchanged.

Comments

CMP compares two operands and sets the flags. CMP is therefore generally followed by a conditional jump instruction. This instruction controls the action of programs. The operands of the CMP instruction cannot both be memory operands or segment registers.

See Also

JA, JNB, JNE, JB, JNAE, JBE, JNA, JC, JE, JZ, JG, JNLE, JGE, JNL, JL, JNGE JLE, JNG, JNC, JNE JNZ, JNO, JNP, JPO, JNS, JO, JP, JPE, JS	To jump under certain conditions
TEST	To test selected bits of operand

Timing and Encoding

Format	Encoding	Examples	Bytes	Clocks	
CMP reg,reg	0011 10dw mod,reg,r/m disp(0 or 2)	cmp ah,al	2-4	8086/88 80286 80386 80486	3 2 2 1
CMP mem,reg	0011 10dw mod,reg,r/m disp(0 or 2)	cmp sum,ax	2-4	8086/88 80286 80386 80486	9+EA 13+EA (w) 7 5 2
CMP reg,mem	0011 10dw mod,reg,r/m disp(0 or 2)	cmp dx,[bx+2]	2-4	8086/88 80286 80386 80486	9+EA !#+EA (w) 6 6 2

CMP mem,immed	1000 00sw mod,111,r/m disp(0 or 2) data(1 or 2)	cmp total,300	3-6	8086/88 10+EA 14+EA (w) 80286 6 80386 5 80486 2
CMP reg,immed	1000 00sw mod,111,r/m disp(0 or 2) data(1 or 2)	cmp bh,1Fh	2-4	8086/88 4 80286 3 80386 2 80486 1
CMP accum,immed	0011 110w data(1 or 2)	cmp al,7Fh cmp ax,7000h	2-3	8086/88 4 80286 3 80386 2 80486 1

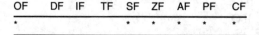

CMPS/CMPSB/CMPSW/CMPSD Compare Strings
86,186,286,386,486

Syntax

```
CMPS destination_string,source_string
```

Function

```
DS:[ESI] - ES:[EDI]
If DF = 0 then
    ESI = ESI + opsize
    EDI = EDI + opsize
else
    ESI = ESI - opsize
    EDI = EDI - opsize

If string is byte then opsize is 1
If string is word then opsize is 2
If string is doubleword then opsize is 4
```

Flags

OF	DF	IF	TF	SF	ZF	AF	PF	CF
*				*	*	*	*	*

Description

The CMPS instruction and its modifications - CMPSB, CMPSW and
(on 386/486) CMPSD - compare the byte, word and doubleword at the address
DS:ES (DS:ESI) (source_string) with the one at the address ES:DI (ES:EDI)
(destination_string). The comparison is performed by subtraction and the flags
are altered according to the result. The index registers SI (ESI) and DI (EDI)
are adjusted according to the size of operands and the status of the Direction
Flag (DF). If DF=0 the index registers are incremented. If not, they are
decremented.

Comments

The CMPS instruction and its modifications are generally used with the repeat prefixes REP, REPE, REPNE, REPNZ or REPZ to repeat the comparison by the number of times placed in CX (ECX). If the REP/REPE/REPZ prefixes are used, CMPS repeats the comparison while CX (ECX) is not equal to zero and the strings are equal (ZF=1). If the REPNE/REPNZ prefixes are used, CMPS repeats the comparison while CX (ECX) is not equal to zero and the strings are *not* equal (ZF=0). CX (ECX) must contain a maximum number of items for comparison.

If the CMPS forms of instruction are used, a segment override prefix can be used for the source_string, but not for the destination_string.

See Also

LODS, LODSB, LODSW, LODSD	To copy DS:SI to AX or AL
MOVS, MOVSB, MOVSW, MOVSD	To copy from DS:SI to ES:DI
SCAS, SCASB, SCASW, SCASD	To compare ES:DI with AX or AL
STOS, STOSB, STOSW, STOSD	To copy AX or AL to ES:DI
REP, REPE, REPZ, REPNZ	To repeat an instruction

Timing and Encoding

Format	Encoding	Examples	Bytes	Clocks	
CMPS	1010 011w	cmps sourc,es:dest	2	8086/88	22 30 (w)
				80286	8
				80386	10
				80486	8

CWD Convert Word To Doubleword   86,186,286,386,486

Syntax

```
CWD
```

Function

```
If AX <  8000h then DX = 0h
If AX >= 8000h then DX = 0FFFFh
```

Flags

OF	DF	IF	TF	SF	ZF	AF	PF	CF

Description

The CWD instruction converts the signed word in AX to a signed doubleword in DX:AX. It does this by copying the sign bit of AX into all bits of DX.

Comments

The CWD instruction can be used before performing the IDIV instruction which divides a signed word in AX by another signed word. The CWD instruction will create a signed doubleword copy of the dividend in the registers DX:AX.

See Also

CBW To convert a byte into a word

IDIV To divide one signed integer by another signed integer

Timing and Encoding

Operands	Encoding	Examples	Bytes	Clocks	
CWD	1001 1001	cwd	1	8086/88	5
	mod,reg,r/m			80286	2
	disp(0 or 2)			80386	2
				80486	3

CWDE Convert Word To Extended Double   386,486

Syntax

CWDE

Function

```
If EAX <  8000h then EAX = EAX & 0000FFFFh
If EAX > = 8000h then EAX = EAX OR 0FFFF0000h
```

Flags

OF	DF	IF	TF	SF	ZF	AF	PF	CF

Description

The CWDE instruction converts a signed word in AX to a signed doubleword in EAX by copying the sign bit of AX into the higher word of EAX.

Comments

The CWDE instruction can be used before performing the IDIV instruction, which divides a signed word in AX by another signed word. CWDE will create a signed doubleword copy of the dividend in the EAX register.

See Also

CBW To convert a byte into a word

IDIV To divide one signed integer by another

Timing and Encoding

Operands	Encoding	Examples	Bytes	Clocks	
CWDE	1001 1001	cwde	1	8086/88	-
				80286	-
				80386	3
				80486	3

DAA Decimal Adjust For Addition 86,186,286,386,486

Syntax

DAA

Function

```
If ((AL & 0Fh) > 9 OR AF = 1) then
    AL = AL + 6
    AF = 1
else
    AF = 0
If ((AL > 9Fh) OR CF = 1) then
    AL = AL + 60h
    CF = 1
else
    CF = 0
```

Flags

OF	DF	IF	TF	SF	ZF	AF	PF	CF
?				*	*	*	*	*

Description

The DAA instruction converts the result of a previous BCD addition operation in AL (if it is less then 100) into a pair of packed BCD digits.

Comments

The DAA instruction adjusts the result when two packed BCD numbers are added together. The DDA instruction must be performed to obtain a valid result.

See Also

AAA To adjust the result of the addition of two unpacked BCD digits

AAS To adjust the result of the subtraction of one unpacked BCD number from another

DAS To adjust the result of the subtraction of one packed BCD number from another

Timing and Encoding

Operands	Encoding	Examples	Bytes	Clocks	
DAA	0010 0111	daa	1	8086/88	4
				80286	3
				80386	4
				80486	2

DAS Decimal Adjust AL After Subtraction86,186,286,386,486

Syntax

```
DAS
```

Function

```
if (AF=1 | ((AL & 0Fh)) >9) then
    AL = AL - 6
    AF = 1
else
    AF = 0
endif
if (CF=1 | (AL >9Fh) then
    AL = AL -60h
    CF = 1
else
    CF = 0
endif
```

Flags

OF	DF	IF	TF	SF	ZF	AF	PF	CF
?				*	*	*	*	*

Description

The DAS instruction adjusts the result in the AL register after the subtraction of two valid packed BCD numbers. After this operation, the AL register contains two valid packed decimal digits.

Comments

The packed BCD number (less than 100) stores the least significant decimal digit in the lower nibble and the most significant decimal digit in the upper nibble.

After the division and multiplication of packed BCD numbers, it is not possible to correct the result. In this case, it is better to use unpacked decimal numbers.

See Also

AAS   To correct the result of the subtraction of one unpacked BCD number from another

DAA   To correct the result of the addition of two packed BCD numbers

SUB   To subtract two operands

SBB   To subtract two operands with borrow

Timing and Encoding

Format	Encoding	Bytes	Clocks	
DAS	0010 1111	1	8086/88	4
			80286	3
			80386	4
			80486	2

Example

```
MOV  AL,31h      ; 35 in packed decimal
SUB  AL,12h      ; placed 1Fh in AL
DAS              ; corrects AL to 19h
```

DEC Decrement   86,186,286,386,486

Syntax

```
DEC operand
```

Function

```
Operand = Operand - 1
```

Flags

OF	DF	IF	TF	SF	ZF	AF	PF	CF
*				*	*	*	*	

Description

The DEC instruction subtracts 1 from the operand which is treated as an unsigned number.

Comments

The segment register cannot be used in this instruction. The Carry Flag is not affected.

See Also

SUB   To subtract one operand from another

INC   To increment an operand

Timing and Encoding

Format	Encoding	Examples	Bytes	Clocks	
DEC reg8	1111 111w mod,001,r/m disp(0or2)	dec bl	2	8086/88 80286 80386 80486	3 2 2 1
DEC reg16	0100 1reg mod,001,r/m disp(0or2)	dec ax	2	8086/88 80286 80386 80486	3 2 2 1
DEC reg32	0100 1reg mod,001,r/m disp(0or2)	dec eax	2	8086/88 80286 80386 80486	3 2 2 1
DEC mem	1111 111w mod,001,r/m disp(0or2)	dec sum	1	8086/88 80286 80386 80486	15+EA 23+EA 7 6 3

DIV Division (Unsigned)   86,186,286,386,486

Syntax

```
DIV divisor
```

Function

If the divisor is a byte then the result is equal to AX/divisor.
AL contains the quotient, AH contains the remainder.

If the divisor is a word then the result is equal to DX:AX/divisor.
AX contains the quotient and DX contains the remainder.

If the divisor is a doubleword then the result is equal to EDX:EAX/
divisor. EAX contains the quotient and EDX and contains the
remainder.

Flags

OF	DF	IF	TF	SF	ZF	AF	PF	CF
?				?	?	?	?	?

Description

DIV performs an unsigned division of unsigned integers contained in AX (if
the divisor is a byte) or DX:AX (if the divisor is a word). If the specified divisor
is 16 bits wide, the dividend is placed in register pair DX:AX. The quotient
overwrites the contents of AX and the remainder is placed in DX. If the divisor
is a byte wide, the dividend is placed in AX. The quotient is left in AL and
the remainder is placed in AH. On 80386/486, if the divisor is EAX, the quotient
is placed in EAX and the divisor is placed in EDX.

Comments

If the quotient is too large to be placed in the destination register (AX for 8-bit division, DX:AX for 16-bit division or EDX:EAX for doubleword division) an interrupt 0 is generated. This usually happens when division by zero is attempted. In this case the quotient and remainder are undefined. Non-integer quotients are truncated to integers.

See Also

IDIV To divide one signed integer by another
IMUL To multiply two signed integers
MUL To multiply two unsigned integers

Timing and Encoding

Operands	Encoding	Examples	Bytes	Clocks	
DIV reg	1111 011w			8086/88	2
	mod,110,r/m			80286	9-20
	disp(0 or 2)			80386	varies
				80486	
DIV mem	1111 011w			8086/88	2
	mod,110,r/m			80286	9-20
	disp(0 or 2)			80386	varies
				80486	

HLT Halt   86,186,286,386,486

Syntax

HLT

Function

None

Flags

OF	DF	IF	T	SF	Z	AF	PF	CF

Description

The HLT instruction stops the work of the CPU until the processor is reset. It can be restarted if the Interrupt Flag (IF) is set to 1 and a nonmaskable interrupt occurs, or if IF is set to 1 and a maskable interrupt is requested by the INTR instruction.

Comments

The HLT instruction stops the CPU and leaves it waiting with CS and IP pointing to the instruction that follows HLT.

See Also

STI	To enable interrupts
CLI	To disable interrupts

Timing and Encoding

Operands	Encoding	Examples	Bytes	Clocks	
HLT	1111 0111	hlt	1	8086/88	2
	(F4h)			80286	2
				80386	5
				80486	4

IDIV Integer Division (Signed)　　　　86,186,286,386,486

Syntax

```
IDIV divisor
```

Function

If the divisor is a byte then the result is equal to AX/ divisor. AL contains the quotient and AH the remainder.

If the divisor is a word then the result is equal to DX:AX/ divisor. AX contains the quotient and DX the remainder.

Flags

OF	DF	IF	T	SF	ZF	AF	PF	CF
?				?	?	?	?	?

Description

The IDIV instruction performs a signed division of signed integers contained in AX (if the divisor is a byte) or DX:AX (if the divisor is a word). If the specified divisor is 16 bits wide, the dividend is placed in the register pair DX:AX. The quotient overwrites the contents of AX and the remainder is placed in DX. If the divisor is a byte wide, the dividend is placed in AX. The quotient is left in AL and the remainder is placed in AH. On 80386/486, if the divisor is EAX, the quotient is placed in EAX and the divisor is placed in EDX.

Comments

If the quotient is too large to be placed in the destination register (AX for 8-bit division and DX:AX for 16-bit division) an interrupt 0 is generated. This usually happens when division by 0 is attempted. In this case the quotient and the remainder are undefined. Non-integer quotients are truncated to integers.

When interrupt 0 is generated on 80286 and 80386/80486, the value saved in CS:IP points to the failed IDIV instruction. However on 8086/88 the value saved in CS:IP points to the instruction following the failed IDIV instruction.

See Also

DIV   To divide one unsigned integer by another
IEW   To divide one signed integer by another
IMUL To multiply signed integers
MUL   To multiply two unsigned integers

Timing and Encoding

Operands	Encoding	Examples	Bytes	Clocks	
IDIV reg	1111 1100	idiv bl	2	8086/88	b=101-112,w=165-184
	mod,111,r/m	idiv cx		80286	b=17,w=25
				80386	b=19,w=27,d=43
				80486	b=19,w=27,d=43
IDIV mem	1111 1100	idiv [bx]	2-4	8086/88	b=107-118,w=171-191+EA*
	mod,111,r/m	idiv cx		80286	b=20,w=28
				80386	b=22,w=30,d=46
				80486	b=20,w=28,d=44

IMUL Integer Multiplication (Signed)   86,186,286,386,486

Syntax

```
IMUL source
IMUL reg,immed                      - 80186-80386 only
IMUL reg16,reg_or_memory,immed      - 80186-80386
IMUL reg,reg                        - 80386
```

Function

```
if source is byte then AX=AL*source(signed)
if source is word then AX,DX=AX*source(signed)
```

Flags

OF	DF	IF	TF	SF	ZF	AF	PF	CF
*				?	?	?	?	*

Description

The IMUL instruction performs multiplication of signed numbers.

If the source operand in the first syntax is a byte, it is multiplied by the value in AL and the product is placed in AX. If the single operand is a word, it is multiplied by the value in AX and the product is placed in DX:AX. On 80386 or 80486 processors the operand can be a word in which case it is multiplied by the value in EAX and the result is placed in EDX:EAX. The Carry and Overflow Flags are cleared unless the product is too large to fit into the register where the second multiplier was located (AL, AX, EAX respectively), in which case these flags are set.

On 80186 and later processors there are two additional forms of this instruction - with either two or three operands.

If there are two operands, the number stored in the destination is multiplied by a constant, i.e. the second operand. The product is placed in the destination operand.

If there are three operands, the second and third operands are multiplied and the product is placed in the first operand.

On the 80386 and later processors any general 32-bit or 16-bit register can serve as the destination, the source must be a register or memory operand of the same size as the destination operand.

In all three cases the Overflow and Carry Flags are cleared unless the product is too large to fit in the first operand, in which case they are set.

See Also

AAM To convert a number in AL into BCD digits in AH and AL (least significant digits in AL)

MUL To multiply two signed integers

Timing and Encoding

Format	Encoding	Examples	Bytes	Clocks	
IMUL reg	1111 011w mod,101,r/m disp(0 or 2)	imul dl imul dx	2	8086/88 80286 80386 80486	b=80-98 w=128-154 b=13 w=21 b=9-14 w=9-22 d=9-38* b=13-18 w=13-26 d=13-I42
IMUL mem	1111 011w mod,101,r/m disp(0 or 2)	imul sum	2-4	8086/88 80286 80386 80486	(b=86-104 w=134-160)+EA* b=16 w= d=24 b=12-17 w=12-25 d=12-41 b=13-18 w=13-26 d=13-42
IMUL reg,immed	0110 10s1 mod,reg,r/m disp(0 or 2)	imul ax,10	2-4	8086/88 80286 80386 80486	(b=86-104 w=134-160)+EA* b=16 w= d=24 b=12-17 w=12-25 d=12-41 b=13-18 w=13-26 d=13-42
IMUL reg,reg, immed	0110 10s1 mod,reg,r/m disp(0 or 2)	imul ax,cx,2	2-4	8086/88 80286 80386 80486	(b=86-104 w=134-160)+EA* b=16 w= d=24 b=12-17 w=12-25 d=12-41 b=13-18 w=13-26 d=1
IMUL reg,reg	1111 011w mod,101,r/m disp(0 or 2)	imul ax,bx	2-4	8086/88 80286 80386 80486	(b=86-104 w=134-160)+EA* b=16 w= d=24 b=12-17 w=12-25 d=12-41 b=13-18 w=13-26 d=13-42
IMUL reg,mem	0110 10s1 mod,reg,r/m disp(0 or 2)	imul bx,var	2-4	8086/88 80286 80386 80486	(b=86-104 w=134-160)+EA* b=16 w= d=24 b=12-17 w=12-25 d=12-41 b=13-18 w=13-26 d=13-42

IN Input Byte From I/O Port   86,186,286,386,486

Syntax

```
IN   accumulator,port_address_byte
IN   accumulator,DX
```

Function

If byte: AL=data from i/o port number or AL=data is addressed by register DX.

If word: AX=data from i/o port number or AX=data is addressed by register DX.

Flags

OF	DF	IF	TF	SF	ZF	AF	PF	CF

Description

The IN instruction reads data (a byte, word or on 80386/80486 - a doubleword) from a specified port to the accumulator register. The port address is specified by an 8-bit constant from 0 to 255 or by the value placed in the DX register - from 0 to 65535. In protected modes, a general-protection error occurs if the IN instruction is used when the current privilege level is greater than the value of the IOPL Flag.

Comments

The IN instruction allows the data to be read from serial and parallel ports accessed via the input port addresses. On IBM PCs the port numbers are from 0 to 3FFh. If a port number is less than 256 it can be specified as a constant, but a port number greater than 255 must be placed in the DX register.

See Also

INS,INSB,INSD,INSW	To transfer a string from an I/O port.
OUT	To send a byte or word to an I/O port.
OUTS,OUTSB,OUTSD,OUTSW	To send a string to an I/O port

Timing and Encoding

Operands	Encoding	Example	Byte	Clocks	
IN accum,immed	1110 010w	in AL,20h	2	8086/88	10 14
	data (1 byte)	in ax,20h		80286	5
				80386	12,pm=6.26*
				80486	14 pm=9.29'
IN accum,DX	1110 110w	in al,dx	1	8086/88	8 12 (w)
		in ax,dx		80286	5
				80386	13 pm=7.27*
				80486	14 pm=8.28'

* - protect-mode timing: CPL<=IOPL. Second timing: CPL>IOPL

INC Increment Operand   86,186,286,386,486

Syntax

```
INC  operand
```

Function

```
Operand = operand + 1
```

Flags

OF	DF	IF	TF	SF	ZF	AF	PF	CF
*				*	*	*	*	

Description

The INC instruction adds 1 to the operand.

Comments

The operand of the INC instruction is treated as an unsigned integer and does not affect the Carry Flag (CF). The segment registers cannot be incremented. It is better to use the 16-bit register as the operand, because the instruction is encoded in 1 byte.

See Also

ADD   To add two operands.
DEC   To decrement an operand.

Timing and Encoding

Operands	Encoding	Examples	Bytes	Clocks	
INC reg8	1111 111w	inc al	2	8086/88	3
	mod,000,r/m	inc cl		80286	2
	disp(0 or 2)			80386	2
				80486	1
INC mem	1111 111w	inc total	2-4	8086/88	15+EA 23+EA (w)
	mod,000,r/m			80286	7
	disp(0 or 2			80386	6
				80486	3
INC reg16	0100 0reg	inc ax	1	8086/88	3
				80286	2
				80386	2
				80486	1

INT Software Interrupt   86,186,286,386,486

Syntax

```
INT int_number
```

Function

```
SP = SP - 2; Flags pushed; IF = 0; TF = 0; SP = 0; CS pushed;
SP = SP - 2;
IP pushed;
CS = data at memory address (type * 4 + 2)
IP = data at memory address (type * 4)
```

Flags

OF	DF	IF	TF	SF	ZF	AF	PF	CF
		0	0					

Description

The INT instruction generates the software interrupt of the CPU, specified by the *int_number*. The *int_number* must be from 0 through 255. When the INT instruction is performed in the real mode, the flags, CS and IP are pushed onto the stack (in that order) and the Interrupt Flags TF and IF are set to 0. The processor then jumps to the instruction whose address (offset and segment address) is stored in the Interrupt Vector Table (IVT) at a location equal to the *int_number* * 4. The IVT starts at segment 0, offset 0. The doubleword entry for the *int_number* is calculated by multiplying the *int_number* by 4.

Comments

Note that procedures called by INT must end with the IRET instruction.

If the *int_number* value is equal to 3 then Assembler encodes INT 3 as one byte of CCh. This is the interrupt which is used by debuggers to set a breakpoint.

See Also

CALL,RET	To call and return from procedures
INTO	To generate interrupt 4 if Overflow Flag is set
IRET	To return from interrupt

Timing and Encoding

Operands	Encoding	Examples	Bytes	Clocks	
INT 3	1100 1100 (CCh)	int3	1	8086/88	72 56 (w)
				80286	23+m
				80386	33
				80486	26
INT immed8	1100 1101 data(1 byte)	int 21h	2	8086/88	51/71
				80286	23+m
				80386	37
				80486	30

INTO Software Interrupt   86,186,286,386,486

Syntax

```
INTO
```

Function

```
If OF = 1, then
   SP = SP - 2
   Flags are pushed
   SP = SP - 2
   CS pushed
   SP = SP - 2
   IP pushed; CS = data at memory location 12h;
   IP = data at memory location 10 h.
```

Flags

OF	DF	IF	TF	SF	ZF	AF	PF	CF
		*	*					

Description

The INTO instruction is used for handling arithmetic overflow. If the Overflow Flag (OF) is set, INTO generates interrupt 4, otherwise it does nothing. The Interrupt Flag (IF) and Trap Flag (TF) are set.

Comments

If INTO is used for handling arithmetic overflow, you must write an interrupt handler for interrupt 4 and place it in a doubleword at address 10h. In MS-DOS the default handler for this interrupt is returned without doing anything.

See Also

INT   To generate a software interrupt for a specified number
IRET   To return from interrupt

Timing and Encoding

Operands	Encoding	Examples	Bytes	Clocks	
INTO	1100 1110	into	1	8086/88	53 73 (w) noj=4
	(CEh)			80286	24+m,noj=3
				80386	35 noj=3
				80486	26 noj=3

IRET Interrupt Return   86,186,286,386,486

Syntax

```
IRET[F]
```

Function

```
IP popped from stack
SP = SP + 2
CS popped from stack
SP = SP + 2
Flags popped from stack
SP = SP + 2
```

Flags

OF	DF	IF	TF	SF	ZF	AF	PF	CF
*	*	*	*	*	*	*	*	*

Description

The IRET instruction returns control back to the instruction after which the interrupt occurred, by popping IP, CS and the flags from the stack.

See Also

INT   To generate a software interrupt for a specified number
RET   To return from procedure
CALL To call procedure

Timing and Encoding

Format	Encoding	Examples	Bytes	Clocks	
IRET	1100 1111	iret	1	8086/88	32 /44
IRETF				80286	17+m pm=(31,55)+m*
				80386	22 pm=38,82*
				80486	15 pm=20,36

JA/JNBE Jump If Above/Jump If Not Below Or Equal
86,186,286,386,486

Syntax

```
JA/JNBE label
```

Function

If CF=0 and ZF=0 then IP=IP+Disp8. Displacement disp8 is
sign-extended to 16 bit.

If CF=0 and ZF=0 then IP=IP+Disp16 (Only for 80386/486).

Flags

OF	DF	IF	TF	SF	ZF	AF	PF	CF

Description

The JA instruction and its functional analog JNBE transfer control to the operand
address (IP+displacement) if the first unsigned operand is greater than the
second unsigned operand. If not, JA/JNBE transfers control to the next
instruction. The operand address must be from -127 to 127 bytes from the next
instruction.

Comments

The JA/JNBE instruction is used after CMP and SUB instructions.

See Also

JAE   To jump to specified label if above or equal
JBE   To jump to specified label if below or equal

Timing and Encoding

Format	Encoding	Examples	Bytes	Clocks	
JA 8-bit disp	0111 0111	ja label	2	8086/88	16 noj=4
	disp(1byte)			80286	7+m noj=3_
				80386	7+m noj=3
				80486	3 noj=1
JA 16-bit disp	0000 0111	ja sign	4	8086/88	--
(80386/486)	1000 0111			80286	--
	disp(2byte)			80386	7+m noj=3
				80486	3 noj=1

JAE/JNB/JNC Jump If Above Or Equal/Not Below/No Carry
86,186,286,386,486

Syntax

```
JAE/JNB/JNC label
```

Function

```
If CF=0 then
   IP = IP + Disp8. Displacement disp8 is sign-extended to
   16 bit.

If CF=0 then IP=IP+Disp16 (Only for 80386/486).
```

Flags

OF	DF	IF	TF	SF	ZF	AF	PF	CF

Description

The JAE instruction and its functional analogs JNB and JNC transfer control to the operand address (IP+displacement) if the first unsigned operand is less than or equal to the second unsigned operand. If not, JNB/JNC transfers control to the next instruction. The operand address must be from -128 to 127 bytes from the next instruction. On 80386/486 processors displacement can be 16-bits or 32-bits wide; the operand address must therefore be from -32768 to +32767 bytes from the current instruction.

Comments

The JAE/JNB/JNC instruction is used after the CMP and SUB instruction.

See Also

JGE	To jump to specified label if greater or equal
CMP	To compare two operands and set the flags
JMP	To jump unconditionally
TEST	To test the operand and set the flags

Timing and Encoding

Format	Encoding	Examples	Bytes	Clocks	
JAE 8-bit disp	0111 0011	jae total	2	8086/88	16 noj=4
JNB 8-bit disp	disp(1byte)	jnb sum		80286	7+m noj=3
JNC 8-bit disp		jnc resul		80386	7+m noj=3
				80486	3 noj=1
JAE 16-bit disp	0000 1111	jae huge	4	8086/88	--
JNB 16-bit disp	1000 0011	jnb bit		80286	--
JNC 16-bit disp	disp(2byte)	jnc res		80386	7+m noj=3
(for 80386/486)				80486	3 noj=1

JB/JNAE/JC Jump Below/Not Above Or Equal/Carry
86,186,286,386,486

Syntax

```
JB/JNAE/JC label
```

Function

```
If CF=1 then
    IP = IP + Disp8. Displacement disp8 is sign-extended to
    16 bit.

If CF=1 then IP = IP + Disp16 (Only for 80386/486).
```

Flags

OF	DF	IF	TF	SF	ZF	AF	PF	CF

Description

The JB instruction and its functional analogs JNAE and JC transfer control to the operand address (IP+displacement) if the first unsigned operand is less than or equal to the second unsigned operand. If not, JB/JNAE/JC transfers control to the next instruction. The operand address must be from -128 to 127 bytes from the next instruction. On 80386/486 processors displacement can be 16-bits or 32-bits wide; the operand address must therefore be from -32768 to +32767 bytes from the current instruction.

Comments

The JB/JNAE/JC instruction is used after the CMP and SUB instructions.

See Also

JAE	To jump to specified label if above or equal
JGE	To jump to specified label if greater or equal
CMP	To compare two operands and set the flags
JMP	To jump unconditionally
TEST	To test operand and set the flags

Timing and Encoding

Format		Encoding	Examples	Bytes	Clocks	
JB	8-bit disp	0111 0010	jbe total	2	8086/88	16 noj=4
JNAE	8-bit disp	disp(1byte)	jnae sum		80286	7+m noj=3
JC	8-bit disp				80386	7+m noj=3
					80486	3 noj=1
JB	16-bit disp	0000 1111	jbe huge	4	8086/88	--
JNAE	16-bit disp	1000 0010	jnae bit		80286	--
JC	16-bit disp	disp(2byte)			80386	7+m noj=3
(for 80386/486)					80486	3 noj=1

JBE/JNA Jump If Below Or Equal/Jump If Not Above
86,186,286,386,486

Syntax

```
JBE/JNA label
```

Function

```
If CF=1 or ZF=1 then
    IP = IP + Disp8. Displacement disp8 is sign-extended to
    16 bit.

If CF=1 or ZF=1 then IP = IP + Disp16 (Only for 80386/486).
```

Flags

OF	DF	IF	TF	SF	ZF	AF	PF	CF

Description

The JBE instruction and its functional analog JNA transfer control to the operand address (IP+displacement) if the first unsigned operand is less than or equal to the second unsigned operand. If not, JBE/JNA transfers control to the next instruction. The operand address must be from -128 to 127 bytes from the next instruction. On 80386/486 processors displacement can be 16-bits or 32-bits wide; the operand address must therefore be from -32768 to +32767 bytes from the current instruction.

Comments

The JBE/JNA instruction is used after the CMP and SUB instructions.

See Also

JGE	To jump to specified label if greater or equal
CMP	To compare two operands and set the flags
JMP	To jump unconditionally
TEST	To test the operand and set the flags

Timing and Encoding

Format	Encoding	Examples	Bytes	Clocks	
JBE 8-bit disp	0111 0110	jbe total	2	8086/88	16 noj=4
JNA 8-bit disp	disp(1byte)	jnae sum		80286	7+m noj=3
				80386	7+m noj=3
				80486	3 noj=1
JBE 16-bit disp	0000 0111	jbe huge	4	8086/88	--
JNA 16-bit disp	1000 0110	jnae bit		80286	--
(for 80386/486)	disp(2byte)			80386	7+m noj=3
				80486	3 noj=1

JCXZ Jump If CX Register Zero   86,186,286,386,486

Syntax

```
JCXZ label
```

Function

```
If CX=0 then
    IP = IP + Disp8. Displacement disp8 is sign-extended to
    16 bit.

If CF=1 then IP=IP+Disp16 (Only for 80386/486).
```

Flags

OF	DF	IF	TF	SF	ZF	AF	PF	CF

Description

The JCXZ instruction transfers control to the operand address (IP+displacement) if the CX register is 0. The operand address must be from -128 to 127 bytes from the next instruction. On 80386/486 processors displacement can be 16-bits or 32-bits wide; the operand address must therefore be from -32768 to +32767 bytes from the current instruction.

Comments

The JCXZ instruction is often used to avoid the execution of a loop.

See Also

LOOP	To loop if CX does not equal 0
LOOPE	To loop while CX equals 0 and ZF is set to 1
LOOPZ	To loop while CX equals 0 and ZF is set to 1
LOOPNZ	To loop while CX does not equal zero and ZF is clear
LOOPNE	To loop while CX does not equal zero and ZF is clear

Timing and Encoding

Format	Encoding	Examples	Bytes	Clocks	
JCXZ 8-bit disp	1110 0011 disp(1byte)	jcxz total	2	8086/88	18 noj=6
				80286	8+m noj=4
				80386	9+m noj=5
				80486	8 noj=5

JE/JZ Jump If Equal/Jump If Zero   86,186,286,386,486

Syntax

```
JE/JZ label
```

Function

```
If ZF=1 then
    IP = IP + Disp8. Displacement disp8 is sign-extended to
    16 bit.

If ZF=1 then IP = IP + Disp16 (Only for 80386/486).
```

Flags

OF	DF	IF	TF	SF	ZF	AF	PF	CF

Description

The JE instruction and its functional analog JZ transfer control to the operand address (IP+displacement) if the first unsigned operand is equal to the second unsigned operand. If not, JE/JZ transfers control to the next instruction. The operand address must be from -128 to 127 bytes from the next instruction. On 80386/486 processors, displacement can be 16-bits or 32-bits wide; the operand address must therefore be from -32768 to +32767 bytes from the current instruction.

Comments

The JE/JZ instruction is used after the CMP and SUB instructions.

See Also

JNE	To jump to specified label if not equal
CMP	To compare two operands and set the flags
JMP	To jump unconditionally
TEST	To test operand and set the flags

Timing and Encoding

Format	Encoding	Examples	Bytes	Clocks	
JE 8-bit disp	0111 1100	je tota	2	8086/88	16 noj=4
JZ 8-bit disp	disp(1byte)	jz sum		80286	7+m noj 3
				80386	7+m noj=3
				80486	3 noj=1
JE 16-bit disp	0000 1111	je huge	4	8086/88	--
JZ 16-bit disp	1000 1100	jz sum		80286	--
(for 80386/486)	disp(2byte)			80386	7+m noj=3
				80486	3 noj=1

JG/JNLE Jump If Greater/Jump If Not Less Than Or Equal
86,186,286,386,486

Syntax

```
JG/JNLE label
```

Function

```
If SF=OF AND ZF=0 then
   IP = IP + Disp8. Displacement disp8 is sign-extended to
   16 bit.

If SF=OF AND ZF=0 then IP = IP + Disp16 (Only for 80386/486).
```

Flags

OF	DF	IF	TF	SF	ZF	AF	PF	CF

Description

The JG instruction and its functional analog JNLE transfer control to the operand address (IP+displacement) if the first signed operand is greater than the second signed operand. If not, JN/JNLE transfers control to the next instruction. The operand address must be from -128 to 127 bytes from the next instruction. On 80386/486 processors displacement can be 16-bits or 32-bits wide; the operand address must therefore be from -32768 to +32767 bytes from the current instruction.

Comments

The JG/JNLE instruction is used after the CMP or SUB instructions.

See Also

JA	To jump to specified label if above
JLE	To jump to specified label if less than or equal to
CMP	To compare two operands and set the flags
JMP	To jump unconditionally
TEST	To test operand and set the flags

Timing and Encoding

Format	Encoding	Examples	Bytes	Clocks	
JG 8-bit disp	0111 1111	jg total	2	8086/88	16 noj=4
JNLE 8-bit disp	disp(1byte)	jnle sum		80286	7+m noj 3
				80386	7+m noj=3
				80486	3 noj=1
JG 16-bit disp	0000 1111	jg huge	4	8086/88	- -
JNLE 16-bit disp	1000 1100	jnle sum		80286	- -
(for 80386/486)	disp(2byte)			80386	7+m noj=3
				80486	3 noj=1

JGE/JNL Jump If Greater Or Equal/Jump If Not Less Than
86,186,286,386,486

Syntax

```
JGE/JNL label
```

Function

```
If SF=OF then
IP = IP + Disp8. Displacement disp8 is sign-extended to
    16 bit.

If SF=OF then IP = IP + Disp16 (Only for 80386/486).
```

Flags

OF	DF	IF	TF	SF	ZF	AF	PF	CF

Description

The JGE instruction and its functional analog JNL transfer control to the operand address (IP+displacement) if the first signed operand is greater than or equal to the second signed operand. If not, JG/JNL transfers control to the next instruction. The operand address must be from -128 to 127 bytes from the next instruction. On 80386/486 processors displacement can be 16-bits or 32-bits wide; the operand address must therefore be from -32768 to +32767 bytes from the current instruction.

Comments

The JG/JNL instruction is used after the CMP or SUB instructions.

See Also

JNE	To jump to specified label if not equal
CMP	To compare two operands and set the flags
JMP	To jump unconditionally
TEST	To test operand and set the flags

Timing and Encoding

Format	Encoding	Examples	Bytes	Clocks	
JGE 8-bit disp	0111 1101	jge total	2	8086/88	16 noj=4
JNL 8-bit disp	disp(1byte)	jnl sum		80286	7+m noj3
				80386	7+m noj=3
				80486	3 noj=1
JGE 16-bit disp	0000 1111	jge huge	4	8086/88	--
JNL 16-bit disp	1000 1101	jnl sum		80286	--
(for 80386/486)	disp(2byte)			80386	7+m noj=3
				80486	3 noj=1

JNE/JNZ Jump If Not Equal/Not Zero   86,186,286,386,486

Syntax

```
JNE disp
JNZ disp
```

Function

```
If ZF=0 then ip=ip+disp8
```

Flags

OF	DF	IF	TF	SF	ZF	AF	PF	CF

Description

If the first unsigned operand is not equal to the second unsigned operand, the JNE instruction and its functional analog JNZ transfer control to the operand address (IP+displacement). If operands are equal, control is passed to the next instruction. The operand address must be from -128 to +127 bytes from the next instruction. On 80386/486 the displacement can be up to 16-bits wide; the operand address must therefore be from -32768 to +32767 bytes from the next instruction.

Comments

The JNE/JNZ instruction is usually used after the CMP and SUB instructions.

See Also

CMP	To compare two operands and set the flags
JMP	To jump unconditionally
TEST	To test operand and set the flags

Timing and Encoding

Format	Encoding	Bytes	Clocks	
JNE displ8	0111 0101 disp(1)	1	8086/88 80286 80386 80486	16, noj=4 7+m,3nj 7+m,3nj 3,noj=1
JNE displ16	0000 1111 1000 0101 disp(2)	1	8086/88 80286 80386 80486	-- -- 7+m,noj=3 3,noj=1

LAHF Load Flags Into AH   86,186,286,386,486

Syntax

```
LAHF
```

Function

```
AH=EFLAGS & 00Fh
```

Flag

OF	DF	IF	TF	SF	ZF	AF	PF	CF

Description

The LAHF instruction writes the low-order byte of the flag register into AH. This byte includes the SignFlag (SF), Zero Flag (ZF), Auxiliary Flag (AF), Parity Flag (PF) and Carry Flag (CF).

Comments

The LAHF instruction is used to emulate the PUSH PSW instruction of the 8080 microprocessor or to save the SF, ZF, AF, PF and CF Flags without using the stack.

Timing and Encoding

Format	Encoding	Bytes	Clocks	
LAHF	1001 1111	1	8086/88	4
			80286	2
			80386	2
			80486	3

Example

```
LAHF            ; Load low-order byte of the flag register
SHR   AH,7      ; Select the SF from AH
AND   AH,1      ; AH contains the SF Flag
```

LDS Load Pointer Using DS   86,186,286,386,486

Syntax

```
LDS   destination,source
```

Function

```
destination=source
seg=source+2
```

Flags

OF	DF	IF	TF	SF	ZF	AF	PF	CF

Description

The LDS instruction places the segment address of the source operand into DS and the offset of the source operand into the destination register.

Comments

This instruction is useful for placing the address of a far pointer to any register.

See Also

LEA   To load offset of operand into a register

Timing and Encoding

Format	Encoding	Bytes	Clocks	
LDS reg,mem	1100 0101	2-4	80086/88	24+EA (w88=16+EA)
	mod,reg,r/m		80286	7
	disp(2)		80386	7
			80486	7

Example

LDS   sx,Pointer1   ; Load a pointer

LEA Load Effective Address   86,186,286,386,486

Syntax

LEA destination,source

Function

destination=address(source)

Flags

OF	DF	IF	TF	SF	ZF	AF	PF	CF

Description

The LEA instruction loads the offset of the source operand into the destination operand.

Comments

The destination operand cannot be a segment register.

See Also

LDS   To load segment and offset of a far pointer
LES   To load segment and offset of a far pointer

Timing and Encoding

Format	Encoding	Bytes	Clocks	
LEA reg,mem	1000 1101	2-6	8086/88	2+EA
	mod,reg,r/m		80286	3
	disp(2)		80386	2
			80486	2

Example

LEA   dx,message

LES Load Pointer Using ES   86,186,286,386,486

Syntax

LES dest_register, source

Function

ESI=[source]
dest_register=[sourse+4]

Flags

OF	DF	IF	TF	SF	ZF	AF	PF	CF

Description

This instruction loads the offset (upper 2 bytes of the doubleword) into the destination register and the selector (lower word) into the segment register which is specified as the operand by the instruction statement. The source memory operand specifies a 48-bit pointer (32-bit in real mode). A pointer consists of a 32-bit offset and a 16-bit selector.

See Also

LEA   To load offset of the operand into a register.

Timing and Encoding

Format	Encoding	Bytes	Clocks	
LDS reg,mem	1100 0100	2-4	8086/88	16+EA (=24 + EA)
	mod,reg,r/m		80286	7,pm=21
	disp(2)		80386	7,pm=22
			80486	6,pm=12

Example

```
LES ESI,Pointer 1
```

LFS Load Pointer Using FS   386,486

Syntax

```
LFS dest_register,source
```

Function

```
FS=[source]
```

Flags

OF	DF	IF	TF	SF	ZF	AF	PF	CF

Description

The LFS instruction loads the offset of a 32-bit or a 48-bit pointer which is placed in a source operand (upper 2 bytes of the doubleword) into the destination register and the segment (low word) into FS.

See Also

LEA   To load the offset of the operand into a register

Timing and Encoding

Format	Encoding	Bytes	Clocks	
LFS reg,mem	0000 1111	4-6	8086/88	-
	1011 0100		80286	-
	mod,reg,r/m		80386	7
	disp(2,4)		80486	7

Example

```
LFS EDI,far_pointer
```

LGS Load Pointer Using GS   386,486

Syntax

```
LGS dest_register,source
```

Function

```
GS=[source]
dest_register=[source+4]
```

Flags

OF	DF	IF	TF	SF	ZF	AF	PF	CF

Description

The LGS instruction loads the offset of a 32-bit or a 48-bit pointer which is placed in a source operand (upper 2 bytes of the doubleword) into the destination register and the segment (low word) into the GS register.

See Also

LEA To load the offset of the operand into a register

Timing and Encoding

Format	Encoding	Bytes	Clocks	
LDS reg,mem	0000 1111	4-6	8086/88	-
	1011 0101		80286	-
	mod,reg,r/m		80386	7
	disp(2 or 4)		80486	6

Example

LGS bx,far_pointer

LOCK Assent BUS LOCK Signal\Signal Prefix
86,186,286,386,486

Syntax

LOCK

Description

The LOCK instruction prefix is used to prevent other processors in the multiprocessor hardware configuration from accessing the BUS for the duration of the instruction.

Comments

The LOCK instruction must only precede one of the following instructions: BT, BTS, BTR, BTC, XCHG, AND, OR, SBB, SUB, XOR, DEC, INC, NEG, or NOT at any one time. LOCK is used as a prefix for an instruction that performs an operation on a shared memory location. Other processors cannot access this location for the duration of the instruction. The XCHG instruction does not require the LOCK prefix because the CPU always activates the BUS LOCK signal during a memory XCHG.

See Also

ESC To send an instruction to the coprocessor

Timing and Encoding

Format	Encoding	Bytes	Clocks	
LOCK	1111 0000		8086/88	2
			80286	0
			80386	0
			80486	1

Example

```
LOCK
XCHG AL, Location
```

LODS,LODSB,LODSW Load String   86,186,286,386,486

Syntax

```
LODS  string
LODSB
LODSW
LODSD (only 80386/486)
```

Function

```
if opcode is LODSB then n=1
if opcode is LODSW then n=2
if opcode is LODSD then n=4
accumulator=DS:[ESI]
if DF=0 then
   ESI=ESI+n
   if not
      ESI=ESI-n
```

Flags

OF	DF	IF	TF	SF	ZF	AF	PF	CF

Description

The LODS instruction places the byte, word or doubleword from DS:SI (DS:SI for 32-bit addresses) into the accumulator. If the Direction Flag (DF) is clear, SI is incremented by the size of the operand. If DF is set, SI is decremented by the size of the operand.

Comments

LODSB, LODSW, and LODSD do not use an operand. The LODS operand is used to indicate whether a byte, word or dword is loaded and whether the segment register is to be overridden. The LODS instruction is not usually used with a repeat prefix, because it is used to repeatedly overwrite the contents of the accumulator with the value from the memory.

See Also

MOVS,MOVSB,MOVSD,MOVSW   To copy from DS:SI to ES:DI
STOS,STOSB,STOSW,STOSD   To copy from AL to ES:DI

Timing and Encoding

Format	Encoding	Bytes	Clocks	
LODS	1010 110w	1	8086/88	12 16(w)
			80286	5
			80386	5
			80486	2

Example

LODS STR   ; next character into AL

LOOP/LOOPW/LOOPD   Loop   86,186,286,386,486

Syntax

```
LOOP  label
LOOPW label
LOOPD label
```

Function

```
ECX=ECX-1
   if (ECX!=0) then
   EIP=EIP+offset
```

Flags

OF   DF   IF   TF   SF   ZF   AF   PF   CF

Description

The LOOP (LOOPW) instruction decrements the CX register and, if the result does not equal 0, transfers control to the address specified by the operand. The LOOPD instruction works in the same way but deals with the ECX register of 80386/80486 microprocessors.

Comments

The operand of the LOOP instruction must be from -128 to +127 bytes from the instruction next to LOOP.

See Also

JMP   To jump unconditionally
JCXZ   To jump when CX is 0

Timing and Encoding

Format	Encoding	Bytes	Clocks
LOOP	1110 0010 disp(1byte)	2	8086/88 17,noj=5 80286 8+m,noj=4 80386 11+m 80486 7,noj=6

Example

```
        MOV  EC,count    ; Load counter in CX
        LEA  SI,array    ;
clear:  LODSB            ;
        LOOP clear       ;
```

LOOPE/LOOPEW/LOOPED Loop On Condition
86,186,286,386,486

Syntax

```
    LOOPE  label
    LOOPEW label
    LOOPED label
```

Function

```
ECX=ECX-1
    if (ECX!=0 & ZF=1) then
    EIP=EIP+offset
```

Flags

OF	DF	IF	TF	SF	ZF	AF	PF	CF

Description

The LOOPE (LOOPEW) instruction decrements the CX register and tests whether the Zero Flag (ZF) has been set. If CX does not equal 0, it transfers control to the address specified by the operand. The LOOPED instruction works in the same way but deals with the ECX register of 80386/80486 microprocessors and overrides the default instruction.

Comments

The operand of the LOOP instruction must be from -128 to +127 bytes from the next LOOPE instruction.

See Also

```
    LOOP        To loop
    JMP         To jump unconditionally
    JCXZ        To jump when CX is 0
```

Timing and Encoding

Format	Encoding	Bytes	Clocks	
LOOPE	1110 0001	2	8086/88	18,noj=6
	disp(1byte)		80286	8+m,noj=4
			80386	11+m
			80486	9,noj=6

Example

```
LOOPE     again
```

LOOPNE/LOOPNEW/LOOPNED Loop On Condition
86,186,286,386,486

Syntax

```
LOOPNE  label
LOOPNEW label
LOOPNED label
```

Function

```
ECX=ECX-1
    if (ECX!=0 & ZF=0) then
    EIP=EIP+offset
```

Flags

OF	DF	IF	TF	SF	ZF	AF	PF	CF

Description

The LOOPNE (LOOPNEW) instruction performs a similar operation to LOOPE. It decrements the CX register and tests whether the Zero Flag (ZF) has been cleared. If CX does not equal 0, LOOPNE transfers control to the address specified by the operand. The LOOPNED instruction works in the same way but deals with the ECX register of 80386/80486 microprocessors and overrides the default instruction.

Comments

The operand of the LOOP instruction must be in the range -128 to +127 bytes from the instruction next to LOOP.

See Also

LOOP	To loop
LOOPE	To loop when ZF=1
LOOPZ	To loop when ZF=1
JCXZ	To loop when CX is 0

Timing and Encoding

Format	Encoding	Bytes	Clocks	
LOOPNE	1110 0000	2	8086/88	19,noj=5
	disp(1byte)		80286	8,noj=4
			80386	11+m
			80486	9,noj=6

Example

        LOOPNE again

LOOPNZ/LOOPNZW/LOOPNZD Loop If Not Zero
86,186,286,386,486

Syntax

        LOOPNZ   label
        LOOPNZW label
        LOOPNZD label

Function

        ECX=ECX-1
            if (ECX!=0 & ZF=0) then
            EIP=EIP+offset

Flags

        OF   DF   IF   TF   SF   ZF   AF   PF   CF

Description

The LOOPNZ (LOOPNZW) performs the same operation as LOOPNE. It decrements the CX register and tests whether the Zero Flag (ZF) has been cleared. If CX does not equal 0, LOOPNZ transfers control to the address specified by the operand. The LOOPNZD instruction works in the same way but deals with the ECX register of 80386/80486 microprocessors and overrides the default instruction.

Comments

The operand of the LOOPNZ instruction must be from -128 to +127 bytes from the next LOOPNZ instruction.

See Also

LOOP	To loop
LOOPE	To loop when ZF=1
LOOPZ	To loop when ZF=1
JCXZ	To loop when CX=0

Timing and Encoding

Format	Encoding	Bytes	Clocks	
LOOPNZ	1110 0000	2	8086/88	19,noj=5
	disp(1byte)		80286	8,noj=4
			80386	11+m
			80486	9,noj=6

Example

        LOOPNZ   again

LOOPZ/LOOPZW/LOOPZD Loop On Condition
86,186,286,386,486

Syntax

        LOOPZ   label
        LOOPZW label
        LOOPZD label

Function

        ECX=ECX-1
          if (ECX!=0 & ZF=1) then
          EIP=EIP+offset

Flags

OF	DF	IF	TF	SF	ZF	AF	PF	CF

Description

The LOOPZ (LOOPZW) instruction performs the same operation as LOOPE. It decrements the CX register and tests whether the Zero Flag (ZF) has been set. If CX does not equal 0, LOOPZ transfers control to the address specified by the operand. The LOOPZD instruction works in the same way but deals with the ECX register of 80386/80486 microprocessors and overrides the default instruction.

Comments

The operand of the LOOP instruction must be from -128 to +127 bytes from the next LOOPE instruction.

See Also

LOOP	To loop
JMP	To jump unconditionally
JCXZ	To jump when CX is 0

Timing and Encoding

Format	Encoding	Bytes	Clocks	
LOOPZ	1110 0001	2	8086/88	18,noj=6
	disp(1byte)		80286	8+m,noj=4
			80386	11+m
			80486	9,noj=6

Example

```
find   LODSB          ; Load symbol
       CMP   AL,CH     ; Compare symbol with CH
       LOOPZ    find   ; Continue until CH equals 0
```

MOV   Move Data   86,186,286,386,486

Syntax

```
MOV destination,source
```

Function

```
Destination = Source
```

Flags

OF	DF	IF	TF	SF	ZF	AF	PF	CF

Description

The MOV instruction copies the data from the source to the destination operand.

Comments

The CS register cannot be used as a destination operand. If the destination operand is SS, interrupts are disabled until the next instruction is executed (in early versions of 8088 and 8086 processors this feature was not implemented). The moving of data between two memory locations or segment registers requires an intermediate step. In this case you should use a nonsegment register as an intermediate storage for the data.

See Also

MOVS   To copy a string from DS:SI to ES:DI

Timing and Encoding

Format	Encoding	Examples	Bytes	Clocks	
MOV reg,reg	1000 10dw mod,reg,r/m disp(0 or 2)	mov dh,bh mov dx,cx	2	8086/88 80286 80386 80486	2 2 2 1
MOV mem,reg	1000 10dw mod,reg,r/m disp(0 or 2)	mov count,cx mov array[di],bx	2-4	8086/88 80286 80386 80486	9+EA 13+EA (w) 3 2 1
MOV reg,mem	1000 10dw mod,reg,r/m disp(0 or 2)	mov dx,bx[si]	2-4	8086/88 80286 80386 80486	8+EA 12+EA (w) 5 4 1
MOV mem,immed	1100 011w mod,000,r/m disp(0 or 2) data(1 or 2)	mov data,7 mov [bx],7fffh	3-6	8086/88 80286 80386 80486	10+EA 14+EA (w) 3 2 1
MOV reg,immed	1011 w reg data(1 or 2)	mov ax,17	3-6	8086/88 80286 80386 80486	4 2 2 1
MOV mem,accum	1010 00dw disp(0 or 2)	mov sum,ax	3	8086/88 80286 80386 80486	10 14 (w) 3 2 1
MOV accum,mem	1010 00dw disp(0 or 2)	mov ax,sum	3	8086/88 80286 80386 80486	10 14 (w) 5 4 1
MOV segreg,reg16	1000 11d0 mod,sreg,r/m disp(0 or 2)	mov ds,a	2	8086/88 80286 80386 80486	2 2,pm=17 2,pm=18 3,pm=9
MOV segreg,mem16	1000 11d0 mod,sreg,r/m disp(0 or 2)	mov es,psp	2-4	8086/88 80286 80386 80486	8+EA 12+EA (w) 5,pm=19 5,pm=19 3,pm=9
MOV reg16,segreg	1000 11d0 mod,sreg,r/m disp(0 or 2)	mov ax,ds	2	8086/88 80286 80386 80486	2 2 2 2
MOV mem16,segreg	1000 11d0 mod,sreg,r/m disp(0 or 2)	mov old_st,ss	2-4	8086/88 80286 80386 80486	9+EA 13+EA (w) 3 2 3

MOVS/MOVSB/MOVSW/MOOVSD Move String
86,186,286,386,486

Syntax

```
MOVS    dest,source
MOVSD   dest
MOVSW   dest
MOVSD   dest
```

Function

```
if opcode is MOVSB then n=1
if opcode is MOVSW then n=2
if opcode is MOVSD then n=4
ES:[EDI]=DS:[ESI]
if DF=0 then
    ESI=ESI+n
    EDI=EDI+n
else
    ESI=ESI-n
    EDI=EDI-n
```

Flags

OF	DF	IF	TF	SF	ZF	AF	PF	CF

Description

The MOVS (MOVSB, MOVSW, MOVSD) instruction copies the source string pointed to by DS:SI to the destination address pointed to by ES:DI. Once the string has been copied, DI and SI are incremented (if DF has been cleared) or decremented (if DF has been set). The operand of the MOVS instruction determines the size of the data elements to be transferred. MOVSD works in the same way but deals with the ECX register of 80386/80486 microprocessors.

Comments

The MOVS instruction and its modifications (the version depends on the size of the operand) may be used with the REP prefix. A segment override can be applied to the source operand of the MOVS instruction.

See Also

LODS,LODSB,LODSW,LODSD	To copy from DS:SI to AX,AL or EAX
STOS,STOSB,STOSW,STOSD	To copy from DS:SI to ES:DI
REP,REPNZ,REPZ	To repeat an instruction

Timing and Encoding

Format	Encoding	Bytes	Clocks	
MOVS	1010 010w	1	8086/88	18 26
			80286	5
			80386	7
			80486	7

Example

```
      LEA   SI,string   ; Get source string
      LES   DI,buf      ; Destination address
      MOV   CX,100      ; Size of string
      CLD               ; Set Direction Flag DF
REP   MOVSB             ; MOV 100 bytes
```

MUL Multiply (Unsigned)   86,186,286,386,486

Syntax

```
MUL source
```

Function

```
if source is byte then AX = AL * source(unsigned)
if source is word then AX,DX = AX * source(unsigned)
```

Flags

OF	DF	IF	TF	SF	ZF	AF	PF	CF
*				?	?	?	?	*

Description

MUL multiplies an unsigned number in AL (if the operand is a byte) or in AX (if the operand is a word) by the operand. The result overwrites the contents of AX register, if the operand is a byte and the DX:AX registers (the 16 most significant bits in DX), if it is a word. On the 80386/486 if the operand is EAX, the result is returned in EDX:EAX. Both operands are treated as unsigned binary numbers. If the higher part of the result (AH for byte source, DX for word source) is non-zero, flags CF and OF are set. If not, they are cleared.

See Also

IMUL To multiply two signed integers

Timing and Encoding

Format	Encoding	Examples	Byte	Clocks	
MUL reg	1111 011w	mul dl	2-4	8086/88	b=70-77 w=118-133
	mod,100,r/m			80286	b=13 w=21
	disp(0 or 2)			80386	b=9-14 w=9-22 d=9-38
				80486	b=13-18 w=13-26 d=13-42
MUL mem	1111 011w	mul sum	2-4	8086/88	16+EA 24+EA (w)
	mod,100,r/m			80286	7
	disp(0 or 2)			80386	7
				80486	3

NEG Two's Complement Negation   86,186,286,386,486

Syntax

```
NEG operand
```

Function

```
operand=0 - operand
```

Flags

OF	DF	IF	TF	SF	ZF	AF	PF	CF
*				*	*	*	*	*

Description

The NEG instruction subtracts the operand from 0 and places its two's complement into the operand. If the operand is 0 then the Carry Flag (CF) is cleared.

If the operand contains the maximum possible negative value (-128 for a byte operand or -32768 for words) the operand does not change but the Carry Flag and Overflow Flags are set.

See Also

NOT   To toggle all bits of the operand
SUB   To subtract one operand from another
SBB   To subtract one operand from another with borrow

Timing and Encoding

Format	Encoding	Bytes	Clocks	
NEG reg	1111 011w	2-4	8086/88	3
	mod,011,r/m		80286	2
	disp(0 or 2)		80386	2
			80486	1
NEG mem	1111 011w	1	8086/88	16+EA (w88=24+EA)
	mod,011,r/m		80286	7
	disp(0 or 2)		80386	6
			80486	3

Example

```
NEG  AX
```

NOP No Operation   86,186,286,386,486

Syntax

```
NOP
```

Function

```
This command has no effect
```

Flags

OF	DF	IF	TF	SF	ZF	AF	PF	CF

Description

The NOP instruction performs no operation.

Comments

The NOP instruction is often used for a timing delay or for alignment.

Timing and Encoding

Format	Encoding	Bytes	Clocks	
NOP	1001 0000	1	8086/88	3
			80286	3
			80386	3
			80486	3

Example

```
       MOV   CX,100      ; Size of timing delay
delay: NOP               ; Nothing occurs - 3 cycles
       LOOP  delay       ; Repeats the cycle
```

NOT One's Complement Negation   86,186,286,386,486

Syntax

```
NOT operand
```

Function

```
operand=~(operand)
```

Flags

OF	DF	IF	TF	SF	ZF	AF	PF	CF

Description

The NOT instruction inverts each bit of the operand. The operand can be a word or a byte.

See Also

AND   To perform a bitwise AND of two operands
NEG   To negate a number
OR   To perform a bitwise OR of two operands
XOR   To perform a bitwise exclusive OR of two operands

Timing and Encoding

Format	Encoding	Bytes	Clocks	
NOT reg	1111 011w	1	8086/88	3
	mod,010,r/m		80286	2
	disp(0 or 2)		80386	2
			80486	1
NOT mem	1111 000w	1	8086/88	16+EA (w88=24+EA)
	mod,010,r/m		80286	7
	disp(0 or 2)		80386	6
			80486	3

Example

NOT   AH   ; complement all bits in AH

Inclusive OR   86,186,286,386,486

Syntax

OR destination,source

Function

destination=destination | source

Flags

OF	DF	IF	TF	SF	ZF	AF	PF	CF
0				*	*	*	*	0

Description

The OR instruction performs a bitwise OR of the source and destination operands and places the result in the destination operand.

Comments

A bitwise OR instruction sets each bit of the result to 1 if the corresponding bit of the source operand or destination operand, or both, is 1.

See Also

AND To perform a bitwise AND of two operands
NOT To perform a bitwise NOT of operand
XOR To perform a bitwise exclusive OR of two operands

Timing and Encoding

Format	Encoding	Bytes	Clocks	
OR reg,reg	0000 10dw	2	8086/88	3
	mod,reg,r/m		80286	2
	disp(0 or 2)		80386	2
			80486	1
OR mem,reg	0000 10dw	2-4	8086/88	16+EA (w88=24+EA)
	mod,reg,r/m		80286	7
	disp(0 or 2)		80386	7
			80486	3
OR reg,mem	0000 10dw	2-4	8086/88	9+EA (w88=13+EA)
	mod,reg,r/m		80286	7
	disp(0 or 2)		80386	6
			80486	2
OR mem,immed	1000 10sw	3-6	8086/88	b=17,w=25+EA
	mod,001,r/m		80286	7
	disp(0 or 2)		80386	7
	data(1 or 2)		80486	3
OR reg,immed	1000 10sw	3-4	8086/88	4
	mod,001,r/m		80286	3
	disp(0 or 2)		80386	2
	data(1 or 2)		80486	1
OR accum,immed	0000 110w	2-3	8086/88	4
	data(1 or 2)		80286	3
			80386	2
			80486	1

Example

OR   AH,80H   ; Set high bit of AH

OUT Output To Port   86,186,286,386,486

Syntax

    OUT port,accumulator

Function

    port = accumulator

Flags

OF	DF	IF	TF	SF	ZF	AF	PF	CF

Description

The OUT instruction sends the byte stored in the accumulator register to the specified I/O port. If the port address is an immediate operand, its value may be in the range 0-255. A port address greater than 255 must be placed in the DX register and this register used as the operand.

See Also

IN	To read a byte or a word from an I/O port
INS,INSB,INSD,INSW	To read a string from an I/O port
OUTS,OUTSB,OUTSD,OUTSW	To send a string to an I/O port

Timing and Encoding

Format	Encoding	Bytes	Clocks	
OUT immed,acc	1110 011w	2	8086/88	10 (w88=14)
	data(1)		80286	3
			80386	10
			80486	16
OUT DX,acc	1110 111w	1	8086/88	8 (w88=12)
	data(2)		80286	3
			80386	11
			80486	16

Example

```
MOV  DX,289h    ; set port address
OUT  DX,AX      ; send word in AX to port 289h
```

POP Pop Value Off Stack   86,186,286,386,486

Syntax

```
POP  destination
```

Function

```
destination=SS:[SP]
SP=SP+2
destination=SS:[ESP]      (only for 80386/486
ESP=ESP+4                 in 32-bit mode)
```

Flags

OF	DF	IF	TF	SF	ZF	AF	PF	CF

Description

The POP instruction pops the top of the stack into the destination operand. The SP is incremented by 2 to point to the new top of the stack (ESP is incremented by 4 if a 32-bit value popped).

Comments

The destination operand of the POP instruction can be any 16-bit register, memory location or segment register, except CS.

See Also

PUSHF,POPF To push and pop the flag register
RET   To pop an address from the stack and jump to it

Timing and Encoding

Format	Encoding	Bytes	Clocks	
POP reg	0101 1reg	1	8086/88	8 88=12
			80286	5
			80386	4
			80486	1
POP mem	1000 1111	2-4	8086/88	17+EA (88=25+EA)
	mod,000,r/m		80286	5
	disp(2)		80386	5
			80486	6
POP segreg	000,sreg,111	1	8086/88	8 (88=12)
	mod,reg,r/m		80286	5,pm=20
	disp(0 or 2)		80386	7,pm=21
			80486	3,pm=9
POP segreg*	0000 1111	2	8086/88	--
	10,sreg,001		80286	--
	disp(0 or 2)		80386	7,pm=21
	data(1 or 2)		80486	3,pm=9

* 80386/486 only

Example

POP DS

POPA Pop All General Registers   186,286,386,486

Syntax

```
POPA
```

Function

```
POP DI
POP SI
POP BP
ADD ESP,2
POP BX
POP DX
POP CX
POP AX
```

Flags

OF	DF	IF	TF	SF	ZF	AF	PF	CF

Description

The POPA instruction pops the top 16 bytes of the stack into the 8 general registers: DI, SI, BP, SP, BX, DX, CX and AX.

Comments

The instruction discards the value for the SP register rather than destroying the stack pointer.

See Also

POP	To pop a single word from the top of the stack
PUSHA	To push all the registers onto the stack
PUSHF,POPF	To push and pop the flags

Timing and Encoding

Format	Encoding	Bytes	Clocks	
POPA	0110 0001	1	8086/88	--
			80286	19
			80386	24
			80486	9

Example

```
POPA
```

POPAD Pop All General Registers   386,486

Syntax

```
POPAD
```

Function

```
POP EDI
POP ESI
POP EBP
ADD ESP,4
POP EBX
POP EDX
POP ECX
POP EAX
```

Flags

OF	DF	IF	TF	SF	ZF	AF	PF	CF

Description

The POPAD instruction pops all of the 32-bit general registers except ESP from the stack into the 8 general registers: EDI, ESI, EBP, ESP, EBX, EDX, ECX, and EAX.

Comments

The instruction discards the value for the ESP register rather than destroying the stack pointer.

See Also

POP	To pop a single word from the top of the stack
POPA	To pop all the registers from the stack
PUSHA	To push all the registers onto the stack
PUSHF,POPF	To push and pop the flags

Timing and Encoding

Format	Encoding	Bytes	Clocks	
POPAD	0110 0001	1	8086/88	--
			80286	19
			80386	24
			80486	9

Example

```
POPAD
```

POPF Pop Stack Into FLAGS   86,186,286,386,486

Syntax

```
POPF
```

Function

```
FLAGS=SS:[ESP]
ESP=ESP+2
```

Flags

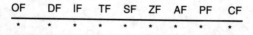

OF	DF	IF	TF	SF	ZF	AF	PF	CF
*	*	*	*	*	*	*	*	*

Description

The POPF instruction pops the top word on the stack into the FLAGS register.

On 80386/486 processors use the POPFD instruction to pop the 32-bit EFLAGS register.

See Also

PUSH,POP   To push and pop a 16-bit value
PUSHF   To push the flags on the stack

Timing and Encoding

Format	Encoding	Bytes	Clocks	
POPF	1001 1101	1	8086/88	8 (88=12)
			80286	5
			80386	5
			80486	9,pm=6

Example

```
POPF
```

POPED Pop Stack Into EFLAGS   386,486

Syntax

```
POPED
```

Function

```
EFLAGS=SS:[ESP]
ESP=ESP+4
```

Description

The POPED instruction pops the top 32-bit value of the stack into the FLAGS register.

See Also

PUSH, POP	To push and pop a 16-bit value
PUSHF, POPF	To push and pop the flags

Timing and Encoding

Format	Encoding	Bytes	Clocks	
POPED	1001 1101	1	8086/88	-
			80286	-
			80386	5
			80486	9, pm=6

Example

POPED

PUSH,PUSHW,PUSHD Push Value Onto Stack
86,186,286,386,486

Syntax

```
PUSH   operand
PUSHW  operand
PUSHD  operand
```

Function

```
if (size of(operand)=16) then
    ESP=ESP-2
if not
    ESP=ESP-4
SS:[ESP]=operand
```

Flags

OF	DF	IF	TF	SF	ZF	AF	PF	CF

Description

The PUSH instruction and its modifications copy the operand onto the stack. The stack pointer is decreased and the source value is copied to the top of the new stack. The operand may be a segment register, a memory location, or a general purpose 16-bit register. On 80186 - 80486 processors the operand can be a constant. As usual, the size of the operand specifies the version of PUSH - PUSHW or PUSHD, push a word (2 bytes) or a double word (4 bytes) respectively. On 80386/486 processors a 32-bit value can be pushed by specifying a 32-bit operand.

Comments

On 8086/8088 processors PUSH SP pushes the value of SP after it has been decremented, but on 80186 - 80486 processors, PUSH SP pushes the value of SP before it is decremented. This fact can be used to distinguish between 8086/88 and the rest of the i80x86 family of processors.

See Also

POP	To pop a 16-bit value from the stack
PUSHF,POPF	To push and pop the flags

Timing and Encoding

Format	Encoding	Bytes	Clocks	
PUSH reg16	0101 0reg	1	8086/88	11(88=15)
PUSH reg32*			80286	3
PUSHW reg16			80386	2
PUSHD reg16*			80486	1
PUSHD reg32*				
PUSH mem16	0101 0reg	2-4	8086/88	16+EA(88=24+EA)
PUSH reg32*	mod,110,r/m		80286	5
	disp(2)		80386	5
			80486	4
PUSH segreg	00,sreg,110	1	8086/88	10(88=14)
PUSHW segreg			80286	3
PUSHD segreg*			80386	2
			80486	3
PUSH segreg	0000 1111	2	8086/88	-
PUSHW segreg	10,sreg,000		80286	-
PUSHD segreg*			80386	2
			80486	3
PUSH immed	0110 10s0	2-3	8086/88	-
PUSHW immed	data(1or2)		80286	3
PUSHD immed*			80386	2
			80486	1

* 80386/486 only

Example

POPED

PUSHA Push 16-bit GENERAL Registers   186,286,386,486

Syntax

```
PUSHA
```

Function

```
temp=SP
PUSH AX
PUSH CX
PUSH DX
PUSH BX
PUSH temp
PUSH BP
PUSH SI
PUSH DI
```

Flags

OF	DF	IF	TF	SF	ZF	AF	PF	CF

Description

The PUSHA instruction pushes the eight general purpose 16-bit registers onto the stack.

Comments

On 8086/8088 processors the PUSHA instruction can be used to push the 32-bit registers.

See Also

PUSH	To push a word onto the stack
POPA	To pop all registers
PUSHF,POPF	To push and pop the flags

Timing and Encoding

Format	Encoding	Bytes	Clocks	
PUSHA	0110 0000	1	8086/88	-
			80286	3
			80386	2
			80486	1

PUSHAD Push 32-bit General Registers   186,286,386,486

Syntax

    PUSHAD

Function

    temp=ESP
    PUSH EAX
    PUSH ECX
    PUSH EDX
    PUSH EBX
    PUSH temp
    PUSH EBP
    PUSH ESI
    PUSH EDI

Flags

OF	DF	IF	TF	SF	ZF	AF	PF	CF

Description

The PUSHAD instruction pushes all eight general purpose 32-bit registers onto the stack.

Comments

The ESP value pushed onto the stack is the contents of the register before execution of the PUSHAD instruction.

See Also

PUSH,PUSHA	To push a word onto the stack
POPA	To pop all registers
PUSHF,POPF	To push and pop the flags

Timing and Encoding

Format	Encoding	Bytes	Clocks	
PUSHAD	0110 0000	1	8086/88	-
			80286	17
			80386	18
			80486	11

Example

    PUSHAD

PUSHF Push 16-bit FLAGS Registers   86,186,286,386,486

Syntax

```
PUSHF
```

Function

```
SP=SP-2
SS:[SP]=FLAGS
```

Flags

OF	DF	IF	TF	SF	ZF	AF	PF	CF

Description

The PUSHF instruction pushes the Flags register onto the stack.

Comments

On 80386/486 processors the PUSHFD instruction can be used to push the 32-bit EFLAGS register onto the stack.

See Also

PUSH,POP   To push and pop a single 16-bit value
POPF   To pop the top of the stack into the flags register

Timing and Encoding

Format	Encoding	Bytes	Clocks	
PUSHF	1001 1100	1	8086/88	10(88=14)
			80286	3
			80386	4
			80486	4,pm=3

PUSHFD Push EFLAGS Register   386,486

Syntax

```
PUSHFD
```

Function

```
ESP=ESP-4
SS:[ESP]=EFLAGS
```

Flags

OF	DF	IF	TF	SF	ZF	AF	PF	CF

Description

The PUSHFD instruction pushes the EFLAGS register onto the stack.

See Also

| PUSH,POP | To push and pop a single 16-bit value |
| PUSHF,POPF | To push and pop the top of the stack into the flags register |

Timing and Encoding

Format	Encoding	Bytes	Clocks	
PUSHFD	1001 1100	1	8086/88	-
			80286	-
			80386	4
			80486	4,pm=3

Example

PUSHFD

RCL Rotate Through Carry Left   86,186,286,386,486

Syntax

```
RCL destination,count
```

Function

```
temp=max(count,31)
if temp=1 then
    OF=(highbit(destination)!=CF)
if not
    OF=?
value=concatenate(CF,destination)
while(temp!=0)
    x=highbit(value)
    value=(value<<1)+x
    temp=temp-1
end
CF=highbit(value)
destination=value
```

Flags

OF	DF	IF	TF	SF	ZF	AF	PF	CF
*								*

Description

The RCL instruction rotates the bits of the destination operand to the left by the number of the bit position specified by the second operand, count. On 8086/88 processors the count operand must be 1 or equal to the value in the CL register. On 80186 - 80486 processors, the count operand can be an 8-bit immediate constant. This instruction concatenates the Carry Flag (CF) with the destination operand and shifts it to the position of the least significant bit of the destination operand. It replaces the CF with the most significant bit of the destination operand.

The Overflow Flag is set if the count is 1 and the Carry Flag (CF) is not equal to the most significant bit of the destination operand. For all other values of the count operand the Overflow Flag is undefined.

Comments

Processors 80186 through 80486 limit the rotation count to 31. If you use a count operand with a larger value, these microprocessors only use the 5 least significant bits. On 8088 and 8086 processors however, the count can have a value from 1 through 255.

See Also

RCR	To rotate bits right through the Carry Flag
ROL	To rotate bits left
ROR	To rotate bits right

Timing and Encoding

Format	Encoding	Bytes	Clocks	
RCL reg,1	1101 000w	2-4	8086/88	2
	mod,010,r/m		80286	2
	disp(0 or 2)		80386	9
			80486	3
RCL mem,1	1101 000w	2-4	8086/88	15+EA (w88=23+EA)
	mod,010,r/m		80286	7
	disp(0 or 2)		80386	10
			80486	4
RCL reg,CL	1101 001w	2	8086/88	8+4n*
	mod,010,r/m		80286	5+n
	disp(0 or 2)		80386	9
			80486	8-30
RCL mem,CL	1101 001w	2-4	8086/88	20+EA+4n (w88=28+EA+4n)
	mod,010,r/m		80286	8n
	disp(0 or 2)		80386	10
			80486	9-31
RCL reg,immed8	1100 000w	2-5	8086/88	--
	mod,010,r/m		80286	5+n
	disp(0 or 2)		80386	9
	data(1)		80486	8-30
RCL mem,immed8	1100 000w	2-5	8086/88	--
	mod,010,r/m		80286	8+n
	disp(0 or 2)		80386	10
	data(1)		80486	9-31

Example

```
RCL    AX,3
```

RCR Rotate Through Carry Right   86,186,286,386,486

Syntax

```
RCR destination,count
```

Function

```
temp=max(count,31)
if temp=1 then
    OF=highbit(destination)!=highbit(destination)<<1))
else
    OF=?
value=concatenate(destination,CF)
while(temp!=0)
    x=value & 1
    value=(value>>1)
    highbit(value)=x
    temp=temp-1
end
CF=highbit(value)
destination=value
```

Flags

OF	DF	IF	TF	SF	ZF	AF	PF	CF
*								*

Description

The RCR instruction rotates the bits of the destination operand to the right by the number of the bit position specified by the second operand, count. On 8086/88 processors the count operand must be 1 or equal to the value in the CL register. On 80186 - 486 processors the count operand can be an 8-bit immediate constant. This instruction concatenates the Carry Flag (CF) with the destination operand and shifts it to the position of the most significant bit of the destination operand. It replaces the CF with the least significant bit of the destination operand. The Overflow Flag is set if the count operand is 1 and the Carry Flag is set to XOR of two most significant bits of the destination operand. For the all other values of the count operand the OF is undefined.

Comments

Processors 80186 through 80486 limit the rotation count to 31. If you use a count operand with larger values these microprocessors only use the 5 least significant bits. On 8088 and 8086 processors however, the count can have a value from 1 through 255.

See Also

RCL   To rotate bits left through the Carry Flag
ROL   To rotate bits left
ROR   To rotate bits right

Timing and Encoding

Format	Encoding	Bytes	Clocks	
RCR reg,1	1101 000w	2	8086/88	2
	mod,011,r/m		80286	2
	disp(0 or 2)		80386	9
			80486	3
RCR mem,1	1101 000w	2-4	8086/88	15+EA (w88=23+EA)
	mod,010,r/m		80286	7
	disp(0 or 2)		80386	10
			80486	4
RCR reg,CL	1101 001w	2	8086/88	8+4n*
	mod,011,r/m		80286	5+n
	disp(0 or 2)		80386	9
			80486	8-30
RCR mem,CL	1101 001w	2-4	8086/88	20+EA+4n (w88=28+EA+4n)
	mod,010,r/m		80286	8n
	disp(0 or 2)		80386	10
			80486	8-31
RCR reg,immed8	1100 000w	2-5	8086/88	--
	mod,011,r/m		80286	5+n
	disp(0 or 2)		80386	9
	data(1)		80486	8-30
RCR mem,immed8	1100 000w	2-5	8086/88	--
	mod,011,r/m		80286	8+n
	disp(0 or 2)		80386	10
	data(1)		80486	9-31

Example

RCR   AX,3

REP Repeat String Prefix   86,186,286,386,486

Syntax

```
REP string_instruction
```

Function

```
when opcode is (INS,LODS,MOVS,OUTS,STOS) then
   while(CX!=0)
      execute string_instruction
      CX=CX-1
   end
when opcode is (CMPS,SCAS) then
   while(CX!=0)
      execute string_instruction
      CX=CX-1
      if ZF=0 then break
   end
```

Flags

OF	DF	IF	TF	SF	ZF	AF	PF	CF

Description

The repeat prefix REP can be applied to any string instruction (CMPS, INS, LODS, MOVS, OUTS, SCAS, STOS). The number of times the instruction is repeated is based on the value in the CX (ECX) register. If CX (ECX) is 0 the string instruction is not performed.

Comments

The ZF Flag cannot be initialized before using repeated string instructions.

When CMPS and SCAS are performed however, these instructions and the ZF Flag must be tested and the ZF Flag must be set. If you interrupt a repeated string instruction and then return to it, it will resume processing from the point of interruption. However, if you interrupt an operation when using other prefixes on a single instruction in addition to REP, when you return to the operation all prefixes will be lost, except the one that preceded the string instruction. To avoid this happening, you should disable all interrupts before performing the instruction and enable them again afterwards.

See Also

REPNE	To repeat an instruction while not equal
MOVS	To copy a string
STOS	To store a character into memory
CMPS	To compare two strings
SCAS	To scan a string
LODS	To load a character into the accumulator

Timing and Encoding

Format	Encoding	Bytes	Clocks	
REP MOVS dest,src	1111 0011	2	8086/88	8+17n (w88=9+25n)
	1010 010w		80286	5+4n
			80386	7+4n
			80486	12+3n
REP STOS dest	1111 0011	2	8086/88	9+10n (w88=9+14n)
	1010 101w		80286	4+3n
			80386	5+5n
			80486	7+4n
REP LODS dest	1111 0011	2	8086/88	--
	1010 101w		80286	--
			80386	--
			80486	7+4n
REP INS dest,DX	1111 0011	2	8086/88	--
	0110 110w		80286	5+4n
			80386	13+6n,pm=(7,27)+6n
			80486	18+8n,pm=(10,30)+8n

REP OUTS DX,src	1111 0011	2	8086/88 --
	0110 111w	2	8086/88 5+4n
			80386 12+5n,pm=(6,26)+5n***
			80486 17+5n,pm=(11,31)+5n***

* 5 if n=0b 13 if n=1
** 5 if n=0
*** First protect-mode timing:CPL<=IOPL. Second timing: CPL>IOPL

Example

    REP   MOVS AX,string

RET/RETN Near Return From Procedure

Syntax

    RET num_value

Function

    EIP = pop();
    ESP = ESP + num_value

Flags

OF	DF	IF	TF	SF	ZF	AF	PF	CF

Description

The RET instruction has two forms: RETN and RETF which denote the NEAR and FAR returns, respectively. The RETN instruction restores the instruction pointer that had been saved by the previous CALL instruction and returns control to the instruction that follows the CALL instruction.

See Also

    CALL To call a procedure
    JMP   To jump unconditionally

Timing and Encoding

Format	Encoding	Bytes	Clocks	
RETN	1100 0011	1	8086/88	16 (w88=20)
			80286	11+m
			80386	10+m
			80486	5
RETN immed16	1100 0010	3	8086/88	20 (w88=24)
	data(2)		80286	11+m
			80386	10+m
			80486	5

Example

```
RET   4      86,186,286,386,486
```

RET/RETF Far Return From Procedure   86,186,286,386,486

Syntax

```
RETF num_value
```

Function

```
EIP = pop();
ECS = pop();
ESP = ESP + num_value
```

Flags

OF	DF	IF	TF	SF	ZF	AF	PF	CF

Description

The RETF instruction performs a FAR return from a procedure which gained control as a result of executing the FAR call. The RETF instruction restores both the command segment and instruction pointer that had been saved by the previous CALL instruction and returns control to the instruction that follows the CALL instruction.

See Also

CALL   To call a procedure
JMP   To jump unconditionally

Timing and Encoding

Format	Encoding	Bytes	Clocks	
RETF	1100 0011	1	8086/88	26 (w88=34)
			80286	15+m
			80386	18+m
			80486	13
RETF immed16	1100 0010	3	8086/88	25 (w88=33)
	data(2)		80286	15+m
			80386	18+m
			80486	14

Example

```
RET   4
```

ROL Rotate Left   86,186,286,386,486

Syntax

```
ROL destination,count
```

Function

```
temp=max(count,31)
if temp=1 then
    OF=(highbit(destination) != CF)
if not
    OF=?
while (temp !=0)
    x=highbit(destination)
    destination=(destination<<1) + x
    temp=temp-1
end
CF=highbit(destination)
```

Flags

OF	DF	IF	TF	SF	ZF	AF	PF	CF
*								*

Description

The ROL instruction rotates the bits of the destination operand to the left by the number specified in the count operand. As the bits are rotated, the most significant bit of the destination operand is copied to the least significant bit of the destination operand. The leftmost bit of the destination operand is copied into the Carry Flag (CF). On 8086/88 processors the count must be 1 or equal to the value in the CL register. On 80186 - 80486 processors the count operand can be an 8-bit immediate constant. The OF is set if the leftmost bit of the destination operand is not equal to the CF.

Comments

Processors 80186 through 80486 limit the rotation count to 31. If you use a count operand with a larger value, these microprocessors only use the 5 least significant bits. On 8086/88 processors however, the count can have a value from 1 through 255.

See Also

RCL   To rotate the bits left through the Carry Flag
RCR   To rotate the bits right through the Carry Flag
ROR   To rotate the bits right

Timing and Encoding

Format	Encoding	Bytes	Clocks	
ROL reg,1	1101 000w	2-4	8086/88	2
	mod,000,r/m		80286	2
	disp(0 or 2)		80386	3
			80486	3
ROL mem,1	1101 000w	1	8086/88	15+EA (w88=23+EA)
	mod,000,r/m		80286	7
	disp(0 or 2)		80386	7
			80486	4
ROL reg,CL	1101 001w	1	8086/88	8+4n
	mod,000,r/m		80286	5+n
	disp(0 or 2)		80386	3
			80486	3
ROL mem,CL	1101 001w	2-4	8086/88	20+EA+4n (w88=28+EA+4t)
	mod,000,r/m		80286	8+n
	disp(0 or 2)		80386	7
			80486	4
ROL mem,immed8	1100 000w	2-4	8086/88	--
	mod,000,r/m		80286	8+n
	disp(0 or 2)		80386	7
			80486	4
ROL reg,immed8	1100 000w	2-4	8086/88	--
	mod,000,r/m		80286	5+n
	disp(0 or 2)		80386	3
			80486	2

Example

```
ROL    AX,5
```

ROR Rotate Right   86,186,286,386,486

Syntax

```
ROR destination,count
```

Function

```
temp=max(count,31)
if temp=1 then
   OF=(highbit(destination)!=highbit(destination<<1))
if not
   OF=?
while (temp !=0)
   x=value & 1
   value=(value>>1)
   highbit(value)=x
   temp=temp-1
end
CF=highbit(value)
destination=value
```

Flags

OF	DF	IF	TF	SF	ZF	AF	PF	CF
*								*

Description

The ROR instruction rotates the bits of the destination operand to the right by the number specified in the count operand. As the bits are rotated, the least significant bit of the destination operand is copied to the most significant bit of the destination operand. The most significant bit of the destination operand is copied into the Carry Flag (CF). On 8086/88 processors the count must be 1 or equal to the value in the CL register, on 80186 - 486 processors the count operand can be an 8-bit immediate constant. The OF is set if the most significant bit of the destination operand is not equal to the bit next to it.

Comments

Processors 80186 through 80486 limit the rotation count to 31. If you use a count operand with a larger value, these processors only use the 5 least significant bits. On 8086/88 processors, however, the count can have a value from 1 through 255.

See Also

RCL   To rotate the bits left through the Carry Flag
RCR   To rotate the bits right through the Carry Flag
ROL   To rotate the bits left.

Timing and Encoding

Format	Encoding	Bytes	Clocks	
ROR reg,1	1101 000w	1	8086/88	2
	mod,000,r/m		80286	2
	disp(0 or 2)		80386	3
			80486	3
ROR mem,1	1101 000w	1	8086/88	15+EA (w88=23+EA)
	mod,000,r/m		80286	7
	disp(0 or 2)		80386	7
			80486	4
ROR reg,CL	1101 001w	1	8086/88	8+4n
	mod,000,r/m		80286	5+n
	disp(0 or 2)		80386	3
			80486	3
ROR mem,CL	1101 001w	2-4	8086/88	20+EA+4n (w88=28+EA+4t)
	mod,000,r/m		80286	8+n
	disp(0 or 2)		80386	7
			80486	4
ROR mem,immed8	1100 000w	2-4	8086/88	--
	mod,000,r/m		80286	8+n
	disp(0 or 2)		80386	7
			80486	4
ROR reg,immed8	1100 000w	2-4	8086/88	--
	mod,000,r/m		80286	5+n
	disp(0 or 2)		80386	3
			80486	2

Example

```
ROR   AX,5
```

SAHF Store AH Into Flags   86,186,286,386,486

Syntax

```
SAHF
```

Function

```
EFLAGS=EFLAGS OR (AH & 0D5h)
EFLAGS = EFLAGS OR (AH & 0D5h)     80386-80486
```

Flags

OF	DF	IF	TF	SF	ZF	AF	PF	CF
				*	*	*	*	*

Description

The SAHF instruction writes the contents of the AH register into the low-order byte of the flag register.

Comments

The SAHF instruction reverses the LAHF instruction and is used to emulate the POP PSW instruction of the 8080 microprocessor. However, the SAHF instruction can also be used to quickly restore five flags - SF, ZF, AF, PF and CF without using the stack.

See Also

CLC,CMC,STC	To manipulate the Carry Flag
CLD,CTD	To manipulate the Direction Flag
CLI,STI	To manipulate the Interrupt Flag
LAHF	To load AH with the low-order byte of the flag register
PUSHF,POPF	To push and pop all 16-bits of the flag register to and from the stack

Timing and Encoding

Format	Encoding	Bytes	Clocks	
SAHF	1001 1110	1	8086/88	4
			80286	2
			80386	3
			80486	2

Example

```
SAHF              ;
```

SAL Left (SHL)   86,186,286,386,486

Syntax

```
SAL destination,count
```

Function

```
temp=count & 001FH
while (temp1=0)
    CF=highorder(destination)
    destination=destination<<1
    temp=temp-1
end
if count=1 then
    OF=highorder(destination)!=CF
else
    OF=?
```

Flags

OF	DF	IF	TF	SF	ZF	AF	PF	CF
*				*	*	?	*	*

Description

The SAL instruction shifts the bits of the destination operand to the left by the number specified in the count operand. Each bit moves one position to the left and the rightmost bit of the destination operand is set to 0. The most significant bit of the destination operand is copied to the Carry Flag (CF). The Overflow Flag (OF) is set if the count is 1 and if the Carry Flag has a different value to the high-order bit of the destination operand. If the count is not equal to 1, the Overflow Flag is undefined. On 8086/88 processors the count must be 1 or equal to the value in the CL register. On 80186 - 80486 processors, the count operand can be an 8-bit immediate constant.

Comments

Processors 80186 through 80486 limit the count to 31. If you use a count with a larger value, these processors only use the 5 least significant bits. On 8086/88 processors the count can have a value from 1 through 255.

See Also

SAR   To shift the bits right while preserving the sign bit

SHR   To shift the bits right with a 0 entering the most significant bit position

Timing and Encoding

Format	Encoding	Bytes	Clocks	
SAL reg,1	1101 100w	2-4	8086/88	2
	mod,100,r/m		80286	2
	disp(0 or 2)		80386	3
			80486	
SAL mem,1	1101 100w	2-4	8086/88	15+EA (w88=23+EA)
mod,100,r/m			80286	7
	disp(0 or 2)		80386	7
			80486	4
SAL reg,CL	1101 001w	2-4	8086/88	8+4n
	mod,100,r/m		80286	5+n
	disp(0 or 2)		80386	3
			80486	3
SAL REG,CL	1101 001w		8086/88	8+4n
	mod,100,r/m		80286	5+n
	disp(0or2)		80386/486	3
SAL mem,CL	---"---		8086/88	20+EA +4n(w88+28+EA +4n)
SAL mem,1	---"---	2-4	8086/88	15+EA(w88=23+EA)
			80286/386	7
			80486	4
SAL mem,CL	---"---		8086/88	20+EA+4n(w88+28+EA+4n)
			80286	8+n
			80386	7
			80486	4
SAL mem,immed8	1100 600w		8086/88	-
	mod,100,r/m		80286	8+n
	disp(0or2)		80386	7
			80486	4
SAL reg,immed	---"---		8086/88	-
			80286	5+n
			80386	3
			80486	2

Example

```
SAL    AL,3
SAL    memop,CL
```

SAR Shift Arithmetic Right   86,186,286,386,486

Syntax

```
SAR destination,count
```

Function

```
temp=count & 001FH
while(temp!=0)
    x=highorder(destination)
    CF=destination & 1
    destination=destination>>1
    highorder(destination)=x
    temp=temp-1
end
if count=1 then
    OF=0
if not
    OF=?
```

Flags

OF	DF	IF	TF	SF	ZF	AF	PF	CF
*				*	*	?	*	*

Description

The SAR instruction shifts the destination operand (word or byte) to the right by the number of the bit position specified by the count operand. Because the leftmost bit (equal to the sign bit) is shifted into the left (high order) end, leaving the sign bit unchanged, that operation is called arithmetic. The Carry Flag (CF) is set equal to the bit shifted off the end of the destination operand. If count equals 1 then the Overflow Flag (OF) is cleared, for the all other values of count it is undefined.

Comments

Processors 80186 through 80486 limit the count to 31. If you use a count with a larger value, these microprocessors only use the 5 least significant bits. On 8088 and 8086 processors however, the count can have a value from 1 through 255.

See Also

SAL,SHL	To shift the bits left
SHR	To shift the bits right
RCL	To rotate the bits left through the Carry Flag
RCR	To rotate the bits right through the Carry Flag
ROL	To rotate the bits left
ROR	To rotate the bits right

Timing and Encoding

Format	Encoding	Bytes	Clocks	
RCR reg,1	1101 000w	2	8086/88	2
	mod,111,r/m		80286	2
	disp(0 or 2)		80386	3
			80486	3
SAR mem,1	1101 000w	2-4	8086/88	15+EA (w88=23+EA)
	mod,010,r/m		80286	7
	disp(0 or 2)		80386	7
			80486	4
SAR reg,CL	1101 001w	2-4	8086/88	8+4n
	mod,111,r/m		80286	5+n
	disp(0,1,2)		80386	3
			80486	3
SAR mem,CL	1101 001w	2-4	8086/88	20+EA+4n (w88=28+EA+4n)
	mod,111,r/m		80286	8+n
	disp(0 or 2)		80386	7
			80486	4
SAR reg,immed8	1100 000w	2-5	8086/88	--
	mod,111,r/m		80286	5+n
	disp(0,1,2)		80386	3
	data(1)		80486	2
SAR mem,immed8	1100 000w	2-5	8086/88	--
	mod,111,r/m		80286	8+n
	disp(0,1,2)		80386	7
	data(1)		80486	4

Example

```
SAR   CX,5
```

SBB Subtraction With Borrow   86,186,286,386,486

Syntax

```
SBB destination,source
```

Flags

OF	DF	IF	TF	SF	ZF	AF	PF	CF
*				*	*	*	*	*

Description

The SBB instruction subtracts the source operand and the value of the Carry Flag (CF) from the destination operand and places the result in the destination operand. Both operands may be bytes or words, but cannot be segment registers or memory locations. Both operands may be signed or unsigned binary values.

Comments

The SBB instruction is used to subtract numbers that are larger than 16-bits.

See Also

SUB	To subtract two operands
DEC	To decrement the operand
NEG	To negate the operand
AAS	To adjust the operand after subtraction
DAS	To adjust the operand after subtraction

Timing and Encoding

Format	Encoding	Bytes	Clocks	
SBB reg,reg	0001 10dw	2-4	8086/88	3
	mod,reg,r/m		80286	2
	disp(0 or 2)		80386	2
			80486	1
SBB mem,reg	0001 10dw	2-4	8086/88	16+EA (w88=24+EA)
	mod,reg,r/m		80286	7
	disp(0 or 2)		80386	6
			80486	3
SBB reg,mem	0001 10dw	2-4	8086/88	9+EA (w88=13+EA)
	mod,reg,r/m		80286	7
	disp(0 or 2)		80386	7
			80486	2
SBB reg,immed	1000 00sw	3-6	8086/88	4
	mod,011,r/m		80286	3
	disp(0,1,2)		80386	2
	data(1 or 2)		80486	2
SBB mem,immed	1000 00sw	3-6	8086/88	17+EA (w88=25+EA)
	mod,011,r/m		80286	7
	disp(0,1,2)		80386	7
	data(1 or 2)		80486	3
SBB accum,immed	0001 110w	3-6	8086/88	4
	data(1 or 2)		80286	3
			80386	2
			80486	1

Example

```
              ; 64-bit subtraction EDX:EAX - EBX:ECX
    SUB   EAX,ECX   ; Subtract low-order bits
    SBB   EDX,EBX   ; Subtract high-order bits
```

SCAS/SCASB/SCASW/SCASD Scan String
86,186,286,386,486

Syntax

    SCAS

Function

```
if (opcode == SCASB) then opsize = 1
if (opcode == SCASW) then opsize = 2
if (opcode == SCASD) then opsize = 4
CMP (accumulator,ES:[EDI])
```

```
if (DF == 0) then
    EDI = EDI + opsize
else
    EDI = EDI - opsize
endif
```

Flags

OF	DF	IF	TF	SF	ZF	AF	PF	CF
*				*	*	*	*	*

Description

The SCAS instruction compares the contents of the accumulator register (AL,AX or EAX) with the operand at the location ES:[DI]. SCAS sets the flags according to the result of the compared operation. After the comparison, the DI register is incremented if the Direction Flag DF is clear, otherwise it is decremented.

Comments

The SCASB processes the byte in AL, the SCASW processes the word in AX and SCASD processes the doubleword in the EAX register (on the 80386/80486 only). With the SCAS instruction you cannot use the segment override prefix but an operand must be present to define the size of the value processed. SCAS and its variations can be used with the REPE and REPNE prefix as normal. The CX register contains the maximum number of times the comparison will be repeated. After the instruction has finished, ES:DI points to an element following the matching or mismatching (depending on prefix used) element.

See Also

CMP,CMPSB,CMPSW	To compare strings
CLD	To clear Direction Flag
STD	To set Direction Flag

Timing and Encoding

Format	Encoding	Bytes		Clocks
scas	1010 101c	1	8086/88	15(w88=19)
			80286	7
			80386	7
			80486	6

Example

```
        LES     EDI,String      ; offset of first byte of string
        MOV     ECX,Str_len     ; string size
        CLD                     ; scan in forward direction
        MOV     AL,'?'          ; character to search
REPNE   SCASB                   ; perform search
        JE      FOUND           ; jump if found
        .
        .
FOUND:
```

STC Set Carry Flag   86,186,286,386,486

Syntax

STC

Function

CF=1

Flags

OF	DF	IF	TF	SF	ZF	AF	PF	CF
								1

Description

The STC instruction sets the Carry Flag (CF).

Timing and Encoding

Format	Encoding	Bytes	Clocks	
STC	1111 1001	1	8086/88	2
			80286	2
			80386	2
			80486	2

Example

STC   ; Carry Flag is set

STD Set Direction Flag   86,186,286,386,486

Syntax

STD

Function

DF=1

Flags

OF	DF	IF	TF	SF	ZF	AF	PF	CF
	1							

Description

The STD instruction sets the Direction Flag.

Comments

If DF is set, the STD instruction causes the string instructions to decrement the SI and/or DI index registers (all subseqent string instructions will process the string from high to low addresses). If DF is clear, the string instructions will autoincrement the registers.

Timing and Encoding

Format	Encoding	Bytes	Clocks	
STD	1111 1101	1	8086/88	2
			80286	2
			80386	2
			80486	2

Examples

```
STD        ; All subsequent string operations process strings backwards
```

STI Set Interrupt Flag   86,186,286,386,486

Syntax

```
STI
```

Function

```
IF=1
```

Flags

OF	DF	IF	TF	SF	ZF	AF	PF	CF
		1						

Description

The STI instruction sets the Interrupt Flag (IF), which enables maskable interrupts.

Timing and Encoding

Format	Encoding	Bytes	Clocks	
STI	1111 1011	1	8086/88	2
			80286	2
			80386	3
			80486	5

Example

```
STI
```

STOS,STOSB,STOSW,STOSD Store String Data
86,186,286,386,486

Syntax

```
LODS    destination_string
```

Function

```
if opcode is STOSB then n=1
    if opcode is LODSW then n=2
if opcode is LODSD then n=4
ES:[EDI]=accumulator
if DF=0 then
     EDI=EDI+n
  if not
     EDI=EDI-n
```

Flags

OF	DF	IF	TF	SF	ZF	AF	PF	CF

Description

The STOS instruction and its modifications (STOSB,STOSW,STOSD) place the contents of the accumulator (AL, AX, or EAX depending on the operation used) in the memory location pointed to by ES:DI (EDI) (even if an operand is given). The STOS instruction then increments or decrements DI(EDI) according to the size of operand and the status of the Direction Flag (DF). You cannot have a segment override prefix with the STOS instruction.

Comments

The STOS instruction and its modifications STOSB (byte), STOSW (word), or STOSD (doubleword - on 80386/486 only) are often used with the REP prefix. The ECX (CX) register must contain the number of times STOS is to be executed.

See Also

MOVS,MOVSB,MOVSW,MOVSD	To copy from DS:SI to ES:DI
LODS,LODSB,LODSW,LODSD	To copy from DS:SI to AL

Timing and Encoding

Format	Encoding	Bytes	Clocks	
LODS	1010 110w	1	8086/88	12 16(w)
			80286	5
			80386	5
			80486	2

Example

```
LODS STR
```

SUB Arithmetic Subtraction (Unsigned)   86,186,286,386,486

Syntax

```
SUB destination,source
```

Function

```
destination=destination-source
```

Flags

OF	DF	IF	TF	SF	ZF	AF	PF	CF
*				*	*	*	*	*

Description

The SUB instruction subtracts the source operand from the destination operand and replaces the destination operand with the result. Both operands must be either unsigned or signed binary numbers.

Comments

When using SUB, the operands cannot be a segment register or two memory operands. If the result does not fit into the destination operand the Carry Flag is set.

See Also

SBB   To subtract integer with borrow

Timing and Encoding

Format	Encoding	Examples	Bytes	Clocks	
SUB reg,reg	0010 10dw	sub ax,bx	2	8086/88	2
	mod,reg,r/m	sub al,dl		80286	3
	disp(0 or 2)			80386	2
				80486	1
SUB mem,reg	0010 10dw	sub sum,cx	2-4	8086/88	16+EA 24+EA (w)
	mod,reg,r/m			80286	7
	disp(0 or 2)			80386	7
				80486	3
SUB reg,mem	0010 10dw	sub cx,sum	2-4	8086/88	9+EA 13+EA (w)
	mod,reg,r/m			80286	7
	disp(0 or 2)			80386	7
				80486	2
SUB mem,immed	1000 00sw	sub sum,3	3-6	8086/88	17+EA 25+EA (w)
	mod,101,r/m			80286	7
	disp(0 or 2)			80386	7
	data(1 or 2)			80486	3

SUB reg,immed	1000 00sw mod,101,r/m disp(0 or 2) data(1 or 2)	sub ax,10	3-4	8086/88 4 80286 3 80386 2 80486 1
SUB accum,immed	0010 110w data(1 or 2)	sub ax,100	2-3	8086/88 4 80286 3 80386 2 80486 1

TEST Logical Compare   86,186,286,386,486

Syntax

```
TEST destination, source
```

Function

```
NULL = destination & source
CF=0
OF=0
```

Flags

OF	DF	IF	TF	SF	ZF	AF	PF	CF
0				*	*	?	*	0

Description

The TEST instruction performs a bitwise AND operation on the destination and source operands. The destination operand is not changed. The flags are set according to the result of the operation.

Comments

The TEST instruction is used to set the flag for a subsequential jump or set instruction. The destination operand usually contains a value to be tested, the other operand contains a bit mask.

See Also

AND   To perform a bitwise AND operation of two operands
CMP   To compare operands
J*   To perform conditional jumps

Timing and Encoding

Format	Encoding	Bytes	Clocks
TEST reg,reg	1000 010w mod,reg,r/m disp(0,1,2)	2-4	8086/88 3 80286 2 80386 2 80486 1
TEST mem,reg	1000 010w mod,reg,r/m disp(0,1,2)	2-4	8086/88 9+EA (88=13+EA) 80286 6 80386 5 80486 2

TEST reg,mem*	1000 010w	2-4	8086/88	9+EA (88=13+EA)
	mod,reg,r/m		80286	6
	disp(0,1,2)		80386	5
			80486	2
TEST reg,immed	1111 011w	2-4	8086/88	9+EA (88=13+EA)
	mod,000,r/m		80286	6
	disp(0,1,2)		80386	5
			80486	2
TEST mem,immed	1111 011w	2-4	8086/88	11+EA
	mod,000,r/m		80286	6
	disp(0,1,2)		80386	5
			80486	2
TEST mem,immed	1010 100w	2-3	8086/88	4
	data(1 or 2)		80286	3
			80386	2
			80486	1

Example

```
TEST   AH,0Fh      ; Check if any bits are set in the high nibble of AH
```

WAIT Wait Until Not Busy   86,186,286,386,486

Syntax

```
WAIT
```

Flags

OF	DF	IF	TF	SF	ZF	AF	PF	CF

XCHG Exchange   86,186,286,386,486

Syntax

```
XCHG operand1, operand2
```

Function

```
temp=operand1
operand2=operand1
operand2=temp
```

Flags

OF	DF	IF	TF	SF	ZF	AF	PF	CF

Description

The XCHG instruction swaps the contents of operands 1 and 2.

Timing and Encoding

Format	Encoding	Bytes	Clocks	
XCHG reg,reg	1000 011w	2-4	8086/88	4
	mod,reg,r/m		80286	3
	disp(0,1 or 2)		80386	3
			80486	3
XCHG reg,mem	1000 011w	2-4	8086/88	17+EA (w88=25+EA)
	mod,reg,r/m		80286	5
	disp(0,1 or 2)		80386	5
			80486	5
XCHG mem,reg	1000 011w	2-4	8086/88	17+EA(w88=25+EA)
	mod,reg,r/m		80286	5
	disp(0,1 or 2)		80386	5
			80486	5
XCHG accum,reg16	1001 0reg	2-4	8086/88	3
	mod,reg,r/m		80286	3
	disp(0,1 or 2)		80386	3
			80486	3
XCHG accum, eg16	1001 0reg	2-4	8086/88	3
	mod,reg,r/m		80286	3
	disp(0,1 or 2)		80386	3
			80486	3

XLAT/XLATB Translate By Table Lookup 86,186,286,386,486

Syntax

```
XLAT
```

Function

```
AL = DS:[EBX + AL]
```

Flags

OF	DF	IF	TF	SF	ZF	AF	PF	CF

Description

The XLAT instruction uses the value in the AL register as an offset from the beginning of the table placed at the memory location DS:BX. The byte at this offset replaces the contents of the AL register.

Comments

You can apply a segment override prefix. The XLATB instruction is a synonym for the XLAT instruction.

Timing and Encoding

Format	Encoding	Bytes	Clocks	
xlat	1101 0111	1	8086/88	11
			80286	5
			80386	5
			80486	4

Example

```
        LEA   EBX,ASCII_TABLE   ; load pointer to ; ASCII_TABLE
        MOV   AL,DIGIT          ; Digit to be translated
        XLAT  TABLE             ; Translate byte
TABLE   db    '0123456789ABCDEF'
```

XOR Boolean Exclusive OR   86,186,286,386,486

Syntax

```
XOR destination,source
```

Function

```
destination=destination XOR source
```

Flags

OF	DF	IF	TF	SF	ZF	AF	PF	CF
0				*	*	?	*	0

Description

The XOR instruction performs a bitwise exclusive OR of two operands and places the result in the destination operand. A bitwise exclusive OR clears each bit of the result if both bits are set or if both bits are cleared. Otherwise, the corresponding bits of the result are set.

Comments

The bitwise exclusive OR is often used to initialize a register to zero. We can say XOR AX,AX. It is slightly faster then using a MOV instruction MOV AX,0, but only on 8086/8088 processors.

See Also

AND   To perform a bitwise AND of two operands
NOT   To perform a bitwise NOT of two operands
OR   To perform a bitwise OR of two operands

Timing and Encoding

Format	Encoding	Bytes	Clocks	
XOR reg,reg	0011 00dw	2-4	8086/88	3
	mod,reg,r/m		80286	2
	disp(0 or 2)		80386	2
			80486	1
XOR mem,reg	0011 00dw	2-4	8086/88	16+EA (w88=24+EA)
	mod,reg,r/m		80286	7
	disp(0 or 2)		80386	6
			80486	3
XOR reg,mem	0011 00dw	2-4	8086/88	16+EA (w88=24+EA)
	mod,reg,r/m		80286	7
	disp(0 or 2)		80386	7
			80486	2
XOR mem,immed	1000 00sw	2-4	8086/88	17+EA (w88=25+EA)
	mod,110,r/m		80286	7
	disp(0 or 2)		80386	7
	data(1 or 2)		80486	3
XOR reg,immed	1000 00sw	3-6	8086/88	4
	mod,10,r/m		80286	3
	disp(0 or 2)		80386	2
	data(1 or 2)		80486	1
XOR accum,immed	0011 010w	1-3	8086/88	4
	data(0 or 2)		80286	3
			80386	2
			80486	1

Example

XOR AX, AX; Set AX to 0

BIOS DATA AREA

Segment Offset Size Description

0040	00h	word	base address of the serial I/O port1 (COM1)
	02h	word	base address of the serial I/O port2 (COM2)
	04h	word	base address of the serial I/O port3 (COM3)
	06h	word	base address of the serial I/O port4 (COM4)
	08h	word	base address of the parallel I/O port1 (LPT1)
	0Ah	word	base address of the parallel I/O port2 (LPT2)
	0Ch	word	base address of the parallel I/O port3 (LPT3)
	0Eh	word	base address of the parallel I/O port4 (LPT4) on non-PS machines, segment address of Extended BIOS Data Segment on PS computers
	10h	word	hardware information

bits 15 -14	number of parallel ports
bit 13	internal modem (Convertible)
bit 12	reserved
bits 11 - 9	number of serial ports
bit 8	reserved
bits 7 - 6	number of diskette drives minus one
bits 5 - 4	initial video mode:
00b	EGA,VGA,PGA
01b	40 x 25 color
10b	80 x 25 color
11b	80 x 25 mono
bit 3	reserved
bit 2	pointing device present (PS), reserved on others
bit 1	math co-processor present
bit 0	diskette available for boot

Segment	Offset	Size	Description
0040	13h	word	size of conventional memory(0-640K bytes)
	17h	byte	keyboard status flags 1

		Description
bit	7	INSert is turned on
bit	6	Caps Lock is turned on
bit	5	Num Lock is turned on
bit	4	Scroll Lock is turned on
bit	3	either Alt key pressed
bit	2	either Ctrl key pressed
bit	1	Left Shift key pressed
bit	0	Right Shift key pressed

Offset	Size	Description
18h	byte	Keyboard status flags 2:

		Description
bit	7	INSert key pressed
bit	6	Caps Lock key pressed
bit	5	Num Lock key pressed
bit	4	Scroll Lock key pressed
bit	3	Pause state is turned on
bit	2	Sys Req key pressed
bit	1	Left Alt key pressed
bit	0	Left Ctrl key pressed

Offset	Size	Description
19h	byte	Alt-nnn input workspace
1Ah	word	keyboard buffer head pointer
1Ch	word	keyboard buffer tail pointer
1Eh	16 words	default keyboard buffer
41h	byte	floppy disk operation status (if successful)

		Description
bit	7	drive not ready
bit	6	seek error
bit	5	general controller failure
bits	4 -0	00h no error
		01h invalid request
		02h address mark not found
		03h diskette write protected
		04h sector not found
		06h diskette change line active
		08h DMA overrun
		09h DMA across 64k boundary
		0Ch media type unknown
		10h CRC error on read

Offset	Size	Description
49h	byte	current video mode
4Ah	word	number of columns on screen
4Ch	word	size of video page (regen buffer) in bytes
4Eh	word	start address of current video page

Segment	Offset	Size	Description
0040	50h	16 bytes	cursor position (col, row) for eight video pages
	60h	word	cursor parameters, high byte - startline, low byte -endline
	62h	byte	current video page number
	63h	word	base address of video controller 3D4h for color adapters, 3B4h for MDA/Hercules
	65h	byte	current setting of video mode select register (ports 3D8h or 3B8h)
	66h	byte	current setting of CGA palette register (port 3D9h)
	6Ch	dword	number of timer ticks since midnight
	70h	byte	Timer overflow, non-zero if it has counted past midnight
	71h	byte	Ctrl-Break flag: bit 7 is set if Ctrl-Break has been pressed
	72h	word	POST reset flag: 1234h to skip memory test (warm boot)
			4321h to preserve memory contents (only for PS/2 MCA)
			64h Burn-in mode
	74h	byte	fixed disk operation status code (non-ESDI drives):
			00h no error
			01h invalid function request
			02h address mark not found
			03h write protect error
			04h sector not found
			05h reset failed
			07h drive parameter activity failed
			08h DMA overrun
			09h DMA data boundary error
			0Ah bad sector flag detected
			0Bh bad track detected
			0Dh invalid number of sectors for Format function
			0Eh control data address mark detected
			0Fh DMA arbitration level out of range
			10h uncorrectable ECC or CRC error
			11h ECC corrected data error
			20h general controller failed

Segment Offset Size Description

Segment	Offset	Size	Description
0040			40h seek failed
			80h time out
			0AAh drive not ready
			0BBh undefined error
			0CCh write fault on selected drive
			0E0h status error/error register is zero
			0FFh sense failed
	75h	byte	number of hard disks attached
	76h	byte	hard disk control byte
	77h	byte	hard disk I/O port offset
	80h	word	offset address of keyboard buffer start
	82h	word	offset address of byte following keyboard buffer end
	84h	byte	number of rows on screen minus one (EGA/MCGA/VGA)
	85h	word	character height in pixels (EGA/MCGA/VGA)
	87h	byte	EGA/VGA status byte (0 for MCGA)
			bit 7 not to clear video buffer when changing video mode (see function 0 of INT 10h)
			bits 6-5 number of 64K bytes blocks of RAM on adapter board minus one
			bit 4 reserved
			bit 3 0 if EGA/VGA video system active
			bit 2 wait for retrace (if 0, you can write to video memory at any time)
			bit 1 mono monitor active (if 0, the color monitor is used)
			bit 0 CGA cursor emulation disabled. If this bit is equal to 0, the CGA cursor size (0 -7) is translated to fit the EGA/VGA character cell.
	88h	byte	EGA/VGA switches settings, reserved for MCGA
			bits 7-4 power-on state of feature connector bits 3-0
			bits 3-0 configuration switches 4-1 (0 means ON, 1 means OFF)

Segment Offset Size Description

0040   8Ch   byte hard disk controller status

8Dh   byte hard disk controller Error Status

8Eh   byte hard disk Interrupt Control

8Fh   byte floppy disk controller information

        bit 7 reserved

        bit 6 drive 1 determined

        bit 5 drive 1 is multi-rate

        bit 4 drive 1 supports 80 tracks

        bit 3 reserved

        bit 2 drive 0 determined

        bit 1 drive 0 is multi-rate

        bit 0 drive 0 supports 80 tracks

90h   byte floppy disk drive 0 media state

91h   byte floppy disk drive 1 media state

        bits 7-6 data transfer rate: 00=500KBps, 01=300KBps, 10=250KBps

        bit 5 if double stepping required (e.g. 360KB disk in 1.2MB drive)

        bit 4 media established

        bit 3 reserved

        bits 2-0 on exit from BIOS disk service:

           000 trying 360KB disk in 360KB drive

           001 trying 360KB disk in 1.2MB drive

           010 trying 1.2MB disk in 1.2MB drive

           011 360KB disk in 360KB drive established

           100 360KB disk in 1.2MB drive established

           101 1.2MB disk in 1.2MB drive established

           110 reserved

           111 all other formats/drives

92h   byte floppy disk drive 0 media state at start of operation

93h   byte floppy disk drive 1 media state at start of operation

94h   byte current number of tracks on floppy disk drive 0

95h   byte current number of tracks on floppy disk drive 1

96h   byte keyboard status byte 3

        bit 7 read-ID in progress

Segment Offset Size Description

0040			bit	6	last code read was first of two ID codes
			bit	5	force Num Lock if read-ID and enhanced keyboard
			bit	4	enhanced keyboard installed
			bit	3	Right Alt key pressed
			bit	2	Right Ctrl key pressed
			bit	1	code E0h was read
			bit	0	code E1h was read
	97h	byte	keyboard status byte 2		
			bit	7	keyboard transmit error flag
			bit	6	LED update in progress
			bit	5	RESEND received from keyboard
			bit	4	ACK received from keyboard
			bit	3	reserved, must be zero
			bit	2	Caps Lock LED
			bit	1	Num Lock LED
			bit	0	Scroll Lock LED
	98h	dword	timer2; on AT and PS except Model 30 points to user wait-complete flag (see INT 15, AX=8300h)		
	9Ch	dword	timer2; on AT and PS except Model 30 contains delay value in microseconds		
	A0h	byte	timer2; on AT and PS except Model 30 contains wait active flag:		
			bit	7	wait time elapsed
			bits	6-1	reserved
			bit	0	function 86h of interrupt 15h has been called
	A8h	dword	points to Video Save Ptr Table for EGA MCGA/VGA adapters		
	0F0h-0FFh		reserved for user purposes		

BIOS Functions

INT 10h   [MDA][CGA][PCjr][EGA][MCGA][VGA]
FUNCTION 00h
Set Video Mode   BIOS

Selects and initializes the video mode and clears the screen.

Input

AH = 00h
AL = Video Mode

Text Resol	Pixel Box	Graphic Resol	Colors	Disp Page	Scrn Addr	MDA	CGA	PCjr	EGA	MCGA	VGA
00h=	40x25	8x8		B&W	8	B800	*	*	*	*	*
01h=	40x25	8x8		16	8	B800	*	*	*	*	*
02h=	80x25	8x8		B&W	4	B800	*	*	*	*	*
03h=	80x25	8x8		16	4	B800	*	*	*	*	*
	80x25	8x8		16	8	B800	*	*	*	*	*
04h=	40x25	8x8	320x200	4	1	B800	*	*	*	*	*
05h=	40x25	8x8	320x200	4gray	1	B800	*	*	*	*	*
06h=	80x25	8x8	640x200	B&W	1	B800		*	*	*	*
07h=	80x25	9x14		mono	1	B800	*		*	*	*
	80x25				8	B800	*	*	*	*	*
08h=	20x25	8x8	160x200	16		B800			*		
09h=	40x25	8x8	320x200	16		B800			*		
0Ah=	80x25	8x8	640x200	4		B800			*		
0Bh= reserved											
0Ch= reserved											
0Dh=	40x25	8x8	320x200	16	8	A800				*		*
0Eh=	80x25	8x8	640x200	16	4	A000				*		*
0Fh=	80x25	8x14	640x350	mono	2	A000				*		*

10h=	80x25	8x14	640x350	4	2	A000	*	
	80x25	8x14	640x350	16	2	A000	*	*
11h=	80x30	8x16	640x480	2		A000		*	*
12h=	80x30	8x16	640x480	16		A000		*
13h=	40x25	8x8	320x200	256		A000		*	*

Output

Nothing

Comments

On a **PC AT, PCjr** or **PS/2**, this function does not clear the video memory of any video adapter if the 7th bit of AL is set (EGA or higher). On a **PC** or **PC XT**, this feature is only available on adapters which have built-in ROM-BIOS such as **CGA, MDA** or **Hercules**.

INT 10h   [MDA][CGA][PCjr][EGA][MCGA][VGA]

FUNCTION 01h

Set Cursor Type   **BIOS**

Sets the start and end lines for the cursor in text modes.

Input

AH = 01h
CH = Start line of cursor
CL = End line of cursor

Output

Nothing

Comments

The ROM BIOS permits the following values for the cursors start and end lines:

monochrome display card:	0-13
color display card (text mode):	0- 7

These values depend on the installed video adapter. For Ega and VGA adapters in some text modes the maximum valid value for the cursor end line is 13 (EGA) or 15 (VGA).

The default values for the cursors start and end lines set by ROM BIOS are:

monochrome display card:	11-12
color display card (text mode):	6- 7

This function is only used to set the cursor within the permitted range. If the cursor is set outside this range, it will be invisible.

In text modes the hardware cursor appears as a constantly blinking rectangle or dash. There is no hardware cursor on the screen in graphic modes. In the graphics video mode, the hardware cursor is not available.

INT 10h   [MDA][CGA][PCjr][EGA][MCGA][VGA]
FUNCTION 02h
Set Cursor Position   **BIOS**

Positions the cursor on the screen.

Input

> AH = 02h
> BH = display page number
> DH = row
> DL = column

Output

> Nothing

Comments

Each video page has a separate cursor that can be set independently.

You can make the blinking cursor disappear by setting the cursor in a position that doesn't exist, for example: column 0, line 25. The co-ordinates x=0 y=0 represent the upper left corner of the screen. The maximum values for the screen co-ordinates (maximum number of rows and columns on the screen) are defined by the selected video mode and the type of video adapter.

See full list of modes in INT 10h Function 00h.

See Also

> INT 10h Function 03h and Function 05h

INT 10h   [MDA][CGA][PCjr][EGA][MCGA][VGA]
FUNCTION 03h
Read Cursor Position   **BIOS**

Reads the position (start and end line) of the cursor on the display.

Input

        AH = 03h
        BH = page number

Output

        CH = start line of cursor
        CL = end line of cursor
        DH = row where the cursor is placed (y coordinate)
        DL = column where the cursor is placed (x coordinate)

Comments

The maximum number of available video pages is defined by the type of current video mode and video adapter.

A separate cursor is maintained for each of 8 display pages.

See Also

        INT 10h Function 03h

INT 10h   [CGA][PCjr][EGA]
FUNCTION 04h
Read Light Pen Position   **BIOS**

Determines the position and current status of the light pen.

Input

        AH = 04h

Output

        AH = 00h light pen not activated
              01h light pen position in registers
        BX = pixel column (graphic x co-ordinate)
        CH = pixel row (graphic y co-ordinate) for modes 04h-06h
        CX = pixel row (graphic y co-ordinate) for modes 0Dh-13h
        DH = row of current cursor position (text y co-ordinate)
        DL = column of current cursor position (text x co-ordinate)

Comments

This function must be called repeatedly until 1 is obtained in the AH register.

The graphics co-ordinates and range of text for this function depend on the current display mode.

In graphics modes, the co-ordinates of the light pen are not continuous. The y co-ordinate is always a multiple of 2 and the x co-ordinate is always a multiple of 4 (320x200 graphics modes) or a multiple of 8 (640x200 graphics modes).

See Also

INT 10h Function 00h

INT 10h   [MDA][CGA][PCjr][EGA][MCGA][VGA]
FUNCTION 05h
Set Display Page   BIOS

Selects the current display page (text mode) for the video display.

Input

AH = 05h
AL = display page

Output

Nothing for the CGA,EGA,MCGA,VGA adapters.

Comments

The number of display pages depends on the video card.

Switching to a new display page doesn't affect the contents. When you switch to a new display page, the screen cursor points to the position of the text cursor on this page.

See Also

INT 10h Function 0Fh

INT 10h   [MDA][CGA][PCjr][EGA][MCGA][VGA]

FUNCTION 06h
Scroll Window Up

BIOS

Scrolls up the text window by a specified number of lines or clears the window (fills it with blank characters).

Input

    AH = 06h
    AL = number of lines to scroll window (if AL is 0, the window is
         cleared)
    BH = attribute to be used for blanked lines
    CH = row of upper left corner of window
    CL = column of upper left corner of window
    DH = row of lower right corner of window
    DL = column of lower right corner of window

Output

    Nothing.

Comments

This function only affects the current video page. Any lines scrolled up beyond the top of the window are lost.

Function 00h of INT 10h clears the screen more effectively.

See Also

    INT 10h Function 07h

INT 10h   [MDA][CGA][PCjr][EGA][MCGA][VGA]

FUNCTION 07h
Scroll Window Down

BIOS

Scrolls down the text window by a specified number of lines or clears the window (fills it with blank characters).

Input

    AH = 07h
    AL = number of lines to scroll window (0 - clear window)
    BH = attribute to be used for blanked lines
    CH = row of upper left corner of window
    CL = column of upper left corner of window
    DH = row of lower right corner of window
    DL = column of lower right corner of window

Output

Nothing.

Comments

This function only affects the current video page. Any lines scrolled up beyond the top of the window are lost.

Function 00h of INT 10h clears the screen more effectively.

See Also

INT 10h Function 06h

INT 10h   [MDA][CGA][PCjr][EGA][MCGA][VGA]
FUNCTION 08h
Read Character and Attribute at Cursor   BIOS

Reads the character and attribute at the current cursor position.

Input

AH = 08h
BH = display page

Output

AL = character
AH = attribute of character
    bits 0-3 foreground color
        0000 black
        0001 blue
        0010 green
        0011 cyan
        0100 red
        0101 magenta
        0110 brown
        0111 light grey
        1000 dark grey
        1001 light blue
        1010 light green
        1011 light cyan
        1100 light red
        1101 light magenta
        1110 yellow
        1111 white

bits 4-6   background color
                000   black
                001   blue
                010   green
                011   cyan
                100   red
                101   magenta
                110   brown
                111   white
        bit 7   blink

Comments

The number of display pages depends on the type of video adapter.

See Also

INT 10h Function 09h, Function 10h Subfunction 03h

INT 10h   [MDA][CGA][PCjr][EGA][MCGA][VGA]
FUNCTION 09h
Write Character and Attribute at Cursor Position   BIOS

Writes an ASCII character and attribute to the screen at the current cursor position.

Input

        AH = 09h
        AL = character
        BH = display page
        BL = Attribute of character (text modes) or color
               (graphics modes)
        CX = number of times character to be written

Output

        Nothing

Comments

In graphics modes if you want the character to be displayed several times (i.e. the value of CX is greater than 1), all characters must be written in the current row.

The control characters (e.g. Bell, Carriage Return, Line Feed) appear as visible ASCII characters and do not affect the cursor position.

This function does not set the cursor in another position.

In graphics modes this function can display characters. The bit patterns for character codes 00-7Fh(0-127) are determined by a table stored in ROM. The bit pattern for character codes 80h-FFh(128-255) is determined by a RAM table, installed by the GRAFTABL command of DOS.

See Also

INT 10h Function 08h

INT 10h   [MDA][CGA][PCjr][EGA][MCGA][VGA]
FUNCTION 0Ah
Write Character at Cursor Position   BIOS

Writes an ASCII character to the screen at the current cursor position for the specified display page and leaves the attribute of the character previously displayed in this position.

Input

AH = 0Ah
AL = character
BH = display page
BL = color character (graphics modes, PCjr
        only)
CX = number of times to write character

Output

Nothing

Comments

In graphics modes if you want the character to be displayed several times (i.e. the value of CX is greater than 1), all characters must be written in the current row.

The control characters (e.g., Bell, Carriage Return, Line Feed) appear as normal ASCII characters and do not affect the cursor position. When the character has been written, the cursor must be set in another position explicitly with INT 10h function.

This function can display a character in graphics modes. The bit pattern for character codes 00-7Fh(0-127) is determined by a table stored in ROM. The address of the table is stored in the vector for INT 43h (for EGA, MCGA, VGA).

If this function writes a character in graphics modes and bit 7 of the BL register is set(1), an exclusive OR(XOR) is performed on the character and current display content for this position. This feature can be used for writing and deleting characters.

See Also

INT 10h Functions 08h and 09h, INT 1Fh, INT 43h, INT 44h

INT 10h   [CGA][PCjr][EGA][MCGA][VGA]

FUNCTION 0Bh
Set Palette, Background or Border Color   BIOS

Selects a palette, background or border color.

Input

AH = 0Bh
BH = 00h
BL = border color (0-15) in text modes and color and background
       color in graphic modes (EGA)
BH = 01h
BL = selects one of two color palettes for the 320x200 graphics

Output

Nothing

Comments

In graphics modes this function defines the color of the screen border and background. In text modes, however, it only defines the color of the border. The background color of each character is defined by the high nibble of its attribute byte.

Two color palettes are available on the CGA and EGA in 320x200 4-color graphics modes. In the 320x200 4-color graphics modes (if register BH=01h) there are the following palettes:

Palette	Pixel value	Color
0	0	same as background
	1	green
	2	red
	3	yellow
1	0	same as background
	1	cyan
	2	magenta
	3	white

See Also

INT 10h Function 10h (used for palettes on PCjr, EGA, MCGA and VGA)

INT 10h   [CGA][PCjr][EGA][MCGA][VGA]
FUNCTION 0Ch
Write Graphics Pixel   **BIOS**

Makes a color dot on the screen at the specified graphics coordinates.

Input

AH = 0Ch
AL = color of dot
BH = display page (ignored if the mode supports only one page)
CX = screen column (graphics x coordinate)
DX = screen row (graphics y coordinate)

Output

Nothing

Comments

The color of the dot (pixel color value) and the graphics coordinates (x,y)
depend on the current graphics mode.

This function performs exclusive OR (denoted by XOR) with the new color
value and the current context of the pixel if bit 7 of AL is set.

This function is only valid in graphics modes.

See Also

INT 10h Function 08h

INT 10h   [CGA][PCjr][EGA][MCGA][VGA]
FUNCTION 0Dh
Read Graphics Pixel on Screen   **BIOS**

Reads a color pixel on the display at the specified graphics coordinates.

Input

AH = 0Dh
BH = display page (ignored if mode supports only one page)
CX = screen column (graphics x coordinate)
DX = screen row (graphics y coordinate)

Output

AL = pixel color value

Comments

The pixel color value and range of permitted values (x,y coordinates) depend on the current video mode.

See Also

INT 10h Function 0Ch

INT 10h   [MDA][CGA][PCjr][EGA][MCGA][VGA]

FUNCTION 0Eh
Write Character and Advance Cursor (Teletype Mode) BIOS

Writes a character to the screen at the current cursor position on the current display page and moves the cursor to the next position. In graphics modes, the color of the new character is the same as the color of the character previously located in the same place.

Input

AH = 0Eh
AL = character
BH = display page
BL = foreground color (graphics modes)

Output

Nothing

Comments

This function recognises special ASCII codes (Bell - 07h, backspace - 08h, Line Feed - 0Ah, Carriage Return - 0Dh) and performs the corresponding actions. All other characters are written on the screen (even if they are control characters). After the function has displayed the character, it moves the cursor to the next position.

This function supports line scrolling and wrapping. When the cursor reaches the last position of one line it is moved to the first position of the next line. If no line follows the current one (the last line on the screen is processed, the screen is scrolled up by one line and a blank line is inserted at the end of the screen

See Also

INT 10h Functions 13h,02h and 0Ah

INT 10h   [MDA][CGA][PCjr][EGA][MCGA][VGA]
FUNCTION 0Fh
Get Current Video Mode   **BIOS**

Reads the number of the current video mode of the active video card.

Input

AH   = 0Fh

Output

AH = number of character columns on the screen
AL = current video mode (see INT 10h Function 00h)
BH = active display page

Comments

If the current mode was set with bit 7 set (no blinking), the same will apply
to the returned mode.

See Also

INT 10h Function 00h and 05h

INT 10h   [PCjr][EGA][MCGA][VGA]
FUNCTION 10h SUBFUNCTION 00h
Set Palette Register   **BIOS**

Sets the values for a palette register to a color which can be displayed.

Input

AH = 10h
AL = 00h
        for PCjr,EGA,VGA
BH = color value
BL = palette register (00-0Fh)
        for MCGA
BX = 0712h

Output

Nothing

See Also

INT 10h Function 10h Subfunctions 02h and 07h

INT 10h   [PCjr][EGA][VGA]
FUNCTION 10h SUBFUNCTION 01h
Set Border Color Register   BIOS

Sets the color of the screen border (overscan) register.

Input

> AH = 10h
> AL = 01h
> BH = color value

Output

> Nothing

See Also

> INT 10h Function 10h Subfunction 01h and 08h

INT 10h   [PCjr][EGA][VGA]
FUNCTION 10h SUBFUNCTION 02h
Set Palette and Border   BIOS

Sets all palette registers and a border color (overscan) with one command.

Input

> AH   = 10h
> AL   = 02h
> ES:DX = segment:offset of 17-byte color list

Output

> Nothing

Comments

The list of palette registers occupies 17 bytes. The first 16 contain the values
of the palette registers 0-15; the 17th byte contains the value of the border
color register.

The default values of the palette registers in 16-color graphics modes are:

Pixel value	Color
01h	blue
02h	green
03h	cyan
04h	red
05h	magenta
06h	brown
07h	white
08h	gray
09h	light blue
0Ah	light green
0Bh	light cyan
0Ch	light red
0Dh	light magenta
0Fh	light white

See Also

INT 10h Function 10h Subfunction 00h,01h and 09h

INT 10h   [PCjr][PS][EGA][VGA]
FUNCTION 10h SUBFUNCTION 03h
Toggle Intensity/Blink Bit   BIOS

Determines whether the 7th bit of the attribute byte of a character enables blinking or displays a character in a bright background colour.

Input

AH = 10h
AL = 03h
BL = blink/intensity status
00h = enable intensity
01h = enable blinking

Output

Nothing

See Also

INT 10h Function 08h

INT 10h [VGA]
FUNCTION 10h SUBFUNCTION 07h
Get Palette Register **BIOS**

Obtains the color from the specified palette register.

Input

    AH = 10h
    AL = 07h
    BL = palette register number

Output

    BH = color

See Also

    INT 10h Function 00h, Function 10h Subfunction 09h

INT 10h [VGA]
FUNCTION 10h SUBFUNCTION 08h
Get Border Color(Overscan) **BIOS**

Obtains a border colour code from the overscan register.

Input

    AH = 10h
    AL = 08h

Output

    BH = value of border color

See Also

    INT 10h Function 10h Subfunction 01h

INT 10h   [VGA]
FUNCTION 10h SUBFUNCTION 09h
Read Contents of All Palette Registers and Overscan
Register   BIOS

Obtains the values of all palette registers and overscan register via one operation.

Input

AH   = 10h
AL   = 09h
ES:DX = segment:offset of 17 byte buffer

Output

Nothing

Comments

The 17 byte buffer has following format:

Offset	Size	Description
00h	16	colors for palette registers 00h-0Fh
16h	1	border colour

See Also

INT 10h Function 10h Subfunctions 02h and 07h

INT 10h   [MCGA][VGA]
FUNCTION 10h SUBFUNCTION 10h
Set Individual DAC Register   BIOS

Sets a single Digital Analog Converter (DAC) register with a red-green-blue
(RGB) combination.

Input

AH   = 10h
AL   = 10h
BX   = color register number
CH   = green color value
CL   = blue value
DH   = red value

Output

Nothing

See Also

INT 10h Function 10h Subfunction 15h

INT 10h   [MCGA][VGA]

FUNCTION 10h SUBFUNCTION 12h
Set Block of Color Registers   **BIOS**

Sets a group of consequiteve Digital Analog Converter (DAC) registers with
a red-green-blue (RGB) combination.

Input

```
AH    = 10h
AL    = 12h
BX    = starting color register
CX    = number of color registers
ES:DX = segment offset of color table
```

Output

Nothing

Comments

The color table consists of 3 byte entries where each 3 byte entry represents
one DAC register. The bytes of each entry represent the red, green and blue
values.

See Also

INT 10h Function 10h Subfunctions 10h and 17h

INT 10h   [VGA]

FUNCTION 10h SUBFUNCTION 13h
Set Color Page State   **BIOS**

Input

```
AH = 10h
AL = 13h
BL = 00h to select paging mode
BH = 00h selects 4 pages of 64 registers
BH = 01h selects 16 pages of 16 register
BL = 01h to select a color register page
BH = page number (0-3) or (0-15)
```

Output

Nothing

Comments

This function is not valid in mode 13h (320x200 256 colors)

See Also

INT 10h Function 10h Subfunction 1Ah

INT 10h   [MCGA][VGA]

FUNCTION 10h SUBFUNCTION 15h
Read Color Register   BIOS

Returns the contents of a color register.

Input

AH = 10h
AL = 15h
BL = palette register number

Output

CH = green value
CL = blue value
DH = red value

See Also

INT 10h Function 10h Subfunction 10h,17h

INT 10h   [MCGA][VGA]

FUNCTION 10h SUBFUNCTION 17h
Get Block of Color Registers   BIOS

Reads the red, green and blue components associated with each set of color
registers in one operation.

Input

AH   = 10h
AL   = 17h
BX   = starting color register
CX   = number of color registers
ES:DX = segment:offset of buffer (3*CX byte in size)

Output

ES:DX = segment:offset of buffer
CX   = number of red, green and blue triples in buffer

Comments

The color list returned in the buffer consists of red, green and blue triples.
Each triple is a 3 byte entry.

See Also

INT 10h Function 10h Subfunction 00h,09h

INT 10h   [VGA]
FUNCTION 10h SUBFUNCTION 1Ah
Get Color Page State   BIOS

Returns the current color page and the color register paging mode.

Input

AH = 10h
AL = 1Ah

Output

BH = current page
BL = paging mode
    00h if 4 pages of 64 registers
    01h if 16 pages of 16 registers

See Also

INT 10h Function 10h Subfunction 13h

INT 10h   [MCGA][VGA]
FUNCTION 10h SUBFUNCTION 1Bh
Get Gray-Scale Values   BIOS

Converts the red, green and blue values of the specified range of color registers
into gray scale equivalents.

Input

AH = 10h
AL = 1Bh
BX = first color register (0-255) to be converted
CX = number of color registers to be converted

Output

Nothing

Comments

When the black and white monitor is used, the factor for each of the three main colors is calculated and written into the color register. The default factor for red is 30%, for green - 59% and for blue - 11%. The value of the factor defines the intensity of gray which corresponds to one of the main colors on the screen. The original values of these colors are lost.

See Also

INT 10h Function 12h Subfunction 33h

INT 10h   [EGA][MCGA][VGA]
FUNCTION 11h SUBFUNCTION 00h AND 10h
Load User Character Set and Reprogram Controller BIOS

Loads a user defined character set table into the specified block of character generator RAM.

Input

AH	= 11h
AL	= 00h or 10h
BH	= bytes per character (eg. 8,14 or 16)
BL	= a number of complete character set (block) to be loaded in map (0-3 [0-7 for VGA])
CX	= number of characters defined by table
DX	= first character ASCII code in table (character offset)
ES:BP	= segment:offset of font table

Output

Nothing

Comments

In text modes this function modifies text display fonts. A maximum of 512 characters can be loaded per character table. When Subfunction 10h is used than page 0 must be active. This function recalculates bytes per character and the row and length of refresh buffer. The controller is reprogrammed as follows:

maximum scan line:	bytes/char - 1
cursor start line:	bytes/char - 2
cursor end line:	0
vertical display end:((rows+1)*(bytes/char))-1	
underline location:	bytes/char - 1

To ensure the operation is successful, the Subfunction 10h should be used directly after the mode has been set (i.e. INT 10h Function 00h).

INT 10h   [EGA][VGA]
FUNCTION 11h SUBFUNCTION 01h AND 11h
Load 8x14 Character Set and Reprogram Controller BIOS

Loads the specified block of the RAM character generator with the default ROM BIOS font 8x14.

Input

       AH = 11h
       AL = 01h or 11h
       BH = block to load

Output

       Nothing

Comments

In text modes this function modifies text display. A maximum of 512 characters can be loaded per font.

When Subfunction 11h is used, page 0 must be active. This function recalculates the bytes per character along with the row and length of the refresh buffer. The controller is reprogrammed as follows:

       maximum scan line: bytes/char - 1
       cursor start line: bytes/char - 2
       cursor end line: 0
       vertical display end:((rows+1)*(bytes/char))-1
       underline location: bytes/char - 1

To ensure the operation is successful the Subfunction 11h should be used directly after the mode has been set (i.e. INT 10h Function 00h).

The function sets the EGA screen to display 25 lines of text and the VGA screen to display 28.

INT 10h   [EGA][MCGA][VGA]
FUNCTION 11h SUBFUNCTION 02h AND 12h
Load 8x8 Character Set and Reprogram Controller BIOS

Loads the ROM BIOS default 8x8 pixel character set into the specified block of character generator RAM.

Input

> AH = 11h
> AL = 02h or 12h
> BH = block to load

Output

> Nothing

Comments

This function provides font selection in text modes. A maximum of 512 characters can be loaded per character table.

When Subfunction 12h is used then page 0 must be active.

This function recalculates the bytes per character along with the row and length of the refresh buffer. The controller is reprogrammed as follows:

> maximum scan line: bytes/char - 1
> cursor start line: bytes/char - 2
> cursor end line: 0
> vertical display end:((rows+1)*(bytes/char))-1
> underline location: bytes/char - 1

To ensure the operation is successful, the Subfunction 11h should be used directly after mode set (i.e. INT 10h Function 00h).

INT 10h   [EGA][VGA]

FUNCTION 11h SUBFUNCTION 03h
Activate Character Set   BIOS

Determines the character set of the four 256 character sets (EGA) or seven 256 character sets (VGA) in text mode.

Input

AH = 11h
AL = 03h
BL = font block specifier (4 bits 0-0Fh for EGA and 6
         bits 0-3Fh for VGA)

Output

Nothing

Comments

On the EGA/MCGA video card, bits 0 and 1 of the BL register specify the character block to use when bit 3 of the character attribute byte is 0. Bits 2 and 3 of the BL register specify the character block to use when bit 3 of the character attribute byte is 1.

On the VGA video card, bits 0, 1 and 4 of the BL register specify the character block to use when bit 3 of the character attribute byte is 0. Bits 2, 3 and 5 of the BL register specify the character block to use when bit 3 of the character attribute byte is 1.

If both fields of the BL register are identical when using a 256 character set, then bit 3 of the character attribute byte controls the foreground intensity. If both fields of the BL register are identical when using a 512 character set, then bit 3 of the character attribute byte selects the upper or lower half of the character set.

INT 10h   [EGA][VGA]

FUNCTION 11h SUBFUNCTION 04h AND 14h
Load 8x16 Character Set and Reprogram Controller BIOS

Loads the specified block of the RAM character with the default ROM BIOS font 8x16 pixel.

Input

AH = 11h
AL = 04h or 14h
BH = block to load (0-7)

Output

Nothing

Comments

This function provides font selection in text modes. A maximum of 512 characters can be loaded per font.

When Subfunction 14h is used then page 0 must be active.

This function recalculates the bytes per character along with the row and length of the refresh buffer. The controller is reprogrammed as follows:

maximum scan line:	bytes/char - 1
cursor start line:	bytes/char - 2
cursor end line:	0
vertical display end:	((rows+1)*(bytes/char))-1
underline location:	bytes/char - 1

To ensure the operation is successful, the Subfunction 14h should be used directly after the mode has been set (i.e. INT 10h Function 00h).

The function sets the VGA screen to display 25 lines of text.

INT 10h   [EGA][MCGA][VGA]
FUNCTION 11h SUBFUNCTION 20h
Set User 8x8 Character Font for Graphics Modes   BIOS

Sets the vector of the interrupt 1Fh to the user-defined 8x8 font table.

Input

AH	=	11h
AL	=	20h
ES:BP	=	segment:offset of user's font table

Output

Nothing

Comments

This function establishes set and display size for text characters. To ensure the operation is successful, the function 20h should be used directly after the mode has been set (INT 10h Function 00h).

INT 10h   [EGA][MCGA][VGA]
FUNCTION 11h SUBFUNCTION 21h
Set INT 43h for User's Font   BIOS

Sets the user graphics character font for graphics modes.

Input

```
AH   = 11h
AL   = 21h
BL   = row specifier
        00h user set
                01h 14 character rows on screen
                02h 25 character rows on screen
                03h 43 character rows on screen
CX   = bytes per character
DL   = number of rows per screen (if BL=00h)
ES:BP = segment:offset of user table
```

Output

Nothing

Comments

This function sets the font and character size in graphics modes. To ensure
the operation is successful, the function 20h should be used directly after the
mode has been set (INT 10h Function 00h).

INT 10h   [EGA][MCGA][VGA]
FUNCTION 11h SUBFUNCTION 22h
Set INT 43h for ROM 8x14 Character Set   BIOS

Sets the vector of the interrupt 43h to the default 8x14 font table without
reprogramming the video controller.

Input

```
AH  = 11h
AL  = 22h
BL  = row specifier
        00h user set
        01h 14 character rows on screen
        02h 25 character rows on screen
        03h 43 character rows on screen
DL  = number of rows per screen (if BL=00h)
```

Output

Nothing

Comments

This function sets the font and character size in graphics modes. To ensure it is successful, the function 22h should be used directly after the mode has been set (INT 10h Function 00h).

INT 10h   [EGA][MCGA][VGA]

FUNCTION 11h SUBFUNCTION 23h
Set INT 43h for ROM 8x8 Character Set   BIOS

In graphics modes, sets the vector of interrupt 43h to the default ROM 8x8 character font table without reprogramming the video controller.

Input

```
AH  = 11h
AL  = 23h
BL  = row specifier
      00h user set
      01h 14 character rows on screen
      02h 25 character rows on screen
      03h 43 character rows on screen
DL  = number of rows per screen (if BL=00h)
```

Output

Nothing

Comments

In graphics modes, this function sets the font and character size..
To ensure the operation is successful, the function 23h should be used directly after the mode has been set (INT 10h Function 00h).

See Also

INT 1Fh, INT 43h

INT 10h   [EGA][MCGA][VGA]

FUNCTION 11h SUBFUNCTION 24h
Set INT 43h for ROM 8x16 Character Set   **BIOS**

Sets the vector of the interrupt 43h to the default ROM 8x16 character font table for graphics modes.

Input

```
AH  = 11h
AL  = 24h
BL  = row specifier
      00h user set
      01h 14 character rows on screen
      02h 25 character rows on screen
      03h 43 character rows on screen
DL  = number of rows per screen (if BL=00h)
```

Output

Nothing

Comments

As above this function sets the font and character size in graphics modes.

To ensure the operation is successful, the function 20h should be used directly after the mode has been set (INT 10h Function 00h).

See Also

INT 1Fh, INT 43h

INT 10h   [EGA][MCGA][VGA]

FUNCTION 11h SUBFUNCTION 30h
Get Font Information   **BIOS**

Returns a pointer to the specified font table and information about the current state of that font.

Input

```
AH  = 11h
AL  = 30h
BH  = pointer specifier
      00h INT 1Fh pointer
      01h INT 43h pointer
      02h ROM 8x14 font table address (EGA,VGA only)
      03h ROM 8x8 font table address (00h-7Fh character)
```

04h ROM 8x8 font table address (80h-FFh character)
05h ROM 9x14 alternative font table address (EGA,VGA only)
06h ROM 8x16 font table address (MCGA, VGA only)
07h ROM 9x16 alternative font table address (VGA only)

Output

CX   = font points (bytes per character)
DL   = screen rows
ES:BP = segment:offset of font table

See Also

INT 10h Function 11h Subfunction 02h & 20h, INT 1Fh INT 43h

INT 10h   [EGA][VGA]
FUNCTION 12h SUBFUNCTION 10h
Read Configuration Information   **BIOS**

Reads the configuration information of EGA/VGA cards.

Input

AH = 12h
BL = 10h

Output

BH = display type (0-color display; 1-monochrome display)
BL = EGA/VGA memory installed
BL = 0   64K
BL = 1   128K
BL = 2   192K
BL = 3   256K
CH = feature bits
CL = switch settings

INT 10h   [EGA][VGA]
FUNCTION 12h SUBFUNCTION 20h
Select Alternative PrintScreen   **BIOS**

Selects an alternative ROM BIOS printscreen handler from the video card BIOS,
which also works properly with EGA and VGA cards and prints as many lines
as are displayed on the screen. The default ROM BIOS handler usually prints
a screen with 25 lines.

Input

    AH = 12h
    AL = 20h

Output

Nothing

See Also

    INT 05h

INT 10h   [VGA]

FUNCTION 12h SUBFUNCTION 30h
Specify Number of Scan Lines   BIOS

Sets the number of scan lines for text modes. If this function is called immediately after Function 11h, it allows you to change the number of rows on the screen (25,28,43 or 50).

Input

    AH = 12h
    AL = vertical resolution
           00h 200 scan lines
           01h 350 scan lines
           02h 400 scan lines (VGA only)
    BL = 30h

Output

    AL = 12h if function is supported (VGA is active)

Comments

This function takes effect when the text mode is changed.

See Also

    INT 10h Function 11h

INT 10h   [EGA][MCGA][VGA]

FUNCTION 12h SUBFUNCTION 31h
Toggle Palette Register Loading   BIOS

Enables or disables the automatic loading of palette registers in VGA BIOS when a video display mode is selected.

Input

AH = 12h
AL = 00h enable default palette loading
      01h disable default palette loading
BL = 31h

Output

Nothing

Comments

AL = 12h if function is supported

INT 10h   [MCGA][VGA]

FUNCTION 12h SUBFUNCTION 32h
Enable/Disable Video   BIOS

Enables or disables video addressing.

Input

AH = 12h
AL = 00h enable video addressing
      01h disable video addressing
BL = 32h

Output

AL   = 12h if function is supported

INT 10h   [MCGA][VGA]

FUNCTION 12H SUBFUNCTION 33h
Enable/Disable Automatic Gray-Scale Summing   BIOS

Toggles using the automatic gray-scale summing. This function is different
from function 10h Subfunction 1Bh which performs *selective* gray-scale summing.

Input

AH = 12h
AL = 00h enables gray-scale summing
      01h disables gray-scale summing
BL = 33h

Output

AL = 12h if function is supported

Comments

If gray scale summing is enabled, it is performed during palette programming, color register loading and display mode selection.

INT 10h   [VGA]

FUNCTION 12h SUBFUNCTION 34h
Enable/Disable Text Cursor Emulation   BIOS

Enables or disables text cursor emulation mode. When cursor emulation is enabled, the ROM BIOS remaps the values of the cursors start and end lines for the current character size.

Input

    AH = 12h
    AL = 00h enables text cursor emulation
          01h disables text cursor emulation
    BL = 34h

Output

    AL   = 12h if function is supported

INT 10h   [MCGA][VGA]

FUNCTION 12h SUBFUNCTION 35h
Switch Active Display   BIOS

Switches between one of two video adapters in system.

Input

    AH   = 12h
    AL   = switching function
           00h off initial video adapter
           01h on system board video adapter
           02h off active video adapter
           03h on inactive video adapter
           80h set system board video active flag
    BL   = 35h
    ES:DX = segment:offset of 128 bytes buffer (if AL=00h,02h and 03h)

Output

    AL   = 12h if function is supported

INT 10h   [VGA]
FUNCTION 12h SUBFUNCTION 36h
Enable/Disable Screen Refresh   **BIOS**

Enables or disables screen refresh for the current display.

Input

    AH = 12h
    AL = screen refresh
         00h enables refresh
         01h disables refresh
    BL = 36h

Output

    AL = 12h if function is supported.

INT 10h   [MDA][CGA][PCJr][EGA][MCGA][VGA]
FUNCTION 13h
Write String   **BIOS**

Transfers the string to the video buffer of the active page and displays it at a specified position on the screen and on the specified display page.

Input

    AH   =13h
    AL   = Output mode (0-3)
            00h attribute in BL, don't update cursor position
            01h attribute in BL, update cursor position after write;
            02h string contains alternating characters and attribute bytes;
            03h string contains alternating characters and attribute bytes;
            update cursor position after write
    BH   = display page
    BL   = attribute, if AL=00h or AL=01h
    CX   = length of string
    DA   = screen row (y coordinate)
    DL   = screen column (x coordinate)
    ES:BP = segment: offset of string to be output

Output

    Nothing

Comments

This function recognises control codes such as Bell(07h), CR (0Dh), LF (0Ah), and BS (08h) and interprets them in the usual way.

See Also

INT 10h Function 09h and Function 0Ah

INT 10h   [PS/2][MCGA][VGA]
FUNCTION 1Ah
Get or Set Display Combination Code   BIOS

Determines the active video card or updates ROM BIOSs variable, indicating the installed adapter.

Input

        AH = 1Ah
        AL = Subfunction
               00h read display combination code
               01h set display combination code
        BH = inactive display code (if AL = 00h)
        BL = active display code (if AL = 01h)

Output

        AL = 1Ah if function is supported
        BH = inactive display code (if AL = 01h)
        BL = active display code (if AL = 01h)

Comments

This function interprets display codes as follows:

        00h no display
        01h MDA with monochrome display
        02h CGA with color display
        03h reserved
        04h EGA with color display
        05h EGA with monochrome display
        06h VGA with color display
        07h VGA with monochrome analog display
        08h VGA with color analog display
        09h reserved
        0Ah MCGA with digital color display
        0Bh MCGA with monochrome analog display
        0Ch MCGA with color analog display
        FFh unknown video card

INT 10h   [PS/2][MCGA][VGA]
FUNCTION 1Bh
Read Functionality/State Information   **BIOS**

Reads the full information about the current display mode and the characteristics of the video adapter and monitor.

Input

AH   = 1BH
BX   = implementation type
       00h return functionality/state information
ES:DI = segment:offset of 64 byte buffer for state
       (see Comments)

Output

AL   = 1Bh if function is supported

Comments

The ES:DI buffer contains state information about the current video mode:

Offset	Size	Content
00h	DWORD	pointer to table with functionality information (see below)
04h	BYTE	current video mode
05h	WORD	number of columns
07h	WORD	length of refresh in bytes
09h	WORD	station address of refresh buffer
0Bh	WORD	cursor position for page 0 (y,x coordinates)
0Dh	WORD	cursor position for page 1 (y,x coordinates)
0Fh	WORD	cursor position for page 2 (y,x coordinates)
11h	WORD	cursor position for page 3 (y,x coordinates)
13h	WORD	cursor position for page 4 (y,x coordinates)
15h	WORD	cursor position for page 5 (y,x coordinates)
17h	WORD	cursor position for page 6 (y,x coordinates)
19h	WORD	cursor position for page 7 (y,x coordinates)
1Bh	WORD	cursor type (start line and end line)
1Dh	BYTE	active display page
1Eh	WORD	adapter base port address
20h	BYTE	current setting of register (3B8h or 3D8h)
21h	BYTE	current setting of register (3B9h or 3D9h)
22h	BYTE	number of rows
23h	WORD	bytes/characters
25h	BYTE	active display code (see INT 10h Function 0Ah)
26H	BYTE	inactive display code (see INT 10h Function 0Ah)

27H	WORD	number of colors supported in current mode (0 for monochrome)
29H	WORD	number of pages supported in current mode
2Ah	BYTE	number of scan lines
		(00h - 200, 01h - 350, 02h - 400, 0Bh - 480)
2Bh	BYTE	primary character black
3Ch	BYTE	secondary character black
2Dh	BYTE	miscellaneous flags

	bit		
	0 = 1	in all modes on all displays (always 0 on MCGA)
	1 = 1	gray-scale summing
	2 = 1	monochrome display attached
	3 = 1	default palette loading disabled
	4 = 1	cursor emulation disabled (always 0 on MCGA)
	5 = 0	intensity; 1 = blinking
	6	reserved
	7	reserved

2Eh	3BYTES	reserved
31h	BYTE	video mode available
		00h=64k, 01h=128k, 02h=192k, 03h=256k
32h	BYTE	save pointer state flag

	bit		
	0 = 1	512 set active
	1 = 1	dynamic save area present
	2 = 1	alfa font override active
	3 = 1	graphics font override active
	4 = 1	palette override active
	5 = 1	DCC (display combination code) override active
	6	reserved
	7	reserved

33h	13BYTES	reserved

Bytes 0-3 of the buffer with state information contain a DWORD pointer to the Static Functionality Table, which contains information about video card and monitor.

Format of Static Functionality Table

Offset	Size	Description
00h	BYTE	video modes are supported
		bit 0 to bit 7 = 1 mode 00h-07h supported
01h	BYTE	video modes are supported
		bit 0 to bit 7 = 1 mode 08h-0Fh supported
02h	BYTE	video modes are supported
		bit 0 to bit 3 = 1 mode 10h-13h supported
		bit 4-7 reserved

| 03h | 4BYTEs | reserved |
| 07h | BYTE | scan lines supported in text modes |

bit 0 to bit 2 = 1, scan lines are 200, 350, 400 respectively
bit 3-7 reserved

08h	BYTE	number of character blocks in text modes
09h	BYTE	maximum number of active character blocks intext modes
0Ah	BYTE	miscellaneous BIOS function flags

bit 0 = 1 all modes on all displays
  1 = 1 gray-scale summing is supported
  2 = 1 character font loading is supported
  3 = 1 mode set default palette loading is supported
  4 = 1 cursor emulation is supported
  5 = 1 EGA palette (64 colours) present
  6 = 1 color palette present
  7 = 1 color paging function is supported

| 0Bh | BYTE | miscellaneous BIOS function key |

bit 0 = 1 light pen is supported
  1 = 1 save/restore state function is supported
  2 = 1 intensity/blinking function is supported
  3 = 1 get/set display combination codeis supported
  4-7 reserved

| 0Ch | WORD | reserved |
| 0Eh | BYTE | save pointer function flags |

bit 0 = 1 512 character set is supported
  1 = 1 dynamic save area is supported
  2 = 1 alpha font override is supported
  3 = 1 graphics font override issupported
  4 = 1 palette override is supported
  5 = 1 DCC extension is supported
  6-7 reserved

| OFh | BYTE | reserved |

See Also

INT 10h function 15h

INT 10h   [PS/2][VGA]
FUNCTION 1Ch
Save or Restore Video State   BIOS

Saves or restores various video state information.

Input

Ah	=	1Ch
AL	=	Subfunction
		00h returns state buffer size
		01h saves video state
		02h restores state
CX	=	requested states
	bit 0	save or restore video hardware state
	1	save or restore video BIOS data state
	2	save or restore video DAC state and color
	3-15	reserved
ES:BX	=	segment:offset of buffer

Output

AL	=	1Ch if function is supported
BX	=	if AL = 00h - number of 64 bytes blocks
		if AL = 01h - state information is in buffer ES:BX
		if AL = 02h - buffer containing previously saved state is ES:BX

INT 11h   [PC][AT][PS/2]
Determine Configuration   BIOS

Reads the system code word of the configuration list from ROM BIOS.

Input

Nothing

Output

AX	= Equipment flag bits
	bit 0 = 1 floppy disk drive(s) is installed
	1 = 1 maths coprocessor is installed
	2 = 1 mouse is installed (PS/2)
	2-3 = system board RAM size (PC,PCjr)
	00 = 16K
	01 = 32K

                    10 = 48K
                    11 = 64K (always on AT and above)
            4-5 = initial video mode
                    00 = reserved
                    01 = 40x25 color text
                    10 = 80x25 color text
                    11 = 80x25 monochrome
            6-7 = number of floppy disk drives (only if bit 0 = 1)
                    00 = 1
                    01 = 2
                    10 = 3
                    11 = 4
            8   0 = DMA present
                    1 = no DMA on system (PCjr)
            9-11= number of RS232 ports
            12 = 1 game adapter is installed
            13 = 1 serial printer is installed (PCjr)
                    1 internal modem is installed (PC and XT
                    only)
            14-15 = number of printers is installed

See Also

INT 12h

INT 12h   [PC][AT][PS/2]
Determine Conventional Memory Size   BIOS

Determines the amount of conventional memory which may be used by MS-DOS and application programs.

Input

Nothing

Output

AX = memory size in KB

Comments

The memory size returned by this function does not include extended memory.

See Also

INT 11h

INT 13h   [PC][AT][PS/2]
FUNCTION 00h
Reset Disk System   **BIOS**

Resets the fixed disk or diskette controller and prepares for disk I/O. If a disk error occurs, you should reset the disk system and retry the operation.

Input

    AH = 00h
    DL = drive
    00h-7Fh floppy disk
    80h-FFh fixed disk

Output

    Carry Flag (CF)=0 (clear) if function successful (AH=00h)
    Carry Flag (CF)=1 (set) Error (AH=Error code)

Comments

The following errors can occur:
    00H - no error
    01H - invalid command
    02H - address mark not found
    03h - write attempt on write protected disk
    04h - sector not found
    05h - reset failed (hard disk)
    06h - diskette changed
    07h - bad parameter table (hard disk)
    08h - DMA overrun (floppy disk)
    09h - DMA across the 64K boundary
    0Ah - bad sector detected (hard disk)
    0Bh - bad track detected (hard disk)
    0Ch - unsupported track (floppy disk)
    0Dh - invalid number of sectors on format (hard disk)
    0Eh - control data address mark detected (hard disk)
    0Fh - DMA arbitration error (hard disk)
    10h - bad CRC/ECC*
    11h - data ECC corrected (hard disk)
    20h - Error in disk controller
    40h - Seek failed
    80h - Time out error (failed to respond)
    AAh - drive not ready (hard disk)
    BBh - undefined error (hard disk)
    CCh - write fault (hard disk)
    E0h - status register error (hard disk)
    FFh - sense operation failed (hard disk)

* CRC - Cyclic Redundancy Check code
  ECC - Error Checking and Correcting code

See Also

INT 13h Functions 0Dh and 11h, INT 21h Function 0Dh

INT 13h   [PC][AT][PS/2]
FUNCTION 01h
Read Disk System Status   BIOS

Reads the current status of the disk drive.

Input

AH = 01h
DL = drive
00h-7Fh floppy disk
80h-FFh fixed disk

Output

Ah = 00h
AL = status of previous disk operation

Comments

The following errors can occur:
00h - no error
01h - invalid command
02h - address mark not found
03h - write attempt on write protected disk
04h - sector not found
05h - reset failed (hard disk)
06h - diskette changed
07h - bad parameter table (hard disk)
08h - DMA overrun (floppy disk)
09h - DMA across the 64K boundary
0Ah - bad sector detected (hard disk)
0Bh - bad track detected (hard disk)
0Ch - unsupported track (floppy disk)
0Dh - invalid number of sectors on format (hard disk)
0Eh - control data address mark detected (hard disk)
0Fh - DMA arbitration error (hard disk)
10h - bad CRC/ECC*
11h - data ECC corrected (hard disk)
20h - Error in disk controller
40h - Seek failed
80h - Time out error (failed to respond)
AAh - drive not ready (hard disk)

BBh - undefined error (hard disk)
CCh - write fault (hard disk)
E0h - status register error (hard disk)
FFh - sense operation failed (hard disk)

INT 13h   [PC][AT][PS/2]
FUNCTION 02h
Read Sector   **BIOS**

Reads one or more disk sectors into a memory buffer.

Input

```
AH   = 02h
AL   = number of sectors to be read
CH   = track (for hard disk bits 8,9 in high bits of CL)
CL   = sector
DH   = head
DL   = drive
       00h-7Fh floppy disk
       80h-FFh fixed disk
ES:BX = segment:offset of buffer
```

Output

```
Carry Flag (CF)    =0   function successful (AH=00h)
AL                 = number of sectors read
Carry Flag (CF)    =1   Error (AH=Error code see AH=01h)
```

Comments

On hard disks, the upper 2 bits of the 10-bit cylinder number are placed in
the upper 2 bits of the CL register.

See Also

INT 13h Functions 03h and 0Ah

INT 13h   [PC][AT][PS/2]
FUNCTION 03h
Write Sector   **BIOS**

Writes one or more sectors to a disk from the memory buffer.

Input

AH	=	03h
AL	=	number of sectors to write
CH	=	low eight bit of cylinder number
CL	=	sector (bits 0-5)
DH	=	head
DL	=	drive
		00h-7Fh floppy disk
		80h-FFh fixed disk
ES:BX	=	segment:offset of buffer

Output

CF	=	0 if function is successful
AH	=	00h
AL	=	number of sectors transfered
CF	=	1 if function is unsuccessful
AH	=	Status (See INT 13h Function 01h)

Comments

On hard disks the bits 8 and 9 of the 10-bit cylinder number are placed in
the upper 2 bits of the CL register.

See Also

INT 13h Function 02h

INT 13h   [PC][AT][PS/2]
FUNCTION 04h
Verify Sector   **BIOS**

Checks that one or more sectors on the disk can be found and read (checking
address fields), and compares the data in the sectors using CRC.

Input

AH	=	04h
AL	=	number of sectors
CH	=	low bit of cylinder number (8-9)

```
CL    =  sector (bits 0-5)
DH    =  head
DL    =  drive
         00h-7Fh floppy disk
         80h-FFh fixed disk
ES:BX =  segment:offset of buffer
```

Output

```
CF    = 0 if function is successful
AH    = 00h
AL    = number of sectors verified
CF    = 1 if function is unsuccessful
AH    = Status (See INT 13h Function 01h)
```

Comments

On the hard disk, bits 8 and 9 of the 10-bit cylinder number are placed in the upper 2 bits of the CL register.

See Also

INT 13h Function 02h

INT 13h   [PC][AT][PS/2]
FUNCTION 05h
Format Track   BIOS

Formats disk sector and initializes the track address fields on the specified track.

Input

```
AH    = 05h
AL    = number of sectors to create on this track
CH    = track
CL    = sector
DH    = head
DL    = drive
         00h-7Fh floppy disk
         80h-FFh fixed disk
ES:BX = segment:offset of address field list
```

Output

```
CF    = 0 (Action successful)
AH    = 00h
CF    = 1 (Action unsuccessful)
AH    = status (See INT 13h Function 01h)
```

Comments

The address field list passed in ES:BX consists of a 4 byte entry. There is one entry for every sector, formatted in the following way:

Byte   Description

0   cylinder
1   head
2   sector
3   number of bytes in the sector
        00h   128 bytes per sector
        01h   256 bytes per sector
        02h   512 bytes per sector
        03h   1024 bytes per sector

This applies to floppy disks.

On PC and PS/2 fixed disks, ES:BX points to a 512 byte format buffer containing 4 byte pairs, F,N, for each sector on the disk as follows:

    F =   00 good sector
         80 bad sector
    N -   sector number

On hard disks the bits 8 and 9 of the 10-bit cylinder number are placed in the upper 2 bits of the CL register.

See Also

    INT 13h Functions 03h and 0Ah.

INT 13h   [PC]
FUNCTION 06h
Format Bad Track   **BIOS**

Initializes a track, writing disk address fields and data sectors, and marks bad sectors by setting bad sector flags.

Input

    AH = 06h
    AL = interleave value
    CH = cylinder number (bits 8,9 in high bits of CL)
    CL = sector number
    DH = head
    DL = drive
        00h-7Fh floppy disk
        80h-FFh fixed disk

Output

CF = 0 (Action successful)
AH = 00h
CF = 1 (Action unsuccessful)
AH = status code (see INT 13h Function 01h)

Comments

This function applies to the PC XT hard disk only.

See Also

INT 13h Functions 01h, 05h and 07h

INT 13h   [PC]
FUNCTION 07h
Format Drive, Starting at Given Track   BIOS

Initializes each sector of the specified cylinder, and writes the disk address
fields and data sectors, starting at the given track.

Input

AH = 07h
AL = interleave value (XT only)
CH = cylinder number (bits 8,9 in high bits of CL)
CL = sector number
DH = head
DL = drive
        00h-7Fh floppy disk
        80h-FFh fixed disk

Output

CF = 0 (Action successful)
AH = 00h
CF = 1 (Action unsuccessful)
AH = status code (see INT 13h Function 01h)

See Also

INT 13h Function 01h

INT 13h   [PC][AT][PS/2]
FUNCTION 08h
Get Drive Parameters   **BIOS**

Reads disk drive parameters for the specified drive.

Input

> AH = 08h
> DL = drive
>   00h-7Fh floppy disk
>   80h-FFh fixed disk

Output

> Carry Flag CF=0 function successful
>   BL   = drive type (AT and PS/2 floppy disks)
>   01h 360K   40 track 5.25"
>   02h 1.2MB   80 track 5.25"
>   03h 720K   80 track 3.5"
>   04h 1.44MB   80 track 3.5"
>   CH   = maximum value of cylinder number
>   CL   = maximum value for sector (bits 0-5 and bits 6-7
>   highest 2   bits of CL)
>   DH   = maximum value for head number
>   DL   = number of drives on first controller
>
> Carry Flag CF=1 function unsuccessful
>   AH   = status code (see INT 13h function 01h)
>   ES:DI = segment:offset of disk drive parameter table

Comments

On PC and PC XT this function is supported on fixed disks only.

INT 13h   [PC][AT][PS/2]
FUNCTION 09h
Initialize Fixed Disk Tables   **BIOS**

Initializes a fixed disk controller using the ROM BIOS disk parameter table.

Input

> AH = 09h
> DL = drive
>   80h-FFh fixed disk

Output

Carry Flag CF=0 function successful
AH = 00h
Carry Flag CF=1 function unsuccessful
AH = status code (see INT 13h function 01h)

Comments

On PC and PC XT, the vector for INT 41h points to fixed disks parameter tables.
On PC AT and PS/2, the vector for INT 41h points to the fixed disk parameter table for drive 0 and the vector for INT 46h points to the fixed disk parameter table for drive 1.

If an error occurs, use function 10h to select the drive and retry operation.

See Also

INT 13h Function 01h

INT 13h
FUNCTION 0Ah
Read Sector Long

[PC][AT][PS/2]

BIOS

Reads one or more sectors into the memory from a fixed disk with a 4 byte entry representing the ECC code for the sector.

Input

AH = 0Ah
AL = number of sectors (1-127)
CH = cylinder (bits 8,9 in high bits of CL)
DH = head
DL = drive
       80h-FFh fixed disk
EX:BX = segment:offset of memory buffer

Output

Carry Flag CF=0 function successful
AH = 00h
AL = number of sector read
Carry Flag CF=1 function unsuccessful
AH = status code (see INT 13h function 01h)

Comments

Function 02h is a more generalized version of the read sector. INT 25h allows you to read absolute sectors from all types of block devices.

If an error occurs while reading a sector, reset the drive and retry the operation at least three times. It may be that the error was caused by the drive motor being off at the time of request.

If an error occurs, use function 10h to select the drive and retry the operation.

See Also

INT 13h Functions 01h and 02h, INT 25h

INT 13h   [PC][AT][PS/2]

FUNCTION 0Bh
Write Sector Long   **BIOS**

Writes one or more sectors from the memory to a fixed disk. A long sector is a sector with information plus 4 bytes representing the ECC code for the sector.

Input

AH	=	0Bh
AL	=	number of sectors (1-127)
CH	=	cylinder (bits 8,9 of 10-bit cylinder address are in high bits of CL)
CL	=	starting sector
DL	=	drive
		80h-FFh fixed disk
EX:BX	=	segment:offset of memory buffer

Output

Carry Flag CF=0 function successful
    AH = 00h
    AL = number of sectors written
Carry Flag CF=1 function unsuccessful
    AH = status code (see INT 13h function 01h)

Comments

This function is only used for diagnostic purposes and only works on the fixed disk. Function 03h is a more generalized version of the write sector. INT 26h allows you to write absolute sectors from all types of block devices.

If an error occurs while reading a sector, reset the drive and retry the operation at least three times. It may be that the error was caused by the drive motor being off at the time of request.

See Also

INT 13h Functions 01h and 03h, INT 26h

INT 13h   [PC][AT][PS/2]
FUNCTION 0Ch
Seek Cylinder   BIOS

Positions the read/write heads at the specified cylinder of the fixed disk. This function does not transfer data and can be performed on the fixed disk only.

Input

    AH = 0CH
    CH = cylinder number (bits 8,9 of 10-bit cylinder address in high
          bits of CL)
    Dh = head
    DL = disk
    DL = drive
          80h-FFh fixed disk

Output

    CF = 0 function successful
    AH = 00h
    CF = 1 function unsuccessful
    AH = status code (see INT 13h function 01h)

Comments

If an error occurs, Function 0h must be used to reset the drive and retry the operation.

See Also

    INT 13h Functions 00h, 02h and 0Ah

INT 13h   [PC][AT][PS/2]
FUNCTION 0Dh
Reset Fixed Disk System   BIOS

Re-initializes the fixed disk controller, resets drivers parameters and sets the read/write heads to cylinder 0.

Input

    AH = 0Dh
    DL = drive
          80h-FFh fixed disk

Output

CF = 0 if function is successful
AH = 00h
CF = 1 if function is unsuccessful
AH = status code (see INT 13h function 01h)

Comments

This function is used on fixed disks only. Function 00h is a more generalized version of this function because it resets the disk controller.

The fixed disk is only reset if the value in the DL register is less than or equal to the last fixed disk in the system.

See Also

INT 13h Functions 00h, 01h and 11h, INT 21h Function 0Dh

INT 13h   [PC][AT][PS/2]
FUNCTION 10h
Test Drive Status   **BIOS**

Returns the status of a specified hard disk and tests whether it is ready to use.

Input

AH = 10h
DL = drive
    80h-FFh fixed disk

Output

CF = 0 function successful
AH = 00h
CF = 1 function unsuccessful
AH = status code (see INT 13h function 01h)

See Also

INT 13h Function 01h

INT 13h   [PC][AT][PS/2]
FUNCTION 11h
Recalibrate Drive   **BIOS**

Returns the status of a specified hard disk and places the read/write head at track 0.

Input

    AH = 11h
    DL = drive
         80H-FFh fixed disk

Output

    CF = 0 function successful
    AH = 00h
    CF = 1 function unsuccessful
    AH = status code (see INT 13h Function 01h)

Comments

If an error occurs, Function 00h must be used to reset the drive and retry the operation.

This function is called by Function 00h and Function 0Dh. Together these functions perform the same actions as Function 11h.

See Also

    INT 13h Functions 00h, 01h and 0Dh

INT 13h   [XT][PS/2]
FUNCTION 12h
Controller RAM Diagnostic   **BIOS**

Performs built-in diagnostic test of hard disk controller.

Input

    AH = 12h
    DL = drive number
         80h first disk
         81h second disk

Output

CF = 0 function is successful
AH = status code (See INT 13h Function 00h)
CF = 1 function is unsuccessful

See Also

INT 13h Functions 13h,14h

INT 13h   [XT][PS/2]

FUNCTION 13h
Controller Drive Diagnostic   **BIOS**

Performs built-in diagnostic test of attached drive.

Input

AH = 13h
DL = drive number
     80h first disk
     81h second disk

Output

CF = 0 function is successful
AH = status code (See INT 13h Function 01h)
CF = 1 function is unsuccessful

See Also

INT 13h Functions 12h,14h

INT 13h   [XT][PS/2]

FUNCTION 14h
Controller Drive Diagnostic   **BIOS**

Performs built-in diagnostic self-test of hard disk controller.

Input

AH = 14h

Output

CF = 0 function is successful
AH = 00h
CF = 1 function is unsuccessful
AH = status (See INT 13h Function 01h)

INT 13h   [AT][PS/2]
FUNCTION 15h
Get Disk Type   BIOS

Returns the type of floppy or fixed disk and also the number of sectors on the drive.

Input

    AH = 15h
    DL = drive
            00h-7Fh floppy disk
            80h-FFh fixed disk

Output

    CF   = 0 function successful
    AH   = disk type code
            00h drive not present
            01h diskette, no change line available
            02h diskette, change line available
            03h fixed disk
    CX:DX= number of 512-byte sectors (If Ah=03h)
    CF   = 1 function unsuccessful
    AH   = status code (see INT 13h Function 01h)

Comments

This function is not available on PCs, PCjrs or XTs.

This function allows you to determine whether a drive supports the Change Line Status function (Function 16h). Change Line Status informs the system whether or not the diskette has been changed since the last operation.

See Also

    INT 13h Functions 01h,16h and 17h

INT 13h   [AT][PS/2]
FUNCTION 16h
Change Line Status   BIOS

Determines whether or not the disk has been changed (or the disk drive door opened) since the last disk access.

Input

    AH = 16h
    DL = drive
            00h-7Fh floppy disk

Output

    CF = 0 function successful (Change Line status is inactive)
    AH = Change Line status
            00H "diskette changed" signal is not active
            01h Invalid diskette parameter
            06h "Diskette changed" signal is active
            80h Drive not ready
    CF = 1 function unsuccessful
    AH = 06h

Comments

This function is not available for PC or PC XT.

If CF is set and AH=01h or 80h, then an error has occurred. If AH=06h and CF is set, then this is not an error: it means the diskette has been changed or the disk drive door has been opened.

This function is only supported for floppy disks.

See Also

    INT 13h Functions 15h, 17h and 01h

INT 13h   [AT][PS/2]
FUNCTION 17h
Set Disk Type for Format   BIOS

Sets a floppy disk type for the specified disk drive.

Input

    AH = 17H
    AL = disk type
            00h no disk
            01h 320/360K floppy disk in 360K drive
            02h 320/360K floppy disk in 1.2M drive
            03h 1.2M floppy disk in 1.2M drive
            04h 720K floppy disk in 720K drive
    DL = drive
            00h-7Fh floppy disk

Output

CF = 0 function successful
AH = 00h
CF = 1 function unsuccessful
AH = status code (see INT 13h Function 01h)

Comments

This function can only be used on diskettes.

This function is not available for floppy disks on PC, PCjrs or PC XT.

See Also

INT 13h Functions 01h, 15h and 16h

INT 13h   [AT][PS/2]
FUNCTION 18h
Set Media Type for Format   **BIOS**

Returns a Diskette Drive Parameter table (DDTP) for the specified drive.

Input

AH = 18h
CH = number of tracks (9,8 bits of 10-bit cylinder address in high
        bits of CL)
CL = sector per track
DL = drive
        00h-7Fh floppy disk

Output

CF = 0 function successful
AH = 00h
ES:DI = segment:offset of 11-byte DDTP
CF = 1 function unsuccessful
AH = status code (see INT 13h Function 01h)

Comments

This function can only be used on diskettes.

This function is not available on PsC or PC XTs. On appropriate machines,
this function is called before calling INT 13h Function 05h.

If Change Status line is active (i.e. the disk has been changed), this function
attempts to recognize the new diskette (i.e., deactivate Change Status Line).
If the function cannot do this, it returns an error - therefore a floppy disk must
be present in the drive.

See Also

INT 13h Functions 05h, 07h and 17h

INT 13h [PS/2]

FUNCTION 19h
Park Heads

BIOS

Moves the read/write heads to prepare for landing. This enables you to turn the drive off, and to move the computer without the surface of the hard disk being damaged.

Input

AH = 19h
DL = drive
    80h-FFh fixed disk

Output

CF = 0 function successful
AH = 00h
CF = 1 function unsuccessful
AH = status code (see INT 13h Function 01h)

See Also

INT 13h Functions 01h, 15h and 16h

INT 13h [PS/2]

FUNCTION 1Ah
Format ESDI Drive

BIOS

Initializes a track, writes disk address fields and data sectors of ESDI fixed disk.

Input

AH = 1Ah
AL = defect table count
CL = format modifiers
    bit 0 ignore primary defect map
    bit 1 ignore secondary defect map
    bit 2 update secondary defect map
    bit 3 perform surface analysis
    bit 4 generate periodic interrupt

DL   = drive
            80h-FFh fixed disk
ES:BX =   segment:offset of defect table

Output

CF = 0 function successful
AH = 00h
CF = 1 function unsuccessful
AH = status code (see INT 13h Function 01h)

Comments

When generic periodic interrupt is selected, then INT 15h Function 0Fh is called after each cylinder has been formatted.

If you want to reflect errors which appear during surface analysis then bit 2 of CL must be set.

When bits 1 and 2 are set, the secondary defect map is replaced.

See Also

INT 10h Functions 07h; INT 15h Function 0Fh

INT 14h   [PC][AT][PS/2]
FUNCTION 00h
Initialize Communications Port Parameters   BIOS

Initializes and configures a serial communications port to the necessary baud rate, parity, stop-bit and word length.

Input

AH = 00h
AL = initializing parameters

	Baud rate	Parity	Stop Bits	Word Length
Bits	7-6-5 4-3	2	1-0	
	000= 110bd	00=none	0=1 bit	00=5 bits
	001= 150bd	01=odd	1=2 bits	01=6 bits
	010= 300bd	10=even		10=7 bits
	011= 600bd			11=8 bits
	100=1200bd			
	101=2400bd			
	110=4800bd			
	111=9600bd			

DX = port number (0 = COM1, 1 = COM2, etc)

Output

```
Ah  = serial port status
      bit    7 = time out error
             6 = transfer shift register empty
             5 = transfer holding register empty
             4 = break discovered
             3 = framing error discovered
             2 = parity error
             1 = overrun error
             0 = data ready
AL  = modem status
      bit    7 = receive line signal detect
             6 = ring indicator
             5 = data set ready
             4 = clear to send
             3 = change in receive line signal detect
             2 = trailing edge ring detector
             1 = change in data set ready
             0 = change in clear to send
```

See Also

INT 14h Function 04h

INT 14h   [PC][AT][PS/2]
FUNCTION 01h
Send Character to Communications Port   BIOS

Sends one character to the communications port.

Input

```
AH  = 01h
AL  = character
DX  = port number (0 = COM1, 1 = COM2, etc)
```

Output

```
AH  = bit 7 = 0 character transmitted
        bit 7 = 1 error
AH  = bits 0-6 serial port status
        bit 6 = transfer shift register empty
             5 = transfer holding register empty
             4 = break discovered
             3 = framing error discovered
             2 = parity error
             1 = overrun error
             0 = data ready
AL  = character(unchanged)
```

Comments

Since bit 7 is used as an error flag, this function cannot detect a time-out error.

See Also

INT 14h Functions 02h and 03h

INT 14h   [PC][AT][PS/2]
FUNCTION 02h
Receive Character from Communications Port   BIOS

Reads a character from the specified serial port.

Input

AH = 02h
DX = port number (0 = COM1, 1 = COM2, etc)

Output

AH = bit 7 = 0 character received
          bit 7 = 1 error
AH = bits 0-6 serial port status
          bit 6 = transfer shift register empty
               5 = transfer holding register empty
               4 = break discovered
               3 = framing error discovered
               2 = parity error
               1 = overrun error
               0 = data ready
AL = character (unchanged)

Comments

This function waits for a character.

See Also

INT 14h Functions 01h and 03h

INT 14h   [PC][AT][PS/2]
FUNCTION 03h
Get Communications Port Status   BIOS

Returns the line status and modem status of the specified serial communications port.

Input

AH = 03h
DX = port number (0 = COM1, 1 = COM2, etc)

Output

AH = line status (see INT 14h Function 00h)
AL = modem status (see INT 14h Function 00h)

See Also

INT 14h Function 00h

INT 14h   [PS/2]
FUNCTION 04h
Extended Initialize Communications Port   **BIOS**

Establishes the necessary parameters of the designated communications port baud rate, parity, stop bit and word length.

Input

AH = 04h
AL = break
    00h none
    01h break
BH = parity
    00h none
    01h odd
    02h even
    03h stick parity odd
BL = stop bit
    00h stop bit
    01h 2 stop bits if word length=6-8 bits
    02h 1.5 stop bits if word length=5 bits
CH = word length
    00h 5 bits
    01h 6 bits
    02h 7 bits
    03h 8 bits
CL = baud rate
    00h   110 bd
    01h   150 bd
    02h   300 bd
    03h   600 bd
    04h 1200 bd
    05h 2400 bd

              06h   4800 bd
              07h   9600 bd
              08h 19200 bd
        DX = port number (0 = COM1, 1 = COM2, etc)

Output

        AH = line status (see INT 14h Function 00h)
        AL = modem status (see INT 14h Function 00h) error

See Also

        INT 14h Functions 00h and 02h

INT 14h   [PS/2]
FUNCTION 05h
Extended Communications Port Control   BIOS

Reads/writes the MCR (modem control register) of the designated
communication port.

Input

        AH = 05h
        AL = Subfunction
              00h reads modem control register
              01h writes modem control register
        BL = modem control register (if AL=01h)
              bit 0 data terminal ready
                   1 request to send
                   2 out1
                   3 out2
                   4 LOOP (for testing)
                   5-7 reserved
        DX = port number (0 = COM1, 1 = COM2, etc)

Output

        AH = port status (see INT 14h Function 00h)
        BL = modem control register (see above) (if AL=00h)
        AL = modem status (see INT 14h Function 00h) (if AL=01h)

Comments

This function reads and writes more operational values for the designated
communication port than INT 14h Function 00h.

See Also

        INT 14h Function 00h

INT 15h [PS/2]
FUNCTION 0Fh
Format ESDI Drive Periodic Interrupt BIOS

Called by the ROM BIOS during ESDI drive formatting after each cylinder
is formatted.

Input

> AH = 0Fh
> AL = phase code
>> 00h reserved
>> 01h surface analysis
>> 02h formatting

Output

> CF = 0 if formatting should continue
> CF = 1 if formatting should be terminated

See Also

> INT 13h Function 1Ah

INT 15h [PS/2]
FUNCTION 4Fh
Keyboard Intercept BIOS

Invoked by the handler of the keyboard hardware Interrupt (09h), at the end
of its work. This function can be used for changing or removing scan codes
returned by the Interrupt 09h handler.

Input

> AH = 4Fh
> AL = scan code
> CF = set

Output

> CF = 0 (scan code is removed or ignored)
> CF = 1 (scan code is not used)
> AL = scan code or new scan code

Comments

If you wish to change the scan code then place the new scan code in AL and
set the Carry Flag.

To determine the machines that support this function, use INT 15h Function 0C0h.

See Also

INT 09h

INT 15h   [AT][PS/2]
FUNCTION 80h
Device Open   BIOS

Informs the operating system that a process uses a logical device.

Input

AH = 80h
BX = device ID
CX = process ID

Output

CF = 0 function is successful
AH = 00h
CF = 1 function is unsuccessful
AH = status
   80h invalid command (PC,PCjr)
   86h function not supported (XT and later)

Comments

A multitasker which wishes to keep track of arbitrate usage of device by multiple process, should capture this function because the default BIOS routine simply returns successfully (CF = 0 and AH = 00h).

See Also

INT 15h Functions 81h and 82h

INT 15h   [AT][PS/2]
FUNCTION 81h
Device Close   BIOS

Informs the operating system that the process has finished using a logical device.

Input

AH = 81h
BX = device ID
CX = process ID

Output

CF = 0 function is successful
AH = 00h
CF = 1 function is unsuccessful
AH = status
      80h invalid command (PC,PCjr)
      86h function not supported (XT and later)

Comments

A multitasker which wishes to keep track of arbitrate usage of device by multiple processes, should capture this function because the default BIOS routine simply returns successfully (CF = 0 and AH = 00h).

See Also

INT 15h Functions 80h and 82h

INT 15h   [AT][PS/2]
FUNCTION 82h
Process Termination   BIOS

Closes all logical devices for a process that were opened with Function 80h.

Input

AH = 82h
BX = process ID

Output

CF = 0 function is successful
AH = 00h
CF = 1 function is unsuccessful
AH = status
      80h invalid command (PC,PCjr)
      86h function not supported (XT and later)

Comments

A multitasker which wishes to keep track of arbitrate usage of device by multiple process, should capture this function because the default BIOS routine simply returns successfully (CF = 0 and AH = 00h).

See Also

INT 15h Functions 80h and 81h

INT 15h [AT][PS/2]

FUNCTION 83h
Event Wait

BIOS

Establishes the amount of time in microseconds at the end of which it sets the semaphore.

Input

AH = 83h
AL = subfunction
    00h set interval (if requesting event wait)
        CX:DX = microseconds of delay
        ES:BX = segment:offset of semaphore byte whose 7th
                bit is to be set
    01h cancel wait interval

Output

CF = 0 function is successful
CF = 1 function is unsuccessful
AH = status
    80h invalid command (PC,PCjr)
    86h function not supported (XT and later)

Comments

The duration of a wait period is always a multiple of 976 microseconds because on most systems the BIOS 1/1024 second date/clock interrupt is used.

See Also

INT 15h Functions 86h

INT 15h [AT][PS/2]

FUNCTION 84h
Joystick Support

BIOS

Reads the joystick switch status if joystick and game ports are avalaible.

Input

AH = 84h
DX = subfunction
    00h read joystick switches
    01h read position of joysticks

Output

CF   = 0 function is successful
AL   bits 4-7 switch setting if DX=00h
        bit 4 = 1 second joystick's second switch enabled
        bit 5 = 1 second joystick's first switch enabled
        bit 6 = 1 first joystick's second switch enabled
        bit 7 = 1 first joystick's first switch enabled
If DX = 01h
AX   = X position of first joystick
BX   = Y position of first joystick
CX   = X position of second joystick
DX   = Y position of second joystick
CF   = 1 function is unsuccessful
AH   = status
        80h invalid command (PC,PCjr)
        86h function not supported (XT and later)

Comments

If no game port is installed, Subfunction 00h returns AL = 00h (all switches open). Subfunction 01h returns AX=00h, BX=00h, CX=00h and DX=00h = 00h.

INT 15h   [AT][PS/2]
FUNCTION 86h
Wait   BIOS

Delays execution of calling program for a specified interval of time in microseconds.

Input

AH   = 86h
CX:DX= microseconds of delay

Output

CF   = 0 function is successful
CF   = 1 function is unsuccessful
AH   = status
        80h invalid command (PC,PCjr)
        83h wait already in progress
        86h function not supported (XT and later)

Comments

The duration of a wait period is always a multiple of 976 microseconds because on most systems BIOS 1/1024 second date/clock interrupt is used.

See Also

INT 15h Functions 83h

INT 15h   [AT][PS/2]
FUNCTION 87h
Move Extended Memory Block   BIOS

Moves a block of extended memory.

Input

```
AH    = 87h
CX    = number of words to move (max 8000h)
ES:SI = segment:offset - Global Descriptor Table(GDT)
```

Output

```
CF  = 0 function is successful
AH  = 00h source copied to destination
CF  = 1 function is unsuccessful
AH  = status
         01h parity error
         02h interrupt error
         03h address line 20 gating failed
         80h invalid command (PC,PCjr)
         86h function not supported (XT and later)
```

Comments

The Global Descriptor Table has the following format:

Offset	Size	Description
00h	16	reserved(zeros)
10h	2	source segment length in bytes (2*CX-1 or greater)
12h	3	24-bit linear source address, low byte first
15h	1	access right byte(93h) of source
16h	2	zero
18h	2	destination segment length in bytes (2*CX-1 or greater)
1Ah	3	24-bit linear destination address, low byte first
1Dh	1	access right byte (93h) of destination
1Eh	18	zeros

Extended memory can be accessed only in protected mode and therefore copying is done in protected mode.

The block move is performed when all interrupts are disabled.

See Also

INT 15h Functions 88h and 89h

INT 15h [AT][PS/2]

FUNCTION 88h
Get Extended Memory Size

BIOS

Reads amount of extended memory in the system.

Input

AH = 88h

Output

CF = 0 function is successful
AX = amount of extended memory in Kb
CF = 1 function is unsuccessful
AH = status
80h invalid command (PC,PCjr)
86h function not supported (XT and later)

Comments

Extended memory can be used only in protected mode, but MS-DOS can work only in real mode. Therefore the extended memory can only be used under MS-DOS for data storage.

See Also

INT 15h Functions 87h

INT 15h [AT][PS/2]
FUNCTION 89h
Enter Protected Mode
BIOS

Switches the system from real mode into protected mode.

Input

AH	= 89h
BH	= interrupt number for IRQ8 (IRQ9-F use next 7 interrupt)
BL	= interrupt number for IRQ0 (IRQ1-8 use next 7 interrupt)
ES:SI	= segment:offset of Global Descpitor Table (GDT)

Output

CF	= 0 function is successful (CPU in protected mode)
AH	= 00h
CF	= 1 function is unsuccessful
AH	= FFh error enabling address line 20

Comments

The Global Descriptor Table (GDT) has the following format:

Offset	Description
00h	null descriptor (initialized to 0)
08h	GDT descriptor
10h	Interrupt Descriptor Table (IDT)
18h	user's data segment (DS)
20h	user's extra segment (ES)
28h	user's stack segment (SS)
30h	user's code segment (CS)
38h	BIOS code segment

Value in BL and BH registers must be multiples of 8.

See Also

INT 15h Functions 87h and 88h

INT 15h [AT][PS/2]
FUNCTION 90h
Device Wait BIOS

Notifies the operating system that a device is waiting for I/O completion.

Input

AH = 90h
AL = device type
    00h-7Fh Serially reusable devices
    80h-BFh Re-entrant devices
    C0h-FFh Wait-only calls, no corresponding Post functions
ES:BX = segment:offset of requested block for device types 80h
    through BFh

Output

CF = 0 drive must perform wait
AH = 00h
CF = 1 wait is performed

Comments

Device types are:

00h   disk (may time-out)
01h   floppy disk (may time-out)
02h   keyboard (no time-out)
03h   PS/2 pointing device (may time-out)
80h   network (no time-out)
FCh   fixed disk reset (PS/2 may time-out)
FDh   diskette motor start(may time-out)
FEh   printer(may time-out)

A multitasker which wishes to allow another task to be executed while the BIOS is waiting for I/O completion should capture this function, because the default BIOS routine returns successfully (CF = 0 and AH = 00h).

See Also

INT 15h Functions 91h

INT 15h   [AT][PS/2]

FUNCTION 91h
OS Hook - Device Post

BIOS

Notifies the operating system that a device is ready and I/O operation is complete.

Input

```
AH   = 91h
AL   = device type
       00h-7Fh Serially reusable devices
       80h-BFh Re-entrant devices
       C0h-FFh Wait-only calls, no corresponding Post functions
ES:BX = segment:offset of requested block for device types 80h
        through BFh
```

Output

```
AH  = 00h
```

Comments

Device types are:

```
00h    disk (may time-out)
01h    floppy disk (may time-out)
02h    keyboard (no time-out)
03h    PS/2 pointing device (may time-out)
80h    network (no time-out)
```

A multitasker which wishes to allow another task to be executed while the BIOS is waiting for I/O completion should capture this function, because the default BIOS routine returns successfully (CF = 0 and AH = 00h).

See Also

INT 15h Functions 90h

INT 15h   [AT][PS/2]

FUNCTION C0h
Get System Environment

BIOS

Returns a pointer to a configuration table in ROM BIOS, filled with information about the system.

Input

AH = C0h

Output

CF   = 0 function is successful
ES:BX = segment:offset of configuration table
AH   = status
      00h successful
      86h unsupported function
CF   = 1 function is unsuccessful

Comments

The System Configuration Table has the following format:

Offset	Size	Description
00h	2	length of table
02h	1	model (See below)
03h	1	submodel (See below)
04h	1	BIOS revision: 0-first...
05h	1	features:

bit 7 =	DMA channel 3 used
bit 6 =	2nd 8259 present
bit 5 =	Real Time clock installed
bit 4 =	INT 15h Function 4Fh called upon INT 9h
bit 3 =	wait for external event is supported
bit 2 =	extended BIOS data area allocated
bit 1 =	bus is Micro Channel
bit 0 =	reserved

Offset	Size	Description
06h	2	reserved (0)
08h	2	reserved (0)

Values for model/submodel are following:

Machine	Model Byte	Submodel Byte
PC	FFh	
PC/XT	FEh	
PC/XT	FBh	00h or 01h
PCjr	FDh	
PC/AT	FCh	00h or 01h
PC/XT-286	FCh	02h
PC Convertible	F9h	
PS/2 Model 30	FAh	00h
PS/2 Model 50	FCh	04h
PS/2 Model 80	F8h	00h or 01h
PS/2 Model 70	F8h	04h,09h,0Bh,1Bh

INT 15h   [PS/2]
FUNCTION C1h
Get Address of Extended BIOS Data Area   **BIOS**

Gets the segment address of the extended BIOS data area. The offset address
is always 0000h.

Input

AH = C1h

Output

CF = 0 function is successful
ES = segment of Extended BIOS data area
CF = 1 function is unsuccessful

INT 15h   [PS/2]
FUNCTION C2h SUBFUNCTION 00h
Enable/Disable Pointing Device   **BIOS**

Enables/disables system pointing device.

Input

AH = C2h
AL = 00h
BH = enbale/disable flag
    00h = disable
    01h = enable functions

Output

CF = 0 function is successful
AH = 00h
CF = 1 function is unsuccessful
AH = status
    01h invalid function
    02h invalid input
    03h interface error
    04h resend
    05h no device handler installed

See Also

INT 33h

INT 15h [PS/2]
FUNCTION C2h SUBFUNCTION 01h
Reset Pointing Device   **BIOS**

Resets a mouse or other pointing device.

Input

    AH = C2h
    AL = 01h

Output

    CF = 0 function is successful
    AH = 00h
    CF = 1 function is unsuccessful
    AH = status
         01h   invalid function
         02h   invalid input
         03h   interface error
         04h   resend
         05h   no device handler installed

See Also

    INT 33h

INT 15h [PS/2]
FUNCTION C2h SUBFUNCTION 02h
Set Sampling Rate   **BIOS**

Sets the polling rate of the systems mouse or other pointing device.

Input

    AH = C2h
    AL = 02h
    BH = sampling rate
         00h   10/second
         01h   20/second
         02h   30/second
         03h   60/second
         04h   80/second
         05h   100/second
         06h   200/second

Output

CF = 0 function is successful
AH = 00h
CF = 1 function is unsuccessful
AH = status
    01h   invalid function
    02h   invalid input
    03h   interface error
    04h   resend
    05h   no device handler installed

See Also

INT 33h Function 1Ch

INT 15h   [PS/2]

FUNCTION C2h SUBFUNCTION 03h
Set Resolution   BIOS

Sets the resolution level of the systems mouse or other pointing device.

Input

AH = C2h
AL = 03h
BH = resolution
    00h   1 count per millimeter (25 dpi)
    01h   2 count per millimeter (50 dpi)
    02h   4 count per millimeter (100 dpi)
    03h   8 count per millimeter (200 dpi)

Output

CF = 0 function is successful
AH = 00h
CF = 1 function is unsuccessful
AH = status
    01h   invalid function
    02h   invalid input
    03h   interface error
    04h   resend
    05h   no device handler installed

Comments

Default for the sensitivity level is 4 count per millimeter.

See Also

INT 33h Function 1Ch

INT 15h   [PS/2]

FUNCTION C2h SUBFUNCTION 04h
Get Pointing Device Type   **BIOS**

Reads the identification type for the systems mouse or other pointing device.

Input

    AH = C2h
    AL = 04h

Output

    CF = 0 function is successful
    BH = device ID
    CF = 1 function is unsuccessful
    AH = status
         01h   invalid function
         02h   invalid input
         03h   interface error
         04h   resend
         05h   no device handler installed

See Also

    INT 33h

INT 15h   [PS/2]

FUNCTION C2h SUBFUNCTION 05h
Initialize Pointing Device Interface   **BIOS**

Initialize the data package size and other parameters for the systems mouse
or other pointing device.

Input

    AH = C2h
    AL = 05h
    BH = data package size D(1-8 byte)

Output

    CF = 0 function is successful
    CF = 1 function is unsuccessful
    AH = status
         01h   invalid function
         02h   invalid input

    03h   interface error
    04h   resend
    05h   no device handler installed

See Also

INT 15h Function C2h Subfunction 01h

INT 15h   [PS/2]

FUNCTION C2h SUBFUNCTION 06h
Set Scaling or Get Status   BIOS

Reads the current status or specifies the scaling factor for the systems mouse or other pointing device.

Input

AH = C2h
AL = 06h
BH = subfunction
    00h   return device status
    01h   set scaling factor at 1:1
    02h   set scaling factor at 2:1

Output

CF = 0 function is successful
AH = 00h
BL = status byte (if BH = 00h)
    bit 0 = 1 right button pressed
    bit 1   reserved
    bit 2 = 1 left button pressed
    bit 3   reserved
    bit 4 = 0 if 1:1 scaling factor
        = 1 if 2:1 scaling factor
    bit 5 = 0 device disabled
        = 1 device enabled
    bit 6 = 0 stream mode
        = 1 remote mode
    bit 7   reserved
CL = resolution
    00h   1 count per millimeter (25 dpi)
    01h   2 count per millimeter (50 dpi)
    02h   4 count per millimeter (100 dpi)
    03h   8 count per millimeter (200 dpi)
DL = sample rate (reports per second)
    00h   10/second
    01h   20/second
    02h   30/second

       03h   60/second
       04h   80/second
       05h   100/second
       06h   200/second
CF = 1 function is unsuccessful
AH = status
       01h   invalid function
       02h   invalid input
       03h   interface error
       04h   resend
       05h   no device handler installed

See Also

INT 33h

INT 15h   [PS/2]

FUNCTION C2h SUBFUNCTION 07h
Set Device Handler Address   **BIOS**

Establishes the address of the pointing device handler routine for the ROM BIOS pointing device driver.

Input

AH   = C2h
AL   = 07h
ES:BX = segment:offset of user device handler

Output

CF = 0 function is successful
CF = 1 function is unsuccessful
AH = status
       01h   invalid function
       02h   invalid input
       03h   interface error
       04h   resend
       05h   no device handler installed

See Also

INT 33h Function 0Ch

INT 15h   [PS/2]
FUNCTION C3h
Enable/Disable Watchdog Timeout   BIOS

Enables or disables automatic watchdog timer which generates an NMI interrupt.

Input

AH = C3h
AL = Subfunction
    00h   disable
    01h   enable
DX = timer counter

Output

CF = 0 function is successful
CF = 1 function is unsuccessful
AH = status
    80h   invalid function (PC,PCjr)
    86h   unsupported function   (XT,PS/2 30)

Comments

This interrupt is avalaible on all PS/2 models, except model 25 and 30.

See Also

INT 33h Function 0Ch

INT 15h   [PS/2]
FUNCTION C4h
Programmable Option Select   BIOS

Changes the systems internal configuration registers and reads the address of the Programmable Option Select (POS) register.

Input

AH = C4h
AL = Subfunction
    00h   return base POS register address
    01h   enable slot
    02h   enable adapter
BL = slot number (if AL = 01h)

Output

CF = 0 function is successful
DX = base POS register address (if function AL=00h)
CF = 1 function is unsuccessful

Comments

This function is avalaible only for PS/2 model 50 and above with Micro Channel
Architecture

INT 16h   [PC][AT][PS/2]

FUNCTION 00h
Read Character from Keyboard   BIOS

Reads the keyboard buffer and returns the character and the corresponding
scan code.

Input

AH = 00h

Output

AH = keyboard scan code
AL = ASCII character code

Comments

This function waits until a character has arrived. After reading the character,
the function removes it from the buffer.

See Also

INT 16h Function 10h, INT 09h

INT 16h   [PC][AT][PS/2]

FUNCTION 01h
Get Keyboard Status   BIOS

Reads the keyboard buffer and determines whether a character is ready to be
entered. If one is ready, it returns the character and a flag.

Input

AH = 01h

Output

ZF = 0 (Character available in keyboard buffer)
AH = scan code
AL = character
ZF = 1 (No character in keyboard buffer)

Comments

The character remains in the keyboard buffer if ZF clear.
This character can be returned by calling either function 00h or this function again.

See Also

INT 16h Functions 00h and 11h

INT 16h   [PC][AT][PS/2]
FUNCTION 02h
Get Keyboard Flags   **BIOS**

Reads and returns the current ROM BIOS keybord status byte that describes the status of various control keys and various keyboard modes.

Input

AH = 02h

Output

AL = shift status bits

bit	description (if bit is set)
00h	Right Shift key pressed
01h	Left Shift key pressed
02h	CTRL key pressed
03h	ALT key pressed
04h	SCROLL LOCK active
05h	NUM LOCK active
06h	CAPS LOCK active
07h	INSERT active

Comments

The keyboard status byte is stored in one byte at memory location 0000:0417h.

The keyboard status byte for an enhanced keyboard can be obtained by calling Function 12h.

See Also

INT 16h Function 12h

INT 16h   [PC][AT][PS/2]
FUNCTION 03h
Set Typematic Rate   **BIOS**

Modifies the ROM BIOS initial typematic (repeat) rate and delays the keyboard.

Input

     AH = 03h
     AL = subfunction
         00h reset default typematic and delay (PCjr)
         01h increase initial delay (PCjr)
         02h increase continuing delay (PCjr)
         03h increase delay and decrease typematic by one half (PCjr)
         04h turn off typematic (PCjr)
         05h set typematic rate (AT and PS/2)
     BH = repeat delay (PC and PS/2)
         00h 250 ms
         01h 500 ms
         02h 750 ms
         03h 1000 ms
     BL = repeat rate (PC and PS/2)
         00h-1Fh character per seconds for 30cps down to 2cps

Output

     Nothing

Comments

Subfunctions 00h - 04h are not supported on PC and PC/XT. Subfunction 05h can be used on all PS/2s and on ATs having ROM BIOS version 15 November 1985 or later.

See Also

INT 16h Function 10h; INT 09h

INT 16h   [AT][PS/2]
FUNCTION 05h
Push Character and Scan Code   **BIOS**

Pushes a scan/character code combination into the keyboard buffer.

Input

     AH = 05h
     CH = scan code
     CL = character

Output

CF = clear (function successful)
AL = 00h
CF = set (function unsuccessful)
AL = 01h

See Also

INT 16h Functions 00h and 10h

INT 16h   [AT][PS/2]
FUNCTION 10h
Read Character from Enhanced Keyboard   BIOS

Reads a scan/character code combination from the keyboard buffer.

Input

AH = 10h

Output

AH = keyboard scan code
AL = ASCII character code

Comments

This function waits until a character has arrived.

This function provides support for the enhanced keyboard (101/102 keys). After the character has been extracted from the keyboard buffer, the keyboard buffer head pointer is increased by 2. If the pointer is already beyond the end of the buffer, it is reset to the start of the buffer.

This function removes the scan code and character from the keyboard buffer.

See Also

INT 16h Functions 00h and 05h

INT 16h   [AT][PS/2]
FUNCTION 11h
Check Extended Keyboard Status   BIOS

Checks whether a character is available in the buffer and reads it if one is waiting.

Input

AH = 11h

Output

ZF = clear (if character is available)
AH = scan code
AL = character
ZF = set (if character is not available)

Comments

This function does not remove the character from the keyboard buffer.

See Also

INT 16h Functions 01h and 10h

INT 16h   [AT][PS/2]
FUNCTION 12h
Get Extended Special Key Status   **BIOS**

Gets the current keyboard flags information from the enhanced keyboard.

Input

AH = 12h

Output

AL = Shift Status
  Bit   Description (if set)
  00h   right Shift key is pressed
  01h   left Shift key is pressed
  02h   either Ctrl key is pressed
  03h   either Alt key is pressed
  04h   Scroll Lock key is locked
  05h   Num Lock key is locked
  06h   Caps Lock key is locked
  07h   Insert key is locked
AH = Extended Shift Status
  bit   Description (if set)
  00h   left CTRL is pressed
  01h   left ALT key is pressed
  02h   right CTRL key is pressed
  03h   right ALT key is pressed
  04h   Scroll Lock key is locked
  05h   Num Lock key is locked
  06h   Caps Lock key is locked
  07h   SysReq key is locked

Comments

The Extended Shift Status reports that keys are being pressed.

See Also

INT 16h Function 02h

INT 17h   [PC][AT]
FUNCTION 00h
Write Character to Printer   BIOS

Writes a character to the specified printer and returns the current status of the specified printer port.

Input

AH = 00h
AL = character
DX = printer number (0=LPT1, 1=LPT2, 2=LPT3)

Output

AH = status bits
  bit 0 time out
  1 unused
  2 unused
  3 I/O error
  4 printer selected
  5 printer out of paper
  6 printer mode seleted
  7 not busy

INT 17h   [PC][AT][PS/2]
FUNCTION 01h
Initialize Printer   BIOS

Initializes the specified printer parallel port. This function must be performed before function 00h.

Input

AH = 01h
DX = printer number (0=LPT1, 1=LPT2, 2=LPT3)

Output

AH = Status bits (see function AH=00h INT 17h)

INT 17h   [PC][AT][PS/2]
FUNCTION 02h
Get Printer Status   **BIOS**

Returns the current status of the specified printer parallel port.

Input

AH = 02h
DX = printer number (0=LPT1, 1=LPT2, 2=LPT3)

Output

Ah = Status bits (see Function AH=00h INT 17h)

INT 19h   [PC][AT]
Reboot System   **BIOS**

Reboots the operation system from the floppy disk or fixed disk.

Input

Nothing

Output

Nothing

Comments

The bootstrap routine will usually try to read sector 1, head 0, track 0 from drive A: or the first hard disk installed in the computer configuration into the memory location 0000:7C00h. It then transfers control to the same address in the master bootstrap loader. To perform a warm boot equivalent to Ctrl-Alt-Del, you should place 1234h into memory location 0040: 0072h and jump to FFFFh:0000h.

To perform a cold boot equivalent to a reset, you should place 0000h into the memory location 0040h:0072h and jump to FFFFh:0000h.

INT 1Ah   [AT][PS/2]
FUNCTION 00h
Read Clock Count   **BIOS**

Reads the current clock count. The clock count is incremented 18.2 times per
second and is the cumulative number of clock ticks since midnight.

Input

AH = 00h

Output

AL = rolled-over flag
   = 00h if clock has been read since midnight
   <>00h otherwise

Comments

The rolled-over flag is only set once per day - after 1573040 clock ticks. After
this the counter is cleared to zero.

On a PC XT without a battery powered realtime clock, the clock counter is
set to 0 during a boot , and on a PC AT with a battery powered realtime
clock, the clock counter is set to the current time during a boot.

See Also

INT 1Ah Function 02h; INT 21h Function 2Ch

INT 1Ah   [AT][PS/2]
FUNCTION 01h
Set Tick Count   **BIOS**

Places a 32-bit value in the current clock count.

Input

AH   = 01h
CX:DX= clock count(high word of clock count in CX)

Output

Nothing

Comments

This function clears the rolled-over flag. PC users can use this function to set
the current time.

See Also

INT 1Ah Function 00h

INT 1Ah   [AT][PS/2]
FUNCTION 02h
Read Realtime Clock   **BIOS**

Reads the current time from the CMOS time chips with realtime clock.

Input

AH = 02h

Output

CH = hours in BCD (binary coded decimal)
CL = minutes in BCD
DH = seconds in BCD
DL = daylight saving time
    00h = if standard time
    01h = if daylight saving time
CL = 0 clock running
CL = 1 clock stopped (dead clock battery)

See Also

INT 1Ah Function 00h

INT 1Ah   [AT][PS/2]
FUNCTION 03h
Set Realtime Clock   **BIOS**

Sets the time in the realtime clock.

Input

AH = 03h
CH = hours in BCD (binary coded decimal)
CL = minutes in BCD
DH = second in BCD
DL = daylight-saving time code
    00h if standard time
    01h if daylight saving time

Output

Nothing

See Also

INT 1Ah Function 01h

INT 1Ah   [AT][PS/2]
FUNCTION 04h
Read Date from Real Time Clock   **BIOS**

Reads the current date from real time clock.

Input

AH = 04h

Output

CH = century (19 or 20) in BCD
CL = year in BCD
DH = month in BCD
DL = day in BCD
CF = 0 if clock running
CF = 1 if clock is dead

See Also

INT 1Ah Function 05h; INT 21h Function 2Ah

INT 1Ah   [AT][PS/2]
FUNCTION 05h
Set Date   **BIOS**

Sets the date in the CMOS calendar.

Input

AH = 05h
CH = century in BCD
CL = year in BCD
DH = month in BCD
DL = day in BCD

Output

Nothing

See Also

INT 1Ah Function 04h

INT 1Ah   [AT][PS/2]
FUNCTION 06h
Set Alarm Time   **BIOS**

Sets an alarm time for the current day.

Input

AH = 06h
CH = hours in BCD
CL = minutes in BCD
DH = seconds in BCD

Output

CF = 0 function successful
CF = 1 if alarm is already set or clock is inoperable

Comments

Only one alarm time can be active at any time. The alarm occurs every 24 hours at the specified time.

If a program uses this function, then you must place the address of the interrupt handler for the alarm in the vector for INT 4Ah. During booting, the interrupt 4Ah points to an IRET command so nothing will happen when the alarm time is reached.

See Also

INT 1Ah Function 07h; INT 4Ah

INT 1Ah   [AT][PS/2]
FUNCTION 07h
Reset Alarm Time   **BIOS**

Cancels an existing alarm request on the CMOS time chip.

Input

AH = 07h

Output

Nothing

See Also

INT 1Ah Function 06h

INT 1Ah   [PS/2]
FUNCTION 0Ah
Read System-Timer Day Counter   BIOS

Reads the contents of the systems day counter.

Input

AH = 0Ah

Output

CF = 1 if function unsuccessful
CF = 0 if function successful
CX = count of days since Jan 1, 1980

See Also

INT 1Ah Function 0Bh

INT 1Ah   [PS/2]
FUNCTION 0Bh
Set System Timer Day Counter   BIOS

Places an arbitrary value in the system's day counter.

Input

AH = 0Bh
CX = count of day since Jan 1, 1980

Output

CF = 0 function successful
CF = 1 function is unsuccessful

Comments

This function clears the rolled-over flag. PC users can use this function to set
current time.

See Also

INT 1Ah Function 00h

INT 1Bh   [PC][AT][PS/2]
Keyboard Break   BIOS

This interrupt is invoked by BIOS on receiving the <Ctrl><Break> key
combination. BIOS initially sets this interrupt to an IRET command. It prevents
any reaction.

Input

Nothing

Output

Nothing

Comments

This interrupt sets an internal DOS Flag. This flag signals that the user has
pressed <Ctrl><Break>. DOS tests this flag occassionally by execution of the
DOS Control Break Check (INT 21h Function 33h). If the flag is set during
a test, the internal flag is reset and INT 23h is called. The current program
stops.

See Also

INT 23h; INT 21h Function 33h

INT 1Ch   [PC][AT][PS/2]
User Timer Interrupt   BIOS

This interrupt is invoked by BIOS on each tick of the hardware clock
(approximately 18.2 times per second). BIOS initially sets this interrupt to an
IRET command in order to prevent any action if the interrupt is called.

Input

Nothing

Output

Nothing

Comments

This interrupt is called by the lower-level hardware timer and is invoked by Interrupt 08h. This interrupt is strictly limited in action, since during execution all other interrupts are disabled (i.e. you cannot get user input). Instead of attempting to hook onto this interrupt, a better approach for a custom handler is to intercept the INT 08h

See Also

INT 08h

GI

DOS Function
Reference - Interrupt 21h

INT 21h   [1.0+]
FUNCTION 00h
Program Termination   **DOS**

Terminates execution of the current process and returns control to the parent
process. MS DOS performs the following actions before passing control to the
calling process:

> Releases all memory belonging to the process.
> Closes all handles for files or devices opened by the process.
> Clears all file buffers.
> Restores the termination handler vector (Int 22h).
> Restores the Ctrl-C handler vector (Int 23h).
> Restores the critical-error handler vector (Int 24h).

Input:

> AH = 00h
> CS = segment address of PSP

Output:

> nothing

Comments:

COM programs store the segment address of the PSP in the CS register
automatically. EXE programs store code and the PSP in two different registers
and you must place the PSP address in the CS register. For this reason you
cannot use this function from an EXE program. Do not use this function for
DOS 2.0 and higher, use INT 21h Function 31h or Function 4Ch instead. These
functions are preferable, since they pass a return code to the current parent
process.

See Also:

INT 21h Function 31h, 4Ch, INT 20h, INT 22h

INT 21h   [1.0+]
FUNCTION 01h
Keyboard Input   DOS

Reads a character from a standard input device and displays it on the standard output device. When the function is called, it waits until a character is available. Since the standard input and output can be redirected, this function can read a character from input devices other than the keyboard and send a character to a device other than the screen. If input is redirected, when the end of the file is reached, the input does not redirect to the keyboard but tries to read data from the file.

Input:

       AH = 01h

Output:

       AL = character read

Comments:

This function must be called twice to read extended ASCII codes on IBM and compatible PCs. The first call returns 0 in the AL register.
If the character being read is the Ctrl-C character and input is not redirected, this function calls interrupt 23h. If standard input has been redirected, a Ctrl-C character is read and BREAK is ON, then this function calls interrupt 23h.

See Also:

INT 21h Functions 06h, 07h, 08h, 0Ah, 0Ch, 3Fh

INT 21h   [1.0+]
FUNCTION 02h
Display Output   DOS

Displays a character on the standard output device. Since output can be redirected, this function can display the character on another output device or send it to a file. This function does not test whether the output device (disk) is full.

Input:

>   AH = 02h
>   DL = character to send to standard output

Output:

>   Nothing

Comments:

If the Ctrl-C combination has been pressed, this function calls the interrupt 23h.

If standard output has not been redirected, then control codes such as backspace, carriage return and linefeed are performed when this function sends characters to the screen. If output has been redirected, these codes are sent to the file as ordinary ASCII codes.

See Also:

INT 21h Functions 06h, 09h

INT 21h   [1.0+]
FUNCTION 03h
Auxiliary Input   DOS

Reads a character from the serial port. The default is the first serial port (COM1). The MODE command can redirect serial access.

Input:

>   AH = 03h

Output:

>   AL = character read

Comments:

In most MS DOS systems the serial device has no internal buffer and is not interrupt driven. This means that it can send data faster than programs can read them. All unread characters may be lost.

Before calling this function you must initialize the serial port by performing the MODE command. When starting up on IBM PC's, MS DOS initializes the serial port to 2400 baud, one stop bit, no parity and 8 data bits.

The ROM BIOS functions of Int 14h are more efficient for accessing the serial port. This interrupt can be used to obtain the status of the auxiliary device, which makes them more flexible than DOS functions.

If the character being sent is a Ctrl-C character, this function calls interrupt 23h.

See Also:

INT 21h Function 04h, INT 14 Function 02h

INT 21h   [1.0+]

FUNCTION 04h
Auxiliary Output   DOS

Sends a character to the serial port. The default is the first serial port (COM1).
The MODE command can redirect serial access.

Input:

> AH = 04h
> DL = character to send

Output:

> Nothing

Comments:

This function transmits the character only when the output device is ready
to accept it.
Before calling this function you must initialize the serial port by performing
the MODE command and set communication parameters (baud rate, number
of stops bit, parity and etc.). When starting up on IBM PC's, MS DOS sets
the serial port to 2400 baud, one stop bit, no parity and 8 data bits.
The functions at ROM BIOS Int 14h are more efficient for accessing the serial
port. This interrupt and its functions can be used to obtain the status of the
auxiliary device, which makes them more flexible than DOS functions.
If the character being sent is a Ctrl-C character, this function calls interrupt
23h.

See Also:

INT 21h Function 03h, INT 14 Function 01h

INT 21h   [1.0+]

FUNCTION 05h
Printer Output   DOS

Sends a character to the standard list device. By default, this is the printer
on the first parallel port (LPT1). The MODE command allows you to redirect
printer access.

Input:

AH = 05h
DL = character to print

Output:

Nothing

Comments:

The function transmits the character only when the output device is ready to accept it.
The functions of the ROM BIOS Int 17h are more efficient for accessing the printer as they are more flexible than DOS functions.
If the character being sent is a Ctrl-C character, this function calls interrupt 23h.

See Also:

INT 17 Function 00h

INT 21h   [1.0+]
FUNCTION 06h
Direct Console I/O Character Output   DOS

Reads a character from the standard input device and writes a character to the standard output device. This function is used to read and write all possible characters and control codes without examining them (e.g., Ctrl-C has no effect on the program). Input and output for standard devices can be redirected. This function doesn't test whether the floppy disk or hard disk is full when it is writing. Neither can it determine whether all the characters have been read from the input device.

Input:

AH = 06h
DL = 00h - FEh sends a character code
DL = FFh - reads a character

Output:

Character output: nothing
Character input: No character ready
        2F = 1: No character ready
        Character received
        2F = 0: No character ready
        AL = character read

Comments:

This function must be called twice to read extended ASCII codes on IBM and compatible PC's. The first call returns 0 in the AL register (this indicates presence of an extended code).

This function cannot display blanks (ASCII code 255) because it interprets the ASCII code 255 as a command to input a character.

If a character is received, it is echoed to STDOUT.

Ctrl-C or Ctrl-Break are NOT checked.

See Also:

INT 21h Functions 01h, 07h, 08h, 09h

INT 21h   [1.0+]
FUNCTION 07h
Unfiltered Character Input Without Echo   DOS

Reads a character from the standard input device without displaying it on the standard output device. If the character is not ready when the function is called, it waits until a character is available. Input to a standard device may be redirected. The operating system does not test the input character (e.g., Ctrl-C has no effect on the program). When input is redirected to a file, this function doesn't test the end of file and continues to try reading data from the file after the end of that file.

Input:

AH = 07h

Output:

AL = Character

Comments:

To read extended ASCII codes on IBM and compatible PC's, the function must be called twice. The first call returns 0 in the AL register. (This indicates the presence of an extended code.)

See Also:

INT 17 Function 00h

INT 21h [1.0+]
FUNCTION 08h
Character Input Without Echo
DOS

Reads a character from the standard input device (the keyboard) without displaying it on the standard output device (the display). If the character is not ready when the function is called, it waits until a character is available. Input to a standard device may be redirected. When input is redirected to a file, this function doesn't test the end of file and continues to try reading data from the file after the end of file.

Input:

AH = 08h

Output:

AL = Character

Comments:

To read extended ASCII codes on IBM and compatible PC's, the function must be called twice. The first call returns 0 in the AL register. (This indicates the presence of an extended code.)

If this function reads a Ctrl-C it calls interrupt 23h.

See Also:

INT 21h Functions 01h, 06h, 3fh, 40h

INT 21h [1.0+]
FUNCTION 09h
Display ASCIIZ String
DOS

Displays a character string to the standard output device. Input to a standard device may be redirected. When input is redirected to a file, this function doesn't test the end of file and continues to try and write the string to file after the end of file.

Input:

AH = 09h
DS:DX = segment:offset of the string

Output:

Nothing

Comments:

If this function reads a Ctrl-C, it calls interrupt 23h.

The string must be terminated with the dollar sign character "$" (ASCII code 36). Control codes such as carriage return, linefeed and backspace can be embedded within the string.

See Also:

INT 21h Function 02h, 06h and 40h

INT 21h [1.0+]

FUNCTION 0Ah
Buffered Keyboard Input

DOS

Reads a string of bytes from the standard input device and sends the characters to a buffer. This function echoes characters to the standard output device. The input ends when it receives a carriage return (0Dh) code. Input on standard device can be redirected. When input is redirected to a file this function doesn't test the end of the file and continues to try reading the character from the file after end of the file.

Input:

AH = 0Ah
DS:DX = segment:offset of the buffer

Output:

Nothing

Comments:

This function uses the buffer in the following format:

Offset	Size	Description
00h	1	maximum number of characters (including the carriage return) buffer can hold
01h	1	number of characters usually read (excluding carriage return)
02h	n	actual characters read from input including the carriage return which terminated the string

This function tests the input and if it reads a Ctrl-C and Ctrl-Break it calls INT 23h.

When the buffer fills to one less than the maximum number of characters it can hold, all subsequent characters are lost and the bell is sounded if you attempt to enter any character other than the carriage return.

The <Backspace> and cursor keys can edit the input without placing these keys in the buffer.

See Also:

INT 21h Function 0Ch

INT 21h   [1.0+]
FUNCTION 0Bh
Check Input Status   DOS

Determines whether a standard input device has a character available for reading. Standard input can be redirected.

Input:

> AH = 0Bh

Output:

> AL = 00h if no character is available
>   FFh one or more characters are available

Comments:

If this function detects Ctrl-C and Ctrl-Break it calls INT 23h.

See Also:

INT 21h Functions 01h, 06h, 07h, 08h, 0Ah, 3Fh, 44h, Subfunction 06h

---

INT 21h   [1.0+]
FUNCTION 0Ch
Flush Input Buffer and Read Standard Input   DOS

Clears the type-ahead input buffer and then performs one of the character input functions 01h, 06h, 07h, 08h, or 0Ah. Standard input may be redirected.

Input:

> AH = 0Ch
> AL = function to be called after clearing buffer
> DS:DX = segment:offset of input buffer(if AL = 0Ah)

Output:

AL = input character (if called with AL = 01h, 06h, 07h, 08h)

Comments:

If AL is not 01h, 06h, 07h, 08h or 0Ah, this function flushes the buffer and passes control to the calling function.

See Also:

INT 21h Functions 01h, 06h, 07h, 08h, 0Ah

INT 21h   [1.0+]
FUNCTION 0Dh
Disk Reset   DOS

Writes all data stored in the internal DOS buffers to the disk.

Input:

AH = 0Dh

Output:

Nothing

Comments:

This function prevents access to new data, since it does not update the directory information for all open files.

See Also:

INT 21h Function 68h; INT 13h Function 00h

INT 21h   [1.0+]
FUNCTION 0Eh
Select Default Disk Drive   DOS

Defines the current or default disk drive and returns the number of available drives.

Input:

AH = 0Eh
DL = Drive number (00h=A, 01h=B, etc)

Output:

>   AL = number of logical drives

Comments:

DOS 1.x supports 16 device codes, DOS 2.x supports 63 device codes and DOS 3.x+ supports 26 device codes(the letters A to Z).
With DOS 3+ this function returns 5 or the drive code corresponding to the LASTDRIVE value in AL.

See Also:

INT 21h Function 19h and 3Bh

INT 21h   [1.0+]
FUNCTION 19h
Get Current Disk   DOS

Determines the number of the current or default disk drive.

Input:

>   AH = 19h

Output:

>   AL = drive (00h=A:, 01h=B:, etc)

See Also:

INT 21h Function 0Eh and 47h

INT 21h   [1.0+]
FUNCTION 1Ah
Set Data Transfer Address (DTA)   DOS

Establishes the address of buffer area in memory to use as the current DTA for FCB-related function calls.

Input:

>   AH = 1Ah
>   DS:DX = segment:offset of DTA

Output:

>   Nothing

Comments:

When the program starts, the DTA is set to a 128 byte buffer at offset 0080h in the Program Segment Prefix (PSP).
MS DOS recognizes an error and aborts disk transfer if DTA is at the end of a segment and disk transfer exceeds the end of the segment.

MS DOS does not test the length of the DTA. You must create a DTA of any size, less than 64k, that is large enough for any disk operation that will use it.

See Also:

INT 21h Function 11h, 12h, 2Fh, 4Eh and 4Fh

INT 21h   [1.0+]
FUNCTION 1Bh
Get Default Drive Data   DOS

Gets information about the size of the default disk drive.

Input:

    AH = 1Bh
    AL = sector per cluster
    CX = bytes per sector
    DX = number of clusters
    DS:BX = segment:offset of media ID byte
            The media ID byte has the following values
            FFh - double-sided disk drive, 8 sectors per track
            FEh - single-sided disk drive, 8 sectors per track
            FDh - double-sided disk drive, 9 sectors per track
            FCh - single-sided disk drive, 9 sectors per track
            F9h - double-sided disk drive, 15 sectors per track
            F8h - hard disk
            F0h - other

    Under DOS 2+ DS:BX points to a copy of the media ID byte of the
        FAT.

See Also:

INT 21h Function 1Ch and 36h

INT 21h   [2.0+]
FUNCTION 1Ch
Get Disk Data   **DOS**

Gets information about the size of a specified disk drive.

Input:

> AH = 1Ch
> DL = drive (00h=default, 01h=A:, etc)

Output:

> AL = sector per cluster
> CX = bytes per sector
> DX = number of clusters
> DS:BX = segment:offset of media ID byte

Comments:

This function is identical to INT 21h Function 1Bh, except that this function designates a specific disk drive.

The media ID byte has the following values

> FFh - double-sided disk drive, 8 sectors per track
> FEh - single-sided disk drive, 8 sectors per track
> FDh - double-sided disk drive, 9 sectors per track
> FCh - single-sided disk drive, 9 sectors per track
> F9h - double-sided disk drive, 15 sectors per track
> F8h - hard disk
> F0h - other

Under DOS 2+ DS:BX points to a copy of the media ID byte of the FAT.

See Also:

INT 21h Function 1Bh and 36h

INT 21h [1.0+]
FUNCTION 1Fh
Get Drive Parameter Block for Default Drive DOS

Gets information about the disk parameters for the current drive.

Input:

AH = 1Fh

Output:

AL = 00h if function is successful
DS:BX = segment:offset of Drive Parameter Block (DPB)
AL = FFh invalid drive

Comments:

The DPB has following format:

Offset	Size	Description
00h	1	Drive number (0=A:,1=B:,etc)
01h	1	unit number within device driver
02h	2	bytes per sector
04h	1	highest sector number within cluster
05h	1	shift count to convert clusters into sectors
06h	2	number of reserved sectors at beginning of drive
08h	1	number of FATs
09h	2	number of root directory entries
0Bh	2	number of first sector containing user data
0Dh	2	highest cluster number (number of data cluster + 1)

DOS 2.x - 3.x

Offset	Size	Description
0Fh	1	number of sectors per FAT
10h	2	sector number of first directory sector
12h	4	address of device driver header
16h	1	media ID byte
17h	1	00h if disk is accessed, FFh if not
18h	4	pointer to next DPB

DOS 3.x

Offset	Size	Description
1Ch	2	cluster at which to start search for free space when writing
1Eh	2	number

DOS 4.0 - 5.0

0Fh	2	number of sectors per FAT
11h	2	sector number of first directory sector
13h	4	address of device driver header
17h	1	media ID byte
18h	1	00h if disk is accessed, FFh if not
19h	4	pointer to next DPB
1Dh	2	cluster at which to start search for free space when writing
1Fh	2	number of free cluster on drive, FFFFh = not known

See Also:

INT 21h Function 1Bh and 36h

INT 21h   [1.0+]
FUNCTION 25h
Set Interrupt Vector   **DOS**

Sets a specified interrupt vector to point to another handling routine.

Input:

AH = 25h
AL = interrupt number
DS:DS = segment:offset address of new interrupt handler

Output:

Nothing

Comments:

This function is a better way to change interrupt handlers than direct modification of the interrupt vector table.
Before this function is performed, the initial contents of the interrupt vector to be edited must be read using INT 21h Function 35h, then saved. After termination of the program, the original interrupt vector should be restored.

See Also:

INT 21h Function 35h, INT 27h

INT 21h [1.0+]
FUNCTION 26h
Create New PSP
DOS

Copies the Program Segment Prefix (PSP) from the PSP of the executing program to a specified address in the memory.

Input:

AH = 26h
DX = segment address of new PSP

Output:

Nothing

Comments:

This function creates a new PSP from the PSP of the current executing program at a specified address in the memory and then updates the new PSP with the current INT 22h, INT 23h and INT 24h interrupt handlers. It prepares an overlay for execution.
This function does not load and execute any program.
This function is now obsolete for DOS 2.0 and higher, and INT 21h Function 4Bh must be used to load and execute any program or overlay.

See Also:

INT 21h Functions 4Bh, 50h, 51h, 55h, 62h and 67h

INT 21h [1.0+]
FUNCTION 29h
Parse Filename into FCB
DOS

Parses a character string and copies into the appropriate fields of an FCB. The string can include drive, filename and file extension.

Input:

AH = 29h
AL = parsing option
    bit 0 = 1 skip leading separators
    bit 1 = 1 set drive specifier in FCB only if the filename is specified on the command line
        0   if the drive specifier will be changed anyway;
            if no drive specifier on the command line, FCB drive code field is set to 0 (default).

bit 2 = 1   set filename only if filename is specified on the command line

0   the filename will be changed; if the filename doesn't present on command line FCB filename is set to ASCII blanks

bit 3 = 1   set extension only if extension specified on the command line

0   the extension will be changed; if the extension doesn't present on command line FCB extension is set to ASCII blanks

bit 4 - 7   reserved (0)

DS:SI = segment:offset of string
ES:DI = segment:offset of file control block (FCB)

Output:

AL = return status
    00h = no wildcard characters encountered
    01h = wildcard present
    FFh = invalid drive specifier
DS:SI = segment:offset of first unparsed character
ES:DI = segment:offset of buffer with unopened FCB

Comments:

If the filename or extension contain asterisks, then they are expanded to question marks in the FCB.

The filename must terminate with an end character (ASCII code 0).

This function cannot be used with a file specification which includes a path.

See Also:

INT 21h Functions 4Bh, 50h, 51h, 55h, 62h and 67h

INT 21h   [1.0+]

FUNCTION 2Ah
Get Date   **DOS**

Gets the current system date from the system calendar.

Input:

AH = 2Ah
CX = year (1980-2099)
DH = month (1-12)
DL = day
AL = day of week (0=Sunday, 1=Monday, etc)

See Also:

INT 21h Functions 2Bh, 2Ch, 2Dh, INT 1A Function 04h

INT 21h   [1.0+]

FUNCTION 2Bh
Set Date   **DOS**

Changes the current system date to a specified date.

Input:

AH = 2Bh

Output:

CX = year (1980-2099)
DH = month (1-12)
DL = day
AL = 00h date set successful
    FFh invalid date
This function does not change the system time.

See Also:

INT 21h Function 2Ah and 2Dh, INT 1Ah Function 05h

INT 21h   [1.0+]

FUNCTION 2Ch
Get Time   **DOS**

Reads the current system time.

Input:

AH = 2Ch

Output:

CH = hours (0-23)
CL = minutes (0-59)
DH = seconds (0-59)
DL = 1/100 seconds (0-99)

Comments:

On most IBM PC compatible systems, the resolution of the real-time system clock is about 5/100 sec, so the values returned in the DL register cannot be incremented by 1.

See Also:

INT 21h Functions 2Ah, 2Dh, INT 1Ah Functions 00h, 02h

INT 21h [1.0+]

FUNCTION 2Dh
Set Time   DOS

Sets the current system time.

Input:

> AH = 2Dh
> CH = hours (0-24)
> CL = minutes (0-59)
> DH = seconds (0-59)
> DL = 1/100 seconds

Output:

> AL = 00h if function is successful
>   FFh invalid time (ignored)

See Also:

INT 21h Functions 2Ah, 2Bh, 2Ch; INT 1Ah Functions 01h, 03h

INT 21h [1.0+]

FUNCTION 2Eh
Set Verify Flag   DOS

Toggles the disk write verification flag. This flag determines that data must be verified once it has been written.

Input:

> AH = 2Eh
> AL = 00h Do not verify data
>   01h Verify data
> DL = 00h (DOS 1.x/2.x only)

Output:

Nothing

Comments:

When the system boots, the default state of the verify flag is OFF because verification is a slow disk operation.
This flag can also be toggled by the MS DOS commands VERIFY ON and VERIFY OFF.

See Also:

INT 21h Function 51h

INT 21h [2.0+]

FUNCTION 2Fh
Get Disk Transfer Address (DTA)   DOS

Determines the address of a current disk data buffer for all FCB file read and write operations.

Input:

AH = 2Fh

Output:

ES:BX = segment:offset of DTA

Comments:

The default DTA starts at offset 80h in the Program Segment Prefix (PSP) and has a length of 128 bytes.

See Also:

INT 21h Function 1Ah

INT 21h [2.0+]

FUNCTION 30h
Get MS DOS Version Number   DOS

Determines the MS DOS version number.

Input:

AH = 30h
AL = Determines information returned in BH.

00h - Manufacturers ID
01h - Flag

Output:

AL = major version number (MS DOS 4.01=4, etc) (if MS DOS 1.0
    AL=00h)
AH = minor version number (MS DOS 4.01=01, etc)
BH = Original Equipment Manufacturer's (OEM) serial number
    00h IBM PC DOS
    FFh MS DOS
BH = version flag (DOS 5+ only)
    08h DOS in ROM
    10h DOS in XMA

See Also:

INT 21h Function 33h Subfunction 06h

INT 21h   [1.0+]
FUNCTION 31h
Terminate and Stay Resident   **DOS**

Terminates the program currently being executed and passes control to the
calling program, without releasing resources allocated to the current process.
The current program stays resident in the memory and waits for another call.

Input:

AH = 31h
AL = return code
DX = number of paragraph to be kept resident

Output:

Nothing

Comments:

The parent process can read the return code in the AL register with INT 21h
Function 4Dh. It can then be tested in a batch file by the ERRORLEVEL and
IF statements. A non zero return code usually indicates an error.
The number of the 16-bit paragraph in the DX register indicates the initial
memory allocation block, beginning with the PSP. This memory cannot be
released by INT 21h Function 48h. This memory can only be released by INT
21h Function 49h.

See Also:

INT 21h Functions 00h, 4Ch, 4Dh; INT 22h; INT 27h

INT 21h   [2.0+]

FUNCTION 32h

Get DOS Drive Parameter Block for Specific Drive   DOS

Gets information about disk parameters for a specific drive.

Input:

AH = 32h
DL = drive (0=current, 1=A:,etc)

Output:

AL = 00h if function is successful
DS:BX = segment:offset of Drive Parameter Block (DPB)
AL = FFh invalid drive

Comments:

The DPB has following format:

Offset	Size	Description
00h	1	Drive number (0=A:,1=B:,etc)
01h	1	unit number within device driver
02h	2	bytes per sector
04h	1	largest sector number within cluster
05h	1	shift count of the cluster size to convert clusters into sectors
06h	2	number of reserved sectors at beginning of drive
08h	1	number of copies FATs
09h	2	number of root directory entries
0Bh	2	number of first sector with user data
0Dh	2	largest cluster number (number of data cluster + 1)

DOS 2.x - 3.x

Offset	Size	Description
0Fh	1	number of sectors per FAT
10h	2	sector number of first directory sector
12h	4	address of device driver header for this device
16h	1	media ID byte
17h	1	00h if disk is accessed, FFh if not
18h	4	address of next DPB

		DOS 3.x
1Ch	2	cluster at which to start search for free space when writing
1Eh	2	number of free clusters on drive, FF if not known

		DOS 4.0 - 5.0
0Fh	2	number of sectors in FAT
11h	2	sector number of first directory sector
13h	4	address of device driver header for this device
17h	1	media ID byte
18h	1	00h if disk is accessed, FFh if not
19h	4	address of next DPB
1Dh	2	cluster at which to start search for free space when writing
1Fh	2	number of free clusters on drive, FFFFh = if not known

See Also:

INT 21h Functions 1Fh

INT 21h   [2.0+]
FUNCTION 33h SUBFUNCTION 00H AND 001h
Get or Set Break Flag   DOS

Reads and changes the state of the Ctrl-Break check flag.

Input:

AH = 33h
AL = 00h if getting break flag
    01h if setting break flag
DL = 00h if turning break flag OFF
    01h if turning break flag ON

Output:

DL = current state
    00h break flag is OFF
    01h break flag is ON

Comments:

When the system break flag is on, this function determines whether DOS should check the keyboard for the activation of Ctrl-C or Ctrl-Break keys, or any DOS function call when operating system input/output is performed. When this flag is off, it checks for traditional character input/output.

Since the Ctrl-Break flag is not part of the environment block of the current program, it affects all programs which use DOS functions for character input/output and which check Ctrl-C and Ctrl-Break.

See Also:

INT 21h Function 33h Subfunction 02h

INT 21h   [3.0+]

FUNCTION 33h SUBFUNCTION 02h
Get and Set Extended Control-Break Checking State   DOS

Obtains and changes the state of the Control-Break flag.

Input:

> AH = 33h
> AL = 02h
> DL = 00h if checking OFF
>   01h if checking ON

Output:

> DL = old state of extended break checking

Comments:

This function is fully re-entrant.

See Also:

INT 21h Function 33h Subfunction 01h

INT 21h   [4.0+]

FUNCTION 33h SUBFUNCTION 05h
Determine Boot Drive Number   DOS

Reads the system boot drive.

Input:

> AH = 33h
> AL = 05h

Output:

> DL = boot drive (1=A, 2=B, etc)

INT 21h [5.0]
FUNCTION 33h SUBFUNCTION 06h
Get Actual Version Number
DOS

Reads the actual version of MS DOS.

Input:

AH = 33h
AL = 06h

Output:

BL = major version
BH = minor version
DL = revision
DH = version flag
     bit 3=1 DOS is in ROM
     bit 4=1 DOS is in HMA

Comments:

This function returns the actual version of MS DOS even if the DOS command
SETVER has changed the version.

See Also:

INT 21h Function 30h

INT 21h [2.0+]
FUNCTION 34h
Get Address of InDOS Flag
DOS

Reads the address of Critical Section (InDOS) flag. This flag indicates that INT
21h function is working.

Input:

AH = 34h

Output:

ES:BX = segment:offset of InDOS flag

Comments:

The value of the InDOS flag is incremented when an INT 21h function begins to work and decremented when it is completed.

During INT 28h call, the value InDOS flag may be 01h instead of zero. But in this case the functions from 01h to 0Ch INT 21h only may be called.There may, however, be occasions when DOS is busy but the InDOS flag is zero. This is possible because during its operation, the critical error handler decrements InDOS and increments the critical error flag.

The Critical error flag is the byte before the InDOS flag in DOS 3+.

This function may be called once at the beginning of a program only.

See Also:

INT 21h Function 5Dh Subfunction 06, 0Bh; INT 28h

INT 21h   [2.0+]
FUNCTION 35h
Get Interrupt Vector   DOS

Gets the address of the interrupt service routine for the specified interrupt vector.

Input:

> AH = 35h
> AL = interrupt number

Output:

> ES:BX = segment:offset of interrupt handler

Comments:

This function must be used to ensure compatability with future versions of DOS.

See Also:

INT 21h Function 25h

INT 21h   [2.0+]
FUNCTION 38h
Get or Set Country Specific Information   DOS

Obtains country specific information or sets the current country parameters.

Input:

> To get country information (DOS 2)
> > AH = 38h
> > AL = 0
> > DS:DX = segment:offset of buffer for returned information
>
> To get country information (DOS 3+)
> > AH = 38h
> > AL = 00h for current country
> > > 1-FEh for specific country with code<255
> > > FFh   for specific country with code>=255
> >
> > BX = country code if AL=FFh
> > DS:DX = segment:offset of buffer for returned information.
>
> To set current country code (MS DOS versions 3+)
> > AH = 38h
> > AL = 1-FEh for specific country with code<255
> > > FFh   for specific country with code>=255
> >
> > BX = country code, if AL=0FFh
> > DX = FFFFh

Output:

> CF = 0 function is successful
> BX = country code
> DS:DX = segment:offset of buffer filled with information as follows
> (for MS DOS 2.x, DOS 3+ country information)

Offset	Size	Description
00h	2	date format
		0=USA mm dd yy
		1=Europe dd mm yy
		2=Japan yy mm dd
02h	5	ASCIIZ currency symbol string
07h	1	Thousand separator character
08h	1	00h
09h	1	decimal separator character
0Ah	1	00h
0Bh	1	date separator character
0Ch	1	00h
0Dh	1	time separator character
0Eh	1	00h
0Fh	1	currency format
		bit 0=0 if currency symbol precedes value
		1 if currency symbol follows value
		bit 1=0 if no space between value and currency symbol
		1 if one space between value and currency symbol

			bit 2=0	if currency symbol and decimal are separate
		1	if currency symbol replaces decimal separator
10h	1	number of digits after decimal in currency value
11h	1	time format:
		bit 0 = 0 if 12-hour clock
		1 if 24-hour clock
12h	4	address of case map routine (FAR CALL)
16h	1	data list separator character
17h	1	00h
18h	10	reserved

CF = 1 function is unsuccessful
AX = error code

Comments:

The case map address in 12-15h is the offset:segment address of the FAR procedure which is used for performing country specific conversion of character codes from 80h through 0FFh. This procedure must be called with the character which should be converted to a capital letter in the AL register. If a capital letter already exists for this character in the AL register, it is returned in AL after the function call, otherwise the contents of AL remain unchanged.

See Also:

INT 21h Function 65h

INT 21h
FUNCTION 39h
Create Directory

[2.0+]

DOS

Creates a new subdirectory in a specified drive.

Input:

AH = 39h
DS:DX = segment:offset of ASCIIZ pathname

Output:

CF = 0 function is successful
CF = 1 function is unsuccessful
AX = error code
    03h Path not found
    05h Access denied

Comments:

An error will occur if:
>Any element in the pathname does not exist.
>A subdirectory with the same name already exists.
>A subdirectory is to be created in a root directory which is already full.

See Also:

INT 21h Function 3Ah, 3Bh

INT 21h   [2.0+]
FUNCTION 3Ah
Delete Directory   DOS

Deletes a subdirectory on a specified drive.

Input:

>AH = 3Ah
>DS:DX = segment:offset of ASCIIZ pathname

Output:

>CF = 0 function is successful
>CF = 1 function is unsuccessful
>AX = error code
>>03h = Path not found
>>05h = Access denied
>>06h = Directory
>>10h = Attempt to remove current directory

Comments:

An error will occur if:
>Any element on the pathname does not exist.
>The specified directory is a current directory.
>T45he specified directory contains no files.

See Also:

INT 21h Functions 1Bh, 1Ch

INT 21h   [2.0+]
FUNCTION 3Bh
Set Current Directory   **DOS**

Changes current or default directory for a specified path and drive.

Input:

    AH = 3Bh
    DS:DX = segment:offset of ASCIIZ pathname

Output:

    CF = 0 function is successful
    CF = 1 function is unsuccessful
    AX = error code
            03h Path not found

Comments:

An error will occur if any element of pathname does not exist.
If the new pathname includes a drive letter, the default drive is not changed.

See Also:

INT 21h Function 47h

INT 21h   [2.0+]
FUNCTION 3Ch
Create File   **DOS**

Creates a new empty file on a specified drive with a specified pathname.

Input:

    AH = 3Ch
    CX = file attribute
            bit 0 = 1 read-only file
            bit 1 = 1 hidden file
            bit 2 = 1 system file
            bit 3 = 1 volume label (ignored)
            bit 4 = 1 reserved (0) - directory
            bit 5 = 1 archive bit
            bit 6 - 15 reserved (0)
    DS:DX = segment:offset of ASCIIZ pathname

Output:

CF = 0 function is successful
AX = handle
CF = 1 function is unsuccessful
AX = error code
03h Path not found
04h No available handle
05h Access denied

Comments:

Wildcards are not permitted in the filename.
An error will occur if any element of pathname does not exist; the file is to be created in a root directory which is full; or a file with the same name and read-only attribute already exists in the current directory.
If a file with the same name exists, it is truncated to zero length.

See Also:

INT 21h Functions 16h, 5Ah and 5Bh

INT 21h   [2.0+]
FUNCTION 3Dh
Open File   DOS

Opens an existing file for reading, writing or appending on the specified drive and specified pathname.

Input:

AH = 3Dh
AL = access mode
bits 0-2   access mode
                000 = read only
                001 = write only
                010 = read/write
bit   3   reserved (0)
bits 4-6   Sharing mode (DOS 3+)
                000 = compatibility mode
                001 = deny all (only current program can access file)
                010 = deny write (other programs can only read from file)
                011 = deny read (other programs can only write into file)
                100 = deny none (other programs can read and write the file)
DS:DX = segment:offset of ASCIIZ pathname

Output:

CF = 0 function is successful
AX = handle
CF = 1 function is unsuccessful
AX = error code
    01h missing file sharing software
    02h file not found
    03h path not found or file does not exist
    04h no handle available
    05h access denied
    0Ch access mode not permitted

Comments:

Wildcards are not permitted in the filename. If the drive or path are omitted in the filename, DOS accesses the current drive or directory.

An error will occur if any element of pathname does not exist, or if the file has the read-only attribute and is opened in the read/write access mode.

The file pointer is set to the first byte of file.

File handlers which are inherited from a parent process by a child process also inherit all sharing and access restrictions from the parent process.

See Also:

INT 21h Function 0Fh and 3Ch, Function 5Dh Subfunction 00h

INT 21h   [2.0+]
FUNCTION 3Eh
Close File   DOS

Writes all information in internal DOS buffers associated with the file to disk and updates directory information, then closes the file.

Input:

AH = 3Eh
BX = handle

Output:

CF = 0 function is successful
AX = destroyed
CF = 1 function is unsuccessful
AX = error code - 06h File not opened or unauthorized handle

Comments:

Do not call this function with a zero handle because the standard input device may close and you won't be able to enter characters from the keyboard.

See Also:

INT 21h Function 10h, 3Ch and 3Dh

INT 21h   [2.0+]
FUNCTION 3Fh
Read File or Device   DOS

Reads a given number of bytes at the current file pointer position, from a previously opened file, with a given valid handle or device, to a buffer.

Input:

AH = 3Fh
BX = handle
CX = number bytes to be read
DS:DX = segment:offset of buffer

Output:

CF = 0 function is successful
AX = number of bytes read
CF = 1 function is unsuccessful
AX = error code
    05h access denied
    06h illegal handle or file not opened

Comments:

If the Carry Flag CF is clear after the function call and AX = 0, it means that the file pointer was already at the end of the file and the file cannot be read.

If the Carry Flag CF is clear after the function call and the value in AX is smaller than the value in CX, it means that only part of the record was read, either because the end of file was reached or an error occurred.

If the reading is successful, the file pointer position is updated after the function call.

If this function is used to read from a file with handle 0 (standard input device - keyboard), it stops reading after the first CR, or once a specified number of characters have been read.

See Also:

INT 21h Function 27h and 40h

INT 21h   [2.0+]
FUNCTION 40h
Write File or Device   DOS

Writes a given number of bytes at the current file pointer position, to a previously opened file, with a given valid handle or device from a buffer.

Input:

> AH = 40h
> BX = handle
> CX = number of bytes to write
> DS:DX = segment:offset of buffer

Output:

> CF = 0 function is successful
> AX = number of bytes written
> CF = 1 function is not successful
> AX = Error Code
>> 05h Access denied
>> 06h Illegal handle of a file which is not open

Comments:

This function writes to a file with a valid handle or to a standard output device, for example the screen with a handle equal to 1.

If the Carry Flag is clear after the function call and AX < CX, it means that only part of the record was written, either because the end of the file was reached, or there was a DOS error (disk full).

If the Carry Flag is clear after the function call and CX = 0 it means that no data is written and the file is truncated or extended to the current position of the file pointer.

If the writing is successful the file pointer position is updated after the function call.

See Also:

INT 21h Function 27h and 40h

INT 21h [2.0+]

FUNCTION 41h
Delete File

DOS

Erases a specified file

Input:

AH = 41h
DS:DX = segment:offset of ASCIIZ pathname

Output:

CF = 0 if function is successful
CF = 1 if function is not successful
AX = Error Code
    02h file not found
    03h path not found or file does not exist
    05h access denied

Comments:

This function cannot delete subdirectories or volume names. This function does not erase data in a file. It only replaces the first symbol in the filename in the directory entry with the hex code 0E5h and marks the FAT Chain for this file as "free".

Wildcards are not permitted in file specification.

An error occurs if an element in the pathname does not exist, or the file has the Read-only attribute.

See Also:

INT 21h Function 13h and 60h

INT 21h [2.0+]

FUNCTION 42h
Set File Pointer

DOS

Moves the file location pointer to a specified position in the file.

Input:

AH = 42h
AL = offset code

      00h absolute offset from start of file
      01h signed offset from current file pointer
      02h signed offset from end of file
BX = handle
CX = most significant part of offset
DX = least significant part of offset

Output:

CF = 0 function is successful
DX = high word of the file pointer
AX = low word of the file pointer
CF = 1 function is unsuccessful
AX = error code
      01h illegal offset code
      06h illegal handle of file not open

Comments:

This function always returns the resulting absolute byte offset from the start of the file in DX:AX.

For offset codes 01h and 02h, the file pointer may be positioned before the start of the file. The file pointer can also be set after the end of the file. No error will be returned at this point, but a subsegment attempt to read or write the file will create errors.

You can get the size of the file using the offset code 02h and the offset of 0 after calling the INT 21h Function 42h and examining the file pointer location.

See Also:

INT 21h Function 24h

INT 21h   [2.0+]

FUNCTION 43h SUBFUNCTION 00h - 01h
Get or Set File Attributes   **DOS**

Determines or sets file attributes for a specified file.

Input:

AH = 43h
AL = 00h to get attributes
      01h to set attributes
CX = file attributes (if AL = 01h)

bit 0 = 1 read-only
bit 1 = 1 hidden
bit 2 = 1 system
bit 3 = 1 volume label
bit 4 = 1 directory
bit 5 = 1 archive
bits 6-15 reserved (0)
DS:DX = segment:offset of ASCIIZ pathname

Output:

CF = 0 function is successful
CX = file attribute
    bit 0 = 1 read-only
    bit 1 = 1 hidden
    bit 2 = 1 system
    bit 3 = 1 volume label
    bit 4 = 1 directory
    bit 5 = 1 archive
    bits 6-15 reserved (0)
CF = if function is unsuccessful
AX = error code
    01h unknown function code
    02h file not found
    03h path not found
    05h attribute cannot be changed

Comments:

Wildcards are not permitted in the pathname. This function cannot change
the volume label or directory attributes.
An error occurs if an element in the pathname does not exist.

INT 21h   [2.0+]

FUNCTION 44h   SUBFUNCTION 00h
IOCTL (I/O control): Get Device Information   DOS

Gets information about a specified file or device.

Input:

AH = 44h
AL = 00h
BX = handle

Output:

CF = 0 if function is successful
DX = device information world
      character device if bit 7 is set
      bit 0 = 1 if standard input
      bit 1 = 1 if standard output
      bit 2 = 1 if NUL device
      bit 3 = 1 if clock device
      bit 4 = 1 reserved
      bit 5 = 0 if the handle is in the ASCII mode
            1 if the handle is in the binary mode
      bit 6 = 0 if end of file on input
      bit 7 = 1 indicating device
      bits 8 - 10 reserved
      bit 11 = 1 drive supports Open/Close calls
      bits 12-13 reserved
      bit 14 = 0 if IOCTL subfunctions 02h and 03h are not
                                   supported
            1 if IOCTL subfunctions 02h and 03h are supported
      bit 15 reserved
      disk file if bit 7 is clear
          0-5 drive number (0 = A, 1 = B, etc.)
          6 = 0 if file has been written
            1 if file has not been written
          7 = 0 indicates a file
          8-15 reserved
CF = 1 if function is unsuccessful
AX = error code
      01h unknown function code
      05h access denied
      06h handle not opened or does not exist

Comments:

DH corresponds to the high byte of the attribute word of the handle for the character device.

In the binary ("raw") mode, MS DOS treats all characters as data. In the ASCII ("cooked") mode, MS DOS checks the character stream and performs the relevant function, if a special character Ctrl-C, Ctrl-S, Ctrl-P, Ctrl-Z or CR is detected.

See Also:

INT 21h Function 44h Subfunction 01h

INT 21h   [2.0+]
FUNCTION 44h SUBFUNCTION 01h
IOCTL: Set Device Information   **DOS**

Sets specific characteristics of the character device.

Input:

    AH = 44h
    AL = 01h
    BX = handle
    DX = device information word
        bit 0 = 1 if standard input
        bit 1 = 1 if standard output
        bit 2 = 1 if NUL device
        bit 3 = 1 if clock device
        bit 4 = 1 reserved (0)
        bit 5 = 0 ASCII mode (cooked)
                1 binary mode (raw)
        bit 6 reserved (0)
        bit 7 = 1 indicating device
        bits 8 - 15 reserved (0)

Output:

    CF = 0 function is successful
    CF = 1 function is unsuccessful
    AX = error code
        01h = unknown function code
        05h = attribute cannot be changed
        06h = handle not opened or handle does not exist
        0Dh = invalid data

Comments:

This function is useful for switching between ASCII (cooked) and binary (raw)
modes, when the handle is associated with a character device.

See Also:

INT 21h Function 44h Subfunction 01h

INT 21h   [2.0+]

FUNCTION 44h   SUBFUNCTION 02h
IOCTL: Read Control Data from Character Device Driver DOS

Reads data specific to each character device driver from a character device.

Input:

AH = 44h
AL = 02h
BX = handle
CX = number of bytes to be read
DS:DX = segment:offset of buffer

Output:

CF = 0 function is successful
AX = number of bytes read
CF = 1 function is unsuccessful
AX = error code
>01h unknown function code
>05h access denied
>06h handle not opened or does not exist
>0Dh invalid data

Comments:

The character device driver defines the structure and type of control data.

This function can be used for reading hardware dependent information and status information of the character device, if this device supports this function. This information cannot usually be obtained by other DOS functions.

See Also:

INT 21h Function 44h Subfunction 00h, 03h and 04h

INT 21h   [2.0+]

FUNCTION 44h SUBFUNCTION 03h
IOCTL: Write Control Data to Character Device Driver   DOS

Writes control data specific to each character device from an application directly to a specified character device.

Input:

AH = 44h
AL = 03h

BX = handle
CX = number of bytes to be written
DS:DX = segment:offset of data

Output:

CF = 0 function is successful
AX = number of bytes sent
CF = 1 function is unsuccessful
AX = error code
    01h = unknown function code
    05h = attribute cannot be changed
    06h = handle not opened or does not exist
    0Dh = invalid data

Comments:

If this function is supported by a character device driver, it can be used to perform certain hardware dependent operations. These operations are not usually supported by other MS DOS function calls.

See Also:

INT 21h Function 44h Subfunction 00h, 02h and 05h

INT 21h   [2.0+]
FUNCTION 44h SUBFUNCTION 04h
IOCTL: Read Control Data from Block Device Driver   DOS

Reads control data directly from the block device into the buffer.

Input:

AH = 44h
AL = 04h
BL = drive code (0=default, 1=A, etc.)
CX = number of bytes to be read
DS:DX = segment:offset of buffer

Output:

CF = 0 function is successful
AX = number of bytes read
CF = 1 function is unsuccessful
AX = error code
    01h = unknown function code
    05h = attribute cannot be changed
    06h = handle not opened or does not exist
    0Dh = invalid data

Comments:

This function can be used if the block device driver supports the IOCTL call.

INT 21h   [2.0+]
FUNCTION 44h SUBFUNCTION 05h
IOCTL: Write Control Data to Block Device Driver   DOS

Writes data specific to each character device control from an application program directly to a block device. The format and structure are specific to each device.

Input:

AH = 44h
AL = 05h
BL = device code (0=default, 1=A, etc.)
CX = number of bytes to be written
DS:DX = segment:offset of data

Output:

CF = 0 function is successful
AX = number of bytes sent
CF = 1 function is unsuccessful
AX = error code
    01h = unknown function code
    05h = attribute cannot be changed
    06h = handle not opened or does not exist
    0Dh = invalid data

Comments:

If this function is supported by a character device driver, it can be used to perform certain hardware dependent operations. These operations are not usually supported by other MS DOS function calls.

See Also:

INT 21h Function 44h Subfunction 03h and 04h

INT 21h   [2.0+]
FUNCTION 44h SUBFUNCTION 06h
IOCTL: Check Input Status   DOS

Reads the status of the specified device to determine whether the device can read data.

Input:

        AH = 44h
        AL = 06h
        BX = handle

Output:

        CF = 0 function is successful
        AX = 00h device not ready or EOF on file
                FFh device is ready, if not EOF
        CF = 1 function is unsuccessful
        AX = error code
                01h = unknown function code
                05h = attribute cannot be changed
                06h = handle not opened or does not exist
                0Dh = invalid data

Comments:

This function can be used to check the status of certain character devices that do not have their own MS DOS functions for status checking (for example, serial port).

See Also:

INT 21h Function 44h Subfunction 07h

INT 21h   [2.0+]
FUNCTION 44h SUBFUNCTION 07h
IOCTL: Check Output Status   DOS

Reads the status of a specified device that determines whether this device can write data.

Input:

        AH = 44h
        AL = 07h
        BX = handle

Output:

        CF = 0 function is successful
        AL = 00h device not ready
                01h device is ready
        CF = 1 function is unsuccessful
        AX = error code

> 01h = unknown function code
> 05h = attribute cannot be changed
> 06h = handle not opened or does not exist
> 0Dh = invalid data

Comments:

This function always returns the ready status indicating that all files are ready for output, even if the disk is full or there is no disk in the drive.

See Also:

INT 21h Function 44h Subfunction 06h

INT 21h   [2.0+]

FUNCTION 44h SUBFUNCTION 08h
IOCTL: Check if Block Device is Removable   DOS

Determines whether the block device media (disk, hard disk, etc.) of the specified block device can be changed.

Input:

> AH = 44h
> AL = 08h
> BL = device number (0=default,1=A, etc.)

Output:

> CF = 0 function is successful
> AL = 00h if media is removable
>   01h if media is not removable
> CF = 1 function is unsuccessful
> AX = error code
>   01h = unknown function code
>   0Fh = invalid drive number

See Also:

INT 21h Function 44h Subfunction 00h and 09h

INT 21h   [3.1+]

FUNCTION 44h SUBFUNCTION 09h
IOCTL: Check if Block Device is Remote   DOS

Determines whether the specified block device is local (part of the PC that is used as a workstation) or remote (part of a network server).

Input:

AH = 44h
AL = 09h
BX = drive number (0=default, 1=A, etc.)

Output:

CF = 0 if function is successful
DX = device attribute word
bit 15=1 drive is SUBSTituted
12=0 drive is local
1 drive is remote
CF = 1 function is unsuccessful
AX = error code
01h = unknown function code
0Fh = attribute cannot be changed

Comments:

This subfunction can be used if network software has been installed previously.

See Also:

INT 21h Function 44h Subfunction 00h and 08h

INT 21h   [3.1+]
FUNCTION 44h SUBFUNCTION 0Ah
IOCTL: Check if Handle Is Remote   DOS

Determines whether the specified handle refers to a file on a remote or local device.

Input:

AH = 44h
AL = 0Ah
BX = handle

Output:

CF = 0 function is successful
DX = attribute word for file or device
bit 15=0 if local
1 if remote
1 drive is remote

CF = 1 function is unsuccessful
AX = error code
01h = unknown function code
06h = handle not opened or does not exist

Comments:

This subfunction can be used if network software has been installed previously.

See Also:

INT 21h Function 44h Subfunction 00h and 09h, Function 052h

INT 21h   [3.1+]
FUNCTION 44h SUBFUNCTION 0Bh
IOCTL: Change Sharing Retry Count   DOS

Sets the number of attempts which MS DOS will perform after the SHARE utility fails to open or lock a file.

Input:

```
AH = 44h
AL = 0Bh
CX = pause between attempts (default=1)
DX = number of attempts (default=3)
```

Output:

```
CF = 0 function is successful
CF = 1 function is unsuccessful
AX = error code
    01h = unknown function code
```

Comments:

This subfunction can be used if network software has been installed previously.

The value in the CX register defines the delay which is performed by executing empty cycles:

```
xor         cx,cx
loop        $        ; repeat this command 65536 times
```

Consequently, the value of the delay depends on the processor speed.

See Also:

INT 21h Function 44h Subfunction 52h

INT 21h [3.2+]
FUNCTION 44h SUBFUNCTION 0Ch
IOCTL: Generic I/O Control for Character Device DOS

Various calls for a character from an application.

Input:

AH = 44h
AL = 0Ch
BX = handle
CH = category code
    00h = unknown (DOS 3.3+)
    01h = Cond, Com2, Com3 or Com4(Dos 3.3+)
    03h = CON(Dos3.3+)
    05h = LPT1,LPT2 or LPT3(Dos 3.2+)
a = function
    45h = Set Iteration Count
    4ah = Select Code Page
    4ch = Set Code Page Preparation
    40h = End Code Page Preparation
    5fh = Set Display Information
    65h = Get Iteration Count
    6ah = Query Selected Code Page
    6bh = Query Prepared List
    7fh = Get Display Information
DS:DX = segment:offset of parameter block

Output:

CF = 0 if function is successful
DS:DX = segment:offset of parameter block if CL = 65h, 6ah, 6bh
or 7fh
CF = 1 function is unsuccessful
AX = error code

Comments:

The parameter block for CL = 45h has the following format:

Offset	Size	Description
00h	2	number of times the device driver will wait before the driver assumes that the device is busy

The parameter block for functions 4A and 6Ah has the following format:

Offset	Size	Description
00h	2	length of data
02h	2	code page ID
04h	2N bytes	DCBS (Double Byte Character Set) lead byte range start/end for each N range (MS DOS 4.01)

The parameter block for function 4ch has the following format:

Offset	Size	Description
ooh	2	font type bit 0 = 0 downloaded
		= 1 cartridge
		bits 1-5 reserved (0)

See Also:

INT 21h Function 44h Subfunction 52h

INT 21h   [3.2+]

FUNCTION 44h SUBFUNCTION 0Dh
IOCTL: Generic I/O Control for Block Device   DOS

Transfers miscellaneous requests from application programs to block device drivers.

Input:

```
AH = 44h
AL = 0Dh
BX = drive number (00h=default, 01h=A, etc.)
CH = category code
     08h = disk drive
CL = function
     40h = set device parameters
     41h = write logical device track
     42h = format and verify track
     46h = set volume serial number (DOS 4.0)
     47h = set access flag (DOS 4.0)
     60h = get device parameters
     61h = read track
     62h = verify track
     67h = get access flag (DOS 4.0)
DS:DX = segment:offset of parameter block
```

Output:

CF = 0 function is successful
DS:DX = segment:offset of parameter block if CL=60h or 61h
CF = 1 function is unsuccessful
AX = error code

Comments:

The parameter block for functions 40h and 60h has the following format:

Offset	Size	Description
00h	1	special functions:
		bit 0 = 0 Device BIOS Parameter Block (BPB) contains a new default BPB
		bit 0 = 1 Function uses current BPB
		bit 1 = 0 Function uses all fields in the parameter block (if CL=60h)
		bit 1 = 1 function uses track layout field
		bit 2 = 0 sectors in track may be different sizes
		bit 2 = 1 sectors in track are all the same size
		bits 3 - 7 reserved (0)
01h	2	device type:
		00h = 320/360k disk
		01h = 1.2M 5.25 inch disk
		02h = 720k 3.5 inch disk
		03h = single density 8-inch disk
		04h = double density 8-inch disk
		05h = fixed disk
		06h = tape drive
		07h = 1.44M 3.5 inch disk
		08h = other type of block device
02h	2	device atributes:
		bit 0 = 0 removable storage medium
		bit 0 = 1 nonremovable storage medium
		bit 1 = 1 door lock is not supported
		bit 1 = 0 door lock is supported
		bits 2 - 15 reserved (0)
04h	2	number of cylinders
06h	1	media type:
		00h = 1.2M 5.25 inch disk (default)
		01h = 320/360k 5.25 inch disk
07h	31	device BPB
26h	2	number of sectors per track
28h	2N	number, size of each sector per track

The parameter block for functions 41h and 61h has the following format:

Offset	Size	Description
00h	1	special function (must be 0)
01h	2	number of disk head
03h	2	number of disk cylinder
05h	2	number of first sector to read/write
07h	2	number of sector to transfer
09h	4	transfer buffer address

The parameter block for functions 42h and 62h has the following format:

Offset	Size	Description
00h	2	special function field
		for DOS<3.2 must be 0
		bit 0 = 0 format/verify track
		bit 0 = 1 format status call (DOS 3.2+)
		bits 1-7 reserved (must be 0 on return in MS DOS 4.0)
01h	2	number of disk head parameters 03h
	2	number of disk cylinders

The parameter block for functions 46h and 66h has the following format:

Offset	Size	Description
00h	2	info level (00h)
02h	4	disk serial number (binary)
06h	11	volume label or "NONAME"
11h	8	file system type "FAT12" or "FAT16" (CL=66h only)

The parameter block for functions 47h and 67h has the following format:

Offset	Size	Description
00h	1	special function field must be 0
01h	1	disk access flag

The device BPB field has the following format:

Offset	Size	Description
00h	2	number of bytes per sector
02h	1	number of sectors per cluster
03h	2	number of reserved sectors at the start of the disk
05h	1	number of FATs
06h	2	number of entries in the root directory

08h	2	total number of sectors: (for DOS 4.0 0 if partition >32M)
0Ah	1	media ID byte
0Bh	2	number of sectors per FAT DOS 3+
0Dh	2	number of sectors per track
0Fh	2	number of heads
11h	4	number of hidden sectors
15h	11	reserved
		DOS 4+
15h	4	total number of sectors if word at 08h contains zero
19h	6	unknown
1Fh	2	number of cylinders
21h	1	device type
22h	2	device attribute (removable or not, etc.)

See Also:

INT 21h Function 44h Subfunction 0Ch and 11h, Function 69h

INT 21h   [3.2+]

FUNCTION 44h SUBFUNCTION 0Eh
IOCTL: Get Logical Drive Map   DOS

Reads the last logical drive used to reference a specific block device.

Input:

    AH = 44h
    AL = 0Eh
    BL = drive number (00h=default, 01h=A, etc.)

Output:

    CF = 0 function is successful
    AL = 00h block device has only one logical drive assigned
         1-26 the letter corresponding to the last logical device on the
         drive (1=A, etc.)
    CF = 1 function is unsuccessful
    AX = error code
         01h invalid function number
         0Fh invalid disk drive

See Also:

INT 21h Function 44h Subfunction 0Fh

INT 21h   [3.2+]
FUNCTION 44h SUBFUNCTION 0Fh
IOCTL: Set Logical Drive Map   DOS

Assigns the drive letter to a specified block device.

Input:

> AH = 44h
> AL = 0Fh
> BL = drive number (00h=default, 01h=A, etc.)

Output:

> CF = 0 function is successful
> AL = mapping code
>> 00h block device has only one logical drive assigned 1-26
>> the last letter used to reference the drive (1 = A, etc)
>> 01h - 0Ah logical drive code (1 = A. 2 = B, etc.) mapped to
>> the block device
> CF = 1 function is unsuccessful
> AX = error code
>> 01h invalid function number
>> 0Fh invalid disk drive

Comments:

This function treats a single physical floppy drive as both A: and B:.

See Also:

INT 21h Function 44h Subfunction 0Eh

INT 21h   [5.0+]
FUNCTION 44h SUBFUNCTION 10h
Query Generic IOCTL Capability (Handle)   DOS

Tests whether a character device drive will support a miscellaneous IOCTL
request to character device driver.

Input:

> AH = 44h
> AL = 10h
> BX = handle for device
> CH = category code
>> 00h unknown (DOS 3.3+)

01h COMn: (DOS 3.3+)
02h CON   (DOS 3.3+)
05h LPTn:
CL = function code
45h set iteration count
65h get iteration count

Output:

CF = 0 function is successful
AX = 0000h specified IOCTL function is supported
CF = 1 function is unsuccessful
AL = IOCTL capability not available

Comments:

Character device driver must support a Generic IOCTL Check call.

See Also:

INT 21h Function 44h Subfunction 0Ch and 11h

INT 21h   [5.0+]

FUNCTION 44h SUBFUNCTION 11h
Query Generic IOCTL Capability (Drive)   DOS

Tests whether a block device drive supports a miscellaneous IOCTL request.

Input:

AH = 44h
AL = 11h
BL = drive number (0=default,1=A:,etc)
CH = category code
08h disk drive
CL = function code

Output:

CF = 0 function is successful
AX = 0000h specified IOCTL function is supported
CF = 1 function is unsuccessful
AL = IOCTL capability not available

Comments:

A block device driver must support a Generic IOCTL Check call.

This function may be used if you wish to use a Generic IOCTL call beyond
the set of calls defined for DOS 3.2.

See Also:

INT 21h Function 44h Subfunction 0Dh and 10h

INT 21h [2.0+]

FUNCTION 45h
Duplicate Handle   DOS

Creates a new file handle that refers to the same currently operating device or file as an existing file handle.

Input:

AH = 45h
BX = file handle

Output:

CF = 0 function is successful
AX = new handle
CF = 1 function is unsuccessful
AX = error code
    04h = no additional handle available
    06h = handle not opened or does not exist

Comments:

This function is used to force DOS to clear the file buffers by closing the duplicate handle. It is faster than closing and reopening a disk file. A better way of doing this in DOS 3.3+ is using Function 68h.

This function can also be used for updating the directory entry of a file that has changed in length without closing and reopening a file.

See Also:

INT 21h Functions 3Dh and 46h

INT 21h [2.0+]

FUNCTION 46h
Force Duplicate File Handle   DOS

Forces the second handle to become a duplicate of the first handle.

Input:

AH = 46h
BX = first file handle
CX = second file handle

Output:

> CF = 0 function is successful
> CF = 1 function is unsuccessful
> AX = error code
>> 04h = no additional handle available
>> 06h = handle not opened on does not exist

Comments:

This function closes first file handle if it is still open.

An I/O operation that changes the position of the file pointer for the file connected to the first handle, and moves the file pointer for the second file.

See Also:

INT 21h Functions 3Dh and 45h

INT 21h   [2.0+]

FUNCTION 47h
Get Current Directory   DOS

Gets current working directory of a specified device.

Input:

> AH = 47h
> DL = drive number (0=default, 1=A, etc.)
> DS:SI = offset:segment of a 64 byte long buffer with ASCIIZ
> pathname

Output:

> CF = 0 function is successful
> CF = 1 function is unsuccessful
> AX = error code
>> 0Fh = invalid drive specification

Comments:

This function returns the path description without the drive letter and the initial backslash.

See Also:

INT 21h Functions 19h and 3Bh

INT 21h   [2.0+]
FUNCTION 48h
Allocate Memory   **DOS**

Allocates memory to the current program.

Input:

>   AH = 48h
>   BX = number of paragraphs to be requested

Output:

>   CF = 0 function is successful
>   AX = pointer to allocated block
>   CF = 1 function is unsuccessful
>   AX = error code
>   07h = memory control block destroyed
>   08h = insufficient memory
>   BX = size of largest available memory block in paragraphs

Comments:

This function always fails when it is executed within COM-format programs.
This is because they initially occupy the largest available block of memory.
Therefore you must free some memory before using this function.

See Also:

INT 21h Functions 49h, 4Ah, 4Bh and 58h

INT 21h   [2.0+]
FUNCTION 49h
Release Memory   **DOS**

Releases memory blocks previously obtained using function 48h.

Input:

>   AH = 49h
>   ES = segment of block to be freed

Output:

>   CF = 0 function is successful
>   CF = 1 function is unsuccessful
>   AX = error code

07h = damaged memory control block
09h = incorrect memory block address

See Also:

INT 21h Functions 48h, 4Ah and 4Bh

INT 21h [2.0+]
FUNCTION 4Ah
Modify Allocated Memory Block   DOS

Changes the size of a memory block previously allocated by function 48h.

Input:

AH = 4Ah
BX = new memory size in paragraph
ES = segment of block address

Output:

CF = 0 function is successful
CF = 1 function is unsuccessful
AX = error code
    07h = damaged memory control block
    08h = insufficient memory
    09h = incorrect memory block address
BX = maximum number of paragraphs available

See Also:

INT 21h Functions 48h and 49h

INT 21h [2.0+]
FUNCTION 4Bh SUBFUNCTION 00H-03h
Load and/or Execute   DOS

Loads and executes (optionally) another program.

Input:

AH = 4Bh
AL = 00h load and execute
    01h load but do not execute (5.0)
    03h load overlay
DS:DX = ASCIIZ string of pathname
ES:BX = segment:offset address of parameter block

Output:

CF = 0 function is successful
BX = destroyed
DX = destroyed
CF = 1 function is unsuccessful
AX = error code
     01h invalid function number
     02h file not found
     03h path not found
     05h access denied
     08h insufficient memory
     10h invalid environment block
     11h invalid format

Comments:

This function loads a sub-program, creates PSP and runs the sub-program.
The parameter block for AL=00h, 01h has the following format:

Offset	Size	Description
00h	2	segment pointer to environment block
02h	4	pointer to command line tail
06h	4	pointer to first FCB to be copied into new PSP
0Ah	4	pointer to second FCB to be copied into new PSP

The parameter block for Subfunction 00h has the following format:

Offset	Size	Description
00h	2	segment address in which to load overlay
02h	2	relocation factor to apply to overlay

If the segment address of the enviroment block is 0, then a child process has
the same environment block as the parent process.
The environment strings must be paragraph aligned and consist of a sequence
of ASCIIZ strings. The strings must be followed by the byte 00h.
The command tail parameter string contains a count byte which represents
the number of characters in the command string. This is followed by ASCII
characters. The string ends with a carriage return (the carriage return is not
included in the count byte). The first character of the string should be a space.
Before using this function, you must ensure that there is enough unallocated
memory available for the child process. If necessary, you must release all the
memory to load the child process.
When this function loads and runs a sub-program, all open files of the parent
process are available to the child process; therefore, if the parent process redirects
standard input or output, it also affects the child process.

See Also:

INT 21h Function 44h Subfunction 0Ch and 11h, Function 69h

INT 21h   [5.0+]
FUNCTION 4Bh SUBFUNCTION 05h
Set Execution State   DOS

Prepares new programs for execution.

Input:

AH = 4Bh
AL = 05h
DS:DX = segment:offset of execution state structure

Output:

CF = 0 function is successful
AX = 00h
CF = 1 function is unsuccessful
AX = error code

Comments:

This function may be used by progams which want to bypass the normal
EXEC function. All DOS, BIOS and other software interrupts cannot be used
after returning from this function and before the start of the child process.

See Also:

INT 21h Function 4Bh Subfunction 00h-03h

INT 21h   [2.0+]
FUNCTION 4Ch
Terminate with Output Code   DOS

Ends the current process and passes an exit code to the parent process.

Input:

AH = 4Ch
AL = return code

Output:

Nothing

Comments:

This function is the proper method for terminating programs in DOS versions 2.0 and above. It releases all the memory belonging to the parent process, flushes all file buffers and closes all open file handles of the parent process. It also restores the contents of the interrupt vectors for the terminate handler (INT 22h), the Ctrl-C handler (INT 23h) and the critical error handler (INT 24h). After this, control is passed to the parent process. All files that have been opened using FSBs must be closed before executing this function.
All network file locks should be removed before this function is performed. Batch files can test the return code with an ErrorLevel and IF statement. The return code zero indicates that the function was successful.

See Also:

INT 21h Functions 00h, 26h, 4Bh and 4Dh; INT 20h; INT 22h

INT 21h   [2.0+]

FUNCTION 4Dh
Get Output Code   DOS

Reads the exit code and termination type of the child process after execution of the EXEC call.

Input:

AH = 4Dh

Output:

AH = termination type
00h . normal termination (INT 20h, INT 21h Function 00h or INT 21h Function 4Ch)
01h Ctrl-C or Ctrl-Break abort
02h termination by critical error handler
03h terminate and stay resident (INT 21h Function 31h or INT 27h)
AL = return code

Comments:

This function can only retrieve the return code once, because the word where DOS stores this code is cleared once the function has read it.

See Also:

INT 21h Functions 48h, 4Ah and 4Bh

INT 21h   [2.0+]
FUNCTION 4Eh
Find First Matching File   DOS

Searches for the first file that matches a specified filename in the default or
specified directory on the default or specified drive.

Input:

AH = 4Eh
CX = file attribute mask (bits may be combined)
    bit 0=1 read only
    bit 1=1 hidden
    bit 2=1 system
    bit 3=1 volume label
    bit 4=1 directory
    bit 5=1 archive
    bits 6-15 reserved (0)
DS:DX = segment:offset of ASCIIZ pathname

Output:

CF = 0 function is successful
[DTA] Disk Transfer Area = FindFirst data block

The DTA has the following format:

Offset	Size	Description
00h	1	drive letter (MS DOS 3.2/3.3/5.0)
01h	11	search template
0Ch	1	search attribute
0Dh	2	entry count within directory
0Fh	2	cluster number of the start of the parent directory (MS DOS 3.2+)
11h	4	reserved (MS DOS 3.2+) all versions
15h	1	attribute of file found
16h	2	file time
		bits 0 - 4 seconds/2 (0-29)
		bits 5 - 10 minutes (0-59)
		bits 11 - 15 hours (0-23)
18h	2	file date
		bits 0 - 4 day (1-31)
		bits 5 - 8 month (1-12)
		bits 9 - 15 year-1980

| 1Ah | 4 | file size |
| 1Eh | 13 | ASCIIZ filename and extension |

CF = 1 function is unsuccessful (no matching file)
AX = error code
    02h file not found
    08h path not found
    12h no file with same attribute is found

Comments:

This function allows the use of wildcards in the filename. If a wildcard character is included in the filename, only the first matching filename is returned.

If the attribute byte is other than 08h, this function returns all files with the specified combination of attribute bits. If the attribute byte is equal to 08h (the volume label), the function returns the volume label only.

See Also:

INT 21h Functions 11h and 4Fh, Function 43h Subfunction 01h

INT 21h   [2.0+]
FUNCTION 4Fh
Find Next Matching File   **DOS**

Searches for the next file that matches a specified filename in the default or specified directory on the default or specified drive, if the previous call of Function 4Eh was successful.

Input:

AH = 4Fh
DTA points to the data block from the previous FindFirst or FindNext call

Output:

CF = 0 function is successful
CF = 1 function is unsuccessful
AX = error code
    12h no file with attribute found

Comments:

This function is usually used after the function 4Eh. The function 4Fh continues the search performed by the function 4Eh if that function leaves the DTA unchanged.

The original file specification must contain wildcard characters.

See Also:

INT 21h Function 12h and 4Eh

INT 21h [2.0+]
FUNCTION 50h
Set Current Process ID (Set PSP address)   DOS

Sets a new value of PID into "current process" variable

Input:

>   AH = 50h
>   BX = segment address of new PSP

Output:

>   Nothing

Comments:

Under DOS 2.x this function cannot be invoked inside an INT 28h handler without setting the Critical Error flag.

Under DOS 3+ this function does not use any internal stacks and is thus fully re-entrant.

See Also:

INT 21h Function 26h, 51h and 62h

INT 21h [2.0+]
FUNCTION 51h
Get Current Process ID (Get PSP address)   DOS

Reads the segment address of the current PSP.

Input:

>   AH = 51h
>   BX = segment address of PSP for current process

Output:

>   Nothing

Comments:

Under DOS 2.x this function cannot be invoked inside an INT 28h handler without setting the Critical Error flag.

Under DOS 3+ this function does not use any internal stacks and is thus fully re-entrant.

See Also:

INT 21h Function 26h, 50h and 62h

INT 21h   [2.0+]

FUNCTION 53h

Translate BIOS Parameter Block to Drive Parameter Block DOS

Transforms drive parameter information from the BIOS Parameter Block (BPB) which is stored on the disk to the format used by DOS.

Input:

AH = 53h
DS:SI = segment:offset BIOS Parameter Block (BPB)
ES:BI = segment:offset buffer for Driver Parameter Block (DPB)

Output:

ES:BP = address of buffer with information

Comments:

The BIOS Parameter Block has the following format:

Offset	Size	Description
00h	2	number of bytes per sector
02h	1	number of sectors per cluster
03h	2	number of reserved sectors at start of the disk
05h	1	number of FATs
06h	2	number of entries in the root directory
08h	2	total number of sectors
0Ah	1	media ID byte
0Bh	2	number of sectors per FAT
- DOS 3+ -		
0Dh	2	number of sectors per track
0Fh	2	number of heads
11h	4	number of hidden sectors
15h	11	reserved

	- DOS 4+ -	
15h	4	total number of sectors if word at 08h contains zero
19h	6	unknown
1Fh	2	number of cylinders
21h	1	device type
22h	2	device attributes (removable or not, etc.)

INT 21h   [2.0+]

FUNCTION 54h
Get Verify Flag   DOS

Gets the current value of the MS DOS "verify" flag (read after write).

Input:

AH = 54h

Output:

AL = 0 if the verfy flag is OFF
AL = 0 if the verfy flag is ON

Comments:

This function does not permit the wildcard character in any pathname specification.
This function cannot rename open files. DOS 3+ allows you to rename directories but not to move them.
An error occurs if the root directory is full and a file is moved to it.

See Also:

INT 21h Function 2Eh

INT 21h   [2.0+]

FUNCTION 56h
Rename File   DOS

Changes the name of a file or moves a file from one directory to another on the same logical drive.

Input:

AH = 56h

Output:

> AL = 0 if the verfy flag is OFF
> AL = 0 if the verfy flag is ON

Comments:

This function does not allow the wildcard character in any pathname specification.

This function cannot rename open files. DOS 3+ allows you to rename directories but not to move them.

An error occurs if the file is moved in the root directory and it is full, or a file with a new pathname exists.

See Also:

INT 21h Function 2Eh

INT 21h   [2.0+]
FUNCTION 57h SUBFUNCTION 00h
Get File's Date and Time   DOS

Reads the date and time of the creation or last modification of a file.

Input:

> AH = 57h
> AL = 00h
> BX = file handle

Output:

> CF = 0 function is successful
> CX = file's time
> > bits 0 - 4 seconds/2 (0-29)
> > bits 5 - 10 minutes (0-59)
> > bits 11-15 hours (0-23)
> DX = file's date
> > bits 0 - 4 day (1-31)
> > bits 5 - 8 month (1-12)
> > bits 9 - 15 year-1980
> CF = 1 function is unsuccessful
> AX = error code
> > 01h invalid function
> > 06h invalid handle

Comments:

This function can only be called after the file has been created or opened using one of the handle functions.

See Also:

INT 21h Function 57h Subfunction 01h

INT 21h   [2.0+]
FUNCTION 57h SUBFUNCTION 01h
Set File's Date and Time   DOS

Modifies the date and time information of a file to given values.

Input:

```
AH = 57h
AL = 01h
BX = file handle
CX = new time
        bits  0 - 4 seconds/2 (0-29)
        bits  5 - 10 minutes (0-59)
        bits 11 - 15 hours (0-23)
DX = new date
        bits  0 - 4 day (1-31)
        bits  5 - 8 month (1-12)
        bits  9 - 15 year-1980
```

Output:

```
CF = 0 function is successful
CF = 1 function is unsuccessful
AX = error code
        01h invalid function
        06h invalid handle
```

Comments:

This function can only be called after the file has been created or opened using one of the handle functions.

See Also:

INT 21h Function 57h Subfunction 00h

INT 21h   [2.0+]

FUNCTION 58h SUBFUNCTION 00h
Get Allocation Strategy   DOS

Reads the control byte which indicates the current MS DOS method for allocating memory blocks.

Input:

> AH = 58h
> AL = 00h

Output:

> CF = 0 function is successful
> AX = current method code
>> 00h first fit
>> 01h best fit
>> 02h last fit
> CF = 1 function is unsuccessful
> AX = error code
>> 01h = function number is invalid

Comments:

DOS has three methods of allocating memory blocks:
First fit: DOS begins searching the available memory blocks at the start of the memory and allocates the first block which is large enough.
Best fit: DOS searches all available memory blocks and allocates the smallest memory block which meets the requested size.
Last fit:DOS begins searching the available memory block at the end of the memory and allocates the first block which is large enough.
The default strategy is the last fit.

See Also:

INT 21h Functions 48h, 49h and 4Ah

INT 21h   [2.0+]

FUNCTION 58h SUBFUNCTION 01h
Set Allocated Strategy   DOS

Writes the control byte which indicates the current MS DOS strategy for allocating memory blocks.

Input:

>   AH = 58h
>   AL = 01h
>   BX = desired strategy code
>   00h = first fit
>   01h = best fit
>   02h = last fit

Output:

>   CF = 0 function is successful
>   CF = 1 function is unsuccessful
>   AX = error code
>   01h = Invalid function number

See Also:

INT 21h Functions 48h, 49h and 4Ah

INT 21h   [5.0+]

FUNCTION 58h SUBFUNCTION 02h
Get Upper-Memory Link   DOS

Defines whether use of Upper Memory Blocks is enabled or disabled.

Input:

>   AH = 58h
>   AL = 02h

Output:

>   AL = 00h UMB is not part of DOS memory chain
>   01h UMB is in DOS memory chain

See Also:

INT 21h Functions 48h, 49h and 4Ah

INT 21h   [5.0+]
FUNCTION 58h SUBFUNCTION 03h
Set Upper Memory Link   **DOS**

Sets the indicator that enables/disables use of UMBs

Input:

        AH = 58h
        AL = 03h
        BX = 0000h remove UMBs from DOS memory chain
             00001 add UMBs to memory chain

Comments:

Before using this function, you must save the indicator of allocation of UMBs
and before termination of process, restore it.

See Also:

INT 21h Functions 48h, 49h and 4Ah

INT 21h   [2.0+]
FUNCTION 59h
Get Extended Error Information   **DOS**

Gets information about errors that occur after an unsuccessful INT 21h function
call.

Input:

        AH = 59h
        BX = 00h

Output:

        AX = extended error code
             01h   function number invalid
             02h   file not found
             03h   path not found
             04h   too many open files
             05h   access denied
             06h   handle invalid
             07h   memory control block destroyed
             08h   insufficient memory

09h	invalid memory address
0Ah	environment invalid
0Bh	format invalid
0Ch	access code invalid
0Dh	data invalid
0Eh	unknown unit
0Fh	disk drive invalid
10h	current directory cannot be removed
11h	different device
12h	no more files
13h	disk write-protected
14h	unknown unit
15h	drive not ready
16h	unknown command
17h	data error(CRC)
18h	bad request structure length
19h	seek error
1Ah	unknown media type
1Bh	sector not found
1Ch	printer out of paper
1Dh	write fault
1Eh	read fault
1Fh	general failure
20h	sharing violation
21h	lock violation
22h	disk change invalid
50h	file already exists
52h	cannot make directory
53h	fail on INT 24h (critical error)
54h	too many redirections
55h	duplicate redirection
56h	invalid password
57h	invalid parameter
5Ah	required system component not installed

BH = error class

01h	out of resource (storage or handles)
02h	temporary problems that can be expected to end
03h	authorization problem
04h	internal error in system software
05h	hardware problems
06h	system software failure (bad or missing CONFIG.SYS)
07h	application error
08h	file or other item not found
09h	file or other item of invalid type or format
0Ah	file or other item locked
0Bh	media problem (wrong disk in drive etc.)
0Ch	item already exists
0Dh	unknown error

BL = suggested action
- 01h   retry a few times
- 02h   pause, then retry
- 03h   ask user to resupply input
- 04h   abort application with cleanup
- 05h   immediate abort without cleanup
- 06h   ignore error
- 07h   retry after user intervention

CH = source of error
- 01h   unknown
- 02h   block device(disk)
- 03h   network
- 04h   serial device
- 05h   memory

ES:DI = ASCIIZ volume label of disk to insert if AX = 022h (MS DOS 3.0+)

See Also:

INT 24h

INT 21h   [3.0+]

FUNCTION 5Ah
Create Temporary File   DOS

Creates a temporary file with a unique name using the current date and time.

Input:

AH = 5Ah
CX = file attribute (bits may be combined)
DS:DX = segment:offset of ASCIIZ path ending with at least 13 zero bytes

Output:

CF = 0 function is successful
AX = handle
DS:DX = segment:offset of complete ASCIIZ pathname
CF = 1 function is unsuccessful
AX = error code
- 03h path not found
- 04h too many open files
- 05h access denied

Comments:

The ASCIIZ pathname contains a drive specification and a path designation. If the pathname does not include either a drive specification or a path designation, this function creates a temporary file in the current directory of the default drive.

This function does not automatically delete temporary files after execution. This function is used by COMMAND.COM for creating a temporary "piping" file, used for redirection of input/output.

See Also:

INT 21h Functions 3Ch and 5Bh

INT 21h   [3.0+]

FUNCTION 5Bh
Create New File   DOS

Creates a file in the specified or default directory if it does not already exist.

Input:

        AH = 5Bh
        CX = file attribute (bits may be combined)
                bit   0 00h read-only
                        1 01h hidden
                        2 02h system
                        3 03h volume label
                        4 04h reserved(0)
                        5 05h archive
                bits 6-15   reserved(0)
        DS:DX = segment:offset of ASCIIZ pathname

Output:

        CF = 0 function is successful
        AX = handle
        CF = 1 function is unsuccessful
        AX = error code
                03h path not found
                04h too many open files
                05h access denied
                50h file exists

Comments:

An error occurs when:

        Any element of the path designation does not exist.
        A filename already exists in the specified directory.
        The file is to be created in the root directory, but this is already full.

When a file is created, it usually has a normal read/write attribute (0).

See Also:

INT 21h Function 3Ch and 5Ah

INT 21h   [3.0+]
FUNCTION 5Ch
Lock or Unlock File Region   **DOS**

Prevents or allows access to the specified region of a file.

Input:

    AH = 5Ch
    AL = 00h lock region of a file
         01h unlock region of a file
    BX = file handle
    CX = high word of region offset
    DX = low word of region offset
    SI = high word of region length
    DI = low word of region length

Output:

    CF = 0 function is successful
    CF = 1 function is unsuccessful
    AX = error code
    01h invalid function code
    06h invalid handle
    21h all or part of region is already locked

Comments:

Every call to lock a region of a file must be followed by a call to unlock the
same region.
A child process created by an EXEC system call does not inherit access to the
locked region of a file which has been locked by its parent.
If a program is terminated by INT 23h or INT 24h, you must release the locked
regions of the open file, otherwise the result is undefined.

See Also:

INT 21h Functions 3Dh and 59h

INT 21h   [3.0+]

FUNCTION 5Eh SUBFUNCTION 00h
Get Machine Name   DOS

Returns the ASCIIZ name of a local computer within a Microsoft Network.

Input:

> AX = 5Dh
> AL = 00h
> DS:DX = segment:offset of buffer (16 bytes) with computer name

Output:

> CF = 0 function is successful
> CH = 00h name not defined
>   <>00h name is defined
> CL = netBIOS name number (ifch<>0)
> DS:DX = segment:offset of computer name (if CH<>0)
> CF = 1 function is unsuccessful
> AX = error code
>   01h invalid function code

Comments:

The computer type is a 16-byte ASCIIZ string. Spaces are added to make it
this length.

See Also:

INT 21h Function 5Eh Subfunction 01h

INT 21h   [3.0+]

FUNCTION 5Eh SUBFUNCTION 01h
Set Redirection Mode   DOS

Sets current redirection mode (printer/disk).

Input:

> AX = 5Dh
> AL = 01h
> DS:DX = segment:offset of buffer (16 bytes) with computer name

Output:

CF = 0 function is successful
CH = 00h name not defined
     <>00h name is defined
CL = netBIOS name number (if CH<>0)
DS:DX = segment:offset of computer name (if CH<>0)
CF = 1 function is unsuccessful
AX = error code
     01h invalid function code

Comments:

The computer type is a 16-byte ASCIIZ string. Spaces are added to make it this length.

See Also:

INT 21h Function 5Eh Subfunction 01h

INT 21h   [3.0+]

FUNCTION 5Eh SUBFUNCTION 02h
Set Printer Setup String   DOS

Specifies the printer setup string which precedes all output to a network printer. This string allows network users to specify their own individual mode to the network printer.

Input:

AH = 5Eh
AL = 02h
BX = redirection list index
CX = length of setup string
DS:DI = segment:offset of setup string

Output:

CF = 0 function is successful
CF = 1 function is unsuccessful
AX = error code
     01h invalid function code
     System redirection list assigns local names to network
     printers, files and directories.

See Also:

INT 21h Function 5Eh Subfunction 03h

INT 21h [3.1+]

FUNCTION 5Eh SUBFUNCTION 03h
Get Printer Setup String DOS

Gets the printer setup string used by a network printer which is running in the Microsoft Network.

Input:

AH = 5Eh
AL = 03h
BX = redirection list index
ES:DI = segment:offset 64 byte setup string

Output:

CF = 0 function is successful
CX = printer setup string length
ES:DI = segment:offset address of buffer is filled with Setup String
CF = 1 function is unsuccessful
AX = error code
01h invalid function code

See Also:

INT 21h Function 5Eh Subfunction 02h

INT 21h [3.1+]

FUNCTION 5Fh SUBFUNCTION 00h
Get Redirection Mode DOS

Reads current redirection mode (printer/disk).

Input:

AH = 5Fh
AL = 00h
BL = redirection type
03h printer
04h disk drive

Output:

CF = 0 function is successful
BH = redirection state
00h off
01h on

Appendix G1

        CX = printer setup string length
        CF = 1 function is unsuccessful
        AX = error code

Comments:

This function is available when Microsoft NetWork is installed.

See Also:

INT 21h Function 5Fh Subfunction 01h

INT 21h   [3.1+]
FUNCTION 5Fh SUBFUNCTION 01h
Set Redirection Mode   DOS

Sets the current redirection mode (printer/disk).

Input:

        AX = 5Fh
        AL = 01h
        BL = redirection type
                03h printer
                04h disk drive
        BH = redirection state
                00h off
                01h on

Output:

        CF = 0 function is successful
        CF = 1 function is unsuccessful
        AX = error code

Comments:

This function is available when Microsoft NetWork is installed. If redirection
is off, then local device is used.

See Also:

INT 21h Function 5Fh Subfunction 01h

INT 21h   [3.1+]
FUNCTION 5Fh SUBFUNCTION 02h
Get Redirection List Entry   DOS

Reads the system redirection list. This list assigns local names to network files, directories or printers.

Input:

> AH = 5Fh
> AL = 02h
> BX = redirection list index
> DS:SI = 16 byte buffer for ASCIIZ device name
> ES:DI = 128 byte buffer for ASCIIZ network name

Output:

> CF = 0 function is successful
> BH = device status flag
> > 00h valid
> > 01h invalid
> BL = device type
> > 03h printer
> > 04h disk drive
> CX = parameter value stored in memory
> DX = destroyed
> BP = destroyed
> DS:DI = segment:offset of ASCIIZ local device name
> ES:DI = segment:offset of ASCIIZ network name
> CF = 1 function is unsuccessful
> AX = error code
> > 01h invalid function code
> > 12h no more files available

See Also:

INT 21h Function 5Fh Subfunction 03h

INT 21h   [3.1+]
FUNCTION 5Fh SUBFUNCTION 03h
Redirect Device   DOS

Redirects a specified device to a specified network name.

Input:

    AH = 5Fh
    AL = 03h
    BL = device type
            03h if printer
            04h if drive
    CX = user data to save
    DS:DI = segment:offset of ASCIIZ local device name
    ES:DI = segment:offset of ASCIIZ network name and ASCIIZ
            password

Output:

    CF = 0 function is successful
    CF = 1 function is unsuccessful
    AX = error code
            01h invalid function code
            03h path not found
            05h access denied
            08h insufficient memory
            0Fh invalid drive
            12h no more files available

Comments:

Device names can be drive specifiers (such as "D:"), printer names (i.e., LPT1,
PRN, LPT2 or LPT3) or null string. If the device name is a null string and
password, then DOS attempts to gain access to the network directory with
the specified password.

See Also:

INT 21h Function 5Fh Subfunction 02h

INT 21h   [3.1+]
FUNCTION 5Fh SUBFUNCTION 04h
Cancel Device Redirection   DOS

Cancels the current redirection for the specified local device with a network
of printers, files or directories.

Input:

AH = 5Fh
AL = 04h
DS:DI = segment:offset of ASCIIZ local device name

Output:

CF = 0 function is successful
CF = 1 function is unsuccessful
AX = error code
01h invalid function code
03h path not found
05h access denied
08h insufficient memory
0Fh invalid drive
12h no more files available

Comments:

This function is available when Microsoft Network is running.
Device names can be drive specifiers (such as "D:"), printer names (i.e.,LPT1, LPT2, LPT3 or PRN) or a string beginning with two back slashes which terminates the connection between the local computer and the network directory.

See Also:

INT 21h Function 5Fh Subfunction 03h

INT 21h   [3.0+]
FUNCTION 62h
Get Current PSP Address   DOS

Reads the segment address of the PSP for the current program.

Input:

AH = 62h

Output:

BX = segment of PSP for current process

Comments:

This function is identical to the undocumented function 51h.

INT 21h   [3.3+]
FUNCTION 65h
Get Extended Country Information   **DOS**

Reads country-dependent information.

Input:

AH = 65h
AL = subfunction
    01h get general international information
    02h get pointer to uppercase table
    04h get pointer to filename uppercase table
    05h (DOS 3.3+) get pointer to filename terminator table
    06h get pointer to collating table
    07h get pointer to Double-byte Character Set (DBCS) Vector
        (MS DOS 4+)
BX = code page (-1 = active CON device)
CX = size of buffer to receive information
DX = country ID (-1 = default)
ES:DI = address of buffer to receive information

Output:

CF = 1 function is unsuccessful
AX = error code
CF = 0 function is successful
CX = size of country information returned
ES:DI = address of country information

Comments:

This function returns an extended version of the information which is returned
by INT21h function 38h

INT 21h   [4.0+]
FUNCTION 65h SUBFUNCTION 20-22h
Country Dependent Character Capitalization   **DOS**

Capitalizes a text in a country dependent fashion.

Input:

AH = 65h
AL = subfunction
    20h Capitalize character
DL = character to capitalize

21h Capitalize string
DS:DX = segment:offset of the string to capitalize
CX = length of the string
      22h Capitalize ASCIZ string
DS:DX = segment:offset of ASCIZ string to capitalize

Output:

CF = 0 function is successful
DL = capitalize character if AL = 20h
CF = 1 function is unsuccessful
AX = error code

INT 21h   [4.0+]

FUNCTION 65h SUBFUNCTION 23h
Determine if Character Represents Yes/No Response   DOS

Determines if a typed character is a "yes/no" response for current country.

Input:

AH = 65h
AL = 23h

Output:

CF = 0 function is successful
AX = type
    00h no
    01h yes
    02h neither yes or no
CF = 1 function is unsuccessful

INT 21h   [3.3+]

FUNCTION 66h
Get or Set Code Page

DOS Reads or sets the current code page.

Input:

AH = 66h
AL = subfunction
    01h Get code Page
    02h Select code Page
BX = select code page (if AL=02h)

Output:

> CF = 0 function is successful
> if AL = 01h
> BX = active code page
> DX = default code page
> CF = 1 error code

Comments:

MS DOS, via the function COUNTRY.SYS, supplies a new code page if AL = 02h, but the device must be prepared for this by the directive DEVICE in CONFIG.SYS and NLSFUNC and MODE CP PREPARE commands in AUTOEXEC.BAT

INT 21h   [3.3+]
FUNCTION 67h
Set Handle Count   DOS

Sets the maximum number of handles currently available to the calling programs.

Input:

> AH = 67h
> BX = number of desired handles

Output:

> CF = 0 function is successful
> CF = 1 function is unsuccessful
> AX = error code

Comments:

The default table of the PSP for the current process can control only 20 handles. An error occurs if the number of handles in the BX register is greater than 20 and there is no free memory available to allocate a block for the enlarged table.

If the number of requested files in the BX register is greater than the available number of entries controlled by the FILES entry in CONFIG.SYS file, no error occurs.
However, an attempt to open a file or device will fail if all file entries are in use, even if not all the file handles have been used by the program.

INT 21h   [3.3+]

FUNCTION 68h
Commit File   **DOS**

Forces all data in DOS buffers associated with a specific handle to be written immediately to the specified device. If the handle points to a file which has been updated, the file's directory entry is also updated.

Input:

AH = 68h
BX = handle

Output:

CF = 0 function is successful
CF = 1 function is unsuccessful
AX = error code

Comments:

This function closes and reopens a file or duplicates a handle and then closes it. This function maintains control of the file in multitasking and networking applicatons.Although this function does not perform any actions when it accesses a character device, it sets the Carry Flag.

INT 21h   [4.0+]

FUNCTION 69h
Get/Set Disk Serial Number   **DOS**

Reads or writes the volume label and serial number of the specified disk.

Input:

AH = 69h
AL = subfunction
      00h = get serial number
      01h = set serial number
BL = drive (0=default, 1=A,2=b,etc)
DS:DX = segment:offset disk serial number info

Output:

CF = 0 function is successful
AX = destroyed
AL = 00h   buffer is filled with value from extended DPB
       01h   extended DPB on disk set to values from buffer
CF = 1 function is unsuccessful

AX = error code
- 01h   function number invalid (network driver)
- 05h   access denied (no extended DPB on disk)

Comments:

This function does not generate critical errors.

This function does not work on network drivers.

The format of disk serial number info has the following format:

Offset	Size	Description
00h	2	info level(zero)
02h	4	disk serial number (binary)
06h	11	volume label or "NO NAME"
11h	8	(AL=00h only) filesystem type storing "FAT12 " or "FAT16 "

See Also:

INT 21 Function 44 Subfunction 0Dh

INT 21h   [4.0+]

FUNCTION 6Ch
Extended Open/Create Number   DOS

Combines functions "create", "open" and "commit" into a common function.

Input:

AH = 6Ch
AL = 00h
BL = open mode

bit 0-2	access type	
	000=read-only	
	001=write-only	
	010=read/write	
bit 3	reserved	
bits 4-6	sharing mode	
	000=compatibility	
	001=deny all	
	010=deny write	
	011=deny read	
	100=deny none	
bit 7	inheritance	

BH = flags

bit 0-4	reserved	
bit 5	critical error handling	
	0	execute INT 24h

	1	return error to process
	bit 6	auto commit on write
	0	write may be buffered
	1	physical write at request time
	bit 7	reserved

CX = create attribute (bits may be combined)

	bit 0	read-only
	bit 1	hidden
	bit 2	system
	bit 3	volume label
	bit 4	reserved
	bit 5	archive
	bits 6-15	reserved

DX = open flag

	bits 0-3	action if file exists
		0000=fail
		0001=open file
		0010=replace file
	bits 4-7	action if file does not exist
		0000h=fail
		0001h=create

DS:SI =segment:offset of ASCIZ filename

Output:

CF = 0 function is successful
AX = file handle
CX = 1 file openend
   = 2 file created
   = 3 file replace
CF = 1 function is unsuccessful
AX = error code

See Also:

INT 21h Function 3Ch and 3Dh

APPENDIX
GII

Mouse Service
Reference - Interrupt 33h

FUNCTION 00h
Reset Driver and Get Status

Initializes the mouse driver and reads its current status. This function first removes the mouse pointer from the screen, then places it in the centre of screen.

Input

AX = 0000h

Output

AX = status
    FFFFh mouse driver/hardware is installed
    0000h mouse driver/hardware not installed
BX = number of mouse buttons
    FFFFh two buttons
    0000h more or less than two buttons
    0003h Mouse Systems/Logitech mouse

Comments

The status of the driver after initialization is as follows:
    Mouse pointer at screen centre
    Mouse pointer is hidden
    Display page for mouse pointer set to zero
    Mouse pointer set to default arrow shape in graphics modes
    Mouse pointer set to reverse block in text modes
    Light pen emulation is enabled
    Vertical mickeys to pixel ratio at 16/8
    Horizontal mickeys to pixel ratio at 8/8
    User mouse masks set to zero
    Minimum horizontal and vertical pointer position set to zero
    Maximum horizontal and vertical pointer position set to include the entire screen in current display mode

See Also

INT 33h Function 21h

INT 33h   [PC][AT][PS/2]
FUNCTION 01h
Show Mouse Cursor

Makes the mouse cursor/pointer visible.

Input

AX = 0001h

Outputs

Nothing

Comments

This function increments the counter (if it is non zero). If counter is zero, the mouse pointer is displayed.
The initial value of the counter is equal to -1 and the mouse pointer is hidden. The mouse pointer must be hidden before performing an action which changes the video display.

See Also:

INT 33h Function 02h and 10h

INT 33h   [PC][AT][PS/2]
FUNCTION 02h
Hide Mouse Cursor

Hides the mouse cursor/pointer.

Input

AX = 0002h

Output

Nothing

Comments

This function decrements the counter.
The cursor is hidden, but the driver continues to track the mouse position.

This function must always be called before an action which changes the video mode.

See Also:

INT 33h Function 01h and 10h

INT 33h   [PC][AT][PS/2]
FUNCTION 03h
Get Mouse Position and Button Status

Reads the current mouse pointer position and button status.

Input

AX = 0003h

Output

BX = button status
bit   Description (if set)
    0   left button is pressed
    1   right button is pressed
    2   middle button is pressed (Mouse Systems or Logitech Mouse)
    3-15 reserved
CX = horizontal (X) co-ordinate in pixels
DX = vertical (Y) co-ordinate in pixels

See Also

INT 33h Function 04h and 0Bh

INT 33h   [PC][AT][PS/2]
FUNCTION 04h
Set Mouse Pointer Position

Sets the mouse pointer to a specified position.

Input

AX = 0004h
CX = horizontal (X) co-ordinate in pixel
DX = vertical (Y) co-ordinate in pixel

Output

Nothing

Comments

This function displays the mouse pointer within specified horizontal and vertical limits for the current virtual display of the mouse.

The co-ordinates of the mouse pointer are obtained by dividing the value of the row (column) by the character cell size. The result is truncated to the next lower multiple of the cell size.

See Also

INT 33h Function 03h

INT 33h   [PC][AT][PS/2]
FUNCTION 05h
Get Button Press Information

Reads the location where the specified mouse button was last pressed after the last call to this function, and reads the current button status and the number of clicks.

Input

        AX = 0005h
        BX = button
        00h left button
        01h right button
        02h middle button (Mouse System/Logitech Mouse)

Output

        AX = button status
        bit   Description (if set)
            0   left button has been pressed
            1   right button has been pressed
            2   middle button has been pressed (Mouse Systems or
                 Logitech Mouse)
        BX = number of times button has been pressed
        CX = horizontal co-ordinate (X) of last button pressed
        DX = vertical co-ordinate (Y) of last button pressed

Comments

This function sets the press counter to zero.

See Also

INT 33h Function 06h

INT 33h   [PC][AT][PS/2]
FUNCTION 06h
Get Button Release Information

Reads the location where the specified mouse button was last released, the current button status and the number of clicks since the last call to this function.

Input

AX = 0006h
BX = button
    00h left button
    01h right button
    02h middle button (Mouse System/Logitech Mouse)

Outputs

AX = button status
bit   Description (if set)
  0   left button is pressed
  1   right button is pressed
  2   middle button is pressed (Mouse Systems/Logitech Mouse)

BX = number of times button has been released
CX = horizontal co-ordinate (X) of last button press
DX = vertical co-ordinate (Y) of last button press

Comments

This function sets the release counter to zero.

See Also

INT 33h Function 05h

INT 33h   [PC][AT][PS/2]
FUNCTION 07h
Set Horizontal Cursor Range

Defines the horizontal boundaries for the mouse pointer.

Input

AX = 0007h
CX = minimum horizontal co-ordinate (column)
DX = maximum horizontal c-oordinate (column)

Outputs

Nothing

Comments

If the horizontal co-ordinate of the mouse pointer was outside the specified range before this function was called, then the mouse pointer moves within the specified range.

If the minimum value of the horizontal co-ordinates is greater than the maximum value, then this function swaps these values.

See Also

INT 33h Function 08h and 10h

INT 33h   [PC][AT][PS/2]
FUNCTION 08h
Set Vertical Cursor Range

Defines the vertical boundaries for the mouse pointer.

Input

AX = 0008h
CX = minimum vertical co-ordinate (row)
DX = maximum vertical co-ordinate (row)

Output

Nothing

Comments

If the vertical co-ordinate of the mouse pointer was outside the specified range before this function was called, then the mouse pointer moves to the appropriate border of the specified range.

If the minimum value of the vertical co-ordinate is greater than the maximum value, then this function swaps these values.

This function re-calculates the current vertical co-ordinate of the mouse pointer so that it refers to the vertical range for displaying the mouse pointer on the screen.

See Also

INT 33h Function 07h and 10h

INT 33h   [PC][AT][PS/2]

FUNCTION 09h
Define Graphic Cursor

Defines bitmap and color of mouse pointer for graphics modes.

Input

> AX = 0009h
> BX = columns of the graphics cursor hot spot in bitmap
> CX = row of cursor hot spot in bitmap
> ES:DX = offset:segment of bitmap

Output

> Nothing

Comments

The mouse pointer is formed in a cell of 16x16 pixels and is defined by two bit masks - a 16 word screen mask and a 16 word cursor mask. Each word of the mask defines 16 pixels of a row, the least significant bit is rightmost.

The co-ordinates of the hot spot mouse pointer must be in the range 0 - 16.

See Also

INT 33h Function 0Ah and 12h

INT 33h   [PC][AT][PS/2]

FUNCTION 0Ah
Set Text Pointer Type

Modifies the appearance of the mouse pointer in text modes.

Input

> AX = 000Ah
> BX = pointer type
>   0 software pointer
>   1 hardware pointer
> CX = AND mask (if BX=0) or cursor start line (if BX=1)
> DX = XOR mask (if BX=0) or cursor end line (if   BX=1)

Output

> Nothing

Comments

This function lets you use the hardware cursor (the standard blinking cursor) as the mouse pointer.
In this case, the values CX and DX define the shape of the the mouse pointer. The start and end line values for the mouse pointer depend on the current screen mode and video adapter type:

    CGA = 0 - 7
    EGA = 0 - 13
    VGA = 0 - 15

If the software cursor is selected (BX=0) then the value of char/attribute at the mouse pointer is ANDed with the AND mask and then XORed with the XOR mask.

The high byte of both masks affects the attributes and the low byte of both masks affects the character code.

See Also

INT 33h Function 09h; INT 10h Function 10h

INT 33h   [PC][AT][PS/2]
FUNCTION 0Bh
Determine Motion Distance

Obtains the distance between the current mouse position and the mouse position following the last call to this function.

Input

    AX = 000Bh
    CX = horizontal distance since last call in mickeys
    DX = vertical distance since last call in mickeys

Output

    Nothing

Comments

The obtained values are given in mickeys. (1 mickey = 1/200 inch).

The values of the CX and DX registers are interpreted as signed values. Positive values indicate downward motion, or movement to the right border of the screen, and negative values indicate motion upward or to the left border of the screen.

See Also

INT 33h Function 0Ah and 12h

INT 33h   [PC][AT][PS/2]
FUNCTION 0Ch
Set Mouse Event Handler

Installs a custom mouse event handler. Sets the address of an event handler
called by the mouse driver when a specified mouse event occurs.

Input

> AX = 000Ch
> CX = event mask
>> bit 0 = mouse movement
>> bit 1 = left button pressed
>> bit 2 = left button released
>> bit 3 = right button pressed
>> bit 4 = right button released
>> bit 5 = centre button pressed
>> bit 6 = centre button released
>> bits 7-15 unused
>
> ES:DX = offset:segment address of your event handler

Output

> Nothing

Comments

See Also

Int 33h Function 18h

INT 33h   [PC][AT][PS/2]
FUNCTION 0Dh
Enable Light Pen Emulation

Enables emulation of lightpen and simulates a lightpen for programs which
require a light pen.

Input

> AX = 000Dh

Output

Nothing

Comments

The light pen emulation must be used with programs which support a light pen (e.g. using the PEN function of Basic).
When enabled, the position of the mouse pointer is directly related to the lightpen's position and pressing the left and right mouse button is taken as pressing the pen button of the lightpen.

See Also

INT 33h Function 0Eh

INT 33h   [PC][AT][PS/2]
FUNCTION 0Eh
Disable Light Pen Emulation

Disables light pen emulation.

Input

AX = 000Eh

Output

Nothing

See Also

INT 33h Function 0Dh

INT 33h   [PC][AT][PS/2]
FUNCTION 0Fh
Set Pointer Speed

Sets the mickeys to pixel rate. This sets the speed at which the mouse pointer moves around the screen.

Input

AX = 000Fh
CX = horizontal mickeys (1-32767, default per 8 pixels)
DX = vertical mickeys (1-32767, default per 16 pixels)

Outputs

Nothing

See Also

INT 33h Function 0Bh and 1Ah

INT 33h   [PC][AT][PS/2]
FUNCTION 10h
Set Mouse Pointer Exclusion Area

Sets a rectangular area on the screen in which the mouse pointer will not be displayed.

Input

AX = 0010h
CX = upper left X co-ordinate of exclusion area
DX = upper left Y co-ordinate of exclusion area
SI = lower right X co-ordinate of exclusion area
DI = lower right Y co-ordinate of exclusion area

Output

Nothing

Comments

All X and Y co-ordinates are virtual co-ordinates rather than physical co-ordinates.

See Also

INT 33h Function 01h, 02h and 07h

INT 33h   [PC][AT][PS/2]
FUNCTION 13h
Set Speed-Doubling Threshold

Sets the maximum threshold for doubling the mouse pointer speed. If the mouse moves quickly, the mouse driver doubles the pointer motion. By default the mouse moves 64 mickeys per second (about 1/3 inch).

Input

AX = 0013h
DX = Limit of speed in mickeys per second

Output

Nothing

Comments

To avoid doubling the mouse speed, set the threshold to a large value, such as 10000.

See Also

INT 33h Function 0Fh and 1Bh

INT 33h   [PC][AT][PS/2]
FUNCTION 14h
Exchange User Defined Mouse Event Handler

Installs a custom mouse event handler and obtains the address and event mask of the previously installed mouse event handler.

Input

AX = 0014h
CX = event mask
      bit 0 = mouse movement
      bit 1 = left mouse pressed
      bit 2 = left mouse released
      bit 3 = right mouse pressed
      bit 4 = right mouse released
      bit 5 = centre button pressed
      bit 6 = centre button released
      bits 7-15 unused
ES:DX = FAR segment:offset address of event handler

Output

CX = event mask of the previous event handler
ES:DX = FAR segment:offset address of the previous event handler

Comments

When any of the specified events occur, the event handler is called by the mouse driver via a FAR CALL. The mouse driver passes the following information on entry to a custom event handler:
AX = mouse event flag
BX = mouse button status
      bit 0 = left button is pressed
      bit 1 = right button is pressed
      bit 2 = centre button is pressed

CX = horizontal mouse position
DX = vertical mouse position
SI = distance of last horizontal mouse movement (mickeys)
DI = distance of last vertical mouse movement (mickeys)
DS = data segment of the mouse driver

The custom event handler must be exited via a FAR RET instruction, not an IRET instruction.

The mickey value of all co-ordinates must be a signed value. Positive values denote motion downward, or to the right border of the screen, and negative values denote motion upwards, or to the left border of the screen.

See Also

INT 33h Function 18h

INT 33h [PC][AT][PS/2]

FUNCTION 15h
Get Mouse Save Status Buffer Size

Obtains the size of the mouse status buffer with the current status of the mouse driver.

Input

AX = 0015h

Output

BX = Mouse status buffer size (bytes)

Comments

Function 16h (Store mouse driver state) saves the mouse status in the buffer.

See Also

INT 33h Function 16h and 17h

INT 33h [PC][AT][PS/2]

FUNCTION 16h
Save Mouse Driver State

Loads the current mouse driver status information in a user's data area.

Input

> AX = 0016h
> ES:DX = segment:offset address of mouse status buffer

Output

> Nothing

Comments

This function is used to save the status of the mouse driver, allowing you to restore it later. The size of the mouse status buffer is determined by calling Function 15h.

This function is called before performing a programm using DOS Function 4Bh EXEC.

See Also

INT 33h Function 15h and 17h

INT 33h   [PC][AT][PS/2]
FUNCTION 17h
Restore Mouse Driver Status

Reads the mouse driver status from the user buffer where it has been loaded by a previous call to INT 33h Function 16h.

Input

> AX = 0017h
> ES:DX = segment:offset address of buffer

Output

> Nothing

See Also

INT 33h Function 15h and 16h

INT 33h   [PC][AT][PS/2]
FUNCTION 18h
Set Alternate Mouse User Handler

Reads the mouse driver status from the user buffer where it has been loaded by a previous call to INT 33h Function 16h.

Input

AX = 0018h
ES:DX = segment:offset address of buffer

Outputs

Nothing

See Also

INT 33h Function 15h and 16h

INT 33h   [PC][AT][PS/2]

FUNCTION 19h
Get Address of Alternate Mouse Event Handler

Obtains the address and mask of a specified alternate event handler which has been installed previously.

Input

AX = 0019h
CX = event mask of event handler (see Function 24h

Output

CX = event mask (00h = no handler is installed)
ES:DX = segment:offset address of matching event handler

Comments

This function attempts to obtain the address and mask of a user event handler whose mask matches the one specified in the CX register.

See Also

INT 33h Function 18h

INT 33h   [PC][AT][PS/2]

FUNCTION 1Ah
Set Mouse Sensitivity

Combines the threshold for sensitivity for horizontal and vertical mouse motion and the threshold for doubling the mouse pointer speed on the screen.

Input

AX = 001Ah
BX = horizontal speed in mickeys per pixel (1-32767)
CX = vertical speed in mickeys per pixel(1-32767)
DX = double speed threshold in mickeys per second

Output

Nothing

Comments

Default value is 8 horizontal mickeys and 16 vertical mickeys.

See Also

INT 33h Function 1Fh,13h and 1Bh

INT 33h   [PC][AT][PS/2]
FUNCTION 1Bh
Determines Mouse Sensitivity

Obtains the current relationship between mouse motion and pointer motion and the threshold for doubling the mouse speed.

Input

AX = 001Bh

Output

BX = horizontal speed in mickeys per pixel (1-32767)
CX = vertical speed in mickeys per pixel(1-32767)
DX = double speed threshold in mickeys per second

See Also

INT 33h Function 13h ,0Fh and 1Ah

INT 33h   [PC][AT][PS/2]
FUNCTION 1Ch
Set Mouse Interrupt Rate

Sets the rate at which the mouse hardware produces interrupts for the mouse driver for the current mouse position and mouse button status.

Input

> AX = 001Ch
> BX = interrupt rate code (if bit is set)
> > bit 0 none
> > bit 1 30 interrupt per second
> > bit 2 50 interrupt per second
> > bit 4 100 interrupt per second
> > bits 5-15 unused

Output

> Nothing

Comments

This function is only relevant to the Inport Mouse.

If more than one bit is set in the AX register, the mouse driver takes the least significant bit only into consideration.

INT 33h   [PC][AT][PS/2]
FUNCTION 1Dh
Set Mouse Display Rate

Sets the display page on which the mouse pointer should appear.

Input

> AX = 001Dh
> BX = page

Output

> Nothing

Comments

The default display page is 0.

See Also

INT 33h Function 1Eh

INT 33h   [PC][AT][PS/2]
FUNCTION 1Eh
Get Pointer Page

Gets the current display page for the mouse pointer.

Input

AX = 001Eh

Output

BX = display page

See Also

INT 33h Function 1Dh

INT 33h   [PC][AT][PS/2]
FUNCTION 1Fh
Disable Mouse Driver

De-activates the mouse driver and releases the address of the previous interrupt handlers, other than INT 33h and INT 10h Function 71h (for 8086), or Function 74h (for 80286/386).

Input

AX = 001Fh

Output

AX = error status
        001Fh if function is successful
        FFFFh if function is unsuccessful
ES:BX = Segment:offset address of previous event handler of
            INT 33h

Comments

The application program can restore the original contents of the interrupt vector of INT 33h using the address in the register pair ES:BX. This effectively eliminates all mouse support.

See Also

INT 33h Function 20h

INT 33h   [PC][AT][PS/2]
FUNCTION 20h
Enables Mouse Driver

Activates the mouse driver and resets all the interrupts that were removed by function 1Fh.

Input

AX = 0020h

Output

Nothing

See Also

INT 33h Function 1Fh

INT 33h   [PC][AT][PS/2]
FUNCTION 21h
Reset Mouse Driver

Resets the mouse driver and sets all internal variables to default values. Removes the mouse pointer from the screen. Disables the currently installed mouse event handler.

Input

AX = 0021h

Output

AX = error status
    0021h mouse driver not installed
    FFFFh mouse driver is installed
BX = 2 if mouse driver is installed

Comments

This function is identical to Function 00h but does not initialize the mouse hardware.

See Also

INT 33h Function 00h

DOS Services
Reference - Interrupt 20h
Through 2Fh

INT 20h [1.0+]
Terminate Program DOS

Ends the currently running process and returns control to the parent process (usually MS DOS command interpreter).

Input:

> CS=segment address of PSP

Output:

> nothing

Comments:

This interrupt performs the following actions:

> Restores the termination handler vector (INT22h), Ctrl-C handler vector (INT23h) and critical-error handler vector (INT24h) from the PSP.
> Releases all memory belonging to the process,
> Clears all data buffers and closes any open handlers for files and devices of the process.
> Returns control to the termination handler.

Do not use this interrupt for DOS 2 and higher to terminate a process. You must use INT 21h Function 31h or Function 4Ch. These functions are preferable, since they pass a return code to the parent process.

See Also:

> INT 21h Function 00h, 4Ch, INT 22h

INT 22h   [1.0+]
TERMINATE ADDRESS   DOS

Specifies the address of the routine that DOS uses after a program is terminated by INT 20h, INT 27h or INT 21h Function 00h, 31h or 4Ch. This interrupt should never be used directly.

Comments

MS DOS stores this vector in PSP at offset 0Ah through 0Dh during termination and then performs a far jump to the address in INT 22h.

See Also

INT 20h, INT 21h Functions 00h, 31h and 4Ch

INT 23h   [1.0+]
Ctrl-C/Ctrl-Break HANDLER ADDRESS   DOS

Specifies the address of the routine that DOS uses when a Ctrl-C or Ctrl-Break is detected.

Comments

This interrupt should never be used directly.

MS DOS stores this vector at offset 0Eh through 11h in PSP during termination and then performs a far jump to the address in INT 23h.

If Break flag is off, DOS detects Ctrl-Break only during console, printer and serial device input/output.

When DOS detects a Ctrl-Break, the keyboard buffer is cleared and performs INT 1Bh. When DOS detects Ctrl-C, the scan-code of Ctrl-C is placed into keyboard buffer.

Any DOS function may be used within the INT 23h handler.

See Also

INT 1Bh

INT 24h [1.0+]
CRITICAL-ERROR HANDLER ADDRESS   DOS

Specifies the address of the routine that DOS uses when a critical error occurs.
This error is usually a hardware error.

Input

```
AH = error information
        bit 7 = 0    disk I/O error
                1    bad FAT image in memory (if block device)
                     error code in DI (if char device)
        bit 6 = unused
        bit 5 = 1    ignore not allowed
                0    ignore allowed
        bit 4 = 1    retry not allowed
                0    retry allowed
        bit 3 = 1.   fail allowed
                0    fail not allowed
        bits 1-2     00 DOS area
                     01 FAT
                     10 root directory
                     11 data area
        bit 0 = 1    if write
                0    if read
AL  =   drive number (if bit 7 of AH clear)
BP:SI = device driver header (BP:[SI+4] bit 15 is set if char device)
DI  =   error code in low byte (if AH bit 7 is set)
        00h          write-protect error
        01h          invalid drive number
        02h          drive not ready
        03h          invalid command
        04h          CRC error
        05h          bad request structure length
        06h          seek error
        07h          unknown media type
        08h          sector not found
        09h          printer out of paper
        0Ah          write error
        0Bh          read error
        0Ch          general error
        0Fh          invalid disk change
        13h          out if input (DOS 4+)
        14h          insufficient disk space (DOS 4+)
```

STACK has the following structure:

size	contents
dword	return address for INT 24h call
word	flags pushed by INT 24h
word	program AX on entry to INT 24h
word	program BX
word	program CX
word	program DX
word	program SI
word	program DI
word	program BP
word	program DS
word	program ES
dword	return address of INT 24h call
word	flags of program pushed by DOS service

Output

AL = DOS action

00h	ignore the error
01h	retry the operation
02h	abort the program through INT 23h
03h	fail system call in progress

Comments

This interrupt should never be used directly.

MS DOS automatically attempts to retry the operation before using the DOS critical error handler INT 24h. The number of attempts is usually three.

The INT 24h handler uses INT 21h Functions 01h-0Ch and 59h only. It must preserve the content of SS,SP,DS,ES,BX,CX and DX registers.

INT 25h   [1.0+]
ABSOLUTE DISK READ   DOS

Reads one or more consecutive sectors from a specified disk to a specified Data Transfer Area.

Input

AL = drive number (0=A, 1=B, etc.)
CX = number of sectors to write
DX = DOS beginning sector number

DS:BX = segment:offset of source buffer
For access on DOS 4.0+ extended partition (>32_B):
AL = drive number (0=A, 1=B, etc.)
CX = -1
DS:BX = segment:offset of parameter block

Output

CF = 0 function is successful
CF = 1 function is unsuccessful
AX = error code
AL = device error (0-Ch). It is the same as bits 0-7 in the lower
      byte of DI upon INT 24h
AH = status
      01h bad command
      02h bad address mark
      03h write protected disk
      04h requested sector not found
      08h DMA error
      10h bad CRC
      20h disk controller error
      40h seek error
      80h device does not respond

Comments

The contents of all registers except the segment registers may be destroyed.

 This interrupt leaves the original CPU flags on stack which must be cleared by the caller to prevent stack overflow.

This function uses a parameter block following format when accessing large partition (>32MB):

Bytes	Size	Description
00h	4	sector number
03h	2	number of sector to read
06h	2	offset to buffer
08h	2	segment buffer

See Also

INT 13h Function 02h, INT 26h

INT 26h   [1.0+]
ABSOLUTE DISK WRITE   DOS

Writes one ore more consecutive sectors to a specified disk from specified Data
Transfer Area.

Input

      AL = drive number (0=A, 1=B, etc.)
      CX = number of sectors to write
      DX = DOS beginning sector number
      DS:BX = segment:offset of source buffer
      For access on DOS 4.0+ extended partition (>32_B)
      AL = drive number (0=A, 1=B, etc.)
      CX = -1
      DS:BX = segment:offset of parameter block

Output

      CF = 0 function is successful
      CF = 1 function is unsuccessful
      AX = error code
      AL = device error (0-Ch). It is the same as bits 0-7 in the lower
           byte of DI upon INT 24h
      AH = status
           01h bad command
           02h bad address mark
           03h write protected disk
           04h requested sector not found
           08h DMA error
           10h bad CRC
           20h disc controller error
           40h seek error
           80h device does not respond

Comments

The content of all registers except the segment registers may be destroyed.

This interrupt leaves the original CPU flags on stack and the stack must be
cleared by the caller to prevent stack overflow.

This function uses a parameter block following format when accessing large
partition (>32MB):

Bytes	Size	Description
00h	4	sector number
03h	2	number of sector to read
06h	2	offset to buffer
08h	2	segment buffer

See Also

INT 13h Function 03h, INT 25h

INT 27h   [1.0+]
TERMINATE AND STAY RESIDENT   DOS

Terminates the currently executing program and exits to DOS leaving part or
all memory allocated so that it will not be overwritten by subsequent programs.

Input

DX = number of byte + 1 to keep resident
CS = segment of PSP

Output

Nothing

Comments

After receiving control MS DOS performs the following actions:
flushes all file buffers
closes any open handles for files and devices used by the program
restores terminal handler vector INT 22h from PSP
restores Ctrl-C handler vector INT 22h from PSP
restores the critical error handler INT 24h from PSP

This function does not work properly if during the call the value in the DX
register is in range 0FFF1h-0FFFFh.

This function is not suitable for calling from an .EXE program.

You are advised to use INT 21h Function 31h instead of this interrupt because
it can pass return and codes, and reserves a larger block of memory.

See Also

INT 21h Function 31h

INT 28h   [2.0+]
DOS IDLE INTERRUPT   DOS

Executed by DOS character input functions 01h - 0Ch and 50h-51h, 59h while
waiting for input.

Comments:

This interrupt is used by the PRINT.COM and other TSR programs.

The default INT 28h handler is an IRET command.

See Also

INT 21h Function 34h

INT 2Fh   [3.0+]
FUNCTION 01
PRINT SPOOLER   DOS

This interrupt determines whether PRINT.COM is installed, and performs
various other functions on the Que.

Input

```
        AH = 01h
        AL = subfunction
              00h = get PRINT.EXE installed state
              01h = add file to queue
              02h = remove file from print queue
              03h = cancel print jobs in queue
              04h = hold print jobs to read job status
              05h = release print queue after status read
        DS:DX = segment:offset of submit packet (Subfunction 01h)
                 segment:offset of ASCIIZ pathname (Subfunction 02h,
                 wildcards allowed)
```

Output

```
        CF = 0 function is successful
        if called with AL = 00h
        AL = status
              00h not installed
              01h not installed, but not OK to install
              FFh installed
         if called with AL = 01h
```

```
AL = status
       01h added to queue
       9Eh now printing
 if called with AL = 04h
DX = error count
DS:SI = segment:offset of print queue
CF = 1 function is unsuccessful
if called with AL = 01h,02h,03h,04h
AX = error code
       01h invalid function
       02h file not found
       03h path not found
       04h out of file handles
       05h access denied
       08h print queue full
       09h spooler busy
       0Ch name too long
       0Fh invalid drive
```

Comments:

The packet is submitted to Subfunction 01h which has the following format:

Offset	Size	Description
00h	1	level (must be 00h)
01h	4	segment:offset of _SCIIZ pathname (no wildcards)

The print queue is a list of 64 byte entries. Each entry contains an ASCIIZ pathname. The list is terminated by an empty filename; the first filename in the list is the file currently being printed.

INT 2Fh   [3.0+]

FUNCTION 06h SUBFUNCTION 00h
ASSIGN Installation State   **DOS**

Determines whether resident part of ASSIGN.COM is installed.

Input

```
AH = 06h
AL = 00h
```

Output

```
AL = status
       00h not installed, OK to install
       01h not installed, but not OK to install
       FFh installed
```

See Also

INT 2Fh Function 06h Subfunction 06h

INT 2Fh   [3.0+]
FUNCTION 06h SUBFUNCTION 01h
Get Drive Assignment Table   **DOS**

Obtains the drive assignment.

Input

    AH = 06h
    AL = 01h

Output

    ES = segment of assignment table of ASSIGN

Comment:

Assignment Table starts at ES:0103h. It specifies which drive from A: through
Z: is mapped to. Initial values are 01h, 02h, 03h,...,1Ah.

See Also

INT 2Fh Function 06h Subfunction 00h

INT 2Fh   [3.2+]
FUNCTION 10h
SHARE   **DOS**

Checks whether SHARE.EXE is loaded.

Input

    AH = 10h
    AL = Subfunction
        00h Get installed state

Output

    CF = 0 function is successful
    AL = status
        00h if not installed, OK to install
        01h if not installed, not OK to install
        FFh if installed
    CF = 1 function is unsuccessful
    AX = error code

See Also

INT 21h Function 52h

INT 2Fh   [3.3+]
FUNCTION ADh SUBFUNCTION 80h
Installation Check   DOS

Checks whether KEYB.COM is installed.

Input

> AH = ADh
> AL = 80h

Output

> AL = FF if installed
> BH = major version
> BL = minor version
> BX = 00h if not installed

See Also

INT 2Fh Function ADh Subfunction 81h

INT 2Fh   [3.3+]
FUNCTION ADh SUBFUNCTION 81h
Set Keyboard Code Page   DOS

Sets translation set for keyboard.

Input

> AH = ADh
> AL = 81h

Output

> CF = 0 function is successful
> CF = 1 function is unsuccessful
> AX = 0001h code page not available

Comments

This function is called by DISPLAY.SYS

See Also

INT 2Fh Function ADh Subfunction 82h

INT 2Fh   [3.3+]

FUNCTION ADh SUBFUNCTION 82h
Set Keyboard Mapping   DOS

Input

> AH = ADh
> AL = 82h
> BL = 00h US keyboard
>   FFh foreign keyboard

Output

> CF = 0 function is successful
> CF = 1 function is unsuccessful
> BL = not 00h or FFh

Comments

Pressing keys Ctrl-Alt-F1 or Ctrl-Alt-F2 is equal to performing this function.

This function works when KEYB.COM is installed.

See Also

INT 2Fh Function ADh Subfunctions 81h and 83h

INT 2Fh   [5.0+]

FUNCTION ADh SUBFUNCTION 83h
Get Keyboard Mapping   DOS

Obtains current keyboard mapping.

Input

> AH = ADh
> AL = 83h

Output

> BL = 00h US keyboard
>   FFh foreign keyboard

Comments:

Pressing keys Ctrl-Alt-F1 or Ctrl-Alt-F2 is equal to performing this function.

This function works when KEYB.COM is installed.

See Also:

INT 2Fh Function ADh Subfunctions 81h and 83h

INT 2Fh   [3.3+]

FUNCTION B7h SUBFUNCTION 00h
APPEND Installation Check   DOS

Tests whether APPEND is installed.

Input

    AH = B7h
    AL = 00h

Output

    AL = status
         00h not installed, OK to install
         01h not installed, but not OK to install
         FFh installed

INT 2Fh   [4.0+]

FUNCTION B7h SUBFUNCTION 02h
Append Version Check   DOS

Gets version number of APPEND, if APPEND is installed.

Input

    AH = B7h
    AL = 02h

Output

    AX = FFFFh if not DOS 4.0 Append or DOS 5.0
    AL = major version
    AH = minor version

See Also

INT 2Fh Function B7h Subfunction 10h

INT 2Fh   [3.3+]

FUNCTION B7h SUBFUNCTION 04h
Get Append Path   DOS

Obtains the path which is the current APPEND path for date files.

Input

AH = B7h
AL = 04h

Output

ES : DI = segment:offset of active APPEND path

INT 2Fh   [4.0+]

FUNCTION B7h SUBFUNCTION 06h
Get Append Function State   DOS

Obtains current state of APPEND.

Input

AH = B7h
AL = 06h

Output

AX = Append State:
     bit 0 = 1   APPEND enabled
     bit 12= 1   (DOS 5+) drive is specified, but APPEND
                    applies directory search
     bit 13= 1   if /PATH flag active
     bit 14= 1   if /E flag active
     bit 15= 1   if /X flag active

INT 2Fh   [4.0+]

FUNCTION B7h SUBFUNCTION 07h
Set Append Function State   DOS

Sets state of APPEND.

Input

> AH = B7h
> AL = 07h
> BX = APPEND state bits (See Subfunction 06h)

Output

> Nothing

INT 2Fh   [3.3+]

FUNCTION B7h SUBFUNCTION 10h
Get Version Info   DOS

Gets version number of APPEND, if APPEND is installed.

Input

> AH = B7h
> AL = 10h

Output

> DL = major version
> DH = minor version

See Also

INT 2Fh Function B7h Subfunction 02h

INT 2Fh   [4.0+]
FUNCTION B7h SUBFUNCTION 11h
Set Return Found Name String   DOS

Writes the fully qualified filename and returns it if the next INT 21h call is function 3Dh, 43h, or 6Ch.

Input

> AH = B7h
> AL = 11h

Output

> Nothing

Comments

The application must provide a sufficiently large buffer, because the name is placed at the same address of ASCIIZ parameter string. The State is reset after APPEND has processed the INT 21h call.

Clipper Modifications

Using Macros for Clipper-MASM Interface
with MASM 6.0 and 6.1

In this book we have given examples of how to use macros for interfacing between Clipper and Assembler modules. These macros are stored in the file EXTENDA.INC which comes with the Clipper compiler and works well with MASM 5.1. Unfortunately, as we mentioned in Chapters Seven and Nine, these macros do not work with MASM 6 and TASM, even if you specify the compatibility feature provided in MASM 6. This continues to be the case even in Clipper 5.0 and 5.01. The file EXTENDA.INC is the same as in Clipper Summer 87 and doesn't work with MASM 6 and MASM 6.1.

However, you can use the modules that you created using the Clipper interfacing macros with more recent versions of Clipper, MASM and TASM.

Since Clipper 5 supports the technique of passing and returning parameters used in its earlier versions, all object modules generated by MASM 5 are suitable for use with Clipper 5. This means, of course, that you can continue to use your old object libraries.

You can also use Clipper interface macros with MASM 6 by slightly altering your EXTENDA.INC file. The main reason why the results generated by MASM 5.1 and MASM 6 are different, is that these versions of assembler treat nested calls of macros in different ways. We'll now recommend how to make macros stored in the EXTENDA.INC file work with MASM versions 6.0 and higher.

First of all you need to provide the compatibility mode, either by including the corresponding OPTION directive, or by specifying the /Zm parameter in the command line for calling assembler. The OPTION directive in an assembler subprogram must include the corresponding parameter, as below:

```
option      oldmacros
```

The command line parameter /Zm has the same effect as the directive

```
option      m510      "Full" compatibility
```

If you use the BAT-files from your program disk, you can specify the /Zm parameter using the DOS environment variable:

```
Set PrmAsm= /Zm
```

The EXTENDA.INC file needs to be edited to provide compatibility with MASM 6. This modification involves two steps:

Moving definitions of macros $import -$x_far to the beginning of the file
Changing macros $p_char - $p_date

The first step is aimed at ensuring that text macros are defined before they are used. The definitions of the following macros need to be placed before the definitions of the SES macro:

```
$import,
$x_byte,
$x_log
$x_long
$x_double
$x_cptr
$x_far
```

The second step involves changing the following macros:

```
$p_char
$p_int
$p_long
$p_double
$p_log
$p_date
```

In these macro definitions, you need to replace an occurrence of the single parameter denoted by *p1* with a sequence of several parameters.

This is needed because MASM 6 treats the blank character as a separator. We'll illustrate this by providing the changed text of the $p_char macro:

```
$p_char macro p1, p2, p3, p4, p5, p6, p7, p8, p9, p10
    LOCAL noparam
    $gen <          MOV     WORD PTR p1 p2 p3 p4 p5 p6 p7 p8 p9 p10, 0>
    $gen <          MOV     WORD PTR p1 p2 p3 p4 p5 p6 p7 p8 p9 p10[2], 0>
    $gen <          CMP     AX, PCOUNT>
    $gen <          JA      noparam>

    $chktype $$CHARACTER
    $gen <          JZ      noparam>

    Ccall _parc <AX>
    $gen <          MOV     WORD PTR p1 p2 p3 p4 p5 p6 p7 p8 p9 p10, AX>
    $gen <          MOV     WORD PTR p1 p2 p3 p4 p5 p6 p7 p8 p9 p10[2], DX>
noparam:
endm
```

The original text of this macro looks like this:

```
$p_char macro p1
    LOCAL noparam
    $gen <          MOV     WORD PTR p1, 0>
    $gen <          MOV     WORD PTR p1[2], 0>
    $gen <          CMP     AX, PCOUNT>
    $gen <          JA      noparam>

    $chktype $$CHARACTER
    $gen <          JZ      noparam>

    Ccall _parc <AX>
    $gen <          MOV     WORD PTR p1, AX>
    $gen <          MOV     WORD PTR p1[2], DX>
noparam:
endm
```

As you can see, the first text is created from the second one by replacing the text "p1" with the text "p1, p2, p3, p4, p5, p6, p7, p8, p9, p10" in the macro header. Within the macro body, the text"p1" must be replaced everywhere by the string "p1 p2 p3 p4 p5 p6 p7 p8 p9 p10". After this, the new EXTENDA.INC file can be used with the program in MASM 5.1, MASM 6.0, MASM 6.1 and TASM.

Index

Symbols

$ 144
4DOS   222

A

absolute addresses   34
accumulator AX   23
active TSR programs   519
Ada   147
   CALL statement   575
adapter, video   319
   determine type   340
   types   321
ADD   60, 70
ADDINT macro   191
addition
   boolean and logical   131
address bus
   defining width   97
address counters   20
address range   99
addresses   112
   20-bit   96
   absolute   34
   connecting with variable name   118
   creating 20-bit with 16-bit registers   97
   data   120
   effective addresses   96
   for accessing objects in segments   107
   instruction addresses   11
   of bytes in RAM   95
   real   16
   relative   16, 34
   segment   113, 122
   storing return addresses   109
addressing   148
   types of   120
   using different types   145
algorithms   57
Align
   column   35
allocation table   19
ALU (arithmetic logical unit)   22
AND   129
ANSI.SYS   339, 346

clearing screen using   361
screen control   365
anti-virus programs   511
arguments
   passing   179
arithmetic constructions   23
arrays   42, 141
   and strings   145
   defining   117
   information about   143
   instructions for manipulating   148
   of bytes   142
   of words   142
   size of elements in   148
   VAR   147
ASCII
   character set   280
   codes for characters 0-9   118, 127
   conversion   206
   conversion to by BIOS   266
   displaying a table   374
   introduction to   266
ASCIIZ   143
   outputting   161
ASM   44
ASM (.ASM)   27, 32
ASM procedure   48, 49
assembly language   11
assembly-time directives   201
ASSUME   109, 196
attribute byte   328
AutoCode   263

B

base indexed addressing   148
base registers   120, 148
base relative addressing mode   147
BASIC   15, 17
   calling sub-programs   577
   COL program   587
   interfacing with   604
   passing parameters   576, 587
   restoring the stack   577
BAT-files
   on your disk   39
bauds   466
BCD numbers
   AF Flag   65
BELL   244
bi-listing   34

Expert programming from the CIS

Pascal from the ground up using progressive examples and easy instructions, for both beginners and users with some experience of programming. Introduces Borland Turbo Pascal, covering the fundamental concepts of the language. Introduces OOP through a series of sample programs.

The Revolutionary Guide to Turbo Pascal
Borodich, Valvachov and Leonenko
ISBN 1 874416 11 7
£27.98 (inc VAT) NET
$34.95

The Revolutionary Guides

Introduces C++ with practical applications, using graduated examples and simple diagrams to introduce the concepts of OOP. The accompanying disk includes the source code for the examples contained within the book and an interactive animated tutorial to make the task of learning the language as easy as possible.

Revolutionary Guide to
o C++
ry Sklyarov
N 1 874416 10 9
98 (incl. VAT) NET
95

REVOLUTIONARY GUIDES TO
WORLD CLASS PROGRAMMING